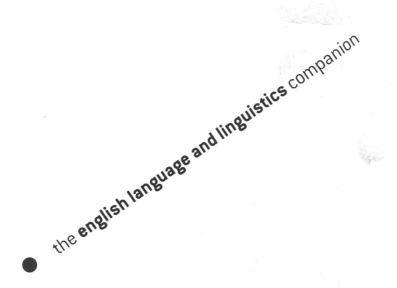

the **english language and linguistics** companion

**Palgrave Student Companions** are a one-stop reference resource that provide essential information for students about the subject – and the course – they've chosen to study.

Friendly and authoritative, **Palgrave Student Companions** support the student throughout their degree. They encourage the reader to think about study skills alongside the subject matter of their course, offer guidance on module and career choices, and act as an invaluable source book and reference that they can return to time and again.

**Palgrave Student Companions** – your course starts here ...

**Published**

The English Language and Linguistics Companion
The MBA Companion
The Politics Companion
The Psychology Companion
The Social Work Companion

**Forthcoming**

The Anthropology Companion
The Health Studies Companion
The English Literature Companion
The Media Studies Companion
The Nursing Companion
The Sociology Companion
The Theatre, Drama and Performance Companion

*Further titles are planned*
www.palgravestudentcompanions.com

About the Authors

KEITH ALLAN is Professor of Linguistics at Monash University, Australia. His research focuses on aspects of meaning in language and his publications include *Natural Language Semantics*, *Forbidden Words: Taboo and the Censoring of Language* (with Kate Burridge), *The Western Classical Tradition in Linguistics* and *The Concise Encyclopedia of Semantics*.

JULIE BRADSHAW is Lecturer in Linguistics at Monash University, Australia. Her main interests are in the sociolinguistic aspects of second language acquisition and use.

GEOFF FINCH retired from Anglia Ruskin University in 2006, where he was Senior Lecturer in English Language and Literature, and now works as a freelance lecturer and writer. His is the author of *How to Study Linguistics*, *A Guide to Understanding Language*, *Key Concepts in Language and Linguistics* and *Word of Mouth: A New Introduction to Language and Communication*.

GEORGINA HEYDON was Research Fellow in the Linguistics Program at Monash University and is now Senior Lecturer in Criminal Justice Administration at RMIT University, Australia. She is the author of *The Language of Police Interviewing*.

KATE BURRIDGE is both Professor and Chair of Linguistics in the Linguistics Program at Monash University. She is the author of *Blooming English: Observations on the Roots, Cultivation and Hybrids of the English Language*, *Weeds in the Garden of Words: Further Observations on the Tangled History of the English Language*, *Gift of the Gob: Morsels of English Language History*, co-author, with Keith Allan, of *Forbidden Words: Taboo and the Censoring of Language*, with Kersti Borjars, of *Introducing English Grammar* and is also a regular presenter of language segments on ABC Radio and television.

# the **english language and linguistics** companion

keith allan • julie bradshaw
geoffrey finch • kate burridge • georgina heydon

palgrave
macmillan

First published 2010 by
PALGRAVE MACMILLAN

Palgrave Macmillan in the UK is an imprint of Macmillan Publishers Limited, registered in England, company number 785998, of Houndmills, Basingstoke, Hampshire RG21 6XS.

Palgrave Macmillan in the US is a division of St Martin's Press LLC, 175 Fifth Avenue, New York, NY 10010.

Palgrave Macmillan is the global academic imprint of the above companies and has companies and representatives throughout the world.

Palgrave® and Macmillan® are registered trademarks in the United States, the United Kingdom, Europe and other countries.

ISBN 978–1–403–98971–0

This book is printed on paper suitable for recycling and made from fully managed and sustained forest sources. Logging, pulping and manufacturing processes are expected to conform to the environmental regulations of the country of origin.

A catalogue record for this book is available from the British Library.

A catalog record for this book is available from the Library of Congress.

10  9   8   7   6   5   4   3   2   1
19 18  17  16  15  14 13 12 11 10

Printed and bound by
Thomson Litho, East Kilbride, Scotland

# contents

List of figures     xiii
Preface     xv
Acknowledgements     xvii

## 1    studying language    1

### 1.1    approaching language    3

What is language?     3
Linguistics is the study of language     7
Why study language?     11
Key points     13
References     14

### 1.2    study skills    15

Introduction     15
Observing language in use     15
Note-taking     16
Effective reading     17
Coping with new linguistic jargon     18
Essay writing     18
Guidelines for presenting work     20
Plagiarism     24
Writing exams     25
Oral presentations     26
A final note     27
References and additional readings     27
Some useful online resources     28

## 2    studying language: core topics    29

### 2.1    phonetics – the science of speech sounds    31

Phones and the organs of speech     31
The International Phonetic Alphabet     34
Articulation     35
Vowels     35
Consonants     37
Key points     39
References     39

| 2.2 | **phonology – sound systems in languages** | **40** |
|-----|---|---|
| | Phonemes | 40 |
| | The difference between phones and phonemes | 42 |
| | Assigning allophones to phonemes | 42 |
| | Alternative analyses | 44 |
| | Phonotactics | 44 |
| | Syllable structures | 45 |
| | Stress and tone | 46 |
| | Intonation | 46 |
| | Disjuncture | 47 |
| | Key points | 48 |
| | References | 48 |
| | | |
| 2.3 | **morphology – word structures** | **49** |
| | Problems with the notion 'word' | 49 |
| | Morphemes, allomorphs, and lexemes | 50 |
| | Morphosyntactic classes | 51 |
| | Inflectional and derivational morphology | 52 |
| | Morphological analysis | 53 |
| | Word formation | 54 |
| | Morphological typology | 54 |
| | Key points | 55 |
| | References | 56 |
| | | |
| 2.4 | **syntax** | **57** |
| | Introduction – types of grammar | 57 |
| | Linguistic competence – what speakers 'know' | 58 |
| | Generative grammar | 61 |
| | Constituency tests | 63 |
| | Universal grammar | 64 |
| | Key points | 64 |
| | References | 66 |
| | | |
| 2.5 | **fundamentals of semantics and pragmatics** | **67** |
| | Defining semantics and pragmatics | 67 |
| | Meaning is compositional | 67 |
| | Context and common ground | 69 |
| | Key points | 74 |
| | References | 74 |
| | | |
| 2.6 | **meaning, maxims, and speech acts** | **75** |
| | Sense, denotation, reference, and connotation | 75 |
| | Entailment | 77 |
| | Conversational implicature | 77 |
| | Mutual entailment | 78 |
| | Contradictories and contraries | 79 |
| | Hyponymy and antonymy | 79 |

The cooperative maxims 79
Speech acts 81
Key points 83
References 84

**2.7 sociolinguistics 86**
Language variation 86
Regional variation 87
Social variation 87
Linguistic ethnography 89
Language and power 91
Address terms 91
Standard languages 92
Language attitudes 92
Sexist language 93
Critical discourse analysis (CDA) 93
Language, gender and sexuality 94
Conversational style 96
Explanations for gender differences in politeness 96
Discursive construction of gender and sexuality 97
Language contact 97
Pidginization and creolization 98
Language death 99
Key points 100
References 100

**2.8 psycholinguistics 103**
Psycholinguistics 103
Neurolinguistics 103
Lateralization 104
Language comprehension 104
Language production 105
Models of linguistic processing 105
Cognitive development 106
Clinical linguistics 106
Developmental disorders 107
Acquired disorders 108
First language acquisition 108
Learning and interaction 109
Acquiring words 110
Syntactic development 111
Theories of language acquisition 112
Key points 113
References 113

**2.9 applied linguistics 115**
Second language acquisition 115

Are the processes of acquiring a first and second language different? 116
Behaviourism and contrastive analysis 116
Universal grammar 116
Interlanguage 117
Input 118
Interaction and negotiation of meaning 118
Noticing 119
Foreign language teaching 119
Language teaching theory and methods 119
Learner-centred approaches 121
Immersion 121
Translation 122
The problem of equivalence 122
Key points 124
Further reading 125
References 125

**2.10    historical linguistics                                        127**
Languages don't stay the same – language evolution 127
Some facts about language evolution 129
Language families – establishing genetic relationship 129
Attitudes to language change 131
Key points 132
References 133

**2.11    stylistics                                                    134**
Stylistics 134
Literary stylistics 138
Key points 140
References 140

**2.12    discourse and conversation                                    141**
Analysing two stories 141
Critical discourse analysis 144
Conversation analysis 144
Turn-taking in Anglo environments 145
Adjacency pairs 146
Key points 148
References 149

**2.13    corpus linguistics                                            150**
Introduction 150
Development of corpus linguistics 150
Creating a language corpus 151
Using a language corpus 153
Corpus-based dictionaries 153
Key points 154

Resources and further reading 155
References 155

**2.14    digital tools in linguistics**                                    **156**
Overview 156
Counting, concordance, collocation, spell-checking 156
Analysis by computer 158
Machine translation 159
Speech recognition 160
Speech synthesis and text generation 160
Expert systems 161
Computer languages 161
Key points 162
References 162

**2.15    forensic linguistics**                                             **164**
Introduction 164
An early example of forensic linguistic analysis 165
Identification 165
Spoken data 165
Written data 166
Discourse analysis 167
Language of origin 168
Commercial applications 168
Lie detection 168
Summary of key issues 168
Key points 169
References 169

**2.16    from pictures to writing**                                         **170**
From pictures to writing 170
The origin of the English alphabet 172
*Scripta continua* 173
Learning to read in Ancient Greece 174
Linguistics and the invention of writing 175
Key points 175
References 176

**3      key terms and concepts in linguistics**                            **177**

**4      some key linguists**                                                **245**

**5      conducting research and identifying resources**                     **267**

**5.1    doing ethical research**                                            **269**
Collecting data through observation and introspection 271
Questionnaires and interviews 272

Recording and transcribing language data     272
Corpus data     273
Statistics     275
Overview     275
Key points     275
References     276

**5.2**    **researching general and theoretical linguistics**     **277**
Ferdinand de Saussure     277
Noam Chomsky     279
John Lyons     281
Key points     281
References     281
Resources     282

**5.3**    **researching phonetics and phonology**     **283**
Key points     285
References     285
Resources     286

**5.4**    **researching morphology**     **287**
Key points     289
References     289
Resources     290

**5.5**    **researching syntax**     **291**
Structuralism     291
Anthropological linguistics     292
Transformational generative grammar     293
Systemic functional grammar     294
Key points     294
References     294
Some useful resources     295

**5.6**    **researching the history of language(s)**     **297**
Sir William Jones     298
Sound laws     298
Diachrony and synchrony     299
Grammaticalization     299
Linguistic universals     300
Variation as a sign of language change     301
Into the twenty-first century     301
Key points     302
References     302
Resources     303

| 5.7 | **researching semantics and pragmatics** | **305** |
|---|---|---|
| | Introduction | 305 |
| | Lexical semantics | 306 |
| | Pragmatics – meaning in context | 307 |
| | Key points | 307 |
| | References | 307 |
| | Resources | 308 |
| | | |
| 5.8 | **researching sociolinguistics** | **310** |
| | Correlational sociolinguistics | 310 |
| | Linguistic ethnography | 313 |
| | Narrative, and negotiation of power | 315 |
| | Language and gender | 316 |
| | Key points | 317 |
| | References | 318 |
| | Resources | 319 |
| | | |
| 5.9 | **researching psycholinguistics** | **320** |
| | Experimental or observational methods | 320 |
| | Neurolinguistic research | 321 |
| | Key points | 322 |
| | References | 322 |
| | Resources | 322 |
| | | |
| 5.10 | **researching applied linguistics** | **323** |
| | Researching second language acquisition | 323 |
| | Researching translation | 324 |
| | Key points | 325 |
| | References | 325 |
| | Resources | 325 |
| | | |
| 5.11 | **researching cognitive linguistics** | **326** |
| | The anthropocentricity of language | 326 |
| | Categorization, prototypes, and stereotypes | 327 |
| | Metaphor | 329 |
| | Figure and ground | 329 |
| | Key points | 330 |
| | References | 330 |
| | Resources | 330 |
| | | |
| 5.12 | **researching functionalist approaches to language** | **332** |
| | Saussure and the Prague School | 332 |
| | Systemic functional grammar | 334 |
| | Other functionalist theories | 334 |
| | Key points | 335 |
| | References | 335 |
| | Resources | 336 |

| | | |
|---|---|---:|
| **5.13** | **researching discourse and conversation** | **337** |
| | Conversation analysis | 337 |
| | Discourse analysis | 338 |
| | Critical discourse analysis (CDA) | 338 |
| | Key points | 339 |
| | References | 339 |
| | Resources | 340 |
| | | |
| **5.14** | **researching forensic linguistics** | **341** |
| | Authentification | 342 |
| | Legal language and discourse analysis | 342 |
| | Key points | 343 |
| | References | 343 |
| | Resources | 343 |
| | | |
| **6** | **career pathways** | **345** |
| | | |
| **6.1** | **career pathways** | **347** |
| | Using your linguistics | 347 |
| | Linguistics and education | 348 |
| | Linguistics, medicine, and therapy | 350 |
| | Linguistics and the law | 350 |
| | Linguistics and writing | 351 |
| | Linguistics in your degree | 352 |
| | The voice of experience – the careers linguists have | 353 |
| | Useful career websites | 356 |
| | A final note | 357 |
| | References | 357 |

# list of figures

1.1    The three-tier system of language    5
1.2    The three tiers of language and linguistics    9

2.1    A visual analysis of *Sit down will you?*    31
2.2    The International Phonetic Alphabet    32
2.3    Organs of speech    33
2.4    The glottis (larynx)    33
2.5    Degree of lip-rounding    35
2.6    Vowel-making area    35
2.7    The cardinal vowel quadrilateral    36
2.8    Diphthong and triphthong (Australian English)    36
2.9    Tree diagram (1)    59
2.10    Tree diagram (2)    59
2.11    In (10) Max and his Rolls occupy the same (real) world    70
2.12    Speaker's model of the two worlds evoked in (7)    70
2.13    Network diagram for part of the Clonard network, showing 100% density    88
2.14    Receptive linguistic processing    105
2.15    Germanic cognates of BROTHER    130
2.16    Classification of Indo-European languages    131
2.17    Collocations of the noun taboo    157
2.18    Text mark-up from ICE-GB    159
2.19    Data entry using Shoebox (Toolbox)    159
2.20    King Narmer defeats his enemies (Egyptian, 3100 BCE)    170
2.21    The Sumerian logograph *sag* "head"    171
2.22    Sumerian c 3000 BCE    171
2.23    Smileys    171
2.24    Ptolemy cartouche from the Rosetta Stone    172
2.25    Normal right-to-left    172
2.26    Left-to-right    172
2.27    The /l/ graphemes in related scripts    173
2.28    Semitic ʔālep "ox", the symbol for ʔ comes to be used for A in Greek    173
2.29    Fragment of the Greek inscription in *scripta continua* on the Rosetta Stone    173

3.1    Labelled tree diagram for *The man ran through the park*    193
3.2    Labelled tree diagram for *feet* /fit/    232

5.1    Class stratification of a linguistic variable in process of change    312
5.2    The Wug Test    320

list of figures

# preface

*The English Language and Linguistics Companion* is designed to aid and enlighten the student in the final year of secondary school, the beginning undergraduate who is contemplating or embarking on the study of linguistics and languages, or anyone who is curious to know about studying language. The *Companion* is highly suitable for those in language programmes, media and communication programmes, teacher training and other educational programmes who need to know about the study of language. Because the book is written in English, most – though by no means all – of the exemplification comes from the English language, making the *Companion* readily accessible to all readers.

*The English Language and Linguistics Companion* offers basic information on the study of language and languages and on the key terms and concepts found in the discipline of linguistics. Part 1 talks about studying language and offers practical advice on reading and note-taking, dealing with technical terminology, writing essays and exams, time-management, and other basic study skills. Part 2 introduces the core topics and concepts of linguistics and the study of language. These include the study of the sounds used in human languages, analysis of the structure of words, phrases, sentences and longer texts, and exploration of the ways in which meaning is expressed in language. The social and psychological aspects of language are also dealt with in detail, along with the applications of linguistics in various fields, including language teaching and the law. Part 3 of the *Companion*, on key terms and key concepts in linguistics, is intended to function as a glossary-cum-encyclopedia that may be referred to when reading Parts 1, 2, 4 and 5, and it can also be read for its own sake. Part 4 identifies some of the key researchers in linguistics and reviews their work. Part 5 of the *Companion* describes the nature of linguistic research in the past and present, and recommends various resources for linguistic inquiry and the study of language and languages suitable for students of these disciplines. Finally, Part 6 consists of a valuable chapter on career pathways that identifies job opportunities for people who have been students of language and linguistics.

The original idea for this book came from Geoff Finch, who was to have been one of the editors. Sadly, Geoff had to withdraw from the project for personal reasons after drafting the outline and three chapters. This left Keith Allan as editor in chief and he was joined by Julie Bradshaw as co-editor. As the project progressed, its content and structure diverged a little from Geoff's original plan which, nevertheless, remains a strong component. Of the 34 chapters in *The English Language and Linguistics Companion*, Geoff Finch wrote two and half, Georgina Heydon wrote four, Kate Burridge wrote six, Julie Bradshaw wrote seven, and Keith Allan wrote 14 and a half.

The editors warmly thank Harvey Mitchell for his astute reading of the manuscript, which helped expunge many infelicities. Responsibility for any faults still remaining lies with Keith Allan and Julie Bradshaw.

KA and JB, Melbourne 2009

# acknowledgements

The authors and publisher wish to thank the following for permission to use copyright material:

Blackwell Publishing Ltd., for the following figures: 'Network diagram for part of the Clonard network, showing 100% density', from *Language and Social Networks*, by Lesley Milroy (Blackwell, 1980); 'Class stratification of a linguistic variable in process of change', from *Sociolinguistic Patterns*, by William Labov (Blackwell, 1972: 114, Figure 4.2).

Cambridge University Press, for the table 'Typical development sequence', from *How Children Learn Language*, by William O'Grady (Cambridge University Press, 2005).

International Phonetic Association, at the Department of Theoretical and Applied Linguistics, School of English, Aristotle University of Thessaloniki, for the reproduction of The International Phonetic Alphabet (2005).

Pearson Education Inc., for the figure 'Receptive linguistic processing', from *Language Development: An Introduction*, by Robert E. Jr. Owens, © 2005, reproduced by permission of Pearson Education, Inc.

Every effort has been made to trace all the copyright holders but if any have been inadvertently overlooked the publishers will be pleased to make the necessary arrangements at the first opportunity.

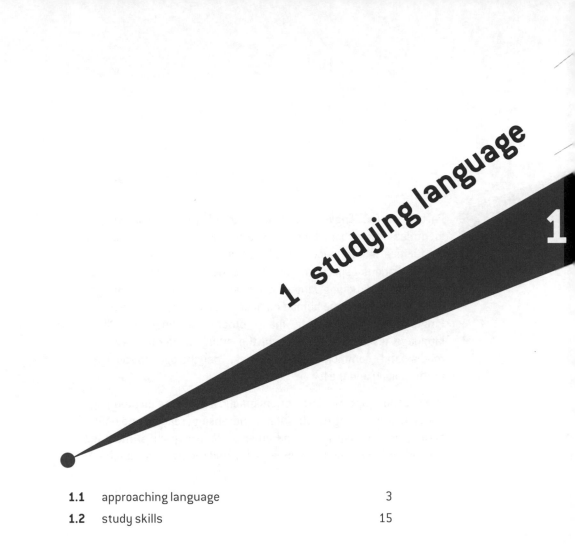

# 1 studying language

**1**

**1.1** approaching language      3

**1.2** study skills      15

Part 1 of *The English Language and Linguistics Companion* identifies the characteristic features of human language. Linguistics is introduced as the empirical study of language, and its various aspects are briefly described. The benefits to be gained from studying language include insights into language itself, the nature of the human mind and human social interaction. Linguistics is relevant to many other disciplines including language teaching and research, the study of literary devices, media and communications studies, psychology, sociology, anthropology and the law.

The second chapter in Part 1 offers practical guidance on studying linguistics, including essay writing, referencing, reading and note-taking, time-management, and other basic study skills. There is also advice on methods for undertaking and reporting research.

# 1.1 approaching language

## chapter contents

> What is language? 3
> Linguistics is the study of language 7
> Why study language? 11
> Key points 13
> References 14

## What is language?

The term *language* is frequently applied to a range of human and non-human activities loosely linked to communication. Zoologists will frequently talk about 'animal language', for instance, and psychologists about 'body language'. Such usages have their own rationale, but they all take their cue from human verbal language, the language we speak and write. The verbal language of humans is special in the animal kingdom. There is nothing which duplicates it in terms of either its form or its function. This chapter aims to describe some of the features which make it so distinctive. We will show what verbal language shares with other language-like forms, as well as identifying what is unique about it.

Verbal language is the most complex and sophisticated form of communication to have evolved on this planet.

Verbal language is not the only form of communication. As human beings we communicate in a host of ways, through images, drawings and music, but all these achievements are subtly dependent on language. An artist has to think how to arrange the objects on his or her canvas, and such thinking can employ language. We also communicate, of course, through gestures and expressions, so called 'non-verbal communication'. This in itself is capable of great subtlety. We can sometimes learn more from someone's body language than we can from what they say. Certainly, if we wish to discover whether a person is lying to us then the tell-tale signs will often be small physical movements, such as rapid blinking or eye movement, which are largely unconscious. Experts refer to these micro-gestures as 'leakage'. Our bodies are constantly leaking information to others, whether we like it or not. Animals, of course, communicate in this way too. A dog can tell from the way another dog approaches whether its intentions are hostile or friendly. In addition, animals also have their own systems of communication, systems which often operate in a similar way to human language. Research in this area has been prolific over the past decade, and, as a consequence, we know a lot about the different sorts of pant hoots emitted by chimpanzees, and the varieties of song used by birds to signal to each other.

Such language-like activity does not always consist of noises made by the mouth. Bees, for example, tell each other by dancing where a good store of nectar is to be found (see Frisch 1966; Wenner 1990).

However, it is one thing for us to know that a bee dance is communicating travel information to its fellow bees, and quite another to be able to decipher the information itself. No researcher has yet been able to observe a bee dance and from that work out where the source of nectar is. This is because we cannot fully interpret the code the bees are using. Every form of communication relies on a code to transmit meaning. This is true of body language as well. We have to know what a shrug means in order to interpret it properly. What distinguishes human verbal language from any other variety is that the code it uses is much more complex. As a consequence, the range of meaning it can communicate is far greater. An animal gesture, or pant hoot, may convey feelings of great subtlety, but, as far as we know, cannot tell a fellow animal about feelings experienced yesterday, or hopes and fears for tomorrow, or next week. But the language that we humans speak can. Only human language can range freely over time and space. This is a phenomenon known as 'displacement', and it is one of the distinguishing features of the language we speak. Every other form of language-like activity is tied to the here and now.

But there is another crucial difference between human language and other systems of communication. We not only use language to communicate to other people, we also use it to communicate to ourselves. As already mentioned, language helps us to think. Most of us have an internal monologue running inside our heads which enables us to debate whether we should do the shopping now or later. This is not to say that thought is not possible in the absence of language. Quite a lot of thinking can go on in images and daydreams, and, of course, we would not want to say that animals can't think. But there is a certain type of thought which is dependent on language. Language enables us to reason about the world. It has what linguists and philosophers call an 'ideational' function. We may not need language in order to conceptualize experience; but we do need it to communicate those concepts to others. Concepts such as time, love, and honesty, are abstract. Language helps clarify them as ideas that we can manipulate and use to construct our lives.

One of the reasons language is able to do this is because it has a naming function. Learning the names of things is an enormous step forward for children in the process of language acquisition. But equally significant is learning that things are attributed with names. As far as we know, animal cries do not have a similar naming function. Vervet monkeys, for example, have warning cries that seem to mean 'Look out, here comes a leopard' or 'Look out, there's a snake' as the case may be. But although the cries vary according to the nature of the predator, they are not pure acts of naming. There doesn't seem to be an isolable bit that means 'leopard' or 'snake'. The cries are rather like the holophrastic utterances of very small children. These are one-word utterances, like *shoe* or *daddy*, but the individual words function as whole sentences, such as 'I want my shoe', or 'Here comes daddy'. At about 18 months a naming explosion occurs with children and they realize that the word *shoe* doesn't mean 'I want my shoe', but that it stands for the thing to put their foot into. This is a revelation to them and from then onwards their vocabulary expands very quickly.

## the power of names

Helen Keller became deaf and blind at the age of 18 months, after a brief illness, possibly meningitis. In this extract from her autobiography she describes her discovery of the meaning of the word water.

As the cold stream gushed over one hand she spelled into the other the word water, first slowly, then rapidly ... and somehow the mystery of language was revealed to me. I knew then that 'w-a-t-e-r' meant the wonderful cool something that was flowing over my hand. That living word awakened my soul, gave it light, hope, joy, set it free! ... Everything had a name, and each name gave birth to a new thought ... every object which I touched seemed to quiver with life. That was because I saw everything with the strange new sight that had come to me. [Keller 1908]

The 'stands for' relationship is a vital feature of language. Children learn that language is a symbolic code, that the word *tree*, for example, represents something in the outside world. They also learn that words represent the world in different ways. A word like *throwing* names an activity, while *big* names an attribute. Such intuitions will later form the basis of parts of speech or **lexical classes**. Of course, other communication codes, such as those of animals, also operate symbolically. The 'stands for' relationship is not unique to verbal language. Part of the bee dance, for example, stands for the direction in which the other bees must go. But the relationship operates in a significantly different way in human language. We know that the three sounds /tri/, which make up *tree*, don't stand for the thing itself, but for the word *tree*.

/tri/ is the phonemic representation of the word *tree* using IPA characters. See Chapter 2.2.

In between us and the world lies a system of words. Animal cries tend to represent the world directly, much in the way the early utterances of children do. But human speech sounds represent words. Animal cries do not appear to have anything equivalent to words. In consequence, they can't be segmented, as we said above. Users of a language, however, know that the sounds of any word can be used over and over again in different combinations to make new words. The sounds in the word *pit* can be recycled to form *tip*, for example, or they can be combined with other sounds to form *cockpit* and *Pitcairn*. In other words, between us and the world lies a **grammar**. A grammar stipulates the rules for combining sounds into words, and for combining words into meaningful strings, that is, **phrases**, **clauses**, and **sentences**. Another way of putting this is to say that human language is a three-tier system of communication, whereas animal signalling is a two-tier system. The linguist Michael Halliday refers to two-tier systems as proto-language (Figure 1.1).

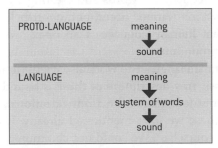

*Figure 1.1 The three-tier system of language (from Halliday 1985)*

The distinction between proto-language and language proper is a useful one because it enables us to separate verbal language not only from the signals of animals, but also from the early cries of children. At some stage in his/her development a child leaves the two-tier system and adopts the three-tier one. It is this leap which is unique to humans. Some animals in captivity have been taught the rudiments of a three-tier system, but the limited repertoire they have acquired suggests they haven't fully understood the principles on which it is based. The construction of words depends on a principle that is quite special to human language, known as **double articulation**. As we have seen, many animals can produce sounds that have definable meanings, such as 'there's a leopard coming', or 'feed me', but what they cannot do is detach those sounds from their immediate context and recombine them to make new meanings. Humans can do this effortlessly. On their own, sounds such as *b* or *t* mean nothing but we can string them together, along with other meaningless sounds, to create a boundless number of words. Because of this, the words themselves bear no natural relationship to the things they represent. So the word *tree*, for example, only refers to the object tree because that's the way English works. In French the same object is represented by a different word, *arbre*, in German by *Baum*. The relationship between word and object is arbitrary (though bound by convention). The only systems that seem to compare with this in the animal world are the songs of some birds and some whales. As with language, each note in the song of a robin or thrush is meaningless. It is the sequence as a whole which is important. Interestingly, it has been found that these sequences sometimes vary regionally within a single species, rather in the manner of human dialects, so that a sparrow in one part of the country may not sing exactly the same sequence as a sparrow elsewhere. But, crucially, the principle of double articulation has very limited application in bird (and whale) communities. Bird songs appear to be restricted to two basic messages, either 'This is my territory', or 'I fancy you'. By contrast, the forty or so speech sounds that compose human languages can be recombined almost endlessly to generate new words. Not only that, but we can put the words together to make strings of words which are entirely novel. Most of the sentences in this book have never been written or uttered before in the whole of human history.

What separates our human system from that of birdsong, then, is a second principle, which is equally important: creativity. Within a finite set of rules for composing new sequences we are able to generate an infinite number of fresh utterances. The nearest equivalent to this is chess, in which a fixed number of pieces are moved in accordance with the rules of the game to create an endless number of actual games. Creativity and double articulation enable a system to advance from contextually bound and fixed meanings to those which are constrained by the conventions of particular languages. There is nothing to stop us inventing a new word or sequence of words and creating a genuine innovation. Incidentally, this is not how most innovations occur, but, nevertheless, the fact that it is conceivable demonstrates that human language is an open system as opposed to the closed systems of animal communication.

The unique design features that enable human language to work also enable it to fulfil a very broad range of functions and purposes. Any description of these is bound to be partial, but linguists conventionally talk about four macro-functions: ideational, interpersonal, textual, and poetic. The first of these we have mentioned already. It is the function by which we represent the world to ourselves. We could not communicate our conceptions of the world without language. In a very important sense, language endows the world with meaning. The second function, the interpersonal, is concerned with the use we make of language to represent ourselves, that is, our feelings, emotions, thoughts, and beliefs in our interactions with other people. A great deal of our time is spent servicing our relationships whether with friends, lovers, or strangers. The textual function has to do with the way language can be used to form texts or discourses, in either written or oral form. Effective communication means being able to string utterances (sentences), together, so that the overall effect is cohesive and coherent. Language has a special set of devices to enable this to happen. The last function, the poetic, has a much broader meaning than the description might imply. It is that side of language which exists purely for the sake of pleasure and delight. In that respect it relates to the creation of jokes, and riddles, as well as aesthetic devices such as rhythm and rhyme.

Language, as we have described it in this section, is a code-like system with design features that make it unique in the animal kingdom. As such, it is fundamental to our sense of ourselves as human beings. The capacity for language is an essential part of our humanity.

## Linguistics is the study of language

Linguistics is the systematic empirical study of language. Its principal concern is with the way we understand, acquire, and use language, both in spoken and in written form. By empirical we mean that the methodology is evidence-based. Linguists do not approach language with a prior belief that any particular use of language is necessarily better or worse than another. Saying *bugger off*, for example, is no worse linguistically than saying *please go away*, simply different; just as Dinka, French, or Serbo-Croat are neither better nor worse as systems of communication than is English. The connotations of so-called 'bad language' are socially conditioned (see Allan and Burridge 2006 for a detailed discussion; such social domains of language are explored by pragmaticists and sociolinguists). Linguists look at language the way a botanist examines a plant, no matter whether a gardener would regard it as prized specimen or a weed. In the terminology of Noam Chomsky, the linguist's task is to 'observe', 'describe', and 'explain'.

It is also true that the aim of linguistic investigation is to determine the rules that govern linguistic behaviour. We need to be very careful here about what we mean by 'rules'. There are all sorts of rules that people may appeal to in order to regulate linguistic usage, from 'Never start a sentence with a conjunction such as *and* or *but*' to 'Don't speak with your mouth full'. For linguists these are issues of etiquette, much in the way deciding what to wear at a wedding or how to address an archbishop are. Linguistic rules are not based on conventions of this kind, but on the principles that unconsciously govern the way in which native speakers of a language talk and write. For example, if you give native speakers of English the sequence *Got n't have any I money* and ask them to arrange it into a proper sentence, they will have no problem in doing so – *I haven't got any money*. Yet no one will have explicitly taught them this. It's just something they will have acquired naturally. But they couldn't have acquired it without understanding the hidden structure on which the sequence is based. Though they may be ignorant of the technical terms used by a linguist, native speakers will know that *I* functions as the subject of the sequence, that *any money* functions as the object, and that *have got* is the verb group that functions as the predicate. They will also know that *n't* is the negative particle and always attaches itself to the auxiliary verb. In other words, they must possess, in their unconscious minds, concepts such as subject of a sentence and auxiliary verb. Without this elementary knowledge they would never be able to construct sentences themselves. Native speakers, therefore, know at least two things: first, that language is structure-dependent; and second, that language is category-based, i.e. that it consists of different classes of items such as nouns, verbs, adjectives, and so on, each with their own rules governing their use.

Our ability to form grammatically acceptable sequences is what, following Chomsky 1965, linguists refer to as our linguistic competence. Much of linguistics is concerned with investigating this and with explaining the principles on which it is based. How do we know, for example, in the following two sentences from Chomsky 2002 that 'he' could be understood as referring to John in (1), but not in (2)?

(1)  John said that he was happy.
(2)  He said that John was happy.

The principle here has to do with co-reference, that is, the ability of the name and the pronoun to refer to the same entity. Co-reference is clearly possible in (1), but not in (2). The interesting thing is that children acquire the rules governing co-reference with a minimum of instruction. Most linguists believe that the reason for this is that we are programmed from birth to acquire language. This is sometimes referred to as the 'innateness hypothesis'. There is a great deal of evidence now to support this, although the question of just how much is innate is still very much open. An important current model of acquisition assumes that our brains resemble computers which are hard-wired genetically to learn language. All we need is access to the particular language, Arrernte, Dutch, English, Japanese, or Maasai, which will become our native tongue. We gain such access through exposure to actual language use by our parents, friends, and other members of the same language community.

Well-formed sequences operate at all levels of language. The examples we have looked at so far illustrate some basic features of the knowledge native speakers possess about the **syntax** (grammar) of English. But before we can arrange words in phrases, clauses, and sentences, we have to be able to form them in the first place, or at least, recognize how they are formed. The structure of words is studied in **morphology**. The term **morphosyntax** refers to the structures of words, phrases, clauses, and/or sentences.

We also have to know the sounds of the language and the acceptable ways in which they can be combined to form words. Study of the sound structure of language is **phonology**. It nearly always comes as a surprise to students to learn that while there are 26 letters of the English alphabet, there are about 44 distinctive sound units or **phonemes** of English. The study of the physical mechanisms that enable us to both make and hear them is **phonetics**. Phonemes are governed by usage rules every bit as complex as those which govern syntax. The sound structure of language involves understanding the way rhythm, stress, pitch, and intonation contribute to utterances. At some stage we also learn, when we learn to write, how these sound units are represented by written symbols. But there is an important difference between speaking and writing. Speaking we acquire naturally, writing we have to be taught. The first is a product of nature, the second, of culture.

Finally, there is something else we need to know about words in addition to how they are pronounced and the structures they can enter into, and that is their meaning. Word meaning is a notoriously slippery area. Words do not have meaning, we have meanings for words. They have some meaning in isolation, but they also have particular meanings in actual utterances. The word *love*, for example, has a different meaning in the utterance *I love chocolate* than in the utterance *I love my wife*. An essential part of our linguistic competence lies in understanding these shades of meaning and being able to construct and interpret actual sequences. This linguistic level is **semantics** and **pragmatics** (see below). Some children have severe difficulty managing it. Autistic children, in particular, cannot cope with the fact that words are capable of having more than one meaning. Asked to *push the pram* they might very well just give it a shove.

Phonetics, phonology, syntax, and semantics constitute the traditional core of linguistic inquiry. The individual abilities they incorporate effectively constitute our linguistic competence. But there are other competences that are important in enabling us to employ language appropriately. Chief among these is communicative competence. If you asked someone the way to the railway station and got the reply *The eagle has landed* you would not be any the wiser about how to get there. Linguistically the response is perfectly competent, but it doesn't fulfil the requirements for an answer to this request. Knowing the correct way to answer questions, give instructions, make requests, and perform all the many other things we do with language means possessing communicative competence. It is this which tells us how much or how little we need to say on any given occasion, i.e. when we can abbreviate and when we can't. It is also vital in the process of interpreting utterances. If you saw the instruction *Dogs must be carried on escalators* you would get no marks for comprehension if you immediately went out and bought a dog. Understanding the meaning of this utterance means knowing something about the world of which it is a part. Communicative competence is one of those broad areas of cognitive ability which linguists study under the heading of **pragmatics**. This is a relatively new area of linguistics concerned with the contextual, or situational, significance of language.

What we have been describing so far are the staples of linguistics. If we revise part of Halliday's diagram of the three-tier nature of language in Figure 1.1 we can see that it correlates very well (Figure 1.2).

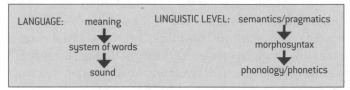

Figure 1.2 *The three tiers of language and linguistics*

In a very broad sense then, linguistics is concerned with studying the way language enables the world of human thought and feeling to be made manifest in a sequence of sounds, or written shapes, and with the way speakers and listeners negotiate this process. There are linguists who choose to focus their attention on a specific level of the subject: phoneticians and phonologists concentrate on the sound level of linguistics, syntacticians on the syntactic level, and semanticists and pragmaticists on the level of meaning. If we think of the discipline of linguistics as a tree, then these levels form the trunk. In addition to the trunk, however, there are numerous branches which have grown up over time. As with any evolving area of research these are being added to all the time. The chief branches are:

> applied linguistics – the study of language teaching and other applications of linguistics
> psycholinguistics – the study of language and mind
> sociolinguistics – the study of society and language use

> historical linguistics – the study of language change over time
> comparative linguistics – the comparative study of different languages and their respective linguistic systems
> computational linguistics – data archiving and the analysis and generation of language using computers
> stylistics – the study of styles of language in different contexts (including literary style)
> discourse and conversational analysis – the study of the structure of written and spoken texts longer than a single sentence.

You will find all these branches discussed in this book. Many of them are sizeable enough to have sprouted branches of their own. Applied linguistics, for example, is a very broad area. It is really an umbrella term for all those aspects of linguistics that involve engaging with real-world language problems, and the application of linguistic theories and procedures to the issues of everyday life. One such application is forensic linguistics, which is concerned with the use of linguistic techniques in connection with the law, and more particularly, in the investigation of crime. Neurolinguistics is the study of brain activity in relation to core linguistic activities such as speaking, listening, writing, reading and signing; and clinical linguistics is the study of language disorders (e.g. speech defects such as stuttering). These sub-disciplines share some interests with psycholinguistics, also a burgeoning field. Sometimes called, albeit loosely, 'the psychology of language', it demonstrates the ability of linguistics to forge links with other disciplines, in this case, psychology. The main concern of psycholinguists is with the way we acquire language, that is, with the mental processes which enable us to understand and use language effectively. In a similar fashion, sociolinguistics has been forged from the interface between linguistics, anthropology and sociology. For sociolinguists, a major concern is with the way language use varies socially from speaker to speaker, and geographically from region to region and also with the way speakers use language to claim identity and negotiate social relations. Sociolinguistics also investigates national and societal language tensions, in which resolution is sought through language planning (a deliberate effort to influence the function, structure, or acquisition of a language or language variety within a speech community).

From a different perspective, language variation is also the concern of historical linguistics and comparative linguistics. In historical linguistics, the focus is on the way languages have evolved over time, and on the reconstruction of older linguistic forms from which they have descended. One of the main research goals of such study is to discover the principles which govern language change through time. In comparative linguistics, linguists study similarities and differences between languages. All languages differ in their structure, vocabulary, and semantic range. By comparing these differences in a systematic way it becomes possible to see what universal features exist in the design of language, and how individual languages express them in terms of their structure, vocabulary, and semantic range.

Of the remaining three branches explored in this volume, the focus of computational linguistics is broadly on the use of computers in the study of language. This has many offshoots, from the development of systems capable of speech processing, i.e. speech synthesis (the conversion of written text into spoken output) and speech recognition (the conversion of speech input into written form), to the creation of computerized banks of language material for linguistic study (corpus linguistics). Stylistics focuses on the deployment of linguistic approaches in the analysis of styles of language used in different contexts. Every time we use language we necessarily adopt a style of some sort, by making a selection from a range of syntactic and lexical possibilities available to us. This is so whether we are writing a job application or a note to a friend, or composing a poem. Stylistics refers to that broad range of methodologies which derive from the insights of linguistics into the various genres of language use. Discourse analysis examines and constructs theoretical and methodological approaches to the analysis of discourse and texts. It examines the way different kinds of texts are constructed in spoken, written, and electronic discourse; the ways that institutions such as the media, education and the judiciary ordain appropriate structures in their discourses; and the ways texts differ cross-culturally. Conversation analysts study the structure of conversations and the resources that speakers manipulate in conversation.

As a discipline, linguistics has grown rapidly. Historically it is one of the newer academic disciplines – before the nineteenth century it didn't really exist as an academic discipline. This is not to say that people didn't study language; clearly they did (see Robins 1997; Koerner and Asher 1995; Allan 2009), but they studied it within disciplines such as philosophy, grammar, philology, or rhetoric. However, since the pioneering work of people like Wilhelm von Humboldt, Franz Bopp, William Whitney, Hermann Paul, Ferdinand de Saussure, Edward Sapir, Leonard Bloomfield, and Noam Chomsky (to name just a few), linguistics has emerged as a discipline in its own right. It has succeeded in penetrating the major domains of human thought and activity, and in contributing considerably to our understanding of them. But despite this, the essence of the discipline remains fundamentally clear. Its principal preoccupation is with enabling us to have a firmer, more systematic, and in that sense, more scientific understanding of what is, arguably, our chief invention as a species: language.

## Why study language?

Much of what we have to say in this section will already be apparent from the previous two sections. As we have already seen, linguistics is a very extensive discipline, and, consequently, it should come as no surprise that there are many reasons for studying language. Probably, if we asked people in general what they considered the main reason for studying language to be they would reply 'in order to use it better'. Certainly this will form part of most people's early education. We are taught at school how to write acceptable sentences, compose written texts, and become better communicators. This kind of study continues throughout life, and there are all sorts of self-help manuals available in shops and libraries to assist us. But this represents only a small and very narrow reason for studying language. The sort of study that we have been discussing in this chapter has very little to do with enabling us to write and speak better, and more to do with enabling us to appreciate how the study of language will provide greater insights into language, ourselves, and the world around us. There are many practical offshoots from studying language in this way, some of which we have touched on already; very many disciplines taught at colleges and universities contain aspects of linguistic study within them just because of this. If you take courses in media, communications, teacher education, psychology, anthropology, sociology, neuroscience, speech therapy or criminology, you can expect at some point to engage with some aspect of linguistics. This is in addition to those courses where it is made explicit, such as, for example, courses in linguistics per se, or in English or other languages.

One small example may help to illustrate the contribution which an understanding of language can make to everyday life. We are used to thinking of racial tension as a consequence of simple prejudice, either about colour, or cultural practices such as religion, but quite often it rests on a miscomprehension about language use. John Gumperz 1982 discusses the example of a West Indian bus driver in London whose routine was to greet passengers with the request *exact change please*. If any passenger couldn't comply with this request he would repeat it, leaving a gap between *change* and *please*, and emphasizing *please* with a higher pitch. To British English speakers, the intonation pattern here would suggest rudeness, since it is excessively direct and implies the passenger is too stupid to have listened properly. But, according to Gumperz, in West Indian speech the norms of intonation are different. Speaking in this manner is a way of being extra polite by isolating the politeness word *please* for special emphasis. In other words, the different language practices of different speech communities can lead to miscommunication and inadvertently cause offence.

An example such as this would be useful to students studying the ethnography of communication, a branch of sociolinguistics which looks at the social conventions of language use. The power of language to influence and persuade, often below the level of conscious awareness, is something most of us are prepared to acknowledge, but unless we study the language of journalism, or advertising, or politics, we are unlikely to understand the techniques upon which this rests. As has already been said, there are many contexts in which knowing something about language is invaluable. Often these contexts are the bases of the branches of linguistics we talked about earlier. In addition, however, it's important to recognize that language is an important subject of study in its own right, as is studying the structure of rocks or the anatomy of animals. It provides an insight into human culture and society, but, more importantly, into the way in which life is organized: the capacity for language is just as basic to us as the capacity to walk. Understanding language is crucial to understanding the human mind. In many ways this is the heartland of linguistics. This is where the contributions of linguists such as Chomsky have been so seminal in the development of the discipline. And here of course, we encounter a problem. There is no way we can observe the operations of language directly. Were we to look into the human brain we would not be able to see nouns or verbs. All we would identify would be electrical impulses. The task of the linguist therefore is to look at the output, at the actual utterances of people in order to reconstruct the mental program that has created them. If we think back to an earlier point, the question is always 'What are the rules which allow us to say so and so?' The rules may be of a purely linguistic character, but equally they may contain elements of other systems within them. There are rules governing successful conversations, just as there are for pronouncing the *s* sound.

We study language in order to study ourselves, because we live, and move, and have our being in language. It is the cornerstone of every other subject, since they are all essentially inexpressible without language, and it is the foundation of all civilized life. The philosopher Ludwig Wittgenstein has said 'The limits of my language mean the limits of my world' (Wittgenstein 1922 §5.6). Was he right?

## Key points

> In the section 'What is language?' we identified the design features of language. Formal features include:

▶ Arbitrariness: the use of tokens which bear no natural relationship to the world; for instance, neither the individual sounds in *chair* nor the word itself is motivated by the thing represented, as opposed to animal cries, where the reverse is the case.

▶ Double articulation: the ability to combine essentially meaningless sounds into units of meaning at a higher level, e.g. /h/+/æ/+/t/ = *hat*.

▶ Naming: the ability to use sound sequences to represent things, events and processes, e.g. *water, global warming, driving*.

▶ Displacement: the ability to refer to things, events and processes removed in time and place from the present, e.g. *Caesar, tomorrow, the next President of the United States*.

▶ Creativity: the ability to generate an infinite number of sequences from a finite set of rules; for example, the rules for constructing sentences allow any speaker to utter entirely novel examples.

> There are functional features such as:

▶ The ideational function: the ability to conceptualize the world as an instrument of thought in order to converse about it with others.

▶ The interpersonal function: the ability to service our relationships and express our interests and feelings; that is, to interact with others linguistically.

▶ The textual function: the ability to construct texts and discourses from utterances, to string linguistic items together to form connected discourse as in narratives, whether oral or written.

▶ The poetic function: the ability to manipulate forms for our own pleasure using sound symbolism (alliteration, onomatopoeia, puns, eccentric spellings) in order to express our delight in novelty and verbal play.

> In the section 'Linguistics is the study of language' we established that linguistics is the empirical study of language (i.e. the methodology is evidence-based). Its principal concern is with the way we understand, acquire, and use language, both in spoken and in written form. The study of linguistics will enable you to have a firmer, more systematic, more rigorous ('scientific') understanding of what is, arguably, our chief invention as a species: language.

> The aim of linguistic investigation is to determine the rules that govern linguistic behaviour; that is, the underlying principles which govern the way in which native speakers of a language talk and write.

> Language is structure-dependent and category-based.

> Our linguistic competence as native speakers of a language L (for instance English or Maasai) is our ability to form grammatically acceptable sequences of L.

> Communicative competence is our ability to use language to communicate effectively.

> A noun phrase and pronoun are coreferential if they refer to the same entity, e.g. in *The old man scratched his itchy nose* 'The old man' and 'his' are coreferential if it is the old man's nose which is scratched.

> The syntactic structure of a language is the arrangement of words into phrases, clauses, and sentences.

> The structure of words is studied in morphology; the structure of the sounds of a language is studied in phonology. Phonetics is the study of the sounds humans make. Semantics and pragmatics study aspects of meaning in language.

> We briefly reviewed some of the sub-disciplines of linguistics such as applied linguistics, psycholinguistics, sociolinguistics, historical and comparative linguistics, computational linguistics, stylistics, discourse and conversational analysis.

> In the section 'Why study language?' we focused on the benefit from the insights to be gained into language itself, ourselves as human beings, and perhaps the world around us. Understanding language is crucial to understanding the human mind.

> The ethnography of communication is a branch of sociolinguistics which looks at the social conventions of language use. It enables us to uncover cross-cultural differences in language use that can cause miscommunication among people from different language/cultural backgrounds.

> Linguistics is relevant to many other disciplines including language teaching and research, the study of literary devices, media and communications studies, psychology, sociology, anthropology and the law.

## References

Allan, Keith 2009. *The Western Classical Tradition in Linguistics*. 2nd edn. London: Equinox.

Allan, Keith and Kate Burridge 2006. *Forbidden Words: Taboo and the Censoring of Language*. Cambridge: Cambridge University Press.

Chomsky, Noam 1965. *Aspects of the Theory of Syntax*. Cambridge MA: MIT Press.

Chomsky, Noam 2002. *On Nature and Language*. Ed. by Adriana Belletti and Luigi Rizzi. Cambridge: Cambridge University Press.

Frisch, Karl von 1966. *The Dancing Bees: An Account of the Life and Senses of the Honey Bee*. Transl. by Dora Isle and Norman Walker. 2nd edn. London: Methuen.

Gumperz, John J. 1982. *Discourse Strategies*. Cambridge: Cambridge University Press.

Halliday, Michael A.K. 1985. *Spoken and Written Language*. Waurn Ponds: Deakin University Press.

Keller, Helen 1908. *The World I Live In*. London: Hodder & Stoughton.

Koerner, E.F. Konrad and Ronald E. Asher (eds) 1995. *Concise History of the Language Sciences: From the Sumerians to the Cognitivists*. Oxford: Pergamon.

Robins, Robert H. 1997. *A Short History of Linguistics*. 4th edn. London: Longman [First edn 1967].

Wenner, Adrian M. 1990. *Anatomy of a Controversy: The Question of a 'Language' among Bees*. New York: Columbia University Press.

Wittgenstein, Ludwig 1922. *Tractatus Logico-Philosophicus* (Introduction by Bertrand Russell). London: Kegan Paul, Trench, Trübner.

# 1.2 **study skills**

## chapter contents

| | | |
|---|---|---|
| › | Introduction | 15 |
| › | Observing language in use | 15 |
| › | Note-taking | 16 |
| › | Effective reading | 17 |
| › | Coping with new linguistic jargon | 18 |
| › | Essay writing | 18 |
| › | Guidelines for presenting work | 20 |
| › | Plagiarism | 24 |
| › | Writing exams | 25 |
| › | Oral presentations | 26 |
| › | A final note | 27 |
| › | References and additional readings | 27 |
| › | Some useful online resources | 28 |

## Introduction

When you first come to a tertiary institution for further study you suddenly find you have to acquire a whole lot of new skills. Even understanding the timetable and the calendar that sets out lecture and tutorial times can present a challenge. You will find that you do not receive the same detailed directions you did at school; suddenly, you have to be much more self-motivated. You will also find yourself in quite a different culture where the expectations are not always clear. In the case of linguistics you will be introduced to a specific kind of scientific inquiry. In investigating the structure of language, for instance, you will be taught how to identify patterns and to formulate and test hypotheses. You will also be taught what constitutes an adequate description and explanation. During the process you will have to learn to interpret the specialist language, the codes, and the abstract concepts that are peculiar to the discipline. This will also mean mastering new and often arcane terminology. We begin this chapter by looking at some of the very practical things you need to think about as you engage in the study of language and language phenomena.

## Observing language in use

Linguistic analysis is based on descriptions of how a language is used. By observing and collecting data we are able to produce hypotheses about the system of phonological, grammatical or other rules underlying a speaker's usage. We can then test these hypotheses by producing new utterances using these rules to see if they are acceptable to the speaker. All linguistic work is dependent on first collecting good data. In your studies you will often be given language data collected by other researchers, and asked to identify patterns and underlying rules. As you go on, however, you will find you need to provide examples and collect data of your own. It is important therefore that from the beginning you develop skills in observing and collecting language data.

A good place to start in developing linguistic skills is to describe your own use of language and that of people around you. Carry a notebook with you and make notes of any interesting language forms you notice. Look for patterns and oddities. Notice when people in the media or in your daily interactions use pronunciations, sentence constructions, idioms and so on which differ from your own. Then try to observe carefully how you encode the same words or meanings. Try to find reasons for any similarities or differences. Carrying out observations of this sort will develop your skills in noticing, describing and explaining language phenomena.

For example, you might overhear someone on a bus say *That's the guy that I don't know where he lives.* If this strikes you as odd or interesting put it in your notebook and listen out for any similar utterances. You might hear the following conversation between a brother and sister in a video shop.

Brother:     Philip Seymour Hoffman isn't in this film.
Sister:      Freakoid! It was like his first film.

This exchange has a number of interesting points: you might find the term *freakoid* novel, and think about how it was formed. You might reflect on the role of insults in intimate relationships, and you might want to consider the function of *like*.

Keeping a data notebook will help you hone your observational skills, and also provide a good source of material for your assignments. Many linguistics tutors will encourage you to provide your own examples as evidence of your insights into a topic you are writing about.

We now move on to handy hints for other aspects of your studies, including lectures and tutorials, project/essay writing and exams.

## Note-taking

You certainly don't need to write down everything the lecturer or tutor says in class, but it is important to note down main points, themes, and key readings. Don't just rely on the lecturer's handouts or PowerPoint slides. Your own lecture notes are an important source for exam revision at the end of semester or term. They also help you to keep your attention focused on what the person is saying. You are far less likely to become distracted or to doze off if you are listening actively. Pay attention to **signal statements** that tell you that what the lecturer is about to say is important. Examples of signal statements are 'The most important point…' and 'Remember that…'. Use abbreviated words such as *cf.* "compared", *ca.* "about", *b/f* "before"; *viz* "namely"; *et al.* "and others") and symbols (such as → "causes, leads to, results in"; ← "is caused by, is the result of"; ↑ "an increase"; ↓ "a decrease"; ⇔ "is related to". This will help you to write or type quickly. Remember that during a class, lecturers and tutors often drop hints and helpful advice, especially with respect to assessment tasks. Listen out for these clues and note them down. A useful exercise is to later rewrite your notes to make them more complete and change abbreviations into whole words, and shortened sentences into longer sentences. You can then take the opportunity to make your notes more accurate by using your textbook or reference sources to follow up anything that wasn't clear during class. If something is not clear, ask your tutor or lecturer for guidance.

If for some reason you are not able to attend class, then check with fellow students and lecturers to see what you might have missed. You may be studying in a university where lectures are recorded and made available online. This is a useful resource, but when it is possible to attend the live lecture this is always a better option. The lecturer's body language may provide important information, and make his or her comments memorable, and you will have the opportunity to ask questions. If something is unclear in a lecture, don't assume that everyone else understands it. Students who ask questions in lectures often find they speak for a grateful cohort of equally confused classmates.

## Effective reading

A major part of your job as a student is to make sense of set readings, and extract key or relevant ideas or arguments. You need to keep in mind your purpose: what question(s) are you trying to answer; what problem are you addressing; what evidence are you seeking. Note-taking is an important part of effective reading, and can serve as the basis of accurate and well-argued writing. It is not enough to simply photocopy a work and then mark-up the text with a highlighter. You can use the margins of your own copy for brief notes and questions. You should also jot down on a separate sheet the main ideas and arguments of the text and how these relate to your own concerns. Make sure that you record the full bibliographic information (i.e., the details to appear in your reference list, see below) for each book or article that you read. If possible, use a bibliographic database program such as Endnote™. As you write your summaries of the most relevant information, record the page number for each note taken. All this work comes in very handy when you need to cite, reference and compile bibliographies for later essays.

You will also be expected to read critically – to identify the strengths and weaknesses in a text. This sort of critical approach to reading means asking yourself many questions about the text. These questions might include for example:

> What is the author saying? What are the main themes and key points?
> Are these clearly conveyed and well developed?
> Are there any inconsistencies in the author's arguments?
> Is there anything missing from the text? Has the author omitted any points?
> Have the data been adequately analysed?
> Are there problems with the methodology? Is it appropriate for the task at hand?
> Are the ideas presented always relevant?
> What is the theoretical perspective of the author?
> What are the supporting data and information that the author draws on? Is the material adequate?
> Has the author answered all the questions there are to be answered?
> Have the author's opinions been grounded adequately within the wider debates of the discipline?
> Has the author oversimplified the issues?
> Has the conclusion been clearly drawn? Is it convincing?

Finally, you will find you don't always need to read every book or article thoroughly.

Sometimes skimming a text is enough to get the general idea (gist) of a text. You can do this by reading the table of contents and chapter or section headings and then selecting the most relevant parts. You can get the general picture by reading the first and last paragraphs, and perhaps glancing over the first few sentences of the other paragraphs. You might even just scan a page (with your eyes) for crucial expressions.

## Coping with new linguistic jargon

Linguists will rightly claim that ordinary non-specialist language cannot adequately capture all the precision that linguisticese (the jargon of linguistics) can. Outside the discipline of linguistics there already exists an extensive non-technical vocabulary used by the lay public when talking about language; but unfortunately, the terminology is often too imprecise to be of real use within the discipline of linguistics. Linguists are therefore faced with having to narrow and redefine everyday terms like *sentence, word, syllable* and *grammar*, as well as add a number of new terms to overcome imprecision and to distinguish things that non-linguists ignore: items or concepts for which ordinary language lacks terms. For example, linguists find the term *word* insufficiently precise for all their purposes, and so occasionally need to distinguish between *grammatical, orthographic,* and *phonological words* as well as introducing new terms like *lex, lexeme, morph* and *morpheme* to capture additional distinctions.

To non-linguists this practice can seem unnecessarily pedantic. The technical language is perceived as intellectual hocus-pocus, and all the more offensive precisely because it deals with familiar subject matter. Sociologists and psychologists have to deal with the same problem. When you are faced with a barrage of new terminology, just remember that if this were quantum mechanics and not linguistics, you would not question the right to furnish the discipline with this sort of technical vocabulary. In your reading, note any unfamiliar terms and their definition. If the author does not define the term, attempt to write your own definition, based on the way it is used in the text. You can check this in the dictionaries of linguistics and applied linguistics listed at the end of this chapter.

## Essay writing

Essay writing forms an important part of the assessment in most disciplines within the humanities and social sciences. Most of the essays you write in linguistics will probably require between 1,500 and 4,000 words. More than anything else, they are an exercise in planning and time management. It is not possible to write a good essay two days before the submission date. You should allow for at least one to two weeks to plan, read and research the essay topic, and you will also need plenty of time for the actual writing process, so start work early.

Academic essays vary from discipline to discipline, but in linguistics they will always be scientifically based pieces of writing in which you aim to evaluate often contradictory claims, and persuade your readers of a specific point of view. To be persuasive you need to back up your ideas with supportive evidence from credible and relevant sources. Linguistics essays require analytical skills and an ability to summarize, compare, and contrast. They should:

> answer a question or carry out a task
> have a structured argument

> present and develop a hypothesis or a set of closely related points by reasoning and by evidence

> be strengthened by examples and supporting facts from academic texts or other reliable materials, supplemented, where relevant, by your own observations

> be written in a style that is appropriately academic and not too chatty or informal.

The following set of bullet points is a basic guide to planning, reading, researching, and – finally – writing your essay. Let us emphasize, however, that writing is not the linear process that these bullet points might suggest. In the course of writing an essay you will probably work through several of these stages a number of times. For example, you might uncover another useful text and need to go back to the reading and note-taking stage or perhaps you will need to seek out specific information or further supporting examples. We should also emphasize that even for the best writers there are usually many (sometimes painful) rewritings before the final version emerges.

> Choose a topic that appeals to you – this makes the writing process easier and helps you to engage readers and to present a solid argument and a clear point of view.

> Spend some time examining the wording of the essay question and determine exactly what the essay requires you to do.

> Take note of the words and concepts used in the question, especially the directive words such as 'discuss', 'compare', 'describe'.

> Ensure that you have interpreted the question correctly by talking to fellow students, the tutor, or the lecturer.

> Determine your point of view and line of argument; note down your initial ideas and thoughts as a list.

> Research the topic. Seek out relevant materials from credible academic sources such as books, journals, and websites for support and evidence. Databases in libraries and the internet are obvious starting points, but remember that not everything on the web can be believed, and online materials may not be as reliable as specialist books and journal articles.

> Make sure you make detailed bibliographic notes of all your resources – it can be very time-consuming chasing these up after writing the essay. Note the name of the author(s), date, article title, journal or book title, page range, place of publication, publisher; and the page from which you took each of the notes or quotes. Put quotes in inverted commas to avoid later accidental plagiarism.

> Read, think, and then make notes – at this stage you should be looking for examples and any compelling quotations to support your views.

> Write your plan of the essay and organize the main ideas.

> Write your first draft. This should include your introduction, body and conclusion (see below).

> Wait a day or two before you read the essay through and edit it.

> Write a second draft. At this stage it may help to have a friend, parent, or fellow student read it through.

> Many writers find it useful to read their work out aloud. This way they are more likely to pick up typographical errors and any infelicities of style or grammar. You will also find that it helps you in checking that your arguments and points are logically and coherently arranged. (Most people find it more accurate to read hard copy than to read on the screen.)

> Make sure you check your references and bibliography, and ensure that all quoted and paraphrased material is appropriately acknowledged (see the discussion of referencing procedures below).
> Complete the final draft and submit it.
> It is a good idea to keep a copy of the work submitted, and even copies of all stages of planning and drafting.

The basic shape of your essay should consist of an introduction, body, and conclusion.

### The introduction – say what you're going to say

A good strong opening paragraph helps you to structure the essay well, and it also sets up the reader to read knowing what to expect. At this stage you need to engage your reader and establish your authority. Here you introduce the topic of your essay and focus on what you understand to be the central issues. You also need to include a statement of your hypothesis.

### The main body – say it

This part of the essay is divided into topic sections. The first might be a backdrop to the history of the problem. You then analyse the current problem before moving on to present your point of view. Remember to support your opinions with the evidence you uncovered when researching the essay topic. You should also situate your opinions within the wider debates of the discipline. Compare your hypothesis with other existing propositions, and show the reader that what you have to offer is the best solution.

As a rule of thumb remember 'one idea = one paragraph'. Each main point requires its own separate paragraph. But be heedful that essays should flow. Make sure the paragraphs unfold in some sort of logical order. Make sure you include enough pointers to guide your reader through the discussion.

### Conclusion – say what you've just said

At the end of your essay you should summarize your main ideas. A strong conclusion reinforces your thesis statement by providing a persuasive summary of the evidence and arguments that you have provided. You might also point out wider implications and scope for further investigation.

You do not need to write the essay in this order. Many people find it easier to plan the conclusion first, and in fact the introduction is often the last section to be written.

## Guidelines for presenting work

The following are some guidelines that might help you to organize and present material in essays and other written work that is to be submitted for marking.

### Format

Essays or assignments should be typed or printed – most departments will not accept work that is handwritten. When you are proofreading your work, bear in mind that marks will sometimes be deducted for words or symbols that are not explained or are not readily decipherable.

Conventions vary from place to place in actual layout, so you should check with your tutor or lecturer for their preferences. The following are generally accepted guidelines. Line spacing of 20 point (= 1.5 lines) is acceptable when typing or printing (provided that your tutor can write comments between the lines); it is customary to use one side of the paper only (though this is ecologically unsound); leave a clear margin of at least 3 centimetres on the left-hand side of the page; number all pages; either staple them together or use folders and plastic envelopes. Do not use pins.

Do not forget to include your name and/or student ID number. Some departments require specific cover sheets (with your name, your tutor's name, and other pertinent details). If you are able to submit online, make sure you use a document name that clearly identifies your work, including your surname, subject code and assignment number. Assignments labelled 'linguistics essay' may disappear if eighty students submit work with the same document name.

The style used in your written work should be that of an academic paper. If in doubt, check the style in a journal such as *Language; Journal of Linguistics* or *Australian Journal of Linguistics*. Formal standards of grammar, spelling, and punctuation are to be observed. Misspelling a linguist's name, for instance, never leaves a good impression. Aim for a plain, informative style which avoids the rhetorical flourishes of journalistic or creative writing. In general, the style used in the articles you read should serve as a good model.

## Referencing procedure (within the text)

Part of any academic work means reading widely and drawing on the work of researchers and writers. Indicating the sources you have drawn on to construct your piece of work demonstrates your scholarship and your familiarity with the literature. If you use the ideas or words of others without acknowledgement in your essays and assignments, then you are stealing other people's ideas (see the note on plagiarism below), so it is important to document carefully all the materials that you use. This means including details such as the author's surname, the year of publication and the page numbers (mandatory for direct quotations). For example, in drawing on Chomsky's work, one might say:

According to Chomsky (1965: 4), ...
At this point, one can invoke the notion of subjacency (Chomsky 1981: 14–23) in order to ...

The full bibliographic details for Chomsky (1965, 1981) are then placed in the references section (bibliography) at the end of the essay. This same procedure is used when acknowledging quotations. For example:

If we adopt illocutionary point as the basic notion on which to classify uses of language, then there are a rather limited number of basic things we do with language; we tell people how things are, we try to get them to do things, we commit ourselves to doing things, we express our feelings and attitudes, and we bring about changes through our utterances. Often we do more than one of these at once in the same utterance. (Searle 1979: 29)

If you quote, you must quote exactly (including the original spelling and punctuation). Note that quotes of fewer than about 40 words are normally marked at the boundaries by quotation marks (inverted commas); those longer than that are normally presented without quotation marks in indented paragraphs like the one above. A quote gives credence to your ideas. What is more, when used effectively, it can give them a far more brilliant, a far more catchy expression than you could manage. For example, you might begin a discussion on quotation by writing something like:

> As linguist David Crystal writes: '[a] quotation is a fragment of socially embalmed language. It is language which has been placed on a pedestal, freely available for anyone to use, but readily sensitive to abuse' (2003: 184).

Crystal captures the idea well; but as he also warns, do not misuse quotations. A good rule of thumb is to quote sparingly. Remember that your tutor wants to see that you can understand (and not just reproduce) important ideas. This means you will often need to summarize or paraphrase other people's ideas. It is important that you do this entirely using your own words, while trying to represent the ideas as accurately as possible. As with quoting, you need to cite the source in the text. Ideas or citations from secondary sources can be handled as follows:

> According to Wilkins 1968 (cited in Allan 1986: 170), ...

Note that the convention used by linguistics is the Harvard system of in-text referencing; that is, the author and date (and page number when quoting) of all references to books, articles and other sources appear at an appropriate point in the text and full details are then given at the end of the essay in a reference list. In this system bibliographic details are not given in footnotes (notes relating to the text that are placed at the bottom of the page) or endnotes (notes placed at the end of the whole work). If you are using a bibliographical software program such as Endnote to compile your references, make sure you select the style of a well-known linguistics journal as your reference style.

You need to be aware that some other disciplines (e.g. English literature, History) use footnotes for referencing. Learn and use the appropriate referencing convention for linguistics as indicated in the set reading for linguistics. If in doubt consult your tutor or lecturer. You should only use footnotes or endnotes to indicate or expand upon a relevant idea where to do so inside the text would distract the reader or disturb in some way the balance of the argument being presented. Be aware that going to a footnote can break the reader's attention to the argument, so use them sparingly.

## Presenting language examples

Any language expression cited as an example within the text is to be underlined or (preferably) italicized, e.g.:

> On the other hand, <u>the</u> is the definite article.

> The sentence *It is clear that this is so* contains an instance of extraposition.

Sentence examples, and sets of examples that are presented to contrast with one another, should normally be separated from text and numbered from (1). For example:

(1) It is obvious that this must be so.
(2) It was obvious that it was so.
(3) It will be obvious that it will be so.

Ungrammatical/unacceptable expressions are conventionally asterisked, e.g. *a chairs*; dubious expressions are annotated by '?', e.g. ?*a scissors*.

Glosses (translations) within examples should be presented as illustrated below. The second line gives the literal meaning, in order, of each lexical and grammatical element. The overall meaning (the third line) is usually given within double quotes (although alternative conventions are possible):

(4) M        -toto       a       -me      -ni      -lip    -a
    c1s       -child      3ssu     -PERF    -1sOB    -pay    -INDIC
    "The child has paid me"

(5) Mtoto                amenilipa
    c1s.child            3ssu.PERF.1sOB.pay.INDIC
    "The child has paid me"

## Reference list

Always attach at the end of your essay a reference list or bibliography listing all (and only) the works referred to in the text. These should be arranged in alphabetical order by the author's surname. Record each work only once, regardless of how many times you have referenced it in your essay. Where you have referred to several works by the same author, list these in chronological order. You need to give the following details in the following order:

author's surname
author's initials or first name
year of publication
title of article
title of journal or book (plus editors, if any)
volume and page number details (for articles)
publication details (for books)
date of access (for web references)

Again conventions will vary from department to department – even publishing houses do not agree on an established set of guidelines. Your department may have guidelines, or you could follow the conventions used in the books and articles you read. The following mini bibliography illustrates one of the widely used methods:

Cole, Peter and Jerry L. Morgan (eds) 1975. *Syntax and Semantics 3: Speech Acts*. New York: Academic Press.

Jacobsen, Anders 2002. American political correctness the word niggardly. http://www.jacobsen.no/anders/blog/archives/2002/09/03/americanpoliticalcorrectnessthe wordniggardly.html. Accessed October 2004.

Rosenberg, Jay and Charles Travis (eds) 1971. *Readings in the Philosophy of Language*. Englewood Cliffs: Prentice-Hall Inc.

Schiffer, Stephen R. 1972. *Meaning*. Oxford: Clarendon Press.

Schreiber, Peter A. 1972. Style disjuncts and the performative analysis. *Linguistic Inquiry* 3: 321–47.

Searle, John R. 1975a. Indirect speech acts. In *Syntax and Semantics 3: Speech Acts*, ed. by Peter Cole and Jerry L. Morgan. New York: Academic Press, pp. 59–82. Reprinted in John R. Searle *Expression and Meaning: Studies in the Theory of Speech Acts*. Cambridge: Cambridge University Press. 1979.

Searle, John R. 1975b. A taxonomy of illocutionary acts. In *Language, Mind, and Knowledge*, ed. by Keith Gunderson. Minneapolis: University of Minnesota Press, pp. 344–69. Reprinted in *Language in Society* 5, 1976: 1–23 and John R. Searle *Expression and Meaning: Studies in the Theory of Speech Acts*. Cambridge: Cambridge University Press. 1979.

Searle, John R. 1979. *Expression and Meaning: Studies in the Theory of Speech Acts*. Cambridge: Cambridge University Press.

A note of caution: some universities will not accept Wikipedia and the like as valid sources for citation in essays because of their unreliability. In our experience Wikipedia <http://www.wikipedia.org/> is more often than not accurate; however, it needs to be used with care. Where possible, information from Wikipedia should be backed up from other sources, because the authors are not strictly vetted.

## Plagiarism

Research is the ongoing enterprise of building on the foundations provided by discoveries already made (and indeed sometimes questioning and improving on these foundations). Thus in your essays and research reports, you will be placing your findings, ideas and interpretations within the academic context of work already done relating to your chosen topic. Your reader needs to see clearly and easily which ideas you are putting forth as your own, and which you have derived from someone else. Researchers have developed the conventions described above to help us in making the necessary distinctions. Plagiarism is the deliberate attempt to pass off work from another source as your own. It represents a serious breach of scholarly convention and is totally unacceptable. The penalties can be harsh, especially for repeat offenders. Of course, lecturers do recognize that at first year level the act may be inadvertent. To avoid plagiarizing unintentionally, always bear in mind that you claim to be the originator of any content that has not been specifically attributed to others.

Usually plagiarism is assumed to have taken place when someone has:

> copied published phrases and passages without quotation marks and without a reference to the author
> presented another person's idea as his or her own
> copied other students' work
> written something together with other students, without the permission of the relevant tutor or lecturer
> submitted a piece of work which has already been submitted for assessment in another course
> downloaded material from the internet without proper citation.

Most institutions will have their own specific guidelines on plagiarism and we advise you to check these out. Meanwhile the following set of hints will help you to avoid plagiarism:

> Make sure you take accurate notes. Always distinguish between your own ideas and the ideas of other writers.
> If you use ideas or opinions from any text (whether they are paraphrased, summarized or in quotation marks) then you must clearly indicate the sources you are using. See the above notes on referencing.
> Working together with other students is a good experience, but always formulate the final product by yourself.
> If you have discussed any aspects of your work with others, you should acknowledge

this contribution in a footnote. For example, 'I discussed this topic in a general way with J. Bloggs'. Thereafter, any specific idea that is not entirely your own would warrant a footnote such as: 'The main idea in this paragraph emerged from a discussion I had with J. Bloggs' or 'This idea was suggested to me by J. Bloggs'.

The following extracts from Burridge and Florey (2002) provide different examples of how to quote your sources, and how to include your own comments:

> The definition of 'intonation unit' which we use here follows Du Bois, Schuetze-Coburn, Cumming, and Paolino (1993: 46): "An intonation unit is a stretch of speech uttered under a single intonation contour. It tends to be marked by cues such as a pause and a shift upward in overall pitch level at its beginning, and a lengthening of its final syllable". Our data revealed occurrences of *yeah-no* within one or two intonation units. ...

> As a number people have discussed (for example, Wierzbicka 1994, Allan and Burridge 1991), Anglo culture operates with the idea of harmony in mind, with a strong preference for agreement and compromise. Social interaction is generally non-hostile. Face threats are minimized – in other words, we are conventionally polite, whatever we might be feeling deep down. The frequent coexistence of agreement and disagreement in conversations attests to this. As Wierzbicka (1994: 79) points out, there is an expression in the language that sums it up nicely – "Let's agree to disagree". *Yeah-no* quite obviously forms part of our repertoire of face-work or politeness strategies. But as is usual with these little conversational markers or particles, there are a number of uses involved and their meanings can be very difficult to pin down. This particular marker seems to have both discourse uses (creating cohesive discourse) and also clear pragmatic uses (expressing speaker attitudes and opinions). It therefore fulfils the functions of both discourse marker and pragmatic particle. ...

> Finally, these data point us in the direction of interesting gender-related research questions. Other studies drawing on conversational data suggest significant gender differences in conversational practices. For example, Pamela Fishman's 1989 research claims that women do more of the "conversational shitwork" – women work harder to initiate and maintain conversation than men yet are less successful. Janet Holmes (1995) also asserts that women are linguistically more supportive in interaction and their conversation generally contains more markers of politeness. Given the interactive politeness phenomena of *yeah-no*, we might therefore expect gender differences in our results. However, at this stage of our research these differences are not apparent.

Your task as a student writer is to make clear to the reader/marker how you have used and built on the ideas in your readings to construct your argument.

## Writing exams

If you are studying linguistics at tertiary level, you have already passed a lot of exams. What you now need to ensure is that you carry on doing those things that have been successful for you in the past, and try to get rid of any bad study habits that have not worked for you and may have hampered your success.

In exams you won't be tested simply on what you know and can remember (although that of course is an important part of the assessment process). Your lecturers will also be interested in finding out how well you apply your linguistic knowledge. As with your other assessment tasks, exams give you the chance to demonstrate your understanding of the subjects you have been studying, so in your exam preparation aim not merely to memorize but to understand the materials.

The difficult aspect of exams is always timing. You have to work under restrictive conditions and time constraints and this experience is usually stressful. A useful exercise is to work through past papers. (Some lecturers will make past exams available; often they are stored on library websites.) It is a good exercise to try working through the entire paper. This will give you an idea of how much you can get through within the allotted time.

As in essay writing, the key to success in exams is preparation. Revision for exams should start early in the semester and become more intense towards the end of the semester. Don't believe those who say they only start revision just before exams and yet fly through.

A good idea is to prepare a pre-exam study timetable. Make contact with other students and, if possible, form study groups with them.

On the day of the exam:

> Make sure you arrive in time (even early) – you want to be as relaxed as possible.
> During reading time, read through the entire paper and assign the time proportionally to each question.
> During the exam, keep to your allocated time. You will find that you can complete some questions more quickly, so you have time up your sleeve to revisit any weaker answers.
> Don't forget to read the question carefully so that you know exactly what is required of you and follow the instructions – don't answer three questions when the instructions require two; don't just 'describe' when you are required to 'discuss'; give examples if they are required.
> If you go blank, breathe deeply and don't panic. Sometimes it helps to just skip the question and start working on another one. The act of writing will help to trigger the answer and you can return to it later.
> Don't leave the exam early – use the time to check over your answers. Even good answers will benefit from some final polishing.
> If you run out of time, don't ignore any questions completely. It is far better to jot down an outline or rough plan of the answer – you will usually get some marks for this effort.

## Oral presentations

Many subjects require oral presentations in tutorials or in seminars, and like many students you may find these the most stressful and confronting forms of assessment. Most of us become nervous when we first have to speak in front of an audience. Just remember that with practice you can become an effective presenter.

The following are some useful tips when preparing for a seminar presentation:

> As with essay writing, pick a topic that interests you.
> Read the background material.

> Analyse your audience (decide how much they probably already know).

> Determine your key points (and remember that listening is hard work – your audience may only be able to recall two or three of these points).

> You need a strong introduction to catch the attention of your audience – point out what the main areas of focus will be.

> Select appealing examples and prepare necessary visual aids such as handouts or PowerPoint slides.

> Most presentations have a time limit. To keep within the allotted time, you need to plan carefully and rehearse.

> Audiences need summaries and concluding remarks. Remember that presentations are largely rated on the basis of the quality of their closing comments.

## A final note

Most universities have learning support units that offer workshops, focused study groups, and perhaps individual consultations. They provide a range of language and learning support resources to help students in the core study skills areas – lectures and tutorials, research reading, writing and oral presentations. Make use of these facilities and the resources they offer. Locate sources for help before you have a problem.

## References and additional readings

Allan, Keith and Kate Burridge 1991. *Euphemism and Dysphemism: Language Used as Shield and Weapon*. New York: Oxford University Press.

Baayen, R. Harald 2008. *Analyzing Linguistic Data: A Practical Introduction to Statistics Using R*. Cambridge: Cambridge University Press.

Brown, James D. 1988. *Understanding Research in Second Language Acquisition: A Teacher's Guide to Statistics and Research Design*. Cambridge: Cambridge University Press.

Brown, James D. 2006. Research methods for applied linguistics. In *The Handbook of Applied Linguistics*, ed. by Alan Davies and Catherine Elder. Oxford: Blackwell, pp. 476–500.

Burridge, Kate and Margaret Florey 2002. 'Yeah-no he's a good kid': a discourse analysis of *yeah-no* in Australian English. *The Australian Journal of Linguistics*, pp. 149–72.

Cadogan, John 1995. *Survive Exams: Study effectively and succeed*. Sydney: Hobsons Press.

Cameron, Deborah, E. Frazer, P. Harvey, M.B.H. Rampton and K. Richardson 1994. The relations between researcher and researched: ethics, advocacy and empowerment. In *Researching Language and Literacy in Social Context*, ed. by David Graddol, Janet Maybin and Barry Stierer. Clevedon: Multilingual Matters in association with the Open University, pp. 18–25.

Crystal, David 2003. *A Dictionary of Linguistics and Phonetics*. 5th edn. Oxford: Blackwell.

Crystal, David 2003. *The Cambridge Encyclopedia of the English Language*. Cambridge: Cambridge University Press.

Dornyei, Zoltan 2003. *Questionnaires in Second Language Research: Construction, Administration, and Processing*. Mahwah NJ: Lawrence Erlbaum.

Dornyei, Zoltan 2007. *Research Methods in Applied Linguistics: Quantitative, Qualitative, and Mixed Methodologies*. Oxford: Oxford University Press.

Hatch, Evelyn and Ann Lazaraton 1991. *Research Manual: Design and Statistics for Applied Linguistics*. New York: Newbury House.

Hillman, Kylie and Julie McMillan 2005. Transition to further education: the first year experience. *Professional Educator* 4/3: 6–9.

Honda, Maya and Wayne O'Neil 2007. *Thinking Linguistically: A Scientific Approach to Language*. Oxford and Malden MA: Blackwell.

Hunston, Susan 2002. *Corpora in Applied Linguistics*. Cambridge: Cambridge University Press.

Johnson, Keith 2008. *Quantitative Methods in Linguistics*. Oxford: Blackwell.

Johnson, Keith and Helen Johnson (eds) 1999. *The Encyclopedic Dictionary of Applied Linguistics*. Oxford: Blackwell.

Li, Wei 2000. Methodological questions in the study of bilingualism. In *The Bilingualism Reader*, ed. by Wei Li. London: Routledge, pp. 438–48.

McEnery, Tony and Andrew Wilson 2001. *Corpus Linguistics*. Edinburgh: Edinburgh University Press.

Oakes, Michael P. 1998. *Statistics for Corpus Linguistics*. Edinburgh: Edinburgh University Press.

Ochs, Eleanor 1999. Transcription as theory. In *The Discourse Reader*, ed. by Adam Jaworski and Nikolas Coupland. London: Routledge, pp. 167–82.

Quinn-Musgrove, Sandra L. 1991. *How to Pass Objective Examinations: And Other Considerations for Study*. Dubuque IA: Kendall/Hunt Publishing Co.

Richards, Jack C. and Richard Schmidt 2002. *Longman Dictionary of Language Teaching and Applied Linguistics*. 3rd edn. London: Longman.

Trask, Robert Lawrence 2000. *The Dictionary of Historical and Comparative Linguistics*. London: Routledge.

Wallace, Andrew, Tony Schirato and Philippa Bright 1999. *Beginning University: Thinking, Researching and Writing for Success*. London: Allen & Unwin.

Wray, Alison and Aileen Bloomer 2006. *Projects in Linguistics: A Practical Guide to Researching Language*. 2nd edn. London: Hodder Arnold.

## Some useful online resources

http://www.monash.edu.au/lls/llonline/index.xml
(Monash University: Language and Learning Online)

http://www.lc.unsw.edu.au/olib.html
(University of New South Wales Learning Centre: Academic Skills Resources)

http://www.fas.harvard.edu/%7Ewricntr/documents/Begin.html
(Beginning the Academic Essay: The Harvard University Writing Centre)

# 2 studying language: core topics

**2.1** phonetics – the science of speech sounds

**2.2** phonology – sound systems in languages

**2.3** morphology – word structures

**2.4** syntax

**2.5** fundamentals of semantics and pragmatics

**2.6** meaning, maxims, and speech acts

**2.7** sociolinguistics

**2.8** psycholinguistics

**2.9** applied linguistics

**2.10** historical linguistics

**2.11** stylistics

**2.12** discourse and conversation

**2.13** corpus linguistics

**2.14** digital tools in linguistics

**2.15** forensic linguistics

**2.16** from pictures to writing

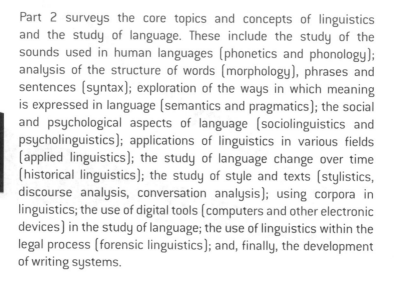

Part 2 surveys the core topics and concepts of linguistics and the study of language. These include the study of the sounds used in human languages (phonetics and phonology); analysis of the structure of words (morphology), phrases and sentences (syntax); exploration of the ways in which meaning is expressed in language (semantics and pragmatics); the social and psychological aspects of language (sociolinguistics and psycholinguistics); applications of linguistics in various fields (applied linguistics); the study of language change over time (historical linguistics); the study of style and texts (stylistics, discourse analysis, conversation analysis); using corpora in linguistics; the use of digital tools (computers and other electronic devices) in the study of language; the use of linguistics within the legal process (forensic linguistics); and, finally, the development of writing systems.

# 2.1 phonetics – the science of speech sounds

## chapter contents

> Phones and the organs of speech     31
> The International Phonetic Alphabet     34
> Articulation     35
> Vowels     35
> Consonants     37
> Key points     39
> References     39

Most of the phones on the International Phonetic Alphabet (IPA) chart (see Figure 2.2 on the next page) can be listened to (in 2009) using an interactive IPA chart online at http://web.uvic.ca/ling/resources/ipa/charts/IPAlab/IPAlab.htm. They are also available on an interactive CD-ROM *The Sounds of the International Phonetic Alphabet* available from the University College London Department of Phonetics and Linguistics: http://www.phon.ucl.ac.uk/shop/soundsipa.php.

## Phones and the organs of speech

Phonetics is the study of speech sounds (**phones**). Most language is spoken and heard, not written and read. Phonetics offers tools to identify, discriminate, interpret, describe and analyse the speech sounds that (if you are a hearing person) constantly surround you. Phonetics has application to language learning and teaching, audiology and speech pathology, sociology, psychology, computer speech recognition, and forensic science.

**Articulatory phonetics** investigates the production of phones and consequently the anatomy and physiology of speech, the process of articulation using vocal organs, and the description and classification of phones based on properties of the speech mechanism. The focus of **acoustic phonetics** is the variations in air pressure that are transmitted as a result of vocal organ activity. **Instrumental phonetics** uses instruments to examine the sound wave characteristics that have been converted to electrical energy, such as frequency (pitch) and intensity (amplitude). **Auditory phonetics** deals with the hearing process.

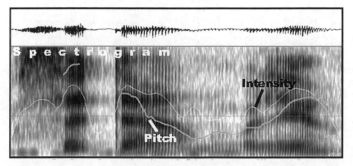

Figure 2.1 *A visual analysis of* Sit down will you?

# THE INTERNATIONAL PHONETIC ALPHABET (revised to 2005)

CONSONANTS (PULMONIC)  © 2005 IPA

| | Bilabial | Labiodental | Dental | Alveolar | Post alveolar | Retroflex | Palatal | Velar | Uvular | Pharyngeal | Glottal |
|---|---|---|---|---|---|---|---|---|---|---|---|
| Plosive | p b | | | t d | | ʈ ɖ | c ɟ | k g | q ɢ | | ʔ |
| Nasal | m | ɱ | | n | | ɳ | ɲ | ŋ | N | | |
| Trill | ʙ | | | r | | | | | R | | |
| Tap or Flap | | ⱱ | | ɾ | | ɽ | | | | | |
| Fricative | ɸ β | f v | θ ð | s z | ʃ ʒ | ʂ ʐ | ç ʝ | x ɣ | χ ʁ | ħ ʕ | h ɦ |
| Lateral fricative | | | | ɬ ɮ | | | | | | | |
| Approximant | | ʋ | | ɹ | | ɻ | j | ɰ | | | |
| Lateral approximant | | | | l | | ɭ | ʎ | L | | | |

Where symbols appear in pairs, the one to the right represents a voiced consonant. Shaded areas denote articulations judged impossible.

## CONSONANTS (NON-PULMONIC)

| Clicks | | Voiced implosives | | Ejectives | |
|---|---|---|---|---|---|
| ʘ | Bilabial | ɓ | Bilabial | ʼ | Examples: |
| ǀ | Dental | ɗ | Dental/alveolar | pʼ | Bilabial |
| ǃ | (Post)alveolar | ʄ | Palatal | tʼ | Dental/alveolar |
| ǂ | Palatoalveolar | ɠ | Velar | kʼ | Velar |
| ǁ | Alveolar lateral | ʛ | Uvular | sʼ | Alveolar fricative |

## OTHER SYMBOLS

ʍ  Voiceless labial-velar fricative

w  Voiced labial-velar approximant

ɥ  Voiced labial-palatal approximant

ʜ  Voiceless epiglottal fricative

ʢ  Voiced epiglottal fricative

ʡ  Epiglottal plosive

ɕ ʑ  Alveolo-palatal fricatives

ɺ  Voiced alveolar lateral flap

ɧ  Simultaneous ʃ and x

Affricates and double articulations can be represented by two symbols joined by a tie bar if necessary.  k͡p t͡s

## VOWELS

Where symbols appear in pairs, the one to the right represents a rounded vowel.

## SUPRASEGMENTALS

| | | |
|---|---|---|
| ˈ | Primary stress | |
| ˌ | Secondary stress | ˌfoʊnəˈtɪʃən |
| ː | Long | eː |
| ˑ | Half-long | eˑ |
| ˘ | Extra-short | ĕ |
| ǀ | Minor (foot) group | |
| ‖ | Major (intonation) group | |
| . | Syllable break | ɹi.ækt |
| ‿ | Linking (absence of a break) | |

## DIACRITICS

Diacritics may be placed above a symbol with a descender, e.g. ŋ̊

| | | | | | | | | |
|---|---|---|---|---|---|---|---|---|
| ̥ | Voiceless | n̥ d̥ | ̈ | Breathy voiced | b̤ a̤ | ̪ | Dental | t̪ d̪ |
| ̬ | Voiced | s̬ t̬ | ̰ | Creaky voiced | b̰ a̰ | ̺ | Apical | t̺ d̺ |
| ʰ | Aspirated | tʰ dʰ | ̼ | Linguolabial | t̼ d̼ | ̻ | Laminal | t̻ d̻ |
| ̹ | More rounded | ɔ̹ | ʷ | Labialized | tʷ dʷ | ̃ | Nasalized | ẽ |
| ̜ | Less rounded | ɔ̜ | ʲ | Palatalized | tʲ dʲ | ⁿ | Nasal release | dⁿ |
| ̟ | Advanced | u̟ | ˠ | Velarized | tˠ dˠ | ˡ | Lateral release | dˡ |
| ̠ | Retracted | e̠ | ˤ | Pharyngealized | tˤ dˤ | ̚ | No audible release | d̚ |
| ̈ | Centralized | ë | ̴ | Velarized or pharyngealized | ɫ | | | |
| ̽ | Mid-centralized | e̽ | ̝ | Raised | e̝ | (ɹ̝ = voiced alveolar fricative) | | |
| ̩ | Syllabic | n̩ | ̞ | Lowered | e̞ | (β̞ = voiced bilabial approximant) | | |
| ̯ | Non-syllabic | e̯ | ̘ | Advanced Tongue Root | e̘ | | | |
| ˞ | Rhoticity | ɚ a˞ | ̙ | Retracted Tongue Root | e̙ | | | |

## TONES AND WORD ACCENTS

| LEVEL | | | CONTOUR | | |
|---|---|---|---|---|---|
| e̋ or ꜛ | Extra high | | ě or ꜜ | | Rising |
| é ꜒ | High | | ê ꜔ | | Falling |
| ē ꜓ | Mid | | e̍ ꜕ | | High rising |
| è ꜔ | Low | | e̩ ꜖ | | Low rising |
| ȅ ꜕ | Extra low | | ᷈e | | Rising-falling |
| ↓ | Downstep | | ↗ | | Global rise |
| ↑ | Upstep | | ↘ | | Global fall |

Figure 2.2 *The International Phonetic Alphabet*

It begins with the vibrations that result from variations in air pressure creating a sound wave; this causes mechanical vibrations in the ear which generate an electrical signal that is carried by the auditory nerve to the brain.

All human speech organs originally had some primary function other than speech. Sound requires an energy source and for speech this is the stream of air that passes in and out of the lungs. When speaking we inhale very quickly and breathe out slowly because almost all speech uses the egressive airstream. Say *This is normal* and then try saying it again while drawing breath in instead of exhaling it: you can only speak on an ingressive airstream for a second or two. Therefore, no language routinely uses an ingressive airstream.

There are phones that don't use pulmonic air (i.e. air from the lungs). For example 'clicks' (heard in the late Miriam Makeba's 'Click Song' of 1960) are sharp suction noises made by the tongue against the teeth and other articulators. Clicks normally use air trapped when the back of the tongue blocks the mouth at the velum (see Figure 2.3, the Organs of speech diagram). Several clicks are found in the Khoisan and Nguni languages of southern Africa. The English sounds written *Tut! Tut!* are clicks; the same phone is used to gee-up horses.

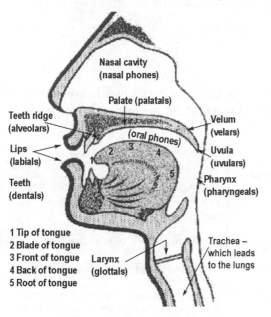

Figure 2.3 *Organs of speech*

Lung air is converted into audible vibrations using speech organs. Located at the top of the trachea in the lowest part of the vocal tract is the larynx or **glottis**, a tube consisting of ligaments and membranes within which are two bands of muscular tissue known as **vocal cords** (the 'sails' in Figure 2.4, adapted from www.wikipedia.org). Air expressed through the trachea from the lungs can vibrate the vocal cords as it passes through. Such vibration creates **voiced** phones. When the vocal cords are open and don't vibrate, a **voiceless** phone results. Touching your throat, utter voiced [zzz] and compare it with voiceless [sss]. Still touching your throat, alternate these phones [zzz sss zzz sss zzz sss] and you should feel the vibration turning on and off. Other familiar voiceless and voiced pairs are [p, b], [t, d], [f, v].

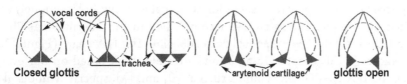

Figure 2.4 *The glottis (larynx)*

## The International Phonetic Alphabet

Writing systems rarely capture the spoken language in a completely consistent and systematic way. Look at the bolded italicized segments of the following words and the comment alongside them.

| | |
|---|---|
| **k**now, **m**nemonic, **g**nome, fo**l**k, **p**neumatic, L**ei**cester | Letters not pronounced |
| **t**alk, soo**t**, na**t**ion, **t**hrough, balle**t** | t pronounced differently in different environments |
| st**ow**, th**ough**, s**ew**, **o**ver, m**oa**t | Same vowel phone, different spellings |
| c**ough**, sl**ough**, thr**ough**, d**ough**, th**ough**t, b**ough** | Same spelling, different pronunciations |
| Edin**burgh**, Lough**borough** | Different spelling, same pronunciation, the vowel before the r not pronounced in most dialects of English. |

Search the web for a copy of *The Chaos* by Gerard Nolst Trenité (1870–1946) describing English spelling. It includes such lines as

Sounds like corpse, corps, horse and worse –
It will keep you, Susy, busy;
Make your head with heat grow dizzy;
Tear in eye your dress you'll tear –
So shall I. Oh hear my prayer.

For more than a millennium there have been attempts to reform spelling or to create a universal alphabet. To properly capture all the sounds that human beings can make there must be a special kind of graphic representation such that each symbol is uniquely associated with just one phone. This is almost accomplished in the International Phonetic Alphabet or **IPA**; see http://www.langsci.ucl.ac.uk/ipa/. The IPA chart (Figure 2.2) is reproduced earlier in this chapter. In addition to Romic script based on our everyday orthography, the IPA uses Greek symbols such as [θ] and [λ], special symbols like [ʃ] and [ʔ], turned symbols like [ʁ] and [ə], digraphs like [ʧ] constructed from two symbols, and it assigns new values to [x] and [q]. By convention, phonetic script is written between square brackets [ ].

## Articulation

Air passing from the lungs through the larynx can be modified by active and passive articulators. The **pharynx** (a continuation of the trachea above the larynx) is a muscular tube that can be widened or narrowed to produce pharyngeal consonants and pharyngealized vowels. The **velum** (soft palate) may be raised against the back wall at the top of the pharynx so that air can escape only through the mouth; most English vowels and consonants are such **oral** phones. The velum is lowered to let air pass through the nasal cavity and out through the nose to produce **nasal** phones. English nasal consonants have the oral cavity blocked at the lips for [m], at the teeth ridge for [n], and at the velum for [ŋ]: compare *dim* [dɪm], *din* [dɪn], *ding* [dɪŋ]. Finally, the velum may be lowered to allow air to escape through both nose and mouth creating **nasal(ized)** vowels, indicated by a DIACRITIC, the superscript '~' (tilde) over the vowel symbol, e.g. French *on*, [õ]. English *nun* and *none* are often pronounced with a nasalized vowel [nʌ̃n] because of the surrounding nasal consonants.

The tongue can move forward, backward, up, or down; it can lengthen, shorten, be made convex, concave or flat; it turns back on itself in retroflex phones (found, for example, in Indian languages, Mandarin, and Polish). It changes shape and position with remarkable speed and accuracy in normal speech. The tongue position is involved in the identification and description of all vowels and most consonants. All changes in configuration serve up to three purposes:

> To block the oral cavity at some point to create **stop** consonants, **flaps, trills**, nasals, and so on.
> To constrict the oral cavity so that air has difficulty passing through, causing it to vibrate noisily, creating **obstruents**.
> To shape the oral cavity, giving rise to different **vowel qualities**.

**unrounded (spread)   close, rounded   open**

*Figure 2.5 Degree of lip-rounding*

The lips can be completely closed to form consonants such as [m] and [p]. They can be held apart in varying degrees; be rounded or spread to create different sounds. They are open and unrounded for [a] as in *ah*; close and unrounded for [i] as in *beat*; close and round for the [w] and the [u] in *woo*.

## Vowels

A vowel is produced when there is no constriction or blockage in the oral cavity. Dialects of a language may differ markedly in the way that vowels are pronounced; there is much less dialectal variation in the pronunciation of consonants. In 1917 Daniel Jones, using X-rays, found that the vowel-making area is a small ellipse about 200 mm across that the highest point of tongue moves through. Tongue

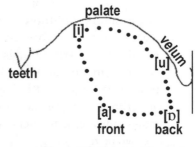

*Figure 2.6 Vowel-making area*

height is determined by movement of the jaw and tongue. The tongue travels through a range of points from **high** or **close** to **low** or **open**. High and close are alternative labels for the location of the tongue nearest the palate; and either low or open for the location furthest away. Articulate an [i] phone (as in *beat*) and contrast it with an [u] phone (as in *boot*). The [i] uses the front of the tongue and oral cavity, whereas the [u] uses the back. Check the notion of height by producing an [a] phone (as in *ah*) followed be an [i] phone. The jaw closes for [i] and opens for [a]; the tongue lies closer to the bottom of the vocal tract for [a] and moves nearer to the alveolar ridge or hard palate (roof of the mouth) for [i].

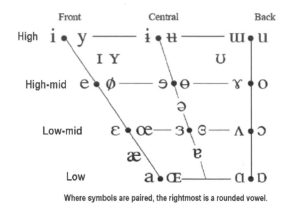

Where symbols are paired, the rightmost is a rounded vowel.

*Figure 2.7 The cardinal vowel quadrilateral*

The vowel boundaries are idealized in the cardinal vowel quadrilateral. [i, e, ɛ, æ, a] are unrounded front vowels; [y, ø, œ, ɶ] are rounded front vowels. [ɯ, ɤ, ʌ, ɑ] are unrounded back vowels; [u, o, ɔ, ɒ] are rounded back vowels. The quadrilateral is a map of the possibilities for the description of vowels that occur in whatever language variety is being described. A vowel is plotted according to (a) the highest point of the tongue between close and open (or high and low); (b) how far forward or back this point is; (c) degree of lip rounding. For example:

[i] is a high front unrounded vowel
[ʊ] is a raised high-mid fronted back rounded vowel (raising = made higher)
[ɔ] is a low-mid back rounded vowel
[ɑ] is a low back unrounded vowel
[ə] is schwa, the central vowel

Vowels are classified into **monophthongs**, where the tongue holds just one position; **diphthongs** such as [ɔɪ] where the tongue moves between two positions; and **triphthongs** like [aʊə] where it moves through three positions (see Figure 2.8). Each of the underlined parts of the words in the tables indicates a distinct vowel (there are two in *apart*).

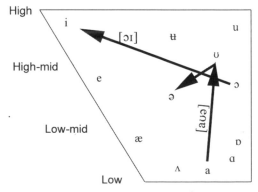

*Figure 2.8 Diphthong and triphthong (Australian English)*

*Monophthongs (the tongue holds just one position)*

| beat | [i] | | bit | [ɪ] |
|------|-----|---|-----|-----|
| bet | [ɛ] | | bat | [æ] |
| apart | [ə] and [a] or [ɑ] | | Bert | [ɜ] |
| Bart | [a] or [ɑ] | | but | [ʌ] |
| pot | [ɒ] | | port | [ɔ] |
| put | [ʊ] | | boot | [u] |

*Diphthongs (the tongue moves through two positions):*

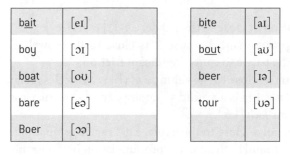

| bait | [eɪ] | | bite | [aɪ] |
|------|------|---|------|------|
| boy | [ɔɪ] | | bout | [aʊ] |
| boat | [oʊ] | | beer | [ɪə] |
| bare | [eə] | | tour | [ʊə] |
| Boer | [ɔə] | | | |

*Triphthongs (the tongue moves through three positions):*

| fire | [aɪə] | | tower | [aʊə] |
|------|-------|---|-------|-------|

Vowels are also classified for length: short as in *bit*, [bɪt]; half-long as in *beat*, [biˑt]; long as in *bead*, [biːd]. Note the symbols · half length, : long.

## Consonants

Consonants result from constriction or blockage in the oral cavity. One criterion for defining a consonant is its **place of artic-ulation**, where the constriction or blockage occurs. A second criterion is **manner of articulation**, what kind of constriction or blockage it is. These are usually the only two parameters used with the class of conson-ants that are normally voiced, known as **sonorants**. The sonorant consonants are, by manner of articulation: **flaps, trills, laterals, glides**, and **nasals**. Members of the class of consonants known as **obstruents** are described in terms of three parameters: **voicing**; **place of articulation**; **manner of articulation**. Obstruents include by manner of articulation: **stops, fricatives**, and **affricates**. (Obstruents are named for being supposedly more obstructive to the air stream than sonorants; but the character of trills and flaps must throw doubt on this claim.)

Starting in the top left corner of the IPA chart (Figure 2.2) and mostly sticking with sounds familiar in English: **Bilabials** (place of articulation) involve both lips. For example, [p] is a voiceless bilabial stop; [b] is a voiced bilabial stop. **Stops** result from complete blockage of the oral cavity (this is the manner of articulation). They are often released with plosion, so stops are also called **plosives**. [m] is a bilabial nasal (nasality is a manner of articulation).

**Labiodentals** (place of articulation) involve the bottom lip and top teeth, e.g. [f] is a voiceless labiodental fricative; [v] is its voiced counterpart. **Fricatives** (manner of articu-lation) result from a narrow constriction that causes significant friction; e.g. the voiceless fricatives [s], [f], [θ] (the initial phones in *sin, fin* and *thin*).

**Dental** fricatives have the tip or blade of the tongue just behind or poked through the teeth: the voiceless dental fricative is [θ]; its voiced counterpart is [ð], 'eth' as in *this*. Many European languages and some Irish dialects have dental stops [t̪] (voiceless) and [d̪], which is voiced. Note the subscripted tooth ̪ under the dental phone. In most English dialects the *t* in *eighth* [eɪt̪θ] is dental (because it is assimilated to the following dental fricative). For the same reason the *n* in *tenth* is also dental [tɛn̪θ].

**Alveolars** have the tip or blade of the tongue on or close to the alveolar ridge behind the top teeth. [s] and [z] are alveolar fricatives; most English *t*s and *d*s are alveolar stops. An alveolar **flap** has the blade of the tongue hit the alveolar ridge, e.g. [ɾ] as in Australian English *better* [bɛɾʌ]; American [bɛɾɚ] or [bɛɾəʲ] also has a **rhotic** (*r*-sounding) final segment [ɚ]=[əˠ]. An alveolar **trill** [r] has the tongue tip set in rapid vibration, e.g. Italian [r] in *Parigi* [pariʤi]. For most English dialects *r*, as in *right* [ɹaɪt], is pronounced [ɹ] an alveolar **approximant** (it is close to the teeth ridge, but not close enough to cause significant friction).

**Postalveolars** (formerly called 'palatoalveolars') have the blade or front of the tongue behind the alveolar ridge but in front of the palate, e.g. [ʃ] as in *shut* [ʃʌt] is a voiceless postalveolar fricative; its voiced counterpart is [ʒ] as in some pronunciations of the final consonant of *garage* (and French *je* [ʒə]). The postalveolar **affricates** have the tongue move from complete blockage to narrow constriction (hence are represented by a digraph of stop+fricative), e.g. *judge* [ʤʌʤ]. [ʤ] is a voiced postalveolar affricate; its voiceless counterpart is found initially in [ʧʌkɫ], *chuckle*.

Alveolar fricatives [s, z], affricates [ts, ʣ], postalveolar fricatives [ʃ, ʒ], and affricates [ʧ, ʤ] are all **sibilants**.

**Palatals** have the front of the tongue on or close to the palate, e.g. [j] as in *yet* [jɛt] is a palatal semivowel (see below) and **approximant**, because it is close to the vowel [i] found in *beat* but not close enough to the palate to cause significant friction.

**Velars** have the back of the tongue on or close to the velum, e.g. [k] is a voiceless velar stop, and [ŋ] a velar nasal as in [kɪŋ] *king*. [g] is a voiced velar stop, and [x] a voiceless velar fricative such as is common in Scots *loch* [lɔx].

**Uvulars** have the back of the tongue on or close to the uvula, e.g. French [ʁ] in *rapide* [ʁapid]. The voiceless uvular stop [q] is found in the correct pronunciation of the Arabic letter *qaf* ق in *al-Qaeda* (القاعدة).

**Pharyngeals** have the root of the tongue close to the wall of the pharynx, e.g. Arabic ح [ħ] is a voiceless pharyngeal fricative as in [ħamala] "carried".

The **glottal stop** [ʔ] is caused by closing then releasing the vocal cords. It is represented in regular orthography by ' as in Arabic *arba'a* "four" and in Cockney pronunciations of the medial and final *t* in, for example, *butter* ⇒ *bu'er* [bʌʔə] and *pot* ⇒ *po'* [pʰɒʔ]. [h] and its voiced counterpart [ɦ] are glottal fricatives (usually with almost no friction).

**Laterals** (L sounds) are made with the tongue tip, blade or front anchored and air passes along one or both sides (i.e. laterally). At the beginning of a word like *lull* the *l* is an alveolar lateral [l] but, in most dialects, at the end of the word, the *ll* is a velarized lateral, symbolized [ɫ]; the back of the tongue approaches the velum (try saying *lull* [lʌɫ] and feel the different tongue positions). Sometimes R and L sounds are grouped as **liquids**, because in many languages they are not differentiated.

**Glides** have the tongue closer to the roof of the mouth than for a vowel but not as close as for a fricative consonant. In many English dialects the initial consonants in *Really you're weird* will be glides [ɹ, j, w]. The palatal glide [j] and the labiovelar glide [w] are often called **semivowels** because of the characteristics they share with the vowels [i] and [u] respectively. **Labiovelars** like [w] involve a **coarticulation**, being part bilabial and part velar.

Superscript ʰ indicates **aspiration**. Thus [tʰ] symbolizes an aspirated voiceless alveolar stop such as is found in most native English dialects in the word *two* [tʰuː]. Other aspirated voiceless stops are found in *pie* [pʰaɪ], and *caught* [kʰɔt]. Stress (see Chapter 2.2) is marked by the stroke before the first syllable of *barter* [ˈbaˑtʰə].

## References

Brown, E. Keith (General editor) 2006. *Encyclopedia of Languages and Linguistics*. 2nd edn. 14 vols. Oxford: Elsevier.

Clark, John, Colin Yallop and Janet Fletcher 2007. *An Introduction to Phonetics and Phonology*. 3rd edn. Malden MA: Blackwell.

Ladefoged, Peter 2006. *A Course in Phonetics*. 5th edn, with CD-ROM. Boston MA: Thomson Wadsworth.

# 2.2 phonology – sound systems in languages

## chapter contents

> Phonemes 40
> The difference between phones and phonemes 42
> Assigning allophones to phonemes 42
> Alternative analyses 44
> Phonotactics 44
> Syllable structures 45
> Stress and tone 46
> Intonation 46
> Disjuncture 47
> Key points 48
> References 48

## Phonemes

Phonetics studies phones (speech sounds); **phonology** examines the relationships among sounds in particular languages.

No matter what language is being used, speakers utter phones in a certain place at a certain time. A phone is not bound to any one language. Human beings can produce an unbounded number of phones, but in any particular language only comparatively few phones are used to indicate meaning differences such as between *bit, beat, pit* and *beak* in English. In these words, /b/ contrasts with /p/, /ɪ/ with /i/, /t/ with /k/: each of these is **a phoneme of English**. Note that phonemes are written between slashes / /.

In the English words *pit* [pʰɪt] and *bit* [bɪt] the 'p' and 'b' contrast with one another to indicate the difference in meaning. However there is no such contrast between [p] and [b] in most Australian Aboriginal languages. In some of them there is a phonemic contrast between dental and alveolar phones with the same manner of articulation, e.g. Kalkatungu /iṯi/ "type of ant" vs /iti/ "to go back". Most English speakers have great difficulty hearing the difference between say [n̪] as in [tʰɛn̪θ] and [n] as in [tʰɛn]. This is because in English there is no phonemic distinction between [n̪] and [n]; but there is phonemic contrast between /p/ and /b/. In the Aboriginal languages referred to above, the converse holds: for them there is a phonemic contrast between /n̪/ and /n/ but none between [p] and [b].

Thai has a phonemic contrast between aspirated /pʰ/ and unaspirated /p/: e.g. /pʰaː/ "split" vs /paː/ "forest". In English there is no such phonemic distinction between aspirated and unaspirated voiceless stops. In most English dialects *pub* is pronounced [pʰʌb], in a few [pʌb]. In English [pʰ] and [p] count as variant realizations (pronunciations) of the same phoneme /p/.

Members of a **minimal pair** differ by just one phone in the same environment resulting in a meaning difference. Earlier we contrasted minimal pairs:

Thai /pʰaː/ and /paː/ "split" vs "forest"   English /pɪt/ and /bɪt/ *pit* vs *bit*

Minimal pairs provide the optimal contrastive environment.

Two phones are allophones of different phonemes in language L if they contrast with one another (i.e. if they indicate a meaning difference) in identical environments. All phones which are realizations of a **phoneme α in language L** are **allophones** of the phoneme α.

The English phonemes /p/ and /b/ contrast initially, medially, and finally in a word:

| /p/ | | /b/ | |
|---|---|---|---|
| /pɪt/ | vs | /bɪt/ | initially |
| /dæpl/ | vs | /dæbl/ | medially |
| /hɒp/ | vs | /hɒb/ | finally |

Two phonetically similar phones, like [pʰ] and [p] in English, are allophones of the same phoneme in L if they can occur in the same environment without indicating a change in meaning.

Where there is more than one allophone for a phoneme, it is usual for the different allophones to be in **complementary distribution**. For most English speakers, the initial /p/ of a stressed syllable is aspirated as in [pʰɪt] whereas following /s/, as in [spɪt], the /p/ is unaspirated. We therefore say that the [pʰ] and [p] allophones of English /p/ are in complementary distribution, that is, they occur in different environments.

The English phonemes /h/ and /ŋ/ do not contrast directly with one another at all, because of their complementary distribution. (Think about *hanger, unhappy, aha, thanks* /ˈhæŋə, ʌnˈhæpɪ, aˈhaː, θæŋks/.) However /h/ and /ŋ/ are not allophones of the same phoneme because they are not phonetically similar (they have very little in common). If there is any phonetic similarity at all between a pair of phonemes, they will always contrast in at least one environment.

In word-final position, English /p/ has the allophones [p], [pʰ], and [p˺] (unaspirated, aspirated, unreleased). Possible pronunciations for /sip/ (*seep*) are [siˑp], [siˑpʰ], and [siˑp˺]. The unreleased stop also occurs before bilabials (cf. *Chapman, clipboard,* and *sharp practice*). What is true for /p/ in this position is also true for /t/ and /k/. Generalizing: the allophones of voiceless stops in word-final position are in **free variation**.

We are now in a position to make a general statement on the allophones of the phoneme /p/ in English:

/p/  →  [pʰ]  initially in stressed syllables
      [p˺]  before bilabials
      [p]  elsewhere
      All allophones of /p/ can occur word-finally.

The first line reads 'the phoneme /p/ is realized as the allophone [pʰ] when it occurs initially in stressed syllables'. The second line: 'the phoneme /p/ is realized as the allophone [p˺] when it occurs before bilabials'. Note that the sequence of rules is significant in that the first line outranks the second and the second outranks the third.

## The difference between phones and phonemes

A phone is a speech sound, irrespective of language. It is an **etic** entity, a natural phenomenon that issues from the mouth of a speaker and, strictly speaking, it can only ever occur once (at a certain time and place). Phonemes, however, are constituents of the systematic description of the phonology of a particular language, L. The phonology of L is a linguist's description of the structure of L's sound system. The phoneme (an **emic** entity) is a theoretical construct, whereas a phone is a physical reality. A phoneme of language L:

> is the smallest unit of sound that distinguishes words in L
> cannot be uttered by a speaker at some particular time, in some particular place, though its allophones are uttered (as phones)
> is an abstract object in the sense that it cannot itself be heard, audio-recorded, or measured acoustically (only an allophone can).

Most languages have between 20 and 50 phonemes, whereas the number of phones is unbounded.

Allophones are phonetically similar phones which are in complementary distribution with each other in at least one environment. An allophone is an etic counterpart to the (emic) phoneme. An allophone is a phone used in a particular language L as the realization of a phoneme in L.

### Symbolizing phonemes

Because phonemes are not themselves pronounced (their allophones are), we could symbolize them any way at all! For example, provided that we distinguish the phonemes /p/, /b/ and /i/ in English we could symbolize them respectively / ♉ /, / ☿ / and / ♒ /. Thus the word *beep* would be phonemically / ☿ ♒ ♉ /. Although theoretically possible, this is not practical; so phonemes are usually symbolized with the same letter as one of their allophones, wherever possible preferring a common alphabet symbol to an exotic one. For instance, the English phoneme which is typically realized by the allophone [ɹ] is usually symbolized /r/ for convenience, e.g. /ræt/. And the standard phonemic representation /bip/ for *beep* is much easier to comprehend than / ☿ ♒ ♉ /.

## Assigning allophones to phonemes

Look at the following phonetically transcribed data and determine from it whether [x] and [ç] are allophones of the same or of different phonemes in German. (Assume you can decide the matter on the data presented here. Find these phones on the IPA chart, Figure 2.2, given in Chapter 2.1. Describe their phonetic characteristics, i.e. voicing, place and manner of articulation.)

| | | | | | | |
|---|---|---|---|---|---|---|
| 1. | [buːx] | book | | 5. | [mɪç] | me |
| 2. | [bɑx] | brook | | 6. | [ziːç] | sickly |
| 3. | [hoːx] | high | | 7. | [pɛç] | pitch |
| 4. | [nɔx] | still | | | | |

(a) In what ways are [x] and [ç] phonetically similar?
(b) How are [x] and [ç] phonetically different?
(c) Are [x] and [ç] more similar than different?
(d) Are [x] and [ç] in complementary distribution?

Check the data 1–7 for minimal pairs; if there are none, **construct a table of comparison** in which to compare the environments in which the two allophones occur. # symbolizes a syllable (and consequently, word) boundary.

| x | ç |
|---|---|
| u # | ɪ # |
| ɑ # | i # |
| o # | ɛ # |
| ɔ # | |

(e) How do the environments of [x] and [ç] differ?
(f) What do the vowels preceding [x] have in common which is different from the vowels preceding [ç]?

You should conclude that in German [x] and [ç] are phonetically similar and that they are in complementary distribution when word-final (from the data given, we don't know what happens in any other location). Consequently, they are allophones of the same phoneme. We shall name this phoneme /x/ (why not /ç/?). Conclusion:

In German, word-finally,
/x/ ⟶ [ç] following a front vowel
[x] following a back vowel

'Word-finally in German, phoneme /x/ is pronounced [ç] following a front vowel, and [x] following a back vowel.' The **phonemic** transcription of the German word for "still" is /nox/ and "pitch" is /pex/.

Consider the phonetic difference between [x] and [ç] – which is closer to the front? Does this suggest any correlation with the fact that, in German, [ç] follows front vowels and [x] back vowels? The answer is YES! Note that a comparison of the phonetic characteristics of the allophones and those of their environments can sometimes prove revealing.

## Alternative analyses

Voiced stops are never systematically aspirated in English. Initial voiceless stops in a stressed syllable are distinguished from homorganic initial voiced stops on two criteria: voicing and aspiration, cf. *pit* [pʰɪt] vs *bit* [bɪt]. (**Homorganic** means that they have the same place of articulation – /p/ and /b/ are both bilabial.) Here is a problem: in the word *spit* the phone represented by the grapheme <p> is an unaspirated voiceless bilabial stop, cf. [spɪt].

> Being voiceless, is this an allophone of the English phoneme /p/?
> Being unaspirated is it an allophone of /b/?

Compare the relevant **distinctive features** of /b/ and [p]:

| /b/ | [p] |
|-----|-----|
| +bilabial | +bilabial |
| –aspirate | –aspirate |
| +voice | –voice |

The only way that the [p] in *spit* could be an allophone of /b/ is by assimilation to the preceding voiceless [s]. Look at the table below in which the subscript ring ˌ indicates voicelessness.

| slither | smooth | snow | play | pray | tray |
|---------|--------|------|------|------|------|
| [sl̥ɪðə] | [sm̥uːð] | [sn̥oʊ] | [pl̥eɪ] | [pɹ̥eɪ] | [tɹ̥eɪ] |

In English, where the first consonant in a syllable-initial consonant cluster is voiceless, the whole cluster is often voiceless. It is, therefore, possible that *spit* is **phonemically** /sbɪt/ in English, and the allophone of /b/ here is [p]. Here # marks a syllable boundary and the slash / links what happens to where it happens.

English /b/ → [p] / [ #s___ ]

We could have written /b/ → [b̥] / [ #s___ ], but [b̥] = [p] so why bother?

We now have two phonemic analyses for *spit*: /spɪt/ and /sbɪt/. The only way to choose between them is on the basis of commonsense. Where a bilabial stop forms part of a syllable initial consonant cluster beginning with /s/, the bilabial stop will be the voiceless allophone [p]. English has a voiceless bilabial stop phoneme /p/, so the simplest solution to our problem is to assign [p] as an allophone of /p/. In linguistic analysis, it is always advisable to use commonsense.

## Phonotactics

In English, the allophones [n] and [ŋ] normally contrast, e.g. in [θɪn] *thin* and [θɪŋ] *thing*, and so we assign them to the different phonemes /n/ and /ŋ/. But [n] and [ŋ] can be interchangeable when the alveolar nasal precedes a velar consonant, e.g. *encrusted* can be pronounced [ɛnˈkɹʌstɪd] or [ɛŋˈkɹʌstɪd] (ˈ marks stress). This variation is

**phonetically conditioned**, so it is not a case of free variation. Instead, we say that the phonemic contrast between /n/ and /ŋ/ in English is, or may be, **neutralized** by a following velar consonant.

/n/ → /ŋ/ / ___ [+velar]

To be read: the phoneme /n/ is changed into /ŋ/ in the environment of (/) a following velar phone (___ [+velar]). Consequently, we can phonemically transcribe *encrusted* two ways: /ɛnˈkrʌstɪd/ or /ɛŋˈkrʌstɪd/. The neutralization of contrast between nasals is found in many languages.

Voiceless phones between voiced ones often get voiced, e.g. *bitter* [bɪrə], *battle* [bært̬], *behind* [bɪˈɦaɪnd]. The rule for this as follows:

[–voice] → [+voice] / [+voice] ___ [+voice]

**Assimilation** is common in all languages, for instance oral vowels may (as we've seen) be nasalized through assimilation to surrounding nasals. A nasal may be assimilated to the place of articulation of the following phone, compare *inexact* [ɪnɪɡˈzækˀt] with *incredible* [ɪŋˈkɹ̥ɛdᵊb̥ɫ]; this is reflected in the spelling of *impossible* and *illiterate* in which the first syllable derives from the negator *in–*. **Elision** occurs where *sixths* is pronounced /sɪkθs/ or /sɪksː/; *do you* → /dju/ and there is **coalescence** when [alveolar] + [palatal] → [postalveolar] such that /dju/ is pronounced [dʒu]. **Epenthesis** (putting in an additional phone) may occur when *tower* /taʊə/ is pronounced /taᵘwə/, *dreamt* is pronounced /drɛmpt/, and *saw him* is /ˈsɔrɪm/. Old English *thymel* is now *thimble*: epenthetic /b/ has been conventionally inserted between /m/ and /l/, not only in pronunciation, but in spelling too.

## Syllable structures

| Metrical feet | Different metrical feet combine strong ('long') and weak ('short') syllables differently. |
|---|---|
| Trochee trips from long to short;<br>From long to long in solemn sort<br>Slow Spondee stalks; strong foot! yet ill able<br>Ever to come up with Dactyl trisyllable.<br>Iambics march from short to long:<br>With a leap and a bound the swift Anapaests throng.<br>(Samuel T. Coleridge) | A trochee is strong+weak;<br>spondee is strong+strong;<br>dactyl is strong+weak+weak;<br>iamb is weak+strong; and<br>anapaests are weak+weak+strong |

All languages have **syllables**. Syllables are pulmonic (chest) pulses that give rhythm to speech.

If C is a consonant, V is a vowel, [+C, +sonorant] is one of /m̩, n̩, l̩, r̩/, and parentheses indicate optionality, then English may have syllables with any combination of (C)(C)(C)V(C)(C)(C)(C) or [+C, +sonorant] such that V or [+C, +sonorant] is the syllable **nucleus**. For example *a* consists of V, /ə/; *an* of VC, /ən/; *band* of CVCC, /bænd/; *kitten* of CVCC̩, /kɪtn̩/. English syllable onsets with three phonemes all consist of

/s/⁀voiceless stop⁀liquid⁀V(C)(C)(C)(C)   e.g. /spleɪ, stræŋgld/.

Other words with four final consonants are /mæntlz, dɪsˈgrʌntld, ɪgˈzɛmpts, strɛŋθnz/.

Syllable structures vary across languages: Swahili *mbwa* /ˈm̩bwa/ has a sequence impossible for English; and Russian consonant в /v/ *to, into* could not function as an English syllable. Japanese syllables are CV([+C, +nasal]), so borrowings from English tend to have vowels inserted into the consonant clusters of the originals, and final consonants have vowels added:

| | | |
|---:|:---:|:---|
| *Let's* [speak] *English!* | ⇒ | Retsu ingurishu |
| *France* | ⇒ | Furansu |
| *privacy* | ⇒ | puraibashii |
| *Smith* | ⇒ | Sumisu |
| *table* | ⇒ | teeburu |

## Stress and tone

Both stress and tone fall on the syllable nucleus. They are emic categories. Phonetically, **stress** is marked movement or sustention of pitch, and this is often accompanied by greater amplitude (loudness) and greater duration (length) in the stressed syllable than is to be found in the adjoining syllables. There is primary and secondary stress, the latter marked by a subscript stroke ˌ . Compare /ˈfoʊtəˌgræf/, /ˌfoʊtəˈgræfɪk/, /fəˈtɒgrəfə/. In many languages stress is phonemic; for instance, Italian contrasts /ˈprintʃipi/ "princes" with /prinˈtʃipi/ "principles"; English contrasts the noun /ˈɛkspɔt/ with the verb /ɛkˈspɔt/.

Phonetically, **tone** is pitch level (measured in Hertz, Hz). Tone is phonemic in tone languages like Chinese. Mandarin has one neutral and four marked tones. The way they sound can be represented as in the following rectangle (left below).

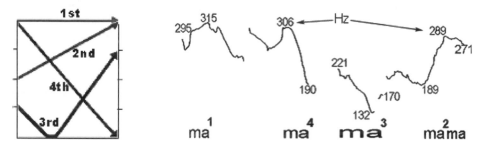

*ma¹* (or *mā*) "mother"
*ma²* (or *má*) "hemp"
*ma³* (or *mǎ*) "horse"
*ma⁴* (or *mà*) "scold"
*ma* [when sentence final] "question marker"
妈妈骂马的麻吗? *ma¹ma ma⁴ ma³ de ma² ma?* "Is mama scolding the horse's hemp?" (which doesn't make much sense).

## Intonation

**Intonation** is the variation in pitch over a sense (meaning) group rather than a syllable. The same word or sequence of words uttered with different intonation patterns conveys different meanings. For instance *Yès!* (fall tone) is assertive; *Yês* (rise-fall) is confirmatory or advisive; *Yěŝ* (fall-rise-fall) means "You've got it absolutely right"; *Yés?* (rise) is inquiring; *Yēs* (level) indicates there is more to say; and so on. And compare the statement

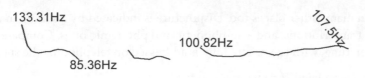

133.31Hz

100.82Hz

107.5Hz

85.36Hz

## John's gone toNew York

with the questioning

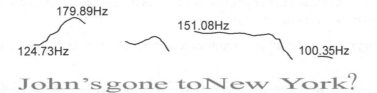

179.89Hz

124.73Hz

151.08Hz

100.35Hz

## John's gone toNew York?

Intonation is also found in tone languages; compare

| 他 在 读书。 | 他 在 读书? |
|---|---|
| Ta zai dushu. | Ta zai dushu? |
| He is reading. [Statement] | He is reading? [Question] |

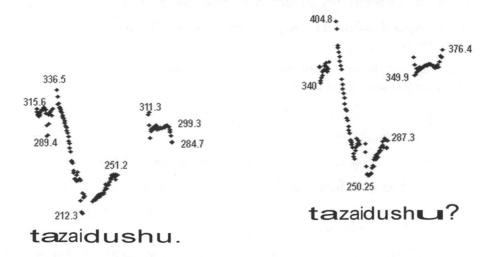

In both English and Chinese, statements tend to having falling intonation, but the same form of words can be turned into a question using rising intonation. This difference is common across languages.

## Disjuncture

Disjuncture is a purposeful brief cessation of the articulatory mechanism (a pause) which is not the accidental consequence of articulating a stop phone. Disjunctures occur not only where punctuation marks like commas, colons, full stops, and so on appear in written texts, but in many other places too. Disjuncture is indicated by a slash / in ordinary orthographic transcriptions, and + in phonetic and phonemic ones. Compare (1), where John has been rung, with (2), where John is addressed on telephoning the speaker.

(1) *Thanks for ringing John.* /ˌθæŋksfərɪŋɪnˈʤɒn/
(2) *Thanks for ringing, / John.* /ˌθæŋksfəˈrɪŋɪŋ + ˈʤɒn/

## Key points

> Whereas phonetics is the study of the phones that human beings can make, phonology is the study of the sound systems of languages.

> A phoneme of language L is the smallest significant unit in the phonological analysis of L.

> A phoneme is a theoretical construct that is realized through utterance of its allophones.

> The allophones of phoneme α in language L are phonetically similar phones in complementary distribution with each other (i.e. occur in different environments).

> Two phones are allophones of different phonemes in L if they contrast (indicate a meaning difference) in identical environments.

> A table of comparison is a useful device for comparing the environments of phones to determine whether they are allophones of the same phoneme.

> In phonological analysis, it is always wise to bear in mind the phonetic characteristics of any phone.

> Look out for phonetic conditioning in the distribution of the allophones of a phoneme (be aware that there may not be any).

> Phonotactics is the effect of phones on their environment.

> The permissible sequences of phonemes in a syllable vary from language to language.

> Stress and tone fall on the syllable nucleus, a sonorant and typically a vowel.

> Word meanings are differentiated by stress in some languages and by tone in others.

> Intonation is variation of pitch over a sense group; it is found in stress languages like English and tone languages like Chinese.

> Additional information may be found at http://www.wikipedia.org/; in Brown 2006; Roca and Johnson 1999; and Clark, Yallop and Fletcher 2006.

## References

Brown, E. Keith (General editor) 2006. *Encyclopedia of Languages and Linguistics.* 2nd edn. 14 vols. Oxford: Elsevier.

Clark, John, Colin Yallop and Janet Fletcher 2006. *An Introduction to Phonetics and Phonology.* 3rd edn. Malden MA: Blackwell.

Roca, Iggy and Wyn Johnson 1999. *A Course in Phonology.* Oxford: Blackwell.

# 2.3 morphology – word structures

## chapter contents

> Problems with the notion 'word'                49
> Morphemes, allomorphs, and lexemes            50
> Morphosyntactic classes                        51
> Inflectional and derivational morphology       52
> Morphological analysis                         53
> Word formation                                 54
> Morphological typology                         54
> Key points                                     55
> References                                     56

## Problems with the notion 'word'

If morphology is about word structure, what is a word? To define it as a **collection of letters separated by spaces** is applicable only to languages with a writing system like ours (not, for instance, to Chinese or Japanese). In Ancient Greece and Rome words were not separated by spaces in the writing system; nor are they in Chinese. Below is part of the Greek inscription from the Rosetta Stone (left) and the Chinese for "He is reading" (right).

ΒΑΣΙΛΕΥΟΝΤΟΣΤΟΥΝΕΟΥΚΑΙΠΑΡΑΛΛΒΟΝΤΟΣ          他在读书。

(See Chapter 2.16 for a discussion of writing systems.)

Furthermore, preliterate language users have a concept of the word (see Sapir 1949: 33f.). And although we use words in speaking, it is certainly not the case that spoken words are bounded by pauses; if you listen to an utterance in an unfamiliar language, it is impossible to distinguish one word from another. It is often the case that **words are isolable constituents of language**. But some words have more than one pronunciation, e.g. *either* can be pronounced /iðə/ or /aɪðə/ and *the* is mostly /ðə/, but /ði/ before vowels. Then there are **homophones** like *too, two, to* and **homographs** like *lead* "metal" /lɛd/ vs "leash" /lid/. Some of these are **distinguished by meaning**, but /iðə/ and /aɪðə/ are in free variation and have the same meaning. And consider the set *happy, unhappy, wrap* and *unwrap*. There are two pairs of words distinguished from each other by meaning and they share a common segment, *un–*. English speakers will support the idea that *un–* has an identifiable meaning – it is a negator – but not that it is a word, because *un–* is unable to **stand on its own**.

So there is no single criterion for identifying a word.

# Morphemes, allomorphs, and lexemes

**A morpheme is the smallest unit of syntactic analysis with semantic specification** (i.e. the smallest unit that is itself meaningful). A word like *unhappy* consists of two morphemes *un + happy*. Each morpheme is associated with a particular meaning but in this case they differ in status. *Happy* is known as a **free** morpheme, that is, it can stand alone as a word, while *un–* is a **bound** morpheme and must be attached to a free morpheme.

> A free form is one that can stand alone in some syntactic structure in the language. Otherwise the form is bound.

The meaning of the English word *rabbits* is transparently composed from the meaning of the noun *rabbit* and the plural morpheme PL indicated by the final *–s*. The plural morpheme in English is instantiated by a variety of **allomorphs**, e.g. the bold italic parts of

cat*s*, bush*es*, th*ese*, ox*en*, m*i*ce, dat*a*, cherub*im*, two sheep (ZERO MORPH)

Whereas the **morph** is a form (an etic category), the morpheme is emic, i.e. an abstract theoretical construct. To introduce some more morphological jargon, consider the structure of the plural noun *undesirables* "people who are undesirable".

| | |
|---|---|
| $[_N$*undesirable-s*$_N]$ <br> STEM-SUFFIX | The suffix *–s* makes the noun stem plural. |
| $[_{Adj}$*undesirable*$_{Adj}]^{-}[_N\emptyset_N]$ <br> STEM-ZERO AFFIX | The zero affix turns the adjective stem into a noun – a process also known as **conversion.** |
| $[_{Adj}$*un-desirable*$_{Adj}]$ <br> PREFIX-STEM | The prefix *un–* negates the adjective stem. |
| $[_V$*desire*$_{V}][_{Adj}$*-able*$_{Adj}]$ <br> ROOT&STEM-SUFFIX | The suffix *–able* turns the root verb into an adjective. |

An **affix** attaches to a **stem**, and the most deeply embedded stem is the **root**. Affixes that precede the stem are **prefixes**, those that follow the stem are **suffixes**. The only **infix** in English is where an expletive such as *bloody* is infixed into the stem, e.g. the bold part of *kanga**bloody**roo*; in this example, the stem is the root, *kangaroo*. The only **circumfix** in English is the causative *en*–ADJ-*en* as in **en**light**en**, **em**bold**en** (there are very few examples). The German past tense is often a circumfix, e.g. *ge**lieb**t* "loved".

At each level in the structure of *undesirables*, it is the rightmost part of the word that determines the syntactic category. At the base level, the suffix *–able* on the verb *desire* creates an adjective. A level above that, *undesirable* remains an adjective because the stem *desirable* is to the right and it is an adjective. At a level higher still, the zero affix is conventionally suffixed to the right in morphological analysis because (in this case) it converts the adjective *undesirable* into a noun. At the top level, the plural suffix shows that the noun is plural. *Undesirables* is, for syntactic and semantic purposes, a plural noun.

Words may consist of:

> a single free morpheme, e.g. *rabbit*
> a combination of free and bound morphemes, e.g. *cat-s*, *re-call*
> a combination of free morphemes, e.g. *chair-person*

> a combination of bound morphemes, e.g. *abb-ess*.

The phrasal verb *put up with* "tolerate" consists of three words but one **lexeme** (see Chapter 3.1). A lexeme is usually referred to by its unmarked or citation form. For instance, in desktop dictionaries and books on language, *give* is normally used to represent the lexeme GIVE. The lexeme is found in a number of different words; see the paradigm below where bound morphemes are glossed to the right.

*Give*      GIVE
*Gives*     GIVE.3.S.SUBJECT      [3 = "third person", s = "singular"]
*Gave*      GIVE.**P**            [**P** = "past tense" (**N** = now, semantic "present tense")]
*Giving*    GIVE.**p**            [**p** = "present participle"]
*Given*     GIVE.**Pp**           [**Pp** = "past participle"]
to give     give.infinitive

The minimal lexeme is a free morpheme.

## Morphosyntactic classes

Words can be classified into **morphosyntactic classes** or, in traditional terms, **parts of speech.** Nouns, verbs, adjectives and adverbs are **open** classes because new items can be added; none can (normally) be added to **closed** classes, which include prepositions, articles, and pronouns. To identify morphosyntactic classes we look at the internal construction of the item, aspects of its meaning and function, and its relationship to other items in a syntactic construction. There is variation between and within languages, but here is a list of typical properties, known as **secondary grammatical categories**, for three open word classes.

| NOUN: | **gender** (e.g. masculine, feminine, neuter) and/or **noun class** (e.g. human, tree-like, mass); **number** (e.g. singular, dual, plural); **case** (e.g. ergative, nominative, accusative, genitive, ablative); **shape** and/or **consistency** (e.g. saliently one-dimensional and rigid, saliently two-dimensional and flexible, round); relative **size**; relative **location**. |
| --- | --- |
| VERB: | **tense** (e.g. past, present, future); **aspect** (e.g. aorist, habitual, progressive, perfective); **voice** (e.g. active, middle, passive); **mood** (e.g. declarative, imperative, interrogative, subjunctive). |
| ADJECTIVE: | **comparative** (e.g. *bigger*); **superlative** (*biggest*). |

Consider the properties of nouns in Dyirbal, an indigenous Australian language. They all refer to things (people, plants, ghosts, tools, and so on). They all have case suffixes, which indicate participant roles in events (such as actor, undergoer, instrument, possessor, location).

| CASES: | Actor | Instrument | Possessor | Location |
| --- | --- | --- | --- | --- |
| man | yaṛa | yaṛaŋgu | yaṛaɲu | yaṛaŋga |
| rainbow | yamani | yamanigu | yamanigu | yamaniga |
| possum | midin | midindu | midinu | midinda |
| bee | gubur | gubuṛu | guburŋu | gubuṛa |

Their syntactic distribution has a noun following a marker that indicates which noun class it belongs to for purposes of grammatical concord (1–4) and the spatial orientation. For example:

| CLASSIFIER NOUN | CLASSIFIER | NOUN |
|---|---|---|
| bayi yaṛa | 1.THERE.VISIBLE | MAN |
| balan djugumbil | 2.THERE.VISIBLE | WOMAN |
| ŋalam mira | 3.THERE.INVISIBLE | BLACK_BEAN |
| yala djawun | 4.HERE.VISIBLE | DILLY_BAG |

This is just a glimpse of the sorts of things that occur in languages; to understand what these terms mean within the grammar of Dyirbal you will need to read Dixon 1972.

## Inflectional and derivational morphology

Morphological processes and word creation play a prominent role in everyday language. Look at the bolded italic items in the following:

> Since its foundation 32 years ago, one of the group's core and inviolable rules had always been non-interference with each other's affairs – for there was much **to non-interfere with**. (Peter Hartcher *Australian Financial Review* Sept. 14, 1999. Bolded italics added.)

> [T]he big hitters Munich **Re**, Gerling **Re** and St Paul **Re** have called for premium rate increases in the January renewal period. (Bernard O'Riordan *Australian Financial Review* Sept. 14, 1999. 'Re' used as an independent word meaning "reinsurance". Bolded italics added.)

Bound morphemes fall into two major categories: inflexional and derivational. The differences between them are summarized in the table below.

| I n f l e x i o n | D e r i v a t i o n |
|---|---|
| (I1)  Adds to the meaning of a lexeme by producing related forms of the same stem lexeme. | (D1) Produces new (derived) lexemes. |
| (I2) Paradigms typically have no gaps. | (D2) Processes typically apply inconsistently to lexemes from the same class. |
| (I3) The combination of stem and inflexion is typically semantically transparent. | (D3) The combination of stem and derivational morpheme is often semantically opaque. |

Under I1, I2, and I3 compare *cat* with *cats*; *kick* with *kicked*: the *–s* and *–ed* are inflexions for plural and past tense respectively. Most nouns can take plural forms; most verbs can be inflected for past tense. Under D1 compare the noun lexeme *helicopter* with the verb lexeme *helicopter*; the verb *admit* with the adjective *admissible*; the adjective *happy* with the noun *happiness*. Under D2 compare *blacken, redden, sadden, widen, fatten* with non-occurring *\*greenen, \*bluen, \*happien, \*narrowen, \*thinnen*. Under D3, compare the relative transparency in meaning of the derivations *legalize* "make legal" and *atomize* "turn into atoms" with the much more opaque derivations *fraternize, revolutionize, computerize, womanize*.

## Morphological analysis

**Morphemes** are abstract constructs realized by **allomorphs** (note the parallel with phonemes and allophones). Consider the plural marking on nouns in English:

| /kæts/ | /kaʊz/ | /hɔsəz/ | cats, cows, horses |
|--------|--------|---------|--------------------|
| /ʃɒps/ | /bɪnz/ | /raɪzəz/ | shops, bins, rises |
| /mɒθs/ | /fulz/ | /fɪʃəz/ | moths, fools, fishes |
| /rifs/ | /waɪvz/ | /ʤʌʤəz/ | reefs, wives, judges |
| /s/ | /z/ | /əz/ | |

The regular plural morpheme in English has three allomorphs /s, z, əz/ – although in some dialects of English the form /ɪz/ is heard instead of /əz/. The context for each of the allomorphs can be described and interpreted according to a phonological rule. Look at the columns above. The words in the left column all end in a voiceless consonant and take the plural allomorph /s/. The nouns in the centre column all end in a voiced phone – either a vowel or voiced consonant. The nouns in the right-hand column end in both voiced and voiceless phones but all the word-final phones in this column are **sibilants** (/s, z, ʃ, ʒ, ʧ, ʤ/). In order to get the rules right we have to order them as follows.

{REGULAR PLURAL} → /əz/ / [+sibilant] ___#
/s/ / [–sibilant, –voice] ___#
/z/ elsewhere

An alternative rule takes the regular plural morpheme to be represented by the morph /z/, in which case there must be another rule that introduces an epenthetic schwa, /ə/, when the noun ends in a sibilant, and a third rule to devoice /z/ when the noun ends in a [–sibilant, –voice] phone, as the result of assimilation.

The third-person singular suffix *–s* of present tense verbs works the same way as the plural suffix. Consider *he eats, it feeds, she pauses* /its, fidz, pɔzəz/.

Thus the allomorphs of the regular plural morpheme in English are **phonologically conditioned**. Obviously some nouns (and the demonstratives *this, that*) need to be marked for irregularity (or at least subregularity) in their plurals; this is called **morphological conditioning**:

th*ese*, th*ose*, ox*en*, m*ice*, dat*a*, phenomen*a*, lacun*ae*, croc*i*, cherub*im*, t*ee*th;
two sheep (has a ZERO MORPH)

Possessive *'s* (and *s'*) is subject to similar phonological conditioning to plural *–s*; but unlike the latter, it is not a suffix, but a **clitic** because in *the man you kissed's sister* it does not attach to the head noun 'man' in the possessive NP nor to 'sister' the head of the possessed NP, but to the verb which comes at the end of the possessive NP; cf. also *the girl you gave it to's brother*.

## Word formation

New open class items can be created using a range of word formation processes: affixation, back-formation, reinterpretation, blending, compounding, functional and semantic shift, reduplication, shortening and sound symbolism. The lexicon can also be extended by borrowing.

For a demonstration of **affixation** see the discussion of *undesirables*. The nouns *actor, driver, cooker* derive by affixation from the verbs *act, drive* and *cook* respectively. By contrast, the verb *edit* was created from *editor* and the adjective *couth* from *uncouth*. This is called **back-formation. Reinterpretation**: the noun *pease* was once used in the singular and plural but around Shakespeare's time came to be reinterpreted as only plural, and so the singular *pea* was coined. *Brunch, workaholic* and *shopathon* are all **blends**, combining parts of exisiting words ("a meal combining aspects of breakfast and lunch", "as addicted to work as an alcoholic is to alcohol", "shopping marathon"). In **compounding**, whole words are combined: *skyscraper, mother-in-law,* and *vacuum cleaner* are all compounds. The lexicon is also extended by **functional and semantic shift**. An example of semantic shift is *bead* which once meant "prayer". Prayers were once counted off on the small pierced balls on the rosary, and the lexeme got transferred to them. Zero derivations exemplify functional shift, e.g. the noun *waitress* converts to the verb. **Reduplication** is common in English baby-talk (*weewee, choochoo*), and quasi-duplications occur in *helter skelter, hanky panky, walkie talkie*. In many languages reduplication indicates plural, e.g. Sundanese *monyet* "monkey", *monyet-monyet* "monkeys". New words are also created by **shortenings** (*TV, ad, e.g., snafu, SOB, pee*) and the use of **sound symbolism**, as in *cuckoo,* Hunanese *niao* "cat", Tzeltal *b'ihš* "squirts of liquid", English *piss* and the common element to *clutter, flutter, scutter, sputter, splutter, stutter,* and so on. Finally, languages expand their lexicons by **borrowing**: foreign words name new entities (*bungalow* from Hindustani, *kangaroo* from an Aboriginal Australian language, *checkmate* from Persian), and they sound better for taboo topics (*faeces* vs *shit, tushy* vs *arse*).

## Morphological typology

Languages can be classified according to the degree of 'separation' or 'inclusion' of meaning into lexemes. Those with greatest separation are called **isolating** or **analytic** where, typically, every morpheme is free. An example is Vietnamese:

| *Khi* | *tôi* | *dến* | *nhà* | *ba* | *tôi,* | *chúng* | *tôi* | *bắt dầu* | *làm* | *bài* |
|---|---|---|---|---|---|---|---|---|---|---|
| WHEN | I | COME | HOUSE | FRIEND | I | PLURAL | I | BEGIN | DO | LESSON |

"When I come to my friend's house, we begin to do lessons."

Languages with greatest inclusion are **polysynthetic**: the word contains many bound morphemes. Chinook is an example.

*aniā'lōt* "I give him to her"

| a– | –n– | –i– | –ā– | –l– | –ō– | –t |
|---|---|---|---|---|---|---|
| TENSE | I | HIM | HER | TO | AWAY FROM | GIVE |

West Greenlandic Eskimo is another: *iqalussuaʁniaʁtuqqusaagaluaqaagunnuuq* "It is said that we have admittedly got a strict order to go out fishing sharks".

In **agglutinative** languages a complex stem will serve as the basis for yet more complex words to a much greater extent than is the case in English. For instance, Turkish *ceplerimizdekilerdenmiş* analyses into

| cep | -ler | -imiz | -de | -ki | -ler | -den | -miş |
|-----|------|-------|-----|-----|------|------|------|
| POCKET | PL | 1.PL.POSSESSIVE | IN | WHICH | PL | FROM | DUBITATIVE |

"[it] is/was supposedly from (among) those that are/were in our pockets"

In Turkish many affixes can reapply, as *göz-lük-çü-lük-çü-lük* "the occupation of being a lobbyist for the oculist profession" based upon *göz* "eye", *-lük* "thing for", and *-çü* "person for".

In **fusional** languages like Russian and Latin an affix may mark a number of secondary grammatical categories. For example the suffix *–am* in Latin *fēminam* marks the noun WOMAN as ACCUSATIVE CASE + FEMININE GENDER + SINGULAR + FIRST DECLENSION; the *–ō* in *puerō* marks BOY as ABLATIVE CASE + MASCULINE GENDER + SINGULAR + SECOND DECLENSION; the *–um* in *sīderum* marks the noun STAR as GENITIVE CASE + NEUTER GENDER + PLURAL + THIRD DECLENSION.

However, all languages have some constructions that fall into each one of these types.

## Key points

> Several criteria were proposed for identifying words; none of them is satisfactory on its own.

> A morpheme of language L is the smallest significant unit in the syntactic analysis of L.

> Morphemes may be free or bound.

> A morpheme is a theoretical construct; it is realized by its allomorphs.

> The allomorphs of a morpheme may be phonologically conditioned; otherwise they are morphologically conditioned. For instance, the forms of the regular past tense in English are phonologically conditioned (think of /kɪkt, kɪst/, /bɒgd, sizd/, /nɒtɪd, nɒdɪd/ – *kicked~kissed, bogged~seized, knotted~nodded*) but irregular *burnt, spilt, caught, went* are morphologically conditioned.

> Affixes (prefix, infix, suffix, circumfix) attach to stems; the most deeply embedded stem is the root. The rightmost part of the word determines the syntactic category.

> The minimal lexeme is a free morpheme; it may consist of more than one word.

> Lexemes (words) fall into morphosyntactic classes (parts of speech) on the basis of their morphological structure, syntactic and semantic functions, and their secondary grammatical categories (e.g. tense for verbs, number for nouns).

> It is usually possible to distinguish inflexional from derivational morphemes.

> Languages fall into several morphological types.

> Additional information may be found in Chapter 5.4 ; at http://www.wikipedia.org/; in Brown 2006; Bauer 2003; Booij 2005; and Carstairs-McCarthy 2002.

# References

Bauer, Laurie 2003. *Introducing Linguistic Morphology*. 2nd edn. Edinburgh: Edinburgh University Press [First edn 1988].

Booij, Geert 2005. *The Grammar of Words: An Introduction to Linguistic Morphology*. Oxford: Oxford University Press.

Brown, E. Keith (General editor) 2006. *Encyclopedia of Languages and Linguistics*. 2nd edn. 14 vols. Oxford: Elsevier.

Carstairs-McCarthy, Andrew 2002. *An Introduction to English Morphology: Words and their Structure*. Edinburgh: Edinburgh University Press.

Dixon, Robert M.W. 1972. *The Dyirbal Language of North Queensland*. Cambridge: Cambridge University Press.

Sapir, Edward 1949. *Language: An Introduction to the Study of Speech*. New York: Harcourt, Brace & World [First published 1921].

2

## 2.4 **syntax**

### chapter contents

> Introduction – types of grammar      57
> Linguistic competence – what speakers 'know'      58
> Generative grammar      61
> Constituency tests      63
> Universal grammar      64
> Key points      64
> References      66

## Introduction – types of grammar

The word **syntax** (from Ancient Greek "arrangement") describes the part of linguistics that examines the way words go together to form sentences. Occasionally, it is also referred to as **grammar**. Linguistic grammars are descriptive, meaning they describe the underlying rules governing how speakers actually use languages. They thus differ from traditional pedagogical grammars, which are often **prescriptive**, i.e. listing value statements about how language ought to be used.

Examples of prescriptive rules include:

Do not use *data* as a singular noun.
Do not end a sentence with a preposition like *to*.
Do not use more than one negative in a sentence.
Do not say *between you and I*.
Do not use *disinterested* to mean "uninterested"

Linguists need to retain an objectively **descriptive** stance and base their theories on observed behaviour in the speech community and not on structures that some prejudiced individual prefers on grounds of aesthetics or faulty logic. For example, a prescriptive view might argue that *data*, the Latin plural of *datum*, needs to be treated as plural in English, as in:

*The data are misleading.*

However observations show that in English we encounter sentences like *The data are misleading* and *The data is misleading*. Both are viable, but in different contexts. These days most ordinary people would say and write *The data is misleading,* except in a piece of academic writing where *data* normally appears as the plural of singular *datum*.

Linguists are interested in the factors that motivate one construction above the other.

They attempt to replace the absolute labels of prescriptive grammar like 'mistake' and 'error' with relative labels like 'appropriate' and 'suitable', taking account of contexts of use, and explain the system that underlies the forms that speakers use.

## Linguistic competence – what speakers 'know'

The main goal of a grammatical theory is to capture what it is that all native speakers know about their language structure; in other words, their **competence**. This competence has a number of aspects.

### Grammaticality judgements

An essential part of a speaker's competence is the ability to understand and produce sentences never before encountered, such as:

> *The druids cooked those large quiches.*

While you are not likely to have ever seen this sentence before, you have no trouble comprehending it. Clearly, this has nothing to do with memory, but must come from the system of rules that underlies this competence. A fundamental property of human language is its 'open-endedness'; speakers can understand and produce an infinite number of sentences. They can also distinguish between grammatical and ungrammatical sentences (the latter indicated by an asterisk).

> *\*Cooked those large quiches the druids.*

### The order of words and morphemes

Part of a speaker's competence is therefore the knowledge that, in a language (as shown here for English), words and morphemes must occur in a special order. When this ordering is not followed, ungrammaticality results, as in *\*Cooked those large quiches the druids.*

### Word classes (parts of speech)

Words belong to **morphosyntactic classes** or what traditionally have been described as 'parts of speech'.

(a)   nouns (N) are (typically) the names of persons, places or things
(b)   verbs (V) are (typically) doing words
(c)   adjectives (Adj) are (typically) describing words (they describe entities, the denotata of nouns)
(d)   adverbs (Adv) are (typically) also describing words (they describe time, manner, place)

Such notional definitions come from traditional grammar and are helpful in identifying word classes across languages, but they cannot always be relied on. Take the nonsense sentence: *This is one of the scrumpiest and most floptastical tapostrophies to be bunked when chumpets are in cropon.* This is a syntactically well-formed sentence that we can break down into word classes, not on the basis of the meaning of the words, but their form and grammatical behaviour. We can identify an adjective, *scrumpy,* which takes two types of inflectional endings: *scrumpier* and *scrumpiest.* We can turn it into an adverb with a derivational ending *–ly* or a noun with *–ness*: *scrumpily* and *scrumpiness.* Moreover, the strict organizational structure of English means that, as an adjective, *scrumpy* will occupy certain positions in the sentence.

Traditionally, nine parts of speech have been identified for English: article, noun, pronoun, adjective, verb, adverb, preposition, conjunction, and interjection (*wow! psst! shhh!*). In many of today's grammars 'article' has been subsumed to **determiner** (which includes demonstratives and possessives along with articles) and a new label has been added for **auxiliaries** (like *have* in *I have eaten*), which were traditionally classified with verbs.

## Constituency

All human languages have a characteristic hierarchical structure. Sentences don't just consist of words, but groups of words that act as units. These are called **constituents**. Consider again the sentence:

*The druids cooked those large quiches.*

Speakers of English will share the intuition that *the* goes with *druids*; that *those* and *large* modify and therefore belong with *quiches* and that the string *those large quiches* forms some sort of structural unit. Some may also feel that *cooked those large quiches* also forms a unit of structure, but intuitions differ on this point. The following **tree diagram** (Figure 2.9) captures this kind of layering of structure:

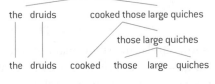

*Figure 2.9  Tree diagram (1)*

Constituents are strings of words that function as a group at some level; they work like linguistic building blocks that combine to make larger and larger constituents. At the top is the highest level of structure, the sentence. The next layer is the **clause**, which is equivalent to a simple sentence (i.e. a sentence containing a single clause). Between the level of clause and word we have intermediate constituents known as phrases. These phrases are always named after the word that is the most important in the string. This word, the core of the phrase, is called the **head**. All the four major word classes of nouns, verbs, adjectives, and adverbs have corresponding phrasal classes; namely, noun phrases (NP), verb phrases (VP), adjective phrases (AdjP) and adverb phrases (AdvP).

We can label the diagram above using abbreviations of the word and phrasal categories like S(entence), N(oun), N(oun) P(hrase), Det(erminer) and so on (Figure 2.10).

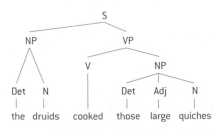

*Figure 2.10  Tree diagram (2)*

An alternative to the tree diagram above is bracketing.

[S [NP [Det *the*] [N *druids*]$_{NP}$] [VP [V *cooked*] [NP [Det *those*] [Adj *large*] [N *quiches*]$_{NP}$]$_{VP}$]$_{S}$]

The tree diagram provides the same sort of information as the bracketing, but shows more clearly the hierarchical arrangement of constituents, which (for most people) makes it easier to understand.

## Functions (or grammatical relations)

Constituents are related to one another in various ways. In the above sentence the **subject** (roughly, that which is performing the action) is *the druids* and the **object** (roughly, that which is undergoing the action) is *those large quiches*. Constituents are members of morphosyntactic classes; functions like 'subject' and 'object' are what constituents do. Grammatical relations can sometimes be very subtle. Compare the constituent *the druid* in the following two sentences:

(a) *The druid is easy to please.* = The druid is easy for anyone to please
(b) *The druid is eager to please.* = The druid is eager to please everyone

Grammatical functions will also account for the fact that examples like the following are ungrammatical.

*The druids disappeared the quiches.
*The druids chased.

Members of the same morphosyntactic class show similar distributional properties and are mutually substitutable, but only up to a point – the verb *disappear* cannot take an object (it is **intransitive**); the verb *chase* requires an object (it is **transitive**).

## Ambiguity

Speakers recognize that a constituent may have more than one meaning, that is, be **ambiguous**. For example, the following sentence is at least two ways ambiguous:

*The druids decided on the village green.*

The ambiguity here is structural and we can represent it with partial brackets (or trees):

(a) The druids [decided on] [the village green]
(b) The druids [decided] [on the village green]

These sentences have more than one syntactic analysis, which can be captured with paraphrase (i.e. we can restate them using different words):

The druids chose the village green.
The druids came to a decision on the village green.

## Paraphrase

Part of our competence is, therefore, that we can recognize sentences that mean the same thing, i.e. where there is a relationship of paraphrase. Here are other examples:

*The druids ate the quiche* vs *The quiche was eaten by the druids.*

*I gave the druids the quiche* vs *I gave the quiche to the druids.*
*I ate up my quiche* vs *I ate my quiche up.*
*Baking quiches is fun* vs *It's fun to bake quiches.*

Language is full of this kind of grammatical richness, and linguists have to be able to capture this feature of grammar in an analytical and rigorous way.

## Generative grammar

As earlier discussed, it is not possible to construct an exhaustive list of all the grammatical constructions in a language, since there is no limit to the number of sentences speakers can produce. (This is not a problem for phonology, since phoneme inventories are finite.) So how can we construct a grammar that will handle the open-ended nature of languages?

Noam Chomsky popularized **generative grammar** – so called because it uses a system of rules that aims to (potentially) generate all possible sentences of a language (much like mathematical rules generate endless sets of values). These are **phrase structure rules** (or **PS-rules**). The following simple PS-rules for English will illustrate.

All sentences of English need an NP (the subject) and a following VP (the verb and potentially other constituents like the object). We can capture this fact in shorthand via the following rule in which the arrow is understood as meaning "consists of" or "expands into".

S → NP VP

There are various rules possible for creating NPs: *druids, the druids, the large druids, the large druids in the picture* and so on.

NP → N
NP → Det N
NP → Det Adj N
NP → Det Adj N PP

We can use an abbreviation convention of parentheses (rounded brackets) to collapse all these rules into one neat NP rule. Whatever appears in ( ) is optional; only the noun (as head of the NP) is obligatory.

NP → (Det) (Adj) N (PP)

We now need another rule to expand the prepositional phrase.

PP → P NP

We also require a rule to expand the verb phrase (allowing for additional optional elements like noun phrases and preposition phrases: *baked those large quiches in the oven*).

VP → V (NP) (PP)

We can continue to expand our PS-rules in this way. For example, NPs can include pronouns (which cannot co-occur with determiners or adjectives): *They baked them.* We can capture this nicely using the convention of curly brackets to indicate the choice 'pick one from inside the brackets':

$$NP \rightarrow \begin{Bmatrix} (Det)\ (Adj)\ N\ (PP) \\ Pro \end{Bmatrix}$$

So far our grammar of English looks like this:

$$S \rightarrow NP\ VP$$
$$VP \rightarrow V\ (NP)\ (PP)$$
$$NP \rightarrow \left\{ \begin{array}{c} (Det)\ (Adj)\ N\ (PP) \\ Pro \end{array} \right\}$$
$$PP \rightarrow P\ NP$$

This mini grammar is already quite powerful. Each simple rule captures both the linear ordering and hierarchical grouping of sentences – specifying the constituents of particular phrases and the order in which these appear. Moreover, the rules are **recursive** – they can apply more than once to generate a structure. Prepositional phrases can keep repeating (*the druids in the picture on the table by the bench in the kitchen*) and our grammar can handle this because one rule feeds another. The PP rule includes an NP that expands to include a PP that expands to include an NP and so on.

This sort of grammar can be used to describe the structure of any language, not just English. Consider the following ten Irish Gaelic sentences (not in standard orthography).

| (i) | tá sé ənso |
| --- | --- |
| | is he here  "He is here" |
| (ii) | tá ən buəxil bjog ənso |
| | is the boy little here  "The little boy is here" |
| (iii) | tá ən kat bjog ənso |
| | is the cat little here  "The little cat is here" |
| (iv) | tá kalín bjog ənso |
| | is girl little here  "A little girl is here" |
| (v) | tá bó vjog ənso |
| | is cow little here  "A little cow is here" |
| (vi) | tá ən vó vjog ənso |
| | is the cow little here  "The little cow is here" |
| (vii) | tá ən van frotəstúnəx ag ən dorəs |
| | is the woman protestant at the door  "The Protestant woman is at the door" |
| (viii) | tá sí ag ən fárk vjog |
| | is she at the park small  "She is at the small park" |
| (ix) | vris sé ən lampə |
| | broke he the lamp  "He broke the lamp" |
| (x) | krúən van frotəstúnəx ən vó vjog |
| | "A Protestant woman milks the little cow (all the time)" |

Two things to notice about the structure of the Gaelic compared with English: (1) the verb comes first in the sentences (no evidence of a VP); (2) adjectives follow nouns. The following rules will generate these ten sentences. (They will also generate sentences that do not appear here like *he broke it*, but it is reasonable to predict that these are grammatical.)

S → V NP (PP)

NP → $\left\{ \begin{matrix} \text{(Det) N (Adj)} \\ \text{Pro} \end{matrix} \right\}$

PP → P NP

Our PS-rules can capture a number of aspects of a speaker's competence (linear ordering, constituency, word classes, grammatical relations). However, it cannot yet capture a relationship of paraphrase between two sentences, as in:

*The druids have eaten the quiche* [active]
*The quiche has been eaten by the druids* [passive]

Deriving these sentences via separate PS-rules would not account for the regular relationship that holds between them. It also does not account for what you probably feel intuitively – the active is the more basic structure. So, rather than generating them independently, we generate the active version via the PS-rules we already have, and derive the passive via another rule known as a **transformational rule** (or **T-rule**). The following is a rough formalization of such a rule. It takes the first structure and converts it into the second structure.

**Active**  $\text{NP}_1 \text{ Aux V NP}_2$
**Passive**  $\text{NP}_2 \text{ Aux+}be \text{ V } by \text{ NP}_1$

The many other English sentences that show such a relationship of paraphrase can also be connected via transformational rules. Although sentences like the following pairs have different surface structures, they have at a deeper (abstract) level the same representation.

*I gave the druids the quiche* vs *I gave the quiche to the druids.*
*I ate up my quiche* vs *I ate my quiche up.*

We have been able to give you just a glimpse of some of the most basic issues and methods of syntactic analysis – however there is much more to structure than appears in this snapshot.

## Constituency tests

So far we have assigned constituency of sentences purely on the basis of intuition. But how can we be so sure that words pattern in this way? Syntax books such as Börjars and Burridge 2001 translate these kinds of intuitions into more formal criteria. In fact, there are a number of different **constituency tests** that can be used to decide whether a particular string (sequence of constituents) forms a (larger) constituent. We will mention just four of these tests.

### Substitution

One thing we can be sure of is that a string of only one word forms a constituent – a word acts as a unit in terms of sentence structure; i.e. in terms of the syntax. This means that if the string of words we are investigating can be replaced by a single word (such as a pronoun), this is an indication that the string is a constituent. Take our original sentence and apply the **substitution** test:

*The druids cooked **those large quiches**.*

*Those large quiches* can be replaced by the pronoun *them* and therefore must form a constituent.

## Movement

Constituents behave distributionally as single units of structure – and as single units they may have the ability to appear in a variety of sentence positions. In short, we can move constituents around in a sentence, but we can't move strings that do not form constituents. It follows then that if a string can be taken out of its place and moved to another part of the sentence, the string functions as a unit. Hence **movement** makes up another of our constituency tests. For example, we can shunt elements to the first position in the sentence for special emphasis or focus. Only constituents can be fronted in this way.

*Those large **quiches** the druids cooked* (not the flans)

The result of moving *those large quiches* to the front is an acceptable, although admittedly rather theatrical-sounding, sentence (such sentences often sound odd out of context). More often than not, movement of one constituent will involve other changes in the sentence. For example, English has another focusing device known as **clefting**. As the name suggests, clefting has the effect of cleaving an original sentence into two clauses. Like fronting, it is another test that we can apply to enable us to discover what the constituents of a sentence are. Here is a clefted version of our original sentence.

*It was **those large quiches** that the druids cooked* (not the flans)

# Universal grammar

Chomsky (Chomsky 1965; 1972; 1986) believes there is a part of the brain that contains innate knowledge of what is a possible language and what is not a possible language. Speakers are said to be born with an **innate grammar** and a task for linguistics is to find out more about this innate grammar. Chomsky and his followers assume the innate grammar is the same for every language, hence there is a **universal grammar**. One goal is therefore to find out more about universal grammar. There is no obvious direct way of studying universal grammar – there is (as yet) no brain scanner that can be used to study it. What linguists who pursue this line of research do is study in great depth the grammars of individual languages. Some people believe that an in-depth study of one language should be enough to discover the abstract structures that make up innate grammar. Others, however, think that a more fruitful way forward is to make in-depth studies of many different languages and compare the results.

## Key points

> If you study the syntax of a language then you have two tasks: you need to break sentences down into their component parts and you need to be able to describe these component parts grammatically.

> The prescriptive approach is one that tells you how you ought to speak and write. The descriptive approach describes how people actually do speak and write.

> Linguistic science must remain objectively descriptive and avoid moral and aesthetic judgement. (But it is appropriate for linguists to focus critically on the particular standards and values being invoked in the prescriptive debates.)

> The following eight features form part of a speaker's linguistic competence:
> (a)   grammaticality judgements
> (b)   ordering of words and morphemes
> (c)   morphosyntactic classes (parts of speech)
> (d)   constituency (the way words group together – there are intervening levels of organization between words and sentences)
> (e)   grammatical relations (how words are related – who's doing what to whom)
> (f)   elements that are either obligatory or prohibited in a sentence
> (g)   structural ambiguity
> (h)   the ability to paraphrase.

> Linguists aim to produce a descriptive grammar (a finite set of rules) that will describe a native speaker's syntactic competence. These rules must:
> (a)   generate all grammatical sentences
> (b)   not produce any ungrammatical sentences
> (c)   account for linguistic knowledge of morphosyntactic classes (like noun and preposition), grammatical relations (like subject and object), paraphrase, ambiguity, and so on.

> There is no limit to the creativity of people's competence. For example, there is theoretically no such thing as the longest sentence, and we can capture this with recursive rules. The limitation on the length of a sentence is imposed by performance constraints on usage, not competence.

> Phrase structure (PS) rules specify constituent structure and can be represented by a labelled tree. PS-rules capture four types of information:
> (a)   linear order
> (b)   hierarchical order (words grouped into constituents)
> (c)   morphosyntactic classes
> (d)   grammatical relations.

> Intransitive verbs can't be followed by an object NP; transitive verbs must be followed by an object NP.

> We can justify whether or not a string is a constituent by tests such as substitution (by one word) and movement (whether the string can appear in different sentence positions).

> Many linguists believe that grammar is innate and is the same for any language; hence that there exists a universal grammar.

> Additional information can be found in Börjars and Burridge 2001; Brown and Miller 1991; Halliday and Matthiessen 2004; Van Valin 2001; Van Valin and LaPolla 1997.

# References

Börjars, Kersti and Kate Burridge 2001. *Introducing English Grammar*. London: Edward Arnold.

Brown, E. Keith and Jim Miller 1991. *Syntax: A Linguistic Introduction to Sentence Structure*. 2nd edn. London: Harper Collins.

Chomsky, Noam 1965. *Aspects of the Theory of Syntax*. Cambridge MA: MIT Press.

Chomsky, Noam 1972. *Language and Mind*. New York: Harcourt, Brace, Jovanovich.

Chomsky, Noam 1986. *Knowledge of Language: Its Nature, Origin, and Use*. New York: Praeger.

Halliday, Michael A.K. and Christian M.I.M. Matthiessen 2004. *An Introduction to Functional Grammar*. 3rd edn. London: Arnold.

Van Valin, Robert D. Jr 2001. *An Introduction to Syntax*. Cambridge: Cambridge University Press.

Van Valin, Robert D. Jr and Randy LaPolla 1997. *Syntax: Structure, Meaning, and Function*. Cambridge: Cambridge University Press.

# 2.5 fundamentals of semantics and pragmatics

## chapter contents

> Defining semantics and pragmatics      67
> Meaning is compositional      67
> Context and common ground      69
> Key points      74
> References      74

## Defining semantics and pragmatics

Within the discipline of linguistics the term *semantics* is not in the least bit pejorative as it is in the colloquial accusation *That's just semantics!* which means "You're just quibbling and prevaricating."

**Semantics** is the study of meaning in human languages. To be more precise, it is the study and representation of the meaning of every kind of constituent and expression in language, and also of the meaning relationships between them.

What about pragmatics?

**Pragmatics** is the context-dependent assignment of meaning to language expressions used in acts of speaking and writing.

Think of pragmatics as the investigation of meaning in language on particular occasions when language is used, whereas semantics studies meaning inherent in the language itself, as already existing in the language for people to make use of. So, where does the semantics come from? Doesn't it – at least partly – derive from the way people use language? And the answer is yes, semantics is to a large extent dependent on pragmatics; but just as the chicken comes from an egg, and the egg comes from the chicken, there is a conundrum: semantics and pragmatics are interdependent, and we shall see some of their mutual influence.

## Meaning is compositional

At the simplest level of analysis, any language is a system of forms paired with meanings. This is most obvious in a language you don't know: you may hear or see the form but not know the meaning, e.g. *Neyam Naiterukop inkituaak are* (Maasai, literally "marry Naiter-ukop women two" – Naiterukop had two wives), and also in dictionaries where forms are listed and their meanings given, e.g.

**bonza/bonzer**

excellent; terrific; very good    (*The Dinkum Dictionary: A Ripper Guide to Aussie English* Lenie Johansen 1988)

Most people in our community hold two true beliefs:

(a)  Meanings are a property of words.
(b)  Word meanings are stored in dictionaries.

The popular notion that words are the basic building blocks for language construction is not precise enough. The defining characteristic of the basic building blocks is that they are form~meaning pairs but their meaning is not determinable from any meaning that can be assigned to their constituent forms. For instance, the meaning of *paddle* cannot be correctly computed from the meaning of *pad–* and the meaning of *–dle*; *paddle* is one of the basic building blocks: a listeme.

> A **listeme** is a language expression whose meaning is not determinable from the meanings (if any) of its constituent forms and which, therefore, a language user must memorize as a combination of form and meaning. A listeme is stored in the dictionary (or lexicon).

A listeme may be:

> ❭  a lexeme such as *the, abbey, put up with, take* (see Chapter 3.1)
> ❭  a morpheme such as *the, give*, PAST TENSE, the nominalizing suffix *–ness* (as in *obtuseness*), the feminine suffix *–ess* (as in *lioness, abbess*), the negative prefix *un–* as in *unbelievable* (and the suffix *–able*)
> ❭  the phonestheme *fl–* that occurs in *flash, flare, flame, flutter, flicker* and many other words; the phonestheme *–utter* that occurs in *flutter, stutter, clutter* and a few other words
> ❭  possibly the stem *–juvenate* that occurs in *rejuvenate* and allows for the creation of, say, *dejuvenate* which could denote the effects of the disease progeria on kids.

If I ask you to construct a meaningful sentence using all the words in (1), you can do so because meaning is compositional.

(1)  *killed, crocodile, hunter, the, the*

We language users combine listemes into words, phrases, sentences, and longer texts. At each level we construct meanings. The meaning of the word *killed* is composed from the listemes KILL and PAST TENSE (*–ed*) and also **the morphosyntactic relationship between the two listemes**. *Bachelors* is composed from BACHELOR and PLURAL (*–s*) and the morphosyntactic relationship between them. The semantics of the combination of the listemes is just as important as the semantics of the listemes themselves. This is partly why dictionaries specify the morphosyntactic class of each entry. *Fly* is many ways ambiguous, but to pick on two senses: the **verb** *fly* means "travel through the air"; the **noun** *fly* "cloth cover for an opening". The **verb** *waitress* means something different from the **noun** *waitress* even if the two are closely connected.

Different combinations of the words in (1) give rise to sentences with vastly different meanings:

(2)  The hunter killed the crocodile.
(3)  The crocodile killed the hunter.

The noun phrases *the hunter* and *the crocodile* have different thematic roles in the two sentences: in (2) *the hunter* is the actor (does the killing), *the crocodile* is the undergoer (gets killed); these roles are reversed in (3).

The **principle of compositionality** is that any complex language expression can be analysed in terms of simpler constituent expressions down to listemes and the structures that combine them. The flip-side of compositionality is **generativity**: language has a structure that permits boundless meanings to be created from a finite set of listemes. Human languages are the objects that we study in semantics. For that reason, the language under investigation is known as the **object language**. The language that a linguist uses to describe and analyse the object language is called the **metalanguage**. The programme for semantic theory includes:

❯ specifying the rules for translating sentences of the object language into a metalanguage that captures their proper semantic components
❯ identifying the rules for combining these components in such a way as to interpret the input sentences of the object language.

The basic requirement for a metalanguage is to satisfactorily communicate the meaning of item $e_{OL}$ – that is, any expression in the object language, whether it is a word, a phrase, or a sentence – in terms of an expression "$e_M$" in the metalanguage. A metalanguage is just another language, often artificial, or perhaps a natural language that is modified in some way. A clue to the difference between a formal and an informal metalanguage is given by comparing (4) with (5).

(4) *dog* means "canine animal"
(5) $\forall x [\textbf{dog}'(x) \leftrightarrow \textbf{animal}'(x) \wedge \textbf{canine}'(x)]$

(5) can be read: "For every x, x is a dog if and only if x is animal and x is canine". We shall not be doing much formal semantics here; it is not absolutely necessary because we can exploit the fact that a metalanguage expression "$e_M$" used in the semantic definition of a natural language expression $e_{OL}$ will always be equivalent to the natural language expression that people use to interpret it.

## Context and common ground

The term **context** denotes any or all of four things:

❯ the world and time spoken of
❯ the co-text, i.e. the text that precedes and succeeds a given language expression
❯ the situation of utterance, and
❯ the situation of interpretation.

The world and time spoken (or written) of is a mental model of the world that we construct in order to be able to produce or understand a phrase, a sentence, or a much longer text. In the course of interpreting any text, Hearer (or Reader) must construct a model of the world and time spoken of. For instance, to interpret a declarative sentence such as (6), Hearer models a world in which it is daytime and the sun is (mostly) shining and there is (at least) one person mowing a lawn.

(6) It's a sunny day and someone is mowing a lawn.

Typically, the world and time spoken of contain people and things Hearer knows or knows of; thus it is a contextualization of the states of affairs referred to by the text producer (Speaker) in terms of place, objects, participants, and so on. It can be (a reconstruction of) the real world, or some other possible world that can be imagined, desired, or supposed. Occasionally people speak of logical impossibilities such as *the largest prime number*; and there may be logically possible worlds no speaker conceives of.

It is often the case that a single utterance evokes more than one world and/or time.

(7) If Max owned a Rolls-Royce, he'd be a lucky man.
(8) Nimoy plays Spock in 'Star Trek'.
(9) President Clinton was a baby in 1946.

(7) evokes an actual world where Speaker presupposes (assumes) that Max does not own a Rolls, but imagines a hypothetical world in which he does. Compare this with (10):

(10) If Max owned a Rolls, he was a lucky man.

(10) means "If indeed it is the case (as you claim) that Max owned a Rolls, then he was a lucky man" in which Speaker maintains a degree of scepticism, but nevertheless accepts Max's Rolls-Royce ownership as a fact – at least for the sake of argument. The important point here is that the model for (10) consists of just one world that contains Max and the Rolls. We can visualize it in Figure 2.11

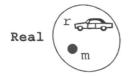

*Figure 2.11 In (10) Max and his Rolls occupy the same (real) world*

In (7) non-factuality is indicated by the initial 'If' plus the verb forms '[woul]d be'. There are two worlds evoked: the reference world of the present in which Max exists, but not the fact of his Rolls-Royce ownership; this is represented by the circle in Figure 2.12. There is also a non-factual or hypothetical world, represented by an ellipse, in which Speaker imagines that Max exists and that he does own a Rolls. Only the non-factual (elliptical) world is actually spoken of; the factual world is implied.

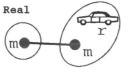

*Figure 2.12 Speaker's model of the two worlds evoked in (7)*

In (8) Speaker refers to the fictional world of 'Star Trek' in which Spock exists and which is to be found (as a series of stories) within the actual world in which Leonard Nimoy exists. In (9) the person who was the baby in 1946 became the US president in 1993.

The same individual may occupy different worlds; two worlds that include the same people and places may exist at different times as in (9) or in different realities as in (7)–(8). Models are therefore defined as world~time pairs. In fact only a part of a world is focused upon in any text, nevertheless the rest of the world (and the universe that contains it) is accessible and can be elaborated upon if need be.

Speaker and Hearer are mutually aware that, normally, their interlocutor is an intelligent being. Speaker does not need to spell out those things which are:

(a) obvious to the sensory receptors of Hearer, or
(b) such that Hearer can very easily reason out on the basis of
    (i) knowing the language and the conventions for its use, and
    (ii) using the knowledge that each of us develops from birth as we experience the world around us.

These constitute what is called **common ground**. Much of our understanding rests on an assumption of common ground: e.g. pointing to something and saying *Isn't that nice?* on the assumption that Hearer understands English and can also see it; or saying *Let's go to Cracow* on the assumption that 'Cracow' will be understood as referring to a certain city. Some common ground is universal, e.g. knowledge of sun, rain, the physiological differences between the sexes. Some common ground is very restricted, e.g. between a couple who use *the Hobgoblin* to refer to the man's first wife. Speaker can usually readily assess the probable common ground with Hearer, and choose his or her words accordingly. Here is a simplified definition of common ground.

Common ground for any community K of two or more people is that:

(a) every member, or almost every member, of K knows or believes some fact or set of facts F
(b) a member is presumed to know or believe F by (almost) every other member of K
(c) a member of K knows that both (a) and (b) are true.

When a member of K applies knowledge of F in order to interpret P, a state of affairs or something said, s/he can presume that others in the community will also apply knowledge of F in order to interpret P. The existence of F, P, and the application of knowledge of F to interpreting P is common ground for members of the community K. Once attended to, P becomes part of F, incrementing the common ground.

Common ground allows meaning to be underspecified by Speaker, so that language understanding is a constructive process in which a lot of inferencing is expected from Hearer (Hearer is defined as the person whom Speaker intends to be the recipient of Speaker's message and consequently to react to it). Take, for example, the following interchange:

(11) [*The doorbell to Maggie and Frank's apartment rings*]
     MAGGIE [voice off]: Did you hear the doorbell, dear? I'm in the bathroom.
     FRANK: I'll get it.

(a) First of all Maggie draws Frank's attention to $P_1$, the fact that the doorbell has been rung, by asking whether Frank has heard it.
(b) By asking the question of him, $P_2$, she demonstrates that she assumes that Frank is not deaf: this is a generalized implicature (i.e. a deniable inference) attached to all spoken questions (part of F).
(c) It also suggests that she thinks that he possibly heard the doorbell himself ($P_1$ becomes part of F): this is a particularized implicature relevant to this particular context.

(d) Maggie could, in principle, justify these implicatures on the basis of what she assumes to be common ground with Frank: he speaks English and knows the conventions for using it (part of F); the doorbell to their apartment has rung ($P_1$) and it is sufficiently noisy that they both have sufficiently good perceptual and cognitive abilities to recognize that if one of them has heard it the other one will probably have done so, too (part of F).

(e) It follows that Maggie expects Frank to infer (as we do) that she is implying that the caller (part of F recognized from $P_1$) needs to be attended to (more of F). This is another generalized implicature, which would usually be described as the point of the question.

(f) Secondly, Maggie announces she is in the bathroom, thereby implying that she is unable to open the door herself (more of F).

(g) Frank takes the hint ($P_3$). Again by a process of implication, we, along with Maggie, recognize the statement 'I'll get it' as a promise (yet more F). If Frank's promise is sincere – which is our normal expectation – he will act upon it.

Note the amount of inferencing that Maggie expects from Frank. This is typical of normal language interchange. We have to conclude: Speaker expects Hearer to make constructive inferences, and Speaker formulates his or her text accordingly. Additional evidence for the constructive nature of text understanding includes:

> Inference and speculation enable Hearer to predict what might happen next, allowing a sentence begun by one participant in conversation to be completed by another.
> Titles and headings set up expectations about the text which follows, and so facilitate understanding.
> Studies of eyewitness testimony and experiments with scrambled stories confirm that we tend to reformulate what we see, hear, and read in terms of what we expect to see, hear, and read.

A text is judged coherent when the world at the time spoken of is internally consistent and generally accords with accepted human knowledge.

In (the model of) the world and time spoken of, states of affairs exist and/or events occur that Hearer is expected to be able to understand or imagine. Chronological coherence is an important aspect of texts; so is coherent unfolding of a storyline. Even an imaginary world is necessarily interpreted in terms of the world of our experience.

The world and time spoken of constitute the most crucial category of context. The **co-text** of language expression $e$ is the text that precedes and succeeds $e$; it is only significant for identifying the world and time spoken of or something within the world. For instance, especially in a written text, a sentence fragment like *By taxi* sends us to the co-text to discover who or what is travelling by taxi. **Anaphora**, which makes successive references to the same entity or kind, is interpreted through co-text (see Chapter 3.1). Most anaphors have co-referential identity with their governing expression; many anaphors are semantically but not co-referentially identical to their governing expression. The typical anaphor is a pronoun. There is only a small set of pronominal anaphors in a language and they have very little semantic content: e.g. in *Max took the beer and Ø thanked him*; the pronoun *him* has the semantic content "the male one". The sentence also contains the zero anaphor (Ø) which has none. This limited semantic content allows each anaphor to be used for a wide range of reference. It also has the consequence that anaphors place especially heavy demands on context to determine their reference. Nevertheless, anaphors exist to make language more efficient than it would be without them. Where there is co-reference, the successive references involve some kind of change to the referent:

(12)  Catch $_[$a chicken$_{1]}$. Kill $_[$it$_{2]}$. Pluck $_[$it$_{3]}$. Draw $_[$it$_{4]}$. Cut $_[$it$_{5]}$ up. Marinade $_[$it$_{6]}$. Roast $_[$it$_{7]}$. When you've eaten $_[$it$_{8]}$, put $_[$the bones$_{9]}$ in the compost.

Thus $_[$it$_{7]}$ refers not to the live chicken in $_{[1]}$, but to the caught, killed, plucked, drawn, cut up, and marinaded pieces of chicken. There is reference to one or more of the same kind in *Ed ordered a lite beer, and I had **one**, too* and *A poodle bit me yesterday; **they**'re horrible dogs*.

The co-text provides information necessary to the proper interpretation of ambiguous forms: e.g. the word *bank* can be a noun (*a bank*) or a verb (*to bank money*); as a noun it can denote a financial institution (*Citibank*) or its buildings (*the bank on High Street*), or a raised earthwork (*river bank*). The co-text will ordinarily disambiguate by permitting only one interpretation to make sense 'in context'. Language expressions not only take from their co-text, they also give to it: what we say or write on any one occasion most often has an important bearing on how a text will continue. Titles and headings facilitate communication through their co-textual function of identifying the topic of the narrative.

In face-to-face interaction the situation of utterance and the situation of interpretation are practically indistinguishable in time, though the locations of Speaker and Hearer are distinct. The **situation of utterance** identifies the place at and the time in which Speaker makes the utterance; it is the world and time spoken IN. The **situation of interpretation** identifies the place at and time in which the utterance is heard, seen, and/or read. These provide anchors for **deictic** (see Chapter 3.1) or **indexical** categories such as tense (time of utterance defines present tense), personal pronouns (Speaker is first person, Hearer second, others third), deictic locatives and demonstratives (*this here* is near Speaker).

In this section we have seen that language understanding is a constructive process, and that Speaker underspecifies meaning knowing that s/he can rely on Hearer's ability to correctly infer Speaker's meaning without every scrap of it having to be made explicit. The fact that people have the ability to use language at all makes it a cognitive entity, and this constructive aspect of understanding exploits human cognitive abilities to the full. The facts that:

> language is used to talk about things in the real and imaginary worlds and times, and
> Hearer must model (construct) the worlds and times spoken of in order to understand an utterance

indicate the crucial significance of context in semantics and pragmatics. If Hearer is to properly understand Speaker's text, Speaker needs to ensure that s/he makes the most accurate assumptions possible about Hearer and the situation of interpretation. Likewise, Hearer needs to take account of what is known about the situation of utterance. Context includes the world and time spoken of, i.e. the content of some mental space; this is normally linked directly to the world and time spoken in, which is defined on the spatio-temporal characteristics of situation of utterance. However, in fictional and imaginative works, the association with the world and time spoken in may be much less substantial – though Speaker's assumptions and beliefs will undoubtedly be influenced by them. The word *context* is often used to refer to the co-text of a given word or longer expression; this is principally because the co-text reveals information about the world and time spoken of.

## Key points

> Semantics is the study and representation of the meaning of every kind of constituent and expression in human languages, and also of the meaning relationships between them.

> Pragmatics is the context-dependent assignment of meaning to language expressions used in acts of speaking and writing.

> In the canonical speech event, Speaker makes an utterance to Hearer at a certain time and place. Hearer is the person whom Speaker intends to be the recipient of Speaker's message, and consequently to react to it.

> A listeme is a language expression whose meaning is not determinable from the meanings of its constituent forms.

> Meaning is compositional. Language has a structure that permits boundless meanings to be constructed from a finite set of listemes.

> The language under investigation is known as the object language. The language that a linguist uses to describe and analyse it is the metalanguage.

> Common ground allows meaning to be underspecified by Speaker, so that language understanding is a constructive process in which a lot of inferencing is expected from Hearer.

> A text is judged coherent if the world at the time spoken of is internally consistent and generally accords with accepted human knowledge.

> The most important category of context is the world and time spoken of – a mental model of the world that we construct in order to be able to produce or understand language. Other categories of context are co-text and the situations of utterance and interpretation. The latter provide anchors for deictic (indexical) categories.

> Anaphora makes successive references to the same entity or kind.

> Additional information may be found at http://www.wikipedia.org/; in Allan 2001; Brown 2006; Cruse 2004; Jaszczolt 2005; Levinson 1983 and Saeed 2003.

## References

Allan, Keith 2001. *Natural Language Semantics*. Oxford & Malden MA: Blackwell.

Brown, E. Keith (General editor) 2006. *Encyclopedia of Languages and Linguistics*. 2nd edn. 14 vols. Oxford: Elsevier.

Cruse, D. Alan 2004. *Meaning In Language: An Introduction to Semantics and Pragmatics*. 2nd edn. Oxford: Oxford University Press.

Jaszczolt, Katarzyna M. 2005. *Default Semantics: Foundations of a Compositional Theory of Acts of Communication*. Oxford: Oxford University Press.

Levinson, Stephen C. 1983. *Pragmatics*. Cambridge: Cambridge University Press.

Saeed, John I. 2003. *Semantics*. 2nd edn. Oxford: Blackwell.

# 2.6 meaning, maxims, and speech acts

## chapter contents

> Sense, denotation, reference, and connotation    75
> Entailment    77
> Conversational implicature    77
> Mutual entailment    78
> Contradictories and contraries    79
> Hyponymy and antonymy    79
> The cooperative maxims    79
> Speech acts    81
> Key points    83
> References    84

## Sense, denotation, reference, and connotation

**Sense** is decontextualized meaning, abstracted from innumerable occurrences (in texts) of the listeme or combination of listemes. Senses are what we find in dictionaries.

> [1]**canine** ... *adj* [L *caninus*. fr. canis dog] **1**: of or relating to dogs or the family (Canidae) including the dogs, wolves, jackals, and foxes **2**: of, relating to, or resembling a dog
> [2]**canine** *n* **1**: a conical pointed tooth; *esp*: one situated between the lateral incisor and the first premolar **2**: dog    (*Webster's New Collegiate Dictionary* 1977)

It is left to you as a dictionary user to decide which of the senses given is relevant to a particular context in which the word is used (because sense is decontextualized meaning). As you see, the sense of a language expression, $e_{OL}$, is a description of its informational content in terms of some other language expression "$e_M$".

The quote in the box above contains the senses of two **homonyms** (words with the same form), [1]**canine** and [2]**canine**, each of which is two ways **polysemous** because each has two senses, numbered **1** and **2**. Two listemes of the same form are homonymous if they warrant separate lexicon entries because the identity of form is coincidental. A listeme is polysemous if it has more than one meaning given within a single lexicon entry.

The sense of (1) is (2):

(1) I totalled my car yesterday.
(2) "Speaker did irreparable damage to his or her car the day before this sentence was uttered."

Sense is a truly semantic category, but **reference** is pragmatic. Referring is something that Speaker does. The reference of a language expression *e* in utterance U is "what

Speaker is talking about when using *e* in U"; e.g. Speaker refers to particular entities, events, places, and times within the world and time s/he is speaking of. The reference of (1) will depend on:

(a) Who utters (1) – which determines between 'his' or 'her' car.
(b) When (1) was uttered – which dates 'yesterday'.

Both reference and **denotation** are relations between expressions in the language and worlds and times spoken of. Denotation is the relation between language expressions and things or events in worlds – not just the world we live in, but any world and time that may be spoken of. To say that a language expression *e* has **extension** in a world $w_i$ at time $t_i$ is equivalent to saying *e* denotes something that exists in the world $w_i$ at time $t_i$. The world spoken of is a mental model of an actual or recalled or imagined world in which it is important to identify what there is and what there isn't (i.e. what doesn't exist). Speaker refers differently to things

> which have extension in the world spoken of
> which do not have extension in the world spoken of, and
> whose existence is uncertain.

> (3) We have a dog [exists], but no cat [doesn't exist]. So we might have mice [existence uncertain].

It is sometimes said that 'referring expressions' identify things that exist, and 'non-referring expressions' identify things that don't; but it is better to define reference as 'what Speaker is talking about' and when dealing with existence to use the term 'extension' instead.

Extension in a world links with the notion of truth in a world at a certain time. Many semanticists think that the purpose of semantic theory is to identify the conditions that must be met for a statement to be assigned one of the truth values from the range {true, false}. In order to understand and evaluate the meaning of *It is raining* or *Koalas are marsupials* you need to know the conditions under which these statements would be true; knowing truth conditions allows you to make inferences such as that you will get wet if you go out into the rain, and that female koalas have pouches. However we also need a semantics for non-truth-functional sentences like *Be quiet!* or *What's your name?* or *Thank you*, or an expressive such as *Shit!* (One can say of a truth-functional sentence such as 'It is raining', *It is true* (or *false*) *that it is raining* but not of non-truth-functional sentences, *\*It is true that be quiet.*)

The **connotations** of a language expression *e* are pragmatic effects that arise from encyclopedic knowledge about the denotation (or reference) of *e* and also from experiences, beliefs, and prejudices about the contexts in which the expression *e* is typically used. Thus *Tom's dog killed Jane's rabbit* has different connotations from *Tom's doggie killed Jane's bunnie*; and dogs can also be referred to by any of *dish-licker, bow-wow, cur, mutt, mongrel, whelp, hound* – all of which have different connotations. Next, consider some connotations of gender in respect of *surgeon, nurse, secretary/receptionist* and *motor mechanic*. Even today there are gendered stereotypes: most surgeons and motor mechanics are male; most nurses and secretary/receptionists are female. The connotations arise from normative conceptions of typical job-holders.

Identifying the connotations of a term is to identify the community attitude towards it. Connotation is intimately involved with notions of appropriateness in language use that condition the choice of vocabulary (including proper names) and style of address. Connotation is involved in choosing expressions that upgrade, downgrade, and insult. Reactions to connotation are pragmatic effects that motivate semantic extension and the generation of new vocabulary, e.g. *sleep with* has been extended to mean "copulate with", *Sugar!* is used as a euphemism for *Shit!*; the neologism *waitperson* has been coined as a unisex term replacing *waiter* and *waitress*; employees are *dehired* and forced into *involuntary retirement* instead of being sacked (see Allan 2007).

## Entailment

Perhaps the most fundamental semantic relation is that of **entailment**. It holds between sentences: If A and B are sentences in the object language, then A entails B (A→B) if, in all possible worlds, B cannot be false when A is true.

(4)  Toro is a bull → Toro is male

If in fact Toro is female, then Toro cannot be a bull. Entailments cannot be cancelled, i.e. to say something like *Toro is a bull, but not a male bull* is nonsense.

## Conversational implicature

The probabilistic character of **conversational implicature** is easier to demonstrate than define. For instance, when you read *Toro is a bull* in (4), the chances are that you conceive of Toro as a bovine animal; but (4) could be referring to a male elephant or my pet male crocodile (because the males of these and a few other large animals are properly called 'bulls'). The fact is that, unless the context makes it unlikely or impossible, to call something a *bull* conversationally implicates that it is a bovine animal.

Conversational implicatures are pragmatic counterparts to the semantic relation of entailment. They are based on stereotyped expectations of what would, more often than not, be the case. In the formula A +> B, B is a conversational implicature of A, B is a part (or perhaps the whole) of Speaker's utterance U made in context C under conventional cooperative conditions. B is a pragmatic inference calculated from the meaning of U as being most probable given the common ground, i.e.

> the cooperative principle (discussed later in this chapter)
> the context C, and
> grammatical and encyclopedic knowledge.

A conversational implicature can be cancelled without contradicting the utterance which implicates it. In both the relations A→B and A+>B, 'B' is an inference from 'A'; the difference is that A→B is a semantic relation in which B is a necessary consequence of A, whereas A+>B is a pragmatic relation in which B is only a probable consequence of A. In (5), (a) entails itself and conversationally implicates (b)–(i) – which constitute the 'restaurant script'.

(5)  (a)  *Sue went to a restaurant last night with her new boyfriend.*
     (b)  Sue intended to eat at the restaurant with her new boyfriend.
     (c)  Sue entered the restaurant, probably with her boyfriend.
     (d)  Sue and her boyfriend sat down.

(e) They ordered food.
(f) The food was brought.
(g) They ate it.
(h) Either Sue or her boyfriend paid the bill.
(i) Then they left the restaurant.

None of the clauses in (b)–(i) describes events that necessarily occurred, but they are all likely given that (a) is true. Any that do not apply can be cancelled, as most are in (6).

(6) Sue went to a restaurant last night with her new boyfriend, but as soon as they'd got inside the door they had a huge fight and left before even sitting down.

In calculating the meaning of an utterance such as (6), the entailments of its constituents take priority over conversational implicatures. (6) entails (7)–(11), each of which has implicatures (e.g. (11) conversationally implicates that they walked out of the restaurant).

(7) Sue went to a restaurant last night with her new boyfriend.
(8) Sue entered the restaurant with her boyfriend ('they'd got inside the door').
(9) Sue and her boyfriend had a huge fight in the restaurant.
(10) Sue and her boyfriend didn't even sit down.
(11) Sue and her boyfriend left the restaurant ('and left').

(7) conversationally implicates (5)(b). (8) supersedes (5)(c). (10) explicitly cancels (5)(d). (11) supersedes (5)(i). (10) and (11) together cancel (5)(e)–(h).

## Mutual entailment

Mutual entailment is represented by ↔. If A and B are sentences in the object language, then A is **synonymous** with B (A ↔ B) if, in all possible worlds, whenever A is true, B is also true; and whenever B is false, A is also false.

(12) Jim is a bachelor ↔ Jim is a man who has never married

If Jim was ever married then he is no bachelor.
*Be wife to* and *be husband to* are **converse predicates**; so are *be taller than* and *be shorter than*.

(13) Jo is Ed's wife ↔ Ed is Jo's husband
(14) Sally is shorter than George ↔ George is taller than Sally

Two predicates P and Q are converse if, and only if, for any pair of well-formed formulae P(x,y) and Q(y,x), P(x,y) ↔ Q(y,x). It is sufficient to understand the term *well-formed formula* to mean something like "grammatical sentence" and that x and y stand for different noun phrases.

Then there are **symmetric predicates** such as *be close to* and *be as tall as*. A two-place predicate P is symmetric if, and only if, for any well-formed formula P(x,y), P(x,y) ↔ P(y,x).

(15) Melbourne is close to Geelong ↔ Geelong is close to Melbourne
(16) Amy is as tall as me ↔ I am as tall as Amy

## Contradictories and contraries

A is the **contradictory** of B when, in all possible worlds, not-A $\leftrightarrow$ B and also not-B $\leftrightarrow$ A. In other words, if A is true then B is necessarily false and also if A is false then B is necessarily true.

(17)  *Harry is not tall* is the contradictory of *Harry is tall* (and vice versa).

It is often said that *true* and *false* are contradictories, and though this is often the case, it is not necessarily so. That which is not-true may be **indeterminable** rather than strictly false. For instance, (18) is complete nonsense and certainly not true. There are no grounds to show that it is false in the way that you can seek to show that (19) is false.

(18)  In 2006 the President of Australia was a colourless green idea.
(19)  In 2006 the Prime Minister of Australia was a woman.

A is the **contrary** of B if, in all possible worlds, A $\rightarrow$ not-B and B $\rightarrow$ not-A, but not-A does not entail B and not-B does not entail A. Contraries are sometimes called 'incompatibles'. Colours are contraries:

(20)  The book has a red cover $\rightarrow$ The book does not have a green cover

*The book does not have a green cover* does not entail that *The book has a red cover* because the cover could be blue or yellow or … .

## Hyponymy and antonymy

**Hyponyms** are contraries that have a common entailment in their **superordinate**. Colour terms (e.g. *red, blue*) are (co-)hyponyms of superordinate *colour*. Within the set of colour terms there are other hierarchies, e.g. *scarlet* and *vermillion* are (co-)hyponyms of superordinate *red*. *Mother* and *father* are (co-)hyponyms of superordinate *parent*.

True **antonyms** are contradictories, but so-called **relational antonyms** are contraries and co-hyponyms on a **relational scale** such as *height* with co-hyponymous relational antonyms *tall* and *short*. There is the temperature scale with co-hyponymous relational antonyms *hot, warm, tepid, cool, cold*. There is a quantity scale ranging through *all, most, many, a few, few, none*. Because they are contraries, *Jo is not short* does not entail that *Jo is tall*, she may be average height. If *the climate there is not-cold*, it does not necessarily follow that it is hot; and if *not many people love talking about contraries* it does not imply that most do!

## The cooperative maxims

The cooperative maxims are fundamental to a proper account of meaning in natural language. Grice 1975 described the **cooperative principle** in terms of four categories of maxims; they can be usefully augmented with the informativeness principle: 'read as much into the utterance as is consistent with what you know about the world' (Levinson 1983: 146f; Atlas and Levinson 1981). The augmented Gricean maxims are as follows.

The maxims of **quantity**: Quantity1 enjoins Speaker to make the strongest claim possible consistent with his/her perception of the facts. Quantity2 enjoins Speaker to give no more and no less information than is required to make his/her message clear to Hearer. Complementing these is a principle of interpretation by Hearer: given the semantic content of the utterance and Hearer's perception of the contextually relevant facts, the strongest inference possible is to be drawn from the utterance. We do not normally say things like *My neighbour, who is a woman, is pregnant* because we know that if the neighbour is pregnant, we must be referring to a woman.

The maxim of **quality**: Speaker should be genuine and sincere. That is, Speaker should state as facts only what s/he believes to be facts; make offers and promises only if s/he intends carrying them out; pronounce judgements only if s/he is in a position to judge and so on. For example it would violate the maxim of quality to assert *This chapter makes good bedtime reading for five-year olds.* Grice referred to 'truth' instead of sincerity. Truth is something independent of human action and belief, though beliefs about what constitutes truth are not. Meaning in language is closely bound to human action and belief. There are many kinds of utterances for which the evaluation of truth is either inapplicable or of secondary consideration to aspects of Speaker credibility and sincerity, for example when giving advice, apologizing, thanking, or congratulating someone. In human communication it is not sufficient to utter a truth: the truth also needs to be credible, and it is often important to modify the truth in order to preserve social harmony. Thus, the maxim of quality emphasizes cooperation in social interaction, which is identified with Speaker's sincerity in believing such things as that the facts are as stated, there is reason to apologize or congratulate Hearer, Speaker will carry out the promise being made, Hearer can accomplish the request being made of him or her, and so forth. If requested to do so, Speaker is under an obligation to provide justification for what is said.

The maxim of **relation** ("be relevant"): In general, an utterance should not be irrelevant to the context in which it is uttered, because that makes it difficult for Hearer to comprehend. We presume that Speaker has some reason for making the particular utterance U in context C, in the particular form which s/he uses, rather than maintaining silence or uttering something different.

The maxim of **manner**: Where possible, Speaker's meaning should be presented in a clear, concise manner that avoids ambiguity, and avoids misleading or confusing Hearer through stylistic ineptitude. Thus one should ordinarily avoid saying things like (21) – but I have a particular purpose in saying it here.

(21) There is a male adult human being in an upright stance using his legs as a means of locomotion to propel himself up a series of flat-topped structures some fifteen centimetres high.

We augment Grice's original idea by requiring that the cooperative principle holds whenever Speaker and Hearer mutually recognize Speaker's observance of three things.

> The **communicative presumption**: When Hearer perceives Speaker's utterance to be linguistic, Hearer presumes that Speaker has made the utterance with the intention of communicating some message using the conventions of natural language.

> The **reasonableness condition**: The communicative presumption presupposes that Speaker is acting reasonably, i.e. Speaker has some reason for making that particular utterance $U_a$, at that time $t_a$, in that place $w_a$, rather than maintaining silence or uttering something different.

The communicative presumption and reasonableness condition explain why a reader will make the effort to understand (22) (try reading it aloud).

(22)    Wants pawn term dare worsted ladle gull hoe lift wetter murder inner ladle cordage honour itch offer lodge dock florist. Disc ladle gull orphan worry ladle cluck wetter putty ladle rat hut, end fur disc raisin pimple caulder Ladle Rat Rotten Hut. (Chace 1956)

Furthermore, Speaker normally has some reason for selecting the forms and style used in the utterance.

> The final component of cooperation in language interaction is observance of the **normal conventions pertaining to face effects** (politeness phenomena) of their community.

Face (Brown and Levinson 1987; Brown and Gilman 1989) can be defined as **public self-image** – i.e. the way one perceives oneself to be viewed through the eyes of others. Face has two aspects:

(a) positive face is the want of a person to have their attributes, achievements, ideas, possessions, goals, and so on well regarded by others (*Congratulations on being top of the class. What a beautiful dress you are wearing!*)

(b) negative (or impositive) face is the want of a person not to be imposed upon by others (*I need you to stay on after closing time to clear up the cellar. Can you lend me ten quid? Get out of here, asshole!*).

Face can be lost (affronted), gained (enhanced), or just maintained. In virtually every utterance, Speaker needs to take care that what is said will maintain, enhance, or affront Hearer's face in just the way s/he intends to affect it, while at the same time maintaining or enhancing Speaker's own face. There is a general presumption that Speaker will be polite except when intending to affront Hearer's positive face; and Speaker will not normally impose on Hearer without good reason, lest Hearer's negative face be affronted. The meaningful effects of an utterance (and longer texts) that result from the Gricean maxims and other face effects are conversational implicatures. A theory of meaning must take account of normal conventions pertaining to face effects within a language community because utterance meaning is partly determined by reference to them; they form part of the common ground.

## Speech acts

Normal utterance involves a hierarchy of **speech acts**. To begin with, there is the act of **utterance**. This is recognizable even in an unknown language in which we cannot distinguish the sentences used, and what Speaker's message is. Utterance is recognized by brute perception: hearing the utterance spoken, seeing it signed or written, or feeling it impressed in braille. Linguistics is concerned with utterances in which Speaker uses a language expression and thereby performs a **locutionary act** (and more). Producing the locution demands that Speaker has knowledge of the grammar, lexicon, semantics, and phonology of L; to understand it, requires that Hearer has comparable knowledge. Speaker uses the locution to **refer** to things. Different Speakers using different locutionary and utterance acts can refer to the same thing.

Austin 1962 alerted us to the fact that Speaker DOES something when making an utterance. Some examples are: Speaker

| states a fact or an opinion | *Semantics can be difficult.* |
|---|---|
| confirms or denies something | *Marilyn Monroe did not commit suicide.* |
| makes a prediction | *It'll rain tonight.* |
| makes a promise | *I'll be with you in five minutes.* |
| makes a request | *What's the time?* |
| offers thanks or an invitation | *Can you come to dinner next Saturday?* |
| issues an order or an umpire's decision | *Out!* |
| gives advice or permission | *Yes, of course you can leave early today.* |
| names a child or a ship | *I name this ship 'QE3'.* |
| swears an oath | *I swear allegiance to the Crown.* |

In making an utterance, Speaker performs an **illocutionary act** by using a particular locution with the **illocutionary force** of a statement, a confirmation, a denial, a prediction, a promise, a request, and so on. Although an utterance has more than one illocutionary force, it will usually have only one message to convey; the illocutionary force that carries this message is said to be the **illocutionary point** of the utterance. In (23) the locution is what you see following the example number.

(23)  I'll make the bed.

Context of utterance will determine the reference of 'I' and 'the bed'. The primary illocutionary force is a statement about a future act. It may be used with a second illocutionary force: to make a promise. If this promise is taken to be Speaker's illocutionary intention, (23) has the illocutionary point "Speaker is promising to make the bed."

Typically, the illocutionary point of (24) is to have Hearer recognize that Speaker is offering a bet. The acceptance or refusal of the challenge is the **perlocutionary effect** of the utterance.

(24)  I bet you five quid Tony Blair will get a knighthood.

A perlocutionary act is the act of achieving a particular perlocutionary effect on Hearer as a result of Hearer recognizing (what s/he takes to be) the locution and illocutionary forces in Speaker's utterance. A perlocution is Hearer's behavioural response to the utterance – not necessarily a physical or verbal response, perhaps merely a mental or emotional response of some kind. Other perlocutions are such things as:

> alerting Hearer by warning Hearer of danger
> persuading Hearer to an opinion by stating supporting facts
> intimidating Hearer by threatening
> getting Hearer to do something by means of a suggestion, a hint, a request, or a command.

Perlocutions are extremely significant within a theory of communication, because the normal reason for speaking is to cause an effect in Hearer, and Speaker typically strives to achieve this by any means s/he can. However, perlocutionary effects fall beyond the boundary of linguistics because they are not part of language but behavioural and/or cognitive and/or emotional responses to the illocutionary forces in utterances. Instead, linguists can properly look at Speaker's **illocutionary intention** to have Hearer recognize the illocutionary point of Speaker's utterance in order to achieve a particular perlocutionary effect.

A promise may be made by using a **performative verb**, one that spells out the illocutionary point of the utterance.

(25)  I promise not to be late.

Whereas (25) makes a promise, (26), which uses past tense, reports one made.

(26)  I promised not to be late, but I was.

A promise is indirectly made in (27) (because Speaker commits to buying an ice-cream for Hearer if s/he stops crying); there is also a direct demand in the first clause.

(27)  Stop crying and I'll buy you an ice-cream.

(28) is directly making a statement, but perhaps indirectly suggesting that either Speaker or Hearer or both (depending on context) go shopping at Harrods.

(28)  They're having a sale at Harrods.

## Key points

> Sense is decontextualized meaning, abstracted from innumerable occurrences of the listeme. It is a semantic category.

> Two listemes of the same form are homonymous if they warrant separate lexicon entries because the identity of form is coincidental. A listeme is polysemous if it has more than one meaning given within a single lexicon entry.

> The reference of a language expression $e$ in utterance U is "what Speaker is talking about when using $e$ in U".

> Denotation is the relation between language expressions and things or events in worlds – not just the world we live in, but any world and time that may be spoken of. For example, the verb *kiss* denotes an act involving the lips; the noun *kiss* denotes the product of such an act.

> A language expression $e$ has extension in a world $w_i$ at time $t_i$ when $e$ denotes something that exists in the world $w_i$ at time $t_i$.

> The connotations of a language expression $e$ are pragmatic effects that arise from encyclopedic knowledge about the denotation (or reference) of $e$ and also from experiences, beliefs, and prejudices about the contexts in which the expression $e$ is typically used.

> We defined the semantic relations of entailment (including linguistic tautology) and conventional implicature (A$\longrightarrow$B), synonymy, converse and symmetric predicates (A$\longleftrightarrow$B); contradictories (not-A$\longleftrightarrow$B) and (not-B$\longleftrightarrow$A), and contraries not(A&B).

> Hyponyms are contraries that entail the same superordinate.

> True antonyms are contradictories. Relational antonyms are contraries and co-hyponyms on a relational scale.

> Sentences may be true or not-true. That which is not-true is either false or indeterminable.

> We defined the pragmatic relation of conversational implicature (A+>B). Whereas A⟶B is a semantic relation in which B is a necessary consequence of A, A+>B is a pragmatic relation in which B is only a probable consequence of A, and so the implicature is defeasible (can be cancelled).

> The cooperative principle of language interchange comprises the four cooperative maxims of quality, quantity, relation, and manner; the communicative presumption; the reasonableness condition; and normal conventions pertaining to face effects in the language community.

> Face is one's public self-image.

> A speech act consists of an act of utterance, a locutionary act, an act of referring, and an illocutionary act that may comprise a number of illocutionary forces; the illocutionary force that carries Speaker's message is the illocutionary point of the utterance. Speakers have the illocutionary intention to have a perlocutionary effect of some kind on Hearer.

> A performative verb spells out the illocutionary point of an utterance. The illocutionary point may be indirectly made and perhaps result through inference from common ground.

> Additional information may be found at http://www.wikipedia.org/, and in Allan 2001; Asher 1994; Brown 2006; Jaszczolt 2005; Levinson 2000; and the other works cited in this chapter.

# References

Allan, Keith 2001. *Natural Language Semantics*. Oxford & Malden MA: Blackwell.

Allan, Keith 2007. The pragmatics of connotation. *Journal of Pragmatics* 39: 1047–57.

Asher, Ronald E. (ed.) 1994. *Encyclopedia of Languages and Linguistics*. 10 vols. Oxford: Pergamon Press.

Atlas, Jay and Stephen C. Levinson 1981. It-clefts, informativeness, and logical form. In *Radical Pragmatics*, ed. by Peter Cole. New York: Academic Press, pp. 1–62.

Austin, John L. 1962. *How to Do Things with Words*. Oxford: Clarendon Press.

Brown, E. Keith (General editor) 2006. *Encyclopedia of Languages and Linguistics*. 2nd edn. 14 vols. Oxford: Elsevier.

Brown, Penelope and Stephen Levinson 1987. *Politeness: Some Universals in Language Usage*. Cambridge: Cambridge University Press.

Brown, Roger W. and Albert Gilman 1989. Politeness theory and Shakespeare's four major tragedies. *Language in Society* 18: 159–212.

Chace, Howard L. 1956. *Anguish Languish*. Englewood Cliffs NJ: Prentice-Hall Inc.

Grice, H. Paul 1975. Logic and conversation. In *Syntax and Semantics 3: Speech Acts*, ed. by Peter Cole and Jerry L. Morgan. New York: Academic Press. pp. 41–58. Reprinted in H. Paul Grice *Studies in the Way of Words*. Cambridge MA: Harvard University Press. 1986.

Jaszczolt, Katarzyna M. 2005. *Default Semantics: Foundations of a Compositional Theory of Acts of Communication*. Oxford: Oxford University Press.

Levinson, Stephen C. 1983. *Pragmatics*. Cambridge: Cambridge University Press.

Levinson, Stephen C. 2000. *Presumptive Meanings: The Theory of Generalized Conversational Implicature*. Cambridge MA: MIT Press.

# 2.7 **sociolinguistics**

## chapter contents

> Language variation     86
> Regional variation     87
> Social variation     87
> Linguistic ethnography     89
> Language and power     91
> Address terms     91
> Standard languages     92
> Language attitudes     92
> Sexist language     93
> Critical discourse analysis (CDA)     93
> Language, gender and sexuality     94
> Conversational style     96
> Explanations for gender differences in politeness     96
> Discursive construction of gender and sexuality     97
> Language contact     97
> Pidginization and creolization     98
> Language death     99
> Key points     100
> References     100

## Language variation

Sociolinguistics is the study of language in its social context. Speakers and hearers use language to present an identity or multiple identities and to locate each other socially. On hearing an unknown speaker on the radio or the telephone, we can usually make an assessment of the person's gender, age (i.e. whether a child, adult, elderly person), first language, country or region of origin, and education level. We use this assessment, whether accurate or not, to help us interpret what the person is saying. Thus language use encodes social information, and sociolinguists seek to understand the nature of this encoding. This entails describing variation between individuals (**interspeaker variation**), based on their affiliations with different social groups or categories.

Sociolinguists are also interested in **intraspeaker variation**. It is clear that we all have more than one way of speaking. At home with family members we speak in a more relaxed style than in a classroom or a job interview. We all have a range of speech styles, from very formal to very casual, and we choose our style depending on the formality of the context and our relationship with our interlocutors. Sociolinguists also identify specific domains or functions that make use of specialist language use, jargons or registers, as for example in the language of public notices (e.g. *Camping prohibited on foreshore*). Register variation will be discussed in more detail in Chapter 2.11, Stylistics. The style shifting associated with formality of social context will be taken up in the discussion below.

## Regional variation

A striking form of interspeaker variation is regional variation. Two speakers from different geographical areas are likely to speak different languages or different dialects of the same language. **Dialects** are regional varieties of the same language which differ in lexis, syntax and phonology. For example, speakers of British or American English arriving in Australia will find most of the language used familiar to them, but they will need to learn some new lexical items, such as *hoon*, a derogatory term for a young male (usually) who engages in dangerous driving. Language adapts to the local context, and changes over time, as speakers coin terms for new concepts and objects. Thus we can identify distinct varieties of English spoken, for example, in Scotland, the United States, India, South Africa and New Zealand; and within most countries there is regional variation as well.

Most languages have regional dialects as a result of the distance between communities and separation over time. In some cases geographical barriers, such as mountain ranges or oceans, or political or national boundaries will contribute to the separation. Small differences will often be treated as significant by speakers. Bob Dixon writes of his fieldwork with speakers of Australian indigenous languages:

> On the second day of my fieldwork in North Queensland, in October 1963, I was talking to Chloe Grant in her house on the southern bank of the Murray River. She explained that there were two local languages – Jirrbal, on the northern side of the river had *bana* for 'water' and *buni* for 'fire' while Girramay, on the southern side, had *gamu* for 'water' and *yugu* for 'fire'. (This is one of the places where a tribal boundary actually runs along the river, for a few miles.) However, on further investigation it became apparent that there was relatively little difference between Jirrbal and Girramay – they have almost identical grammars and over 80 per cent of their vocabularies are the same. In linguistic terms, Jirrbal and Girramay are mutually intelligible dialects of one language; they differ about as much as do Scottish English and English English.

> But those differences that do exist between Jirrbal and Girramay are looked upon as highly significant, and taken as indices of tribal affiliation. (Dixon 1980: 33)

Regional dialects have been surveyed using questionnaire techniques, sampling speakers across geographical areas and constructing maps of usage (see Chapter 5.8). A line, called an **isogloss**, is drawn on the map to indicate where a usage changes, and if a number of isoglosses occur in the same place we recognize a dialect boundary. Dialect maps allow historical linguists to reconstruct likely population movements and contact between languages in the region.

## Social variation

When you want to describe someone who has drunk too much alcohol you might describe them as *inebriated, under the influence, drunk, merry, blotto, pissed, tired and emotional,* or *legless,* and you may have other terms in your **repertoire** (the inventory of all your knowledge of the language). While these terms have roughly the same referential meaning, they have different connotations because they convey different social information. By your choice of term you are telling the hearer how formal you think the situation is and how seriously you take the behaviour. You may also be signalling information about your education, social class, and group affiliation. Thus the choice of variant conveys social meaning.

Sociolinguistic research shows that social class (usually identified by income, occupation and education) correlates with a particular frequency of use of sociolinguistic variables. In many varieties of English the final consonant in the progressive morpheme *–ing* (e.g. in *going, thinking, talking*) varies between a velar nasal [ŋ] and an alveolar nasal [n]. In most of these communities middle-class speakers tend to use the velar nasal more frequently than working-class speakers do. Thus it is possible to identify **sociolects** (social class varieties) on the basis of frequency of use of such variables.

Labov 1972b has shown that in more formal settings, speakers tend to shift towards the sociolect of the next highest social class, indicating that usage by higher social groups bestows **prestige** on a variant. For example in New York City, the use of /r/ after the vowel in words such as *fourth* and *floor* has prestige as a result of being more frequently used by speakers from higher social classes (see also Chapter 5.8).

Labov assumes that members of a speech community share the social value of a variable. However, if certain variables such as post-vocalic (r) have high prestige but are used very little by lower-class speakers, to what extent can we be sure that these speakers share the community's norms? That is, why don't more lower-class speakers change their behaviour towards the high prestige norm? (Note that Labov uses the convention of a round bracket, e.g. (r), to indicate the abstract notion of a sociolinguistic variable.)

One factor is gender. In Norwich, in the south-east of England, Trudgill 1974; 1983 compared usage with self-report and found that women overstate their use of the prestige variant (e.g. [ɪə] in *ear, hear, idea*) while men tended to overstate their use of the non-standard, low prestige variant [ɛ:] (i.e. *ear* is homophonous with *air*). This suggests that there are two contrasting forms of prestige: **overt prestige** associated with standard variants used in education and formal settings, particularly by higher social groups, and **covert prestige** associated with local vernacular forms. Men, especially from lower socioeconomic groups, valued the tough masculinity projected by the use of non-standard forms, while women oriented to the overt, socially sanctioned norm, as part of their claim to social status.

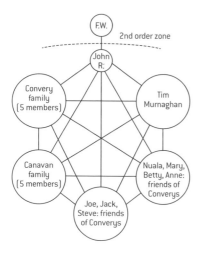

*Figure 2.13 Network diagram for part of the Clonard network, showing 100% density (from Milroy 1980: 58)*

Another possible factor is membership of social networks. Milroy 1980 studied Belfast neighbourhoods. In some working-class neighbourhoods people interact with each other in a number of roles, as for example when a relative is also a neighbour and works in the same place (Milroy calls these **multiplex** networks). Such networks are often also **dense** (i.e. the people one knows also know each other). Figure 2.13 is a partial network for Milroy's participants in the Clonard area, showing a maximally dense and multiplex network.

Milroy argues that the dense, multiplex networks of the Belfast neighbourhoods she studied provided strong reinforcement for local non-standard norms. Speakers orient to and identify with the local groups with whom they interact most extensively, rather than to an abstract notion such as social class or prestige.

Contemporary work in sociolinguistics seeks to explain dialect maintenance or change in terms of the affiliation of individuals with local social groups. Le Page and Tabouret-Keller 1985 argued on the basis of their research in the Caribbean that, in order to account for the complex patterning of variation in speech, we need to see each linguistic choice as an **act of identity,** where speakers model their language behaviour on the language behaviour of a group or groups with whom they may wish to be identified. This may include the addressee, or others who are not present (see also the model of **audience design** in Bell 1984). For example, if I want to report what someone else has said I might use the quotative phrase *she said* (e.g. *I asked Kerry to lend me her car and she said 'No way!'*). Younger speakers in Australia and Britain can also use the verb *go* ( ... *and she goes 'No way!'*) but increasingly also they draw on a form which is widespread in youth culture in North America: *is like* ( ... *and she's like 'No way!'*). We can see the choice of this form as an identity marker, allowing speakers to claim affiliation with cool, highly valued youth culture, and separate themselves from the older generations. Recent work in Britain (Cheshire and Fox 2008) also finds a quotative *This is X: ' ... '* where X is the speaker being quoted, e.g. *This is me 'what ... what's your ... what's your problem?'*

Current work draws on the notion of **community of practice** (Lave and Wenger 1991). When people come together for a joint enterprise and develop shared practices and a common repertoire, they constitute a community of practice. Individuals may be central or peripheral members of a group. Eckert 1989 showed how one group of students in a Detroit school (the 'Jocks'), who oriented towards the school culture of study, sport and leadership, and had plans to go to college, used language differently from another group who were anxious to leave school and go into blue-collar or manual jobs in the local community (the 'Burnouts'). Burnouts displayed affiliation to their community of practice with extensive swearing, the use of non-standard grammar (e.g. multiple negation as in *I don't know nothing*) and the greeting *How ya doing?* Jocks greeted with *Hi,* and used standard grammar. A sound change in progress (the backwards shift of the vowel in words such as *lunch,* moving it closer to the vowel in *launch*) was being led by the Burnouts. Eckert showed that the use of Jock or Burnout linguistic features correlated with peer affiliation rather than parents' social class.

## Linguistic ethnography

The **ethnography of communication** is the study of situated language use, and ethnographers aim to document language behaviour in context, and understand the meanings and values assigned to such behaviours within a **speech community** (people who share norms of language use). Unlike Chomsky, who argued that '[l]inguistic theory is primarily concerned with an ideal speaker-listener in a completely homogeneous speech community' (Chomsky 1965: 3), Hymes 1972b rejected the goal of understanding the language system abstracted from its context of use. His focus was on **communicative competence,** that is, what one needs to know to speak appropriately and be a properly functioning member of a speech community. Contemporary linguistic ethnography adds to this a concern with describing the sociopolitical context itself (Rampton 2007).

Communicative competence is culture-dependent: communities differ in the rules governing speech, and the value attached to different forms of language use. For example, Reisman 1974 contrasted communicative competence in Antigua and Sweden. In Antigua, speech was seen as a form of self-expression and great value was attached to 'making noise' in conversation (i.e. boasting, cursing, and arguing). People talked simultaneously, with no norm of turn-taking nor constraints against interruption. Very different norms apply in the Lapp community of northern Sweden, where long silences are normal in friendly conversation.

Ethnographic work is important in understanding problems of cross-cultural communication, as was shown by the Gumperz work discussed in Chapter 1.1. For example, when responding to a compliment (*That's a beautiful jacket*) we can accept it (*Yes, isn't it*) or express thanks, perhaps with some deflection of the compliment (*Thanks. It was a birthday present*), or reject the compliment (*No, it's just an old thing*). Japanese women are more likely to reject the compliment, while English speakers tend to accept with deflection. Leech 1983 argues that for Japanese women the norm of modesty outweighs the norm of agreement with the interlocutor, whereas the opposite is true for most English speakers.

Hymes 1972a uses the word SPEAKING as a mnemonic device to outline the elements that need to be described in an ethnography of communication (cf. also Saville-Troike 1982). The table on the following page summarizes the elements and illustrates them with a commonplace example of an unsolicited telemarketing phone call.

Changing an element of the cultural context can change the language behaviour. For example, if the telemarketer and receiver of the call were friends, or if the receiver wanted financial advice, the interaction would unfold very differently, and different norms would apply.

Speech events across a wide range of societies have been described using ethnographic approaches. Ethnographers describe what happens using a combination of methods, including participant observation over an extended time frame, and recording and analysis of speech events, and supplementing these with participant interviews to help to establish the meaning of acts or events.

Ethnographic approaches attempt to make visible the taken-for-granted aspects which form the hidden framework for everyday events. Important ethnographic work has examined children's acquisition of literacy (Heath 1983, and see Chapter 5.8), and more recent ethnographic work has brought critical discourse analytic insights to the study of literacy events. Street 1995 highlights the role of ideology in privileging dominant constructions of discourse (see discussion of critical discourse analysis below). Eckert's work in Detroit schools combined variationist and ethnographic approaches, and a number of other scholars have conducted important ethnographic studies in schools (Heller 1999; Rampton 1995; 2006, and see Chapter 5.8). This work recognizes the importance of adolescence as a time of identity formation, and of language innovation. Schools are also sites of multilingual encounters and contact between cultures of conformity and resistance. Recent sociolinguistic and ethnographic approaches have shifted from a structuralist paradigm, which locates an individual's language use as a product of his or her socialization and social position in a culture, to a more constructivist or post-structuralist paradigm which assigns a greater role to human agency, and highlights the role of power in configuring social space.

| S | Setting; Scene | Time, place, physical setting; psychological setting | Friday evening, at home, telephone; private sphere |
|---|---|---|---|
| P | Participants | Roles and relationships | Caller (male, adult) Receiver (male, adult) Caller and receiver are strangers |
| E | Ends, purposes, outcomes, goals | a) Conventional expectations of outcome b) Participants' goals (if different from a) | a) Civil cooperative interaction b) C's goal: to sell a banking product; R's goal: to preserve privacy and not engage in a commercial transaction |
| A | Acts | The sequence of speech acts | 1. C: Phone rings. 2. R: Hello? 3. C: Good evening. You are paying off a mortgage, aren't you? 4. R: No, I'm bloody not. 5. C: Have a good day! [R slams down the phone] |
| K | Key | Tone, manner or spirit of interaction | C: semi-formal, assertive R: curt, offensive |
| I | Instrumentalities | The channel (spoken, written, etc.), code and variety used | Spoken, via telephone Semi-formal and informal English |
| N | Norms of interaction and interpretation | Rules governing speech and how it is interpreted | Turn-taking rules apply Caller raises topic Caller assumes cooperative principle, uses conventional polite forms Receiver assumes a norm of non-invasion of privacy; considers invasion of privacy justifies non-use of politeness conventions |
| G | Genre | The textual category or type of language (e.g. poem, sermon) | Telemarketing |

## Language and power

Earlier studies of language and power described the social construction and linguistic encoding of inequality, at either the personal or the institutional level. Contemporary work takes a **critical discourse analysis** focus, analysing how interlocutors negotiate power. Critical approaches aim to reveal the role of ideology in constructing taken-for-granted conventions and meanings, and allow participants to challenge these assumptions, from a Marxist, feminist or other perspective. Such work draws on the insights of Bakhtin 1981; Bourdieu 1991; Foucault 1981 and other post-structuralist theorists.

## Address terms

In early work Brown and Gilman 1960 developed a framework for analysing the use of second-person pronouns in European languages. French, for example, makes a distinction between *tu* ("you" singular), and *vous* ("you" plural), and many European languages do the same (though English has lost the singular *thou* form, and uses the earlier plural form *you* for both singular and plural address). In addition to the primary meaning of singular or plural, an overlay of social rules developed in French, Spanish, German, and Russian and other European languages, so that when speaking to a stranger or a superior it was considered appropriate to use the plural form (the **V form**) while the **T form** was confined to addressing an intimate or social inferior. Brown and Gilman modelled the rules using two dimensions: power and solidarity. In situations of unequal power, the inferior uses V to the superior, and receives T; in situations of equality, strangers use reciprocal V, while friends use reciprocal T. The precise nature of the social rules varies from one society to another, and is changing over time as social circumstances change (cf. Allan and Burridge 2006: 133ff; Clyne, Kretzenbacher, Norrby et al. 2006).

Brown and Ford 1964 applied this model of power and solidarity to the study of address terms in American English, and showed that the choice of addressing an inter-locutor using first name (e.g. *Lee*) or title plus last name (*Dr Rankin*) was similarly governed by the factors of power and solidarity. The model also helps to explain polite-ness systems and multilingual code choice (see discussion below).

## Standard languages

The role of power is also evident in the way languages and dialects are organized socially. In a society where more than one language or dialect is spoken, the social status and power of groups of speakers attach to the language or dialect they speak. In this way the dialect of the powerful group comes to be seen as better than other dialects or languages, and may acquire a gatekeeping function. In multiracial and multilingual Singapore, four languages (English, Mandarin Chinese, Malay, and Tamil) are given official language status. Official languages are recognized by the state and can be used in formal public functions (government business, the media, education, and so on). Other languages used in the community (such as Hokkien, Hakka, Baba Malay, and Arabic) cannot be used in formal domains. Official recognition thus privileges speakers of the designated languages, giving them ready access to formal domains, while minority language speakers need to learn the official languages in order to function effectively in the community. Bourdieu 1991 challenges the legitimation attached to a state's official language and the imposition of its norms on the community as a whole. By critically examining the historical proc-esses that make some languages dominant, while others are assigned minority status or stigmatized, we can avoid the perception of natural authority and legitimacy associated with official languages (May 2005).

The privileging of some dominant languages (or dialects) has led to calls for protec-tion and **language rights** to be granted to speakers of minority languages, particularly those suffering from the **linguistic imperialism** of global English (Philippson 1992); however May 2005 suggests that such calls ignore the natural processes of language contact (see below) which lead to **hybridity.** Purists lament the loss of minority languages, but they can leave their mark on the dominant language which can be trans-formed, as has happened with Singapore English. A distinctive local variety has emerged in which a hybrid Singaporean identity can be vibrantly expressed.

## Language attitudes

Languages or dialects that are spoken by the elite, and chosen for official functions, become more developed than others. Dictionaries and grammars are written for those varieties, codifying the grammar and phonology and designating them as **standard**. Thus the notion of a standard language is a political construct, based on unequal power between groups. In this way the variety of English spoken in the south-east of England came to be seen as the standard variety of English, and other regional dialects were seen as **non-standard**. Thus differences in power and prestige between social groups lead to the development of **language attitudes**, that is, judgements made about dialects or languages, and thence also about speakers.

Studies of language attitudes in the UK by social psychologists (Giles and Powesland 1975) were conducted using **matched guise** techniques, where one actor would read the same text using different accents. Recordings were played to participants who were told they were listening to different speakers and were asked to judge each speaker using Likert scales. For example, they might be asked to rank the speaker's intelligence (or competence, trustworthiness, and so on) on a five-point scale ranging from *very trust-worthy* to *very untrustworthy*. Findings indicated that speakers using prestigious accents, such as Received Pronunciation (the educated Southern British accent), were seen as more intelligent and competent, but less friendly and trustworthy than speakers of non-standard varieties. There have been challenges to the validity of matched guise techniques, but the findings are striking. One important insight from language attitude studies is that we make judgements of others based on their speech style, without being aware that we are doing so.

## Sexist language

Critical approaches to sociolinguistics argue that we need to make speakers aware of the values we have unconsciously absorbed from the hierarchical organization of society, and further that we need to challenge the operation of power in language. Fairclough 1995; 1999 and others have argued that oppression is transmitted and constructed through the language of the powerful. A good example of this comes from the feminist challenge to the use of sexist language. It was argued that the encoding of male gender in supposedly neutral references (*The committee needs to elect a chair***man**; *when a child is born,* **he** *... ; Anthropology is the study of* **man**; and so on) made women invisible as active participants in society. This was reinforced by examples such as **man's** *basic needs include food and shelter for* **himself** *and* **his wife** *and children* (Spender 1990). Proponents of non-sexist writing argued that it was possible to make generic language gender neutral, and use gendered reference only in relation to particular individuals (thus *the committee* **chair**, *or* **chairper-son**; *When children are born,* **they** *... ; Anthropology is the study of* **human beings** *... ;* **people's** *basic needs include food and shelter for* **themselves** *and their* **families,** *and so on*).

Argument remains about whether particular forms of language (e.g. sexist language) can structure the way we perceive the world (drawing on a hypothesis developed by Sapir and refined by Whorf, see Chapter 4.1).

## Critical discourse analysis (CDA)

[L]anguage indexes power, expresses power, is involved where there is contention over and a challenge to power. Power does not derive from language, but language can be used to challenge power, to subvert it, to alter distributions of power in the short and long term. ... Power is signalled not only by grammatical forms within a

> text, but also by a person's control of a social occasion by means of the genre of a text. It is often exactly within the genres associated with given social occasions that power is exercised or challenged. (Wodak 2001: 11)

CDA assumes that power is central to language use; examines the political assumptions underlying discourse; explores power, history and ideology in relation to spoken and written texts, and includes an examination of the social and historical processes leading to their production, and shaping the way participants derive meaning from them (Wodak 2001). Dominant structures establish conventions and make them appear natural. CDA attempts to reveal the hidden, ideological foundations for conventions, and the nature of resistance. This approach has been used extensively in studies of gender, identity, and media language.

Studies of identity construction are increasingly making use of personal history narratives to analyse how speakers make sense of social change, and locate themselves in terms of competing 'social and historical voices' (Bakhtin 1981). Using a variety of social languages or discourses, writers or speakers express different points of view, drawing on different ideologies. Fairclough 1999 and others have called this *interdiscursivity*.

## Language, gender and sexuality

> Women's language has been said to reflect their (our) conservatism, prestige consciousness, upward mobility, insecurity, deference, nurturance, emotional expressivity, connectedness, sensitivity to others, solidarity. And men's language is heard as evincing their toughness, lack of affect, competitiveness, independence, competence, hierarchy, control. (Eckert and McConnell-Ginet 1998: 485)

The work of Labov and Trudgill revealed that gender was a significant social factor in sociolinguistic variation, and subsequent studies have shown that gender difference is common across the world's languages. In general these are differences in frequency of use of linguistic forms, rather than exclusively female or male language. Yanyuwa, a now endangered Australian indigenous language, is unusual in having distinctive male and female dialects (Bradley 1998). Word stems are shared in the two dialects, but prefixes marking grammatical class on nouns, pronouns, and verbs are different. An example below gives the same sentence as spoken by a woman and a man. The sentence includes nouns and pronouns from three of Yanyuwa's seven noun classes: male (M), masculine (MSC) and arboreal (ARB). In the example, DAT indicates dative, and ALL is allative, indicating movement 'to' a location. We have used bold type to highlight the shared material between the two dialects. It is clear that the stems and suffixes are shared, while most of the prefixes differ. For example, the women mark male class items (adjective, noun, name of the man referred to) with *nya–* while men use a zero allomorph. With nouns in the masculine class, *–wamarra–*, *–walya–*, women use the prefix *ji–* while men use *ki–*.

### Women's Dialect

*Nya-ja   nya-**wukuthu**   nya-**rduwarra**      niya-**wini**   nya-**Wungkurli**      kiwa-**wingka***
This-M    M-short      M-initiated man   his-name   M-personal name     he go

***wayka-liya   ji-wamarra-lu   niwa-yirdi   na-ridiridi      ji-walya-wu***
down-wards   MSC-sea-ALL   he-bring   ARB-harpoon   MSC-dugong/turtle-DAT

**Men's Dialect**

| *Jinangu* | *Ø-wukuthu* | *Ø-rduwarra* | *na-wini* | *Ø-Wungkurli* | *ka-wingka* |
|-----------|-------------|--------------|-----------|---------------|-------------|
| This | short | initiated man | his-name | personal name | he go |

| *wayka-liya* | *ki-wamarra-lu* | *na-yirdi* | *na-ridiridi* | *ki-walya-wu* |
|--------------|-----------------|------------|---------------|---------------|
| down-wards | MSC-sea-ALL | he-bring | ARB-harpoon | MSC-dugong/turtle-DAT |

"The short initiated man whose name is Wungkurli, went down to the sea, taking a harpoon with him for dugong or sea turtle." (Bradley 1998: 14)

Sex exclusive forms are rare. More usual across a wide range of communities is a difference in the frequency with which women and men use certain forms, particularly those which correlate with different sociolects. Labov in his study of New York's Lower East Side (Labov 1972a) found a complex interaction between gender and social class: women in each social class use a higher frequency than men of the prestige variants, such as post-vocalic (r), thus appearing to orient more strongly towards the social class above. In Trudgill's Norwich study (Trudgill 1974; see also Trudgill 1998) a similarly complex interaction between social class and gender was revealed. As noted earlier in this chapter, he argued that women were more oriented to overt, socially sanctioned norms, while men were more oriented to covert, non-standard norms. In his view, women were using language to claim social status, men to express masculinity.

However, the association between social class, gender, and choice of linguistic variant may not be so straightforward. Milroy 1980 in her work in Belfast (discussed earlier) found that language choice depended on the nature of network ties, suggesting that there is a need to look more locally at the networks and life patterns of women and men in order to discover what might motivate them to use certain variants. Susan Gal 1998 studied a bilingual Austrian peasant community and found that gender was associated with language shift from Hungarian to German. Women preferred to use German because Hungarian was associated with peasants rather than urban workers, and marriage to a peasant would give them a harsher life. The male peasants had to look for wives outside the village, and these wives were often German-speaking, reinforcing the shift of the community towards German.

Another perspective comes from work in New Zealand (Gordon 1997) which suggests that women shift to more standard language to avoid being labelled as sexually loose, a labelling based on stereotypes of working-class behaviour (see Chapter 5.8). Eckert 1989 in the Detroit school study, emphasizes the pressure on girls to present themselves in the appropriate image of their community of practice. Jock girls risk being labelled as 'sluts' and Burnout girls as 'snobs' if they don't conform to the appropriate norms. She argues that while men can construct identity through action, women need to perform identity symbolically, through language use.

> A star varsity athlete, for instance, regardless of his character or appearance, can enjoy considerable status. There is virtually nothing, however, that a girl lacking in social or physical gifts can do that will accord her social status. In other words, whereas it's enough for a boy to have accomplishments of the right sort, a girl must be a certain sort of person. (Eckert 1989: 256)

Eckert's work was concerned with use of sociolinguistic variables, but considerable attention has also been paid to conversational style.

## Conversational style

Research in Britain, the United States, and New Zealand shows gender differences in conversational style (Holmes 1994). Women seem to be cooperative, facilitative participants, using more politeness markers, showing concern for their conversational partners, while men tend to dominate the talking time, interrupt more often than women, and focus on the task at hand rather than the addressee. Some differences between typical male and female conversational style are shown in the transcript extract below. (Transcription conventions have been modified: (.) indicates a short pause, (..) a slightly longer pause, items in square brackets indicate simultaneous speech.)

| 1 | Max: | I got a phone call from Pat's mother saying you (.) c– you're a complete bastard Pat's told us what you did to her (..) you're so inconsiderate (.) |
|---|------|---|
| 2 | Nell: | oh dear |
| 3 | Max: | especially when she's been under such stress (..) well what was I supposed to say (.) what did they want |
| 4 | Nell: | mm (.) tricky (.) did [you ask her   ] |
| 5 | Max: | [I didn't know ] what to say (.) I mean I have no idea what story Pat told them (..) |
| 6 | Nell: | mm |
| 7 | Max: | she's got a vivid imagination when she gets started who know w– (.) who knows what fabrication they had been treated to |
| 8 | Nell: | well she was pretty stressed out (.) maybe they were just over-reacting from worry [about her d'you think] |
| 9 | Max: | [not them not them   ] they just hate my guts (..) any excuse to abuse me (.) I'm not good enough for their daughter |

(Holmes 1995: 30)

In this extract Nell indicates that she is listening by using backchannel signals (*oh dear, mm*). There is some evidence that women make more use of these than men. Men are more likely than women to interrupt, and Max does this to Nell at lines 5 and 9. Interruptions violate current speaker turn and are a sign of relative power.

## Explanations for gender differences in politeness

Early studies of women's style (e.g. Lakoff 1975) suggested that men's language is prestigious and women's speech differed from it because of their insecurity. Female style was seen as a sign of subordination and self-denial. Women have less power in patriarchal society and seek to raise their status by showing deference, being polite and using the standard language. Maltz and Borker 1982 related the differences to culture rather than power (see also Tannen 1990). They argued that women and men belong to different subcultures, which are based on the different socialization patterns of the predominantly single sex playgroups of their childhood. Cameron 1997 has shown that our preconceptions lead us to see what we expect to see, so, for example, the use of gossip by men is overlooked. We read all behaviour through a more general discourse on gender difference which may itself construct that difference.

## Discursive construction of gender and sexuality

Heller 1999; 2001, using ethnographic methods, studied bilingual language behaviour in a French language secondary school in Ottawa, Canada (see Chapter 5.8). Her observations showed that boys controlled the public discourse in the school, while girls had marginal roles. However, one group of girls resisted the marginality, and the silent, passive, nurturing and decorative roles assigned to girls in the school culture, by designating themselves as the 'Nerds'. They displayed their resistance by speaking out in class and in the corridors, choosing to use English rather than French, and proclaiming themselves lesbians in opposition to the dominant romantic ideology of girls as passive objects of male pursuit.

Gender and sexuality are now generally seen as performance, as unstable and subject to variation. Work on gay, lesbian and transgendered identity construction shows how different ways of speaking may be drawn on to present a speaker as straight, effeminate or butch. For example the adjective *gay* may be used pejoratively (*that's so gay*) to present the speaker as heterosexual (cf. Cameron and Kulick 2003).

## Language contact

Colonization, migration or political boundary changes bring speakers of different languages or dialects into contact with each other. Some speakers will become bilingual or bidialectal and the varieties in contact are likely to change. Depending on the sociopolitical context there may be rapid flux and instability, or the communities may settle into a relatively stable arrangement of rights and expectations.

Where bilingualism is widespread in a society, speakers are likely to use the languages in different **domains** and for different functions. Domains are areas of social life that differ in terms of participants and their relationships, and the nature and function of their interactions. Examples of different domains are family, friendship, religion, employment, or education. Ferguson 1959 described **diglossia**, the patterned use of formal and colloquial forms of the same language by speakers of Arabic, Swiss-German, Greek, and Haitian Creole (Greek diglossia has changed since Ferguson's study). Speakers of Arabic, for example, acquire the local colloquial variety (the **L**, or low variety) at home, and use it in personal or informal domains such as the family or friendship, and in folk literature, personal letters, and radio soap operas, while the standard, classical variety (the **H**, or high variety) is learnt at school and used in formal domains (education, government, administration, and so on). The H has prestige and status, while the L is seen as ungrammatical. Fishman 1967 observed that a similar distribution may develop between two different languages. For example, in Paraguay the indigenous language, Guaraní, functions as the L, and Spanish is the H.

In diglossic communities everyone shares the same home variety, and those who are educated also learn the formal variety. In many bilingual or multilingual communities speakers from different ethnolinguistic groups with different home languages need to interact, perhaps at work or in everyday transactions. In order to communicate, speakers will need to make choices from among the codes or languages available in their individual linguistic repertoires. An Italian-Australian family may use Italian at home but **codeswitch** to English when talking to a non-Italian-speaking neighbour. Within the household, while everyone knows both Italian and English, some topics may trigger a switch to English (e.g.

children talking about mathematics homework), or to Italian (e.g. discussing the election of a representative to the Italian parliament). The grandparents are likely to be more comfortable in Italian, while the grandchildren are more likely to use English. Members of the household will choose their code to suit their interlocutor. Thus changes in the situation (topic, setting or participants) are likely to trigger codeswitching. There are also rhetorical triggers for codeswitching. Blom and Gumperz 1972 described **metaphorical codeswitching** where speakers signal a change in communicative purpose. A speaker may codeswitch to indicate humorous intent, or to quote another person.

Codeswitching may occur at sentence boundaries (**intersentential codeswitching**) or within a sentence (**intrasentential codeswitching**, sometimes called **codemixing**). Myers-Scotton 1993 suggests that intrasentential codeswitching is systematic: one language will supply the grammar for a sentence and this should be seen as the **matrix language**. She illustrates this with the following example from the Wei 1998 Chinese/English corpus (Myers-Scotton 2002):

1   *Ni* **paper** *hai mei* **finish** *a?*               *wode san-fen*
    you paper yet not finish PART/AFFIRM    my three-CLASSIF
2   **term paper** *qiantian*                    *yijin*
    term paper  the day before yesterday  already
3   *jiaoshangqu le.*             *Ni   tai* **slow** *le.*
    turn in    PART/PERF        you too slow  PART/AFFIRM

"You haven't finished your paper yet? My three term papers were already turned in the day before yesterday. You are too slow."

In this example, the grammatical framework is Chinese. This is clear from word order and the use of Chinese affirmative and perfective particles (PART/AFFIRM, PART/PERF) and noun classifier (CLASSIF). Into this Chinese matrix are slotted English lexical items (*paper, finish, term paper, slow*).

## Pidginization and creolization

Contact between speakers of different languages arises through trade, or social upheavals and the mass relocation of people. In extreme circumstances, people are thrust into situations where they need to find a common code to survive, but none exists. In these situations a new variety is created from the language resources of the participant groups, to serve as a **lingua franca**. The slave trade brought speakers of a range of West African languages into contact with each other on plantations owned by speakers of English, French, Spanish, or Portuguese in the Americas. Contact with the slave owners was too limited for full language learning to take place, but lexical items from the dominant (or **superstrate**) language were grafted onto the grammatical systems of the slaves' native languages, to create improvised codes for simple communication.

Bickerton 1981 studied the language of labourers brought to work on the Hawaiian plantations in the early twentieth century, and showed that English or Hawaiian words were used with speakers' native Japanese, or Chinese or Philippine language syntax, or sometimes with no identifiable syntax at all. An improvised code that becomes stabilized through extended contact is called a **pidgin**. It has a simple grammar that does not correspond to any of the input languages. When pidgin-speaking communities become established, and particularly when they have children, who are native speakers of the new code, the pidgin expands, developing systematic syntax and new vocabulary to meet a full range of expressive needs. The resulting language is called a **creole**. Pidginization is a process of simplification and reduction, while creolization is a process of expansion and grammaticalization.

Thomason 2001 notes that not all creoles develop through the prototypical pathway described above. In some cases of extensive trade and contact (e.g. West African Pidgin English or Tok Pisin in New Guinea), a pidgin may expand its resources without necessarily acquiring native speakers (there are some native speakers of both these languages, but many of the changes are attributed to non-native speakers).

The pronominal system of Tok Pisin shows how grammatical influence from the **substrate** indigenous languages and lexical items from the superstrate language, English (*me, you, him, two, fellow (>fella > pela), three* and *all (> ol)*, may together contribute to the new language system (see the table below, adapted from Thomason 2001: 171).

|  | *singular* | *dual* | *trial* | *plural* |
|---|---|---|---|---|
| 1st exclusive | mi | mitupela | mitripela | mipela |
| 1st inclusive |  | yumitupela | yumitripela | yumipela |
| 2nd | yu | yutupela | yutripela | yupela |
| 3rd | em | tupela | tripela | ol |

Thomason 2001: 171 notes that the system follows Austronesian languages in distinguishing between inclusive and exclusive first person forms (for example, in *we hope you'll come again soon*' 'we' does not include the addressee, whereas in *we're alone at last* it does), and while English distinguishes only singular and plural forms, Tok Pisin has singular, dual, trial, and plural forms.

Grammatical features of pidgins and creoles formed in contact with different superstrate languages are often strikingly similar. For example, they often mark aspect (completive, progressive, and so on), while tense marking is optional or absent. This has led to debate about whether the similarities are a result of a shared ancestor pidgin such as Sabir, the original Mediterranean lingua franca, which has been spread around the world and been **relexified** (its vocabulary replaced) in contact with new superstrate languages. Opposed to this theory is the notion that the similarities occur because creole genesis draws directly on features of shared universal grammar. Thomason 2001 argues that both theories oversimplify the complexity and variability of the ways in which different pidgins and creoles emerge. She believes that the processes involved in second language acquisition (i.e. negotiation of meaning and transfer, see Chapter 2.9) are sufficient to explain the emergence of contact languages. More recently Mufwene 2001 has argued that the notions of pidginization and creolization are racist constructs: white scholars' views of black people's languages undergoing the processes of change and contact that affect all languages.

## Language death

Another consequence of language contact is that minority languages may be replaced by dominant languages, causing speakers to lose their ancestral languages. It is predicted that somewhere between 50% and 90% of the world's 6,000 languages will be dead or dying by 2100 (Thomason 2001: 241–2). There is a gradual process of attrition, as the language loses speakers, and is used in a narrower range of domains. All too rapidly it will become endangered and eventually cease to exist. Scholars in the field of endangered languages are working to describe languages that are threatened with extinction, to preserve them as part of human heritage, but also to provide materials to help with language revitalization.

## Key points

> Linguistic variation conveys social meaning; we assign people to social categories depending on the way they speak.

> Differences in language use reflect different social affiliations.

> Speakers vary their language use to mark their relationships to interlocutors and events.

> Gender is increasingly seen as socially constructed: speakers use language as one way of signalling how they wish to be seen.

> Language use is governed by implicit cultural rules, which are studied using ethnographic methods.

> Power (equal or unequal) and solidarity (low or high social distance) are important factors in shaping interlocutors' language choices.

> A critical analysis of talk and text allows us to recognize how power shapes the organization of meaning.

> Bilingual speakers use codeswitching to express social meanings.

> Language contact may lead to language change, shift and loss.

> Some scholars have argued that when languages come into contact in a situation where speakers have limited exposure to the dominant language there may be pidginization and creolization, with a new language emerging.

## References

Allan, Keith and Kate Burridge 2006. *Forbidden Words: Taboo and the Censoring of Language*. Cambridge: Cambridge University Press.

Bakhtin, Mikhail M. 1981. *The Dialogic Imagination: Four Essays*, ed. by Michael Holquist; transl. by Caryl Emerson and Michael Holquist. Austin: University of Texas Press.

Bell, Alan 1984. Language style as audience design. *Language in Society* 13: 145–204.

Bickerton, Derek. 1981. *Roots of Language*. Ann Arbor: Karoma.

Blom, Jan-Petter and John J. Gumperz 1972. Social meaning in linguistic structures: code-switching in Norway. In *Directions in Sociolinguistics: The Ethnography of Communication*, ed. by John J. Gumperz and Dell H. Hymes. New York: Holt, Rinehart and Winston, pp. 407–34.

Bourdieu, Pierre 1991. *Language and Symbolic Power*, ed. by John B. Thompson; transl. by Gino Raymond and Matthew Adamson. Cambridge: Polity Press.

Bradley, John 1998. Yanyuwa: 'Men speak one way, women speak another'. In *Language and Gender: A Reader*, ed. by Jennifer Coates. Oxford: Blackwell, pp. 13–20.

Brown, Roger W. and Marguerite Ford 1964. Address in American English. In *Language in Culture and Society: A Reader in Linguistics and Anthropology*, ed. by Dell Hymes. New York: Harper & Row, pp. 234–44.

Brown, Roger W. and Albert Gilman 1960. The pronouns of power and solidarity. In *Style in Language*, ed. by Thomas A. Sebeok. Cambridge MA: MIT Press, pp. 253–76. Reprinted in *Language and Social Context*, ed. by Pier P. Giglioli. Harmondsworth: Penguin, 1972: 252–82.

Cameron, Deborah 1997. Performing gender: young men's talk and the construction of heterosexual masculinity. In *Language and Masculinity*, ed. by Sally Johnson and Ulrike H. Meinhof. Oxford: Blackwell, pp. 47–64.

Cameron, Deborah and Don Kulick 2003. *Language and Sexuality*. Cambridge: Cambridge University Press.

Cheshire, Jenny and Sue Fox 2008. Performed narrative: The pragmatic function of 'this is me' and other quotatives in London adolescent speech. Paper presented at Sociolinguistics Symposium 17: Micro and Macro Connections, Amsterdam, April 2008.

Chomsky, Noam 1965. *Aspects of the Theory of Syntax*. Cambridge MA: MIT Press.

Clyne, Michael, Heinz-Leo Kretzenbacher, Catrin Norrby and Doris Schüpbach 2006. Perceptions of variation and change in German and Swedish address. *Journal of Sociolinguistics* 10: 287–319.

Dixon, Robert M.W. 1980. *Languages of Australia*. Cambridge: Cambridge University Press.

Eckert, Penelope 1989. *Jocks and Burnouts: Social Categories and Identity in the High School*. New York: Teachers College Press.

Eckert, Penelope and Sally McConnell-Ginet 1998. Communities of practice: where language, gender and power all live. In *Language and Gender: A Reader*, ed. by Jennifer Coates. Oxford: Basil Blackwell pp. 484–94.

Fairclough, Norman 1995. *Critical Discourse Analysis: The Critical Study of Language.* London: Longman.

Fairclough, Norman 1999. Linguistic and intertextual analysis within discourse analysis. In *The Discourse Reader*, ed. by Adam Jaworski and Nikolas Coupland. London: Routledge, pp. 183–211.

Ferguson, Charles A. 1959. Diglossia. *Word* 15: 325–40.

Fishman, Joshua A. 1967. Bilingualism with and without diglossia: diglossia with and without bilingualism. *Journal of Social Issues* 23 (2): 29–38.

Foucault, Michel 1981. The order of discourse. In *Untying the Text: A Post-Structuralist Reader*, ed. by Robert Young. London: Routledge & Kegan Paul, pp. 48–68.

Gal, Susan 1998. Peasant men can't get wives: language change and sex roles in a bilingual community. In *Language and Gender: A Reader*, ed. by Jennifer Coates. Oxford: Basil Blackwell, pp. 147–59.

Giles, Howard and Peter F. Powesland 1975. *Speech Style and Social Evaluation*. New York: Academic Press.

Gordon, Elizabeth 1997. Sex, speech and stereotypes: why women use prestige forms more than men. *Language in Society* 26: 47–63.

Heath, Shirley Brice 1983. *Ways with Words: Language, Life and Work in Communities and Classrooms*. Cambridge: Cambridge University Press.

Heller, Monica 1999. *Linguistic Minorities and Modernity: A Sociolinguistic Ethnography*. London: Longman.

Heller, Monica 2001. Gender and public space in a bilingual school. In *Multilingualism, Second Language Learning and Gender*, ed. by Aneta Pavlenko, Adrian Blackledge and Marya Teutsch-Dwyer. Berlin: Mouton de Gruyter, pp. 257–82.

Holmes, Janet 1994. Improving the lot of female language learners. In *Exploring Gender: Questions and Implications for English Language Education*, ed. by Jane Sunderland. London: Prentice-Hall, pp. 156–62.

Holmes, Janet 1995. *Women, Men and Politeness*. Harlow: Longman.

Hymes, Dell H. 1972a. Models of interaction of language and social life. In *Directions in Sociolinguistics: The Ethnography of Communication*, ed. by John J. Gumperz and Dell H. Hymes. New York: Holt, Rinehart and Winston, pp. 35–71.

2

Hymes, Dell H. 1972b. On communicative competence. In *Sociolinguisticsx*, ed. by John B. Pride and Janet Holmes. Harmondsworth: Penguin, pp. 269–93.

Labov, William 1972a. *Language in the Inner City*. Philadelphia: University of Pennsylvania.

Labov, William 1972b. *Sociolinguistic Patterns*. Oxford: Basil Blackwell.

Lakoff, Robin T. 1975. *Language and Woman's Place*. New York: Harper Colophon.

Lave, Jean and Etienne Wenger 1991. *Situated Learning: Legitimate Peripheral Participation*. Cambridge: Cambridge University Press.

Le Page, Robert B. and Andrée Tabouret-Keller 1985. *Acts of Identity: Creole-based Approaches to Language and Ethnicity*. Cambridge: Cambridge University Press.

Leech, Geoffrey N. 1983. *Principles of Pragmatics*. London: Longman.

Maltz, Daniel N. and Ruth A. Borker 1982. A cultural approach to male–female miscommunication. In *Language and Social Identity*, ed. by John J. Gumperz. Cambridge: Cambridge University Press, pp. 195–216.

May, Stephen 2005. Language rights: moving the debate forward. *Journal of Sociolinguistics* 9: 319–47.

Milroy, Lesley 1980. *Language and Social Networks*. Oxford: Basil Blackwell.

Mufwene, S.S. 2001. *The Ecology of Language Evolution*. Cambridge: Cambridge University Press.

Myers-Scotton, Carol 1993. *Duelling Languages: Grammatical Structure in Code-Switching*. Oxford: Clarendon.

Myers-Scotton, Carol 2002. *Contact Linguistics: Bilingual Encounters and Grammatical Outcomes*. Oxford: Oxford University Press.

Philippson, Robert 1992. *Linguistic Imperialism*. Oxford: Oxford University Press.

Rampton, Ben 1995. *Crossing: Language and Ethnicity among Adolescents*. London: Longman.

Rampton, Ben 2006. *Language in Late Modernity: Interaction in an Urban School*. Cambridge: Cambridge University Press.

Rampton, Ben 2007. Neo-Hymesian linguistic ethnography in the United Kingdom. *Journal of Sociolinguistics* 11: 584–607.

Reisman, Karl 1974. Contrapuntal conversations in an Antiguan village In *Explorations in the Ethnography of Speaking*, ed. by Richard Bauman and Joel Sherzer. Cambridge: Cambridge University Press, pp. 110–24.

Saville-Troike, Muriel 1982. *The Ethnography of Communication: An Introduction*. Oxford: Blackwell.

Spender, Dale 1990 *Man Made Language*. London: Pandora.

Street, Brian 1995. *Social Literacies: Critical Approaches to Literacy in Development, Ethnography and Education*. London: Longman.

Tannen, Deborah 1990. *You Just Don't Understand: Women and Men in Conversation*. New York: William Morrow/Milsons Point NSW: Random House.

Thomason, Sarah G. 2001. *Language Contact: An Introduction*. Edinburgh: Edinburgh University Press.

Trudgill, Peter 1974. *The Social Differentiation of English in Norwich*. Cambridge: Cambridge University Press.

Trudgill, Peter 1983. *On Dialect: Social and Geographical Perspectives*. Oxford: Blackwell.

Trudgill, Peter. 1998. Sex and covert prestige. In *Language and Gender: A Reader*, ed. by Jennifer Coates. Oxford: Basil Blackwell, pp. 21–8.

Wodak, Ruth 2001. What CDA is about – a summary of its history, important concepts and its developments. In *Methods of Critical Discourse Analysis*, ed. by Ruth Wodak and Michael Meyer. London: Sage, pp. 1–13.

# 2.8 psycholinguistics

## chapter contents

> Psycholinguistics 103
> Neurolinguistics 103
> Lateralization 104
> Language comprehension 104
> Language production 105
> Models of linguistic processing 105
> Cognitive development 106
> Clinical linguistics 106
> Developmental disorders 107
> Acquired disorders 108
> First language acquisition 108
> Learning and interaction 109
> Acquiring words 110
> Syntactic development 111
> Theories of language acquisition 112
> Key points 113
> References 113

## Psycholinguistics

Drawing on linguistics, psychology, neuroscience and other disciplines, psycholinguists study psychological aspects of language, with a particular focus on language acquisition, comprehension, and production (Carroll 2008). They attempt to understand cognitive processes and brain functions which play a role in language use.

## Neurolinguistics

Neurolinguistics is the study of how the brain processes language. The lower part of the brain, the **brainstem,** keeps us alive by managing involuntary functions such as breathing, while the upper part of the brain, the **cerebrum**, manages the relationship between the brain and the environment (Aitchison 1992). The cerebrum is divided into two **hemispheres,** left and right, which play different roles in language processing and production, while extensive connections between the two hemispheres via the **corpus collosum** integrate these processes (Peng 2005). Information is transmitted among the millions of neurons of the brain by chemical-electric impulses which pass along white fibrous connective tracts, creating neural pathways.

Each hemisphere consists of four lobes: the **frontal**, **parietal**, **occipital**, and **temporal** lobes, and within these are areas which seem to have specific language processing functions. In most right-handed people, and 60% of left-handers, the left hemisphere is specialized for language, particularly for processing sequential information (such as a sequence of phonemes). The right hemisphere is dominant in holistic processing, integrating information and processing visual and spatial information of the sort needed to recognize letter shapes in reading. Speech prosody and metaphor are also typically processed in the right hemisphere (Owens 2005).

Language development is related to the process of brain maturation, and possibly to specialization of hemispheres. In the first two years of life the brain triples in weight as a result of chemical changes, the growth in size (but not number) of neurons, and the development of a dense web of connections between parts of the brain. The nerves develop a protective sheath in a process called **myelination**, and this speeds the transmission of neural information. Oestrogen contributes to myelination, so the process happens faster in girls than boys. As the neural pathways are used they become stronger. The links between the areas of the brain that manage auditory processing and motor skills mature around the age of two, allowing infants to imitate speech sounds and intonation contours. The development of neural connections may be inhibited by malnutrition, disease or sensory deprivation (Owens 2005).

## Lateralization

Lateralization of language to the left hemisphere begins *in utero* and develops rapidly through childhood, though some scholars contend that lateralization is completed before birth. Children with brain injuries in early childhood will develop language processing functions in other areas of the brain, suggesting that the young brain possesses a plasticity which it loses as lateralization develops. Lenneberg 1967 argued that the period before lateralization is completed is a **critical period** for language acquisition, during which a child can directly access innate processes for acquiring a language. After puberty, when brain lateralization is complete, the child no longer has access to these innate processes and must learn a language more consciously and with more effort. Debate continues about the existence of a critical period, and how long it might last. In particular, scholars are interested in whether second language acquisition after lateralization is a different process from children's first language or early bilingual acquisition.

## Language comprehension

In order to comprehend speech, we need to perceive an auditory signal and decode it. The area known as **Heschl's gyrus** (see Figure 2.14) draws on past experience to distinguish speech sounds from other noises. Paralinguistic information is sent to the right temporal lobe for processing, while the left temporal lobe handles the linguistic data. Sentences are stored in working memory in Broca's area, while being analysed in Wernicke's area.

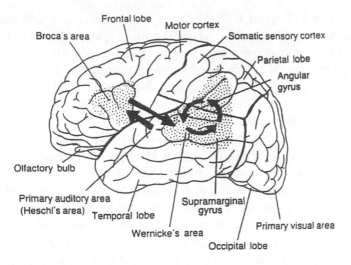

*Figure 2.14 Receptive linguistic processing (from Owens 2005: 111)*

## Language production

Peng 2005: 258 argues that animals and humans may see something such as a house on fire in similar ways, with a similar proto-meaning. The animals may respond by fleeing, but humans have another possible response: shouting *fire*. This requires additional neural processing, changing the proto-meaning into a linguistic meaning and an acoustic image.

In preparing to produce speech the message is formed conceptually in Wernicke's area, and then sent to Broca's area, where it is put into words. Scholars identify the areas involved by examining people with brain injury: different aspects of speech processing seem to be impaired by injuries to different parts of the brain. However some caution is required, as experiments examining blood flow in the brain show that a number of areas are involved in tasks such as word retrieval or sentence processing. Neuro-imaging studies have attempted to provide answers to questions of localization of function, but the findings remain unclear (Paradis 2004).

## Models of linguistic processing

**Information processing theory** suggests that all healthy people have the same fixed structures of the brain, but they manage information using processes which vary depending on the individual and the task involved. In order to process linguistic information, we use five functions: **attention**, **discrimination**, **organization**, **memory**, and **transfer**. In processing unfamiliar information we need first to attend to it, and this depends on motivation. Discrimination is the process of holding sentences in working memory while we check for words already known, perform syntactic analysis, and identify meaning. New information needs to be organized so that it can later be retrieved from memory, and this is done by **mediation** (connecting a new symbol, such as a word, to information or an existing image) or **association** (linking the symbol to another symbol). According to Owens, memory consists of **working memory** where input is held while actions are performed on it, **short-term memory** where it is analysed and decoded by comparing it with existing knowledge, and **long-term memory**, where it is retained unless we choose to discard it. 'Memory is best when information is deep-processed, which includes semantic interpretation and elaboration and relating to prior experience and knowledge' (Owens 2005: 115). Transfer is the process of using stored information to interpret new information. Initial processing takes effort and concentration, but with familiarity it becomes automated and requires less cognitive space (Owens 2005: 113).

Peng 2005 challenges this model, and argues that there is no evidence for the existence of working memory. He argues that memory and cognition cannot be separated but are two sides of the same information-processing activity. Experiences, stored as images, form the content of memory and serve as the basis for cognition. We can actively engage in processing, as for example when consciously storing a word or phrase in memory using mnemonic devices. Paradis 2004 notes the importance of metalinguistic knowledge, along with pragmatics and motivation, to language comprehension and production. Foreign language learners develop techniques for learning new vocabulary, for example by finding related L1 words to link to the new words. These are **metacognitive** processes (Owens 2005).

Information-processing theory needs to be supplemented with additional models of processing to explain how language is handled in the brain. Some linguistic processing follows the retrieval and analysis of low-level bits of information, and builds from identifying phonemes, to words, to sentences, to overall meaning. This is called **bottom-up processing**. However it is clear that we approach some speech events or texts with a set of expectations of how they will be structured and what sorts of meanings will be transmitted. Evidence for this comes from research on reading, which shows that we anticipate the overall structure and the sequence of information in sentences, and we read to confirm our prediction. This form of processing is called **top-down**.

## Cognitive development

There is debate about whether cognitive development precedes linguistic development, but it is clear that infants need to develop perceptual skills and auditory memory in order to begin developing language. The brain is activated by early experiences which develop neural pathways. Piaget 1954 argued that the child's developing brain organizes information into systems, and adapts with increasing exposure, either by incorporating new information into existing structures, or by modifying these, or developing new ones.

As infants interact repeatedly with familiar entities in the world they learn to respond to particular signals with action; for example, they learn to respond to a feeding bottle by drinking. By 8 months they begin to imitate a limited range of actions of others, and learn to recognize that actions have purposes. They can also recognize prosodic patterns in language. By 8–9 months they can set goals and act to achieve them, thus developing intentionality. Between 6 and 12 months they gradually develop the concept of causality. Children's first words appear around 12 months, and by 18 months they are able to represent objects in the mind, and solve problems (Owens 2005).

## Clinical linguistics

Clinical linguistics is the study and treatment of language disorders. It aims to describe disorders and identify their source, and on the basis of this, develop appropriate treatments. Disorders may include speech problems of people with hearing impairment or cleft palate, or those suffering from neurological disease, deterioration or injury, or developmental delay.

In addition to clinical applications, important theoretical implications stem from this work. The study of language disorders can provide insights into the nature of normal language behaviour and development. If damage to a particular area of the brain affects language behaviour in a specifiable way, this gives us insight into how the normal brain processes language.

In order to identify speech disorders, we need to identify normal and non-normal language use, and explain the cause of the problem. For example, if an English speaker who has had a stroke appears to replace voiceless stops that have short voice-onset time (/p/, /t/, /k/) with voiced stops with longer voice-onset time (/b/, /d/, /g/), the analyst may choose to explain this as a result of the speaker either selecting the wrong phoneme (a phonological selection problem) or inaccurately producing the right phoneme (a phonetic error) (Weismer 2006: 93). Weismer notes the danger of imposing explanatory accounts driven by bias towards a particular linguistic model.

## Developmental disorders

Children with non-normal language development are the focus of work on developmental disorders. Genetic factors, pre- or post-natal traumas, disease, metabolic problems, or deprivation are all factors that are likely to impair children's sensory, motor or cognitive development, and have an effect on language development (Miller and Klee 1995). However, there are many children who have not suffered any of these forms of brain damage, but who nonetheless show impairment in language development, in comparison with normal children. These children progress more slowly than normal children in their language development, and produce more errors. There is considerable variation, and over time the disorder may change in appearance. The manual of the American Psychiatric Association 1987 distinguishes between two groups: children with production difficulties and those with difficulties in both comprehension and production. However Miller and Klee 1995: 548 argue that this classification is too simplistic.

**Specific language impairment** (**SLI**) is measured by tests that address a single dimension of language use, such as mean length of utterance or number of different words. Another measure is to assign particular grammatical constituents a score for grammatical complexity, producing sentence scores. A clinician may compile a profile of the child's areas of strength and weakness, and computer databases have been developed to allow researchers to compare children with or without a language disorder (Miller and Klee 1995). These tests need to be handled carefully, with awareness that impairment of one linguistic level is likely to have effects on other levels.

Phonological impairment may result from hearing problems, autism, mental retardation, or brain lesions, but there are also children who show problems without these causes. Sounds that appear late in language development (e.g. /r/, /l/, /s/) may be problematic for children who have delayed maturation of motor skills (Weismer 2006). Other problems require an understanding of the child's developing linguistic system. Articulatory difficulties may be caused by problems with the organization of speech sounds, shown for example by a child who produces /tip/ for *sheep* and /ʃip/ for *sleep* (Leonard 1995: 574). In some cases it is clear that the child has no problem with perception of sounds, so the explanation is sought in the area of psycholinguistic processes intervening in speech production. Children who consistently produce open rather than closed syllables (e.g. /dɒ/ for *dog* with no final consonant) may be diagnosed as operating a deletion rule (Weismer 2006). The theoretical account of the problem then provides the direction for therapeutic intervention.

In general, the developmental patterns of children with phonological impairment show delay: they resemble those of normal but younger children. In grammar, SLI children also follow a developmental sequence similar to that of normal children, but with a substantial time lag of 2 to 3.5 years, and they also appear to have problems making use of the grammatical patterns and forms they know. Grammatical morphology seems to be an area of particular weakness for SLI English-speaking children, who, for example, have a tendency to use bare verb stems without inflections (Fletcher and Ingham 1995). SLI children may also display pragmatic impairment, but more work needs to be done in this area (Craig 1995). Delayed linguistic development is also found in children with Down syndrome, a chromosomal abnormality which affects cognitive development (Chapman 1995).

## Acquired disorders

Aphasia is the term used for problems with spoken language production or comprehension, usually as the result of brain injury, disease, or dementia, all of which may affect neural processing, and damage aspects of language processing. Attempts have been made to relate specific forms of aphasia to areas of trauma in the brain – this is called **localization**. Damage to Broca's area and Wernicke's area produces distinct types of speech disorder. People with Broca's aphasia suffer from **agrammatism** (the loss of function words and inflections), speech sound errors, lack of fluency, and problems with prosody. They will have trouble interpreting sentences such as *The boy was chased by the girl* where grammatical information is needed to work out who is doing the chasing. However they can use pragmatic strategies to comprehend *The soup was eaten by the girl* (Dabrowska 2004: 40). These symptoms can be produced by lesions in the anterior region of the brain.

People with Wernicke's aphasia have fluent and grammatical speech, but have comprehension problems, difficulty in retrieving vocabulary and deviant speech. For example (in response to a therapist asking why the patient was in hospital):

> What's wrong with me because I ... was myself until the taenz took something about the time between me and my regular time in that time here and that's when the the time took around her and saw me around in it it's started with me no time and then I bekan work of nothing else that's the way the doctor find me that way. (Obler and Gjerlow 1999, cited in Dabrowska 2004: 40)

Field 2004 suggests that Broca's and Wernicke's areas are particularly vulnerable because they are at places where a large number of neural pathways intersect. Some scholars argue that the degree of variation is too great to warrant a theory of precise localization of function (Eisele and Aram 1995; Peng 2005). Dabrowska 2004: 48 suggests that 'linguistic knowledge is represented in a redundant manner in various regions of the brain, with the language areas acting as a kind of central switchboard', and she notes that grammatical and lexical aspects seem to be closely linked.

## First language acquisition

First language acquisition is studied experimentally and observationally. Observational methods involve recording samples of children's naturally occurring speech at regular intervals, and keeping diary notes of the language used. Experimental methods involve eliciting language to test for stages of development (see Chapter 5.9).

## Learning and interaction

Children acquire a first language in interaction with people around them. They need to learn all the levels of language described in this book: the sound system of their mother tongue, words and their meanings, inflectional and derivational morphology, syntactic patterns, pragmatics, discourse structure, and communicative competence. Some scholars argue that humans have an innate capacity to acquire language, but there is evidence that interaction plays a major role. In early interactions, infants learn to attend to the other speaker, to jointly focus attention on a subject of discussion, and to listen and take turns (Clark 2003).

Adults use eye contact and speech modifications to engage infants in conversational exchanges. In most cultures, adults modify their speech to children. English speakers use higher pitch, exaggerated intonation contours, slower pace and pausing, repetition, a small range of simple syntactic structures (*where's X, look at X*), and a semantic focus on present time and place (Clark 2003: 38–43). These modifications serve to attract and retain children's attention. There is evidence, for example, that small children are more sensitive to high pitch. The modifications also serve to make language more comprehensible by using simple forms that provide accessible input, allowing children to begin segmenting the speech continuum into elements such as words and morphemes.

Innatists have argued that given sufficient exposure to a language, the universal grammar faculty will operate and allow the child to acquire the language. However, Clark 2003: 46 cites evidence of a child of deaf parents who was exposed to spoken language through radio and television, but lacked direct interaction. He developed a very small vocabulary, and was far behind other children in syntactic development.

Adults interact with infants as if they are engaging in conversation, as does the mother in example (1) below talking to her daughter Ann, 3 months.

(1)    Ann:     (smiles)
       Mother:  oh, what a nice little smile
                yes, isn't that nice
                there
                there's a nice little smile
       Ann:     (burps)
       Mother:  what a nice little wind as well
                yes, that's better, isn't it?
                yes
                yes
       Ann:     (vocalizes)
       Mother:  there's a nice noise

(from Snow 1972, cited in Clark 2003: 30)

The mother treats Ann as an interlocutor, and models turn-taking behaviour, giving very positive responses to Ann's behaviours, which are constructed as conversational turns. In routine daily interactions, parents regularly treat infants' contributions as meaningful. Gradually they expect vocal responses, as we see in an interaction with Ann at 1 year, 6 months.

(2)     Ann:     (blowing noises)
        Mother:  that's a bit rude
        Ann:     *mouth*
        Mother:  mouth, that's right
        Ann:     *face*
        Mother:  face, yes, mouth is in your face
                 what else have you got in your face?
        Ann:     *face* (closing eyes)
        Mother:  you're making a face, aren't you?

(Snow 1972, cited in Clark 2003: 31)

The mother treats Ann's utterances as initiating exchanges, and responds to them with confirmation, and expansion, making links between items (*mouth is in your face*). As children get older, adults widen the range of things talked about. Adults name objects, explain their functions, and relate the names to other words (Clark 2003: 49–50).

Through this process children learn the phonology of the language, and acquire words and the rudiments of syntax.

## Acquiring words

Children's utterances move through stages. Their first vocalizations are crying or cooing, but around six to eight months they begin **babbling,** producing random repeated sounds, often using consonants that are simple to produce, e.g. *ba-ba-ba, ma-ma-ma, da-da-da*. While these may simply be vocal exercises, parents will attribute interactive meaning to these sounds (*He called me mama!*). Babbling continues over several months, and the sounds will drift towards those found in the language being acquired (Aitchison 1992). The intonation patterns also come to resemble those of the language being acquired, and the child may use these intonation contours to distinguish requests and rejections, even before words have emerged (Clark 2003: 104).

First words appear around 8 to 12 months, and by 18 months children will have about 50 words. There is then a spurt in vocabulary acquisition. By 6 years of age children will have acquired more than 10,000 words. Children need to be able to identify word and morpheme boundaries, separating them out from the continuous stream of sound they hear in adult utterances. Some early vocabulary may be learnt as unsegmented chunks, such as *whassup* for "what's up" or *dowanna* for "I don't want to", and analysed further only when recurrent elements (e.g. *wanna*) are recognized in other syntactic contexts. Evidence for this comes from utterances such as *it's fell* or *it's has wheels*, where the child has not yet recognized that *it's* consists of two morphemes (O'Grady 2005: 10). Some children have a gestalt learning style, acquiring unanalysed chunks, while others have an analytic style, breaking chunks down easily. There is evidence that English children focus very early on the predominant stress pattern of strong followed by weak syllables, and use this to pick out words (O'Grady 2005: 13f).

In early attempts at words children may develop their own phonological schema. David, between 1 year 1 month and 1 year 4 months, produced vocalizations with *d–* (possibly derived from *there*) when showing or pointing to something, *h–* when reaching for something (possibly from *here*) and *b–* when hiding (possibly related to *bye-bye*) (Carter 1979, cited in Clark 2003: 105).

Children gradually learn to produce sounds, for example, *dog/doggy* may first be produced as /dɒ/, then as /dɒdi/, then, as /gɒgi/ as the child masters /g/ but cannot yet manage to produce two different consonants in one word (Clark 2003: 107). Children choose to say certain words whose sounds they are confident they can produce, draw on those sounds to replace others they have not yet mastered, and simplify clusters (cf. Clark 2003: 114f).

As children acquire words they are also acquiring meanings, which initially may not match adult meanings. For example, the word *dog* may be used to refer to dogs, cows and horses, or *moon* to refer to moon, half a grapefruit, a dishwasher dial, or a slice of lemon. This is called **overextension** (O'Grady 2005: 44–5), and it gives us some indication of the semantic properties the child selects as the salient meaning of the word.

## Syntactic development

The first sentences begin to emerge between 18 and 24 months. At this stage they usually consist of two words, e.g. *allgone milk*, and there may be no positional rules, so the same child might produce *milk allgone*. When word order rules emerge there are some differences between children, but they often use semantic categories as the basis, so there may be a rule such as action + object (*eat cookie, throw ball*), or possessor + possession (*Daddy shoe*) (Owens 2005).

The next stage, around 25 months, is the development of three or more word utterances, such as agent + action + object (*Mommy sit chair*). Children at this stage may have fixed frames into which they insert lexical items (*I wanna X*, where *X* = go, eat, play, watch TV, and so on) (O'Grady 2005: 86).

An important aspect of syntactic development is the acquisition of inflectional morphology, for marking number on nouns or pronouns, and tense and aspect on verbs. Roger Brown in the 1970s observed remarkable similarities between children in the order in which they acquired English morphemes. While children differ, many follow the order outlined in the table below (adapted from O'Grady 2005: 94, citing Brown 1973). Such evidence has been used to support an innatist model of language development.

|  | *Item* | *Examples* |
|---|---|---|
| 1 | –ing | *playing* |
| 2–3 | in, on | *in the house, on the bed* |
| 4 | plural –s | *cats, books* |
| 5 | irregular past tense | *ate, ran* |
| 6 | possessive –s | *Cromer's car* |
| 7 | is, are, etc. (uncontractable) | *guess where he is* |
| 8 | the, a | *the apple, a snack* |
| 9 | regular past tense –ed | *walked, jumped* |
| 10 | the verbal ending –s | *she knows* |

# Theories of language acquisition

In the first half of the twentieth century a general theory of learning, **behaviourism**, was applied to language learning. B. F. Skinner 1957 argued that children learn language by imitation. When correct forms were produced they were reinforced by positive feedback. In fact, however, children produce utterances that do not resemble those of people who talk to them.

It is clear from children's utterances that acquiring a language is not simply a process of imitation. The evidence suggests that the process is one of hypothesis testing. Children create rules for plural morpheme formation or past tense marking, or negation, and test these by producing sentences, which initially may not resemble those of adults. As they refine their rules, their utterances move gradually closer to the form of adult utterances, increasing in length and syntactic complexity. This is seen by many as evidence of an innate predisposition to acquire language, using what Chomsky 1965 called the **language acquisition device**.

Chomsky 1959 (and many others) argues that the speed and effectiveness of children's language acquisition, and the impoverished input to which they are exposed, support a theory that they are pre-programmed to acquire language. Children are born with an innate capacity, which dictates the form languages can take, and this innate capacity operates on language data to which the child is exposed.

Chomsky later reformulated this model and argued that the human predisposition to acquire language is based on **universal grammar. UG** consists of a set of **principles** which hold for all languages, and **parameters** which can be set for different languages. An example of a principle is that all constituents contain a head (Meisel 1995: 11). An example of a parameter is that some languages such as Italian omit subject pronouns (**pro-drop**) whereas in languages such as English, they are obligatory: 'I don't know' in Italian is *Non lo so* ('∅ not it know'), where the first person pronoun *io* does not appear; the first person is signalled in the verb form *so* (from *sapere*). Children bring to language acquisition both the pre-programmed principles and the ability to detect and set the appropriate parameters for the language they are acquiring.

Other scholars have argued that general theories of learning can explain language acquisition, and there is no need to posit an innate process. **Sociocultural theory** is an important example of such an approach. Based on the work of the Russian developmental psychologist Lev S. Vygotsky (1896–1934), which was first translated into English in the 1960s (Vygotsky 1962), sociocultural theory sees cognitive development as related to the use of tools to control and interact with the world. In our mental activity, language is a symbolic tool which allows us to control and organize the world. Language is used to guide learners of any activity to become skilled. A novice can perform an activity only through support; their performance is **other-regulated**. As skills are acquired the learner becomes increasingly autonomous (**self-regulated**). A good example of this is the way we learn to drive a car, initially with an instructor's support. As we continue to gain skills we become independent. The process where the more skilled person provides support is called **scaffolding.** Scaffolding allows the learner to perform tasks beyond their current ability, in what is called the **zone of proximal development**. The activity that we can perform with assistance is in the process of being learnt. For Vygotsky all language learning takes place in social interaction through this process of scaffolding.

**Connectionist** models of language acquisition draw on the design of neural processing, and argue that language acquisition operates through a network of associations or connections between multiple inputs and outputs. The system detects regularities in the environment, drawing on patterns of frequency. Learning happens when the output produces the target form, which strengthens the neural pathway. The networks of associations become progressively richer and more complex, and this increases the ability to solve problems (see Plunkett 1995; Bialystok 2001).

Psycholinguistic research attempts to test and validate competing theories of language, of cognition and of brain function.

## Key points

> Psycholinguists study language acquisition, comprehension and production in normal and non-normal children and adults.

> Evidence from brain injury suggests that areas of the brain have specialized functions related to different aspects of language processing.

> There may be a critical period for language acquisition: after brain lateralization is complete, language acquisition appears to be more difficult.

> Language development accompanies cognitive development, and both emerge in interaction.

> Innatists argue that the human brain is hard-wired to acquire language.

## References

Aitchison, Jean 1992. *Introducing Language and Mind*. London: Penguin English.

American Psychiatric Association 1987. *Diagnostic and Statistical Manual of Mental Disorders: DSM III R*. 3rd edn. Washington DC: American Psychiatric Association.

Bialystok, Ellen 2001. *Bilingualism in Development: Language, Literacy and Cognition*. Cambridge: Cambridge University Press.

Brown, Roger W. 1973 *A First Language: The Early Stages*. London: Allen and Unwin.

Carroll, David W. 2008. *Psychology of Language*. 5th edn. Belmont CA: Wadsworth.

Carter, Anne L. 1979. Prespeech meaning relations: an outline of one infant's sensorimotor morpheme development. In *Language Acquisition: Studies in first Language Development*, ed. by Paul Fletcher and Michael Garman. Cambridge: Cambridge University Press, pp. 61–92.

Chapman, Robin S. 1995. Language development in children and adolescents with Down Syndrome. In *The Handbook of Child Language*, ed. by Paul Fletcher and Brian MacWhinney. Oxford: Blackwell, pp. 641–63.

Chomsky, Noam 1959. Review of 'Verbal Behavior' by Burrhus F. Skinner (1957). *Language* 35: 26–58. Reprinted in *The Structure of Language: Readings in the Philosophy of Language* ed. by Jerry A. Fodor and Jerrold J. Katz. Englewood Cliffs: Prentice-Hall. 1964: 547–78.

Chomsky, Noam 1965. *Aspects of the Theory of Syntax*. Cambridge MA: MIT Press.

Clark, Eve 2003. *First Language Acquisition*. Cambridge: Cambridge University Press.

Craig, Holly K. 1995. Pragmatic impairments. In *The Handbook of Child Language*, ed. by Paul Fletcher and Brian MacWhinney. Oxford: Blackwell, pp. 623–40.

Dabrowska, Eva 2004. *Language, Mind and Brain: Some psychological and neurological constraints on theories of grammar*. Edinburgh: Edinburgh University Press.

Eisele, Julie A. and Dorothy M. Aram 1995. Lexical and grammatical development in children with early hemisphere damage: a cross-sectional view from birth to adolescence. In *The Handbook of Child Language*, ed. by Paul Fletcher and Brian MacWhinney. Oxford: Blackwell, pp. 664–89.

Field, John 2004. *Psycholinguistics: The Key Concepts*. London: Routledge.

Fletcher, Paul and Richard Ingham 1995. Grammatical impairment. In *The Handbook of Child Language*, ed. by Paul Fletcher and Brian MacWhinney. Oxford: Blackwell, pp. 603–22.

Lenneberg, Eric H. 1967. *Biological Foundations of Language*. New York: Wiley.

Leonard, Laurence B. 1995. Phonological impairment. In *The Handbook of Child Language*, ed. by Paul Fletcher and Brian MacWhinney. Oxford: Blackwell, pp. 573–602.

Meisel, Jürgen M. 1995. Parameters in acquisition. In *The Handbook of Child Language*, ed. by Paul Fletcher and Brian MacWhinney. Oxford: Blackwell, pp. 10–35.

Miller, Jon F. and Thomas Klee 1995. Computational approaches to the analysis of language impairment. In *The Handbook of Child Language*, ed. by Paul Fletcher and Brian MacWhinney. Oxford: Blackwell, pp. 545–72.

O'Grady, William 2005. *How Children Learn Language*. Cambridge: Cambridge University Press.

Obler, Loraine K. and Kris Gjerlow 1999. *Language and the Brain*. Cambridge: Cambridge University Press.

Owens, Robert E. Jr 2005. *Language Development: An introduction*. 6th edn. Boston: Pearson Education.

Paradis, Michel 2004. *A Neurolinguistic Theory of Bilingualism*. Amsterdam: John Benjamins Publishing Company.

Peng, Fred C.C. 2005. *Language in the Brain: Critical Assessments*. London: Continuum.

Piaget, Jean 1954. *The Construction of Reality in the Child*. Transl. by Margaret Cook. London: Routledge & Kegan Paul.

Plunkett, Kim 1995. Connectionist approaches to language acquisition. In *The Handbook of Child Language*, ed. by Paul Fletcher and Brian MacWhinney. Oxford: Blackwell, pp. 36–72.

Skinner, Burrhus F. 1957. *Verbal Behavior*. New York: Appleton-Century-Crofts.

Snow, Catherine E. 1972. Mother's speech to children learning language. *Child Development* 43: 549–65.

Vygotsky, Lev S. 1962. *Thought and Language*. Cambridge MA: MIT Press.

Weismer, Gary 2006. Speech disorders. In *Handbook of Psycholinguistics*, ed. by Matthew J. Traxler and Morton Ann Gernsbacher. 2nd edn. Amsterdam: Elsevier, pp. 93–124.

# 2.9 **applied linguistics**

## chapter contents

> Second language acquisition     115
> Are the processes of acquiring a first and second language different?     116
> Behaviourism and contrastive analysis     116
> Universal grammar     116
> Interlanguage     117
> Input     118
> Interaction and negotiation of meaning     118
> Noticing     119
> Foreign language teaching     119
> Language teaching theory and methods     119
> Learner-centred approaches     121
> Immersion     121
> Translation     122
> The problem of equivalence     122
> Key points     124
> Further reading     125
> References     125

## Second language acquisition

All normal humans acquire a first language without apparent effort, but subsequent language learning is often arduous, particularly in formal classroom settings. Yet bilingualism and multilingualism are common around the world, and in many communities the second, third and subsequent languages are often acquired in similar ways to the first language, namely, through daily use. Can classroom language instruction be made easier, possibly by identifying and replicating what happens when languages are acquired naturally? The main goal of second language acquisition research is to discover how second (and subsequent) languages are learnt. Linguists working in this field wish to understand the process of **second language acquisition** (henceforth **SLA**) and discover whether it resembles first language acquisition or is fundamentally different. Using experimental and observational data, scholars test hypotheses in order to confirm or disconfirm competing theories of SLA. The goals of SLA research are both theoretical (to construct explanatory models of SLA), and applied (to improve the teaching and learning of languages). We will outline key concepts and summarize some of the main theories which have been used to explain the process of SLA.

# Are the processes of acquiring a first and second language different?

Studying another language in class can be very demanding, and progress often seems slow. Many students give up, and those who continue may find that after many years of study they are still unable to use the language comfortably. Few achieve native-like competence in grammar, and even fewer will sound like a native speaker. This contrasts dramatically with the ease with which we all learned our first language. Can we explain this by arguing that second language learning is different in nature from first language acquisition? If so, why are they different? Or could the apparent differences be attributed to other factors such as the nature of formal language instruction? The languages themselves do not differ, as any living language may be either a first language or a second language. The differences must lie in the nature of the learner or the context of learning.

## Behaviourism and contrastive analysis

One of the first attempts to construct a theory of SLA drew on behaviourism (discussed in more detail below) which saw learning as a process of habit formation. In this model, it was argued that language forms are acquired through repetition. Unlike children acquiring a first language, second language learners already have a set of established language habits. It was suggested that when the new language habits are the same as the old ones the learner will easily learn the L2 form, but where there are differences the old habits will **interfere** with the ready acquisition of the new ones. For example, Italian and French both classify nouns by gender (masculine and feminine) and distinguish articles accordingly, while English does not distinguish nouns by gender in the same way.

| English | Italian | French |
|---------|---------|--------|
| **the** car | **la** macchina (f.) | **la** voiture (f.) |
| **the** cat | **il** gatto (m.) | **le** chat (m.) |

The **contrastive analysis hypothesis** (Lado 1957) predicted that, for example, an English-speaking student would have more difficulty in mastering the appropriate use of French articles than would an Italian student. Thus difficulties in learning a second language were attributed to differences between the first language and the target language. Linguists wrote comparative grammars, for example, of English and Spanish, in order to reveal the areas in which speakers of each language were likely to have problems learning the other. By comparing the two languages, researchers hoped to provide an inventory of similarities and differences which could serve as the basis for syllabus design. Teachers could then ignore the similarities and focus classroom teaching on the areas of difference. Unfortunately the predictions of contrastive analysis were not accurate: contrastive analyses do not reliably predict learners' actual errors.

## Universal grammar

The behaviourist model of SLA was challenged by Chomsky 1959, who showed that children do not acquire a first language by imitation, but creatively construct novel utterances based on their developing internal grammatical systems. They move through developmental stages, as revealed by the increasingly complex utterances they produce.

The stages are common across children and across languages, leading Chomsky and his followers to infer the existence of an innate predisposition to acquire language. This innate faculty was initially labelled the **language acquisition device**, and subsequently called **universal grammar**. ('Grammar' here is not restricted to syntax but used in the broad sense of the rule system underlying all aspects of language.) Evidence for this innate system comes from the relative ease with which children acquire their mother tongue, despite exposure to limited and debased input data, and their creative construction of novel but increasingly complex utterances.

SLA researchers were influenced by this work on first language acquisition, and asked whether similar innate processes might operate in second language learning. Evidence from children growing up in bilingual households suggests it is possible for children to acquire two native languages perfectly. Why then do later learners have difficulty? One possibility, proposed by Lenneberg 1967, was that the language acquisition device atrophies with age, possibly as a result of brain lateralization (see Chapter 2.8), so that while young children can apply innate processes to all languages they encounter, after puberty the language acquisition device is no longer available. This would explain the apparent ease with which young children pick up a second language, compared with the difficulties many older second language learners encounter. This **critical age hypothesis** has been extensively researched in SLA, with conflicting results. Different ages have been proposed for the cut-off, and some work has suggested that the decline is gradual rather than abrupt. Whether or not the innate language faculty continues to be available to learners, researchers agree that learners move through a series of developmental stages.

## Interlanguage

Descriptions of developmental stages in first language acquisition led to a search for similar patterns in SLA. Selinker 1972 and others argued that second language learners develop a series of models which move increasingly closer to the target language. **Interlanguage** is the term used for the learner's language system at any point of time, as he or she moves along the interlanguage continuum towards mastery of the target language. The concept of **hypothesis testing** was used to explain how the L2 learner progressed along the interlanguage continuum, in much the same way as it is used to explain L1 acquisition.

According to Selinker, interlanguage is the result of 5 processes:

> **Language transfer**
> Learners transfer aspects of the first language (L1) into the second language (L2). Unlike interference, which is only negative, transfer may also be positive.

> **Overgeneralization of L2 rules**
> A learner may fail to recognize the exceptions to a rule. For example, having learnt the English noun plural morpheme –s, a learner may produce *sheeps*.

> **Transfer of training**
> The way in which teachers present material may distort the input data. For example, Japanese male and female speakers use different first-person singular pronouns. A male teacher who uses only the male form, may mislead female students into using the same form.

> **Strategies of L2 learning**
> Learners may simplify the L2 data as a strategy to deal with complexity. For example, the learner may choose to use the present continuous for all verbs (*I am not knowing the answer*).

> **Communication strategies**
> A learner may leave out communicatively redundant grammatical items (*It was nice car*).

Learner errors offer important evidence of the learner's developing target language competence, or interlanguage. Morpheme acquisition order studies (Dulay and Burt 1974) showed that there is a consistent sequence in which learners acquire second language morphology, a sequence which is similar but not identical to the first language morpheme acquisition order (see Chapter 5.8).

Not all learners will move all the way along the interlanguage continuum. Some learners will reach a plateau beyond which they seem unable to move. This is known as **fossilization**. It is likely that attitude and identity factors play a role in fossilization – a learner may feel sufficiently able to communicate, or may not want to go further and be mistaken for a native speaker of the target language. Other factors may include age, lack of learning opportunity, or the nature of feedback the learner receives (Ellis 1994: 354). De Bot, Lowie and Verspoor 2005: 3) argue that people who continue to use their language are constantly developing, while those who stop using it may stagnate or lose language skills.

## Input

One of the most influential models of SLA was Krashen's Monitor Model, and in particular the **input hypothesis** (Krashen and Terrell 1983). In this model, a fundamental distinction was made between **acquisition** and **learning**. Acquisition makes use of innate mental processes, and it happens when the learner is exposed to **comprehensible input**. The language spoken to the learner needs to be simplified to a level that makes it comprehensible, but also needs to be one stage above the learner's current interlanguage level (Krashen calls this i+1). Anxiety may raise the learner's **affective filter**, blocking the flow of input data to the language acquisition device. Students who find language classes stressful are thus unable to acquire language. The model suggests that if we are relaxed and under no pressure to speak before we are ready, and have access to comprehensible input, we will be able to acquire the language in the same way as a child does. What we acquire can be processed by our innate linguistic faculty and the rules are constructed without conscious awareness.

Krashen 1982 contrasts the natural and unconscious process of acquisition with the formal process of **learning**. Language learning is a conscious process of making sense of language data, following explicit rules. If teachers or textbooks give us information about the language rather than comprehensible input, we learn only a set of **metalinguistic rules**. We can apply these consciously to **monitor** and revise the output of our unconscious rules, but they do not form part of the underlying interlanguage grammar. This model offers a very powerful explanation of why the immense effort of classroom language learning so often seems ineffective. However SLA scholars now argue that its claims cannot be supported.

## Interaction and negotiation of meaning

For Krashen, input is the key. However, this raises a question: how is input made comprehensible? Long 1983 and others have addressed this by analysing recordings of language learners interacting with each other and with native speakers. They argue that participants adapt and simplify their language in interaction, based on feedback they receive from the interlocutor. Speakers can check that their utterances are understood using comprehension checks (e.g. *yeah?*), and seek to make sense of the interlocutor's utterances by requesting repetition (*sorry? what was that? you went where?*) or using clarification requests (*do you mean … ? what's a … ?*). Using these and other conversational devices, speakers are able to negotiate meaning, making the input comprehensible.

## Noticing

Subsequent work has shown that while Krashen's input hypothesis contributes enormously to our understanding of the process of SLA, it is not the whole story. Swain and Lapkin 1995 examined the language competence of students in Canadian French immersion schooling (discussed again later in this chapter). English-speaking children who do their schooling entirely in French, and are thus exposed to enormous amounts of comprehensible input, become extremely competent in French, but their language production is not perfect. Persistent errors in their output attest to limitations in the input model, suggesting that input does not necessarily turn into intake. In addition to comprehensible input, students also need to produce L2 **output** in order to test and refine their underlying grammatical rules.

Schmidt 1990 suggests that in order to turn input into intake, learners need to **notice** the difference between the target form and their own attempt. This **consciousness-raising** is particularly useful in drawing learners' attention to structures that are not possible in the target language by providing negative evidence. Thus while Krashen saw unconscious learning as the key to acquisition, it is now clear that noticing and focusing on form have an important role to play.

## Foreign language teaching

A distinction is sometimes made in the language teaching profession between **second** and **foreign** language teaching, depending on whether the target language is being learnt in a community where it is widely spoken. Thus speakers of other languages will learn English as a second language in the UK or India, for example, but as a foreign language in Japan. The difference is that learners in second language contexts can encounter the language outside the classroom, and may need to use it for daily interactions, whereas in foreign language contexts the teacher is often the sole source of language input (though in an increasingly globalized world with internet access this difference is becoming less meaningful). While the social context of learning is important, approaches to teaching languages other than the mother tongue are sufficiently similar to be discussed under one heading.

## Language teaching theory and methods

Post-Renaissance approaches to foreign language teaching, based on methods associated with studying classical Greek and Latin texts, employed the method known as **grammar-translation**. Students worked with written texts, learning vocabulary and prescriptive grammar rules which were then applied to translating target language texts into the first language, or vice versa. Teaching was conducted in the first language, so learners had little experience of listening and speaking, except in reading written texts aloud. While this method may have served well in learning to read classical languages, it had limitations for those who wished to learn to speak modern languages.

In the late nineteenth century, there was a shift to teaching in the target language; this approach is known as the **direct method.** While some listening and speaking practice was seen as desirable, the mastery of written language was still the primary goal of foreign language learning.

In the first half of the twentieth century, the development of psychological theories of learning offered the possibility of developing a theoretical basis for language teaching. The work of Pavlov, Skinner and other behaviourists proposed that learning, including learning a language, was a process of habit formation. It was important to encourage and reinforce good habits, and avoid errors. Learners were encouraged to repeat carefully modelled correct sentence patterns.

At the same time a **structuralist** model of language was being developed in linguistics. This emphasized grammatical patterns, and the primacy of spoken language over the written form. A new method of language teaching, **audiolingualism**, combined insights from behaviourist learning principles and structuralist linguistics. The principles of audiolingualism included the separation and ordering of the **four skills:** listening, speaking, reading, and writing. Teachers modelled words or sentences. Learners were expected to listen and then repeat what they had heard, thus avoiding errors. Oral drilling was a favoured method designed to instil correct pronunciation, including stress and intonation. Students were then allowed to insert supplied lexical items into sentence patterns being studied, but the opportunities for such creativity were very limited. A written stage involved writing sentences already acquired orally. In this model, the target language was seen as a set of grammatical structures, pronunciation patterns, and words.

Chomsky's scathing review (Chomsky 1959) of Skinner's book *Verbal Behavior* (1957) had a profound impact on language teaching, as well as on first and second language acquisition theory. As we have shown, he argued that first language acquisition must involve creativity and the construction of underlying rules. This insight was embraced by second language theorists, and freed language teaching from its fear of error. Errors came to be seen as evidence of stages in effective rule creation. Language teaching retained its focus on spoken language, and grammatical structure, but there was a shift away from repetition. A new concern was with presenting language input in line with the hypothesized natural order of acquisition.

Developments in sociolinguistics, in particular Hymes's notion of communicative competence (Hymes 1972, see Chapter 2.7), led to more changes in language teaching methods. Communicative language teaching grew out of the emerging awareness of language users as social beings. The recognition that language is used in a certain context led to the development of situation-based teaching (e.g. *at the post office*). As the field of pragmatics developed, language teaching moved to a more functional approach (e.g. how to make a request, or apologize). Situational and functional methods involved students learning dialogues or performing role plays. However, it became clear that these approaches were asking students to mimic communication rather than to actually communicate.

The focus shifted to creating classroom activities which generate real communication. Task-based methods put students in situations where they have to draw on the linguistic resources they have available to solve problems. The notion of authenticity is central to this approach. As far as possible authentic materials are used, to give students exposure to real language used naturally, without the stereotyping and standardizing usually applied to purpose-written materials. Authentic materials prepare students for the language variation they will encounter in target language communities.

Task-based approaches move away from the old teacher-centred classroom, organizing students into small groups that work together to solve problems, using the target language to achieve goals. The teacher's role has shifted to that of classroom organizer and facilitator. The old behaviourist fear that learners would acquire each other's errors was replaced by an awareness of the importance of scaffolding (see Chapter 2.8). Learners were able to work together to achieve a level of accuracy that would not have been possible if they had worked alone.

## Learner-centred approaches

The focus on the learner that grew out of task-based approaches led to the recognition of different learning styles. Some learners may prefer analytic approaches, while others learn more holistically. Personality factors such as extroversion or anxiety may affect how students respond to classroom activities. Classroom teaching needs to provide a range of resources that will give learners autonomy and allow them to use different strategies. The importance of learner motivation has also been recognized. Gardner and Lambert 1972 distinguished two forms of orientation underpinning language learning motivation: instrumental and integrative. Instrumentally oriented learners have goals such as passing exams, getting into a particular tertiary course, or achieving career ambitions, while integratively oriented learners are drawn to the speakers and culture of the target language and wish to identify with them in some way. In addition, learners' success or failure may affect their integrative orientation (resultative motivation) and teachers may be able to stimulate or stifle motivation by their choice of classroom activities. More recent work (Dörnyei, 2001; 2005; 2006) shows that learners respond to a range of factors, inside and outside the classroom, in a cycle of changing motivation.

Cultural differences may also play a role in language learning. In some communities rote learning is highly valued, and students will respond positively to tasks such as learning vocabulary lists. It has been noted that teachers who are not native speakers of the target language are often uncomfortable with communicative methods.

## Immersion

Communicative approaches to language teaching have changed learners from passive recipients of information about the target language to active agents in their own learning. The target language is increasingly seen as the means of achieving other goals (such as, for example, completing tasks or solving problems), rather than as a body of knowledge to be memorized. This shift has been most effectively achieved in **immersion programmes**. In Canada, for example, many English-speaking children undertake their primary and secondary schooling in French-medium schools designed specifically for them. English-speaking children adapt very readily to learning all their regular subjects through the medium of French, and become nearly bilingual (see earlier comments on residual syntactic errors), with no negative effects on their academic performance. What these schools show is that we learn language most effectively when we use it as a tool to learn and communicate with others.

# Translation

Translation studies as a research discipline grew out of contrastive analysis (discussed above) and comparative literature (Munday 2001). It is a field that has undergone rapid change in the last decades under the influence of critical theory, and feminist and Marxist perspectives, leading to a gap between theorists and practitioners (Kuhiwczak and Littau 2007). Scholars draw on linguistics, literary theory, and philosophy to reflect on insider and outsider perspectives on languages, cultures, and histories.

Translating is the process of taking a **source text** in one language or code (the source language, or SL), and producing an equivalent text, the **target text**, in another language or code (the target language, or TL). Jakobson 1959 distinguished three forms of translation: interlingual (between different languages), intralingual (between dialects, codes or varieties of the same language) and intra-semiotic (transmuting verbal into non-verbal encoding, such as music or film). In general, translation studies focus on interlingual translation. The key issue in translating is what counts as equivalent (see discussion below).

A distinction is usually made between translating written texts, and **interpreting** speech; however, translators and interpreters face similar linguistic problems. Although in this chapter the discussion will focus on translation, we recognize that the same concerns apply to interpreting. The term translation may refer either to the process or the product, i.e. the target text. There are specialized sub-types of translation – literary or technical translation, subtitling, and machine translation (Hatim and Munday 2004).

Holmes 1988 is credited with founding the discipline of translation studies and specifying its goals, which are to describe the phenomena involved in translation, and to identify general principles which underlie these phenomena. For example, Holmes argued that (i) translations will inevitably be more standardized (i.e. have less variability) and have more cohesion than source texts, but (ii) some irregularities of the source language will be transferred into the target text, creating odd patterns. These are posited as universals of translation (Hatim and Munday 2004: 7).

The source text is produced in one sociocultural context and will be read in a different sociocultural context. This raises questions of **equivalence** and **translatability**. A translator is faced with the task of accurately rendering the content or meaning and the style of a source text into the target language. Jakobson 1959 suggests that the importance of style in a poem may make it untranslatable.

A distinction is made between **literal** and **free** translation, the latter placing its emphasis on representing the sense rather than the form of the original text. Translation that is too literal tends to produce a stilted and incomprehensible text. Recent work in translation has attempted to provide operational definitions for these terms (Munday 2001): translation that takes the word as the unit of translation tends to be literal, while free translation takes a longer element (clause, phrase or sentence) as the unit. Hatim and Munday (2004: 14) characterize the distinction as a continuum, and argue that text type, audience and purpose influence how literal the translation needs to be.

## The problem of equivalence

Jakobson 1959 drew on Saussure's notion of the **linguistic sign** (Saussure 1931) to describe the problem of equivalence. As discussed elsewhere in this text (e.g. Chapter 3.1), a linguistic sign involves a relationship between a **signifier**, i.e. a (spoken or written) word, and the **signified**, i.e. the concept that it represents. This is an arbitrary relation-ship. The signified, for which the signifier *tree* is used in English, is called *arbre* in French and *shajara* in Arabic. However, we cannot assume that signifieds are identical. For example, the English signifier *brown* refers to a range of hues, some of which can be referred to by the French signifier *brun*. However, French also has the signifier *marron* referring to chestnut-coloured hues, which are thus distinguished lexically from *brun*. In English these would all be called *brown*, and to make the distinction we would have to use modifiers, as in *chestnut-brown*.

Languages also differ structurally, for example in the way they assign gender to nouns, or in how aspect is encoded in verb phrases. Translators need to identify the meaning of the message (the signified) and how it is encoded, and then attempt to translate that meaning, rather than the word (the signifier). However this is not unproblematic. For example, the distinction between polite (V) and intimate (T) forms of the second-person pronoun in many European languages (see Chapter 2.7) poses a problem for translators. The choice of pronoun signals the tenor of the relationship between interlocutors, in a manner which cannot so easily be conveyed in English. The closest equivalent would be the use of *mate* or *sir* as a form of address. There is no straightforward way of translating the implicit social message obligatorily expressed by pronoun choice, without making clumsy metalinguistic comments. Readers of French literature in translation may notice the attempts by translators to represent the shift from V to T when characters become more intimate.

Translation studies draw on approaches from structural linguistics such as componential analysis (Nida 1964; 1975) to identify meaning distinctions. This involves specifying meanings in terms of a series of attributes, so *girl* (+human, –male, –adult) is contrasted with *woman* (+human, –male, +adult) or *boy* (+human, +male, –adult). (In response to feminist critiques, the simple binary classification +/– male in componential analysis has been changed, so women are now represented as +female rather than –male.) Nida distinguishes translations that stay as close as possible to the form and meaning of the source text, with a focus on accuracy (**formal equivalence**), and those that attempt to capture the spirit or effect of the text with a focus on naturalness (**dynamic equivalence**). The morpheme by morpheme glossing used by linguists (see Chapter 2.3) is an example of formal equivalence (Munday 2001). **Adjustment** is the process of adapting the target language form to achieve dynamic equivalence (Hatim and Munday 2004).

Malmkjær 2005: 37 compares two translations into English of a Hans Christian Andersen story. The first version tries to stay as close as possible to the original. The second (Mary Howitt's 1846 translation, Andersen 1846) shows the effect of adjustment.

From *Ole Lukøie* (1842)

[A]nd they all talked about themselves, except the spittoon, which stood silent, cross that they could be so vain as to only talk about themselves and only think about themselves and have no thought for it, even though it stood so humbly in the corner and let itself be spat on.

Andersen 1846, *Olé Luckioè* (4–5):

Everything talked except the old door mat, which lay silent, and was vexed that they should all be so full of vanity as to talk of nothing but themselves, and think only about themselves, and never have one thought for it which lay so modestly in a corner and let itself be trodden upon.

Since the 1980s, studies of translation have highlighted the importance of culture, gender and power in interpreting texts and translating meanings (Bassnett 2002). Two translators will produce different versions of the same text, partly because of different selections made between words from the same semantic field (e.g. *good, fine*, and so on), and partly because translators may manipulate translations to take account of cultural sensitivities or expectations of the target language culture. For example, Mary Howitt brought nineteenth-century religious sensibilities to her translation of Hans Christian Andersen texts, removing or replacing anything she considered inappropriate or offensive (Malmkjær 2005: 66).

Bassnett 2002: 27–30 cites the example of the French ritual phrase *bon appetit* (literally "good appetite") exchanged at the start of a meal, and imagines a text about a family conflict before a wedding banquet. The family members sit down at the table, and the angry silence is broken by the head of the family uttering this phrase. An English translator cannot use a literal translation, because it would not sound natural in English. None of the available English expressions such as *Dig in, Tuck in, Do start, I hope you enjoy it, I hope it's alright* have the same effect. According to Bassnett 2002: 29f, in deciding what to do the translator has to:

> Accept the untranslatability of the SL phrase in the TL on the linguistic level.
> Accept the lack of a similar cultural convention in the TL.
> Consider the range of TL phrases available, having regard to the presentation of class, status, age, sex of the speaker, his relationship to the listeners, and the context of their meeting in the SL.
> Consider the significance of the phrase in its particular context – i.e. as a moment of high tension in the dramatic text.
> Replace in the TL the invariant core of the SL phrase in its two referential systems (the particular system of the text and the system of culture out of which the text has sprung).

This suggests there is an underlying meaning of a text that can be identified, and Bassnett 2002: 33 argues that different translations of the same text will share what Popovič 1976 has called an invariant core, that is a commonality of meaning, beneath the different expressive forms. This is a contentious notion in translation studies (Hatim and Munday 2004).

Linguistic studies of discourse and genre have influenced translation studies, with an increasing awareness of the importance of text type and function. Much of this work draws on Halliday's Systemic Functional Grammar, which links text and context (see Chapters 2.11 and 5.12).

Translation studies is a field characterized by interdisciplinarity: it changes rapidly as changes occur in cultural studies, linguistics, and other fields. Scholars and practitioners need to be aware of this trajectory. Malmkjær 2005: 185 stresses the need to be 'deferential to future users' of a text, while being mindful of the corpus of past usage.

## Key points

> Second language learners move along an interlanguage continuum: their developing grammatical systems increasingly approximate to the target language system.

> It has been argued that humans are innately equipped to construct a grammar of the language they are exposed to; it is not clear whether the language acquisition device is available for second language learning.

> The critical age hypothesis argues that after brain lateralization is complete there is no further access to the language acquisition device. Debate remains about when and if this happens.

> Successful acquisition of a second language requires comprehensible input.

> Input is made comprehensible through negotiation of meaning between interlocutors.

> Input is necessary but not sufficient: learners need to produce output, and notice how it differs from the target language.

> Language teaching methods draw on second language acquisition theory, which in turn draws on theories in linguistics and psychology.

> Contemporary language teaching methods use the target language for instruction, encourage communication and interaction between learners by providing problem-solving tasks, and recognize errors as evidence of interlanguage development.

> Effective language classrooms are learner-centred and encourage autonomy, to allow scope for different learning styles.

> Translators seek to produce a target language text which is equivalent to the source language text; however, texts such as poems in which style is very significant may be untranslatable.

> Translations may be literal (based on the form of the source language text) or free (based on the sense).

> Cultural differences may impede translatability; the notion of an invariant core that can be preserved in cross-cultural translation is contentious.

## Further reading

Carter, Ronald and David Nunan (eds) 2001. *The Cambridge Guide to Teaching English to Speakers of Other Languages.* Cambridge: Cambridge University Press.

Doughty, Catherine and Michael H. Long (eds) 2003. *The Handbook of Second Language Acquisition.* Oxford: Blackwell.

Ellis, Rod 1997. *Second Language Acquisition.* Oxford: Oxford University Press.

Gass, Susan M. and Larry Selinker 2001. *Second Language Acquisition.* 2nd edn. Mahwah NJ: Lawrence Erlbaum.

Hedge, Tricia 2000. *Teaching and Learning in the Language Classroom*. Oxford: Oxford University Press.

Lightbown, Patsy and Nina Spada 2006. *How Languages are Learned.* 3rd edn. Oxford: Oxford University Press.

Mitchell, Rosamond and Florence Myles 2004. *Second Language Learning Theories.* 2nd edn. London: Hodder Arnold.

Saville-Troike, Muriel 2006. *Introducing Second Language Acquisition.* Cambridge: Cambridge University Press.

## References

Andersen, Hans C. 1846. *Wonderful Stories for Children*. Transl. by Mary Howitt. London.

Bassnett, Susan 2002. *Translation Studies*. 3rd edn. London: Routledge.

Chomsky, Noam 1959. Review of 'Verbal Behavior' by Burrhus F. Skinner (1957). *Language* 35: 26–58. Reprinted in *The Structure of Language: Readings in the Philosophy of Language*, ed. by Jerry A. Fodor and Jerrold J. Katz. Englewood Cliffs: Prentice-Hall. 1964: 547–78.

De Bot, Kees, Wander Lowie and Marjolijn Verspoor 2005. *Second Language Acquisition: An Advanced Resource Book*. London: Routledge.

Dörnyei, Z. 2001. *Teaching and Researching Motivation*. Harlow, Essex: Pearson Education.

Dörnyei, Z. 2005. *The Psychology of the Language Learner: Individual Differences in Second Language Acquisition*. New York: Lawrence Erlbaum Associates.

Dörnyei, Z. 2006. Individual differences in second language acquisition. *AILA Review* (Bardovi-Harlig, K. and Z. Dörnyei (eds) *Themes in SLA Research*) 19: 42–68.

Dulay, Heidi C. and Marina K. Burt 1974. Natural sequence in child second language acquisition. *Language Learning* 24: 37–53.

Ellis, Rod 1994. *The Study of Second Language Acquisition*. Oxford: Oxford University Press.

Gardner, Robert C. and Wallace E. Lambert 1972. *Attitudes and Motivation in Second Language Learning*. Rowley MA: Newbury House.

Hatim, Basil and Jeremy Munday 2004. *Translation: An Advanced Resource Book*. London: Routledge.

Holmes, James S. 1988. *Translated! Papers on Literary Translation and Translation Studies*. Amsterdam: Rodopi.

Hymes, Dell H. 1972. On communicative competence. In *Sociolinguisticsx*, ed. by John B. Pride and Janet Holmes. Harmondsworth: Penguin, pp. 269–93.

Jakobson, Roman 1959. On linguistic aspects of translation. In *On Translation*, ed. by Reuben Brower. Cambridge MA: Harvard University Press, pp. 232–9.

Krashen, Stephen D. 1982. *Principles and Practice in Second Language Acquisition*. Oxford: Pergamon.

Krashen, Stephen. D. and Tracy D. Terrell 1983. *The Natural Approach: Language Acquisition in the Classroom*. Oxford: Pergamon.

Kuhiwczak, Piotr and Karin Littau 2007. Introduction. In *A Companion to Translation Studies*, ed. by Piotr Kuhiwczak and Karin Littau. Clevedon: Multilingual Matters, pp. 1–12.

Lado, Robert 1957. *Linguistics Across Cultures: Applied Linguistics for Language Teachers*. Ann Arbor: University of Michigan Press.

Lenneberg, E. H. 1967. *Biological Foundations of Language*. New York: Wiley.

Long, Michael H. 1983. Linguistic and conversational adjustments to non-native speakers. *Studies in Second Language Acquisition* 5: 177–93.

Malmkjær, Kirsten 2005. *Linguistics and the Language of Translation*. Edinburgh: Edinburgh University Press.

Munday, Jeremy 2001. *Introducing Translation Studies: Theories and Applications*. London: Routledge.

Nida, Eugene A. 1964. *Toward a Science of Translating: With Special Reference to Principles and Procedures Involved in Bible Translating*. Leiden: E.J. Brill.

Nida, Eugene A. 1975. *Componential Analysis of Meaning: An Introduction to Semantic Structures*. The Hague: Mouton.

Popovi , Anton 1976 *Dictionary for the Analysis of Literary Translation*. Edmonton: Department of Comparative Literature, University of Alberta.

Saussure, Ferdinand de 1931. *Cours de Linguistique Générale*. Publié par Charles Bally et Albert Sechehaye avec la collaboration de Albert Riedlinger. 3rd edn. Paris: Payot [First edn published 1916].

Schmidt, Norbert 1990. The role of consciousness in second language learning. *Applied Linguistics* 11: 129–58.

Selinker, Larry 1972. Interlanguage. *International Review of Applied Linguistics* 10: 209–31.

Skinner, Burrhus F. 1957. *Verbal Behavior*. New York: Appleton-Century-Crofts.

Swain, Merrill and Sharon Lapkin 1995. Problems in output and the cognitive processes they generate: a step towards second language learning. *Applied Linguistics* 16: 371–91.

# 2.10 **historical linguistics**

## chapter contents

> Languages don't stay the same – language evolution       127
> Some facts about language evolution       129
> Language families – establishing genetic relationship       129
> Attitudes to language change       131
> Key points       132
> References       133

## Languages don't stay the same – language evolution

Step back around 600 years to the time of medieval England. To give you an idea of the language at this time, here is a fourteenth-century recipe for rabbit stew. Try reading it out aloud: strange spelling often makes language look more bizarre than it really is, and reading it aloud helps to overcome this problem. Note, the letters <u> and <v> are used interchangeably here for both the vowel and the consonant, compare "grauey" *gravey* with "vp" *up*.

> Conynggys in grauey schul be sodyn & hakkyd in gobettys; and grynd gyngyer, galingale & canel, & temper it vp wyth god almand mylk & boyle it. & nym macys and clowys and kest theryn, & the conynggis also, & salt hym & serue it forthe.

The following is a literal translation.

> Rabbits in gravy shall be sodden and hacked into gobbets; and grind ginger, galingale [= an aromatic root] and cinnamon and temper it up with good almond milk and boil it. And take mace and cloves and cast (these) therein, and the rabbits also, and salt them and serve it forth.

There is no doubt that recipes for rabbit stew have changed appreciably over the years, as has the English language. For example, the vocabulary has changed, and some words here will be totally unfamiliar to you. The word for "rabbits", *connynges*, no longer exists. During the nineteenth century English speakers started to feel uneasy about this word because its shortened form *coney* rhymed with *honey* reminded them too much of the taboo word for a female body part that still occurs in *cunnilingus*. (The modern pronunciation of, for example, Coney Island was a deliberate dissimilation from the tabooed term.)

There are other words here with interesting histories, especially those whose meanings have altered over the years. An example is the word for "gravy". In medieval times gravy was a sauce made from broth, thickened with almonds and usually heavy with spices and herbs (often to disguise the smell and flavour of rotting meat). It was nothing like the modern-day gravy made from juices produced by roasting. The word is also interesting because it should actually be spelt something like *graney*. Someone translating the original French word misread the letter "n" for "u/v"and the change stuck.

When we track the origin and development of words in this way, we are studying the etymology of these words. In the case of *gravy*, it is as if the word outgrew its original meaning. The method of making the sauce changed, but the word remained. This is an example of external change – the same word is used but in a brand new world. More usually, the meanings themselves alter over time and this accounts for much of what is curious in the recipe here, such as the strange reference to "sodden rabbits". These rabbits are not soaked to the skin. At that time *sodden* was the past participle of the verb *seethe* (meaning "to boil"), but *seethe* and *sodden* parted company and are no longer connected. There is still something curious about an instruction to "seethe rabbits" because nowadays we can only *seethe* figuratively, as in *I seethed with fury*. Thus the meaning of the verb has narrowed to a specific, once metaphorical use.

We are also advised here to "hack" the rabbits into "gobbets"; other recipes around this time suggested "smiting" or "hewing" them. All this hacking, hewing and smiting of small rabbits seems excessive to us today, because these verbs now have more violent meanings: "sever into pieces with violent cutting blows". In fact, both *hew* and *smite* are archaic and survive only in biblical contexts (*smiting the enemy*) and in idioms like *hew asunder* and *smitten with love*. It is typical for lexical changes to leave relics in the form of frozen expressions.

We have only considered lexical and semantic change so far, but aspects of phonology, morphology, and syntax are also in a constant state of flux. The branch of linguistics that investigates these changes is known as **historical and comparative linguistics**. It is historical because it deals with the history of languages; it is comparative because it compares languages and also looks at the relationship between them. You might also see it occasionally referred to as **comparative philology**, although this term more usually now describes the scholarly study of literature.

When linguists examine change in language, they have to consider three different aspects:

> What?
> How?
> Why?

The first point refers to the change itself: what changes into what; and what are likely and unlikely changes? The second refers to the process of change: how is it implemented; how does it sneak through the language; how does it sneak through the speech community? The last aspect – the "why" of change – is perhaps the most interesting. What factors trigger language change? Is it predictable or is it more like the changing fashions, say, of clothing? We might wear baggy trousers one year, and leggings the next. At least one linguist, Paul Postal 1968, has suggested that changes in language are stylistic, and as eccentric as fashions in clothing. However, most linguists argue that they are more systematic and the triggers far more complex.

The clue to observing language change is variation – what some see as slipshod pronunciations, mistakes in grammar, coinages, or new-fangled meanings. These are what provide the basis for real change. Some features will drop by the wayside, some will remain as variation, while others will catch on, be used more and more, and eventually become established.

## Some facts about language evolution

> All linguistic change in progress shows up as variation.
> Change proceeds gradually over a geographical area; for example, different regional dialects can be at different stages in a sound change and this is what causes variation of accent (see Chapter 2.7).
> Change proceeds gradually through the language; for example, a sound change slowly spreads through the vocabulary, affecting different groups of words at different times.
> All change occurs in the presence of socially relevant variation; a change may first affect the speech of some members of the speech community and then may spread to other groups of speakers (see Chapter 2.7).

## Language families – establishing genetic relationship

Below are the forms in Dutch, Swedish, English and German for the words "father", "brother", "you" and "that". You'll notice that the English word for "you" is *thou*, a word that has now disappeared from ordinary everyday language.

| Dutch | Swedish | English | German |
|-------|---------|---------|--------|
| broer | broder | brother | Bruder |
| vader | fader | father | Vater |
| du | du | thou | du |
| dat | det | that | das |

Here is a set of words that are not only the same in meaning, but also phonetically very close. We can rule out borrowing here because there are hundreds of such sets, all strikingly similar in meaning and in sound. Borrowings do not normally occur on such a large scale. Secondly, these are everyday words. Speakers would not need to borrow a term for "brother" or a personal pronoun like "you". Nor is it likely that the similarities are due to chance. The speakers of these different languages could not have arrived independently at the same sound patterns to represent these concepts. Languages might have some vocabulary based on sound symbolism, but generally speaking the correlation between the form and the meaning of language expressions is arbitrary – there is no natural and no necessary connection between the physical shape of a word and what it denotes. Shakespeare was correct: 'That which we call a rose, by any other name would smell as sweet' (*Romeo and Juliet* II.ii). So borrowing and chance cannot account for groups of words like those in the table above.

We have no choice but to assume that these words are connected in origin. Their similarity is due to the fact that they have evolved from the same source and can be traced back to a single parent language, or proto-language (*proto* = "original"). The parent language in this case is **Proto-Germanic**. It was spoken about 2,500 years ago, but unfortunately left behind no written evidence. Either the Proto-Germanic people had not developed a writing system, or perhaps no written texts survived. Despite this, we do have some idea of the original shape of these four words. Via a technique known as the **comparative method**, we can reconstruct *\*brōðer; \*fader; \*ðū;* and *\*ðat*. (The macron – line over the vowel

– indicates that the vowel was long; the "ð" represents a voiced dental fricative; the asterisk is used here to show that these are hypothetical forms.)

The ancestral words in Proto-Germanic represent a relationship between sound and meaning that is carried through to each of the modern Germanic languages, despite at times drastic sound changes. These kinds of words are called **cognates**.

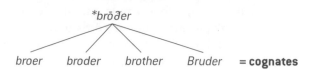

Figure 2.15 *Germanic cognates of* BROTHER

Cognates are words similar in form and in meaning because they are historically (or etymologically) related; as we go back in time, the more striking the similarities become. Listed below are versions of English, Swedish, and German from around one thousand years ago. Old Norse is the parent of Swedish. Middle Dutch is not as old as these; it dates only from the Middle Ages – very little has survived of original Old Dutch. If we were really serious about reconstructing the parent of the modern Germanic languages, it would make our task easier to work backwards from these earlier cognates.

| Middle Dutch | Old English | Old Norse | Old High German | Modern English |
|---|---|---|---|---|
| Broder | brōðer | broðer | bruoder | brother |
| Fader | fæder | faðir | fater | father |
| Ðū | ðū | ðū | dū | you |
| Dat | ðæt | ðat | daz | that |

Via the ordinary processes of language change, a single language can split into dialects and over a long enough period of time these dialects can turn into distinct languages. Proto-Germanic did exactly this. Eventually it diverged into Dutch, Swedish, English, and German. Because there is less time-depth separating the languages above, they have had less time to diverge; hence the similarities are even more striking. As you turn the clock back, so you undo the changes and the languages become closer. Around one thousand years ago these were more like varieties of the same language. Eighth-century speakers of so-called Old English and Old Norse, for example, would have been able to understand one another's languages.

It was in the eighteenth century that the concept of genetic relatedness emerged. During a famous lecture in 1786, Sir William Jones (1746–94) argued that the classical languages Sanskrit, Ancient Greek, and Latin were related and could be traced back to a common language that no longer exists. Jones was arguing for the existence of Proto-Indo-European, the parent of most of the languages of Europe, south-western Asia and northern India. It has left us no written records, but is assumed to have been spoken sometime around 5,000 years ago. In an interesting article that originally appeared in the *Scientific American*, Thieme 2001 shows what reconstructing Proto-Indo-European can tell us about the history and culture of the contemporary speakers of Indo-European languages.

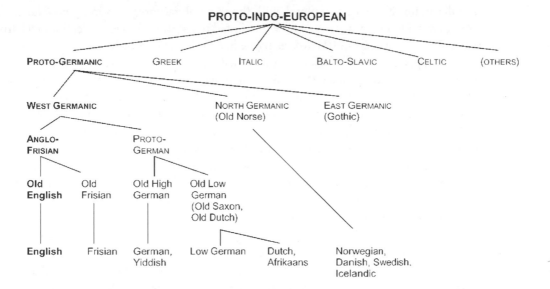

Figure 2.16 *Classification of Indo-European languages*

Other scholars adopted Jones's idea, and before long the systematic study of language evolution was undertaken for the first time. The work carried out by European linguists during the nineteenth century led to the classification of all the Indo-European languages into the family tree shown in Figure 2.16. The modern Germanic languages represent the diverse continuation of Proto-Germanic, and the bolded nodes on the left indicate the development of English through to modern times.

## Attitudes to language change

For the majority of people, change is fine as long as it is in the past. Curiously, most speakers are interested in word origins and the stories behind the structures that they find in their language, but they dislike any change that is happening now– invariably it is viewed as change for the worse. So why is it that people react this way?

To take a straightforward example, English can convert words to other parts of speech without adding any sort of affix. This is **conversion** (aka zero-derivation) and it is something that people have been doing for centuries (see Chapter 2.3). Despite this, many (usually older) speakers are quick to condemn usages like *a big ask* and *to stretcher*. Complaints about new conversions are commonplace and it has always been this way. The verb *to contact* (created from a noun) was once colloquial jargon and in the early twentieth century there was ferocious resistance to it. An outraged public used descriptions like 'lubricious barbarism' and 'abomination' for this new arrival on scene. The *Oxford English Dictionary* has a small entry for the verb *to contact* with quotations like the following from 1927: 'Dreiser should not be allowed to corrupt his language by writing "anything that Clyde has personally contacted here"'. It is hard for us today to understand what possible objection people could have had to the verb *to contact*. In fact, this is not a language issue, but a social one. When it first appeared as a verb, *to contact* smacked of pretentious jargon (much like the verb *to impact on* today) and many people did not want to be identified with the kinds of speakers who used that sort of jargon.

In 1653 the grammarian John Wallis railed against the use of the word *chicken* as a singular noun (it was once a plural, with the same plural morph as in *oxen, children*). In 1755 Samuel Johnson described how he wanted to rid the language of 'colloquial barbarisms'. The sort of 'colloquial barbarisms' he had in mind were words like *novel* in place of *new* and *capture* in place of *take*. Jonathan Swift, author of *Gulliver's Travels*, complained bitterly about contemporary shortenings like *mob* from the Latin phrase *mobile vulgus* and *pozz* from *positive*. Swift blamed changes like these on the 'loose morals' of the day. However, the social significance of all these usages is lost to us today, and the objections to them now seem puzzling and trivial. With time, recent newcomers like *to stretcher* and *a big ask* will sound as everyday as venerable forms like *to contact* (verb from noun), *an attempt* (noun from verb) and *a comic* (noun from adjective) and the next generation of English speakers will be puzzling over what possible objections there could be to these words. Of course by then there will be other linguistic battles to wage.

As linguists will always point out (Aitchison 2001; Burridge 2005), flux and variance are natural and inevitable features of any language. If King Alfred the Great had chanced upon the language of Chaucer over 500 years later, he would have been shocked at the changes – changes that we now see another 600 years on as part of the richness and versatility of the language. The only languages that do not change are ones that are well and truly dead.

## Key points

> All aspects of the linguistic system are constantly changing: lexicon, phonology, syntax and semantics.

> Historical (and comparative) linguistics is that branch of the discipline that investigates change.

> All linguistic change will take place in the presence of socially relevant variation.

> Change is slow. It proceeds gradually over a geographical area and also through the linguistic system.

> The process of change and geographical separation inevitably gives rise to regional variation. Over a long enough period of time, regional dialects will diverge further to become mutually unintelligible; in other words, become distinct languages.

> Sound correspondences are said to exist when sounds regularly occur in corresponding positions in sets of words which are similar in shape and meaning.

> Words that are historically related are cognates. Cognates represent the continuation of a single lexical item in the parent (or proto) language.

> The symbolic nature of language and the orderliness of sound change are what give us the licence to compare languages and establish genetic relationships.

> Proto-Indo-European is the hypothetical common ancestor of the modern languages stretching from India to Europe.

> Attitudes to linguistic change are usually negative – change is viewed as change for the worse. It is the social setting of language that gives rise to these feelings.

# References

Aitchison, Jean 2001. *Language Change: Progress or Decay?* 3rd edn. Cambridge: Cambridge University Press.

Burridge, Kate 2005. *Weeds in the Garden of Words: Further Observations on the Tangled History of the English Language*. Cambridge: Cambridge University Press.

Postal, Paul M. 1968. *Aspects of Phonological Theory*. New York: Harper & Row.

Thieme, Paul 2001. The Indo-European language. In *Linguistics at Work: A Reader of Applications*, ed. by Dallin D. Oaks. Cambridge MA: Heinle & Heinle.

# 2.11 stylistics

## chapter contents

> Stylistics                134
> Literary stylistics       138
> Key points                140
> References                140

## Stylistics

Stylistics is the study of the linguistic choices that speakers and writers make to produce contextually appropriate utterances or texts. In each of the examples given below it is likely that you will be able to identify the contexts in which they were written or spoken.

(1)  Is there any pain when I press here?

(2)  Cream together butter, sugar and beaten yolks until smooth.

(3)  New Elastube. The tubular dressing retention bandage. No sticking. No tying. No pinning.

(4)  gotta go im l8 4 class. cu l8tr

(5)  The palate is ripe and harmonious with spicy dark cherry fruit, good length and finely tuned tannins.

(6)  Hon, are you gonna answer that?

As hearers and readers, we use cues such as the choice of vocabulary, grammatical patterns, and interactive features, such as address terms, to recognize the probable contexts of use. For example email messages may employ emoticons, also called smileys, such as ☺, to convey interpersonal information, and mobile phone text messages compress words to fit limited space (e.g. *cu l8r* instead of *see you later*). Textual cues suggest the likely contexts of the examples above are (1) a doctor–patient consultation, (2) a recipe, (3) an advertisement, (4) a mobile phone text message, (5) a wine bottle label, and (6) an interaction between family members when the phone rings. In many cases we can attach a simple label to the event or text-type (e.g. *recipe, advertisement*), indicating that members of the speech community share norms which identify context-specific language behaviour.

Contexts have been described using the three dimensions of **field**, **mode** and **tenor** (Halliday 1985). Field refers to what is going on: the nature of the activity performed and the topic discussed by the text. In example (5) above, the topic is wine. If it appears on the label of a bottle, it is a form of wine marketing, while if it appears in a wine column in a newspaper it is part of a wine review. Mode refers to the form of transmission of the text. This includes the channel (phonic or graphic) and the medium (the style of language normally associated with speech or with writing). Example (5) is graphic and uses normal written style, unlike example (4) which, though also graphic, uses an innovative style that draws on aspects of spoken language, given a new graphic representation. Tenor refers to the interpersonal relationship between interlocutors, including relative power or status and degree of intimacy. The participants in example (6) are clearly intimates and probably of equal status, whereas in example (1) we might infer unequal status and a low level of intimacy. A specific configuration of field, mode and tenor constitutes a **register**, and will require a particular text-type.

There is a style of language typically associated with writing, especially in formal contexts, and this can be contrasted with the style associated with spoken language and informality. These differences are usually seen as forming a continuum of features rather than two discrete styles. The written and spoken styles may be associated with different channels of transmission, so a written text may be delivered orally, or a film script may give a written representation of informal spoken language.

The tables below, adapted from Baron 2000: 21, contrast the physical features of oral and graphic texts, and the stylistic properties of the two ends of the continuum of written and spoken language style.

### Physical properties of graphic and oral

| Graphic text | Oral text |
|---|---|
| durable | ephemeral |
| scannable | only linearly accessible |

### Stylistic properties of written and spoken language styles

| Written style | Spoken style |
|---|---|
| objective | interpersonal |
| a monologue | a dialogue |
| planned | spontaneous |
| highly structured | loosely structured |
| concerned with past and future | concerned with present |
| formal | informal |
| expository | narrative |
| argument-oriented | event-oriented |
| decontextualized | contextualized |
| abstract | concrete |

Halliday 1989 argues that a key difference between spoken and written style is the use in the latter of **grammatical metaphor** (encoding an object, process or attribute using a grammatical form which doesn't match the real world). The most common form of this is **nominalization**, where processes are encoded as nouns rather than verbs. For example, the verb *argue*, in the clause *I argue that this is not so* may be replaced with a noun, as in *the argument to the contrary...*. As a result of nominalization the language becomes more formal and more impersonal, with the removal of the subject pronoun *I*, which has no place in the nominal version. It also leaves space in the sentence for more information, as the examples (7)–(8)from Halliday and Matthiessen 2004: 656 show.

**Written style**

   (7)  The argument to the contrary is basically an appeal to the lack of synonymy in mental language.

**Spoken style**

   (8)  In order to argue that [this] is not so [he] simply points out that there are no synonyms in mental language.

This device of nominalization allows the development of impersonal writing of the sort deplored by the Plain English movement. The use of passive forms also contributes to an impersonal effect. For example, Iedema 1997:74 describes administrative language such as (9) in which the source of the directive is not identified, and the recipient is referred to in the third person (*all registered agents ... they*), rather than directly as *you*.

   (9)  From 21 September 1992 all registered agents will be required to complete a declaration (Form 932) in relation to every application with which they assist.

Other aspects of text that are important in explaining stylistic effects include the way in which cohesion and coherence are managed (Halliday and Hasan 1976). Cohesion is the use of language to indicate links between items in the texts, as in example (9) above where the pronoun *they* is used to refer to *all registered agents*. Coherence is the way ideas in the text are interconnected thematically. This depends on how the text is interpreted. Recent work has focused on modality (expressing probability, obligatoriness, willingness, usuality) (Toolan 1996), deixis (locating aspects of the utterance or text in time and space), and the use of evaluation to express the author's point of view (McRae and Clark 2004).

Systemic functional linguistics has developed techniques for describing the relationships between texts and contexts. In any language and culture there are textual means to achieve particular goals. Martin 1984 describes a **genre** as a purposeful activity, producing a text consisting of culturally appropriate stages and specific elements of **lexico-grammar** (a term used to highlight the interrelation between the linguistic levels of lexis and grammar). This allows a contrast to be made between, for example, narrative and explanatory text.

Labov and Waletzky 1967 describe the structure of personal narratives told in the course of casual conversation, and identify obligatory and optional elements, which occur in a specifiable sequence. A narrative is defined as 'one method of recapitulating past experience by matching a verbal sequence of clauses to the sequence of events which (it is inferred) actually occurred' (Labov 1999: 225).

### Labov's model of spoken narrative

| | |
|---|---|
| **Abstract**: | summarizes the whole story in a clause or two (i.e. what was this about?) |
| **Orientation**: | locates the event in time and place, and identifies the participants (i.e. who, when, what, where?) |

| | | |
|---|---|---|
| **Complicating action**: | describes the sequence of events (i.e. then what happened?) | |
| **Evaluation**: | reports the orientation of the storyteller at different points (i.e. so what?) | |
| **Result or resolution**: | reports the outcome (i.e. what finally happened?) | |
| **Coda**: | signals the story is finished, and indicates the impact of the events on the narrator. (Labov 1999: 227, 234) | |

Some of these elements, such as abstract, coda and evaluation are optional, and evaluation can occur throughout the recounting of the event. We recognize a stretch of talk as a narrative simply on the basis of the sequence of events given in the complicating action. Narratives also occur in written texts, but, as we would expect, differences of field, mode and tenor lead to differences of text-type (see the discussion of written narratives in Chapter 2.12).

In the following conversation Angie and Jill produce a collaborative narrative which consists of complicating action, resolution and coda. They do not need to supply an orientation, as this is established by Dan's comment. Transcription conventions: (.) indicates a pause, [ ] indicates overlapping/simultaneous text.

| | | |
|---|---|---|
| | Dan: | You guys are <u>exactly</u> where I left you this morning |
| Complicating action | Angie: | Yeah but I (..) had a shower and got dressed and cleaned the whole hou:se (.) cleaned the whole hou[se from top to bottom so (.) yeah |
| | Jill: | [hehh hahh |
| | | We mopped and vacuumed and (.) swept and (...) yeah (.) cool and watched a <u>lot</u> of Futurama (.) and fell asleep fo:r many hours. |
| | Angie: | Hehh hahh |
| | | <u>I</u> didn't fall asleep for long, [it's– probably like an hou[r |
| | Jill: | [Yeah you did] [and a half] |
| | Angie: | Okay an hour and a half [hehh hahh] |
| | Jill: | [hehh hahh] |
| Resolution | Angie: | and then I woke up and I was drooling everywhere |
| | Dan: | hehh hahh |
| | Angie: | hehh hahh And Dad was like (.) hehh hahh |
| Coda | | so that was funny (.) hehh hahh |

This story finishes with an evaluation *so that was funny* which tells the hearer the point of the story, and serves as the coda, signalling the end of the story. Toolan 2001 notes the importance of the relationship between teller, tale, and addressee in constructing a narrative.

Labov 1999: 228 gives an example of a story told by Larry, a member of the Jets street gang in New York's Harlem, which includes an abstract and orientation. (Some of the complicating action has been omitted here.)

| | |
|---|---|
| Abstract | An' then three weeks ago I had a fight with this other dude outside He got mad 'cause I wouldn't give him a cigarette. Ain't that a bitch? |
| | (Oh yeah?) |
| Orientation | Yeah, you know, I was sitting on the corner an' shit, |

| | smoking my cigarette, you know |
|---|---|
| | I was high, an' shit. |
| Complicating action | He walked over to me, |
| | 'Can I have a cigarette?' |
| | He was a little taller than me, |
| | but not that much. |
| | 'I said I ain't got no more man.' |
| | [Larry goes on to recount a series of verbal exchanges, followed by physical aggression] |
| | An' boy, let me tell you, |
| | I beat the shit outa that motherfucker. |
| | I tried to *kill* 'im – over one cigarette. |
| | I tried to kill 'im. Square business! |
| | After I got through stompin' him in the face, man |
| | You know all of a sudden I went crazy! |
| | I jus' went crazy. |
| | An' I jus' wouldn't stop hittin' im, man, |
| | Till the teacher pulled me off o' him. |
| Resolution | An' guess what? After all that I gave the dude the cigarette, after all that. |
| | Ain't that a bitch? |

Evaluation is found throughout the story, as the narrator presents his stance. For example, Larry uses the phrase *Ain't that a bitch?* twice to indicate his judgement of the irrational nature of his behaviour. Other forms of evaluation include the contrast created in the utterance *I tried to kill 'im – over one cigarette*. All these serve to indicate the point of the story.

An important observation is that there are systematic linguistic choices made in different parts of the narrative: complicating action is typically told in a series of simple past tense clauses, which follow the temporal sequence in which they occur. By contrast, the orientation in the Labov text above uses a progressive form *was sitting*. Codas often use present tense or present perfect forms to indicate that the narrative is closed and the focus is returning to the present (e.g. *And ever since then I've been afraid of dogs*).

Stylistics is concerned with specifying the linguistic patterns that allow us to label a register or genre. This may include labelling the optional and obligatory elements of the text, describing the linguistic choices available to the writer or speaker in constructing those elements, and the effects of those choices. There are culturally established norms governing appropriate language use in context. McRae and Clark 2004 note that writers and speakers need to take account of the way different readers and hearers are likely to interpret the text.

## Literary stylistics

Stylistics has its origins in the study of literary texts. Scholars use the techniques of linguistic description in order to reveal how poets and other writers create their effects, and what choices they have made from the range of forms available at any point. The aim is to describe empirically the way the elements of the text function, and how linguistic elements contribute to aesthetic judgements (Thornborrow and Wareing 1998).

Carter 1997 argues that there is no clear boundary between literary and non-literary texts. Instead there is a continuum based on the way the text is written and read. Texts at the literary end of the continuum can be interpreted without support from other media such as photographs or a key to abbreviations. That is, they exist to be read as self-contained texts.

The genres or registers described above draw on specific lexico-grammatical features. No such constraints apply to literary texts: any words or grammatical patterns may be woven in. Literary texts employ a more complex patterning of different linguistic levels, drawing, for example, on contrast between simple and complex syntax, between lexical items of different origins and diverse syllabic structures, and semantic contrasts (Carter 1997; Carter and Nash 1990). There are often complex links between sentences, creating a chain of meaning.

Literary writers, particularly poets, exploit the phonological properties of the language to create effects using devices such as **rhyme**, where the nucleus (vowel) and coda (final consonant) are the same (e.g. *treat~feet*), **alliteration**, where the same initial segments are used (e.g. *shell~shoe*), **assonance**, where the same vowel is found in the nucleus (e.g. *swim with him*), or **consonance**, where the final consonants are the same (e.g. *good old Dad*). There is also **reverse rhyme**, where the onset and nucleus are the same (e.g. *hat~Harry*), and **pararhyme**, where the onset and coda are the same, but the nucleus is different (e.g. *pen~pain*). Poets also use repetition. Word and sentence stress are used to create the rhythmic patterns of poetry, which are called **metre**. English poetry frequently makes use of the **iambic pentameter** (a line of poetry consisting of ten syllables, with alternating unstressed and stressed syllables; see Chapter 2.2) (Thornborrow and Wareing 1998).

Lexical choice is also important in the creation of literary effect. Toolan 1996 describes as a paradox the writer's need to choose the most fitting word, yet one that the reader might not have predicted. In other domains, writers strive to avoid ambiguity, but in creative writing, singularity of meaning is not necessarily valued: polysemy is an important feature of literary writing, as the multiple senses of a word or phrase are exploited to suggest layers of meaning. Writers draw on both denotation and connotation (see Chapter 3.1) to create this interpretive richness. Meanings are not always overtly presented, and readers need to seek possible alternative meanings (Carter 1997). Original metaphors and other forms of figurative language (e.g. irony, hyperbole, understatement) are used to create additional depth of meaning, and the sense of both unexpectedness and rightness that Toolan describes. The field of pragmatics thus has an important role to play in stylistic analysis of texts (Black 2006; see Chapter 2.6).

Literary writers often allude to the language of other texts to create meaning links, and draw on the resonances produced by these allusions. This is known as **intertextuality**.

Critical discourse analysis has had a major influence on the approach taken in stylistics. There has been a shift from attempting to present 'objective' analysis of text to an increasing recognition of the role of ideology in interpreting meanings (McRae and Clark 2004). Recent work has also drawn on insights from cognitive science to assist in understanding how a literary text creates particular emotional effects for the reader (Stockwell 2006).

## References

Baron, Naomi S. 2000. *Alphabet to Email: How Written English Evolved and Where It's Heading*. London: Routledge.

Black, Elizabeth 2006. *Pragmatic Stylistics*. Edinburgh: Edinburgh University Press.

Carter, Ronald 1997. *Investigating English Discourse: Language, Literacy and Literature*. London: Routledge.

Carter, Ronald and Walter Nash 1990. *Seeing Through Language: A Guide to Styles of English Writing*. Oxford: Blackwell.

Halliday, M.A.K. 1985. *Spoken and Written Language*. Geelong: Deakin University Press.

Halliday, Michael A.K. 1989. *Spoken and Written Language*. 2nd edn. Oxford: Oxford University Press [First edn 1985].

Halliday, Michael A.K. and Ruqaiya Hasan 1976. *Cohesion in English*. London: Longman.

Halliday, Michael A.K. and Christian M.I.M. Matthiessen 2004. *An Introduction to Functional Grammar*. 3rd edn. London: Arnold.

Iedema, Rick 1997. The language of administration: organizing human acitivity in formal institutions. In *Genre and Institutions: Social Processes in the Workplace and School*, ed. by Frances Christie and James R. Martin. London: Continuum, pp. 73–100.

Labov, William 1999. Narrative structure. In *The Discourse Reader*, ed. by Adam Jaworski and Nikolas Coupland. London: Routledge, pp. 221–35.

Labov, William and Joshua Waletzky 1967. Narrative analysis: oral versions of personal experience. In *Essays on the Verbal and Visual Arts*, ed. by June Helm. Seattle: American Ethnological Society, pp. 12–44.

Martin, James R. 1984. Language, register and genre. In *Children Writing: Reader*, ed. by Frances Christie. Geelong: Deakin University Press, pp. 21–30.

McRae, John and Urszula Clark 2004. Stylistics. In *The Handbook of Applied Linguistics*, ed. by Alan Davies and Catherine Elder. Oxford: Blackwell, pp. 328–46.

Stockwell, Peter 2006. Language and literature: stylistics. In *The Handbook of English Linguistics*, ed. by Bas Aarts and April M.S. McMahon. Oxford: Blackwell, pp. 742–58.

Thornborrow, Joanna and Shân Wareing 1998. *Patterns in Language: An Introduction to Language and Literary Style*. London: Routledge.

Toolan, Michael J. 1996. *Language in Literature: An Introduction to Stylistics*. London: Arnold.

Toolan, Michael J. 2001. *Narrative: A Critical Linguistic Introduction*. 2nd edn. London: Routledge.

# 2.12 discourse and conversation

## chapter contents

> Analysing two stories     141
> Critical discourse analysis     144
> Conversation analysis     144
> Turn-taking in Anglo environments     145
> Adjacency pairs     146
> Key points     148
> References     149

## Analysing two stories

Let's investigate two very short stories with a view to tracking the way in which a theme is signalled and maintained, and persons or things are identified and re-identified in the course of the narrative. I will refer to the first story as 'the Clapton story' and the second as 'the Jag story'.

## Practise that guitar, Clapton told

LONDON: Guitar great Eric Clapton was told he could have two months to practise before being allowed to play at his local church — by a vicar who didn't recognize him.

Millionaire Clapton was visited by his local vicar Rev. Dennis Ackroyd on a house-to-house visit in Surrey, on London's southern out-skirts.

'When I knocked at the door a very nice chap answered, invited me in and told me his name was Eric,' Mr Ackroyd said.

'I noticed a guitar lying in a corner, he said he played, so I asked him if he would come and do something at our family service.

'I told him I would give him a couple of months to practise,' he said.

Mr Ackroyd said Clapton dropped a few hints before the bell finally rang. Clapton eventually played at the local church, singing hymns for the congregation.

Clapton, a veteran of 1960s supergroups including the Yardbirds and Cream, is regarded as Britain's finest blues guitarist.

(Brisbane *Courier Mail*, Thursday February 10, 1994, p.10)

## The Jag story

One morning Tom found his Jaguar wouldn't start. He phoned Ed and asked him to come and look at it. Ed didn't really want to, but he came anyway. He saw that the plugs were worn, and advised Tom to fit some new ones. Tom did so. After that the car worked perfectly.

If you've read these stories you will know what they are about. Let's investigate some of what you understand.

One short cut to identifying what a story is about is to look at the title. A title is often a mini-summary of the story. At best it will identify the major theme in the story, or at least indicate one of the major themes that will establish in the reader's mind what is relevant to understanding the point of the story. In the title of 'the Clapton story', the proper name 'Clapton' sends the reader to his/her internalized encyclopedia (knowledge base) to check for information about the referent. A few readers may have no entry for 'Clapton' at the outset, though such readers will do so after reading the story. Yet even at this stage they can infer that Clapton plays (or tries to play) the guitar. Why should this be newsworthy? All (would-be) musicians need to practise, so what is **unordinary** is that someone thinks that Clapton needs to be told to practise. Notice the assumption that a story must be about something out of the ordinary. The question of newsworthiness arises equally for readers who already know that Eric Clapton is a professional musician said to have fine technique and to be a great blues/rock guitarist. The difference between the two kinds of readers is that the latter will know that Clapton does not need to be told to practise; they will conclude either that Clapton is not the guitarist he used to be, or that his abilities have not been recognized for some reason. For all readers, it is the news-worthiness of a (would-be) musician being told to practise that motivates the story. It also sets up the kind of world being spoken of.

'The Jag story' is evidently a story about (a) Jag. That much will be obvious to someone without the further information that *a Jag* (note the initial capital letter) refers to a certain car marque. The more knowledgeable reader will set up the correct frame for a story about a car. The less knowledgeable reader will activate that frame only after reading the first sentence.

For both stories, we have established a thematic subject. The main protagonist in the first is (Eric) Clapton and in the second it is a Jaguar car – or to those who didn't guess this, someone or something called (a) Jag. In most stories and anecdotes, the thematic subject is human, simply because stories are created by humans for humans. Humans figure extensively even in the many stories, books, and anecdotes that are not principally about humans. The Jag story is one such. In the Clapton story the theme is summarized in a capsule statement in the first paragraph. This functions in a similar way to the 'abstracts' of academic papers; so we call these openers **abstracts**. Their function is to expand upon the title by explicitly identifying the writer's goal and perhaps giving some indication of the means by which it is achieved. There are two purposes. One is to whet the reader's appetite; if successful s/he reads on, or s/he may decide the piece is of no further interest. The second is to establish common ground with the reader through developing the frame or mindset evoked in the title in order to prepare the reader for what is to come.

In the Clapton story, Clapton is the grammatical as well as the thematic subject of a main clause in the first, second, fourth, sixth and seventh paragraphs; the grammatical subject of one finite and four non-finite subordinate clauses in the first paragraph; three finite subordinate clauses in the third paragraph; one subordinate finite and two non-finite clauses in the fourth paragraph; and one finite and one non-finite clause in the sixth paragraph. (If you don't understand terms like *main clause, subordinate clause, finite clause, non-finite clause* look them up under entries for **clause** and **finite** in Chapter 3.1 'Key terms and concepts'.) The only other grammatical subject is the Rev. Dennis Ackroyd: he is the subject of one main clause in the third paragraph, two in the fourth, two in the fifth, and one in the sixth. He is also the subject of a finite subordinate clause in the first, second, and third paragraphs and a non-finite subordinate clause in the fifth paragraph. A guitar is subject of one non-finite subordinate clause in the fourth paragraph. The weight of evidence is clear: in addition to Clapton being mentioned in the title, he is grammatical subject in 18 clauses and so there are 18 things predicated of him. By comparison, Ackroyd is a bit player, being subject of only 10 clauses, and most predications are reports of his interaction with Clapton. As befits an inanimate object, the guitar is even less prominent; its relevance is as an appendage to Clapton. Note that *Clapton* and *Ackroyd* are proper names (nouns), whereas *a guitar* is not. The more important something or somebody is, the more likely it is to get a proper name. To sum up, we recognize Clapton as the thematic subject because references to him pervade the story.

The Jag story is much shorter. It is a story about a car and, unless it is to be a fantasy, about some person's car. Although it is the thematic subject of the story, the Jaguar, is the grammatical subject only of a non-finite clause in the first sentence; its spark-plugs are subject of a finite clause in the fourth sentence but the car itself is the subject of a finite clause only in the final (sixth) sentence. By contrast, Tom is the grammatical subject of one finite clause in the first sentence; two in the second sentence; one in the fifth. Tom is also the subject of a non-finite clause in the fourth sentence. Ed is the subject of two non-finite clauses in the second sentence; two finite and at least one non-finite clause in the third sentence; and two finite clauses in the fourth sentence. Humans are more grammatically prominent than the Jaguar, so how does the latter come to be a thematic subject?

A significant difference between the two stories is that the Clapton story is about real people, and the Jag story is not; so it is not a story about, say, my brother Tom. Even if it were, the story has the classic story format:

Title
Setting
There is a problem
A protagonist seeks (help) to resolve it
A resolution is found (there is a dénouement)
Outcome

It is **resolving the problem** that gives the story a **plot**; and in longer stories than this one there are usually several attempts – think of a Raymond Chandler or Agatha Christie story (or a myriad others). In the Jag story, the problem is that the car won't start, and the whole story is about getting it running again. The humans serve to achieve this end. Note that there is no characterization: you can change the names at will. Both humans could just as well be women as men. Thus the fact that the humans have proper names is of no importance to this story except as a means of distinguishing them as participants. The humans are therefore bit parts; the main character is the Jag.

We have seen that titles and abstracts establish common ground by activating a frame or mindset for what follows (i.e. the world spoken of). We also reviewed what characterizes the thematic subject in a story. In the human-interest news story about Eric Clapton we found that references to Clapton dominate the piece; his name is overwhelmingly the grammatical subject of clauses within the story, thus more is predicated of him than of anything else. Any business concerning other people revolved around him. This analytical method did not transfer to the Jag story, where the Jag is at the centre of the story structure, because its failure to start is the problem that the story seeks to resolve. The question arises whether the Clapton story fits the same format as the Jag story. It does. In the Clapton story, the setting is somewhere in Surrey; the problem is that Ackroyd fails to recognize Clapton; therefore, when he asks Clapton to play guitar in church, he makes an outrageously inappropriate remark that reveals he doubts Clapton's abilities are up to performing the task. The resolution is found when 'the bell finally rang'; the outcome is that Clapton plays in church. The final paragraph functions as a **coda**; it is characterized by a certain autonomy from the discourse theme, often links past events to the present by reflecting on some current situation deriving from events or participants in the discourse theme; and it often takes the hearer or reader back to something mentioned at the outset of the story. The Jag story has neither abstract nor coda. Looking at the Clapton story from the aspect of its rhetorical structure, we conclude that it is not simply Clapton that is the thematic subject, but Clapton the great blues/rock guitarist.

## Critical discourse analysis

Our analysis of the two stories focused on their narrative structure. Critical discourse analysis (CDA) focuses on the social constructs of written and spoken texts. Every speaker or writer has an ideological position, which is more often covert and unconscious than explicit. This viewpoint affects the evaluations of participants, states, and events that are referred to in the text. Consequently it portrays social relations in a particular way (or ways), including the relation between speaker and hearer, or writer and reader. Moreover, it does not merely reflect such relations and evaluations, it constructs and develops them. From a CDA perspective, the Jag story is of little or no interest, while the Clapton story is far meatier. In the latter, the author presents an admired celebrity as a man who has achieved greatness, yet all that is required for the story to work is that Eric is an unrecognized celebrity and a professional musician. Thus, the view that he is a '[g]uitar great' and 'Britain's finest blues guitarist' is something that a reader may wish to dispute, and that some other writer would not report in this favourable way. Though the Rev. Ackroyd is not maliciously pilloried in the Clapton story, he is presented as the slow-off-the-mark fall guy at whom the author gently pokes fun. As the door-knocker, Ackroyd already has a status inferior to that of the householder, though this could easily change, because a vicar will be of higher social status than many of his parishioners. However, in this story Ackroyd remains the one with lower status and less power because Clapton is an admired celebrity. But note that 'before the bell finally rang' Ackroyd did assume the higher status that he believed his role as vicar allows him in many social situations; it sanctions him to issue a command: 'I told him I would give him a couple of months to practise.' Clapton's reported reaction is not that of someone as insulted as Clapton had the right to be, instead he politely 'dropped a few hints' about who he was. We don't know whether this report is Ackroyd's or the journalist's, but at least one of them is presenting Clapton in a favourable light – an evaluation reconfirmed by Clapton's generosity in freely donating his time in service to the vicar's congregation.

CDA reveals how the discourse practices in the text reproduce, reflect, and help construct an evaluation of sociocultural practices (see also Chapter 2.7).

## Conversation analysis

Conversation is the basic and commonest communicative activity and we receive little if any instruction on how to converse. Conversation is not as orderly as written discourse, but it is not unstructured. There are procedural conventions that work to manage relatively smooth, clear, and minimally interrupted interaction. These are the study of **conversation analysis** (CA). CA developed within **ethnomethodology** which emphasizes the influence of everyday knowledge on social activity. CA seeks to identify, for example,

> how to initiate conversation
> why interruptions are relatively rare
> how we know to respond to our interlocutor, and
> how to end conversation.

It is knowledge of the organizational structure of conversation that CA tries to make explicit.

In language use, knowledge and action are deeply linked and mutually constitutive. When we engage in conversation we demonstrate that we know how to conform with and reinforce the procedural conventions. CA differs from some other approaches to discourse analysis in being pragmatic rather than theoretical, focusing on naturally occurring conversation. A central aspect of analysis is transcription of collected data (see Chapter 5.2). The transcription records in written form all words and utterance fragments spoken; identifies the speakers, times, and sequences of utterances; and includes prosodic features such as loudness, stress, disjuncture, intonation. It also records fluctuations in tempo, pause, and lengthening; non-verbal noises such as laughter, throat-clearing, and inhalation; and non-utterance events that become relevant to the interaction (e.g. thunder). Additionally, it must include comments from the transcriber indicating anything else that is relevant to the record of conversation, such as inability to make out the words spoken.

The transcription of conversations must be concise yet accessible to other analysts. Many different people put speech into written form: journalists, oral historians, phoneticians, and conversation analysts. Each does it differently. So far as CA is concerned, a good transcription system should be able to accommodate everything from friendly conversation to a political speech. Every transcription should be accompanied by a key to the symbols used for such things as overlap between speakers, latching (when there is no gap between one line and the next), length of disjuncture (pause), cut-offs, inhalation and exhalation, amplitude, tempo, and so on.

## Turn-taking in Anglo environments

As already mentioned, everyday conversation is not disorganized. Overwhelmingly, one party (TH, the turn holder) talks at a time, though backchannelling from the addressees is common. Backchannelling includes head nods and shakes; perfunctory, face-maintaining verbal acknowledgements like *yes, no, mhm, uhuh*; utterance completions; requests for clarification; and brief restatements. Most transitions between THs are without significant intervening pause. Turn order varies as does turn size. The content of a conversation is not normally specified in advance, nor is the distribution of turns. There may be deviation from a topic that is later returned to, and there are repair mechanisms to use when things go awry.

TH can select NTH (next TH), but NTHs often self-select (Sacks, Schegloff and Jefferson 1974). When NTH self-selects s/he often shifts posture, leans forward or back, straightens or crosses legs, twists feet, and so on. Most turn exchanges occur when LTH (last TH) and NTH exchange mutual gaze; or when NTH is looking at LTH. When only TH gazes at someone, it is often with the intention to select NTH. Otherwise NTH self-selects or LTH continues. NTH usually takes the floor at the next **TRP** (**transition relevance place**, i.e. potentially a place for smooth turn exchange).

NTH often indicates the intention to speak with increased body tension, audible intake of breath, and gazing at TH. Current TH signals TH-ing by speech (except, perhaps, when accepting backchannelling). Typically, TH looks away immediately the turn begins, unless asking a question. TH may exchange gaze to accept backchannelling but otherwise tends to look away much of the time when speaking. TH expresses body tension and movement, including gesturing. Gesturing is tied to sense groups; it always ceases prior to the close of a phrase or clause, and at a TRP.

Pauses occur between exchanges but also within turns. Pauses with turn-initial **fillers** such as *No, last year he uh ... he* or *Well ... I mean ...* are unchallenged. Idiosyncratic speech patterns are recognized and allowed for. Planning or breathing pauses are positioned after minor category elements such as *and, but, the, is ...* or elsewhere within sense groups, so as not to relinquish the turn. TH holds onto the turn by the use of level or rise tones at TRPs (which may nonetheless result in overlap with a would-be NTH) or by increased ampli-tude, especially over a challenge for the turn (and occasionally over a backchannel remark). The end of the turn is typically marked by grammatical completeness, posing a question, falling intonation, less amplitude, pause, laughter, relaxation of body and cessation of gesture, and changed facial expression (including gaze). Hearers tend to gaze at TH more than TH gazes at hearers; hearers backchannel in low amplitude and have relaxed bodies.

## Adjacency pairs

Adjacency pairs (occasionally triples) partially determine the structure of spoken discourse.

> Greeting

  (1) X greets Y
  (2) Y greets X

> Phoning

  (1) X telephones Y
  (2) Y answers the phone and thereby responds to X
  (3) X identifies him/herself to Y

> Question and answer

  (1) X asks Y a question
  (2) Y answers X

The first part may be preceded by a **presequence**, an attempt to check that unknown parts of the preparatory conditions on the speech act (see Chapter 2.6) are in place by, e.g., *If you've got the time, [could we have a chat?] Do you know ....* or *You know that book Harry was talking about, ...* There are presequences to answering, particularly when the answer is giving permission, e.g.

(1) *Can I go out with Harry tonight, Dad?*
      PreAnswer 2'     *What time will you be home?*
      PreAnswer 1'     *Eleven.*
(2) *OK.*

> Order/request and compliance/refusal

(1) X requests that Y do A   OR   X orders Y to do A
(2) Y does A and usually states the intention to do A prior to doing A  OR
     Y states refusal to do A

A pre-order might be an attention getter, e.g. *Hey you, [get off my land]*. Pre-requests check whether item requested is available, whether Y is able and willing to do A, e.g., *Do you have any Stilton? [Give me 200 grams]*. Y will often reply to the question that functions as a pre-request.

> Offer/invitation and acceptance/rejection

(1) X offers/invites Y to do A
(2) Y accepts and thanks X   OR   Y thanks X but rejects the offer

A pre-invitation will often check Y's ability and/or willingness; e.g. *If you are free Friday night, [how about coming to dinner?]* A pre-offer: *If you need any help, [I'll be only too happy to oblige.]*

> Proposal/announcement and acceptance/challenge

(1) X proposes something to Y (can be either information or opinion)
(2) Y accepts X's proposal and perhaps develops it   OR   Y challenges X

Pre-announcements use introducers like *Guess what?* and *I forgot to tell you that ...; Did you know that ....*

> Challenge and uptake/avoidance

(1) X challenges Y
(2) Y takes up the challenge   OR   Y dismisses the challenge

A pre-challenge would be something like *Do you **really** think that the world is flat?* Or more combatively, *What **the hell do you think** you are doing with my wife?* – which is itself a challenge.

There are **preferred** and **dispreferred** second pair parts. Silence is always dispreferred (except perhaps in response to the command *Shut up!*). Dispreferred seconds include no response to a summons or greeting; a negative answer to a question when a positive is sought; refusal to comply with an order or request; rejection of an offer; and disagreement with X's opinion. Dispreferreds (other than silence) are often marked by a longish pause before delivery, prevarications, hedges, expressions of doubt, prefaces like *uh, well*; token agreement before disagreement, appreciations, apologies, and careful explanation of the purported reason for the dispreferred second, e.g. *Thank you so much for asking, we ... er ... we'd love to come to dinner, but ... er ... Margaret's mother is visiting and we've promised to take her out to a movie.*

## Key points

> A title gives a mini-summary of the text.

> A story must be about something unordinary (newsworthy).

> A thematic subject is essentially who or what the story is about; it is the subject matter of the problem resolution in a story. References to the thematic subject usually pervade the story.

> In most stories and anecdotes, the thematic subject is human, simply because stories are created by humans for humans.

> An abstract summarizes the story at the beginning in order to whet Hearer's appetite and to establish common ground by setting the frame to facilitate understanding.

> Many stories have the structure:

> Title
> Abstract
> Setting
> There is a problem
> A protagonist seeks (help) to resolve it
> A resolution is found (there is a dénouement)
> Outcome

> The two core constituents are 'There is a problem' and 'A resolution is found'.

> Critical discourse analysis (CDA) reveals how the discourse practices in spoken or written text reproduce, reflect, and help construct an evaluation of sociocultural practices.

> Conversation analysis (CA) seeks to make explicit the organizational structure of conversation.

> CA attempts to represent every aspect of utterance in transcriptions of conversation.

> Turn-taking has clear procedural conventions to facilitate turn transitions from one participant to another.

> The end of a turn is indicated partly through syntax, but also through body language.

> Much conversation (and other language interchange) is partly determined by adjacency pairs.

> Additional information may be found at http://www.wikipedia.org/; in Brown 2006; Brown and Yule 1983; Drew and Heritage 2006; Fairclough 1995; 2003; Gee 2005; Hutchby and Wooffitt 1998; Johnstone 2008; Mandler 1984; Schiffrin 1994; and Wodak and Meyer 2002.

# References

Brown, E. Keith (General editor) 2006. *Encyclopedia of Languages and Linguistics*. 2nd edn. 14 vols. Oxford: Elsevier.

Brown, Gillian and George Yule 1983. *Discourse Analysis*. Cambridge: Cambridge University Press.

Drew, Paul and John Heritage (eds) 2006. *Conversation Analysis*. 4 vols. London: SAGE.

Fairclough, Norman 1995. *Critical Discourse Analysis: The Critical Study of Language*. London: Longman.

Fairclough, Norman 2003. *Analysing Discourse: Textual Analysis for Social Research*. London: Routledge.

Gee, James P. 2005. *An Introduction to Discourse Analysis*. 2nd edn. New York: Routledge.

Hutchby, Ian and Robin Wooffitt 1998. *Conversation Analysis: Principles, Practices, and Applications*. Cambridge: Polity.

Johnstone, Barbara 2008. *Discourse Analysis*. 2nd edn. Malden MA: Blackwell [First edn 2002].

Mandler, Jean M. 1984. *Stories, Scripts, and Scenes: Aspects of Schema Theory*. Hillsdale NJ: Lawrence Erlbaum.

Sacks, Harvey, Emmanuel Schegloff and Gail Jefferson 1974. A simplest systematics for the organization of turn-taking for conversation. *Language* 50: 696–735.

Schiffrin, Deborah 1994. *Approaches to Discourse*. Oxford: Blackwell.

Wodak, Ruth and Michael Meyer (eds) 2002. *Methods of Critical Discourse Analysis*. London: Sage.

# 2.13 **corpus linguistics**

## chapter contents

> Introduction                              150
> Development of corpus linguistics         150
> Creating a language corpus                151
> Using a language corpus                   153
> Corpus-based dictionaries                 153
> Key points                                154
> Resources and further reading             155
> References                                155

## Introduction

Corpus linguistics is a term that refers broadly to the use of large quantities of 'raw' text to analyse language. Samples of language, written or spoken, are collected and coded for predetermined features, so that they can then be usefully analysed, yielding results that are based on evidence of usage, rather than intuition. Language corpora can vary considerably in size, content and purpose. This chapter will present an overview of the many ways in which a corpus can contribute to the development of linguistic applications, whether it is teaching students of a foreign language or teaching a computer to 'speak' a first language.

## Development of corpus linguistics

The first successful attempt to create a machine-readable language corpus resulted in the 'Brown University Standard Corpus of present day American English', which consists of over one million words of American English, drawn from texts published in 1961 (Kučera and Francis 1967). It was compiled by Nelson Francis and Henry Kučera and made available for linguistic research in 1964 in the form of a magnetic tape and a manual of information. At the time, the use of such a corpus to provide an empirical basis for language description was unpopular in the dominant Chomskyan school of linguistics, which held that the analyst's intuition about his or her native language was sufficient evidence of grammatical features. This division between traditional linguistics and corpus-based approaches to language was also a topic for academic discussion and debate across the Atlantic, at the University of Birmingham in the United Kingdom. Here, another foundational corpus was being created under the name of COBUILD – Collins Birmingham University International Language Database – by a team of linguists and lexicographers led by John Sinclair. The argument for using a corpus of linguistic data to analyse language is clearly articulated by Sinclair himself:

> [The] contrast exposed between the impressions of language detail noted by people, and the evidence compiled objectively from texts is huge and systematic. ... The language looks different when you look at a lot of it at once. (Sinclair 1991)

Following the Brown Corpus, a number of similar language corpus projects were begun, such as the Lancaster-Oslo/Bergen (LOB) Corpus (1970–78), which was intended to replicate the work of Francis and Kučera but using British English texts published during 1961. Other corpora focused on the English of Australia (Australian Corpus of English), India (Kolhapur Corpus), New Zealand (Wellington Corpus) and 1990s North American English (the Brown Corpus). One of the largest and most well-known corpora is the British National Corpus, the BNC, which includes approximately 100 million words of spoken and written texts.

## Creating a language corpus

The description of a linguistic corpus as 'a collection of texts' makes the process of creating such a database sound fairly straightforward. However, the design of a corpus involves a complex and highly theoretical methodology, to ensure that the resulting tool can provide users with accurate data in the most appropriate format. Meyer 2002 suggests that there are many aspects of the process to consider, such as the following.

### Overall length

In theory, the overall length of the corpus should be decided according to the users' requirements: creating dictionaries, for example, requires much larger corpora than analysing the grammar of different regional varieties of English. However, the overall length of the corpus is likely to be limited to some extent by the resources available, as the labour involved in entering texts into a database remains a considerable hurdle despite advances in information technology and automatic text processing.

### The range of genres

The texts collected will need to represent a broad range of genres if the data are to be used for a wide variety of purposes (e.g. language learning, grammatical analysis, and regional variation). However, texts from a narrow range of genres may be sufficient if the corpus is to have a more specific purpose. The Michigan Corpus of Academic Spoken English (MICASE) can be used to explore the features of speech used in an academic environment, which makes it a more useful tool for teaching English for Academic Purposes than a general purpose corpus like the BNC.

### Length of samples

Like the overall length of the corpus, the length of each text sample will be determined to a large extent by the proposed use for the corpus. Most corpora contain text fragments rather than entire texts; it is simply not practical to include entire books, for example, because of restrictions of space, copyright, and resources (the COBUILD corpus is an exception to this, including entire books in its database). On the other hand, many text fragments can be considered sufficiently complete such that similar sized units of text can be compared with each other. In a set of written texts, such units might be journal article abstracts, recipes for Christmas pudding, or opening paragraphs of novels. Spoken units of text that might be interesting to study are telephone greetings, retail shopping transactions, or judges' instructions to juries in court cases. Of course, if the corpus is to be used to study variations in the pronunciation of vowels in different parts of England, then very short text samples will probably suffice.

### Sampling methods for texts and speakers or writers

Clearly it is desirable for the corpus to be properly representative of the range of data it seeks to cover. If we created a corpus of British newspaper editorials that included samples from only three papers, or included only editorials published on 12 September 2001, it would be unrepresentative of British newspaper editorials in general. Sampling methods developed by social scientists can help to get the balance right by calculating the number of samples needed from a given dataset if the corpus is to be representative of that 'data population'. There are also linguistic issues to be taken into account, such as the level of internal variation of a genre to be represented. Some genres, such as academic writing, contain many subcategories and varieties, while others, such as scripted speeches, are quite homogeneous and unvarying (see Biber, Conrad and Reppen 1998). A representative corpus of academic writing would need to include a much larger number of samples than a corpus of scripted speeches in order to capture a set of data that cover all the varieties of that genre.

### Sociolinguistic variables

A number of variables may be relevant to future users of a linguistic corpus, and this must be acknowledged when sampling the texts. It is quite likely, for example, that researchers will need to know basic demographic features of the speakers or writers, such as age, sex, education, employment, place of birth, regional and social dialect, and social networks. When collecting text samples, it will be necessary to take these factors into account and ensure that each is adequately and evenly represented.

### Timing the data collection

Some corpora will be designed to include a set of samples that range across a given time period. These corpora will allow the study of language use across time (diachronic study). Other corpora consist of texts collected at a specific time, and they can be used for studies of language as it is being used at that time (synchronic studies). Because language is constantly changing, this is an important consideration in selecting the criteria for sampling texts to build a corpus.

As the samples are collected, they must be prepared for collation using a system of tagging and coding. If the data are to be searchable, they must be appropriately identified within the system according to the features relevant to the searcher. Imagine that a user intends to search a database for instances of the use of swearwords by female speakers over the age of 60. Each sample would need to be identified according to whether or not it contains a swearword (which could be done in a variety of ways), whether it is a (transcribed) spoken text or a written text, and in terms of the age and gender of the speaker. While it is beyond the scope of this chapter to give detailed technical information on linguistic tagging, there are many publications and websites dedicated to the subject; some of these are listed below as a springboard for further reading and research.

## Using a language corpus

From a twenty-first century perspective, the notion that the specialist's own intuition might be a better tool for the study of language than a massive database of 'raw' text may seem a narrow view, given that the corpus can be coded and queried in almost any way imaginable. However, it must be recalled that when projects such as the Brown Corpus of American English and the COBUILD corpus were begun, there was not the computing power or expertise available that today we take for granted. It was rare to find linguists with the necessary technological background needed to build theories of computational linguistics (see Moon 2007: 162). Thus the application of these databases to any theoretical problem seemed very limited. More obvious, though not uncontroversial, was their usefulness in the complex task of writing dictionaries and providing exemplification of words, particularly for those learning a language.

The history and development of corpus-based dictionaries make an interesting case study of the use of a language corpus, but this is merely representative of the enormous variety of work in corpus linguistics. Linguistic corpora can be used:

> to document the grammatical features of endangered languages and establish linguistic family trees
> to undertake comparative studies of literature or discourse, so as to track collocations such as the occurrence of *stormy* together with *relationship, weather, and* or *sea.*
> Corpora are used in forensic linguistics to establish the likelihood of authorship or to assist in speaker identification.
> Computers can be trained to recognize features of grammar using a corpus.
> Study materials for students learning to distinguish between genres of English can be based on the statistical analysis of genre features within a corpus.

In fact, the uses of linguistic corpora for studying language are as widely varying as linguistics itself and in many cases extend the application of linguistic theory to domains previously considered beyond the scope of linguistics.

Industries such as marketing and professional communications training are more receptive to linguistic innovations that are based on statistically valid data drawn from a large and representative dataset. In childhood development studies, a large corpus of child language such as the CHILDES database can be used to establish benchmarks and norms that are useful to general practitioners and allied health professionals who do not have speech pathology training. Critical studies of political movements and social attitudes can be greatly enhanced by analyses of texts that highlight the use of language in particular circumstances, such as the collocation of *Islam* and *terrorism* in newspaper editorials pre- and post-11 September 2001.

## Corpus-based dictionaries

The publication of the *Collins COBUILD English Language Dictionary* (*CCELD*) in 1987 represents a milestone in the history of corpus linguistics because it sought to change both the way that dictionaries are compiled and the approach to language description in general (see Moon 2007 for a history of the *CCELD* project and the theoretical debates it provoked). As a result of the corpus-based approach used in its production, the *CCELD* differed from existing English language dictionaries in a number of aspects. As in the *Oxford English Dictionary* 1989, definitions were written based on real language texts, rather than concocted examples, but priority was given to those senses that occurred more frequently in the database, even though they might be more abstract or less significant historically. This was in contrast with traditional dictionaries, which had tended to order the various senses for a word according to their role in the historical or semantic development of the headword. In short, the guiding principle of the *CCELD* was that it should be based on actual language usage.

The reliance on actual texts has further challenged lexicographic theory in areas such as substitutability – is it possible to accurately substitute one word for another when providing a definition? Consider the following ways of defining *serve* (adapted from Moon 2007):

(1)  *serve* 'give something that is required (esp. to a customer in a shop)' (from the *Collins English Learner's Dictionary* 1974)

(2)  'If someone **serves** customers in a shop, bar, etc, they help them and provide them with what they want to have or buy.' (*CCELD*)

The difference between these examples demonstrates the impact of the corpus-based approach on the principles of substitutability in definitions. Whereas the first example seeks to provide a phrase that might be exactly substituted for the headword in a sentence without disrupting the syntax of that sentence, the second example does not assume that such precise duplication of meaning is possible. In the second example, the meaning is explained through usage, rather than substitution.

It should be noted that the use of language corpora to create a dictionary is not without its limitations. Although such databases are now commonly used by lexicographers compiling dictionaries, it makes the task hugely time-consuming; hundreds or even thousands of examples of a single word must be processed and analysed in order to decide on the form of the definition and differentiate between idiomatic and formulaic constructions. Nonetheless, corpus-based dictionaries in general and Sinclair's work in particular have drawn attention to the centrality of usage and typicality to definitions, especially for language learners, and marked a shift away from an emphasis on artificial examples which Sinclair 1984 claims may in fact be atypical.

## Key points

> Corpus linguistics is a term that refers broadly to the use of large quantities of 'raw' text to analyse language.

> By relying on real texts as a data source, corpus linguistics differs significantly from traditional methods of language analysis and description, which relied on the analyst's own perceptions and intuitions about language.

> Language corpora can vary considerably in size, content, and purpose.

> When researchers create a language corpus they must consider carefully how it will be used, as this will dictate its parameters, such as the overall size, the range of texts used for samples, and the type of genres represented by the samples.

> One of the largest and most celebrated corpora is the British National Corpus (the BNC) which includes approximately 100 million words of spoken and written texts.

## Resources and further reading

Three international peer-reviewed journals dedicated to corpus linguistics are the *International Journal of Corpus Linguistics*, *Corpora*, and *Corpus Linguistics and Linguistic Theory*.

Both Biber, Conrad and Reppen 1998 and Meyer 2002 provide accessible introductions to corpus linguistics.

For a gateway to web-based resources on corpus linguistics, see http://www.corpus-linguistics.com/

## References

Biber, Douglas, Susan Conrad and Randi Reppen 1998. *Corpus Linguistics: Investigating Language Structure and Use*. Cambridge: Cambridge University Press.

Kučera, Henry and W. Nelson Francis 1967. *Computational Analysis of Present-day American English*. Providence: Brown University Press.

Meyer, Charles F. 2002. *English Corpus Linguistics: An Introduction*. Cambridge: Cambridge University Press.

Moon, Rosamund 2007. Sinclair, lexicography, and the Cobuild Project: the application of theory. *International Journal of Corpus Linguistics* 12: 159–81.

*Oxford English Dictionary*. 1989. 2nd edn. Oxford Clarendon Press [Abbreviated to *OED*]. Also available on Compact Disc.

Sinclair, John 1984. Naturalness in language. In *Corpus Linguistics: Recent Developments in the Use of Computer Corpora in English Language research* ed. by Jan Aarts and Willem Meijs. 2 vols. Amsterdam: Rodopi, pp. 1: 203–10.

Sinclair, John 1991. *Corpus, Concordance, Collocation*. Oxford: Oxford University Press.

# 2.14 **digital tools in linguistics**

## chapter contents

> Overview                                                    156
> Counting, concordance, collocation, spell-checking          156
> Analysis by computer                                        158
> Machine translation                                         159
> Speech recognition                                          160
> Speech synthesis and text generation                        160
> Expert systems                                              161
> Computer languages                                          161
> Key points                                                  162
> References                                                  162

## Overview

Modern computer programming was conceived in the late 1930s and the digital revolution was boosted by the rapid development of electronic circuitry during World War II. After 1950, second generation computers with transistors and printed circuits appeared; then in the late 1970s microcomputers, and in particular the Apple II (1977), brought computing to the general public (the IBM PC appeared in 1981).

The first digital audio recordings appeared in the 1970s, digital CDs in 1982, DVDs from 1996.

Advantages to linguistics of the digital revolution include:

> Universally available high quality recording and playback of speech; also video capture of language interaction.
> Rare language materials can be made widely available for study.
> Storage facilities for archiving recorded media are cheap and plentiful.
> Large corpora of language data in digital form are readily accessible for research.
> **Data mining** has become much easier. (Data mining is the gathering of relevant information from the large amount of data in a source.)

However, standards need to be established and maintained to make archives universally accessible. At the same time archives need to be constantly updated to ensure that they do not become impossible to access because their encoding format is no longer supported by the latest computer programs and playback devices.

## Counting, concordance, collocation, spell-checking

Computers are of practical help in very rapidly recognizing strings of symbols for the purposes of **counting** the instances of a word or phrase in a document (see Manning and Schütze 1999). This also enables the construction of **concordances**, identifying where and how often in a set of texts (e.g. the Bible, Shakespeare) an item occurs. The environment in which the term occurs, i.e. its **collocation**, can also be readily identified. For instance, the Corpus Concordance Sampler at http://www.collins.co.uk/Corpus/CorpusSearch.aspx in January 2010 generated the list in Figure 2.17 for 40 occurrences of the noun *taboo* in the 56 million word Collins Wordbanks *Online* English corpus.

```
thay maybe people shouldn't wirte songs about.  Taboo subjects." Because they're taboo? [p] Because
      on my cutting room floor, to DJ for the club  Taboo, which he was setting up with Jeffrey Hinton.
        to invest in magazines like Heavy Metal and  Taboo-both forums for underground and foreign
    but sex between children and adults is still  taboo Maybe it's even more difficult. when I was
     married couples, the topic is something of a  taboo amongst friends and family before it happens,
 informers. Sex outside marriage has always been  taboo in northern Sudan. Now that Islamic law is
       in the melting pot? [p] Doing It With You Is  Taboo meets women, men, gays and lesbians who have
         series on Channel 4, To Do It With You Is  Taboo. Produced by Stella Orakwue's SOI Film and TV
        of `glasnost open discussion of previously  taboo subjects. And with it came POLITICAL reform -
 of Japanese militarism, usually regarded as a  taboo subject at these gatherings, were raised. The
     permissive, and who goes from permissivity to  taboo. The book reflects the fact that nowadays a
      daughter would speak out publicly on such a  taboo subject as a sexually transmitted disease?
    the `heavenly Kingdom" was therefore to avoid a  taboo. [p] Hsien Feng Eighth Year Almanac (1858).
   father. Sadly many fathers do not respect this  taboo, despite its deep roots stretching back to
  in the international drugs trade - the ultimate  taboo subject for Western governments, even more
 of fewer and fewer taboos, the word still had a  taboo quality to it. It sounded defeatist and
     recently been hunter gatherers, believing it  taboo to grow crops, but sadly deforestation has
 is an example of the National Lottery going one  taboo too far.  [p] There have long been
 broader political debate in Japan on previously  taboo subjects such as sovereignty, national
     was another step towards addressing the last  taboo". But Touvier was small fry in the
      2.99 4.99 12.99 9.99 5.25 4.99 8.99 12.99 [p]  Taboo Boardgame 19.99 19.97 19.99 19.99 26.95 19.97
 last 20 years and the topic has become almost a  taboo subject within the game.  [p] But Walker blew
      attitudes are shifting.  [p] Sex used to be a  taboo subject but younger women said they had a
    races or religion.  [p] We aim to break the  taboo that surrounds it and bring it out into the
 junk food. There are no foods that are totally  taboo. Therefore, when you indulge in a fudge
    always to be avoided, but now it was strictly  taboo. The Koyemshi had appeared in the village two
         word `absolution." He said, `If a Zun~i  taboo is broken, is there any way to get
 was worrying about whether that had broken the  taboo. There." The priest pointed at the small
    And that Ernesto was afraid he had broken a  taboo by telling George more than you're supposed
 pursuing the man made desirable because he is  taboo. [p] Or perhaps Father Tso [f] was [f]
     Leaphorn frowned again. Killing a frog was a  taboo, but a minor one. A personal chant would cure
     just 5 or 6 years ago, when the topic seemed  taboo. Fundraisers for AIDS research, hosted by
        of this suppression of evidence. [p] The  taboo against discussing race and IQ has not left
 others (but not John Bowlby) complied with this  taboo. As a result, they could not bring to
  Paradoxically, often this process of defining  taboo topics helps dispel myths about acceptable
 business. [p] Marcia Haydee (Ballet Dancer This  taboo that dancers at 30--it's already finished--
  Even discussion of political reforms has been  taboo ever since the crushing of the democracy
 know the parents are [ZF1] th th [ZF0] they're  taboo they've done wrong take these children away
  have come from a political family so that was  taboo.  [ZGY] Er and then another chap he was a bit
     what we've got to do is somehow remove the  taboo because many of the public out there believe
```

*Figure 2.17 Collocations of the noun taboo*

Electronic **spell-checking** matches strings typed against strings in a dictionary (i.e. a lexical database). A well-known problem is the failure to identify inappropriate collocations such as we see in Jerry Zar's 1992 *An Owed to the Spelling Checker* of which the first two stanzas are:

I have a spelling checker
It came with my PC
It plane lee marks four my revue
Miss steaks aye can knot sea.

Eye ran this poem threw it,
Your sure reel glad two no.
Its vary polished in it's weigh
My checker tolled me sew.

(For the rest, see http://www.bios.niu.edu/zar/poem.pdf)

# Analysis by computer

Machine reading of natural language has, since the 1960s, led to the need for computer programs that can parse input text, assigning syntactic analyses (parses) en route to interpreting meaning. The dominant analytical procedure is the 'transition network', a term that reflects the move from the start node (the first item the parser encounters) to the next node. Text is linear, but syntactic and semantic structure is hierarchical; and so:

> There are subroutines that will, for instance, resolve the syntactic function of 'moved' material such as the undergoer 'Who' in *Who did Mary see?* (compare *Mary saw who?*) and the syntax and semantics of a subject noun phrase like *the man who lives next door's son* before proceeeding to resolve its predication *has been sniffing glue* – whose parsing will itself involve subroutines.

> A loop is needed to deal with recursion in, for example, *Mary thinks that Neil thinks that Kate is unhappy* (in which the sentence, $S_1$, *Kate is unhappy* is embedded in the sentence, $S_2$, *Neil thinks that $S_1$* which in turn is embedded in $S_3$, *Mary thinks that $S_2$*).

> Probabilistic criteria are needed to cope with lexical and syntactic ambiguities as in *That bass is wonderful* (fish? singer? string instrument?) and *Pablo Picasso drew the man with the pencil* (who held the pencil?).

The interpretation of meaning required the development of formal semantic parsing. Far more difficult is creating a database that serves to augment the underspecification of normal natural language usage. This branch of artificial intelligence eventually morphed into cognitive science. Among the most convincing of the early attempts was *Scripts, Plans, Goals and Understanding: An Inquiry into Human Knowledge Structures* (Schank and Abelson 1977). The seminal idea is that much of our understanding is based on dynamic knowledge structures named **scripts** which describe expected sequences of events and their participants in stylized everyday situations; we earlier referred to the 'restaurant script' (in Chapter 2.6). In later work Schank 1986 gathered scripts with common features into what he called 'memory organizational packets'. Research on parallel and distributed processing (PDP) in neural networks was described in Rumelhart, McClelland and the PDP Research Group 1986 and McClelland and Rumelhart 1988. In the PDP computational model, units representing neurons connect with other units via a link having a certain weight or strength such that networks of units supposedly correspond to concepts in the mind or brain. Varying activation levels can lead to learning: one system of networks in the computer model was taught English past tense forms with reasonable success (Rumelhart and McClelland 1986).

Text mark-up in the British Component of the International Corpus of English (ICE-GB) is exemplified in Figure 2.18 (the search term was *taboo*). Field linguists can classify their own data in a broadly similar way using such freeware as the Summer Institute of Linguistics' Toolbox (formerly Shoebox); for details see http://www.linguistics.unimelb.edu.au/thieberger/RNLD/IntroductionShoebox.pdf and for a sample of data entry see Figure 2.19 from Peter Austin's 'Developing interactive knowledge bases for Australian Aboriginal Languages' at http://emeld.org/workshop/2003/Malyangapa.pdf (the item in focus is *pula* "two").

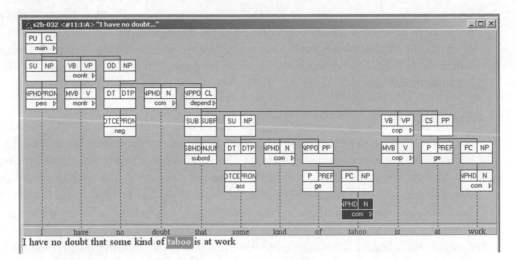

I have no doubt that some kind of taboo is at work

*Figure 2.18  Text mark-up from ICE-GB*

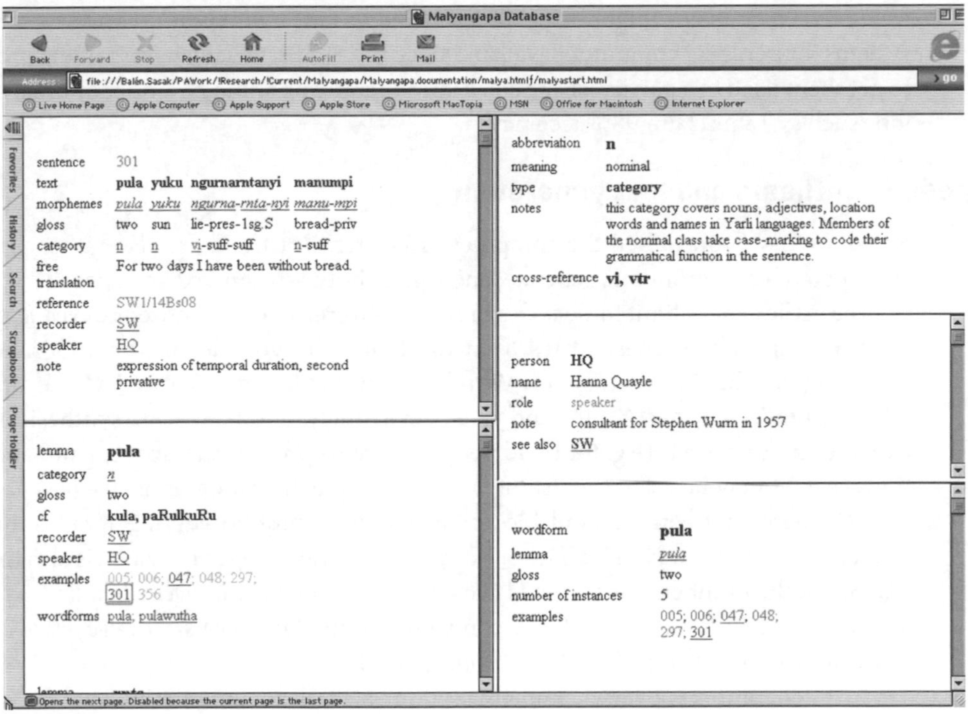

*Figure 2.19  Data entry using Shoebox (Toolbox)*

## Machine translation

Machine translation substitutes words in one natural language for words in another. To access the lexicon, the machine translator needs to be able to handle morphosyntax and to recognize phrases, idioms, proper names and figurative expressions in the source language. Working from established corpora helps by bringing statistical likelihood into play. The Google translator does that; however it turned French *Les liens de cette liste donnent accès à des pages secondaires de ce site* into the very literal "The bonds of this list give access to secondary pages of this site"; a freer translation would be *Listed on this page are links to other sites*. Machine translation is greatly helped by human intervention; at best, machine translation helps the human translator who can refine its output. Of course where there is no human available, as with web pages translated by Google, it is much better than nothing.

## Speech recognition

Speech recognition systems capture an acoustic signal from a microphone or telephone and convert it into either graphic form for a human reader or some other digital form that can be machine-interpreted. Where the system is open to a wide public whose every member pronounces phones differently, the input topic has to be severely restricted to, for instance, uttering numbers in customer service call routing, identifying names for directory assistance or travel booking. Speech recognition systems have problems with recognizing different intonation patterns (e.g. when used to distinguish statement from question). Furthermore, normal speech contains disfluencies and ambiguities that machines find harder to process than scripted speech which is read aloud. For instance *It would recognize speech* might be heard as *It would wreck a nice beach*. However, dictation systems for personal computers, available since the 1990s, usually have training programs to get them used to a particular speaker's idiosyncratic phonology; under optimal conditions such systems claim 98% accuracy.

## Speech synthesis and text generation

So far we have considered the computer as Hearer. But there are also rather primitive attempts to have computers generate language as both written text and speech.

The earliest, very limited, speech synthesizers were created hundreds of years ago; but electronic speech synthesis dates from the Bell Labs Vocoder in the 1930s. A 1939 recording of the Voder (son of Vocoder) can be heard at http://www.cs.indiana.edu/rhythmsp/ASA/partA.html and it is surprisingly good. Speech synthesizers that convert text to speech (e.g. for blind people) have to process the text, expand abbreviations (e.g. *St* may be /strit/ or /seɪnt/), and distinguish homographs like *bow* /boʊ/ vs /baʊ/ (there is freeware available at http://www.naturalreaders.com/). A number sequence like 1215 might be a date or house number *twelve fifteen* – which is also the time 12.15; but the numbers *one thousand two hundred and fifteen* and *twelve hundred and fifteen* are other possibilities. One software company had the US voice say *twelve fifteen* and the UK voice say *one thousand two hundred and fifteen*!

Text generation is overwhelmingly used for factual documentation such as weather reports from raw meteorological data and assembly instructions for knock-down (flat-pack) furniture and the like (though the latter are mostly graphic). Another form of text generation is the creation of abstracts and summaries. Early examples are found in Rumelhart 1977 and Schank 1984. We saw in Chapter 2.13 'Discourse and conversation' that the two core constituents of a story are 'There is a problem' and 'A resolution is found'; it is only to be expected, then, that a summary is based on stating the problem and its resolution. Practical applications of such devices are:

> summarizing news stories and business reports
> summarizing several journal abstracts from papers on a common topic

> summaries made by search engines of mined data
> summaries downloaded from the web to mobile phones.

## Expert systems

Expert systems (Durkin 1994) provide a knowledge base, often accessed through question and answer, that offers a diagnosis of a health or other problem in engineering, the military, and so on. All expert systems are specific to a particular task. The value lies in the fact that the expert system is a more reliable database than a human being will be for any single occasion. It enables the human user to assess a situation on the basis of all knowledge available and will typically offer tested solutions to problems. Expert systems are constructed by a 'knowledge engineer' who obtains both theoretical and practical field expertise from human experts, coding it into accessible categories that can be implemented in a program that is both effective and seemingly intelligent in its behaviour. The expertise of the system is tested by giving it problems to solve, having the domain expert criticize its output, then modifying the program as required. A limitation of expert systems is that they cannot learn: all modifications must be handcrafted.

## Computer languages

Natural language is very forgiving: you can perfectly well make sense of (1), but no computer can.

(1) Aoccdrnig 2 a rsecherear at an Elingsh uinervtisy, it desn't mttaer in waht oredr the ltteers in a wrod r, the olny iprmoetnt tihng is that frist and lsat ltteer is at the rghit pclae. The rset can be a toatl mses and you can sitll raed it wouthit porbelm. Tihs is bcuseae we do not raed ervey lteter by itslef but the wrod as a wlohe.

Computer languages must have the symbols arranged in the expected sequence and no other. In fact, of course, it is wrong to say that computers 'understand' anything; they don't. But they do respond to input. Normally all instructions must be laid out explicitly; the more so in tight languages like Java than in sloppy language like JavaScript or HTML where at least some closing tags can be omitted without generating error. Here is part of a form written in PHP.

```
<?
if ( $name=="" && $ID=="" && $ex=="" && $answer="" ) {
print "<p> </p>
<center><h1>Please return to the form and complete ALL fields</h1>";
}
else {
// $filename="wk01ans.htm";
// $fp = fopen( $filename, "a" );
"<p><hr><table cellpadding=3><tr><td width=25%><p>". date ("G:i, D, j/n/Y" ) .".</td>
<td width=25%><p>".stripslashes( $name )."</td>
<td width=25%><p>$ID</td>
<td width=25%><p>Exercise number: $ex</td>
<tr><td colspan=4><p><i>Answer:</i> ".stripslashes( $answer )."</td></tr></table>";
}
?>
```

Note the pairs of opening and closing tags <? ?>, ( ), { }, <td> </td> and so on, and the fact that the HTML tag <p> can optionally not have a closing </p>. The $ coding marks a field name; the date format will spell out as, for example, 4:44, Thu, 22/7/2004. The .stripslashes command gets rid of slashes and apostrophes from the input text that the program might misinterpret as commands. The lines beginning // are ignored by the program – they could as well have been deleted; this // device is used for the programmer to comment on the source code.

It is easy to see that the language used in computer programming is very different from ordinary language. But it is edging closer.

## Key points

> The impact of the digital revolution on data collection and management in linguistics has been profound.

> Linguists have become familiar with digital recording technology, digital editing techniques, software for transcription, annotation and analysis, and the problems of interoperability and encoding which must be considered in preparing digital material for archiving. In addition, many linguists take advantage of the capabilities of database technology to organize and analyse their data.

> Linguists also need to be adept at data mining from language corpora and other archived material.

> Linguistics, computational science, artificial intelligence, and cognitive science have come together in the development of computational means of linguistic analysis, machine translation, text generation, and speech synthesis.

> Any student contemplating studying Natural Language Processing (NLP) or Computational Linguistics would greatly benefit from taking mathematics up to the final year in secondary school and, at university, studying calculus, probability, and statistics – as well as computing and linguistics.

> Additional information may be found at http://www.wikipedia.org/; in Brown 2006; the very comprehensive Jurafsky and Martin 2000; and the other references cited in this chapter.

## References

Brown, E. Keith (General editor) 2006. *Encyclopedia of Languages and Linguistics*. 2nd edn. 14 vols. Oxford: Elsevier.

Durkin, John 1994. *Expert Systems: Design and Development*. New York: Macmillan – now Palgrave Macmillan.

Jurafsky, Daniel and James H. Martin 2000. *Speech and Language Processing: An Introduction to Natural Language Processing, Computational Linguistics, and Speech Recognition*. Upper Saddle River NJ: Prentice-Hall Inc. [A second edn is appearing piecemeal at http://www.cs.colorado.edu/ffmartin/SLP/Updates/index.html].

Manning, Christopher D. and Hinrich Schütze 1999. *Foundations of Statistical Natural Language Processing*. Cambridge MA: MIT Press.

McClelland, James L. and David E. Rumelhart 1988. *Explorations in Parallel Distributed Processing: A Handbook of Models, Programs, and Exercises*. Cambridge MA: MIT Press.

Rumelhart, David E. 1977. Understanding and summarizing brief stories. In *Basic Processes in Reading: Perception and Comprehension*, ed. by David LaBerge and S. Jay Samuels. Hillsdale NJ: Lawrence Erlbaum, pp. 265–303.

Rumelhart, David E. and James L. McClelland 1986. On learning the past tense of English verbs. In *Parallel Distributed Processing: Explorations in the Microstructure of Cognition. Vol 2: Psychological and Biological Models*, ed. by David E. Rumelhart, James L. McClelland and the PDP Research Group. Cambridge MA: MIT Press, pp. 216–71.

Rumelhart, David E., James L. McClelland and the PDP Research Group (eds) 1986. *Parallel Distributed Processing: Explorations in the Microstructure of Cognition*. 2 vols. Cambridge MA: MIT Press.

Schank, Roger 1984. *The Cognitive Computer*. Reading MA: Addison-Wesley.

Schank, Roger 1986. *Explanation Patterns*. Hillsdale NJ: Lawrence Erlbaum.

Schank, Roger and Robert C. Abelson 1977. *Scripts, Plans, Goals and Understanding: An Inquiry into Human Knowledge Structures*. Hillsdale NJ: Lawrence Erlbaum.

# 2.15 forensic linguistics

## chapter contents

> Introduction     164
> An early example of forensic linguistic analysis     165
> Identification     165
> Spoken data     165
> Written data     166
> Discourse analysis     167
> Language of origin     168
> Commercial applications     168
> Lie detection     168
> Summary of key issues     168
> Key points     169
> References     169

## Introduction

When most people hear the term *forensics* they immediately think of boffins in white coats performing almost magical scientific tests to provide that crucial piece of rock-solid evidence that solves a complex crime. On the rare occasion that a language expert is featured in one of the many television crime dramas, the expert is invariably able to rely on some kind of supercomputer to identify suspects by their 'voiceprint', irrespective of the quality or quantity of data available. Sadly, such an image is strictly limited to the realm of science fiction at this stage, as no one has yet been able to isolate a uniquely distinguishing feature of the human voice upon which to base such a 'voiceprint'. Nonetheless, the student of linguistics, excited by the possibilities of such a real-world application of their skills in analysing language, should not be put off by this gap between myth and reality: the truth is that forensic linguistics is a more varied and fascinating field than could ever be imagined by a lay audience. Forensic linguistics, and the study of language and the law more broadly, requires the analyst to enlist a wide variety of analytic tools and skills, drawing on almost every aspect of core linguistic study, from phonetics to pragmatics, from syntax to sociolinguistics. Forensic linguistic inquiries may form part of criminal investigations by police, or they may be initiated by the defence team on behalf of a client. They may involve trademark disputes or even non-legal concerns, such as selecting the most appropriate brand name for a product to be launched in a specific market.

The International Association of Forensic Linguists and the International Association for Forensic Phonetics and Acoustics were formed in the early 1990s by specialists working in these areas and, while each organization represents a different emphasis in the field, they are both represented by the scholarly publication, the *International Journal of Speech, Language and the Law*.

> The aim and purpose of the International Association of Forensic Linguists, from the website www.iafl.org: 'is to improve the administration of the legal systems throughout the world by means of a better understanding of the interaction between language and the law.'

## An early example of forensic linguistic analysis

The following case study will give some indication of the breadth of scholarship needed by the forensic linguist in providing expert evidence.

> In 1950, Timothy John Evans was hanged for the murders of his wife and child at 10 Rillington Place, London. Evans had maintained his innocence, and accused John Reginald Halliday Christie of committing the crimes, despite the fact that the police were able to produce an allegedly verbatim record of Evans confessing to the murders in his police interview. In a dramatic turn of events, Swedish linguist Jan Svartvik showed, in 1968, that the confession used to convict Evans was most likely the product of police influence and differed sharply in style and structure from the remainder of Evans's statements. Svartvik 1968 was able to show, using linguistic analysis of the discourse structures, that the key sections of the statement, where Evans apparently confesses to the murders, are written using a formal register, typical of police texts, but most atypical of the speech of Evans and inconsistent with the remainder of the interview transcript. Evans was posthumously pardoned and, when several more bodies were discovered at 10 Rillington Place, Christie was hanged.

Svartvik's analysis of the Evans case, often cited as the original forensic linguistic investigation, involved the analysis of syntactic structure, style, register, spoken language versus written language, and knowledge of the specific police register (i.e. jargon) used in statement-taking. It is interesting that this landmark case did not involve the analysis of vocal qualities, which has now become the archetypal forensic linguistic application.

Here are some types of forensic analysis.

## Identification

The types of analysis that are most commonly associated with the practice of forensic linguistics are those that seek to identify the source of a message. This includes the analysis of spoken and written data, and can involve some level of computer or statistical analysis. The data being used in the analysis will almost always include at least one sample of **known data**, where the source has been reliably identified, and one sample of **questioned data**, where the source is unknown. There may be some rare cases where two data samples are compared to establish whether or not they originate from the same source, without either being identified as belonging to a specific speaker. A **scoresheet** may be devised, where each segment from the questioned data is rated against the known data for similarity.

## Spoken data

There is some debate as to whether identifying the source of spoken data should be labelled 'voice identification' or 'speaker identification', but either way, the process for this kind of analysis involves comparing samples of recorded voice data in order to establish the likelihood that they represent samples of the same voice, versus the likelihood that they represent samples of different voices.

Individual sounds as well as longer stretches of talk are usually isolated for comparison across the samples. Nowadays, this is done using some form of digital sound editing software that allows the analyst to isolate very small amounts of speech data, such as one vowel sound, into separate files or segments. In this way, the analyst can collect many tokens of specific sounds or utterances which represent different aspects of the voice(s). For example, the analyst may choose to isolate all the instances of close front unrounded vowels (the vowel in *seen*), and compare them across the samples using either an automated or machine-assisted process or by listening with an expert ear. This process would then be repeated for a range of individual phonemes, as well as for longer stretches of talk.

The approach that is commonly known as forensic phonetics involves the automated or semi-automated processing of vocal data segments according to measurable features, such as formant values (see the box below, and Chapter 2.1), pitch range or the rate of speech. This computer-based analysis may be supported by the expert phonetician's perception of the vocal features in each sample.

During speech production, the air in the vocal tract vibrates at many different frequencies at once and, in the production of vowel sounds, the most dominant frequencies combine and appear as bands on a spectrograph image of the air vibrations. Each of these bands is known as a formant and the different vowels are typically characterized by the different combinations of the first three formants (i.e. the three bands appearing at the lowest frequencies).

When the analysis relies solely on the expert's ear to determine the phonetic qualities of the samples, the term used by some forensic linguists is 'aural-perceptual analysis' (Hollien 2002). The analyst considers the data in terms of various vocal parameters, such as perceived pitch, articulation, and prosody, which can be heard and compared across samples.

The aural-perceptual analysis in particular may also rely on the analyst's knowledge of dialectology and sociolinguistics to compare the data samples. In this kind of analysis it is the presence of certain dialectal features that enables the analyst to distinguish the two speakers.

For the analysis of spoken data in legal cases, the known data samples are very often drawn from a recording of the police interview with the suspect. The unknown data samples are usually some form of covert recording obtained by tapping the suspect's phone, or from a concealed recording device, but in one case well known to the authors, the questioned audio data samples were extracted from video surveillance tapes (CCTV) made during armed robberies allegedly committed by the suspect. While the video footage was of such poor quality that the person committing the crimes could not be identified visually, the audio tracks were of high quality and provided critical evidence in the case.

## Written data

The principles of the forensic examination of written data are essentially the same as for spoken data – that is, samples of known and questioned data are compared according to a set of linguistic parameters. In the case of written texts, the sorts of features that can be systematically analysed include punctuation, sentence structure, verb types, terms of address, spelling and grammatical errors, any idiosyncrasies of the writer, and broader patterns of discourse, such as the development of specific themes.

One of the problems facing prosecutors in legal cases that involve written data is how to obtain known data samples from the suspect. Very often, the questioned material, such as a threatening letter or ransom note, is readily available as it forms the basis for the complaint against the suspect. The known text, where available, often has to be drawn from personal communications signed or otherwise identified as written by the suspect. Email is becoming a major source of this kind of data, but it is important that the impact of the medium of communication is taken into account when comparing email with, say, a handwritten letter. Recently, cases have been undertaken by forensic linguists that involved mobile phone text messages, and the distinctively individual nature of text messages is considered an advantage in author identification.

Handwriting and typeface comparison are not considered part of forensic linguistic practice, but are often carried out by the relevant experts in conjunction with the forensic linguistic analysis.

## Discourse analysis

The area of forensic discourse analysis is concerned with the appropriateness of interviewing techniques, the interpretation of legal texts, suspect profiling and other applications of discourse analysis to a legal case or to law enforcement more broadly. A case study involving the interpretation of a legal text is described below. The expert testimony reads:

> The semantic interpretation of the adjectival phrase *standing to the credit of* rests in the aspect of the verb form *standing*. It is possible to expand the elliptical form of the phrase from *the moneys standing to the credit of* to the full, implied form *the moneys [that are] standing to the credit of*. The structure of *standing* is thus TO BE + stand + ING. This form is the present progressive and is described by Kreidler 1998 as a temporary or bounded form. Kreidler further notes that: 'the present progressive is used for what is temporarily true'. Thus, the activity *standing to the credit of* is confined to a bounded period of time – it does not extend indefinitely as might be the case with the simple present *stands to the credit of*, which would express a durative activity, something that may continue to be true.

> Conclusion. According to the semantic analysis of the questioned text, the phrase *the moneys standing to the credit of* is highly likely to be interpreted by the addressee to mean that the moneys are those standing to the credit of the relevant accounts at the time that the words were written – that is, the date of the Order or, at the latest, the date of the Order being read by the addressee.

In this case, an Order was made by a judge prohibiting the defendant from accessing money held in various bank accounts. The forensic linguistic analysis focused on a phrase used in the Order where it described the relevant funds as 'moneys standing to the credit of [bank accounts held by the defendant and his associates]' and considered whether or not the paragraph would be reasonably interpreted to mean that the word 'moneys' referred only to funds in the relevant accounts at the time that the Order was made, and not to any future funds credited to the accounts.

## Language of origin

Linguists may be called on to identify a speaker's national or regional origin. This is done by analysing elements of their language such as accent, vocabulary and grammatical features. Clearly, this type of analysis has applications in establishing refugee status, where it is commonly used, but as it requires the analyst to have a thorough knowledge of both language acquisition theory and the very specific regional dialect spoken by the subject, its legitimacy is strongly contested by organizations such as the International Association of Forensic Linguists.

## Commercial applications

There are numerous commercial applications of forensic linguistics, but the most common applications are in disputes over trademarks and copyright. Very often a company will require expert testimony as to the extent to which a rival company may have infringed copyright or trademark legislation in naming or promoting a new product.

## Lie detection

Various forms of linguistic analysis are employed by those attempting to establish the veracity of written, and sometimes spoken, statements. Often the analysis includes consideration of personal pronouns, tense, vocabulary items, and sentence structure, but does not usually take account of sociocultural and regional variation in language use. This type of analysis is only loosely classed as forensic linguistics, as its validity is often the focus of disagreement among professionals and academics working in the area.

## Summary of key issues

A major concern for members of the international forensic linguistics community is the reliability of the evidence obtained through forensic linguistic analysis. There continues to be much controversy surrounding almost every aspect of forensic linguistics described in this chapter, primarily due to questions of methodology and expertise. In many instances, the debate focuses on whether the analytic technique is statistically valid, though in some cases, such as lie detection and language of origin analysis, the main concern is that the methods are not based on sound sociolinguistic and/or language acquisition theory in the first place, but are used uncritically by government departments and law enforcement agencies. In such cases, many linguists have considered it their professional duty to inform and educate such agencies about the pitfalls of using unreliable analytic techniques. The controversy over the statistical reliability of analytic methods, especially in the area of voice or authorship identification, is generating intense debate within the forensic linguistic community. There is a clear division between those who reject all analysis that cannot be statistically validated, and those who argue that there is a place for qualitative analysis, such as dialectology and sociolinguistic analysis, in expert testimony.

In cases relating to the analysis of discourse structure, and especially where the dispute centres on the interpretation of a legal text (see the case study above) it is common for the linguistic evidence to be disregarded on the basis that such interpretation is a matter for legal experts, not linguists. In the case presented above concerning the semantic interpretation of the verb *standing*, the judge ruled that the matter was a point of law and therefore not the province of a linguist, irrespective of their expertise. Do you agree?

## References

Coulthard, Malcolm 1997. A failed appeal. *Forensic Linguistics: The International Journal of Speech, Language and the Law* 4: 287–302.

Coulthard, Malcolm 2000. Whose text is it? On the linguistic investigation of authorship. In *Discourse and Social Life*, ed. by Malcolm Coulthard and Srikant Sarangi. Harlow: Longman, pp. 270–87.

Danet, Brenda 1980. Language in the legal process. *Law and Society Review* 15: 445–565.

Gibbons, John (ed.) 1994. *Language and the Law*. London: Longman.

Hall, M.C. and A.M. Collins 1980. The admission of spectographic evidence: A note of Reg v Gilmore. *The Australian Law Journal* 54: 21–4.

Hammarström, Göran 1987. Voice identification. *The Australian Journal of Forensic Sciences* 19 (3): 95–99.

Hollien, Harry F. 2002. *Forensic Voice Identification*. San Diego and London: Academic Press.

Jensen, Marie-Therese 1995. Linguistic evidence accepted in the case of a non-native speaker of English. In *Language in Evidence: Issues Confronting Aboriginal and Multicultural Australia*, ed. by Diana Eades. Sydney: University of NSW Press, pp. 127–46.

Kaplan, J.P., G.M. Green, C.D. Cunningham and J.N. Levi 1995. Bringing linguistics into judicial decision-making: semantic analysis submitted to the Supreme Court. *Forensic Linguistics: The International Journal of Speech, Language and the Law* 2: 81–98.

Kreidler, Charles W. 1998. *Introducing English Semantics*. London: Routledge.

Shuy, Roger W. 1993. *Language Crimes: The Use and Abuse of Language in the Courtroom*. Oxford: Blackwell.

Solan, Lawrence M. 1998. Linguistic experts as semantic tour guides. *Forensic Linguistics: The International Journal of Speech, Language and the Law* 5 (2): 87–106.

Svartvik, Jan 1968. *The Evans Statements: A Case for Forensic Linguistics*. Göteborg: Göteborgs Universitet.

# 2.16 **from pictures to writing**

## chapter contents

> From pictures to writing      170
> The origin of the English alphabet      172
> *Scripta continua*      173
> Learning to read in Ancient Greece      174
> Linguistics and the invention of writing      175
> Key points      175
> References      176

## From pictures to writing

The earliest writing systems date back more than 5,000 years. They provide positive evidence of early linguistic enterprise because the development of a writing system requires the analysis of speech into segments. However, a writing system is created for some practical purpose such as the keeping of records; it does not follow that the creator of the writing system will either undertake, or have any interest in, further analysis of language.

Figure 2.20 *King Narmer defeats his enemies (Egyptian, 3100 BCE)*

Writing is a means of recording events, transactions, agreements, and observations in ways that do not rely entirely on oral transmission. Before writing, events were recorded in pictures. Like writing, pictures use conventional symbols to represent experience – even though pictures are closer likenesses of what they represent than is writing. Notice the symbolism in Figure 2.20: the King is identifiable from his head-dress; the enemies are trampled underfoot.

Writing systems usually began with pictographs. They are back in fashion: 🚹 is the internationally recognized symbol for "women's toilet"; 🚭 "no smoking" consists of a pictograph 🚬 "smoking" and the "forbidden" logograph 🚫. Some people might prefer to call the latter an *ideograph* "graph for a concept"; but all pictographs and logographs are graphs (inscriptions) of concepts. The ideograph is distinguished by having no phonological realization, which renders it less linguistically interesting than the logograph. The earliest writing systems are logographic. A logographic system uses symbols for words:

♂ is a logograph for "male"
4 is a logograph for "four"

A logograph may start out as a pictograph, then get more abstracted as in Figure 2.21:

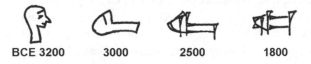

| BCE 3200 | 3000 | 2500 | 1800 |

*Figure 2.21 The Sumerian logograph* sag *"head"*

Sumerian, which is not related to any modern languages, was spoken in Mesopotamia (Iraq). Writing was at first inscribed on wet clay with a pointed stylus (as in Figure 2.22) which was later (*c* 2500 BCE) replaced by a wedge-shaped stylus, giving rise to the description *cuneiform* script (from the Latin *cuneus* "wedge").

*Figure 2.22 Sumerian c 3000 BCE.
Note the graph for drinking (head and cup), bottom left*

The 90° turn *c* 3000 BCE (cf. the left half of Figure 2.21) was systematic and recurs elsewhere; it marks the first stage in abstraction from pictograph to abstract symbol. The emoticons ('smileys') in Figure 2.23 are pictorial, but also conventionalized. When in text format, emoticons are strikingly like the earlier forms of writing, even to the extent of being rotated 90° counterclockwise.

| smile | frown | wink | laugh | surprise | foot-in-mouth |
| :-) | :-( | ;-) | :-D | =-O | :-! |

*Figure 2.23 Smileys*

Note the use of

:    for eyes
)    for up-turned mouth (smiling)
!    for exclamation

O    for open mouth
(    for down-turned mouth

There are cultural differences, for instance a Chinese smile is ( ˆ－ˆ ) or ( ˆ＿ˆ ), a Japanese smile ( －－ ).

Logographs may in fact represent morphemes rather than words. They do not have to be narrowly language specific – many Chinese logographs have different pronunciations in different Chinese languages, and some are used in Japanese and Korean. Logographic systems have usually developed so that some logographs extend to homophones of the original word symbolized, as in a "for sale" sign that uses 4 instead of for. This process was also used in ancient times: it is known as the **rebus** principle. In

**4 SALE**

SMS texting, there are logographic and syllabic effects in e.g. *c u l8r 2nIt*: *c* is a logograph for "see", *8* is the graph for the rhyme of the syllable *late*, i.e. /eɪt/, *2* stands for the initial syllable 'to-' of *tonight*, *I* stands in for the homophonous nucleus /aɪ/ of the syllable *night*.

By and large, ideographs and logographs are as conventional as alphabetic symbols. Our digit for *one* is a single stroke 1, in Arabic script ١, Ancient Greek Ι, Roman I, Chinese 一; but in Devanāgarī it is १, in Thai ๑, and so forth. Our *two* is 2 like Devanāgarī २, the source for Arabic ٢; Ancient Greek used two strokes ΙΙ, so too the Roman II and Chinese 二; the Thai is ๒. There is obviously an ideographic element in some of these systems of digits; but at the same time there is the vertical convention in Greek, Roman, and Arabic that contrasts with the horizontal convention in Chinese, cf. Roman III, Chinese 三.

The Sumerian graph used for both *an* "sky" and *dingir* "god" distinguished between them by adding a 'phonetic complement'. Once a logographic symbol is associated with phonetic form there is scope for its development into either a syllabary representing the syllables in a language or an alphabet based on the phonemes of a language. Syllabaries and alphabets exemplify prehistoric phonological analyses of language. An early syllabary is 'Linear B', the script of Mycenaean Greek of around 2000 BCE; Japanese *kana* is also a syllabary, e.g. the two symbols よ こ spell *yoko* (not the name, but "horizontal").

Egyptian script mostly reads from right to left, but also from the top down. The cartouche for *Ptolemēos* (Ptolemy V, reigned 204–181 BCE) from the Rosetta Stone is shown in Figures 2.24–2.26. One reads down and right-to-left in the Egyptian original, Figure 2.25, and down and left-to-right in the Anglicized Figure 2.26.

Figure 2.24 *Ptolemy cartouche from the Rosetta Stone*

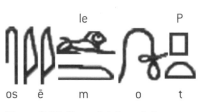

Figure 2.25 *Normal right-to-left*

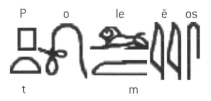

Figure 2.26 *Left-to-right*

## The origin of the English alphabet

The English alphabet derives from the same Semitic alphabet that gave rise to Hebrew and Arabic scripts (although these maintain the right-to-left sequence). Figure 2.27 shows the /l/ graphemes in these related scripts. (The Roman <L> may have come from Etruria or Marsiliana in the north-west or from the Messapii or Picene peoples of the Adriatic in the east.)

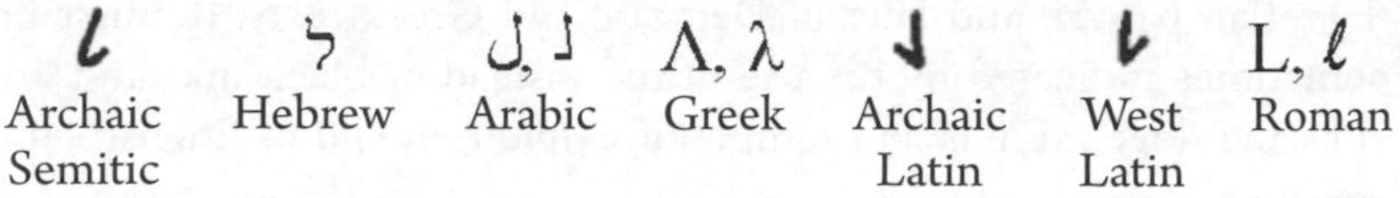

ι̇         ל         ڶ,ل         Λ, λ         ↓         ↙         L, ℓ

Archaic   Hebrew    Arabic      Greek       Archaic     West        Roman
Semitic                                     Latin       Latin

*Figure 2.27 The /l/ graphemes in related scripts*

Perhaps because of the characteristics of Semitic languages, they are consonantal scripts, although vowels may be marked with diacritics, especially for learners. For instance the Arabic consonantal root *k-t-b* has the meaning "marking, inscribing"; vowels are more or less predictable from additional consonants and from context; cf. *kataba* "he wrote", *katabat* "she wrote", *katîb* "writer", *kitâb* "book", *kutub* "books", *kutayyib* "booklet", *kutubî* "bookdealer", *maktaba* "library", *maktab* "office", *miktâb* "typewriter", *maktûb* "letter", *mukâtaba* "correspondence", *istiktâb* "dictation". The original alphabetic symbols were based on pictographic mnemonics for the initial phoneme of a word, e.g. the initial glottal stop of ʔālep "ox" was symbolized initially as on the left in Figure 2.28; then the letter was rotated almost 90° in Archaic Semitic, and another 90° as it became a vowel symbol in Greek and Latin.

∀ ⅄ ∀ A

*Figure 2.28 Semitic ʔālep "ox", the symbol for ʔ comes to be used for A in Greek*

In myth, the Greek alphabet was brought to Greece by a Phoenician prince. The Phoenicians, a Semitic trading nation, used a Semitic script. Like other Indo-European languages, the Greek language needed to be able to write vowels as well as consonants because they are very much less predictable than in Semitic languages. Greeks therefore adapted the old Semitic consonantal alphabet by reassigning symbols for phones that did not occur in Greek. On this basis the glottal stop letter was used for the vowel *A*; *E* (epsilon) was based on *hē*; *H* (eta) on *ħēt* (initial voiceless pharyngeal); *I* (iota) on *jod*; *O* (omicron) on *ʕajin* (initial voiced pharyngeal); *Υ* (upsilon) on *wāw* (which later gave rise to *F* in Latin). Italic alphabets were based on the Greek alphabet, as is the Russian Cyrillic alphabet (Русская кириллица).

## Scripta continua

In the ancient world all texts were handwritten in *scripta continua* (script without spacing between words, also called *scriptio continua*). Sometimes without punctuation as in the Greek inscription on the British Museum's Rosetta stone, part of which looks like Figure 2.29.

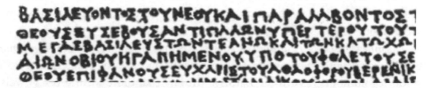

*Figure 2.29 Fragment of the Greek inscription in* scripta continua *on the Rosetta Stone*

In early Egyptian papyri, and later in Demotic and Greek texts, the first line of a stanza was sometimes indicated by the use of red instead of black ink; and line ends were marked by red dots. Here is an example of *scripta continua* in English (line ends marked by grey dots).

ALLTHEWORLDSASTAGE•ANDALLTHEMENANDWOMENMERELYPLAY
ERS•THEYHAVETHEIREXITSANDTHEIRENTRANCES•ANDONEMANIN
HISTIMEPLAYSMANYPARTS•HISACTSBEINGSEVENAGESATFIRSTTHEI
NFANT•MEWLINGANDPUKINGINTHENURSESARMS•THENTHEWHIN
INGSCHOOLBOYWITHHISSATCHEL•ANDSHININGMORNINGFACECRE
EPINGLIKEASNAIL•UNWILLINGLYTOSCHOOL

There were also boustrophedonic (from *bou-strophos* "ox-turning") texts in which text went left-to-right then right-to-left; here is an example in English:

IHAVEADREAMTHATONEDAYTHISNATIONWILLRISEUPANDLIVE
OTSHTURTESEHTDLOHEWDEERCSTIFOGNINAEMEURTEHTTUO
BESELFEVIDENTTHATALLMENARECREATEDEQUAL

In very Ancient Greek new paragraphs were sometimes marked by a stroke, |, speeches by different personae by a dash, –. By the third century BCE three punctuation marks were in use: the high point ˙ marking a full pause (*teleia*), counterpart to our full stop (period); the mid point · (*mesē*) marked a long pause roughly counterpart to our semicolon; and the low point . (*hupostigmē*) was roughly counterpart to our comma. It was common for only majuscules (upper case letters) to be used – as exemplified above. On papyri, cursive script was sometimes used, and it was this that gave rise to minuscules. Initial capital letters were used for proper names, and often to mark the beginning of a paragraph or quotation, but not otherwise sentence initially. It was not until the fifth century CE that regular use was made of word spacing. Modern punctuation arose with the development of printing in the fifteenth century.

## Learning to read in Ancient Greece

Although many people in Ancient Greece could read, all copies of every book were hand-written; consequently reading material was expensive and rare. The public lecture was the prime source of information; silent reading was virtually unknown: poetry was normally recited, dramas acted, songs sung. No two copies of an ancient text were identical; they needed to be cross-checked for differences, especially for scribal omissions, additions, errors, and emendations. The first step towards understanding written text is identifying the letters; in *scripta continua* the second is to identify the word and sentence boundaries. In poems especially, the identification of syllables is necessary for metrical purposes; although at a time when reading aloud was the norm, it was almost as necessary for reciting prose works. The alphabet was learnt in sequence *alpha, beta, ... omega* and backwards *omega, psi, chi, ... alpha* and paired, as in *alpha-omega, beta-psi, gamma-chi*, and so on. Familiarity with the alphabet was important because the Ancient Greeks used letter symbols for numbers (as did the Latins). The fact that there were seven vowels was seen as correlating with the seven notes on their musical scale and the seven celestial bodies known as 'planets', namely the Sun, Moon, Mars, Mercury, Jupiter, Venus, Saturn.

The term *letter* and its translation equivalents were used from ancient times through to the early twentieth century to refer to one or all of three properties: *letter* denoted the combined orthographic form, name, and pronunciation, all of which needed to be known. *Letter* was an abstraction; the orthographic form and pronunciation are manifestations of the abstraction in much the same way as a *phone* is the manifestation of the abstraction we call a *phoneme*.

| GRAMMA (Gk) | LITTERA (Lat.) | LETTER | *example* |
|---|---|---|---|
| onoma | nomen | name | alpha |
| charaktēr | figura | form | <α> |
| ekphōnēsis | potestas | pronunciation | /a/ |

## Linguistics and the invention of writing

The development of writing systems shows prehistoric analysis of language structure and the ability to segment words. An alphabetic writing system (the earliest appeared about 3,000 years ago) demonstrates a measure of phonemic analysis. The creators of writing systems were doing linguistics in at least a primitive way, because they had to segment the spoken language in order to give it visual and more permanent representation. The way in which language came to be represented in writing is intrinsically interesting, but only indirectly relevant to the history of linguistics. It is, however, relevant to the metalinguistic process of devising a means of representing the structure of language. Prehistoric thought about the structure and composition of language is the pretheoretical pathway towards linguistics proper. What characterizes a linguist is that:

> The linguist studies language and/or languages in a methodical way.

It is the methodical study that justifies claiming linguistics to be a science. A 'linguist' is someone who studies and writes about the structure and composition of language.

## Key points

> Writing is a means of recording events, transactions, agreements, and observations in ways that do not rely entirely on oral transmission.

> Before the advent of writing, events were recorded in pictures.

> The earliest writing systems are at the same time pictographic, ideographic, and logographic.

> As pictographs become more abstract, they often turn through 90° counterclockwise.

> Logographs come to be associated with phones; usually the initial phoneme or syllable of the word they symbolize. This gives rise to syllabaries and alphabets.

> The English alphabet is Semitic in origin. The Greeks got their alphabet from the Phoenicians and gave it to the Latins who passed it on to us.

> Semitic scripts are consonantal; Greek adopted unused Semitic consonant symbols for vowels.

> Until about the fifth century CE *scripta continua* was used: there was no spacing between words and sometimes no other punctuation either.

> Before the invention of printing in the fifteenth century everything was hand-written (or carved). Silent reading was almost unknown, because books were rare, treasured, and shared through being read aloud. Most people were illiterate, of course.

> When all documents were hand-written no two were identical. Copies had to be checked for discrepancies.

> Translation equivalents of the term *letter* denoted three things: the name of the letter, its pronunciation, and its graphological form.

> The invention of writing was probably the earliest kind of linguistic analysis.

> Additional information may be found at http://www.wikipedia.org/; and in Brown 2006; Coulmas 2003; Daniels and Bright 1996; and Rogers 2005.

## References

Brown, E. Keith (General editor) 2006. *Encyclopedia of Languages and Linguistics*. 2nd edn. 14 vols. Oxford: Elsevier.

Coulmas, Florian 2003. *Writing Systems: An Introduction to Their Linguistic Analysis*. Cambridge: Cambridge University Press.

Daniels, Peter T. and William Bright (eds) 1996. *The World's Writing Systems*. New York: Oxford University Press.

Rogers, Henry 2005. *Writing Systems: A Linguistic Approach*. Oxford: Blackwell.

Accent [179] ¦ Acceptability [180] ¦ Accommodation [180] ¦ Addresser and addressee [181] ¦ Adjective [181] ¦ Adverb[ial] [182] ¦ Affix, prefix, infix, suffix, circumfix [183] ¦ Allomorph [183] ¦ Allophone [183] ¦ Anaphora [183] ¦ Antonymy [184] ¦ Argument [184] ¦ Aspect [184] ¦ Assemblage error or slip of the tongue [185] ¦ Associative meaning [185] ¦ Caregiver language or motherese [185] ¦ Cataphora [186] ¦ Channel [186] ¦ Clause [186] ¦ Code [188] ¦ Codeswitching [188] ¦ Cognitive linguistics [189] ¦ Coherence and cohesion [189] ¦ Collocation [190] ¦ Common ground [190] ¦ Competence [190] ¦ Conjunction or connective [191] ¦ Connotation [192] ¦ Consonants [192] ¦ Constituent [193] ¦ Context [193] ¦ Contradictories [194] ¦ Contraries or incompatibles [194] ¦ Converse predicates [194] ¦ Cooperative principle [194] ¦ Covert prestige [195] ¦ Creole [196] ¦ Deixis [196] ¦ Denotation [197] ¦ Determiner [197] ¦ Diachrony and synchrony [197] ¦ Diacritic [198] ¦ Dialect [198] ¦ Diglossia [199] ¦ Distribution [199] ¦ Duality of patterning [200] ¦ Elision [200] ¦ Ellipsis [200] ¦ Entailment [200] ¦ Epenthesis [201] ¦ Feature [201] ¦ Finite [202] ¦ Force [202] ¦ Garden-path sentences [203] ¦ Generative grammar [203] ¦ Grammar [203] ¦ Graph and grapheme [204] ¦ Homonymy and polysemy [204] ¦ Hyponymy [205] ¦ Idiolect [205] ¦ Illocutions [206] ¦ Implicature, impliciture, and explicature [206] ¦ Inference [207] ¦ Infix [208] ¦

**3** key terms and concepts in linguistics

International Phonetic Alphabet or IPA [208] ¦ Intonation [209] ¦ Jargon or register [209] ¦ Langue and parole [210] ¦ Lexeme [211] ¦ Lexical classes [211] ¦ Lexicon or dictionary [211] ¦ Liaison [212] ¦ Listeme [212] ¦ Markedness [213] ¦ Medium and mode [213] ¦ Mentalese [214] ¦ Meronymy [214] ¦ Metaphor [214] ¦ Modality [215] ¦ Mood [216] ¦ Morphology, morpheme, allomorph, and morph [216] ¦ Morphosyntactic classes, lexical classes, word classes or parts of speech [217] ¦ Noun [217] ¦ Observer's paradox [218] ¦ Paradigmatic and syntagmatic [219] ¦ Parole [220] ¦ Parts of speech [220] ¦ Performance [220] ¦ Phone, phoneme and allophone [220] ¦ Phonetics and phonology [221] ¦ Phrase [221] ¦ Pidgin [222] ¦ Polysemy [223] ¦ Pragmatics [223] ¦ Prefix [223] ¦ Preposition [223] ¦ Presupposition [223] ¦ Productivity [224] ¦ Pronoun [224] ¦ Prototype semantics [224] ¦ Reference [225] ¦ Register [225] ¦ Sapir-Whorf hypothesis [225] ¦ Schwa (shwa) [226] ¦ Selection restrictions [226] ¦ Semantics [227] ¦ Semantic field [227] ¦ Sense, denotation, and reference [228] ¦ Sentence [229] ¦ Sign, signifier, and signified [230] ¦ Slip of the tongue [231] ¦ Speech Act [231] ¦ Standard variety [231] ¦ Stylistics [232] ¦ Suffix [232] ¦ Syllable [232] ¦ Synchrony [233] ¦ Synonymy [233] ¦ Systemic functional grammar (SFG) [233] ¦ Syntagmatic [234] ¦ Syntax [234] ¦ Tenor [235] ¦ Tense [236] ¦ Theta theory [236] ¦ Transformational generative grammar (TG) [237] ¦ Transitivity [237] ¦ Tree diagram [238] ¦ Truth conditions [239] ¦ Universal grammar [239] ¦ Unmarked [240] ¦ Variety [240] ¦ Verb [240] ¦ Voice [241] ¦ Vowels [242] ¦ Well-formedness [242] ¦ Word [242] ¦ Word classes [243] ¦

You will find useful additional information in the following sources:

Brown, E. Keith (General editor) 2006. *Encyclopedia of Languages and Linguistics.* 2nd edn. 14 vols. Oxford: Elsevier.
Crystal, David 2003a. *The Cambridge Encyclopedia of the English Language*. 2nd edn. Cambridge: Cambridge University Press.
Crystal, David 2003b. *A Dictionary of Linguistics and Phonetics* 5th edn. Oxford: Blackwell.
Frawley, William J. (General editor) 2003. *International Encyclopedia of Linguistics*. 2nd edn. Oxford: Oxford University Press.

In our experience Wikipedia <http://www.wikipedia.org/> is more often than not accurate; however, it needs to be used with care. Where possible, information from Wikipedia should be backed up from other sources because the authors are not strictly vetted.

**Accent** (1) The set of pronunciation features which identify where a person is from, regionally, or socially. Unlike dialect (q.v.) accent is concerned solely with auditory effects; dialect refers to varieties differentiated by grammar and vocabulary but often includes accent. Most accents are regional, or national: so there are, for example, West Country, Manchester, Scottish, General American, Southern (US), and Australian accents. But some social accents relate to the cultural and educational background of the speaker. In Britain, the best example of such an accent is received pronunciation (RP), the regionally neutral accent associated with public schools, the Civil Service and, some decades ago, the BBC. People who use RP often think of themselves as having 'no accent'. As a consequence, accents are popularly conceived of as deviations from the norm, and a social stigma often attaches itself to those accents, usually urban ones, which are considered least elegant. But, for a linguist, all accents are equal and, despite its non-regionality, RP is as much an accent as Cockney. RP is distinctive, however, in being paired with the written Standard English dialect. This is not the case with other accents. A Cockney accent, for example, can be used with either Cockney or Standard English grammar.

Despite its image as the Queen's/King's English, it is clear that RP is as much subject to change as any other accent. Linguists generally distinguish three main types of RP:

> conservative RP, spoken by older RP users, including Queen Elizabeth II, typified by tense vowels and a clipped manner
> advanced RP, spoken by younger members of the Royal Family, with more drawling vowels
> general or mainstream RP, spoken by newscasters, journalists, and professional people generally.

Noticeably, this latter variety seems to be acquiring some of the features of Cockney and it is not uncommon to hear the occasional glottal stop in words like *quite* /kwaɪʔ/ and *alright* /oˈraɪʔ/, spoken by otherwise mainstream speakers. Today the speech of both conservative and advanced RP speakers is likely to seem 'affected', and it may well be that RP itself has lost some of the image it acquired as an icon of 'correct' pronunciation.

**Accent** (2) The emphasis which makes a word or syllable stand out in a stream of speech. This prominence may be the result of loudness and intensity, pitch change or sustention, length, or a combination of such factors, often called **word stress**. English is sometimes referred to as a **stress-timed** language, which means that there is a tendency for accents to fall at fairly regular intervals in speech. It is this which accounts for the particular rhythm of English. In (1), for example, an unmarked pronunciation pattern would alternate accented with unaccented syllables:

(1)  if i've *TOLD* you *ONCE* i've *TOLD* you *TWICE*

There's nothing to stop us, of course, accenting any of the syllables, but in so doing we would be registering a particular meaning. The usual practice of speakers is to accent the lexical items and leave function words unaccented. In this respect it is noticeable that the unaccented items in (1) are all function words (pronouns and auxiliary verbs). The study of this aspect of linguistics is termed **prosody.**

In literary stylistics prosody takes on a special

meaning, particularly in the study of poetry, where analysts are concerned with metre. Even with these more formalized patterns of accentuation, however, it is still the case that the rhythms of English verse are predominantly founded on those of natural speech, and much of the subtlety of poetic writing comes from the interplay between metre and speech rhythm.

*Further reading:*

Bolinger, Dwight 1972. Accent is predictable (if you're a mind-reader). *Language* 48: 633–44.

Hughes, Arthur and Peter Trudgill 1996. *English Accents and Dialects: An Introduction to Social and Regional Varieties of British English*. 3rd edn. London: Arnold.

Wells, John C. 1982. *Accents of English. Volume 1: An Introduction. Volume 2: The British Isles. Volume 3: Beyond the British Isles*. Cambridge: Cambridge University Press.

**Acceptability** The terms 'acceptable' and 'unacceptable' are used to describe native speakers' intuitions about the grammatical correctness, or otherwise, of sentences. Native speakers of English, for example, will automatically know that *Bought he the watch?* is not a well-formed question in contemporary English, because it violates the normal formation rules for English questions. They know this even though they cannot make explicit what the rules for forming a question are. In other words, our knowledge of grammar is largely unconscious. It is this submerged, intuitive sense of grammaticalness – 'the judgement of native speakers' that linguists like Noam Chomsky use as their primary source of evidence in their inquiries into linguistic competence.

The problem with such evidence, however, is that acceptability judgements are not necessarily an accurate reflection of well-formedness (q.v.). Some conservative English speakers would find the sentence *Who did you meet at the party?* unacceptable on the grounds that the 'correct' pronoun form should be *whom*. Linguistically, however, there is nothing ungrammatical (ill-formed) about the use of *who* here. It is simply that, for many speakers, marking the distinction between subject and object has become redundant in this instance. So, while acceptability judgements are important in providing evidence for grammaticality, they have to be treated with caution. They are liable to be influenced by taste, fashion, and social prejudice. Because of this it is necessary for the linguist to compensate by filtering out factors which are perceived to interfere with natural competence. Most linguists, especially those working in the Chomskyan tradition, attempt to do this by assuming that they are working with ideal native speakers whose own use of the language directly mirrors their competence and who, therefore, make perfect well-formedness judgements. This, of course, is a fiction, but arguably a necessary one if we are to arrive at an understanding of the underlying grammatical structure of the language.

The most useful way to regard the notion of acceptability is to see it as a performance concept. Native speakers will comment on the way in which their language is performed, for example, saying something doesn't sound right or look correct, based on their own intuitions. It is up to the linguist, subsequently, to interpret these data and decide to what extent judgements are a reflection of native competence, and how far they reflect personal or social factors.

*Further reading:*

Chomsky, Noam 1965. *Aspects of the Theory of Syntax*. Cambridge MA: MIT Press.

Crystal, David 2003. *The Cambridge Encyclopedia of the English Language*. 2nd edn. Cambridge: Cambridge University Press.

Radford, Andrew 1997. *Syntax: A Minimalist Introduction*. Cambridge: Cambridge University Press.

**Accommodation** A theory associated with the social psychologist Howard Giles, which tries to explain why people modify their style of speaking in order to make it similar to that of their addressees. According to the theory, part of the way in which we cooperate and show our friendliness to others is by altering our manner of speech so as to converge with theirs, much as two people may adopt a reciprocal posture. Thus, a person who normally uses RP may do so less in the company of someone with a regional accent; and vice versa, of course. Alternatively, should we wish to emphasize the difference between us and our addressee, we could achieve this by ensuring that our style of speaking diverges from theirs.

*Further reading:*

Giles, Howard, Justine Coupland and Nikolas Coupland (eds) 1991. *Contexts of Accommodation: Developments in Applied Sociolinguistics*. Cambridge: Cambridge University Press.

Wardhaugh, Ronald 2006. *An Introduction to Sociolinguistics*. 5th edn. Oxford: Basil Blackwell [First edn 1986].

**Addresser and addressee** The two principal participants in any linguistic act of communication. The addresser is the speaker or writer, and the addressee, the intended recipient of the message. The paradigm situation envisaged here is a basic one involving a speaker and a listener, or a writer and a reader. However, complex acts of communication may involve various intermediaries. Erving Goffman referred to *animator, author,* and *principal:*

> One meaning, perhaps the dominant, is that of *animator*, that is, the sounding box from which the utterances come. A second is *author*, the agent who puts together, composes, or scripts the lines that are uttered. A third is that of *principal*, the party whose position, stand, and belief the words attest. (Goffman 1981: 226)

In the case of an advertisement it is unclear whether the author is the advertising company or the organization on whose behalf it is working (the principal). A somewhat sharper distinction exists between author and animator. In the canonical situation these participants are one and the same, but in other circumstances they may not be. At the other end of the spectrum, the concept of addressee requires sharpening in order to distinguish the various recipients of a message. A letter may be read by someone other than the person it's intended for, and so might many advertisements. In such cases, it's helpful to distinguish between the receiver and the addressee. Bell 1984 makes a distinction between addressee, auditor, and overhearer – all of whom affect the speaker's choice of sociolinguistic style – and an eavesdropper of whom the speaker is not aware (see also Bell 2001).

The situation becomes more complex if we try to fit literary communication into this framework. Novels can have a number of different addressers and addressees. The novelist is the animator and author, but there is often a fictional author, within the text. The fictional author is often identified in literary criticism as the 'narrator', although in first-person novels the situation may be even more complex. And just as there are different authors, there are different readers: there is the implied or ideal reader, the reader intended by the author, and the person who actually reads the book. Again, it is helpful here to distinguish between the addressee and the receiver.

*References and further reading:*

Bell, Alan 1984. Language style as audience design. *Language in Society* 13 (2): 145–204.

Bell, Alan 2001. Back in style: reworking audience design. In *Style and Sociolinguistic Variation*, ed. by Penelope Eckert and John R. Rickford. Cambridge: Cambridge University Press.

Goffman, Erving 1981. *Forms of Talk*. Philadelphia: University of Pennsylvania Press.

Toolan, Michael J. 2001. *Narrative: A Critical Linguistic Introduction*. 2nd edn. London: Routledge.

**Adjective** Adjectives are a lexical class of words which specify the attributes of the denotata of nouns (see **Sense, denotation** and **reference**). Typically, they give information about the size, colour, shape, and other properties of entities. In English, we characteristically find adjectives in two places: first, in an **attributive** position within a noun phrase, as in the *lovely* flower; and second, in a post-verbal, or **predicative** position, as in *The flower is* **lovely**. Adjectives that can occur in both of these positions are termed 'central'. We can think of these as the most typical adjectives.

Not all adjectives are central, however. Some, such as *outright, utter, chief* and *former*, will only occur attributively. So while we are able to say *an outright lie*, for example, we cannot normally say *\*The lie was outright*. Other adjectives will only be found predicatively. These include *unwell, loath* and *asleep. The boy was asleep* is fine but not *\*the asleep boy*. These adjectives with more restricted distribution are termed 'peripheral'. The difference between the two positions available for adjectives seems to correlate with a difference in meaning. Attributive adjectives tend to indicate qualities of the noun that are felt to be permanent, like size or colour, whereas predicative adjectives specify features that are considered to be non-permanent, such as being asleep or unwell.

There are two other criteria that distinguish adjectives. First, many adjectives are **gradable**. That is, they can be modified by degree adverbs (q.v.) or intensifiers which indicate intensity (e.g. **very** *beautiful*, **quite** *short*). And second, they have comparative and superlative forms (*lovely, lovelier, loveliest*, or alternatively, *more lovely, most lovely*). But again, not all adjectives can do this. Adjectives like *previous, inherent, former* and *mere* are not normally gradable and do not form the comparative or superlative. However, the instinct to grade is perennial and we sometimes find intensifiers in novel combinations with non-gradable adjectives, e.g. *He's very dead*.

As with other lexical classes, once we start to examine the criteria for membership of the adjective class we tend to find degrees of 'adjectiveness': some adjectives fulfil all the criteria, and others fulfil only some. As a consequence, the subclassification of adjectives is not without its problems. Some grammars, for instance, would label as an adjective everything in attributive position between the determiner (q.v.) in (1) (a possessive pronoun) and the head noun 'barn'.

(1)   my uncle's large old country barn.

To classify nouns such as *country* and *uncle's* as adjectives is not very helpful since it blurs any distinction between them and true adjectives like *large* and *old*. A more satisfactory solution to the difficulty is to recognize a form and function distinction. In other words, while such peripheral items are formally members of another lexical (morphosyntactic) class, nevertheless, when they occur in environments such as (1) they are fulfilling an adjectival function.

The order in which adjectives occur in attributive position suggests an underlying semantic pattern (which may differ in different languages) in which colour terms come before indications of size in proximity to the noun, followed by evaluative terms, as in *his **beautiful small black** cat*. Where nouns used adjectivally are present, they normally either precede or follow the adjectives, e.g. *his **father's** beautiful small black **Manx** cat*.

*Further reading:*
Bolinger, Dwight 1967. Adjectives in English: attribution and predication. *Lingua* 18: 1–24.
Huddleston, Rodney and Geoffrey K. Pullum 2002. *The Cambridge Grammar of the English Language*. Cambridge: Cambridge University Press.
Sinclair, John McH. (ed.) 1990. *Collins COBUILD English Grammar*. London: Collins.

**Adverb(ial)** Adverbs are the most mixed of all the major word classes. Typically, an adverb modifies a verb by giving circumstantial information about the time, place, or manner in which an action, event or process takes place. In English, **manner adverbs** are formed by adding the **suffix** *–ly* onto an adjective, e.g. *beautifully, quickly, sadly*. Beware of *friendly*, however, where the suffix is not an adverb signal, since this is an adjective formed from the noun *friend*. In non-standard grammar the *–ly* suffix is frequently dropped from adverbs altogether, as in *She talked very clever*. Interestingly, manner adverbs can also occur in comparative and superlative form with *more* and *most*, just like many adjectives, and they can usually be graded by intensifiers such as *very* and *quite*.

But not all adverbs are of this form. Into the adverb class also come *here, there, now* and *tomorrow*, words which indicate the place and time of some occurrence but which are not gradable and cannot occur as comparatives or superlatives. The same applies to **degree adverbs** (**intensifiers**) such as *very, quite, extremely*, and *awfully*. These serve to intensify adjectives and other adverbs, e.g. **quite** *bad(ly)*. Lastly, there are **sentence adverbs** such as *maybe, perhaps, however, frankly* and *hopefully*, which instead of modifying a verb, modify a whole clause or sentence. Their function is often signalled by their occurrence in initial position within a clause: ***Frankly**, my dear, I don't give a damn.* At the same time, however, they are extremely mobile and can occur almost anywhere. The adverb *occasionally*, for example, can be inserted into any position in the sentence *I return home*.

The clausal function that adverbs perform is termed **adverbial**. However, this is also a function that can be performed by phrases and clauses. Prepositional phrases and noun phrases, as well as adverbial phrases, can all be used in sentences to give circumstantial information about time, place and manner, e.g. *I am going **in five minutes/ next week/very soon***. The term *adverbial*, as a consequence, has much larger scope than the lexical class adverb. Along with terms like subject, object, predicate, and adjectival, it denotes the function of an element of clause structure, as opposed to a word class.

*Further reading:*
Huddleston, Rodney and Geoffrey K. Pullum 2002. *The Cambridge Grammar of the English Language*. Cambridge: Cambridge University Press.
Sinclair, John McH. (ed.) 1990. *Collins COBUILD English Grammar*. London: Collins.

**Affix, prefix, infix, suffix, circumfix** An **affix** attaches to a **stem**, and the most deeply embedded stem is the **root**. In the plural noun *undesirables* the root is the verb *desire*, the other morphemes are affixes. Affixes that precede the stem are **prefixes** (*im–* is a negative prefix in *improbable*), those which follow the stem are **suffixes** (*–tion* is a suffix in *intention*). The only **infix** in English is where an expletive is infixed into the stem, e.g. the bold part of *fan**fucking**tastic*; in this example, the stem is *fantastic*. The only **circumfix** in English is the causative ***en*–ADJ–*en***.

*Further reading:* Chapter 2.3 and
Bauer, Laurie 2003. *Introducing Linguistic Morphology*. 2nd edn. Edinburgh: Edinburgh University Press [First edn 1988].
Booij, Geert 2005. *The Grammar of Words: An Introduction to Linguistic Morphology*. Oxford: Oxford University Press.
Bubeník, Vít 1999. *An Introduction to the Study of Morphology*. Munich: Lincom Europa.

**Allomorph** See **Morphology, morpheme, allomorph** and **morph**.

**Allophone** See **Phone, phoneme** and **allophone**.

**Anaphora** The term *anaphora* comes from a Greek word meaning "carrying back". It is used in syntax, semantics, pragmatics, discourse analysis, and stylistics to describe the cohesive ties that link a language expression to other items in its co-text. Anaphoric reference is a form of discourse connection that enables the reader to see the sentences s/he is reading as constituting a text, as in (1).

(1)  He caught **the chicken**, wrang **its** neck, plucked **it** and cooked **it**.

A counterpart is cataphora, forward looking reference, as in (2).

(2)  (a) When **he** got back, **Harry** went straight to bed.
(b) **That's** what I like to see, **an empty plate**.

Because of its anticipatory quality, cataphora can be used to create suspense:

(3)  Over in the corner **it** lay, **a small untidy heap**. As Michael approached he saw **a perfectly formed human shape**.

Cataphoric reference is more marked (q.v.) than anaphora, and is less frequently encountered in ordinary discourse.

Anaphoric reference is typically achieved in three ways. First by co-reference, in which pronouns and sometimes determiners refer to items previously mentioned in the text, as in (4) where 'it' refers back to 'Finish your homework'.

(4)  Finish your homework. It will save you being put in detention.

Second, to avoid repetition by substituting a semantically or lexically identical item, as in (5).

(5)  (a) I like his car; it's a new **one**.
(b) His cat scratches. If it **does**, just tap it on the nose.

And third, by **ellipsis** (zero anaphora), for example in (6), where Ø is understood as *I am going*:

(6)  Q.  Where are you going?
A.  [Ø] To the pictures.

Failures of anaphoric reference are frequently encountered in the speech and writing of young children, who will talk about *he* or *she* without having indicated who is being referred to. Novelists may also omit the governing nominal or verb deliberately in order to create the illusion of a pre-existing world, as in the opening sentence of a novel: 'When she was home from her boarding-school I used to see her almost every day sometimes, because their house was right opposite the Town Hall Annexe' (John Fowles, *The Collector*. London: Pan Books. 1963).

*Further reading:*
Huang, Yan 2000. *Anaphora: a Cross-linguistic Study*. Oxford: Oxford University Press.
Huddleston, Rodney and Geoffrey K. Pullum 2002. *The Cambridge Grammar of the English Language*. Cambridge: Cambridge University Press.

**Antonymy** A sense relation that exists between words or sentences which are opposite in meaning (sense, q.v.). True antonyms are **contradictories**: if X and Y are antonymous X = not-Y and not-X = Y. For true (or complementary) antonyms the opposition between the terms is absolute. *Alive* and *dead*, *married* and *single*, have an either/or relationship. To say someone is not alive usually means that they are dead, and vice versa. However, it's quite common to find colloquial instances of grading, for example *He's very much alive*. So called **gradable antonyms** are in fact not contradictories, but contraries (or incompatibles), i.e. X = not-Y, but it is not the case that not-X = Y. For example, *wide* and *narrow*, *old* and *young*, *tall* and *short* are gradable antonyms. In each of these pairs the opposition is not absolute. There are degrees of width, age and height, so that to say a road is not narrow doesn't mean it's wide, and vice versa. Also, our definition of *wide, old,* and *tall* will vary according to the referent: a tall man is shorter than a tall building, for instance. Gradable antonyms normally have one item that can be more widely used, in which case it is said to be unmarked (q.v.). I can say someone is three months 'old' or 60 years 'old' without meaning that they are old, but I can really only refer to them as 'young' if they are indeed young. In this case 'young' is marked whereas 'old' is unmarked.

**Converse predicates** are items like *husband* and *wife* or *above* and *below*, or *lend* and *borrow*. Such relational antonyms exhibit reversibility. This is a logical relationship which allows us to say that if I am your husband then you are my wife, or if you are above me then I am below you, and so on.

*Further reading:*
Allan, Keith 2001. *Natural Language Semantics*. Oxford & Malden MA: Blackwell.
Saeed, John I. 2003. *Semantics*. 2nd edn. Oxford: Blackwell.

**Argument** A term used by logicians and linguists to describe the role played by particular entities in the semantic structure of sentences. All verbs (or, strictly speaking, **predicates**) are said to have arguments. It is the number and nature of the arguments they require which distinguishes them grammatically. A verb like *fall*, which is typically intransitive, requires only one argument, as in ***The man** fell*, whereas a monotransitive verb, such as *kick*, needs two, ***The boy** kicked **the ball***, and a ditransitive verb, needs three *I gave **her** some **flowers***. Expressions that do not function as arguments are described as 'non arguments'. For example, if we added *yesterday* onto the last sentence, *I gave her some flowers yesterday*, we would be adding on a wholly optional element which is not part of the argument structure of the verb. Information about the set of arguments required by verbs is contained in our mental lexicon, and plays a vital part in the construction of well-formed sentences.

The term 'argument' itself comes from predicate calculus. Sentences (clauses) are regarded as propositions in which something is predicated, i.e. claimed, about another entity, or entities. The argument structure of verbs is particularly important in theta theory, which seeks to describe the thematic role arguments fulfil in individual sentences.

*Further reading:*
Allan, Keith 2001. *Natural Language Semantics*. Oxford & Malden MA: Blackwell.
Jackendoff, Ray S. 1990. *Semantic Structures*. Cambridge MA: MIT Press.

**Aspect** A category used in the description of verbs which refers to the internal temporal contour of a situation, part of the development of an event, initiation, inchoativeness (becoming), ongoingness, termination, completeness, habitualness, iteration, punctualness, and so on. It's important to distinguish it from tense, which is primarily concerned with location in time, i.e. when something occurred. There are several types of aspectual contrast: compare *The water sparkled/ is sparkling. The water is cool / \*is being cool. The water cooled slowly / was cooling quickly. The balloon burst suddenly/ \*slowly.* The starred items are unacceptable, for example progressive aspect rarely occurs with statives like the predicate *be cool* though it may occur with the inchoative aspect in the verb *cool*, cf. *the water is cooling rapidly.* The punctual nature of bursting precludes it being slow.

English has a **progressive aspect** that is typically used to indicate continuous activity (some grammars refer to it as the **continuous** aspect). In order to form the progressive we have to use the **auxiliary** verb *be* together with a main, or lexical, verb, as (1) and (2).

(1)  I am walking the dog.
(2)  I was walking the dog.

In both cases the progressive indicates an activity which is continuous or ongoing, whether in the present, as in (1), or the past, as in (2). Not all verbs can readily occur in the progressive. Those that do are characteristically action verbs of some kind, e.g. *kick*, *eat*, *throw*. These are traditionally referred to as dynamic verbs. Stative verbs such as *seem* and *be*, which identify states of being, are not usually found in the progressive:

(3)  He seems nice    \*He is seeming nice
(4)  He is a footballer  \*He is being a footballer

However, there are special contexts in which the progressive is possible with many stative verbs:

(5)  Q.  What game is Tommy playing?
     A.  He's **being** a footballer today.

The so-called perfect aspect is in fact a retrospective tense. Semantically, the present perfect is a present ranging over a past, thus *I have lived in Tucson* is present tense (it is true now) but identifies something the speaker did in the past (lived in Tucson). The past perfect or pluperfect is a past in the past. *Ed had finished eating when Jo came in* refers to the past event of Jo coming in, and when that occurred Ed had, sometime previously (i.e. in the past relative to Jo coming in) finished eating.

*Further reading:*
Allan, Keith 2001. *Natural Language Semantics*. Oxford & Malden MA: Blackwell.

Huddleston, Rodney and Geoffrey K. Pullum 2002. *The Cambridge Grammar of the English Language*. Cambridge: Cambridge University Press.

**Assemblage error or slip of the tongue** A mistake in speaking or writing in which sounds, syllables, or words are mixed up. The most common assemblage errors are slips of the tongue (or pen): *bake my bike* (take my bike); *par cark* (car park). These sorts of errors are known as transpositions, or metatheses. *Bake my bike* contains an anticipation: the early anticipation of the *b* of *bike* interferes with the initial segment of *take*. *Par cark* demonstrates a reversal or spoonerism named after the nineteenth-century clergyman William Spooner, who regularly transposed sounds in this way. Other slips may involve blends, in which the onset of one word is combined with the rhyme of another as in *grastly* (gr[uesome + gh]astly); or selection errors, in which the wrong word is selected as in *he killed the light* (turned off the light) – though such expressions can be used figuratively for expressive effect.

Assemblage errors provide important evidence for the linguist about how language production is planned. For the most part, speakers/writers have the correct items but assembled in the wrong order. This suggests that we do not plan what we are going to say or write word by word, but in the larger chunks of phrases and clauses – because the items must have been chosen in advance of actual production. The problem, then, is largely a processing fault, and the task for the psycholinguist is to investigate what happens in the production programme to cause the errors.

*Further reading:*
Cutler, Anne (ed.) 1982. *Slips of the Tongue and Language Production*. Berlin: Mouton.
Fromkin, Victoria A. (ed.) 1973. *Speech Errors as Linguistic Evidence*. The Hague: Mouton.
Obler, Loraine K. and Kris Gjerlow 1999. *Language and the Brain*. Cambridge: Cambridge University Press.

**Associative meaning** See **Collocation**; **Connotation**; and **Jargon** or **register**.

**Caregiver language or motherese** Loosely called 'baby-talk', this is the language spoken to children by those who look after them. Many people when speaking to very young children adopt marked intonation patterns, speaking slowly, at a higher pitch than normal, and often employing baby-talk such as *moo cow*, *baa lamb*, and *bow wow*. The effect of such language on infants is probably limited to reinforcement of articulatory processes. There's little evidence that young children actually acquire much grammatical or lexical knowledge from such interactions, but they may learn some useful prosody and interactional skills. At a later stage, adults may help by providing children with expansions of their utterances. So, for example, if a child says *Shoes dirty*, a parent may expand this into a complete sentence by replying *Yes, your shoes are dirty*. It used to be thought that expansions are a principal agent of children's development in providing a model for children to aim at, but recent research suggests that recasts are more productive. These are responses in which the parent repeats what the child says in an alternative form and continues the conversation, for example, *They're not very dirty. Let's clean them, shall we?*

*Further reading:*
Aitchison, Jean 1998. *The Articulate Mammal: An Introduction to Psycholinguistics*. 4th edn. London: Routledge.

**Cataphora** See **Anaphora.**

**Channel** The technical means by which a message is transmitted. For some linguists it is synonymous with **medium**, and it is acceptable to use it in that way. However, a useful distinction can be made between them. Medium is more concerned with the physical form a message takes. Speech is the primary medium of linguistic communication and can be transmitted in a number of ways: by telephone, television, radio, or face-to-face. Similarly, writing can appear as marks on paper using a pencil or pen, electronically on a computer screen, or on the printed page of a book. All these technical communication aids are channels.

In stylistics, 'channel' is one of a number of variables which affect the style, register, or jargon we adopt in speaking or writing. Most people, for instance, will speak differently over the phone than face-to-face. Without the visual clues to tell us how a message is being sent or received, we have to pay more attention to phrasing and intonation. Characteristic of much communication today is the use of multiple channels, in which one channel is embedded in another, as in a discussion that is broadcast over the radio. In this case both the primary channel of face-to-face interaction and the secondary, of radio broadcast, would subtly affect the medium of speech. You only have to compare a football commentary over the radio with one transmitted via television to become aware of this.

*Further reading:*
Blommaert, Jan (ed.) 1995. *Handbook of Pragmatics*. Amsterdam and Philadelphia: John Benjamins.
Gregory, Michael and Susanne Carroll 1978. *Language and Situation: Language Varieties and their Social Contexts*. London: Routledge and Kegan Paul.

**Clause** A clause is a simple sentence that may be **finite** (q.v.) as in *Jack died* or **non-finite** as in the first clause of *Falling from the cliff, Jack died*. The distinctive feature of clauses is that they consist of a **predicate** (typically a verb) and one or more **arguments** (q.v.) which are noun phrases: *Jack died* (one argument), *Harry shot Jack* (two arguments), *Suzy gave the book to Harry* (three arguments). A clause or simple sentence has the structure NP VP (noun phrase followed by verb phrase) though in some grammars these are referred to as subject and predicate.

| NP | VP |
|---|---|
| *The boy* | *kicked the ball over the fence* |
| *The tall-masted schooner* | *sank* |
| *She* | *slept* |

All these clauses are also complete sentences in their own right because a **simple sentence** consists of a single clause. **Compound and complex sentences** will consist of more than one clause, e.g. *Sue dated Harry and Edna (dated) George* is a compound sentence, where the clauses are linked by *and, or, but*, and so on. Complex sentences involve embedded clauses typically introduced by subordinators as in *Because she was so small, Sally couldn't reach* *the chocolates on the mantelpiece* or *He'll be very good-looking **when he grows up***.

In Systemic Functional Grammar, clauses are constructed of the elements subject (S) and predicator or verb (V), object (O), complement (C), and adjunct (A). The requirement for a particular element to be present or not depends on the type of clause we are constructing. This, in turn, is largely determined by the character of the verb. Verbs tend to select the elements that accompany them. It's on the basis of these selection restrictions that verbs are said to be subcategorized. In Systemic Functional Grammar there are five principal types of clause structure which result from the possible permutation of elements.

(1) S + V:          *The man died*
(2) S + V + O:      *Max drank the beer*
(3) S + V + O + O:  *Sue gave granny some chocolates*
(4) S + V + C:      *The milk went sour*
(5) S + V + O + C:  *Jack thought the exam hard*

(1) is **intransitive**, it can't be passivized. (2) is **monotransitive**, its single object can become subject of a passive clause: *the beer was drunk by Max.* (3) is **ditransitive**, both objects can be the subject of passive sentences: *Granny was given some chocolates by Sue* and *Some chocolates were given (to) granny by Sue*. In example (4) the subject and complement are linked intransitively together. And finally, (5) is a **complex-transitive** in which the object, *the exam,* needs a complement to complete the sense of the clause – *\*Jack thought the exam* is not well-formed. Notice that none of the clauses requires an adverbial. There are no verbs which are subcategorized by an adverbial.

The clauses we have been considering are exemplars of the default **declarative** type, not **imperative** or **interrogative**, for instance. They are also positive, not negative, and unmarked (q.v.) in terms of word order. This is not how we always encounter clauses, since they are subject to various discourse transformations in the production of actual sentences, but it's useful to take idealized examples like these in order to establish grammatical paradigms. One such transformation is the reduced or verbless clause, as in **When ripe** these oranges are delicious. Here, the omitted elements indicate *when ripe* to be a reduced type (4) structure.

The **declarative** is the default clause-type; it potentially has a truth-value (is either true or false):

(a)  He just wouldn't stop whingeing.
(b)  Bill was shot by Max.
(c)  Bill, Max shot.
(d)  Bill died.
(e)  Max gave the Salvos a donation.
(f)  *It's snowing* is a declarative sentence.
(g)  Mortgage rates down at last.
(h)  Dunno who did it.

**Interrogatives** make requests and look like this:

(a)  Will you stop whingeing?
(b)  Care to come along?
(c)  Which came first? The chicken or the chicken nuggets?
(d)  Why bother? After all, who wants to crash a convivial high by spending an hour at the sink?
(e)  I shouldn't have worn those heels today, should I?
(f)  He's not bad, huh?
(g)  Please may I be excused?
(h)  You were where on the night of eighteenth May?

The third basic clause-type is the **imperative,** which either directs or entreats the addressee(s) to do something:

(a)  Stop your bloody whingeing!
(b)  Move it, Grandma.
(c)  Be warned!
(d)  Get yourself checked by someone qualified.
(e)  You give me that ball, you!
(f)  Nobody move!
(g)  Let the Games begin.
(h)  Let me help.
(i)  Let's eat.
(j)  Have a good day!

English also has a couple of rather archaic sounding **hypothetical** constructions (sometimes called subjunctive or optative): *Would that I were rich. May he rot in hell!* But hypotheticals also occur in declaratives, *Wish I were rich*; interrogatives, *Could you post this letter for me?* and imperatives, *If Harry should call, tell him I'm on my way.* **Exclamatives** occur within the other clause-types and do not count as a distinct clause-type in their own right; they are marked by exaggerated acoustic intensity. There are also certain **expressive idioms** such as *Goodness gracious! Wow! Jesus! Thanks. Congratulations. Hi. Bye. Good luck!* which are not strictly speaking clauses, but which have a similar function.

*Further reading:*

Allan, Keith 2006c. Mood, clause-type and illocutionary force. In *Encyclopedia of Languages and Linguistics*. 2nd edn, ed. by E. Keith Brown. 14 vols. Oxford: Elsevier, pp. 8: 267–71.

Börjars, Kersti and Kate Burridge 2001. *Introducing English Grammar*. London: Edward Arnold.

Halliday, Michael A.K. and Christian M.I.M. Matthiessen 2004. *An Introduction to Functional Grammar*. 3rd edn. London: Arnold.

Sinclair, John McH. (ed.) 1990. *Collins COBUILD English Grammar*. London: Collins.

**Code** In its simplest sense a code is a system of correspondence rules which allows us to transmit information in symbolic form. Human language is often said to be a code because it consists of words which symbolically represent ideas, events, and objects in the world outside, and which, when put together in certain sequences, enable us to communicate. In order to be able to use the code we have to learn a variety of systems of rules governing the phonology, syntax and semantics of language. Some of these are common to all languages and constitute language universals, and others are specific to individual languages.

A code is basically a sign system. Listemes (the morphemes, words, and idioms listed in a dictionary) are signs, a view emphasized by one of the early modern linguists, Ferdinand de Saussure (see Chapter 4.1). A characteristic of sign systems is that messages can be converted from one system, or **primary code**, into another, or **secondary code**. Morse code and semaphore are both secondary codes, being based on language. Linguists sometimes talk about the processes by which we transmit and receive language as **encoding** and **decoding**. This can give the impression that activities such as speaking and listening are largely mechanical. Clearly, understanding what someone is saying to us involves more than simply turning the stream of sound that we are receiving back into words.

We have to be able to interpret prosodic features such as stress and intonation, both of which contribute to meaning.

A limitation on the notion that language is a code is the amount of inferencing normally required in interpreting what is said. Strictly speaking, a code has an algorithmic relation with what is encoded (whether it be one-to-one or one-to-many), but normally language has a heuristic relation to what is spoken of. Common ground (which includes context) will determine the meaning of *He lost his heart* (spoken of a card game, a romance, the cutting up of a cadaver in a mortuary). Similarly *I've had breakfast* normally needs *this morning* to be supplied in order for it to make sense. And *It killed me* needs to be recognized as hyperbolic. Irony like *I'm sure the cat likes you pulling its tail* uttered to a child pulling a cat's tail, is probably meant to get the child to desist. In all these examples, the implied and inferred meaning goes beyond anything that can reasonably be called a code.

It is also worth remembering that language is only one sign system among many. The non-verbal behaviour that accompanies speech, commonly called *body language*, is also a form of signalling, employing its own complex system of communicating. Indeed, in a general sense, all aspects of human behaviour function as signs, from the way we dress to the cars we drive. The study of these sign systems is the concern of **semiotics**. The success of this field of study among modern communications theorists is evident from the way in which most disciplines in the humanities have their respective codes. There are cultural codes, aesthetic codes, theatrical codes, and literary codes. All of them are based on the idea that we make sense of what we see and hear by drawing on an implicit system of signs encoded in a text, painting, play, or social event.

*Further reading:*

Cobley, Paul (ed.) 2001. *The Routledge Companion to Semiotics and Linguistics*. London: Routledge.

**Codeswitching** The shifting by speakers between one language or one dialect, and another, e.g. a Frenchman playing liar dice saying *J'ai trois tens* (I have three tens). Many native English speakers will switch between speaking regional dialect, or non-standard English, casually among friends, and Standard English for professional, or business, purposes. Bidialectalism, as it is sometimes called, has received the overt support of many linguists as a way to approach the difficulty that schools face of giving appropriate recognition to the local dialect of children while at the same time respecting their entitlement to acquire Standard English. Bilingual speakers, of course, do more than simply switch dialects. People who are fluent in two or more languages may regularly switch from one to the other according to the situation, the person being addressed, or even the topic.

*Further reading:*

Bernstein, Basil 1971. *Class, Codes and Control*. London: Routledge and Kegan Paul.

Clyne, Michael G. 2003. *Dynamics of Language Contact: English and Immigrant Languages*. Cambridge: Cambridge University Press.

Holmes, Janet 2001. *An Introduction to Sociolinguistics*. 2nd edn. Harlow: Longman.

Myers-Scotton, Carol 2002. *Contact Linguistics: Bilingual Encounters and Grammatical Outcomes*. Oxford: Oxford University Press.

Romaine, Suzanne 2000. *Language in Society: An Introduction to Sociolinguistics*. 2nd edn. Oxford: Oxford University Press.

**Cognitive linguistics** is the systematic study of language under the assumption that language is constrained and informed by the relations that human beings (a) perceive in nature – particularly in relation to themselves; (b) have experience of in the world they inhabit; (c) conceive of in abstract and metaphysical domains. In other words cognitive linguistics holds that language categories are not randomly created in a completely arbitrary fashion, but reflect human perceptions and conceptions about the things humans use language to refer to.

*Further reading:*

Croft, William and D. Alan Cruse 2004. *Cognitive Linguistics*. New York: Cambridge University Press.

Geeraerts, Dirk 2006. *Cognitive Linguistics: Basic Readings*. Berlin: Mouton de Gruyter.

Taylor, John R. 2002. *Cognitive Grammar*. Oxford: Oxford University Press.

**Coherence and cohesion** It is part of the quality of a text that it is not just a series of disconnected sentences but possesses what Michael Halliday terms 'textuality'. Our ability to create and recognize such sequences, according to Halliday, constitutes our textual competence.

Cohesion signifies the surface ties which link units together. Halliday and Hasan 1976 identified a range of ties at various linguistic levels, phonological, syntactical, lexical and semantic, which serve to hook sentences onto each other. Some of the principal devices here are lexical, involving the use of synonyms or hyponyms: *He turned to the **ascent** of the mountain. The **climb** was steep*; *I bought some **daffodils**. They're very practical **flowers**.* Others involve anaphoric strategies of co-reference, substitution, and ellipsis.

Cohesiveness used to be considered by language teachers as a basic requirement for texts. But coherence is a more significant criterion of textuality. It's possible for a sequence of sentences to be cohesive without being coherent – see the quote below.

> I bought a Ford. A car in which President Wilson rode down the Champs Elysées was black. Black English has been widely discussed. The discussions between the presidents ended last week. A week has seven days. Every day I feed my cat. Cats have four legs. The cat is on the mat. Mat has three letters. (Nils Enkvist, quoted in Brown and Yule 1983: 197)

A text is judged coherent where the model of the world spoken of in the text is internally consistent and generally accords with accepted human knowledge. Even an imaginary world is necessarily interpreted in terms of the world of our experience. A text may in fact be coherent without any cohesive links at all. The following two sentences have nothing to tie them together but are nevertheless logically related in the minds of both speaker and listener: *I must tidy the house. My mother-in-law's coming tomorrow.* This utterance could easily be made cohesive by the insertion of *because* between the sentences but it's not absolutely necessary in such a context. We know the two are causally related partly because of the logical sequence of assertion followed by explanation, which is one of the discourse frames we habitually use, and partly because we know in the real world what a visit by a mother-in-law may entail.

The speech of schizophrenics is characterized by incoherent cohesion:

THERAPIST: A stitch in time saves nine. What does that mean?

SCHIZOPHRENIC: Oh! That's because all women have a little bit of magic in them. I found that out. And it's called, it's sort of good magic. And nine is a sort of magic number. Like, I've got nine colours here you will notice. I've got yellow, green, blue, grey, orange, blue and navy. And I've got black. And I've got a sort of clear white. The nine colours, to me they are the whole universe; and they symbolize every man, woman, and child in the world. (Rochester and Martin 1979: 94f)

These examples would suggest that cohesion doesn't render a text coherent. Rather it seems to signal coherence for purposes of clarity, emphasis, or elegance. Coherence is concerned with the way in which propositions are linked together in a logical and sequential manner. Our expectation of such linkage is a basic convention of communication and underlies the cooperative principle. Coherence depends, crucially, on inference, i.e. our ability to detect and interpret meanings not necessarily present in the text. This is part of our pragmatic knowledge and as a consequence must take into account features such as context and audience. Speaking to someone from a different culture, for example, we may need to use fairly explicit cohesive devices in order to signal actively the logical connections we are making, whereas with someone we know very well we can afford to take all kinds of discourse liberties.

References and further reading:

Allan, Keith 2001. *Natural Language Semantics*. Oxford & Malden MA: Blackwell.

Brown, Gillian and George Yule 1983. *Discourse Analysis*. Cambridge: Cambridge University Press.

Halliday, Michael A.K. and Ruqaiya Hasan 1976. *Cohesion in English*. London: Longman.

Halliday, Michael A.K. and Christian M.I.M. Matthiessen 2004. *An Introduction to Functional Grammar*. 3rd edn. London: Arnold.

Rochester, Sherry and James R. Martin 1979. *Crazy Talk: A Study of the Discourse of Schizophrenic Speakers*. New York: Plenum Press.

**Collocation** We know a word by the company it keeps. *Collocation* refers to the tendency for certain words to occur together. The term itself comes from the verb *collocate*, meaning "to go together". A word like *clear*, for example, can be found with a number of nouns: *clear sky*, *clear conscience*, *clear idea*, *clear road*. In each case the term *clear* has a slightly different meaning because of the word it is modifying. In some instances the difference can be quite marked: *strong* has a completely different meaning in *strong tea* than it does in *strong language*, where it is usually a euphemism for *swearing*. Collocational differences sometimes separate words which are otherwise synonymous: *quiver* and *tremble* are synonyms, but we *tremble* with fear and *quiver* with excitement. The distribution of a word within a language is referred to as its collocational range.

Further reading:
Firth, John R. 1957. *Papers in Linguistics, 1934–1951*. London: Oxford University Press.

Firth, John R. 1968. *Selected Papers of J.R. Firth, 1952–1959*, ed. by Frank R. Palmer. Bloomington: Indiana University Press.

**Common ground** What a speaker assumes that a hearer is most likely to know. That is, things which are obvious to the sensory receptors of both speaker and hearer, or which a hearer can very easily reason out on the basis of knowing the language and the conventions for its use, and drawing on the knowledge that each of us has acquired from experience of the world around us.

Further reading: Chapter 2.5 and
Allan, Keith 2001. *Natural Language Semantics*. Oxford & Malden MA: Blackwell.

Stalnaker, Robert C. 2002. Common ground. *Linguistics and Philosophy* 25: 701–21.

**Competence** A term introduced in *Aspects of the Theory of Syntax* (Chomsky 1965) to describe the knowledge possessed by native users of a language which enables them to speak and understand their language fluently.

This knowledge is internalized by speakers and not necessarily something they are aware of possessing. All English speakers, for example, will know the rules for forming questions, statements, and commands, but, unless they have studied syntax (grammar), will probably be unable to say what they are.

There are two main forms of competence: grammatical, and communicative, the latter named by Hymes 1972. Grammatical competence identifies the linguistic abilities described in the previous paragraph, i.e. our knowledge of language as a grammatical system. Because of it, we know how to pronounce words (phonological competence), how to arrange them in phrases, clauses, and sentences (syntactic competence), and how to assign meanings to them (semantic competence). Communicative competence is concerned with our use of this internalized knowledge to communicate effectively. For example, if you asked someone the time and received the reply *Manchester United won the League in 2000*, the fact that the reply was grammatically competent and a well-formed sentence would be of no use whatever in answering your question. Communicative competence involves knowing what counts as an appropriate reply, and understanding the cultural rules governing the use and interpretation of language. Among other things it means knowing when to abbreviate an utterance – saying simply *The opera*, for example, in reply to the question *Where are you going?* instead of producing the grammatically complete *I am going to the opera*. It also includes knowing when and to whom one can ask questions such as *Where are you going, How old are you?* or *How much did you pay for that?* Knowing how much information to seek or give, how best to arrange it, and generally being aware of the audience and the cultural rules governing language use are all essential features of communicative competence.

Chomsky 1980 refers to 'pragmatic competence', which is almost identical to communicative competence. His own example involves a fellow academic saying *Today was a disaster*, after giving a lecture. Given this context it's possible for the listener to infer that the lecture went down badly. Nothing in the utterance itself makes this explicit, and indeed the interpretation may be incorrect, but we clearly need more than gram-matical competence to understand its meaning completely. It's possible also to distinguish a creative, or poetic, competence: i.e. the ability to use language in a uniquely striking way of the kind we find in significant literature – poems, novels, plays, and so forth.

In describing the dimensions of competence that second language learners need to acquire, Canale and Swain 1980 identified grammatical competence, sociolinguistic competence (the knowledge of rules governing social interaction), discourse competence (the knowledge of rules governing the organization of talk and text), and strategic competence (the ability to repair break-downs in communication).

But however many competences we distinguish, the important point to grasp is that competence describes a cognitive (mental) skill. We are talking here of what native speakers understand of the structure and use of their language. The practical execution of those abilities in terms of actual speaking and writing comes within the scope of the partner term to competence – performance (q.v.).

*References and further reading:*
Canale, Michael and Merrill Swain 1980. Theoretical bases of communicative approaches to second language teaching and testing. *Applied Linguistics* 1: 1–47.
Chomsky, Noam 1965. *Aspects of the Theory of Syntax*. Cambridge MA: MIT Press.
Chomsky, Noam 1980. *Rules and Representations*. New York: Columbia University Press.
Hymes, Dell H. 1972. On communicative competence. In *Sociolinguisticsx*, ed. by John B. Pride and Janet Holmes. Harmondsworth: Penguin, pp. 269–93.
Matthews, Peter H. 1979. *Generative Grammar and Linguistic Competence*. London: Allen & Unwin.
Newmeyer, Frederick J. 1996. *Generative Linguistics: A Historical Perspective*. London: Routledge.

**Conjunction or connective** A conjunction is a linking word whose main function is to connect language expressions together. For example, *bananas **and** cream, the young women **and** old men, Jack went up the hill **but** Jill wouldn't go.*

There are two main kinds of conjunction: **coordinating**, and **subordinating**. Coordinators *and, or, but,* and *yet* link together units which are of equal status. Subordinating conjunctions involve a more complex relationship between the units being joined, where one is thought to be subordinate to, i.e. dependent on, the other. These conjunctions typically occur between two clauses:

[1]  I will do it **if** I can.
[2]  He will come **when** he is ready.
[3]  She asked **whether** he was willing to help.

In each of [1]–[3] the clause following the conjunction elaborates a requirement that has to be fulfilled for the action in the main clause to be accomplished. Other subordinating conjunctions are *while, whether, because* and *since*. Similar to them are adverbial **conjuncts** like *however, meanwhile, moreover, so, nevertheless* and *now*, which serve to provide circumstantial information.

[4]  **Now** I was intending to go home.
      **However**, it was raining as usual.
      **Meanwhile**, we played monopoly.

Conjuncts are principally used as textual devices in developing and staging an argument or narrative.

*Further reading:*
Adamson, Donald 1995. *Practise Your Conjunctions and Linkers*. Harlow: Longman.
Sinclair, John McH. (ed.) 1990. *Collins COBUILD English Grammar*. London: Collins.

**Connotation** The connotations of a language expression are pragmatic effects that arise from encyclopedic knowledge about its denotation (or reference) and also from experiences, beliefs, and prejudices about the contexts in which the expression is typically used. The connotation of a language expression is clearly distinct from its sense, denotation and reference. Connotation is intimately involved with notions of appropriateness in language use that conditions the choice of vocabulary (including proper names) and style of address. For example, *Mike* and *Michael* can have the same reference but different connotations. *John* is an unsuitable name for your newborn daughter; so is *Springtime in Paris* an inappropriate name for a 1200cc Harley-Davidson motorbike or an auto-repair shop. To identify the connotations

of a term is to identify the community attitude towards it. For instance the connotations of English *octopus* and the Japanese translation equivalent *tako* are very different: an octopus is a sinister, alien creature; tako is edible and endearing.

Connotation is intimately involved with notions of appropriateness in language use – i.e. with pragmatic effect. For instance, racist dysphemisms (*Wog, Paki, Honkey, Yid, Coon, Abo*) occur when a speaker refers to or implicates the hearer or some third person's race, ethnicity, or nationality in such terms as to cause a face affront (face is one's public self-image). Many such 'racist' terms can be disarmed by being used, without irony, as in-group solidarity markers by the targeted group; e.g. the use of *Nigger/Nigga* among African Americans.

Reactions to connotation are pragmatic effects that motivate semantic extension and the generation of new vocabulary. The negative connotations of an existing word often lead to its replacement. Connotation is involved in choosing expressions that upgrade, downgrade and insult. It plays a part in the loaded weapon of dysphemism and the euphemistic avoidance of dispreferred expressions judged discriminatory, blasphemous, obscene, or merely tasteless. Although *Jesus Christ!* is blasphemous; the euphemistic forms *Gee whiz* and *By jingo* are not. From a purely rational viewpoint, if one of these is blasphemous, then all of them are. But the pragmatic effects, i.e. connotations, are different.

*Further reading:*
Allan, Keith 2007. The pragmatics of connotation. *Journal of Pragmatics* 39: 1047–57.
Backhouse, Anthony E. 2003. Connotation. In *International Encyclopedia of Linguistics*, ed. by William Frawley. New York: Oxford University Press, pp. 4: 9–10.

**Consonants** are produced by obstructing the air flow as it comes up from the lungs. This distinguishes them from vowels, for which the air flow is unobstructed. Consonants are conventionally described in articulatory terms in respect of three main features: whether they are voiced or not ([s] and [p] are unvoiced, [z] and [b] are voiced); the place of articulation, i.e. where the obstruction occurs (lips, teeth, velum, and so on); and the manner of articulation, i.e. the way the phone is articulated [e.g. a nasal [n], a fricative [z], a stop [d]]. More subtle distinctions can be made between them and form the basis of distinctive feature analysis.

*Further reading:* Chapter 2.2 and

Clark, John, Colin Yallop and Janet Fletcher 2007. *An Introduction to Phonetics and Phonology.* 3rd edn. Malden MA: Blackwell.

Ladefoged, Peter 2006. *A Course in Phonetics.* 5th edn, with CD-ROM. Boston MA: Thomson Wadsworth.

**Constituent** The term **constituent** is a basic term in linguistics for a unit which is a component of a larger one. So a clause (sentence) can be analysed into a series of constituents, such as NP (noun phrase) plus VP (verb phrase). These constituents can be analysed into further constituents, e.g. an NP might consist of a determiner plus a noun, and such analysis can continue until no further subdivision is possible. In the case of individual words it can continue down to the level of particular morphemes, e.g. *undesirables:*

$$\{_{\text{PL.N}}\{_{\text{N}}\{_{\text{NEG.A.}}\{\text{un-}\}+\{_{\text{A}}\{\text{desir}_{\text{VERB}}\}+\{\text{able}\}_{\text{ADJ}}\}_{\text{NEG.}}$$
$$_{\text{ADJ}}\}\varnothing_{\text{NOUN}}\}+\{\text{s}\}_{\text{PLURAL NOUN}}\}.$$

Constituents are always represented hierarchically but the precise form in which they are shown varies among linguists. The most popular representation is in the form of a rooted labelled tree or phrase structure tree (see Figure 3.1).

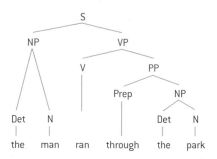

*Figure 3.1 Labelled tree diagram for* The man ran through the park

Alternatively, bracketing can be used:

$$[_{\text{S}}[_{\text{NP}}[\text{the}_{\text{DET}}]\,[\text{man}_{\text{N}}]]\,[_{\text{VP}}[\text{ran}_{\text{V}}]\,[_{\text{PP}}[\text{through}_{\text{P}}]$$
$$[_{\text{NP}}[\text{the}_{\text{DET}}]\,[\text{park}_{\text{N}}]_{\text{NP}}]_{\text{PP}}]_{\text{VP}}]_{\text{S}}]$$

In the analysis, NP and VP are **immediate constituents** of S, V and PP are immediate constituents of VP, Prep and NP are immediate constitutents of PP.

Constituent analysis is an important feature of most grammatical accounts, but it is particularly significant in constituent-structure grammar, which analyses sentences wholly in terms of a hierarchy of structural layers.

*Further reading:* Chapter 2.5 and

Börjars, Kersti and Kate Burridge 2001. *Introducing English Grammar.* London: Edward Arnold.

Brown, E. Keith and Jim Miller 1991. *Syntax: A Linguistic Introduction to Sentence Structure.* 2nd edn. London: HarperCollins.

**Context** is convenient shorthand for four different categories of context: the situation of utterance and the situation of its interpretation, the world spoken of, and the co-text.

The **situation of utterance** identifies the place and the time in which the utterance is made. The **situation of interpretation** of the utterance is the place and time in which it is heard or read. In face-to-face conversation the situation of interpretation is almost identical with the situation of utterance; but telephone and radio conversations take place between people in different places and perhaps in different time zones. With written texts there is even greater scope for temporal and spatial distance between writer and reader. The situation of utterance provides the spatio-temporal coordinates for the utterance, and can be thought of as 'the world spoken in'. It also identifies the speaker and, especially in face-to-face encounters, the hearer. Consequently it provides definitions for deictic categories such as personal pronouns, deictic locatives, and tense. The so-called 'macro-context' assumes a geographical, social, and cultural framework or background of shared values and beliefs which constitute part of the common ground. It remains an indeterminate area of analysis if only because situational context is essentially extra-linguistic in character. As such, it's the point at which language and the world at large interact.

**The world spoken of** (or written of), sometimes called the discourse world or discourse model or scenario, is the mental model of the world which we all construct in order to be able to produce or understand a phrase, a sentence, or much longer text. When reading the sentence *Peter went to the pictures* we might imagine a trip to the movies or some action in an art gallery and perhaps other things. If you ask someone whether they want a cup of coffee and the reply is *Coffee keeps me awake*, then, clearly, in order to know whether this means *yes* or *no*, we need to know more than the simple meaning of the words being used. The ability to interpret utterances correctly involves us in processing not just the words but the world being spoken of. The situation of utterance may also be a factor in determining the world spoken of. A seemingly innocent question about coffee will vary in contextual meaning according to whether it is said in a cafe, on top of a bus, in a time of coffee shortage, or in a culture which regards coffee drinking as decadent.

**Co-text** is significant only for identifying the world spoken of (or something within it); co-text is the text that precedes and succeeds a given language expression. The context for comprehension contains not only all the assumptions explicitly expressed by the preceding utterances in the discourse, but also all the implications of these utterances. A sentence fragment like *Tonight* sends us to the co-text to discover what has or will happen tonight. The interpretation of pronouns and other anaphoric expressions usually requires that they be correlated with names or full noun phrases in their co-text. The co-text provides information necessary to the proper interpretation of ambiguous forms: e.g. the word *head* can be a noun (*a head*) or a verb (*to head the company*); the co-text will ordinarily disambiguate it by permitting only one of these to make sense 'in context'. Language expressions not only take from their co-text, they also give to it: what we say or write at any point most often has an important bearing on how a text will continue.

*Further reading:*

Allan, Keith 2001. *Natural Language Semantics*. Oxford & Malden MA: Blackwell.
Schiffrin, Deborah, Deborah Tannen and Heidi E. Hamilton (eds) 2001. *The Handbook of Discourse Analysis*. Oxford: Blackwell.

**Contradictories** See **Antonymy**.

**Contraries or incompatibles** If X is the **contrary** of Y, it cannot be the case that both X and Y are concurrently true. When X and Y are contraries they are **incompatible**. We cannot say *This instrument is a piano and a violin*, since the sense of *piano* excludes that of *violin* (they are **co-hyponyms** of *musical instrument*). Similarly, in the field of fruit we cannot say *This fruit is an apple and a banana*. And if we say *This book is red and black* it must be part red and part black, because colour terms are contraries. The important fact about contraries is that if X is the contrary of Y, X is not Y and Y is not X, but not-X is not (necessarily) Y, and not-Y is not (necessarily) X: *the bird is black* → the bird is not brown, but *the bird is not brown* ↛ the bird is black.

*Further reading:*

Allan, Keith 2001. *Natural Language Semantics*. Oxford & Malden MA: Blackwell.
Cruse, D. Alan 2004. *Meaning In Language: An Introduction to Semantics and Pragmatics*. 2nd edn. Oxford: Oxford University Press.
Saeed, John I. 2003. *Semantics*. 2nd edn. Oxford: Blackwell.

**Converse predicates** See **Antonymy**.

**Cooperative principle**

> Make your conversational contribution such as is required, at the stage at which it occurs, by the accepted purpose or direction of the talk exchange in which you are engaged. One might label this the cooperative principle. (Grice 1975:45)

Like other social activities, language interchange requires participants to mutually recognize certain conventions.

**Quantity:**

> Make your contribution as informative as is required (for the current purposes of the exchange).
> Do not make your contribution more informative than is required.

This might be revised as follows: a speaker should make the strongest claim possible consistent with his/her perception of the facts, such that what isn't said, isn't relevant. At the same time a speaker should give no more and no less information than is required to make his/her message clear to the hearer, with the effect that what is expressed simply is stereotypically exemplified. Hence *Emma got pregnant and married George* indicates that the marriage took place after Emma got pregnant which is not the situation in *Emma got pregnant and married George – but not in that order.*

**Quality**: Try to make your contribution one that is true. [Be sincere]

> Do not say what you believe to be false.
> Do not say that for which you lack adequate evidence.

In other words the speaker should be genuine and sincere; i.e. should state as facts only what s/he believes to be facts; make offers and promises only if s/he intends carrying them out; pronounce judgements only if s/he is in a position to judge and so on.

**Relation**: Be relevant.
In general, an utterance should not be irrelevant to the context in which it is uttered, because that makes it difficult for the hearer to comprehend.

**Manner**: Be perspicuous.

> Avoid obscurity of expression.
> Avoid ambiguity.
> Be brief (avoid unnecessary prolixity).
> Be orderly.

Where possible, a speaker's meaning should be presented in a clear, concise manner that avoids ambiguity, and avoids misleading or confusing the hearer through stylistic ineptitude. One type of exploitation of this manner principle is that 'What's said in an abnormal way isn't normal' (Levinson 2000); for instance, *Jenny is talented and her sister Madge is not untalented* indicates that Madge is less talented than her sister; *Harry caused his sister's death* indicates that he didn't murder her.

Such maxims are not laws to be obeyed, but reference points for language interchange – much as the points of the compass are conventional reference points for identifying locations on the surface of the earth.

*References and further reading:*
Grice, H. Paul 1975. Logic and conversation. In *Syntax and Semantics 3: Speech Acts*, ed.

by Peter Cole and Jerry L. Morgan. New York: Academic Press, pp. 41–58. Reprinted in H. Paul Grice *Studies in the Way of Words*. Cambridge MA: Harvard University Press. 1986.
Huang, Yan 2007. *Pragmatics*. Oxford: Oxford University Press.
Levinson, Stephen C. 2000. *Presumptive Meanings: The Theory of Generalized Conversational Implicature*. Cambridge MA: MIT Press.

**Covert prestige** A term used in sociolinguistics to describe the way in which non-standard forms belonging to regional or social dialects may be positively valued by some speakers. The existence of such prestige helps to explain why there are not more RP and Standard English speakers than there are. Some communities clearly value non-standard forms, chiefly as a means of reinforcing group solidarity and local identity, even though this is not always a matter of conscious awareness.

Evidence for covert prestige has usually come from what sociolinguists call 'under-reporting', a classic instance of which is detailed in Peter Trudgill's Norfolk study (Trudgill 1974). As part of his analysis of Norfolk dialect, Trudgill asked informants to take part in a self-evaluation test in which they reported on what they believed themselves to be saying, which he compared with what they actually did say. Using a range of linguistic variables he was able to show that perceptions of speech habits were often at variance with actual usage. For instance, in the case of yod dropping (the dropping of /j/ before /u/ in words such as *beauty* and *tune*), as many as 40% of informants claimed to use the non-standard form (*booty, toon*) when in fact the tape recording showed them using the standard form. Even allowing for the influence of tape recorders on linguistic behaviour this represents a remarkable disparity. The conclusion which Trudgill drew from this is that '[s]peakers ... report themselves as using the form at which they are aiming and which has favourable connotations for them, rather than the form which they actually use' (Trudgill 1983: 91).

Trudgill discovered that covert prestige was more common among male speakers, a finding which correlates with the frequently observed phenomenon that women value standard forms of speech more highly than men:

A large number of male speakers, it seems, are more concerned with acquiring *covert prestige* than with obtaining social status (as this is more usually defined). For Norwich men (and we can perhaps assume, for men elsewhere) working-class speech is statusful and prestigious. (Trudgill 1983: 92)

*References and further reading:*
Trudgill, Peter 1974. *The Social Differentiation of English in Norwich.* Cambridge: Cambridge University Press.
Trudgill, Peter 1983. *On Dialect: Social and Geographical Perspectives*. Oxford: Blackwell.

**Creole** A creole develops from a pidgin (q.v.) which has become the mother tongue of a community. For this to happen it needs to acquire native speakers. A classic case is the development of creole in the Caribbean as a consequence of the slave trade. This major upheaval resulted in speakers of very different languages being forced to live together with only a pidgin as a common means of communication. Not surprisingly, children soon acquired it as a native language, as a consequence of which the pidgin underwent creolization. This process involves a considerable expansion of the vocabulary, syntax, and stylistic range of the original pidgin to the point that we can truly talk of it as a distinct language. Such a process has been occurring for a number of years in Papua New Guinea, where there are many different indigenous languages, and where the English-based creole known as 'Tok Pisin' has emerged as the first language of many in the country.

A final stage often occurs if, as sometimes happens, the original 'target' language is reintroduced into the community. In many West Indian countries, for example, since independence, Standard English has become the language of law, government, and in some cases, education. The effect of this is to cause the creole to unravel in a process known as decreolization. This results in a **post-creole continuum** in which we get a range of forms from pure creole at one end of the spectrum to Standard English at the other. So, as O'Donnell and Todd 1991: 52 comment, we find a number of forms in Guyana for the English sentence *I gave him*, ranging from *mi gii am, mi bin gii am, a di gi ii, a giv ii,* and so on up to the Standard English form.

It is likely that Black Vernacular English of the kind we find in America and Britain is not imperfectly learnt English but a decreolized creole.

The process of creole formation enables us to see creoles as languages in their own right, rather than debased or corrupt forms of more prestigious languages. This is important to speakers of these varieties because of the recognition it affords to otherwise stigmatized linguistic forms. But it is equally important for linguists, for whom studying such processes has brought increased understanding of how languages, generally, are formed. It has been powerfully argued by Derek Bickerton, in particular, that creolization provides vital evidence for the genetic inheritance of linguistic ability. According to Bickerton 1981, the rapid expansion that results when children become native speakers of pidgin happens because they are generating vital linguistic material themselves. If this is so it solves the vexed question of why creoles the world over are grammatically so similar. The reason is simply that children are operating what Bickerton calls the same 'bioprogram'. Needless to say, this view is contentious and there are many who have challenged it, but, nonetheless, it provides intriguing evidence as to the continuing importance of this area of linguistics. A recent critique by Mufwene (2001) labels the notions of pidgins and creoles as racist (see Chapter 2.7).

*References and further reading:*
Bickerton, Derek 1981. *Roots of Language*. Ann Arbor: Karoma.
Holm, John 2000. *An Introduction to Pidgins and Creoles*. Cambridge: Cambridge University Press.
Mufwene, Salikoko 2001. *The Ecology of Language Evolution.* Cambridge: Cambridge University Press.
O'Donnell, William R. and Loreto Todd 1991. *Variety in Contemporary English.* 2nd edn. London: HarperCollins.
Sebba, Mark 1997. *Contact Languages: Pidgins and Creoles*. Basingstoke: Macmillan – now Palgrave Macmillan.

**Deixis** From a Greek word meaning "pointing" or "showing". Deixis refers to those features of language which derive from the situation of utterance and orient our utterances in time, space, and speaker's standpoint. So, for example, the tense system is deictic because it locates events in the present, future or past, typically relative to the moment of utterance (*now*). Similarly, words such as *here*, *there*, *this*, and *that*, are normally deictic because they locate items in space relative to the person who is speaking: my *here* is your *there*. The first-person pronouns *I*, *we*, and the second-person pronoun *you* are also deictic in this respect. This form of deixis is **exophoric** in character in that it is situationally rather than co-textually bound.

A secondary form of deixis is **endophoric** and serves to locate items textually: in (1), *this* points forward cataphorically to the next sentence.

(1)  This is important. Don't go out.

Additionally, terms like *this* and *that* can be used to locate things emotionally. Linguists refer to this as 'displacement'. In (2), the demonstrative *that* as well as pointing to the particular animal conveys the speaker's dislike.

(2)  Get that animal out of here.

Similarly, *this* frequently occurs in jokes and anecdotes as a means of indicating familiarity: *There was this man* (i.e. a particular man).

*Further reading:*
Allan, Keith 2001. *Natural Language Semantics*. Oxford & Malden MA: Blackwell.
Fillmore, Charles J. 1997. *Lectures on Deixis*. Stanford: CSLI Publications.
Levinson, Stephen C. 1983. *Pragmatics*. Cambridge: Cambridge University Press.
Lyons, John 1968. *Introduction to Theoretical Linguistics*. London: Cambridge University Press.

**Denotation** See **Sense, denotation** and **reference.**

**Determiner** Determiners are a class of words which always occur with a noun and serve to specify such properties as its number and definiteness. In English the most frequently occurring determiners are the indefinite article *a(n)*, and the definite article *the*. Other words that can have a determiner function include possessives, *my*, *your*, *his*; demonstratives, *this*, *that*, *these*, *those*; and quantifiers, *some*, *many*, *several*.

Many grammars distinguish between central determiners, predeterminers, and postdetermin-

ers. Central determiners, which include the items listed above, can only ever occur singly. We can't say *\*the my book*, or *\*his a dog* (*his many books* is possible, but see below). Predeterminers are a small set of words which occur before central determiners and which characteristically express notions of quantity. They include items such as *all*, *both* and *half*, as in *all* the cats, **both** my brothers, **half** the loaf. Correspondingly, postdeterminers occur after the central determiner. As with predeterminers, they also usually express quantity. Included here are numerals, both cardinals (*the* **three** boys) and ordinals (*the* **first** *time*) as well as quantifiers (*the* **many** cats, *a* **few** people). Notice that these can also occur as central determiners, e.g. **many** cats, **few** people, and also as predeterminers, **many of** the cats, **few of** the people.

The most recent version of X-bar syntax has raised the status of determiners and sees them as forming the heads of the phrases in which they occur. According to this view, which remains controversial, rather than premodifying nouns, determiners are complemented by nouns or noun phrases. Currently, this view remains speculative.

*Further reading:*
Berry, Roger 1997. *Determiners and Quantifiers*. London: HarperCollins.
Huddleston, Rodney and Geoffrey K. Pullum 2002. *The Cambridge Grammar of the English Language*. Cambridge: Cambridge University Press.

**Diachrony and synchrony** Diachrony and synchrony together describe two basic perspectives for the study of language. Diachrony is the historical perspective for studying language, as opposed to synchrony, which is concerned with its state at any one particular time. Studying language diachronically involves analysing the changes which have taken place over time in sounds, syntax and vocabulary.

There was a flowering of diachronic linguistics in the nineteenth century, especially in phonology, when linguists (at that time called 'philologists') were engaged in studying the sound changes that took place in the Indo-European languages and establishing a number of important phonological rules. Since the twentieth century, most innovatory work in linguistics is synchronic in character.

If we think of language as resembling a game of chess, then the linguist who is engaged in studying language synchronically is like an observer who comes in while the game is in play and analyses it from the current distribution of the pieces. The observer is not interested in how they came to be in their respective places on the board, being concerned only with the relationships between the pieces as they currently stand. Considerations of etymology and derivation are consequently irrelevant in synchronic description.

Nonetheless, an awareness of diachronic variation is important for a complete picture of any language, and it is essential for any linguist working on aspects of earlier periods of a language. We should bear in mind that synchronic and diachronic variation are two sides of the same coin. Because language is a dynamic, continuously evolving system, we can arrive at a true understanding of how it operates only by seeing it against the background of its historical development.

*Further reading:*
Allen, Cynthia L. 1980. *Topics in Diachronic English Syntax*. New York: Garland.
Roberts, Ian 2007. *Diachronic Syntax*. Oxford: Oxford University Press.

**Diacritic** A mark or symbol (i.e. a graph) which indicates the pronunciation value of a speech segment. Diacritics are not pronounced themselves but serve simply to provide information about pronunciation. They are predominantly used in conjunction with symbols from the International Phonetic Alphabet (IPA), to indicate allophonic variants. The voiced phonemes /b/, /d/, /g/ for example, often lose their voicing at the ends of words. This can be shown by adding a small symbol, or diacritic, to the phoneme when it occurs, thus /d̥/ indicates a devoiced pronunciation of /d/, namely [t]. Similarly a wavy line through [l] as in [ɫ], informs us that the phone is velarized. In this case it indicates the difference between /l/ in *lip*, and /l/ in *milk*, where the back of the tongue is raised towards the velum (soft palate).

In addition, some letters of the conventional alphabet also function diacritically. The graph <e>, for example, often functions in this way at the end of monosyllables. In the case of *din* /dɪn/ and *dine* /daɪn/, the silent <e> shows that the previous vowel is the diphthong /ai/, rather than a short vowel /ɪ/. As this is the only pronunciation difference between them, the extra graph performs a valuable service. Similarly, double letters can also perform diacritically, as in *red~reed* /rɛd~rid/, showing a difference in pronunciation of the vowel, and *diner~dinner* /daɪnə~dɪnə/, where the second <n>, although not pronounced, provides essential information about the quality of the preceding vowel. In the pair *halo~hallo* /ˈheɪloʊ~hɛˈloʊ/, there is not only a difference in vowel quality between the vowels in the first syllables of these words but also a stress difference.

*Further reading:*
Rogers, Henry 2000. *The Sounds of Language: An Introduction to Phonetics*. Harlow: Longman.

**Dialect** A geographically or socially based language variety with distinct phonological, syntactic and lexical forms. (Dialect is sometimes distinguished from accent (q.v.), which refers solely to features of pronunciation.) The term dialect is used, in a technical sense which differs slightly from its common usage, to refer to all the varieties of a language (see the discussion of Dixon's work in Chapter 2.7). Dialects are historically related and often mutually intelligible. Historical processes of change (see Chapter 2.10), contact and social stratification (see Chapter 2.7) produce different regional varieties (**regional dialects**), socially distinct dialects (**sociolects**) and varieties associated with particular ethnic groups (**ethnolects**).

In England, speakers from Essex, Cornwall and Northumberland have access to distinctive words, phonological patterns and grammatical constructions. Similarly, speakers of Appalachian English can be distinguished from New Yorkers, and Parisian speakers use a different variety of French from that used in Quebec. An example of an ethnic variety is African-American English. Speakers often have access to more than one dialect, and move between these to express different aspects of identity or respond to different contexts.

Early dialectologists studied rural dialects, producing dialect maps of, for example, England, France and India, in the latter case using linguistic criteria to identify dialects of the same language and boundaries between different languages.

Since then the focus has shifted to the study of urban dialects. Principally important here has been the American sociolinguist William Labov, whose work on phonological variation in the speech of New Yorkers influenced a generation of sociolinguists (see Chapters 2.7 and 5.8).

National boundaries add a layer of complexity to the identification of dialects. For example the Dutch–German border cuts across a dialect continuum (see Chapter 2.10). Dialects on either side of the border are closely related but for political reasons people living on the Dutch side will be seen as speaking a dialect of Dutch, and will learn the standard variety of Dutch in school, and the converse on the German side.

Dialects develop in speech, and the advent of written language changes the way we perceive them. Norms emerge for spelling, grammatical conventions are standardized and codified, and dictionaries are produced, and these conventions are typically based on the dialect used by the most powerful group. This variety then becomes established as the appropriate form to be used in education and other formal contexts, and gains considerable prestige. In common usage, this variety is often seen as the 'language', and the non-standard varieties are termed 'dialects'. It is important to recognize how this folk usage differs from the technical sense of the term.

See also **Standard English**.

*Further reading:*
Trudgill, Peter 1983. *On Dialect: Social and Geographical Perspectives*. Oxford: Blackwell.
Trudgill, Peter 2004. *New Dialect Formation: The Inevitability of Colonial Englishes*. New York: Oxford University Press.

**Diglossia** Some languages have two very different varieties co-occurring throughout a speech community, each with a different range of social functions. If you are in Lebanon, for example, you might well find native users of the language using one form, 'Classical Arabic', in writing and formal speeches, but using 'Colloquial Arabic' in everyday speech. Such a situation is diglossic. It's usually the case that one form, sometimes called 'high', is used for the more prestigious purposes of education, politics and commerce, and the other, or 'low' variety, for domestic and informal settings. While the high variety is more prestigious, the low is thoroughly acceptable in the contexts in which it is used. Diglossic situations are also found in Haiti, where both French and a French-based creole are used, in Switzerland, where speakers use High German and Swiss German, and in Singapore, with Standard and colloquial English.

Historically, it is likely that the Romance languages such as French, Spanish, and Italian arose from diglossic situations in which a high variety, Latin, was used for education, religion and politics, whereas a Latin-based vernacular was used in everyday speech. Such situations exist today in communities in the Pacific and Caribbean, where both a standard variety of English and a pidginized or creolized form exist side by side.

*Further reading:*
Crystal, David 2003. *A Dictionary of Linguistics and Phonetics* 5th edn. Oxford: Blackwell.
Ferguson, Charles A. 1959. Diglossia. *Word* 15: 325–40.

**Distribution** The distribution of an item, e.g. a phoneme or morpheme, is the total set of linguistic contexts in which it can occur. Every unit has a characteristic distribution. So, for example, a verb such as *appear* has a range of sentence contexts in which it can be found as a consequence of its grammatical and semantic properties. We describe this range as its 'distribution within the linguistic system'. The notion of distribution was originally developed in phonology and later extended to other linguistic levels. The distribution of phonemes and their allophones in the linguistic system is a major factor in their classification. Allophones of the same phoneme are said to be in 'complementary distribution', i.e. they are found in mutually exclusive environments within syllables.

Distribution is also sometimes used to describe the range of social, rather than linguistic, contexts in which items occur. Sociolinguists, for example, will talk about the distribution of certain linguistic variables within a community.

*Further reading:* Chapter 2.2 and
Harris, Zellig S. 1954. Distributional structure. *Word* 10: 146–62.
Lyons, John 1968. *Introduction to Theoretical Linguistics*. London: Cambridge University Press.

**Duality of patterning** A term which describes one of the defining properties of language, namely, its ability to combine essentially meaningless units into meaningful sequences. So, for example, the sounds represented by the letters *p, t* and *a* are not in themselves meaningful. However, arranged in the sequence *pat*, they are. Not only that, but they can be recombined to make other meaningful sequences: *apt, tap*. Duality of patterning goes up through the linguistic system, with an increase in the range and complexity of meaning as an outcome. Sounds combine to form morphemes, which combine to form words, and so on, up to sentences. This is a crucial design feature of language which allows us to use the same units over and over again in a variety of meaningful patterns.

*Further reading:*
Hockett, Charles F. 1960. The origin of speech. *Scientific American* 203 (3): 88–96.

**Elision** The omission of a vowel, consonant, or whole syllable. Words like *handsome* and *postman* are frequently pronounced with the omission of /d/ in *handsome*, and /t/ in *postman*. The word *sixths* may be pronounced /sɪkθs/ or /sɪkss/ but almost never /sɪksθs/. In rapid casual speech *do you* gets reduced to /dʒʊ/, *vegetable* to /vɛdʒtbl/ and the onsets to *him, her*, and *incredible* are often elided. In French the sequence *tu+ne+as+pas+vu+la+auto* (you have not seen the car) is elided graphemically to *Tu n'as pas vu l'auto* and phonemically to /ta pa vy lɔto/.

*Further reading:* Chapter 2.2 and
Clark, John, Colin Yallop and Janet Fletcher 2007. *An Introduction to Phonetics and Phonology.* 3rd edn. Malden MA: Blackwell.

**Ellipsis** A term used to describe the omission of a word or words from a sentence, where they are recoverable from the context. In the exchange in (1) the full form of Y's answer (*I am feeling fine*) is predictable from the context.

(1)  X:  How are you feeling?
     Y:  Fine.

Ellipsis is a frequent feature of speech. It is generally used for the sake of economy, but also sometimes for emphasis, as in (2).

(2)  X:  Can I go out?
     Y:  No!

Linguists would not normally use the term, however, to apply in the case of abbreviated utterances where the full sense was not predictable, for example, saying *Sorry* after bumping into someone, which could mean *Sorry, I didn't see you* or *Sorry for bumping into you*, or something else.

*Further reading:*
McShane, Marjorie J. 2005. *A Theory of Ellipsis*. Oxford: Oxford University Press.
Stainton, Robert J. 2006. *Words and Thoughts: Subsentences, Ellipsis, and the Philosophy of Language*. Oxford: Clarendon Press.

**Entailment** A logical relationship between two sentences such that the truth of the second sentence necessarily follows from the truth of the first, symbolized X ⟶ Y. So, for example, sentence (1), below, entails sentence (2):

(1)  John killed Bob.
(2)  Bob died.

The entailment here gives rise to the semantic relationship between *kill* and *die*. We know that there are various ways to die and that being killed is one of them. In other words, an important part of the sense of *killed* is the sense of *die*. This kind of entailment, in which the sense of one lexical item is included within another, gives rise to a hierarchical relationship between items, known as **hyponymy**. Notice, however, that the relationship is not reversible. Saying that Bob died does not entail that John killed him. Mutual entailment, such that X ⟷ Y, is **synonymy** as in the case of (2) and *Bob is no longer alive*. The passive version of (1), *Bob was killed by John*, entails and is entailed by (1). These two sentences are paraphrases of one another.

One of the principal difficulties that students regularly have is distinguishing entailment from **presupposition** (q.v.). This is another logical relationship involving statements which are dependent on one another. The big difference is in the nature of that dependence. In the sentences above, negating (1) means that (2) can be either true or false (saying that John didn't kill Bob leaves completely open the question of whether or not Bob died). In other words, the entailment fails.

This would not be so if the relationship were one of presupposition. (3) presupposes (i.e. assumes) the truth of (4); symbolically, (3) ≫ (4).

(3) The King of England left for Peru yesterday.

(4) There is a King of England.

But even if we negate (3) as in (5) the presupposition (4) holds.

(5) The King of England did not leave for Peru yesterday.

Presupposition is an entailment that holds under negation, in other words it looks as if X ≫ Y if and only if X ⟶ Y and not-X ⟶ Y. For various technical reasons this is absurd (see Allan 2001: 204–10 for discussion). Instead it seems that presuppositions are really the conditions that must be in place for any utterance to be made felicitously (in other words, an utterance of (3) or (5) is only felicitous if the speaker correctly believes that (4) is true).

*Further reading:*

Allan, Keith 2001. *Natural Language Semantics*. Oxford & Malden MA: Blackwell.

Gazdar, Gerald 1979. *Pragmatics: Implicature, Presupposition, and Logical Form*. New York: Academic Press.

Levinson, Stephen C. 1983. *Pragmatics*. Cambridge: Cambridge University Press.

Saeed, John I. 2003. *Semantics*. 2nd edn. Oxford: Blackwell.

**Epenthesis** Epenthesis (sometimes called 'liaison') is the putting in of an additional phone (speech sound) for phonotactic reasons. For example, the word *dreamt* is usually pronounced /drɛmpt/ with an epenthetic /p/. The reason is that after making the bilabial nasal, the velum closes while the lips and glottis open to make /t/, and a /p/ results: it has the [+bilabial] feature of [m] and the [–voice] feature of [t]. The stop (plosive) quality arises from the opening of the lips.

Old English *thymel* and *bremel* correspond to modern English *thimble* and *bramble* where epenthetic /b/ has been conventionally inserted between /m/ and /l/, not only in pronunciation, but in spelling too.

Epenthetic *r* is very common in some dialects of English. It does not come from spelling as can be seen in examples like *banana and cream* [bɐˈnãːnɐ̃ɡ̃ŋ ˈkɹiːm] with an epenthetic /r/ before *and*; or *I saw him there* [ʔʌɪˈsɔːɹɪmˈθɛə], with an epenthetic /r/ between *saw* and *him*.

Epenthesis is not uncommon after diphthongs and triphthongs. For example, although *tower* is normally pronounced [taʊə], it may be pronounced [taᵘwə] in which the [w] is either epenthetic or may replace the high(ish) back rounded vowel altogether, [tawə]. There is similar epenthesis or replacement when *How are you?* [haʊˈɑːju] is pronounced [hawˈɑːju] (the [ɑː] may be pronounced [aː] in some dialects; and the vowel in [ju] may be any of [u, ʊ, ʉ, ə]). There is also *You are?* [juˈɑː] which may be pronounced [jᵘwˈɑː].

Similarly a diphthong or triphthong rising towards a front vowel [ɪ, i] may attract an epenthetic semivowel [j] or be replaced by it. Thus we find *higher* [haɪə] pronounced [haɪjə] or [hajə]. We also hear *Come here* [kʌmˈhɪə] being pronounced [kʌm ˈhijə]. Occasionally the emphatic statement of *He is!*, normally [hiˈɪz], is pronounced [hiˈjɪz].

*Further reading:*

Warner, Natasha and Andrea Weber 2001. Perception of epenthetic stops. *Journal of Phonetics* 29: 53–87.

**Feature** A term which refers to any typical or noticeable property of spoken or written language. Like many such terms in linguistics it can be used in either a general or a specific sense. Using it generally, we could say, for example, that a feature of spoken language is the use of intonation because intonation is a typical property of speech, or that complete grammatical structures are a feature of written language. Used more precisely, however, 'feature' refers not simply to typical but to distinctive linguistic properties. Phonologists use it this way in distinctive feature theory. Today the number of distinctive features is reduced from the 25 or so in *Sound Pattern of English* (Chomsky and Halle 1968) to ±sonorant, ±continuant, ±voice, ±nasal, ±lateral, ±ATR (advanced tongue root); additionally there are the unary features labial, dorsal, and coronal (which subcategorizes into ±anterior, ±distributed). In a similar way, some grammarians build up feature specifications for morphology. For instance, the Latin case system can be specified in terms of distinctive features from the categories of case, gender, number, and declension. Componential semantics uses features, e.g. *bull* [+bovine, +adult, +male], *stallion* [+equine, +adult, +male], *ewe* [+ovine, +adult, −male], *foal* [+equine, −adult, ±male]. These features derive from entailments:

> bull —→ BOVINE & ADULT & MALE
> stallion —→ EQUINE & ADULT & MALE
> ewe —→ OVINE & ADULT & FEMALE
> foal —→ EQUINE & YOUNG

*Further reading:*

Allan, Keith 2001. *Natural Language Semantics*. Oxford & Malden MA: Blackwell.

Chomsky, Noam and Morris Halle 1968. *The Sound Pattern of English*. New York: Harper and Row.

Clark, John, Colin Yallop and Janet Fletcher 2007. *An Introduction to Phonetics and Phonology*. 3rd edn. Malden MA: Blackwell.

Jakobson, Roman 1988. *Roman Jakobson Selected Writings VIII: Major Works 1976–1980*. Berlin: Mouton de Gruyter.

Roca, Iggy and Wyn Johnson 1999. *A Course in Phonology*. Oxford: Blackwell.

**Finite** A term used in the grammatical description of independent or main clauses (q.v.) which contain a verb inflected for tense (present, past) and in person and number concord with the sentence subject. Clauses that can't show these contrasts are non-finite. Thus, clauses containing, for instance, only participle forms – the present participle, *–ing* form (e.g. *Swimming strongly, ...* ) or the past participle, *–en* form (e.g. *His wrist broken, ...* ) are non-finite. So are infinitive clauses such as *To be or not to be, ...*.

For participles to appear in finite clauses they must be preceded by one or more auxiliary verbs. It is these, not the participle, which carry the burden of indicating tense, number, person (and mood) as in *I am/was walking; They are/were walking; I have/had walked*. These are all finite clauses in which the participles *walking* and *walked* remain the same whoever is being talked about – *I* or *they* – and whether or not the action is past or present.

Non-finite clauses are **subordinate**, for example, ***Breaking windows** is against the law*, or *It is against the law **to break windows***. In these cases the finiteness of the sentence is the property of the (unbolded) main clause to which the subordinate clause is attached.

*Further reading:*

Börjars, Kersti and Kate Burridge 2001. *Introducing English Grammar*. London: Edward Arnold.

Huddleston, Rodney and Geoffrey K. Pullum 2002. *The Cambridge Grammar of the English Language*. Cambridge: Cambridge University Press.

**Force** The contextual meaning of a linguistic item, frequently signalled by intonation. Force is an aspect of utterance meaning rather than sentence meaning. If, for example, someone says *I like your hat*, we need to know more than the sense and reference of the words in order to interpret them correctly. We need to recognize the intended **illocutionary** point. We have to be alert to the possibility of irony in the speaker's tone, particularly if there is anything odd about the hat, in which case the speaker might actually be implying the reverse of *like*. Indeed, ironical statements characteristically oppose force and sense, as when *Nice one* is meant sarcastically.

The analysis of force is more the concern of pragmatics than semantics. At issue here is not so much linguistic, as extra-linguistic, meaning: in other words, those elements of meaning which are not explicit in the language itself and for which reference to a dictionary would be of only limited help. Intonation plays an essential part here, and so does stress. You have only to think of the ways in which the stress pattern of any simple sentence could be varied to see the differing interpretations possible from an actual utterance. The sense of *I'm not going out tonight* is clear enough, but its force will depend on where we place the nuclear stress, compare:

(1) *I*'m not going out tonight.
  [Someone else is]
(2) I'm *NOT* going out tonight.
  [That's for sure]
(3) I'm not *GOING OUT* tonight.
  [I'm staying in]

(4)  I'm not going out to*NIGHT*.
     [It's tomorrow]

The other main way in which force is communicated is by thematic arrangement. We tend to make the most important parts of our utterances more prominent by thematizing them, i.e. by positioning them at the beginning. Newspapers frequently do this to draw attention to the most dramatic bits of the news, but creative writers also do it. Rearranging *The rain came down* to *Down came the rain*, doesn't alter the sense of the line but it does alter its force because now the emphasis is on the physical descent of the rain rather than its simple existence.

*Further reading:*
Allan, Keith 1986. *Linguistic Meaning*. 2 vols. London: Routledge and Kegan Paul [Reprint edn, Beijing: World Publishing Corporation. 1991].
Leech, Geoffrey N. 1983. *Principles of Pragmatics*. London: Longman.

**Garden-path sentences** These are sentences in which listeners are initially led astray because a sentence is capable of more than one meaning. In (1), for example, the word *punch* would normally be interpreted by most listeners as a blow, until they got to the end and realized that it referred to a drink.

(1)  John reeled from the effect of Bill's powerful punch – though I know he has a high tolerance for alcohol.

Misinterpretations such as these provide linguists with valuable clues about how people process language. Some think that we compute one meaning initially, and go back and compute another only if it becomes implausible or contradictory. This would explain the surprise people get on discovering their original interpretation was wrong. However, research has shown that people take longer to process ambiguous fragments than they do unambiguous ones, which suggests that rather than computing one meaning at a time listeners compute at least two and then immediately pick the most likely one on the basis of context. This is not to say that they are actively aware of ambiguity as such; the assumption is still that there is only one meaning, which the context will clarify.

*Further reading:*
Aitchison, Jean 1998. *The Articulate Mammal: An Introduction to Psycholinguistics*. 4th edn. London: Routledge.
Gernsbacher, Morton Ann 1990. *Language Comprehension as Structure Building*. Hillsdale NJ: Lawrence Erlbaum.

**Generative grammar** is a theory of grammar deriving directly from Noam Chomsky 1957 (though see also Harris 1970) in which grammar is conceived as a set of rules for generating from an initial symbol all and only the sentences of a given language. An expansion rule (rewrite rule) such as S $\longrightarrow$ NP VP expands the initial symbol 'S' (sentence) into its constituents 'NP' (noun phrase) and 'VP' (verb phrase). These constituents are subsequently expanded into the ultimate constituents that are given morphological and then phonetic form by subsequent rules and processes, so as to create or generate all possible sentences of a given language. Supposedly the rules are such as to prohibit the generation of ungrammatical strings – a constraint that has caused no end of so far unsolved problems for grammarians.

*References and further reading:*
Chomsky, Noam 1957. *Syntactic Structures*. The Hague: Mouton.
Freidin, Robert 2007. *Generative Grammar: Theory and its History*. London: Routledge.
Harris, Zellig S. 1970. *Papers in Structural and Transformational Linguistics*. Dordrecht: D. Reidel.

**Grammar** The grammar of a language consists of a set of rules which native speakers intuitively follow in the production of well-formed constructions. So, for example, knowing that English regular verbs form their past tense by adding *–ed*, is a rule of English morphology, and knowing that *–ed* may be pronounced /t/, /ɪd/ or /d/, depending on the environment, is a rule of English phonology. The term 'rule' has a special sense here: we tend to think of rules as externally imposed constraints that everyone has to obey, like *Don't walk on the grass*, but linguistic rules are not of this kind. They are internal, not external, constraints and, as such, are unconsciously present in the minds of native speakers. They are better understood as principles by which the language operates.

Having said that, however, *grammar* is a word which is open to a number of different uses and interpretations. Some linguists, particularly those of a more traditional bent, limit its application to the domains of syntax and morphology, while others use it to encapsulate the entire set of rules for the proper construction of spoken and written language. However, it is true to say that debates over different models of grammar tend to concentrate largely on syntax. Modern grammars are descriptive or theoretical in character, and include theories of cognitive grammar, functional grammar, transformational generative grammar, and universal grammar. Despite the different approaches, for the great majority of contemporary linguists, grammatical knowledge, even though it may be largely unconscious knowledge, is a cognitive (mental) property; i.e. it represents the way in which our minds work. If this is the case, then understanding grammar is an important key to understanding the way in which we make sense of ourselves and the world around us.

*Further reading:*
Brown, E. Keith and Jim Miller 1991. *Syntax: A Linguistic Introduction to Sentence Structure.* 2nd edn. London: HarperCollins.
Pinker, Steven 1994. *The Language Instinct: The New Science of Language and Mind.* London: Allen Lane.
Van Valin, Robert D. Jr and Randy LaPolla 1997. *Syntax: Structure, Meaning, and Function.* Cambridge: Cambridge University Press.

**Graph and grapheme** A graph is the smallest discrete segment in a stretch of writing or print. In English these are popularly called 'letters', but a moment's thought will show the inexactness of this term. If we take the letter *s*, for example, this can be written in a number of different ways, lower case 's', upper case 'S', archaic 'ʃ' or 'ſ'. Clearly these forms are not separate letters, but simply variants. 'Letters' exist both as concepts, traditionally called the **'character'**, and as physical forms (traditionally, the 'letter'), rather like sounds. And as with sounds, we need a more technical vocabulary to describe the relationship between concept and physical substance. In the case of phonology

we have phones and allophones or phonemes. Similarly with written forms, we have graphs and allographs of graphemes. Using this vocabulary we can say that the grapheme <s> is realized by three allographs: 's', 'S', and 'ſ' (or 'ʃ'). The relationships between them are these:

grapheme = individual letter as concept ('character')
allograph = physical representation of the character ('letter')
graph = physical substance

Like phonemes, graphemes are minimal contrastive units. Changing a grapheme in a written word produces a different word whereas merely changing a graph doesn't. It makes no difference whether <soot> is written *Soot*, soot or *soot*, it is still the same word. This is not the case, however, if we substitute <l> for the first segment. Grapheme analysis is the main business of graphemics or graphology. The writing system of language is known as its **orthography**.

*Further reading:* Chapter 2.16 and
Daniels, Peter T. and William Bright (eds) 1996. *The World's Writing Systems.* New York: Oxford University Press.
Rogers, Henry 2005. *Writing Systems: A Linguistic Approach.* Oxford: Blackwell.

**Homonymy and polysemy** Homonymy is a relation that exists between words (or other language expressions) that have the same form but unrelated senses. Homonyms may have the same phonological or graphological form, or both. Examples of the former are *sight/site*, and *rite/right*. These are **homophones**. Examples of the latter are *lead* (of a dog, /liːd/), and *lead* (on the roof, /lɛd/). These are **homographs**. And some homonyms are homophonic and homographic: *mail* (armour) and *mail* (post), *cleave* (cling) and *cleave* (split). The difficulty is to distinguish between homonymy and polysemy.

**Polysemy** is a sense relation in which a listeme has acquired more than one sense (those with only one meaning are monosemic). The listeme *flight*, for example, can mean all of the following: (i) the power of flying; (ii) an air journey; (iii) a series of steps; (iv) a digression; (v) a unit of the air force. These senses are clearly related and it is possible to see how they might have the same origin. Many nouns acquire new meanings by having a literal and a metaphoric meaning, for example parts of the body, *eye*, *leg*, *hand*, *foot*, applied to *needle*, *chair*, *clock*, and *bed*. And some nouns acquire a concrete and an abstract sense. So *text*, *book*, and *thesis*, can be used to refer to a specific item, as in *I've had my thesis bound*, or to a more general one, as in *I agree with your thesis*.

At the theoretical level the distinction between homonymy and polysemy is clear enough in that homonyms are separate listemes such that the relationship between them is accidental. It is similar to discovering that one has a double somewhere to whom one is totally unrelated. In the case of polysemy, however, we are dealing with a single lexical item which has acquired more than one sense. In practice, however, the distinction is often difficult to make. The most straightforward solution is to take word origin, or etymology, as the principal criterion. But that would lead us to decisions which are counter-intuitive. *Pupil* (eye) and *pupil* (student) have a common origin and are therefore, by an etymological criterion, polysemic. But the senses are so unrelated that most people would intuitively classify them as separate listemes, i.e. as homonyms. A similar problem exists with *sole* (fish) and *sole* (shoe). Arguably a more useful approach is to look for a common core of meaning existing between the senses, and to set the matter of etymology aside.

*Further reading:*
Allan, Keith 2001. *Natural Language Semantics*.
Oxford & Malden MA: Blackwell.
Cruse, D. Alan 2004. *Meaning In Language: An Introduction to Semantics and Pragmatics*.
2nd edn. Oxford: Oxford University Press.
Saeed, John I. 2003. *Semantics*. 2nd edn. Oxford:
Blackwell.

**Hyponymy** A hierarchical sense relation that exists between two terms in which the sense of one is included in the other. Terms such as *daisy*, *daffodil* and *rose* all contain the meaning of *flower*. That is to say, they are all hyponyms of *flower*. The more general term is called the **superordinate** or hypernym. Much of the vocabulary is linked by such systems of inclusion: *red* is a hyponym of *colour*,

*flute* of *musical instrument*, and *hammer* of *tool*. Sometimes a word may be superordinate to itself; for instance *dog* has a sexual contrast with *bitch* (in this sense, *dog* and *bitch* are contraries), but both are also hyponyms of *dog*. Hyponymy is a vertical relationship which is fundamental to the way in which we classify things. Most dictionaries rely on it for the provision of definitions ('a chair is a type of furniture', 'a flute is a type of musical instrument', and so on; but see Chapter 2.13). The set of terms that are hyponyms of the same super-ordinate term are co-hyponyms, for example, *red*, *black*, and *yellow*, in the colour system. As such, they are contraries (or incompatibles). That is, if something is red it is not black or green, but if it is not red we don't know what colour it is.

*Further reading:*
Allan, Keith 2001. *Natural Language Semantics*.
Oxford & Malden MA: Blackwell.
Cruse, D. Alan 2004. *Meaning In Language: An Introduction to Semantics and Pragmatics*.
2nd edn. Oxford: Oxford University Press.
Saeed, John I. 2003. *Semantics*. 2nd edn. Oxford:
Blackwell.

**Idiolect** The speech habits of an individual. Each of us is unique in the way in which we use language. Although our speech may predominantly belong to a particular dialect, nonetheless the selection of features we make within that variety will differ from that of other users of the same dialect. In a sense we all have our own dialect: a product of where we were born, our age, sex, education, race, nationality, and personality. Wales 1989 likens it to a fingerprint. When sociolinguists study dialect they are really studying an abstraction made up of the regularly recurring features of speakers in a particular speech community. Idiolect is a useful term, not only in sociolinguistics, but also in stylistics. Authors can be said to have their own idiolect in the sense that each will have their own set of individual stylistic features. Some writers also habitually construct characters with distinctive language traits. Many of Dickens's comic creations, for example, are characterized in this way.

*Reference and further reading:*
Wales, Katie 1989. *A Dictionary of Stylistics*.
London: Longman.

**Illocutions** Austin 1962 alerted us to the fact that the speaker does something when making an utterance. Some examples are that the speaker:

| STATES A FACT OR AN OPINION | *Semantics can be difficult.* |
|---|---|
| CONFIRMS OR DENIES SOMETHING | *It's not true that Marilyn committed suicide.* |
| MAKES A PREDICTION | *It'll rain tonight.* |
| MAKES A PROMISE | *I'll be with you in five minutes.* |
| MAKES A REQUEST | *What's the time?* |
| OFFERS THANKS OR AN INVITATION | *Can you come to dinner next Saturday?* |
| ISSUES AN ORDER OR AN UMPIRE'S DECISION | *Out!* |
| GIVES ADVICE OR PERMISSION | *Yes, of course you can leave early today.* |
| NAMES A CHILD OR A SHIP | *I name this ship 'QE3'.* |
| SWEARS AN OATH | *I swear allegiance to the Crown.* |

In making an utterance, the speaker performs an **illocutionary act** by using a particular locution (the words used with their senses) with the **illocutionary force** of a statement, a confirmation, a denial, a prediction, a promise, a request, and so on. Although an utterance has more than one illocutionary force, it will usually have only one message to convey; the illocutionary force that carries this message is said to be the **illocutionary point** of the utterance. In (1) the locution is what you see following the example number.

(1)  I'll make the tea.

Context of utterance will determine the reference of 'I' and 'the tea'. The primary illocutionary force is a statement about a future act. It may be used with a second illocutionary force: to make a promise. If this promise is taken to be the speaker's illocutionary intention, (1) has the illocutionary point "The speaker is promising to make the tea."

*References and further reading:*
Allan, Keith 1994. Speech act theory – an overview. In *Encyclopedia of Language and*

*Linguistics*, ed. by Ronald E. Asher. Vol. 8. Oxford: Pergamon Press, pp. 4127–38.
Allan, Keith 2001. *Natural Language Semantics*. Oxford & Malden MA: Blackwell.
Austin, John L. 1962. *How to Do Things with Words*. Oxford: Clarendon Press.
Austin, John L. 1975. *How To Do Things With Words*. 2nd edn, ed. James O. Urmson and Marina Sbisà. Oxford: Oxford University Press [First edn 1962].
Bach, Kent and Robert M. Harnish 1979. *Linguistic Communication and Speech Acts*. Cambridge, MA: MIT Press.
Searle, John R. and Daniel Vanderveken 1985. *Foundations of Illocutionary Logic*. Cambridge: Cambridge University Press.

**Implicature, impliciture, and explicature** All of these are kinds of inference. The term implicature derives from Grice 1975, where he identified **conversational implicatures** as inferences which derive from the cooperative principle. Allan 2001 and Levinson 2000 refer to the bolded inferences within square brackets in sentences (1)–(5) below as conversational implicatures. Bach 1994; 2006 called them **implicitures** because the inference is implicit in the words uttered. Carston 2002 (and other relevance theorists) would refer to these same inferences as **explicatures**.

(1)  Harry and Sally got married on Sunday [**to each other**].
(2)  Ralph is ready [**to do something identified through common ground**].
(3)  Bill got drunk and [**as a result**] drove his car into a tree.
(4)  Harry crashed his BMW [**Harry drives (and probably owns) a BMW**].
(5)  If [**and only if**] you stop crying, I'll buy you an ice-cream.

Bach and Carston (and their followers) claim that Gricean conversational implicatures arise only from the circumstances under which an utterance is made, the common ground, as in (6) where the relevance of Y's remark is as a response to X's question.

(6)  X:  What happened to that steak I left out to thaw?
     Y:  Oh dear, the dog was looking very pleased with herself just now.

The point about all of (1)–(6) is that they can usually be cancelled; although relevance theorists claim that explicatures cannot be cancelled – a matter of considerable unresolved controversy.

Grice 1975; 1978 also identified **conventional implicature**. He gave so few examples that there is a great deal of controversy about the nature of conventional implicature. Allan 2001 suggests it is an uncancellable sense relation similar to entailment except that it does not typically hold between propositions (clauses). For instance, the meaning of (7) relies on the conventional implicature of *therefore* being "in consequence".

(7) Ed is an Englishman, therefore he is brave.

This meaning of *therefore* cannot be cancelled despite the fact that such a sentence expresses not a certain truth, but a prejudice that depends on the very word *therefore*. *Two fingers* is a conventional implicature of *four fingers*, thus it follows that if *Max had four fingers amputated* he had two amputated (indeed two lots of two).

*References and further reading:*

Allan, Keith 2001. *Natural Language Semantics*. Oxford & Malden MA: Blackwell.
Bach, Kent 1994. Conversational impliciture. *Mind and Language* 9: 124–62.
Bach, Kent 2006. Impliciture vs. explicature: what's the difference? <http://userwww.sfsu.edu/~kbach/Bach.ImplExpl.pdf>.
Carston, Robyn 2002. *Thoughts and Utterances: The Pragmatics of Explicit Communication*. Oxford & Malden MA: Blackwell.
Grice, H. Paul 1975. Logic and conversation. In *Syntax and Semantics 3: Speech Acts*, ed. by Peter Cole and Jerry L. Morgan. New York: Academic Press, pp. 41–58. Reprinted in H. Paul Grice *Studies in the Way of Words*. Cambridge MA: Harvard University Press. 1986.
Grice, H. Paul 1978. Further notes on logic and conversation. In *Syntax and Semantics 9: Pragmatics*, ed. by Peter Cole. New York: Academic Press, pp. 113–27. Reprinted in H. Paul Grice *Studies in the Way of Words*. Cambridge MA: Harvard University Press. 1986: 41–57.
Jaszczolt, Katarzyna M. 2002. *Semantics and Pragmatics: Meaning in Language and Discourse*. Harlow: Longman.
Levinson, Stephen C. 2000. *Presumptive Meanings: The Theory of Generalized Conversational Implicature*. Cambridge MA: MIT Press.

**Inference** An inference is a reasoned conclusion drawn from one or more assumptions (premises).

Abductive reasoning was championed by the early pragmatist Charles Peirce 1940 as an empirically focused procedure for the construction of classes and categories from observed data. Abductive inferences lead to testable hypotheses about states of affairs. Data are correlated on the basis of their similarity or by analogy with some known system, usually with an eye to their apparent function or relevance within the emerging general description. An example of abductive reasoning in historical linguistics is (1). (In these examples, (a1) = Assumption 1, (a2) = Assumption 2, (c) = Conclusion. An 'assumption' is sometimes called a 'premise'.)

(1) (a1) In the ancient Indic language Sanskrit, words for numbers 2–7 are *dva, tri, catur, pañca, ṣaṣ, sapta*. These are similar to number words in European languages known to be related to one another: e.g Slovak *dva*, Latin *duo* "2"; Slovak *tri*, Italian *tre* "3"; Latin *quattuor* "4"; Welsh *pump*, German *fünf* "5"; Spanish *seis*, English *six* "6"; Latin *septem* "7".

(a2) If Sanskrit were related to these European languages (i.e. they all have a common ancestor), the similarity would be a matter of course.

(c) There is a reason to suspect that Sanskrit is related to European languages.

(1(a2)) is an imaginative leap because Sanskrit is separated by time and thousands of kilometres from the European languages, and it was spoken by a different race. (1(a2)) expresses the intuition underlying the creation of the hypothesis in (1(c)). The essential contribution of intuition to scientific theory is widely recognized among philosophers of science (see Poincaré 1946: 214f, 219; Einstein 1973: 221).

Before Peirce, abduction was included within induction. An example of inductive inference is (2).

(2) (a1) Every day till now the sun has risen in the east.

    (c) If we check tomorrow, the sun will have risen in the east.

The inductive inference (2(c)) is a prediction based on sampling; if the sampling technique is good, the prediction will probably be verified: (2(c)) is highly probable given the assumption (2(a1)), but it is not necessarily going to be the case. Inductive inference is used in linguistics: for instance, if you are told that almost all French nouns ending in *–ion* are feminine then you can inductively infer that the next French noun you encounter that ends in *–ion* will most probably be feminine. Induction uncovers tendencies, but not certainties, and so is open to dispute; so, the problem with inductive reasoning is exactly that it identifies conclusions in which we have some degree of confidence (given the assumptions) but not the kind of confidence that is given to deductions.

In formal semantics and other formal systems (such as logics) deductive reasoning is required because, provided the assumptions are correct and the reasoning process valid, a consistent conclusion is guaranteed. From (a1) *A bachelor is a man who has never married* and (a2) *Max is married*, we can deduce that (c) *Max is not a bachelor*.

An Aristotelian syllogistic is (3).

(3) (a1)    All humans are mortal.
& (a2)    All Greeks are human.

    (c)    All Greeks are mortal.

If we vary this by making premise (3(a1)) false, *All humans are immortal,* the conclusion must be *All Greeks are immortal* – clearly demonstrating that false assumptions will lead by valid argument to consistent but probably false conclusions. Not always, though:

(4) (a1)    All women are cats.
& (a2)    All cats are human.

    (c)    All women are human.

It follows that we must get our assumptions right if we are to use deductive inference to seek true conclusions. Note that valid reasoning is defined within a system (a logic) whereas truth is defined in relation to (models of) worlds.

Pragmatic inference is common in resolving some kinds of anaphora, e.g. *The vet smelled the dog's breath when she bit her*; and for supplying appropriate contextual information to interpret 'jack' in (5) and (6).

(5) John's never gonna get that wheel off, he hasn't got *the jack*.

(6) John's going to lose this trick, he hasn't got *the jack*.

It is also common in the use of scripts or frames to interpret examples such as the italicized definite noun phrases in the following:

She entered the doctor's surgery. As she approached *the receptionist,* she noticed that *the ceiling* was beautiful.

In cases such as this the inferences rely on the general knowledge that surgeries have receptionists and rooms have ceilings.

*References:*
Einstein, Albert 1973. *Ideas and Opinions*. Laurel edn. New York: Dell [First published 1954].
Peirce, Charles S. 1940. *The Philosophy of Peirce: Selected Writings*, ed. by Justus Buchler. London: Routledge and Kegan Paul.
Poincaré, Henri 1946. *The Foundations of Science: Science and Hypothesis, The Value of Science, Science and Method.* Transl. by George B. Halstead. Lancaster PA: The Science Press.

*Further reading:*
Allan, Keith 2001. *Natural Language Semantics*. Oxford & Malden MA: Blackwell.
Allan, Keith 2006b. Inference: abduction, induction, and deduction. In *Encyclopedia of Languages and Linguistics.* 2nd edn, ed. by E. Keith Brown. 14 vols. Oxford: Elsevier, pp. 5: 651–4.
Clark, Herbert H. 1977. Inferences in comprehension. In *Basic Processes in Reading: Perception and Comprehension*, ed. by David LaBerge and S. Jay Samuels. Hillsdale: Lawrence Erlbaum, pp. 243–63.

**Infix** See **Affix, prefix, infix, suffix, circumfix**.

**International Phonetic Alphabet or IPA** In the late nineteenth century it was recognized that in order to properly capture in writing the sounds that human beings can make there needed to be special kind of graphic representation such that each symbol is uniquely associated with just one phone (i.e. one speech sound). This was more or less accomplished when the IPA was established in 1886. In addition to Romic script based on our everyday orthography, the IPA uses Greek symbols such as [θ] and [λ], special symbols like [ʃ] and [ʔ], digraphs like [ʧ], and assigns new values to [x] and [q] (all of which we look at in Chapter 2.1).

*Further reading:* Chapter 2.2; http://www2.arts. gla.ac.uk/IPA/ipa.html.

**Intonation** Intonation is the variation in pitch over a sense (meaning) group rather than a syllable. The same word or sequence of words uttered with different intonation patterns conveys different meanings.

*Further reading:* Chapter 2.2 and
Bolinger, Dwight 1989. *Intonation and Its Uses.*
   Stanford: Stanford University Press.
Clark, John, Colin Yallop and Janet Fletcher 2007.
   *An Introduction to Phonetics and Phonology.*
   3rd edn. Malden MA: Blackwell.

**Jargon or register** In stylistics, sociolinguistics and applied linguistics, **register** refers to a socially, or situationally, defined style of language (see Chapter 2.11). Many fields of discourse, such as religion and medicine, have their own special language varieties. These are professional or technical registers (also known as jargons). **Jargon** is the language peculiar to a trade, profession, or other group; the language used in a body of spoken or written texts dealing with a circumscribed domain in which speakers share a common specialized vocabulary, habits of word usage, and forms of expression. (Many linguists use the term **genre** to designate these field-specific varieties, particularly those with a common purpose.)

   Jargons differ from one another grammatically and sometimes phonologically or typographically, as can be seen by comparing a statement of some of the requirements on the cricket-field with the two-line excerpt from a knitting pattern, then the wedding invitation below it, and all of these with the excerpt from a Wordsworth poem and a text message version of that (such as might be conveyed using the SMS facility on a mobile phone).

Cast on 63 sts: Knit 6 rows plain knitting.
7th row: K4, wl. fwd. K2 tog to the last 3 sts. K3.

A fast-medium right arm inswing bowler needs two or three slips, a deep third man, a gully, a deepish mid-off, a man at deep fine leg and another at wide mid-on.

R.S.V.P. 1st May, 1992

| Earth has not anything to shew more fair: Dull would he be of soul who could pass by A sight so touching in its majesty. <br><br>(Wordsworth *Upon Westminster Bridge*) | erth nt a thng so brill hes dul v soul pssng by sght of mjstic tch. <br><br>(Peter Finch *N Wst Brdg*, a text message version of the Wordsworth lines from http://.guardian.co.uk//// 0,12241,785819,00.html in September 2002 |
| --- | --- |

Jargon has two functions:

> to serve as a technical or specialist language
> to promote in-group solidarity, and to exclude as out-groupers those people who do not use the jargon.

To the initiated, jargon is efficient, economical, and even crucial in that it can capture distinctions not made in the ordinary language. Linguists, for instance, redefine everyday terms like *sentence, word, syllable* and *grammar*, and add a number of new terms to overcome imprecision and to distinguish things that non-linguists ignore and, in consequence, ordinary language lacks terms for. They distinguish between *grammatical, orthographic,* and *phonological words* as well as introducing terms like *lex, lexeme, morph* and *morpheme* to capture additional distinctions.

Because it is founded on a common interest, the most remarkable characteristic of a jargon is its specialized vocabulary and idiom. While jargons facilitate communication among in-groupers on the one hand, on the other they erect communication barriers to keep out-groupers out. It is, of course, out-groupers who find jargon offensive.

A jargon cannot be precisely defined because the boundaries of any one particular jargon are impossible to draw non-arbitrarily.

It is impossible to taboo jargon. Jargon cannot be translated into 'ordinary English' (or whatever language) because there is no such thing. Changing the jargon alters the message: a speaker simply cannot exchange *faeces* for *shit* or *terrorist* for *freedom-fighter* or even *bottlenecks* for *localized capacity deficiencies* without changing the connotations of the message s/he intends to convey. There is no convenient substitute for some jargon: to replace legalese *defendant* with *a person against whom civil proceedings are brought* is communicatively inefficient. It would be inappropriate for a lawyer not to use jargon when creating a legal document: that is exactly what legalese is for. Legal language is difficult because laws are complex and not because lawyers try to obfuscate. Similar remarks apply to other well-motivated uses of jargon.

The term 'jargon' was also used of a pidgin trade language such as Chinook Jargon: see George Gibbs *A Dictionary of the Chinook Jargon, or Trade Language of Oregon* (Washington DC: Smithsonian Institution. 1863).

*Further reading:*

Allan, Keith and Kate Burridge 2006. *Forbidden Words: Taboo and the Censoring of Language*. Cambridge: Cambridge University Press.
Nash, Walter 1993. *Jargon: Its Uses and Abuses*. Oxford: Blackwell.
Wardhaugh, Ronald 2006. *An Introduction to Sociolinguistics*. 5th edn. Oxford: Basil Blackwell [First edn. 1986].

**Langue and parole** *Langue* is the term introduced by Ferdinand de Saussure (Saussure 1931) to refer to the language system shared by members of a speech community. It is comparable with the Chomsky 1965 notion of competence, with the difference that competence is a term which relates to the individual's ability rather than to the linguistic system itself. We could say that part of our competence as native speakers of a language is a knowledge of its *langue*, i.e. its communicative system. Nevertheless Saussure wrote:

> Language [*la langue* ... ] is a system of signs where the most essential thing is the union of sense (meaning) with the acoustic/auditory image, and where the two parts of the sign [signifier and signified] are both psychological entities [*sont également psychiques*]. (Saussure 1931: 32)

If both signifier and signified are psychological categories, how is the signifier $S_x$ of signified $X$ different from the signifier $S_y$ of signified $Y$? The answer lies in the differential value [*valeur*] of each within the system of *langue*: 'each signifier and signified consists of nothing but *difference* from every other signifier and signified in the system' (Joseph 2004: 60).

*Langue*, the system of signs ("language system"), and *parole* ("speech"), together constitute *langage* ("language").

> The study of language [*langage*] has two parts: one, the most important, has for its object the language system [*langue*] which is fundamentally social and independent of individual speakers; its study is exclusively psychological. The other is secondary; the focus of *la parole* is the individual speaker's part in language; it consists of speaking [*phonation*] and is psycho-physical. (Saussure 1931: 37)

The idea probably derives from Hermann Paul 1880; 1891 (see Allan 2009a for discussion of this matter). There are many similarities between Saussure's notion of *parole* and Chomsky's notion of performance.

> The language system [*la langue*] is not a creation of the speaker, it is something that the individual passively assimilates. ... Speech

[*parole*] is, by contrast, an act of individual will and intellect. (Saussure 1931: 30)

*Parole* is the source for language change and development, and so the source for *langue*.

*References and further reading:*
Allan, Keith 2009a. *The Western Classical Tradition in Linguistics*. 2nd edn.London: Equinox.
Chomsky, Noam 1965. *Aspects of the Theory of Syntax*. Cambridge MA: MIT Press.
Joseph, John E. 2004. The linguistic sign. In *The Cambridge Companion to Saussure*, ed. by Carol Sanders. Cambridge: Cambridge University Press, pp. 59–75.
Paul, Hermann 1880. *Prinzipien der Sprachgeschichte*. Halle: Max Niemeyer.
Paul, Hermann 1891. *Principles of the History of Language*. Transl. by Herbert A. Strong. London: Longman, Green, & Co.
Saussure, Ferdinand de 1931. *Cours de Linguistique Générale*. Publié par Charles Bally et Albert Sechehaye avec la collaboration de Albert Riedlinger. 3rd edn. Paris: Payot [First edn published 1916].
Saussure, Ferdinand de 1974. *A Course in General Linguistics*. Glasgow: Fontana/Collins [Transl. by Wade Baskin from the 3rd edition of *Cours de Linguistique Générale*. Paris: Payot, 1931. First edn published in 1916].

**Lexeme** A term frequently used in linguistics instead of *word*. This is because individual words can have different forms while still, in one sense, remaining the 'same word'. So, for example, a word such as *nose* has a written form <nose> and a phonological form /noʊz/. Most people would not want to call these two different words. Neither would they if we put *nose* into the plural, *noses*, since all we have done is grammatically inflect it. The term *lexeme* helps to solve these difficulties by specifying an abstract unit which underlies the physical form. The lexeme *nose* has a number of different forms depending on whether it is transmitted by Morse code, semaphore, speech, or writing. Moreover, as a noun lexeme it has a singular and a plural form. It is the abstract unit lexeme which is listed in the dictionary as a listeme. You won't, for example, find forms such as *walks*, *walking* and *walked* listed among diction-

ary entries because they are simply grammatical variants of the root lexeme, *walk*.

Part of the usefulness of the lexeme/word distinction is that it enables us to deal with items that change their grammatical category through conversion (or zero derivation). If we change *nose* from a noun into a verb, as in *I'll nose around for a bit*, we have clearly altered it quite substantially even though it looks the same. It can now be inflected as a verb: *noses, nosed, nosing, to nose*. It's the abstract unit that has changed: while we still have the same word form, we have a new lexeme.

All this makes clear the inexactness of the term *word*. Most of us don't have to worry very much about the elasticity of it until we come to study linguistics. It's only then that the need for a more precise vocabulary becomes apparent.

*Further reading:* Chapter 2.3 and
Allan, Keith 2001. *Natural Language Semantics*. Oxford & Malden MA: Blackwell.
Bauer, Laurie 2003. *Introducing Linguistic Morphology*. 2nd edn. Edinburgh: Edinburgh University Press [First edn 1988].
Katamba, Francis and John T. Stonham 2006. *Morphology*. 2nd edn. Basingstoke: Palgrave.

**Lexical classes** See **Morphosyntactic classes, lexical classes, word classes** or **parts of speech**.

**Lexicon or dictionary** Most people recognize that meanings are a property of words and that word meanings are stored in dictionaries. But this popular notion that words are the building blocks for language construction is not precise enough. The defining characteristic of the basic building blocks is that they are form~meaning pairs but their meaning is not determinable from any meaning that can be assigned to their constituent forms, e.g. the meaning of *shuttle* cannot be correctly computed from the meaning of *shut–* and the meaning of *–tle*. So, the language user must memorize each basic building block individually, as a form paired with its meaning. All that a grammar can do is list them in the lexicon or dictionary (whether mental or physical). For that reason, Di Sciullo and Williams 1987 dubbed them **listemes**. We language users combine listemes into words, phrases, sentences, and longer texts. At each level we construct meanings. The meaning of the word *bachelors* is composed from at least the listemes *bachelor* and *–s* and also the morphosyntactic relationship between the two listemes.

The **lexis** of a language is its vocabulary or word hoard. You will often come across the term in its adjectival form, *lexical*. A **lexical item** is either a lexeme or a listeme. The complete inventory of all the listemes possessed by native speakers is referred to as a *lexicon*. 'Why not simply use the term "dictionary"?' you might ask. Some say that dictionaries are repositories of information about lexical items whereas lexicons exist in our minds; but this distinction between *lexicon* and *dictionary* is not rigidly maintained. Most linguists agree that we all possess a mental lexicon, in which is stored the mental representation of all that we know about the listemes of our language; 'formal' information about how to pronounce and write them, 'morphosyntactic' information about the word class they belong to and their syntactic properties, and 'semantic' information about what their meaning is. In generative grammars morphosyntactic and semantic properties are often presented as sets of features as a convenient shorthand. Thus the entry for *dog* will look something like:

<dog>, /dɒg/ [+N, +count, +concrete]
[+canine]

This gives the spelling and British/Australasian pronunciation of this concrete count noun for a canine. Since all canines are animate, we rely on some general redundancy rule that [+canine] → [+animate] and we, therefore, don't need to specify both [+animate, +canine].

The morphosyntactic information about verbs typically includes information about their argument structure (also referred to as theta-marking). There is a great deal of controversy about the best way to describe the participant roles (or theta-roles) of arguments. The single argument of the verb *die* for instance is variously described as 'undergoer' and 'patient' which is appropriate for one of the arguments of the verb *kill*, the other one being 'actor' or 'causer' or 'agent'. In *John killed Bill*, John acts to cause the death that Bill undergoes as a result of which his state changes (which makes him a 'patient'). For the three place (ditransitive) verb *give*, the giver is the 'actor' or 'agent', what is given is an 'undergoer', 'theme', or 'patient', and the recipient is 'dative' or 'recipient' (and usually the

'beneficiary'). The verb *know*, as in *Harry knows my uncle*, has an 'experiencer' or 'cognizer' as an 'actor' (the knower) and the person or thing known is the 'undergoer', 'theme' or 'patient'. We need to be able to represent the fact that the activity denoted by *Bill is dying* is of different kind from the act denoted in *John is killing Bill* and that \*John is knowing Bill is not well-formed because *know* does not denote an activity but a state of awareness.

The lexicon is a bin for storing listemes, but it needs to be closely related to an encyclopedia or knowledge base. Whereas a lexicon gives information about listemes, the encyclopedia gives information on their denotata (what the words are used to refer to in real and imaginary worlds). Standard desktop dictionaries normally include some encyclopedic information. There is controversy over how much encyclopedic information the lexicographer should include in the lexicon – both a desktop dictionary and a model of the mental lexicon.

*Further reading:*

Aitchison, Jean 2003. *Words in the Mind: An Introduction to the Mental Lexicon*. 3rd edn. Oxford: Blackwell.

Allan, Keith 2001. *Natural Language Semantics*. Oxford & Malden MA: Blackwell.

Di Sciullo, Anna-Maria and Edwin Williams 1987. *On the Definition of Word*. Cambridge MA: MIT Press.

Dowty, David R. 1991. Thematic proto-roles and argument selection. *Language* 67: 547–619.

Goldberg, Adele E. 1995. *Constructions: A Construction Grammar Approach to Argument Structure*. Chicago: University of Chicago Press.

Jackendoff, Ray S. 1990. *Semantic Structures*. Cambridge MA: MIT Press.

Van Valin, Robert D. Jr 2005. *Exploring the Syntax-Semantics Interface*. Cambridge: Cambridge University Press.

**Liaison** See **Epenthesis**.

**Listeme** A **listeme** is a language expression whose meaning is not determinable from the meanings (if any) of its constituent forms and which, therefore, a language user must memorize as a combination of form and meaning.

(See entry for **Lexicon**.)

*Further reading:*
Allan, Keith 2001. *Natural Language Semantics*. Oxford & Malden MA: Blackwell.
Di Sciullo, Anna-Maria and Edwin Williams 1987. *On the Definition of Word*. Cambridge MA: MIT Press.

**Markedness** The concept of markedness is variously interpreted in linguistics. In generative grammar it refers to a distinction between sets of features, where one is considered to be default or neutral and the other non-neutral. So, for example, there is a formal feature marking the plural in English count nouns, i.e. the addition of –s; the plural is therefore **marked**, and the singular **unmarked**. It is the unmarked form that is the citation form of the listeme (i.e. appears in a dictionary). In describing the singular as unmarked we are identifying it as the default form of the word, free from any modification, and the plural as derived from it by a process of marking. A similar case can be made for the verb inflections –s, –ed, –en, –ing. In feature analysis, +F is marked and –F unmarked, thus in phonology the feature [+voice] identifies a phone marked for voicing.

Other interpretations of marking involve frequency of occurrence rather than presence versus absence. Properties that can be found in many languages count as unmarked whereas those found in just a few are marked; thus, the clause sequence subjectˆverbˆobject is unmarked compared with objectˆverbˆsubject. In discourse analysis, for example, it is sometimes said that a falling intonation pattern is unmarked, because it is more common than a rising one (partly because it requires less air and correlates with breathing out). Yet another interpretation can be found in the semantic analysis of words, where pairs of items are seen as marked or unmarked, respectively, on the grounds that one has a wider distribution, or application, than another, e.g. *old~young*: *How old is John?* is less marked than *How young is John?* because the latter already presupposes he is young to some degree. A related sense has to do with specificity, where one term is more specific than another, e.g. *dog~bitch*: unmarked *dog* can be used to refer to animals of either sex, but *bitch* is marked because it is limited to a female.

The concept of markedness, therefore, can be used in a variety of contexts to distinguish what we can consider as the default, normative, or most common forms of items or features from those which are derived, non-normative, or less frequent.

*Further reading:*
Battistella, Edwin L. 1996. *The Logic of Markedness*. New York: Oxford University Press.
de Lacy, Paul 2006. *Markedness: Reduction and Preservation in Phonology*. Cambridge: Cambridge University Press.
Lyons, John 1968. *Introduction to Theoretical Linguistics*. London: Cambridge University Press.

**Medium and mode** These terms are sometimes used interchangeably in stylistics, although some linguists do attempt to distinguish them. **Medium** refers to the physical means by which a message is transmitted. In communication theory this could be almost anything, from the human body to clothing. As far as language is concerned there are two main media: speech (phonic medium), and writing (graphic medium). Occasionally 'medium' is also used to refer to the channel (q.v.) of communication, i.e. the technical means of transmission. A message in the phonic medium (speech) can be transmitted via several different channels: telephone, television, radio, and so on.

Speech and writing, then, are the distinctively linguistic media. The relationship between them, and the dynamics of speaker~hearer interaction which each involves, have been the subject of much study. Writing is not simply speech in another form; it involves a quite different attitude towards language and a different relationship between participants. Because it's a visual medium, rather than an oral one, it alters the way we perceive ourselves as linguistic beings. Cultures that are wholly oral often have a semi-magical view of language, in which words are part of the objects or people that they name. This is the source of spells and incantations, as well as oaths. The dynamics of orality and literacy are a central feature of communication theory.

At a less theoretical level, however, we have to acknowledge that speech and writing, although separate media, are not entirely discrete forms. A good deal of writing – dramatic dialogue, lectures, and much poetry – is written to be spoken. It is also true that people's speech is frequently influenced by things they have read. Characteristic, then, of advanced literate cultures, are complex media, in which speech and writing are intertwined. It's here that distinguishing between medium and mode can be useful. Those who make this distinction use the term *mode* to indicate the particular format or genre which a piece of writing, or speech, adopts. Letters, monologues, reports, poems, sermons are all constructed according to certain conventions either of speech, or of writing, or both. They have a rhetorical mode. One of the rhetorical conventions of letters, for example, is the greeting formula *Dear Sir/Madam* with its various degrees of informality *Dear Mr Jones/Jim*. When we read these greetings we interpret them conventionally, i.e. according to the rules of the genre.

*Further reading:*
Crystal, David 2003. *The Cambridge Encyclopedia of the English Language*. 2nd edn. Cambridge: Cambridge University Press.
Halliday, Michael A.K. and Christian M.I.M. Matthiessen 2004. *An Introduction to Functional Grammar*. 3rd edn. London: Arnold.


**Mentalese** The hypothetical 'language of thought' in which ideas are considered to exist prior to their expression in linguistic form. The concept of mentalese is an attempt to answer one of the perennial problems of linguistic inquiry concerning the relationship between thought and language. What kind of thought is possible without language is a question that has received a variety of answers. To George Orwell in his novel *Nineteen Eighty Four* (London: Secker & Warburg [First published 1949]), the abolition of words like *freedom* and *equality* was supposed by Big Brother to result in these ideas no longer being thinkable. However, as a consequence of the modern belief in the modular structure of language (see Fodor 1983), many linguists believe that language is a distinct faculty, quite separate from the general ability to think. If thought can exist independently of language, a question arises about its form and structure. It's here that the concept of mentalese comes in. To its exponents, mentalese is a logically based programme which uses symbols to represent concepts. 'People do not think in English or Chinese or Apache,' argues Steven Pinker 1994: 81; 'they think in a language of thought'. Being linguistically competent means 'knowing how to translate mentalese into strings of words and *vice*

*versa*' (*ibid.* p. 82). The concept of mentalese owes much of its currency to the work of the American psychologist Jerry Fodor, who popularized it in his book *The Language of Thought* (Fodor 1975).

*References and further reading:*
Fodor, Jerry A. 1975. *The Language of Thought*. New York: Thomas Crowell.
Fodor, Jerry A. 1983. *Modularity of Mind*. Cambridge MA: MIT Press.
Katz, Jerrold J. 1981. *Language and Other Abstract Objects*. Totowa NJ: Rowman and Littlefield.
Pinker, Steven 1994. *The Language Instinct: The New Science of Language and Mind*. London: Allen Lane.


**Meronymy** A part~whole relationship between the senses of words. *Cover* and *page*, for example, are meronyms of *book*, and *piston* and *valve* are meronyms of *internal combustion engine*. Meronymy is similar to hyponymy in reflecting a hierarchical relationship between words.

*Further reading:*
Allan, Keith 2001. *Natural Language Semantics*. Oxford & Malden MA: Blackwell.
Cruse, D. Alan 2004. *Meaning In Language: An Introduction to Semantics and Pragmatics*. 2nd edn. Oxford: Oxford University Press.
Saeed, John I. 2003. *Semantics*. 2nd edn. Oxford: Blackwell.


**Metaphor** Characteristically, a process in which one semantic field of reference is carried over, or transferred, to another. So, for example, in the sentence *The ship ploughed the water*, the field of farming is transferred to that of sailing through use of the verb *plough*. In traditional literary criticism, the field being described, in this case sailing, is referred to as the 'target' or 'tenor', and the field being used for the comparison, farming, is referred to as the 'source' or 'vehicle'.

There are two main positions on the role of metaphor in language. The first, often called the classical view, can be traced back to Aristotle. Basically, this sees metaphor as a kind of decorative addition to ordinary language. Metaphor is regarded as something outside normal language, requiring special forms of interpretation. A version of this is often adopted in the literal language theory. According to this, metaphor is a form of anomaly, or deviation, which a hearer recognizes as such before employing strategies to construct the figurative, or non-literal meaning. These usually involve lifting the selection restrictions on words. For example, we register the sentence *All our yesterdays have lighted fools the way to dusty death*, as anomalous or deviant, because the verb *light* doesn't normally select *yesterday* as an appropriate subject. As a consequence, we interpret the sentence by suppressing this feature, and any others which block interpretation, and highlight those which don't. In this particular instance one characteristic that a day and a candle could be said to share is transience, in that neither lasts very long.

A second approach views metaphor not as an anomaly requiring special methods of interpretation, but as an integral part of everyday language and thought. From this standpoint there is no real distinction between figurative and non-figurative language since all language is essentially metaphorical. An extension of this view can be found in the work of cognitive semanticists, though they usually adopt a position in which some distinction is made between literal and figurative language. Of principal importance here is the work of George Lakoff and others (Lakoff and Johnson 1980; Lakoff and Turner 1989), who see metaphor as a naturally occurring, everyday feature of language, and a consequence of the way in which we reason and think about the world.

Lakoff and Johnson distinguish three basic kinds of metaphors. With structural metaphors, one thing is experienced and understood in terms of another, e.g. *He defended his argument* ('an argument is war'), *His argument is founded on …* ('an argument is a building') and *His argument includes the idea that* ('an argument is a container'). With orientational metaphors, we transfer the physical environment to metaphysical or emotional experience, e.g. *His spirits rose* ('up is good') *He's feeling down* ('down is bad'). With ontological metaphors, we 'comprehend events, actions, activities and states [as] discrete entities or substances' (Lakoff and Johnson 1980: 5), e.g. *Are you going to the race?* – where an event in time is conceptualized as an object.

Much work has been done by cognitive linguists since 1980 describing the mental schemas which, it is argued, we construct as part of the process of conceptualizing experience. An example of such a schema is the path schema used in 'life is a journey' metaphors.

*References:*
Lakoff, George and Mark Johnson 1980. *Metaphors We Live By*. Chicago: University of Chicago Press.
Lakoff, George and Mark Turner 1989. *More Than Cool Reason. A field guide to poetic metaphor*. Chicago: University of Chicago Press.

*Further reading:*
Dirven, René and Ralf Pörings (eds) 2003. *Metaphor and Metonymy in Comparison and Contrast*. Berlin: Mouton de Gruyter.
Hiraga, Masako 2005. *Metaphor and Iconicity: A Cognitive Approach to Analysing Texts*. New York: Palgrave Macmillan.
Kövecses, Zoltán 2005. *Metaphor in Culture: Universality and Variation*. New York: Cambridge University Press.
Lakoff, George 1987. *Women, Fire, and Dangerous Things*. Chicago: University of Chicago Press.

**Modality** is indicated in English by a set of auxiliary verbs *can~could, may~might, shall~should, will~would* and *must* and modal adjectives and adverbs like *necessary~necessarily, possible~possibly*. The modal auxiliary verbs are always in first position in the verbal group, cf. *He **could** have been being difficult* but not *\*He have could been being difficult*; *\*He have been being could difficult*; and so on. The modal adjective occurs most typically in a cleft construction, e.g. *It's **possible** he was being difficult* and less usually *That he was being difficult is **possible***. The adverb may occur in a number of positions, e.g. ***Possibly** he was being difficult; He was **possibly** being difficult; He was being difficult, **possibly***.

Modal auxiliaries have a **root** or dynamic meaning, e.g.:

(1) Connie will insist on telephoning me at 11.30 at night.
(2) Suzie can speak Swahili.
(3) The President may, at his discretion, grant a reprieve.
(4) She must poke her nose into my business, she can't help herself.

These derive directly from the original meanings of these verbs; respectively: "have a will to", "know how to", "have the power or right to", "circumstances make it happen".

There are **epistemic** meanings. For *will* this is a willingness to commit and hence a prediction as in *Will you do the washing up?* and *Their pool will be about ten metres long.* Epistemic *can* expresses possibility, e.g. *Can you come to lunch on Sunday?* Epistemic *must* expresses necessity as in *The victim must have been shot several days ago.*

Finally there are **deontic** meanings as in the command of the first clause in *You will stop crying or I'll smack you* which may be paraphrased "it is required that you stop crying". The second clause contains an epistemic prediction about what will happen otherwise. Similarly with *Dogs must be on a lead* (are required to be). Deontic *can* and *may* express permission: *Of course your little friend can/may come home for tea.*

*Further reading:*

Allan, Keith 2001. *Natural Language Semantics*. Oxford & Malden MA: Blackwell.
Bybee, Joan L. and Suzanne Fleischman (eds) 1995. *Modality in Grammar and Discourse*. Amsterdam/Philadelphia: John Benjamins.
Coates, Jennifer 1983. *The Semantics of Modal Auxiliaries*. London: Croom Helm.
Huddleston, Rodney and Geoffrey K. Pullum 2002. *The Cambridge Grammar of the English Language*. Cambridge: Cambridge University Press.
Palmer, Frank R. 2001. *Mood and Modality*. 2nd edn. Cambridge: Cambridge University Press.

**Mood** The traditional moods of the classical grammars are indicative (incorporating declarative and interrogative), imperative, and subjunctive. These moods correlate with different clause-types and are in contrast with one another. In English, however, most clauses that have traditionally been named subjunctive do not contrast with the indicative, cf. *I wish I **were** rich; **Could** you post this letter for me? Let it **be brought** here; I **should leave** at once, if I **were** you; I suggest that she **be sacked***. There is a body of opinion that these traditional moods should be abandoned in favour of the polar distinction between **realis** (real) and **irrealis** (not-real) moods, with the traditional

categories ranged between them to accommodate the fact that, whereas this distinction appears to be language universal, different languages locate different clause-types in different locations. At the realis pole are declaratives. Hypotheticals such as subjunctives and optatives are located towards or at the irrealis pole, cf. English *Would that he would drop dead.* In some languages, imperatives, e.g. *Have a good day*, are realis and in others irrealis. Futures and negatives tend to be irrealis.

*Further reading:*

Allan, Keith 2006a. Clause-type, primary illocution, and mood-like operators in English. *Language Sciences* 28: 1–50.
Mithun, Marianne 1995. On the relativity of irreality. In *Modality in Grammar and Discourse*, ed. by Joan L. Bybee and Suzanne Fleischman. Amsterdam/Philadelphia: John Benjamins, pp. 367–88.
Palmer, Frank R. 2001. *Mood and Modality*. 2nd edn. Cambridge: Cambridge University Press.
Palmer, Frank R. 2003. Modality in English: theoretical, descriptive and typological issues. In *Modality in Contemporary English*, ed. by Roberta Facchinetti, Manfred Krug and Frank R. Palmer. Berlin/New York: Mouton de Gruyter, pp. 1–17.

**Morphology, morpheme, allomorph, and morph**
Morphology studies the internal structures of words. A **morpheme** is the smallest unit of syntactic analysis with semantic specification. A word like *unhappy* consists of two morphemes {*un*}+{*happy*}. Each morpheme is associated with a particular meaning and in this case they differ in status. *Happy* is known as a free morpheme, i.e. it can stand alone as a word, while *un*– is a bound morpheme that must be attached to a free (or another bound) morpheme. Morphemes are abstract constructs realized by allomorphs.

An **allomorph** is a variant form of a morpheme. The meaning of the English word *rabbits* is transparently composed from the meaning of the noun *rabbit* and the plural morpheme PL indicated by the final –*s*. The plural morpheme in English is instantiated by a variety of **allomorphs**, e.g. the bold italic parts of

chair*s*, church*es*, th*ose*, ox*en*, l*i*ce, dat*a*, seraph*im*, two deer (ZERO MORPH)

Whereas the **morph** is a form (an etic category), the morpheme is emic, i.e. an abstract theoretical construct.

*Further reading:* Chapter 2.3 and

Bauer, Laurie 2003. *Introducing Linguistic Morphology*. 2nd edn. Edinburgh: Edinburgh University Press [First edn 1988].

Booij, Geert 2005. *The Grammar of Words: An Introduction to Linguistic Morphology*. Oxford: Oxford University Press.

Bubeník, Vít 1999. *An Introduction to the Study of Morphology*. Munich: Lincom Europa.

**Morphosyntactic classes, lexical classes, word classes or parts of speech** The traditional nine parts of speech are: noun, verb, participle, article, pronoun, adverb, preposition, conjunction, and interjection. Today, participles are not normally counted as a separate morphosyntactic (or lexical) class and interjections tend to be ignored altogether. From the time of the Ancient Greeks, these lexical classes have been given syntactic and notional descriptions, such as 'a noun is inflected for case [this was true for Greek and Latin] and denotes a proper name or a common name for person, thing or event.' The same criteria are still used. For present-day English we should not use a syntactic criterion for nouns that refer to case, though it is sometimes incorrectly said that nouns can take the genitive as in *the cat's whiskers* – the possessive is actually marked on noun phrases. Instead we refer to number marking and co-occurrence with a **determiner**. There are also functional criteria such as that nouns are the head elements of noun phrases, and that noun phrases function as the arguments of clause predicates that are typically verbs.

We identify morphosyntactic classes in part by their morphological properties, in part by their distributional possibilities within a **syntagm** (construction). In order to name something we use a noun phrase consisting minimally of a noun, perhaps an adjective, probably a determiner which may be an article or a demonstrative. In order to attribute something to what has been named we will need a predicate consisting, in part at least, of a verb. The verb or its auxiliaries will be inflected for tense and aspect; the verbal group may contain a modal, it will certainly contain

an indication of mood. Adverbs typically modify verbs in some way, e.g. *speak quickly, drive fast*. These single adverbs are effectively functioning as the heads of adverbial phrases, which may consist of certain types of noun (e.g. *tomorrow* in *He's arriving tomorrow*) or may be marked by prepositions as in *He'll be here **at** three o'clock* (which has a spatial followed by a temporal adverbial) or subordinating conjunctions as in ***Because** she was blind, Arabella couldn't find the needle she'd dropped; **When** she arrives, show her to the Green Room.*

Morphosyntactic classes fall into two kinds. There are the major lexical categories, also called open classes because they readily take additions: nouns, verbs, adjectives, adverbs. Then there are minor classes, sometimes called grammatical or closed classes: prepositions, pronouns, articles, and conjunctions.

*Further reading:*

Börjars, Kersti and Kate Burridge 2001. *Introducing English Grammar*. London: Edward Arnold.

Brown, E. Keith and Jim Miller (eds) 1999. *Concise Encyclopedia of Grammatical Categories*. Oxford: Elsevier.

Hurford, James R. 1994. *Grammar: A Student's Guide*. Cambridge: Cambridge University Press.

Katamba, Francis 2005. *English Words: Structure, History, Usage*. London: Routledge.

**Noun** In some school grammars a noun is defined as the 'name of a person, place or thing'. In good traditional grammars (see Allan 2009a), as in modern linguistics, formal, distributional and functional criteria are invoked. According to these criteria a noun is a type of word (part of speech) that behaves in a particular manner and this will vary from language to language (and sometimes from dialect to dialect). In English, nouns may be used countably, in which case they have a zero inflection for the singular and normally some inflection marking the plural, e.g wine~wine**s**, child~child**ren**. Nouns typically function as the heads (essential elements of) **noun phrases**. In English, noun phrases (NP) are often marked by initial articles *the* or *a(n)~some* or by demonstratives *this~these, that~those*. The NP may also have an adjective preceding or following the noun, e.g. *a bright star, the stars visible*. In many languages, nouns take case markings, e.g. Latin *fēmina* ("woman.NOM.S"), *fēminam* ("woman.ACC.S"), *fēminae* (GEN.S or DAT.S or NOM.PL), *fēminā* (ABL.S), *fēminas* (ACC.PL), *fēminārum* (GEN.PL), *fēminīs* (DAT. PL or ABL.PL); but in English, genitive case marking is cliticized to the NP as in *the man next door's cat* (the cat belonging to *the man next door*).

Allan 1980 showed that there are countability preferences among nouns that can be established by a set of tests such as whether the head noun may be quantified by *one*, or the singular may be quantified by *all*, or if a plural head noun is preceded by a fuzzy denumerator such as *(a) few, several, many, a dozen or so, about fifty*, and high rounded numbers. These demonstrate that there are the following degrees of countability, ranged from most countable (*car*) to least countable:

*car < oak < cattle < Himalayas / scissors < mankind < admiration < equipment*

What this proves is that the simplistic binary distinction often made between count versus mass nouns is inept. A similar conclusion probably applies to several other subcategorizations of nouns, such as that a noun always falls into only one gender or noun class. The true picture is more complicated.

From this brief overview of noun subclassifications it should be evident that arriving at a descriptive account of nounness is not without its problems. As with most descriptive phenomena we are forced to rely on a fairly broad range of criteria.

*References and further reading:*

Allan, Keith 1980. Nouns and countability. *Language* 56: 541–67.

Allan, Keith 2009a. *The Western Classical Tradition in Linguistics*. 2nd edn. London: Equinox.

Börjars, Kersti and Kate Burridge 2001. *Introducing English Grammar*. London: Edward Arnold.

Huddleston, Rodney and Geoffrey K. Pullum 2002. *The Cambridge Grammar of the English Language*. Cambridge: Cambridge University Press.

Ross, John R. 1973. Nouniness. In *Three Dimensions of Linguistic Research*, ed. by Osamu Fujimura. Tokyo: TEC Company Ltd, pp. 137–257. Reprinted in Bas Aarts et al. (eds) *Fuzzy Grammar: A Reader*. Oxford: Oxford University Press. 2004: 351–422.

**Observer's paradox** Formulated by the sociolinguist William Labov, this states that: 'The aim of linguistic research in the community must be to find out how people talk when they are not being systematically observed; yet we can only obtain this data by systematic observation' (Labov 1970: 32). Most people will tend to alter their speech if they know they are being observed, thus rendering any systematic analysis of their actual linguistic usage extremely difficult. The obvious solution would be not to tell informants, but this would violate the ethical rules under which linguistic research is conducted (see Chapter 5.1).

The observer's paradox poses a problem for linguists using the classic Labovian method, whereby informants are randomly sampled. Those using a participant observation approach, which involves becoming part of a group and carrying out observations over a substantial period of time, are less likely to encounter it. Labov himself developed a number of strategies for coping with the problem. These included leaving the tape recorder running during natural breaks, such as interruptions or a coffee break, or asking people to talk about some event in their lives which might engender strong feelings and enable them to forget about being recorded. Another technique was to record data from groups of people interacting with each other in their normal settings (e.g. Harlem street gangs): the impact of the observer is lessened by the familiarity of setting and interlocutors. Even so, a researcher might have to wait a long time before the particular dialectal features being researched occur frequently enough to be analysed. S/he might also have to wait a considerable time to observe style shifting, the capacity of speakers to adjust their style of speech to the situation. This is why some researchers ask informants to read a word list, or a passage – tasks which are normally performed with a more self-conscious delivery, and which enable comparison with more casual speech. In his early research, Labov investigated the use of non-prevocalic /r/ in New York speech – whether /r/ was pronounced before a consonant or word-finally (e.g. in *fourth* and *floor*). He would go into a department store and ask about some goods on the fourth floor: 'Excuse me, where are the women's shoes?' Having received the required answer he would then pretend not to have heard and elicit a repetition anticipating a more careful reply. In this way he was able to compare a casual pronunciation of words involving non-prevocalic /r/ with a careful one.

While a carefully designed study such as this may elicit impressive results, most contemporary researchers favour long-term participant observation, although this limits the range and number of people who can be observed and is invariably more time-consuming.

*References and further reading:*
Chapters 2.7, 5.8 and
Labov, William 1970. The study of language in its
    social context. *Studium Generale* 23: 30–87.
Labov, William 1972. *Language in the Inner City*.
    Philadelphia: University of Pennsylvania.
Milroy, Lesley and Matthew Gordon 2003.
    *Sociolinguistics: Method and Interpretation*.
    Oxford: Blackwell.

**Paradigmatic and syntagmatic** The term **paradigmatic** describes the substitutional relationships which a linguistic unit has with other units. In the sentence *I like linguistics*, for example, each of the clause constituents can be exchanged with a number of others without changing the basic syntactic arrangement:

| A real connoisseur | *loves* | good art |
| Kids | *like* | bread |
| I | *'m hating* | linguistics |
| we | *despise* | him |
| Some people | *adore* | these mints |

Substitutability is one of the criteria important in the classification of words into various categories such as noun, verb, adjective, pronoun and so on. Items that can substitute for *I* and *linguistics* will be pronouns, or noun phrases, while those that can substitute for *like* will be verbal groups. Paradigmatic relations of this kind operate at all levels of language. In the sound system, for instance, the phonemes /p/ /k/ and /t/, can all be substituted for /f/ in the context of /＿ɪt/. Indeed, it is on the basis of such possible substitutions that phonologists are able to determine the phonemes of a language. Sets of paradigmatically related items are often referred to as **paradigms** and sometimes as **systems**. The English subject personal pronoun paradigm consists of *I, you, he, she, it, we, they*.

Most of us become aware of paradigmatic relations when we are searching for the right word to use in a particular context (perhaps for this reason Saussure 1931 referred to them as associative relations). We may be seeking a verb with a stronger emotive force than *frightens* and a weaker one than *terrifies*. We try various possibilities until we settle on *scares*.

Paradigmatic relations are best visualized as the vertical dimension of language, but there is also the linear dimension, i.e. the arrangement of words sequentially. These relations are **syntagmatic**. Together with paradigmatic relations they constitute the distributional identity of an item within the linguistic system as a whole. When we construct words and sentences we follow a certain order in arranging the individual items. To form the word /pit/, for example, we are obliged to utter the particular phonemes in that order; any other order would either make an entirely different word, or be nonsense. The phonemes, which in this instance are the constituents of the word, are referred to as **syntagms**, and the relationships that they enter into with the phonemes on either side can be referred to as **syntagmatic relations** (though more usually, **phonotactic relations**). If we identified all the syntagmatic relations which a phoneme was capable of entering into in a particular language it would provide us with a key to the range of possible words which could be formed using that phoneme. Establishing syntagmatic relations is important in the study of phonotactics, which is the study of which sequences of phonemes are permitted in a language. We know, for example, that English does not permit syllables in which /t/ is followed by /b/.

Syntagmatic relationships can be formed at all linguistic levels. Phrases and clauses follow an implicit order in the arrangement of their constituents. These arrangements can often be altered as, for example, when a sentence is rearranged to make something thematically more important. But there is a limit to such rearranging: we can't freely move an item to just any position. In the phrase *the table*, which consists of the definite article and a noun, we can put a variety of items between *the* and *table*, but we are not permitted to reverse them (*table the* is not a noun phrase). Again, if we identified all the syntagmatic relations that a word was capable of entering into within the language, it would provide us with a key to the range of possible constructions that could be formed using it. Syntagmatically related constituents, whether phonemes in a word, or words in a phrase, are referred to as *constructions* or *structures*.

We are most likely to become aware of syntagmatic relationships when we experience difficulties in sequencing sounds in pronunciation or when we don't know how to complete a phrase or clause. Severe difficulties in forming correct sequences of sounds or words in a language may be an indication of some form of linguistic handicap.

*References and further reading:*
Lyons, John 1968. *Introduction to Theoretical Linguistics*. London: Cambridge University Press.
Saussure, Ferdinand de 1931. *Cours de Linguistique Générale*. Publié par Charles Bally et Albert Sechehaye avec la collaboration de Albert Riedlinger. 3rd edn. Paris: Payot [First edn published 1916].

**Parole** See **Langue and parole**.

**Parts of speech** See **Morphosyntactic classes, lexical classes, word classes** or **parts of speech**.

**Performance** A term introduced by Chomsky 1965: 4 to describe 'the actual use of language in concrete situations'. The notion of performance is very similar to Saussure's notion of *parole*. What Chomsky seems to mean by it is the physical execution of the linguistic system in terms of actual utterances (spoken and written). So, for example, if we take the sentence *I love linguistics*, it exists both as an abstract entity, something we are able to construct and understand because of our native competence, and also as a physical entity, a sequence of sounds or letters capable of being uttered (performed) by as many speakers and writers as care to do so. Each utterance of the sentence will be different, because no one speaks or writes in exactly the same way as anyone else and no two utterances by the same speaker are ever completely identical in all respects. Being able to utter sentences correctly is important in communicating successfully but, equally, we should bear in mind that performance errors

do not necessarily reflect a lack of linguistic competence. Everyone makes slips of the tongue occasionally; sometimes these reflect grammatical uncertainty, but more often than not they are due to a variety of performance factors like external distractions, tiredness, boredom, drugs, and so forth. Deciding whether a linguistic difficulty is due to performance or competence is often important in early language learning. A young child's inability to make a certain sound may be because s/he does not have that particular phone (q.v.) in his/her arsenal of sounds, or it may be a motor difficulty to do with the movement of various speech organs (see Chapter 2.8).

The majority of linguists are more interested in competence than in performance, but for some, particularly for those interested in pragmatics and psycholinguistics, performance is a very important concept. The study of performance errors has become increasingly significant in determining how we produce and comprehend utterances. Slips of the tongue (q.v.) typically follow a pattern, and it is also the case that hesitations and repetitions are frequently discourse markers used in the management and planning of utterances. Indeed the boundary between competence and performance becomes increasingly difficult to maintain the more closely we examine particular instances. Most linguistic phenomena can be studied both in terms of their conformity to an abstract system and as concrete realizations. In this sense it is useful to consider the notions of competence and performance (like those of *langue* and *parole*) as complementary.

*References and further reading:*
Chomsky, Noam 1965. *Aspects of the Theory of Syntax*. Cambridge MA: MIT Press.
Steinberg, Danny D. and Natalia V. Sciarini 2006. *An Introduction to Psycholinguistics*. 2nd edn. Harlow: Pearson Longman.

**Phone, phoneme and allophone** A **phone** is a speech sound, irrespective of language. It is an 'etic' entity, a natural phenomenon that issues from the mouth of a speaker, and which, strictly speaking, can only ever occur once (at a certain time and place). **Phonemes**, however, are constituents of the systematic description of the phonology of a particular language, L. The phonology of L is a linguist's description of the structure of L's sound system. The phoneme (an 'emic' entity) is a theoretical construct whereas a phone is a physical reality. Albert Einstein wrote that the relationship between what linguists call the emic and the etic 'is not analogous to that of soup to beef, but rather that of check number [emic] to overcoat [etic]' ('Physics and reality' Albert Einstein in *Ideas and Opinions* p. 294 [Laurel edn. New York: Dell]).

A phoneme of language L is the smallest significant unit of phonological analysis (i.e. the smallest unit of sound that distinguishes words in L). For example the difference between English *pit, bit, bat, cat* and *back* indicates that English has the phonemes /p/, /b/, /t/, /k/, /ɪ/ and /æ/, because these contrast with one another.

**Allophones** are phonetically similar phones which are in complementary distribution with each other in at least one environment. An allophone is an etic counterpart to the (emic) phoneme. An allophone is a phone used in a particular language L as the realization of a phoneme in L.

A phoneme cannot be uttered by a speaker at some particular time, in some particular place, though its allophones are uttered (as phones). This is because a phoneme is an abstract object in the sense that it cannot itself be heard, audio-recorded, or measured acoustically (only an allophone can). If there is any phonetic similarity at all between a pair of phonemes they will contrast in at least one environment.

Most languages have between 20 and 50 phonemes (whereas the number of phones is unbounded).

*Further reading:* Chapter 2.2 and
Clark, John, Colin Yallop and Janet Fletcher 2007.
*An Introduction to Phonetics and Phonology.*
3rd edn. Malden MA: Blackwell.

**Phonetics and phonology** Phonetics studies phones (speech sounds). **Phonology** examines the relationships among sounds in particular languages. No matter what language is being used, speakers utter speech sounds in a certain place at a certain time. These speech sounds are called phones. A phone is a phonetic entity. It is an 'etic' category that has spatio-temporal location – it is a bit of real data. A phone, unlike an allophone, is not bound to any one language. Human beings can produce an unbounded number of phones, but in any language only comparatively few phones are used to indicate meaning differences such as between *bit, beat, pit* and *beak*. In these words /b/ contrasts with /p/, /ɪ/ with /i/, /t/ with /k/: each of these is a phoneme of English. Note that phonemes are written between slashes / /, but phones between square brackets [ ].

Articulatory phonetics investigates the production of phones and consequently the anatomy and physiology of speech, the process of articulation using vocal organs, and the description and classification of phones based on properties of the speech mechanism. There is also auditory phonetics which focuses on hearing, and instrumental phonetics which uses instruments to measure the properties of phones.

*Further reading:* Chapters 2.1–2.2 and
Clark, John, Colin Yallop and Janet Fletcher 2007.
*An Introduction to Phonetics and Phonology.*
3rd edn. Malden MA: Blackwell.

**Phrase** A phrase is a syntactic unit, intermediate between word and clause, and it typically consists of more than one word. In most modern grammars it is regarded as the cornerstone of syntactic theory. In a phrase the individual words cohere together to form a single syntactic entity, capable of being moved around and also of being replaced by another word. In (1)–(3), the words in bold are capable of both of these.

(1) **The man** went **down the hill.**
(2) **Down the hill** went **the man** [Movement]
(3) **He** went **there.** [Substitution]

The two tests that are being applied here are described by Nigel Fabb in the following way:

(i) if a sequence of words can be moved as a group, they may form a phrase (the movement test); (ii) if a sequence of words can be replaced by a single word, they may form a phrase (the replacement test). (Fabb 2005: 3–4)

Phrases are projections of the main lexical word classes, which function as the head of the phrase. So there are noun, verb, adjective, adverbial, and prepositional phrases. The tests mentioned above work better for some types of phrase than for others. Verb phrases, for example, are not very amenable to movement although they can be replaced, albeit in a limited manner:

(4)  The man **went down the hill** and the dog **did** too.

In (4), *did* is substituting for the string *went down the hill*, and as a consequence is evidence that it is a phrase.

You will have noticed from (4) that phrases can contain other phrases within them. The verb phrase *went down the hill* has the adverbial prepositional phrase *down the hill* embedded in it. And indeed we can break this down even further since *the hill* is also capable of being moved and replaced and is therefore a phrase, in fact a noun phrase. The principle of embedding is crucial to the way in which phrases link together to form sentences. In fact, some complex phrases often contain clauses embedded within them as in the noun phrase in (5).

(5)  the man **who is standing by the door** [is exceptionally charming]

In very simple phrases the phrase may just consist of the head word. In (6) 'John' functions as a noun phrase.

(6)  John went home.

But in *John*, **who is an actor**, *went home* the head is modified by the appositive relative clause *who is an actor*. Modification is a process which allows phrases to expand and incorporate a variety of subordinate material. It can occur either before or after the head word and consists of words, phrases and sentences which are dependent in some way on it. Modification that occurs before the head is termed pre-modification, and that which occurs following it is post-modification.

Because of the versatility and importance of the phrase syntactically, it is common nowadays to describe sentences in terms of the phrases which they comprise. Phrase structure grammar provides us with rules for sentence formation which utilize this form of analysis.

*References and further reading:* Chapter 2.4 and
Börjars, Kersti and Kate Burridge 2001. *Introducing English Grammar*. London: Edward Arnold.

Fabb, Nigel 2005. *Sentence Structure*. 2nd edn. London & New York: Routledge [First edn 1994].
Huddleston, Rodney and Geoffrey K. Pullum 2002. *The Cambridge Grammar of the English Language*. Cambridge: Cambridge University Press.

**Pidgin** A pidgin is an auxiliary language which arises to fulfil certain limited communication needs among people who have no common language. The majority of pidgins around the world originated as trade languages; the word *pidgin* is commonly thought to derive from the word *business* as pronounced by Chinese traders. Probably the earliest documented pidgin was Sabir, based on Portuguese and used by the Crusaders in trading with Arabs.

Pidgins are all derived from a so-called 'superstrate' language, such as English, French, or Portuguese. In their initial stages they involve simplifying the superstrate language by reducing the vocabulary and eliminating secondary grammatical categories such as tense and plural inflections. Some argue that the pidginization process is similar to the one we all undergo when learning a foreign language, though with very limited access to the target language. Just as we may import some English words and pronunciation patterns into our newly acquired language, so pidgins often absorb elements of the less dominant (substrate) languages. This is a process known as admixture.

The classic situation for pidgin formation arises from a trading relationship between, say, a group of European seamen and a local community. This results in the formation of a marginal pidgin. A second stage begins when local groups who speak different languages use the pidgin as a **lingua franca**. As it is extended to a wider range of functions, it grows in vocabulary and grammatical structure and becomes an expanded pidgin. These kinds of pidgins exist all over the world where trading has taken place between populations of different countries with no common link language. The principal regions where we find them, however, are in the Pacific basin and along the coast of West Africa. A further stage is the development of expanded pidgins into creoles.

*Further reading:* Chapter 2.7 and

Holm, John 2000. *An Introduction to Pidgins and Creoles*. Cambridge: Cambridge University Press.

Holmes, Janet 2001. *An Introduction to Sociolinguistics*. 2nd edn. Harlow: Longman.

Romaine, Suzanne 2000. *Language in Society: An Introduction to Sociolinguistics*. 2nd edn. Oxford: Oxford University Press.

**Polysemy** See **Homonymy and polysemy**.

**Pragmatics** studies the context-dependent assignment of meaning to language expressions used in acts of speaking and writing. It can be thought of as the investigation of meaning in language on particular occasions of language being used, whereas **semantics** studies meaning inherent in the language itself; i.e. as already existing in the language for people to make use of.

*Further reading:* Chapters 2.5–2.6 and

Huang, Yan 2007. *Pragmatics*. Oxford: Oxford University Press.

Jaszczolt, Katarzyna M. 2002. *Semantics and Pragmatics: Meaning in Language and Discourse*. Harlow: Longman.

Levinson, Stephen C. 1983. *Pragmatics*. Cambridge: Cambridge University Press.

**Prefix** See **Affix, prefix, infix, suffix, circumfix.**

**Preposition** Prepositions are words that link two parts of a sentence together where the relationship is typically one of time, place, or logic, as in the following examples:

(1) Time: He went home **after/during/before** the lecture.
(2) Place: She went **in/to/by/from** the house.
(3) Logic: She went **because of/in spite of** you.

Simple prepositions consist of one word, e.g. *about*, *from*, *at*, *across*, and complex prepositions of more than one word, e.g. *apart from*, *ahead of*, *in front of*.

You will usually encounter prepositions in prepositional phrases. These consist of a preposition plus a complement, most often a noun phrase, but it can also be a clause:

(4) I saw him **at the bus stop**
[preposition + noun phrase]
(5) I stay **with whoever I can**
[preposition + clause]

*Further reading:*

Sinclair, John McH. (ed.) 1990. *Collins COBUILD English Grammar*. London: Collins.

Tyler, Andrea and Vyvyan Evans 2003. *The Semantics of English Prepositions: Spatial Scenes, Embodied Meaning, and Cognition*. Cambridge: Cambridge University Press.

**Presupposition** A term used in both semantics and pragmatics to refer to assumptions implicitly made by speakers and listeners which are necessary for the correct interpretation of utterances. In making the statement *I'm sorry it's raining*, for example, a truthful speaker presupposes that it is raining. The presupposition also holds if the statement is negated: *I'm not sorry it's raining*, also presupposes *it's raining*. But does the presupposition lie in the sense of the sentence or is it (as earlier assumed) what the speaker must hold to be true? Although not all linguists agree, it seems best to determine that presupposition deals with the necessary preconditions for statements to be true, for questions to be answerable, for directives to be carried out, for expressives to be appropriately made, and so on. So the sentence *My cat was run over yesterday* assumes as a necessity the truth of *I had a cat*. The question *Is it raining?* needs to be addressed to someone who can reasonably provide an answer. The directive *Run!* should not be given to a bed-ridden person. The injunction (directive) *Don't put up with back pain*, for example, carries the implicit presupposition *You have back pain*. The expressive *Thank you* presupposes that there is some reason to thank the addressee. This account assumes that presupposition is pragmatic.

Certain presuppositions are the result not of the words used but of intonation. In the following cases, for example, the sentences are exactly the same but uttered with a different stress pattern. The consequence is the production of different presuppositions:

(1) Jenny admired *JOHN*.
(2) *JEN*ny admired John.

In (1) the presupposition is *Jenny admired some-one*, whereas in (2) it is *someone admired John*.

The problem with the account of **semantic presupposition**, which is limited to the sense of sentences, is that it doesn't take full account of presuppositions which clearly depend upon our knowledge of the world. Compare the following sentences:

(3) She tripped before getting in the car.
(4) She died before getting in the car.
(5) She got in the car.

(5) is presupposed by (3) but not by (4). The reason for this is simply that we know that some-one who has died cannot get into a car. The issue here is pragmatic rather than strictly semantic. In any communication there is a certain amount of presumed knowledge independent of purely semantic knowledge. The degree and kind of assumed knowledge depends on a wide range of factors which linguists broadly refer to as **common ground.** Stylistically, presupposition is exploited in a range of discourse types including advertisements, newspapers, and fiction.

*Further reading:*

Allan, Keith 2001. *Natural Language Semantics*. Oxford & Malden MA: Blackwell.

Jaszczolt, Katarzyna M. 2002. *Semantics and Pragmatics: Meaning in Language and Discourse*. Harlow: Longman.

Saeed, John I. 2003. *Semantics*. 2nd edn. Oxford: Blackwell.

**Productivity** Productivity has both a general and a specific sense. In its general sense it refers to the creative capacity of language users to produce an endless number of new sentences, in contrast to the communication systems of animals, which are limited to set formulas and are thus 'unproductive'. Productivity is, therefore, one of the design features of human language. In its more restricted sense it refers to the use made by a language of a specific feature. Features are productive if they are currently used to produce further instances of the same type. For example, the plural suffix *–s*, which is added onto the base form of nouns, is productive because any new noun that is adopted into English will employ it, whereas the change from *foot* to *feet* is unproduc-

tive because it represents a fossilized plural form limited to a small set of nouns. Productivity is a useful concept for establishing the potentiality of particular linguistic patterns. Some, for example the prefix *un–*, are semi-productive, because they are sometimes, but not always, attached to words of Germanic origin to form their opposites, e.g. *lovely > unlovely*, but not *good >\* ungood*.

*Further reading:*

Bauer, Laurie 2001. *Morphological Productivity*. Cambridge: Cambridge University Press.

Plag, Ingo 2003. *Word-formation in English*. Cambridge: Cambridge University Press.

**Pronoun** A word which can be used to substitute for a single noun (non-co-referential) or a complete noun phrase (typically co-referential).

(1) He's got a blue **jacket** and I've got a red **one**. [Replacing a noun]
(2) **Your brother Jack's** here. **He's** over there. [Replacing a noun phrase]

There are many types of pronoun. The following are the ones most usually recognized.

**Personal pronouns:** *I/me, you, he/him, she/her, it, we/us, they/them*

**Possessive pronouns:** *mine, yours, his, hers, ours, theirs*

**Reflexive pronouns:** *myself, yourself, himself, herself, ourselves, themselves*

**Demonstrative pronouns:** *this/that, these/those*

**Interrogative (*wh-*) pronouns:** *why, which, when, where, who, how*

**Relative pronouns:** (substitute for noun phrases in relative clauses): *who, which, whose, that*

**Indefinite pronouns:** *one, one's, anybody, some-body, anything, something*

*Further reading:*

Allan, Keith 2001. *Natural Language Semantics*. Oxford & Malden MA: Blackwell.

Panagiotidis, Phoevos 2002. *Pronouns, Clitics and Empty Nouns: 'Pronominality' and Licensing in Syntax*. Amsterdam: John Benjamins.

Sinclair, John McH. (ed.) 1990. *Collins COBUILD English Grammar*. London: Collins.

**Prototype semantics** selects a particular deno-tatum or a particular sense as the most typical exemplar for a lexeme, e.g. for most people today the prototype for *phone* is probably a mobile (cell) phone. Categories like Rugs and Carpets (corresponding to lexemes *rug* and *carpet*) or Cups and Mugs (corresponding to *cup* and *mug*) or Trees and Bushes seem to merge gradually one into another, although prototypical exemplars of each category are clearly different (see Labov 1978). For example, the prototypical tree is well over twice the height of a human being while the prototypical bush is round about human height.

Lakoff 1972 proposed using fuzzy sets to index the exemplariness of a category member. The prototype (best example) was given the value 1.0, the worst example has a value close to 0.0. Values of fuzzy set membership can be calculated from experiments such as asking informants to list all the birds or fruits they can think of in 30 seconds: items that are highest and most frequent in the lists are taken to be most prototypical. However, these values are only valid for the tested population at the time of the experiment, not for all speakers of the language and not even for the same subjects on a different occasion. For instance, Rosch 1973 claimed that a robin is a good exemplar of the category Bird (lexeme *bird*) for North Americans. It would not be so good for New Zealanders, for whom the kiwi ranks much higher because the kiwi is the national bird. Figures from Battig and Montague 1969 demonstrate that a tomato is more of a vegetable than a fruit — 0.68 vs 0.14 — but this doesn't reveal anything new about the meaning of the lexemes *tomato* or *vegetable* or *fruit*. A tomato is both a fruit and a vegetable, but mostly it is used like a vegetable. Its characteristics are included in the internalized (cognitive) model of the tomato and contribute to the semantic frame of *tomato*. Prototype theory has no means of representing such facts. Even the poorest examples of a category remain within the category: the fact that an onion is a poor exemplar of a vegetable for a tested population does not change their perception that it is a vegetable. The prototype in no way defines the category: no one believes that, just because a carrot is the prototypical vegetable, a vegetable is a carrot!

Furthermore, categories are independent of related categories with respect to prototypicality. For instance, a *guppy* is a good exemplar of the category Pet Fish, but it is not a good exemplar of either of the categories Pet and Fish. All in all, prototype semantics has failed to deliver startling insights into semantics.

*References:*
Battig, William F. and William E. Montague 1969. Category norms for verbal items in 56 categories. *Journal of Experimental Psychology Monograph 80*.
Labov, William 1978. Denotational structure. In *Papers from the Parasession on the Lexicon*, ed. by Donka Farkas, Wesley M. Jacobsen and Karol W. Todrys. Chicago: Chicago Linguistics Society, pp. 220–60.
Lakoff, George 1972. Hedges: a study of meaning criteria and the logic of fuzzy concepts. In *Papers from the Eighth Regional Meeting of the Chicago Linguistics Society*, ed. by Paul M. Peranteau, Judith N. Levi and Gloria C. Phares. Chicago: Chicago Linguistics Society, pp. 183–228. Revised version in *Contemporary Research in Philosophical Logic and Linguistic Semantics*, ed. by D. Hockney, W. Harper, and B. Freed. Dordrecht: Reidel. 1972, pp. 221–71.
Rosch, Eleanor 1973. On the internal structure of perceptual and semantic categories. In *Cognitive Development and the Acquisition of Language*, ed. by Timothy E. Moore. New York: Academic Press, pp. 111–44.

*Further reading:*
Allan, Keith 2001. *Natural Language Semantics*. Oxford & Malden MA: Blackwell.
Lakoff, George 1987. *Women, Fire, and Dangerous Things*. Chicago: University of Chicago Press.
Osherson, Dan N. and Edward E. Smith 1981. On the adequacy of prototype theory as a theory of concepts. *Cognition* 9: 35–58.
Pulman, Stephen G. 1983. *Word Meaning and Belief*. London: Croom Helm.

**Reference** See **Sense, denotation,** and **reference.**

**Register** See **Jargon** or **register.**

**Sapir-Whorf hypothesis** The so-called Sapir-Whorf hypothesis, perhaps better named the **linguistic relativity hypothesis** is expressed in the following quotations.

The fact of the matter is that the 'real world' is to a large extent unconsciously built up on the language habits of the group. No two languages are ever sufficiently similar to be considered as representing the same social reality. The worlds in which different societies live are distinct worlds, not merely the same worlds with different labels attached. (Sapir 1929: 209)

The 'linguistic relativity principle' ... means, in informal terms, that users of markedly different grammars are pointed by the grammars toward different types of observations and different evaluations of externally similar acts of observation, and hence are not equivalent as observers but must arrive at somewhat different views of the world. (Whorf 1956: 221)

A strong version of the Sapir-Whorf hypothesis (that language determines the way we see the world) is untenable, but a weak version is not. This is that a language directs its speakers towards certain aspects of perceived phenomena – but, because perception is independent of language, other aspects of phenomena can be commented upon, if desired, by circumlocution, or by the novel use of a language expression.

The linguistic relativity hypothesis was first proposed in the work of Wilhelm von Humboldt 1836.

*References:*
Humboldt, Wilhelm von 1836. Einleitung. Über die Verschiedenheit des menschlichen Sprachbaues und ihren Einfluss auf die geistige Entwickelung des Menschengeschlechts. In *Über die Kawi-Sprache auf der Insel Java.* Erster Band. Berlin: Druckerei der Königlichen Akademie der Wissenschaften.
Sapir, Edward 1929. The status of linguistics as a science. *Language* 5: 207–14. Reprinted in *Selected Writings of Edward Sapir in Language, Culture and Personality*, ed. by David G. Mandelbaum, Berkeley: University of California Press. 1949, pp. 160–66. Also in *Culture, Language and Society: Selected Essays*, ed. by David G. Mandelbaum, Berkeley: University of California Press. 1956, pp. 65–77.
Whorf, Benjamin L. 1956. *Language, Thought, and Reality: Selected Writings of Benjamin Lee Whorf*, ed. by John B. Carroll. Cambridge MA: MIT Press.

*Further reading:*
Allan, Keith 2009a. *The Western Classical Tradition in Linguistics.* 2nd edn. London: Equinox.
Gumperz, John J. and Stephen C. Levinson (eds) 1996. *Rethinking Linguistic Relativity.* London: Croom Helm.
Niemeier, Susanne and René Dirven (eds) 2000. *Evidence for Linguistic Relativity.* Amsterdam/ Philadelphia: John Benjamins.
Pütz, Martin and Marjolijn Verspoor (eds) 2000. *Explorations in Linguistic Relativity.* Amsterdam/Philadelphia: John Benjamins.

**Schwa (shwa)** symbolized /ə/. The name of the most frequent vowel phoneme in English, the weak and rather colourless unstressed lax vowel produced in the central area of the oral cavity, that occurs in *about* /əˈbaʊt/, and *banana* /bəˈnanə/. It frequently occurs in function words like *the*, *and*, *for*, especially in running speech, and it is often the result of vowel reduction (compare the careful pronunciation of these words in isolation – /ði, ænd, fɔ/). The term 'schwa' comes from the Hebrew epenthetic vowel, 'sheva'.

**Selection restrictions** Selection restrictions are postulated to block anomalies. Language combines the meaning encapsulated in listemes (items listed in a lexicon) into the complex meanings of phrases, sentences, and longer texts. Such combination is conditioned by the rules of syntax and at least four kinds of selectional restrictions. **Category** features (Noun, Verb, ...) determine different morphological and collocational possibilities, e.g. of *waitress*$_{\text{Noun}}$ and *waitress*$_{\text{Verb}}$. **Strict subcategorization** identifies other syntactic categories that collocate with the listeme. Syntactically transitive verbs, for instance, are defined by some notational variant of the strict subcategorization feature [+ __NP] "takes a 1st object"; *open* (as in *Fred opened the box*) has this feature, whereas the intransitive verb in *The door opened easily* has the feature [– __NP]. Supposedly syntactic **inherent** features such as [+human, +female, ...] for *woman*; or [+active, ...] for *go* have a semantic basis. The **selectional** features of one listeme refer to the inherent features of collocated listemes [e.g. for a verb like *admire* [+ [+animate]__[±abstract]] "has an animate subject NP and either a concrete or abstract 1st object NP"]. So there are no grounds for the claim that selectional features are syntactic; they are without any doubt semantically conditioned. It would otherwise be impossible to generate meaningful sentences like (1)–(2).

(1)  Grace me no grace, nor uncle me no uncle. (Shakespeare *Richard II* II.iii.87)
(2)  But me no buts. ([= "don't prevaricate"] Scott *The Antiquary* Ch. XI)

What governs the co-occurrence of listemes is that the collocation has some possible denotation (be it substance, object, state, event, process, quality, metalinguistic statement, or whatever). Consider three examples marked anomalous in McCawley 1968: 265).

(3)  *That electron is green.
(4)  *I ate three phonemes for breakfast.
(5)  *My hair is bleeding.

(3) is judged anomalous because electrons are theoretical constructs that cannot absorb or reflect light, and therefore cannot be predicated as green. But suppose an explanatory model of an atom were constructed in which an electron is represented by a green flash: there would be no anomaly stating *That electron is green* with respect to such a model. Consider (4): phonemes are abstract entities, and one cannot eat abstract entities. Now imagine a situation in which a breakfast cereal is made in the shape of letters (*à la* alphabet soup); this cereal is fed to participants at a Linguistic Society conference and some wag eats a **p**, a **t**, and a **k**, and utters *I ate three phonemes for breakfast*. Such a statement is no more anomalous than Austin (1975: 144) saying *France is hexagonal* – which no one has judged anomalous. Take (5): hair has no blood vessels, so it cannot bleed; but that wouldn't stop a child painting bleeding hair, or a computer game creating bleeding hair somewhere in cyberspace – both cases establishing conditions under which the utterance of (5) would not be anomalous.

Empirical evaluations of sequences of listemes for coherence and sensicalness depend upon what they denote; evaluations must be matched in the grammar by well-formedness conditions,

in part expressed by selection restrictions. To describe the full set of well-formedness conditions for the occurrence of every listeme in a language entails trying every conceivable combination of listemes in every conceivable context, and such a task is at best impracticable and at worst impossible. One alternative is to systematically describe semantic frames for every listeme along the lines of the 'lexical semantic structures' of Pustejovsky 1995.

*References and further reading:*
Allan, Keith 1986. *Linguistic Meaning*. 2 vols. London: Routledge and Kegan Paul. (Reprint edn, Beijing: World Publishing Corporation. 1991.)
Austin, John L. 1975. *How To Do Things With Words*. 2nd edn, ed. James O. Urmson and Marina Sbisà. Oxford: Oxford University Press [First edn 1962].
McCawley, James D. 1968. Concerning the base component of a transformational grammar. *Foundations of Language* 4: 243–69. Reprinted in James D. McCawley *Grammar and Meaning*. Tokyo: Taikushan. 1973: 35–58.
Pustejovsky, James 1995. *The Generative Lexicon*. Cambridge MA: MIT Press.

**Semantics** Within linguistics, semantics is the study and representation of the meaning of every kind of constituent and expression in language, and also of the meaning relationships between them.

*Further reading:* Chapters 2.5–2.6 and
Allan, Keith 2001. *Natural Language Semantics*. Oxford & Malden MA: Blackwell.
Allan, Keith (ed.) 2009b. *Concise Encyclopaedia of Semantics*. Oxford: Elsevier.
Cruse, D. Alan 2004. *Meaning In Language: An Introduction to Semantics and Pragmatics*. 2nd edn. Oxford: Oxford University Press.
Jaszczolt, Katarzyna M. 2002. *Semantics and Pragmatics: Meaning in Language and Discourse*. Harlow: Longman.
Saeed, John I. 2003. *Semantics*. 2nd edn. Oxford: Blackwell.

**Semantic field** The idea of semantic fields derives from the fact that a conceptual field such as colour, kinship, or cooking terms is covered by a number of listemes in a language, each denoting a part of the field. Different languages, and at different times in history any one language, may divide the field differently among listemes. The semantic field of a listeme is determined from the conceptual field in which its denotatum occurs. A semantic field is structured in such a way as to mirror the structure of the conceptual field. Semantic fields are primarily useful in establishing meaning relations among the listemes of a language. Each item in the field was said by Saussure 1931 to have a 'valeur', a differential value which is that part of the conceptual field that it denotes in contrast with the part denoted by other listemes in the same semantic field. Saussure rightly pointed out that the differential value of the English word *sheep* is, by comparison with the French word *mouton*, restricted by the existence of the word *mutton* for sheep meat (which in French is also *mouton*). So English and French divide up the semantic field dealing with aspects of sheep differently. The disparate differential values that so-called 'translation equivalents' have in the different languages is one of the things that makes learning another language difficult.

The notion of semantic field is most useful when the field is readily circumscribed. For instance the semantic field of colour can be exhaustively listed in any language using colour terms that divide up the field completely; it is far more difficult to exhaustively list the field of verbs of motion *walk*, *run*, *skip*, ... or the field of adjectives of emotion *happy*, *angry*, *disappointed*, ....

*References and further reading:*
Backhouse, Anthony E. 1994. *The Lexical Field of Taste: A Semantic Study of Japanese Taste Terms*. Cambridge: Cambridge University Press.
Lehrer, Adrienne 1974. *Semantic Fields and Lexical Structure*. Amsterdam: North Holland.
Lyons, John 1977. *Semantics*. 2 vols. Cambridge: Cambridge University Press.
Saussure, Ferdinand de 1931. *Cours de Linguistique Générale*. Publié par Charles Bally et Albert Sechehaye avec la collaboration de Albert Riedlinger. 3rd edn. Paris: Payot [First edn published 1916].

**Sense, denotation, and reference** Sense is decontextualized meaning, abstracted from innumerable occurrences of the listeme (or combination of listemes) in texts. It is what we find in dictionaries. It is left to you as a dictionary user to decide which of the senses given is relevant to a particular context in which the word is used (because sense is decontextualized meaning). The sense of a language expression is a description of its informational content in terms of some other language expression as can be seen from the *Macquarie Dictionary* online entry for **jargon** in the box below.

> *noun* **1.** the language peculiar to a trade, profession, or other group: *medical jargon*.
> **2.** pretentious language abounding in uncommon or unfamiliar words.
> **3.** unintelligible or meaningless talk or writing; gibberish.
> **4.** *Obsolete*→ pidgin.
> *--verb* (i) **5.** to utter or talk jargon or a jargon.

People talk about things (physical objects, abstract entities, places, states, events) that have existed (happened) in the past, things that exist (are happening) at present, and things that they predict will exist (happen) in the future. They also talk about things that could be or could have been if the world were different than it was, is, or is expected to be. They talk about things in the fictional worlds and times of books and films; about things represented in paintings and photographs; about things that they deny exist; even about impossible things such as *the largest prime number* or *My brother is an only child*. We need to consider how semantic theories meet the challenge of connecting the language expressions used to talk about all these different kinds of things to the very things spoken about. In short, we must look at the way language connects to things in the worlds and times spoken of. **Reference** and **denotation** are relations between expressions in the language and worlds and times spoken of. Unfortunately, there is inconsistency among scholars and textbook writers in their use of the terms reference and denotation. The meaning ascribed to them here is determined by the need to have names for each kind of relationship between 'words and things'.

> **Denotation** is the relation between language expressions and things or events in worlds – not just the world we live in, but any world and

time that may be spoken of. The world spoken of is a mental model of an actual or recalled or imagined world in which it is important to identify what there is and what there isn't.

> The **reference** of a language expression is what the speaker is talking about when using that expression in some particular utterance on some particular occasion. For example, the speaker refers to particular entities, events, places, and times within the world and time s/he is speaking of. Thus, referring is something that a speaker does, and it is intimately connected with speaker meaning.

Consider the example in (1). The sense of (1) is (2):

(1) I spoke to the Prime Minister yesterday.

(2) "Speaker spoke with the chief minister in the parliament of a certain country the day before this sentence was uttered."

Sense is a truly semantic category, and reference is truly pragmatic. Denotation is somewhere in between. (1) denotes a speaker, a Prime Minister, a particular day, and a certain event that occurs in some world. Under normal felicitous conditions of use the speaker of (1) will refer to and thereby identify who the speaker is (for instance George W. Bush in 2006), the prime minister (say, Tony Blair, British PM in 2006) and a particular event of linguistic interaction that occurred on an identifiable date (say, Thursday, 7 December 2006 – the utterance was made on 8 December 2006).

A speaker refers differently to things that have existence in the world spoken of and to things that do not. It is sometimes said that 'referring expressions' identify things that exist, and 'non-referring expressions' identify things which don't; but it is better to define reference as 'what Speaker is talking about' and when dealing with existence use some other term such as **extension** instead.

*Further reading:*

Allan, Keith 2001. *Natural Language Semantics*. Oxford & Malden MA: Blackwell.

Jaszczolt, Katarzyna M. 2002. *Semantics and Pragmatics: Meaning in Language and Discourse*. Harlow: Longman.

**Sentence** Traditional definitions of sentences often describe them as grammatically complete units capable of standing on their own and semantically independent. This is true of many sentences, including the one you have just read. But it is clearly not so for all sentences. In actual speech we often abbreviate utterances and elide elements in order to maintain fluency and avoid pointless repetition as in the exchange in (1).

(1) Q. Where are you going?
    A. To Tim's.

Here the sequence *To Tim's* can only function as a reply because the full meaning is recoverable from the context. Sentence fragments or **subsentences** of this kind are frequent in speech and increasingly common in writing, too. They have always been a feature of novels or short stories, where the aim is to reproduce the utterance flavour of language, but they can also be found in advertisements and even public announcements. Geoffrey Leech (in *English in Advertising*. London: Longman. 1966) has called this style 'public colloquial' and observed its growing frequency in written English as a phenomenon of late twentieth-century culture.

Sentences, then, are units of style as well as grammar. This raises the problem of how we can formally describe them in grammatical terms. How can we arrive at a description which takes account of both the fully independent kind and the sentence fragments? We can make a start by distinguishing, as some linguists do, between sentences and subsentences (sometimes referred to as 'major' and 'minor' clauses or sentences). Subsentences are incomplete in some way. This useful terminological distinction enables us to focus our attention, for purposes of grammatical description, on full sentences, the major variety. It also allows us to discern two sets of rules here: first, the grammatical rules which govern sentence formation, and second, text formation rules, which operate on sentences when they become part of connected discourse.

Sentences may consist of one clause or more. In Chomskyan linguistics, clauses are normally dubbed sentences, the single clause sentence being a simple sentence. A sentence with more than one clause is **compound** if the constituent clauses are linked by conjunctions e.g.

(2) Jack went up the hill **and** Jill followed him.

(3) Harry chose the fish **but** Sue preferred the steak.

The sentence is **complex** if it contains subordinate clauses, e.g.

(4) **When Sue called**, Harry was out **because he needed to buy a screwdriver.**
(5) I sang **while he played the piano**.
(6) **If you sing** I will play the piano.

Sentences have the structure described for clauses (see that entry).

*Further reading:*
Börjars, Kersti and Kate Burridge 2001. *Introducing English Grammar*. London: Edward Arnold.
Sinclair, John McH. (ed.) 1990. *Collins COBUILD English Grammar*. London: Collins.
Stainton, Robert J. 2006. *Words and Thoughts: Subsentences, Ellipsis, and the Philosophy of Language*. Oxford: Clarendon Press.
Van Valin, Robert D. Jr 2001. *An Introduction to Syntax*. Cambridge: Cambridge University Press.
Van Valin, Robert D. Jr and Randy LaPolla 1997. *Syntax: Structure, Meaning, and Function*. Cambridge: Cambridge University Press.

**Sign, signifier, and signified** The term **sign** is frequently used by people studying communication theory to characterize the way in which meaning is communicated symbolically, via certain objects within individual cultures; thus the Cross operates as a sign within Christian cultures. The study of signs is **semiotics**. Not surprisingly, linguistics has been influenced by semiotics to the extent that words are sometimes described as linguistic signs. It's not difficult to see the connection here because it can be argued that words represent the world in a symbolic rather than a literal way, and that understanding these symbolic relationships is what distinguishes speakers from non-speakers of a language. The linguist most closely associated with the concept of linguistic signs is the Swiss Ferdinand de Saussure. He argued that words comprise two elements: a sound image, i.e. a phonological form, which he named 'signifiant' (**signifier**), and its meaning: the 'signifié' (the thing **signified**). To use the example Saussure himself used, the word *tree* is made up of a signifier /tri/ which signifies 'treeness'. The relationship between them is a conventional, not a natural one: there is no reason why society shouldn't use any other sequence of sounds to represent 'treeness' if it so wished (French, which Saussure wrote in, uses *arbre* /aʁbʁ/). The signifier, then, acts as a label, but for a concept, not an actual object. It is the signifier and signified together, the complete word, or sign, which is used by us as speakers of the language to refer to actual trees. This yields two types of meaning which words are capable of: signification (or sense), and denotation.

The notion that words are internally structured as signs and represent the world symbolically has had an important influence on the study of language. Its effect has been most profoundly felt in semantics where the study of sense relationships, i.e. the relationships between signifieds, has led to some important insights into the ways in which words 'mean'. But beyond that, the splitting of the sign in this way between sound image and concept has become part of that movement of thought termed **structuralism**, which has had such a profound impact on interpretative procedures in literature and the arts generally.

> Structuralism may be defined as the trend of linguistics which is concerned with analysing relations between the segments of a language, conceived as a hierarchically arranged whole. (Bohumil Trnka and others 1964)

*References and further reading:*
Bohumil Trnka and others 1964. Prague structural linguistics. In *A Prague School Reader in Linguistics*, ed. by Josef Vachek. Bloomington: Indiana University Press, pp. 468.
Culler, Jonathan (ed.) 2006. *Structuralism*. London: Routledge.
Harris, Roy 2003. *Saussure and His Interpreters*. 2nd edn. Edinburgh: Edinburgh University Press.
Saussure, Ferdinand de 1931. *Cours de Linguistique Générale*. Publié par Charles Bally et Albert Sechehaye avec la collaboration de Albert Riedlinger. 3rd edn. Paris: Payot [First edn published 1916].
Saussure, Ferdinand de 1974. *A Course in General Linguistics*. Glasgow: Fontana/Collins [Transl. by Wade Baskin from the 3rd edition of *Cours de Linguistique Générale*. Paris: Payot, 1931. First edn published in 1916].

**Slip of the tongue** See **Assemblage error**.

**Speech Act** Language results from acts of speaking or writing, when someone says (or writes) something to someone else at a certain time in a certain place – often as part of a longer discourse or interchange. Normal utterance involves a hierarchy of speech acts. To begin with, there's the **act of utterance**. This is recognizable even in an unknown language in which we cannot distinguish the sentences used, and what the speaker's message is. Utterance is recognized by brute perception: hearing the utterance spoken, seeing it signed or written, or feeling it impressed in braille. Linguistics is concerned with utterances in which a speaker uses a language expression and thereby performs a locutionary act (and more).

In performing a **locutionary act** the speaker uses an identifiable sentence or subsentence from a language L. Producing the locution demands that the speaker has knowledge of the grammar, lexicon, semantics, and phonology of L; recognizing it, a hearer requires comparable knowledge. The speaker uses the locution to **refer** to things, i.e. talk about them. Different speakers can refer to the same thing using different locutionary and utterance acts.

Austin 1975 alerted us to the fact that a speaker **does** something when making an utterance. Some examples were given under the entry for **Illocution**: the speaker states a fact or an opinion, denies something, makes a prediction, a promise, or a request; offers thanks or an invitation; issues an order or an umpire's decision; gives advice or permission; names a child; swears an oath. In making an utterance, the speaker performs an **illocutionary act** by using a particular locution with the **illocutionary force** of a statement, a confirmation, a denial, a prediction, a promise, a request, and so on. Although an utterance has more than one illocutionary force, it will usually have only one message to convey; the illocutionary force that carries this message is said to be the **illocutionary point** of the utterance. In (1) the primary illocutionary force is a statement about a future act.

(1) I'll give you a hand.

(1) may be used with a second illocutionary force: to make a promise. If this promise is the speaker's illocutionary intention, then (1) has the illocutionary point "Speaker is promising to help the addressee."

Typically, a speaker has the **illocutionary intention** to create some **perlocutionary effect** on the hearer as a result of the hearer recognizing speaker's illocutionary point. For example, *Got a minute?* would most likely be intended to have the hearer pay attention to something the speaker wishes to say to him or her. A perlocution is the hearer's behavioural response to the utterance – not necessarily a physical or verbal response, perhaps merely a mental or emotional response of some kind. Other perlocutions are such things as: alerting the hearer by warning the hearer of danger; persuading the hearer to an opinion by stating supporting facts; intimidating the hearer by threatening; getting the hearer to do something by means of a suggestion, a hint, a request, or a command; and so forth.

*References and further reading:*

Allan, Keith 1994. Speech act theory – an overview. In *Encyclopedia of Language and Linguistics*, ed. by Ronald E. Asher. Vol. 8. Oxford: Pergamon Press, pp. 4127–38.

Austin, John L. 1975. *How To Do Things With Words*. 2nd edn, ed. by James O. Urmson and Marina Sbisà. Oxford: Oxford University Press [First edn 1962].

Bach, Kent and Robert M. Harnish 1979. *Linguistic Communication and Speech Acts*. Cambridge, MA: MIT Press.

**Standard variety** The variety of a language which is used in education and other formal contexts such as the legal system, government and the news media, and which is described in dictionaries and pedagogic grammars. In developing writing systems for previously unwritten languages, linguists need to engage in status planning (selecting the most appropriate variety as a basis for the writing system) and corpus planning (developing and extending the lexicon, and choosing between variant forms). This is part of a process of standardization.

Long-established standard varieties such as (British) Standard English, Standard Italian or Mandarin Chinese came to prominence as a consequence of a number of social and cultural factors. In Britain, the power of speakers of the local dialect of the region bounded by Oxford, Cambridge, and London gave that dialect prestige and saw it established as the norm provider.

Standard English is the variety of the language which is taught, and used as the medium of education, codified in dictionaries and grammars, and subject to minimum variation of form and maximum variation of function. This means that syntactic and orthographic variation in Standard English is limited (within a speech community there is usually only one way to spell a word, for example), while at the same time it is used in a wide variety of contexts – the law, medicine, the church, politics, and so on. Standard varieties of English vary in small ways: American English spelling, for example, has *color, theater, traveler* where British English has *colour, theatre, traveller,* and there are minor grammatical differences between Standard Englishes (*fit/fitted* as the past tense of *fit*; *got/ gotten,* the use and particularly negation of modals such as *must/should/ought* and so on). The most extensive differences are in the lexicon, particularly in the newer Englishes. While the grammars of different national varieties of Standard English resemble each other very closely, the grammars of non-standard varieties diverge greatly.

Non-standard regional, ethnic and social class dialects are restricted in function and non-standard speech has no fixed orthographic form. This poses a problem, of course, if writers wish to use dialect in novels or poetry, as they sometimes do, to create a sense of authenticity. Usually they resort to eye-dialect, which involves spelling words in an unconventional way to indicate the presence of a dialect speaker. However, because the spelling system is only loosely phonetic, the result is often merely quaint. If we saw the line *Wot e sez is* we might be inclined to think the speaker is a Cockney, but it actually represents the standard pronunciation more accurately than does the conventional orthography. The same problem occurs with attempts by scholars working in conversational analysis to represent the pronunciation of different dialect speakers: General American transcribers, for example, may use the letter 'h' to represent non-use of /r/ in non-rhotic dialects, as in *I left my cah in the Hahvahd yahd,* to represent a Boston speaker saying *I left my car in the Harvard yard*.

*Further reading:*
Allan, Keith 2009a. *The Western Classical Tradition in Linguistics*. 2nd edn. London: Equinox.
Allan, Keith and Kate Burridge 2006. *Forbidden Words: Taboo and the Censoring of Language*. Cambridge: Cambridge University Press.
Leith, Dick 1997. *A Social History of English*. 2nd edn. London: Routledge.

**Stylistics** Stylistics is the study of the linguistic choices that speakers and writers make to produce contextually appropriate utterances or texts. See Chapter 2.11.

**Suffix** See **Affix, prefix, infix, suffix, circumfix.**

**Syllable** All languages have **syllables**. Syllables are pulmonic (chest) pulses that give rhythm to speech. English may have syllables with any combination of (C)(C)(C)V(C)(C)(C)(C) – though there are constraints, see Chapter 2.2. Syllable structures vary across languages. Swahili /ˈn̩dogo/ has a sequence impossible for English, and Russian /#v#/ *in, at* could not function as an English syllable.

A syllable, σ, consists of two major constituents: **onset** and **rhyme**. For instance *feet* /fit/ has the onset /f/ and the rhyme /it/. The rhyme splits into a **nucleus**, which is the vowel /i/ and **coda**, which in this case is /t/. See the tree diagram, Figure 3.2.

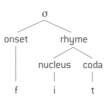

*Figure 3.2 Labelled tree diagram for* feet /fit/

The word *go* /goʊ/ has an onset /g/ and a rhyme /oʊ/; the rhyme has a nucleus (every rhyme has a nucleus), /oʊ/, but no coda. The word *goad* /goʊd/ has the rhyme /oʊd/ with the nucleus /oʊ/ and the coda /d/. The word *photograph* has three syllables: /foʊ/ in which the rhyme has no coda, + /tə/ in which the rhyme has no coda, + /græf/ in which the onset is /gr/, the rhyme is /æf/, of which the /æ/ is the nucleus and the /f/ the coda.

*Further reading:*
Goldsmith, John A. 1999. *Phonological Theory: The Essential Readings*. Oxford: Blackwell.
Roca, Iggy and Wyn Johnson 1999. *A Course in Phonology*. Oxford: Blackwell.

**Synchrony** See **Diachrony** and **synchrony**.

**Synonymy** If X and Y are sentences in the object language, then X is synonymous with Y (X ⟷ Y) if, in all possible worlds, whenever X is true, Y is also true; and whenever Y is false, X is also false. Synonymy is a relation of mutual entailment, hence the double-headed arrow, ⟷.

(1)  Jim is a bachelor ⟷ Jim is a man who has never married

If Jim was ever married then he is no bachelor.

(2)  Diana is now dead ⟷ Diana was once alive

If Diana had never been alive, then she couldn't have died.

Synonymy appears to exist between words which have a similar sense, for example *drunk~intoxicated, mad~insane*. This is because *Jo is drunk* ⟷ *Jo is intoxicated*; *Lear is mad* ⟷ *Lear is insane*. English is particularly rich in synonymous (or near synonymous) lexemes because of the influx into it of words from a variety of languages. *Royal, regal* and *kingly*, for example, are near synonymous terms which have derived from French, Latin, and Anglo-Saxon respectively. Although, theoretically, it is possible for two words to be completely synonymous, that is to say, they entail one another in all contexts, it is very rare for this to happen. Such is the nature of language that there is almost always some difference. In other words, such synonyms frequently differ stylistically and usually have different connotations. *Steed* and *nag* have the same conceptual sense but belong to different styles of English: the first is poetic and rather archaic, the second slang. *Hide* and *conceal, obstinate* and *stubborn, tight* and *stingy*, are all synonyms but most users would feel that they have different nuances of meaning. Near synonyms differ in their collocational range, i.e. the words with which they can co-occur. *Powerful, mighty* and *strong* look interchangeable but they won't all occur with

*tea, ocean* and *language*, and where they do occur the meaning is likely to be different in each case: *powerful language*, for instance, has a different meaning from *strong language*.

*Further reading:*
Allan, Keith 2001. *Natural Language Semantics*. Oxford & Malden MA: Blackwell.

**Systemic functional grammar (SFG)** Michael Halliday developed a polysystemic grammatical theory, originally called System-Structure Grammar, then Scale and Category Grammar, and now Systemic Functional Grammar (SFG): Halliday 1973; 1978; 1994; Halliday, Fawcett and Young 1987–88; Martin, Matthiessen and Painter 1997; Halliday and Matthiessen 2004.

The major clause constituents in SFG are Subject and Finite, which 'combine to form one constituent we call the Mood' (Halliday and Matthiessen 2004: 113); the rest of the clause is referred to as the Residue. The Residue consists of a Predicator (present in all major clauses) and perhaps a Complement, 'an element within the Residue that has the potential of being Subject but is not' (*ibid.* 122); there may also be an Adjunct, 'an element that has not got the potential of being Subject' (*ibid.* 123) and typically identifies the circumstances relevant to the state of affairs (realized by, for example, adverbials and prepositional phrases) – but also what are in other grammars referred to as Indirect Objects. The syntactic analysis at group level is very traditional.

SFG is strong on prosody but weak on other aspects of phonology. There has been little study of morphology within SFG. It explains **lexicogrammar** in terms of a configuration of the functions that language has evolved. By fleshing out the functions of constituent elements SFG does more than provide a mere structural skeleton in rooted labelled trees.

Halliday and his school have always been interested in the grammatical analysis of text and discourse (see Halliday and Hasan 1976; 1989; Halliday and Martin 1993; Fries and Gregory 1995); and the Hallidayan approach has been taken up in Rhetorical Structure Theory by analysts such as William Mann and Sandra Thompson, and by text generation enthusiasts such as Christian Matthiessen (see Mann, Matthiessen and Thompson 1992; Mann and Thompson 1986; Matthiessen and Thompson 1988). Hallidayan theory has also been adopted by critical discourse analysts (such as Hodge and Kress 1988; Kress and Leeuwen 2001).

SFG developed through practical application in language acquisition studies and teaching; and it has proved useful in the textual analysis of language varieties. It is used in both text generation and parsing (e.g. Matthiessen and Bateman 1991; Bateman, Matthiessen and Zeng 1999; Matthiessen, Zeng, Cross et al. 1998).

*References:*

Bateman, John A., Christian M.I.M. Matthiessen and Licheng Zeng 1999. Multilingual language generation for multilingual software: a functional linguistic approach. *Applied Artificial Intelligence: An International Journal* 13: 607–39.

Fries, Peter H. and Michael Gregory (eds) 1995. *Discourse in Society: Systemic Functional Perspectives*. Norwood NJ: Ablex.

Halliday, Michael A.K. 1973. *Explorations in the Functions of Language*. London: Edward Arnold.

Halliday, Michael A.K. 1978. *Language as a Social Semiotic*. London: Edward Arnold.

Halliday, Michael A.K. 1994. *An Introduction to Functional Grammar*. 2nd edn. London: Edward Arnold [First edn 1985].

Halliday, Michael A.K. and Ruqaiya Hasan 1976. *Cohesion in English*. London: Longman.

Halliday, Michael A.K. and Ruqaiya Hasan 1989. *Language, Context, and Text: Aspects of Language in a Social-semiotic Perspective*. 2nd edn. Oxford: Oxford University Press [First edn 1985].

Halliday, Michael A.K. and James R. Martin 1993. *Writing Science: Literacy and Discursive Power*. London: Falmer.

Halliday, Michael A.K. and Christian M.I.M. Matthiessen 2004. *An Introduction to Functional Grammar*. 3rd edn. London: Arnold.

Halliday, Michael A.K., Robin P. Fawcett and David J. Young (eds) 1987–88. *New Developments in Systemic Linguistics*. 2 vols. London: Frances Pinter.

Hodge, Robert and Gunther Kress 1988. *Social Semiotics*. Cambridge: Polity Press.

Kress, Gunther and Theo van Leeuwen 2001. *Multimodal Discourse: The Modes and Media of Contemporary Communication*. London: Arnold.

Mann, William C. and Sandra A. Thompson 1986. Relational propositions in discourse. *Discourse Processes* 9: 57–90.

Mann, William C., Christian M.I.M. Matthiessen and Sandra A. Thompson 1992. Rhetorical Structure Theory and text analysis. In *Discourse Description: Diverse Linguistic Analyses of a Fund-Raising Text*, ed. by William C. Mann and Sandra A. Thompson. Amsterdam/Philadelphia: John Benjamins, pp. 39–76.

Martin, James R., Christian M.I.M. Matthiessen and Clare Painter 1997. *Working with Functional Grammar*. London: Arnold.

Matthiessen, Christian M.I.M. and John A. Bateman 1991. *Text Generation and Systemic Linguistics: Experiences from English and Japanese*. London: Pinter.

Matthiessen, Christian M.I.M. and Sandra A. Thompson. 1988. The structure of discourse and subordination. In *Clause Combining in Grammar and Discourse*, ed. by John Haiman and Sandra A. Thompson. Amsterdam: John Benjamins.

Matthiessen, Christian M.I.M., Licheng Zeng, M. Cross, I. Kobayashi, T. Teruya and C. Wu 1998. The Multex generator and its environment: application and development. *Proceedings of the Ninth International Natural Language Generation Workshop, August 1998*. Niagara-on-the-Lake: ACL SIGGEN, pp. 228–37.

*Further reading:*

Halliday, Michael A.K. 1994. *An Introduction to Functional Grammar*. 2nd edn. London: Edward Arnold [First edn 1985].

Halliday, Michael A.K., Robin P. Fawcett and David J. Young (eds) 1987–88. *New Developments in Systemic Linguistics*. 2 vols. London: Frances Pinter.

Halliday, Michael A.K. and Christian M.I.M. Matthiessen 2004. *An Introduction to Functional Grammar*. 3rd edn. London: Arnold.

**Syntagmatic** See **Paradigmatic** and **syntagmatic.**

**Syntax** The study of rules that govern the structure of sentences and sentence constituents, and that determine the grammaticality of sentences and their parts. Chomsky (from Chomsky 1957 to Chomsky 2006) and his followers believe in the autonomy of syntax: i.e. that syntactic structures are generated without input from semantics, pragmatics, or phonology. Cognitive and functional grammarians do not believe in the autonomy of syntax (e.g. Bresnan 2001; Croft and Cruse 2004; Dik 1997; Goddard and Wierzbicka 2002; Goldberg 1995; Halliday and Matthiessen 2004; Langacker 1987; 1991; Pollard and Sag 1994; Van Valin 2001; Van Valin and LaPolla 1997).

References:

Bresnan, Joan 2001. *Lexical-Functional Syntax*. Malden MA: Blackwell.

Chomsky, Noam 1957. *Syntactic Structures*. The Hague: Mouton.

Chomsky, Noam 2006. *The Architecture of Language*, ed. by Nirmalangshu Mukherji, Bibudhendra Narayan Patnaik, and Rama Kant Agnihotri. New Dehli: Oxford University Press.

Croft, William and D. Alan Cruse 2004. *Cognitive Linguistics*. New York: Cambridge University Press.

Dik, Simon C. 1997. *The Theory of Functional Grammar*, ed. by Kees Hengeveld. 2nd revised edn. 2 vols. Berlin: Mouton de Gruyter.

Goddard, Cliff and Anna Wierzbicka (eds) 2002. *Meaning and Universal Grammar*. Amsterdam/Philadelphia: John Benjamins.

Goldberg, Adele E. 1995. *Constructions: A Construction Grammar Approach to Argument Structure*. Chicago: University of Chicago Press.

Halliday, Michael A.K. and Christian M.I.M. Matthiessen 2004. *An Introduction to Functional Grammar*. 3rd edn. London: Arnold.

Langacker, Ronald W. 1987. *Foundations of Cognitive Grammar. Vol. 1, Theoretical Prerequisites*. Stanford: Stanford University Press.

Langacker, Ronald W. 1991. *Foundations of Cognitive Grammar. Vol. 2*. Stanford: Stanford University Press.

Pollard, Carl J. and Ivan Sag 1994. *Head-driven Phrase Structure Grammar*. Stanford: Center for the Study of Language and Information (CSLI).

Van Valin, Robert D. Jr 2001. *An Introduction to Syntax*. Cambridge: Cambridge University Press.

Van Valin, Robert D. Jr and Randy LaPolla 1997. *Syntax: Structure, Meaning, and Function*. Cambridge: Cambridge University Press.

Further reading: Chapter 2.5 and Brown, E. Keith and Jim Miller (eds) 1996. *Concise Encyclopedia of Syntactic Theories*. Oxford: Pergamon.

Van Valin, Robert D. Jr and Randy LaPolla 1997. *Syntax: Structure, Meaning, and Function*. Cambridge: Cambridge University Press.

**Tenor** In traditional literary criticism 'tenor' is one of a pair of terms – the other is 'vehicle' – which describe the twin parts of a metaphor. In linguistics, however, it's a term used in discourse analysis to describe the relationship between participants in a discourse. 'Tenor' is one of the factors that affect the style of language we adopt. This is particularly evident in situations that call for more, or less, formality. Two lovers will naturally use a different language style from an employee talking to his/her boss. There will be significant differences in intonation pattern, syntactic structure, and the choice of lexical items. The tenor of their relationship is intimate. Complications occur, however, if the boss and employee are also lovers. In this case there is a clash between two separate relationships, each with its own individual tenor. Many linguists cope with this by distinguishing between personal tenor and functional tenor. The first of these involves the degree of personal relationship between participants: whether they are friends, relatives, lovers, or just acquaintances. The second involves the more public relationship they have. The ingredients here have to do with status, rank, and social roles. Wealth and fame are usually felt to increase a person's social standing, as does rising to a higher rank in the commercial world, the armed forces, or the class system. In addition there are subtle nuances of functional tenor between doctor and patient, shop assistant and customer, teacher and student, as a consequence of the particular roles they play.

Situations in which there is a possible conflict of functional and personal tenors can be described as having a complex tenor, as opposed to the simple tenor of those which are controlled by only one set of constraints. Many novels and plays exploit the possibility of functional versus personal clashes. In Shakespeare's *King Lear* a king hands over power to his daughters, and in D.H. Lawrence's *Lady Chatterley's Lover* (Harmondsworth: Penguin. 1960), a lady falls in love with her gardener. Along with context, field, mode or medium, and channel, tenor is one of the main variables determining the style that we adopt in everyday discourse.

*Further reading:*
Crystal, David 2003. *A Dictionary of Linguistics and Phonetics* 5th edn. Oxford: Blackwell.
Gregory, Michael and Susanne Carroll 1978. *Language and Situation: Language Varieties and their Social Contexts*. London: Routledge and Kegan Paul.

**Tense** A secondary grammatical category associated with verbs. Every language has a set of listemes for time locations such as *yesterday, today, tomorrow*, and a boundless set of lexically complex expressions such as *last year, an hour ago, five minutes and forty-three seconds after Ivan arrived*. Not all languages have tense systems, but those that do represent events as ordered relative to one another in time. **Tense** consists of a small number of grammatical morphemes which systematically locate situations in time relative to a deictic centre, most commonly the moment of utterance, *now*.

Morphologically, the English tense system has a **past,** typically marked by *—ed* and an unmarked **non-past**. There is also a retrospective tense, called the **perfect**. Semantically, English has a **present, past,** and **future** as well as a perfect. The present and non-past *Jo lives in Hampstead* contrasts with the past *Jo lived in Hampstead until she got married.* The perfect *Jo has lived in Hampstead for the past ten years* is retrospective in the sense that she is currently doing something that began ten years ago; similarly in *Sue had been eating when Fred called*, Fred's call occurred in the past at a time when Sue was in the middle of eating (which had begun some time previously). The semantic future is indicated by a non-past: *Jo leaves/is leaving/will leave for Paris within the hour.*

The so-called historic present is used to make past events seem more immediate as in *He **comes** in yesterday and he **says** to me 'What've you done to my bloody car?'* The past tense form is used in the semantic present for hypotheticals (often called subjunctives) like *Right now I really wish I **were** rich, so's I **could** buy you that lovely diamond ring.*

What is clear from studies of tense and time is that there is no easily stateable relationship between them. We use the two formal grammatical distinctions, past and present, to perform a number of functions, some of which are purely temporal, and some which are modal, or interpersonal in some way. It's another indication of the way in which the human meanings we have to convey exceed the strictly grammatical means at our disposal.

*Further reading:*
Allan, Keith 2001. *Natural Language Semantics*. Oxford & Malden MA: Blackwell.
Comrie, Bernard 1985. *Tense*. Cambridge: Cambridge University Press.

**Theta theory** Theta or θ-theory is concerned with assigning thematic roles to the arguments of verbs. 'Theta' is the name of the Greek letter θ, which corresponds to *th* in English, and since *thematic* begins with *th* it has become standard to abbreviate the expression 'thematic role' to 'θ-role'. It's important to recognize that 'theme' is being used differently here from its use in functional grammar, where it has largely a discourse meaning as the first item in a clause. In theta theory, 'theme' indicates one of a number of semantic roles which arguments fulfil. Clauses are seen as consisting of propositions which require certain types of arguments in order to be acceptable sentences of English. The essential elements of the theory differ somewhat from linguist to linguist, but the following are the commonly assumed theta-roles:

**Agent** (or **actor**) = instigator of some action: *John threw the ball*.
**Experiencer** = entity experiencing some psychological state: *John was happy*.
**Benefactive** = entity benefiting from some act: *Mary bought some chocolate **for John***.
**Instrument** = means by which something comes about: *Joanna dug the garden **with a spade***.
**Theme** = entity located or moved: ***The ball** rolled off the table*.
**Patient** = entity whose state is changed by the act: ***The vase** was broken in the fall*.
**Locative =** place in which something is situated: *John put the washing **in the bin***.
**Goal or recipient** = entity towards which something moves: *Mary passed the plate **to John***.
**Source** = whence something moves: *John returned **from London***.

The value of incorporating thematic roles into a model of syntax is that it allows us to give a more principled account of the way in which linguistic items behave than if we relied simply on formal grammatical criteria. In the following pair of sentences, the phrase *the vase* fulfils the same grammatical role, that of subject, but two distinct thematic roles:

(1) The vase shattered the glass.
(2) The vase shattered.

In (1) the vase is the cause of the shattering, hence it performs the role of **force** (inanimate actor), whereas in (2) it is the entity which undergoes the effect of shattering, hence it is a patient. The difference of thematic status is reflected in a difference of selection restrictions. In (1) we can replace *the vase* with *the noise*, or *a hidden flaw*, but not in (2).

*Further reading:*
Dowty, David R. 1991. Thematic proto-roles and
    argument selection. *Language* 67: 547–619.
Haiden, Martin 2005. *Theta Theory*. Berlin:
    Mouton de Gruyter.
Van Valin, Robert D. Jr and Randy LaPolla 1997.
    *Syntax: Structure, Meaning, and Function*.
    Cambridge: Cambridge University Press.

## Transformational generative grammar (TG)

Although its foundation is usually associated with the name of Noam Chomsky, TG was actually a creation of his mentor Zellig Harris (Harris 1970). Nonetheless, it was Chomsky 1957 which established TG as a worldwide phenomenon. The basic idea of TG is that context-free phrase structure rules such as the following create output strings that are lexically interpreted (i.e. have items inserted from the lexicon).

$$S \rightarrow NP\,VP$$
$$VP \rightarrow V\,(NP)\,(PP)$$
$$NP \rightarrow \left\{ \begin{matrix} (Det)\,(Adj)\,N \\ Pro \end{matrix} \right\}$$
$$PP \rightarrow P\,NP$$

Items in parentheses are optional; those stacked between braces, { }, are alternative choices. These rules are also known as rewrite rules or expansion rules because, for instance, S[entence] expands into N[oun]P[hrase] and V[erb]P[hrase].

Lexical insertion rules were context-sensitive and did not count as transformations. Lexical insertion was followed by semantic interpretation and phonological spelling-out that gave rise to a semantically interpreted phonetic string (in other words, a sequence of sounds expressing a meaning or meanings). In the 1960s and 1970s there were a host of transformations to apply to these so-called deep structures generated by phrase structure rules. All deep structures were patterned on positive active declarative sentences (*The boy ate the beans*). Passives (*The beans were eaten by the boy*) were generated by a passive transformation, negatives (*The boy didn't eat the beans*) by a negative transformation, interrogatives (*Did the boy eat the beans?*) and imperatives (*Eat those beans, boy!*) also resulted from transformations. In the 1990s the only transformation postulated was 'move-alpha', and by then deep structures have become D-structure and the phrase structure rules were very different.

*References and further reading:*
Bornstein, Diane D. 1977. *An Introduction to Trans-*
    *formational Grammar*. Cambridge MA: Winthrop.
Brown, E. Keith and Jim Miller (eds) 1996.
    *Concise Encyclopedia of Syntactic Theories*.
    Oxford: Pergamon.
Chomsky, Noam 1957. *Syntactic Structures*. The
    Hague: Mouton.
Harris, Zellig S. 1970. *Papers in Structural and
    Transformational Linguistics*. Dordrecht: D.
    Reidel.
Radford, Andrew 1988. *Transformational
    Grammar: A First Course*.
Radford, Andrew 1997. *Syntax: A Minimalist
    Introduction*. Cambridge: Cambridge University
    Press.

## Transitivity

A category used in the grammatical analysis of clause constructions to describe the relationship between the verb and its arguments. **Transitive** verbs are those that can take a **direct object**, i.e. which can **passivize**. In the case of some verbs the object is obligatory, for example, *enjoy*: *\*The man enjoyed* is clearly incomplete as a sentence and needs an object to complete it – *The man enjoyed his meal* (and to form its passive *His meal was enjoyed by the man*). Verbs that can't take an object are referred to as **intransitive**. Into this category come *die*, *fall*, and *digress*. None of these can occur in the passive: *be died by one's killer, *be fallen by the lumberjack, *be digressed by the politician are all impossible. Put another way: we can't die, fall, or digress something or somebody. However, the situation is more complicated than that because many verbs have both a transitive and an intransitive use. Where this occurs there is usually a different meaning being expressed, as in the following.

| intransitive | transitive |
|---|---|
| He's washing (i.e. washing himself) | He's washing the car |
| She's expecting (i.e. pregnant) | She's expecting a letter |
| She's working (i.e. busy) | She's working miracles |

With some verbs, however, such as *read*, and *eat*, the object (the undergoer) can be omitted, but is implicit (an impliciture) as indicated in the square brackets of (1) and (2):

(1) I'm reading [something].
(2) I'm eating [something].

Without the object NP in place, the clause cannot be passivized, e.g. (1) cannot be transformed into *is being read by me. The verb *enjoy* has recently acquired such an intransitive form in the waiter's instruction to diners to *Enjoy* with the implicit object NP *your meal*.

There are also verbs like *open* and *drive* which may be used with undergoer subjects in active (non-passive) clauses as well as undergoer subjects in passive clauses.

(3) The little boy opened **the door** ~
   **The door** was opened by the little boy.
(4) **The door** opened to reveal a richly decorated room.
(5) The police impounded **the car** ~
   **The car** was impounded by the police.
(6) **This car** drives well, doesn't it?

There are active~passive counterparts in the transitive clauses (3) and (5); the clauses in (4) and (6) are active intransitives with undergoer subject NPs.

*Further reading:*
Dixon, Robert M.W. and Alexandra Y. Aikhenvald (eds) 2000. *Changing Valency: Case Studies in Transitivity*. Cambridge: Cambridge University Press.

Næss, Åshild 2007. *Prototypical Transitivity*. Amsterdam: John Benjamins.

**Tree diagram** Rooted labelled tree diagrams are widely used in linguistics as a way of showing the internal hierarchical structure of sentences, i.e. clauses. The 'root' of the tree is at the top of the diagram, labelled by the symbol S ('sentence'). From this topmost point, branches descend which correspond to the categories specified by the rules. For example the phrase structure rules in (1) with the addition of some lexical insertion (Det is either *that* or *my*; N is *boy* or *brother*; V is *is*) are represented in the tree diagram of (2). NP = noun phrase, VP = verb phrase, V = verb, Det = determiner, and N = noun. Each of these is a **node** in the tree diagram of (2).

(1) S → NP VP
    VP → V NP
    NP → Det N

(2)

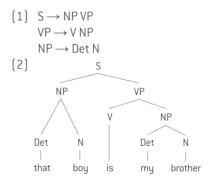

The tree shows that S immediately **dominates** the **sisters** NP and VP; these are said to be **daughters** of S; they are also **immediate constituents** of S. NP immediately dominates Det and N (its daughters or immediate constituents); VP immediately dominates V and NP. S dominates everything else in the tree; VP dominates all the nodes below it in the tree including the lexical items, i.e. V, NP, Det, N, *is, my, brother*.

In Chomskyan grammars since Chomsky's *Aspects of the Theory of Syntax* (1965), the functional relations **subject of** and **direct object of** have been defined in terms of tree structures: the clause or sentence subject is the NP immediately dominated by S, the direct object is the NP immediately dominated by VP. (An indirect object is the NP immediately dominated by a prepositional phrase that is daughter of VP.)

*References and further reading:* Chapter 2.5 and Chomsky, Noam 1965. *Aspects of the Theory of Syntax*. Cambridge MA: MIT Press.

Radford, Andrew 1988. *Transformational Grammar: A First Course*.

**Truth conditions** Many semanticists think that the purpose of semantic theory is to provide an account of how a speaker has the ability to recognize the truth conditions on statements. A truth condition on a statement or proposition is the condition that must be met for it to be assigned one of the truth values from the range {true, false}. In order to understand and evaluate the meaning of *The echidna ambled across the road* you need to know the conditions under which this statement would be true. One problem is to connect the language used to the world being spoken of. A greater problem is providing an acceptable semantics for non-truth-functional sentences like *Excuse me* or *What's the time?* or *Sorry*, or an expressive such as *Whoopee!* (One can say of a truth-functional sentence Φ, *It is true* (or *false*) *that Φ* but not of non-truth-functional sentences, *\*It is true that sorry*.)

Extension in a world (existing in that world) links with the notion of truth in a world at a certain time because, for instance, if my dog Zelda exists then I can truly predicate this of her in the sentence *Zelda exists* or I can presuppose her existence (i.e. take it for granted) and predicate of her *Zelda is a good-natured dog*. This leads to the question: What does it mean for a proposition to be true? The truth of *My brother Bill wasn't bald when he married Cynthia* depends on (at least) the following facts – according to the speaker:

(a) The speaker has (or once had) a brother Bill.
(b) At the time Bill married Cynthia he was not bald (he had a full head of hair).
(c) At a later time, Bill is or was bald, or it has been implied that he is or was bald (even though he may not be).

*Further reading:*
Allan, Keith 2001. *Natural Language Semantics*. Oxford & Malden MA: Blackwell.
Gamut, L.T.F. 1991. *Language Logic and Meaning. Vol. 1, Introduction to Logic. Vol. 2, Intensional Logic and Logical Grammar*. Chicago: Chicago University Press.

**Universal grammar** The notion of universal grammar can be traced back to Aristotle (about 350 BCE) (see Allan 2009a). It was revived among the scholastic grammarians of the Middle Ages, then in slightly different form by the rationalist grammarians of the seventeenth and eighteenth centuries, but was repudiated during the first half of the twentieth century. It came back into vogue with Chomskyan linguistics; and universal grammar as a characteristic of the human mind and brain has been a major area of linguistic research since Chomsky 1965. In *Aspects of the Theory of Syntax* Chomsky wrote:

> Real progress in linguistics consists in the discovery that certain features of given languages can be reduced to universal properties of language and explained in terms of these deeper aspects of linguistic form. (Chomsky 1965: 35)

The celebrated distinction in *Aspects* between 'competence', an idealization of what the individual knows about their language, and 'performance', the manifestation of competence in the use of language but including such features of spontaneous speech as hesitation and slips of the tongue, was later revised into the distinction between 'I-language' (idealized and internalized) and 'E-language' (expressed, externalized). Universal grammar is now abbreviated to UG.

> The statements of a grammar are statements of the theory of mind about the I-language, hence statements about structures of the brain formulated at a certain level of abstraction from mechanisms. ... UG now is construed as the theory of human I-languages, a system of conditions deriving from the human biological endowment that identifies the I-languages that are humanly accessible under normal conditions. (Chomsky 1986: 23)

Chomskyan UG claims to investigate the integration of grammar, mind, and brain.

> The basic assumption ... is that languages have no rules at all in anything like the traditional sense, and no grammatical constructions (relative clauses, passives, etc.) except as taxonomic artefacts. There are universal principles and a finite array of options as to how they apply (parameters). (Chomsky 1995: 388)

Chomsky has moved from the rationalist preoccupation with knowledge of language (in the mind) to the language faculty of the brain, which is a part of the human biological endowment. This incorporates an interest in language acquisition (also found among the seventeenth- and eighteenth-century rationalists) and the neurological mechanisms involved.

The Chomskyan turn to universal grammar has had the effect that all major grammatical theories from the late twentieth century have pretensions to universal applicability.

*References and further reading:*
Allan, Keith 2009a. *The Western Classical Tradition in Linguistics*. 2nd edn. London: Equinox.
Chomsky, Noam 1965. *Aspects of the Theory of Syntax*. Cambridge MA: MIT Press.
Chomsky, Noam 1986. *Knowledge of Language: Its Nature, Origin, and Use*. New York: Praeger.
Chomsky, Noam 1995. Bare phrase structure. In *Government and Binding Theory and the Minimalist Program: Principles and Parameters in Syntactic Theory*, ed. by Gert Webelhuth. Oxford: Blackwell, pp. 383–440.
Cook, Vivian J. and Mark Newson 2007. *Chomsky's Universal Grammar: An Introduction*. 3rd edn. Oxford & Malden MA: Blackwell.

**Unmarked** See **Markedness**.

**Variety** A term used, most commonly in sociolinguistics and stylistics, to describe a particular form of a language. Regional (including national) varieties of English, for example, would include dialects, such as Cockney, Jamaican English, Glaswegian, or British, American, Australian or Singapore English. Sociolects (social dialects) ethnolects (ethnic dialects), and even genderlects, are also varieties of a language.

The term **variety** is also used in relation to different linguistic jargons or registers: religious English, or literary English, which have their own distinctive vocabulary and forms of expression, could be described as varieties of English. Many varieties are the product of a number of different ingredients, such as social class, occupation, age, gender, and context. Not surprisingly, the term has a fairly generous application.

See also **Jargon** or **registers**.

*Further reading:*
Davies, Diane 2005. *Varieties of Modern English: An Introduction*. Harlow: Pearson Longman.

**Verb** A term used in lexical classification to refer to a class of words which typically denote a process or state of being (rather than 'doing' or 'action' words). For instance, *kill, eat, wear* involve action or process, whereas *seem, resemble* and *be* are better described as states. As with other lexical classes, the criteria used by linguists to distinguish verbs are based on their behavioural characteristics. These principally concern the morphology of verbs – the ways in which they change form to indicate contrasts of tense, aspect, person, and number – and their syntactic function. Syntactically, verbs predicate, i.e. assign an attribute or function to someone or something, or relations between things:

(1)   Jack**'s** happy.
(2)   Fred **ate** all the chocolate.
(3)   The door **opened** unexpectedly.
(4)   The photographs **were given** to Maria.
(5)   Harry **loves** Jake.

Verbs are categorized into two main groups, **lexical** (or full), and **auxiliary**. Lexical verbs are those which can act as the main verb in a clause. Auxiliary verbs, popularly known as 'helping verbs', are restricted both in form and in distribution. Many of them, such as *can~could* and *shall~should*, have only the two tense forms. They don't have any participle forms, for instance, such as *be canning~be canned, or *be shalling~*be shalled. More restrictive still is their distribution. With the exception of *be* and *have,* they don't ever serve as main verbs but have to co-occur with a lexical verb. Despite these restrictions, however, they are enormously powerful. In present-day English they are necessary for such operations as asking questions and negation, and for the construction of contrasts of aspect and voice. And, indeed, in verb phrases where they occur, they are also responsible for determining tense.

Lexical verbs can be divided into **regular** and **irregular**. The irregular variety have forms which English has retained from its Germanic parent. The distinction between the two kinds has to do with the formation of the past tense. Regular verbs characteristically form the past tense by adding

−ed to the stem (*show~showed*; *phone~phoned*), whereas irregular ones don't. They have an unpredictable past tense. Many irregular verbs have a separate past tense and past participle form (*take~took~taken*), whereas in the case of regular verbs the −ed form serves for both. There are up to six forms for verb lexemes (and often accompanying spelling changes).

> The unmarked (citation) form: *wish, love, burn, take, break*
> The infinitive form: *to wish, to love, to burn, to take, to break*
> The third-person singular present tense form: *s/he wishes, s/he loves, s/he burns, it takes, it breaks*
> The present participle, made by adding −ing to the unmarked form: *loving, wishing, burning, taking, breaking*
> The past tense, typically made by adding −ed to the unmarked form, but made in a variety of other ways with irregular verbs: *wished, loved, burnt* or *burned* (standard dialects vary), *took, broke*
> The past participle, often identical with the past tense of regular verbs, otherwise typically made by adding −en to the past tense of irregular verbs: *wished, loved, burnt* or *burned, taken, broken*

As you can see, this means, in practice, that regular verbs typically have one form fewer than irregular verbs.

*Further reading:*

Greenbaum, Sidney and Randolph Quirk 1990. *A Student's Grammar of the English Language*. Harlow: Longman.

Huddleston, Rodney and Geoffrey K. Pullum 2002. *The Cambridge Grammar of the English Language*. Cambridge: Cambridge University Press.

**Voice** In English there is only one voice distinction: between active and passive voice. Other languages have more.

(1)  The greedy girl ate the whole cake.
(2)  The whole cake was eaten by the greedy girl.

Only transitive clauses can passivize. We can formulate a passive transformation to show the relationship:

ACTIVE: NP$_1$ V NP$_2$ ⇒ PASSIVE: NP$_2$ *be* V−*en* by NP$_1$

There are a number of things wrong with the formulation of this transformation, but it will suffice for exemplificatory purposes. As can be seen, the sequence of NPs is swapped around in the passive, the actor NP$_1$ falls in the scope of the preposition *by*, and the verb is changed by the insertion of the auxiliary *be* followed by the V as a past participle, see (2). If the verbal group already contains other auxiliaries the passive *be −en* sequence comes after them, cf. *I suppose Harry could have been **be**ing insult**ed** by one of the drunks at the party.*

The English passive with *be* is ambiguously stative or dynamic. The passive using *get* is always dynamic. Compare (3) with (4); only the latter can refer to the state in which the window has been found, but both can refer to a dynamic process, which can be made explicit by adding *when the stone struck it.*

(3)  The window got broken.
(4)  The window was broken.

The English passive is said to be **periphrastic** because of the insertion of *be*; in Latin the passive is an inflection. Compare *Puer librum legit* "the.boy.NOMINATIVE the.book.ACCUSATIVE reads" with the passive *Liber a puero legitur* "the.book. NOMINATIVE+by+the.boy.ABLATIVE+is.read".

English is sometimes said to have a **middle voice** in sentences like *The door opened unexpectedly* or *The bread was baking in the oven* where the syntactic active suggests a semantic passive − implicitly, someone or something opened the door and someone was baking the bread. The reflexive impliciture of *Suzie showered and got dressed* would be translated using middle voice in some languages.

See also **Transitivity**.

*Further reading:*

Huddleston, Rodney and Geoffrey K. Pullum 2002. *The Cambridge Grammar of the English Language*. Cambridge: Cambridge University Press.

Klaiman, Miriam H. 1991. *Grammatical Voice*. Cambridge: Cambridge University Press.

**Vowels** A vowel is produced when there is no constriction or blockage in the oral cavity. Accents of a language may differ markedly in the way that vowels are pronounced; there is much less accent variation in the pronunciation of consonants. The vowel-making area is a small ellipse about 200 mm across that the highest point of tongue moves through. At the extremities of the vowel-making area are made all the peripheral **cardinal** vowels. Tongue height is determined by movement of the jaw and tongue. Opening and closing the jaw controls the size of the gap between the teeth and lips. The tongue travels through a range of points from high (or close) to low (or open). High and close are alternative labels for the location of the tongue nearest the palate; and either low or open for the location furthest away.

Vowels that hold one tongue position are **monophthongs** as in *hat* /hæt/; a glide between two vowel positions results in a **diphthong** as in *hate* /heɪt/ or *boat* /boʊt/, and between three positions a **triphthong** as in *fire* /faɪə/.

*Further reading:* Chapter 2.2 and
Clark, John, Colin Yallop and Janet Fletcher 2007. *An Introduction to Phonetics and Phonology.* 3rd edn. Malden MA: Blackwell.
Ladefoged, Peter 2006. *A Course in Phonetics.* 5th edn, with CD-ROM. Boston MA: Thomson Wadsworth.
Roca, Iggy and Wyn Johnson 1999. *A Course in Phonology.* Oxford: Blackwell.

**Well-formedness** A term derived from systems of logic and applied to the output strings of formal grammars when the outputs are generated according to the rules specified in the grammar. However, the terms *well-formed* and *ill-formed* are loosely used not of outputs of a formal grammatical system but of utterances made by speakers.

A sentence like (1), for example, might well be considered ill-formed according to the rules of Standard English grammar, just as (2) is.

(1) I ain't got no money.
(2) Got ain't money no I.

However, the use in (1) of the double negative and the colloquial term *ain't* is an English dialect form that is syntagmatically comparable with Standard English (NP Aux V NP), whereas the word-salad

in (2) is not. If we examine the dialect in which utterances like (1) regularly occur, we may well wish to say that, within that dialect, (1) is well-formed. But we should also wish to say that it is not well-formed in Standard English and therefore unacceptable in a situation for which Standard English is required.

The sentence *My brother is a girl* is perfectly well-formed in terms of its syntax, but, if it is taken literally as referring to my brother's sex, it is ill-formed semantically because it is manifestly a contradiction. However, if it is meant to refer to his sexuality, his imputed effeminacy, it is perhaps appropriate as a figurative expression. Much figurative language is, from a literal viewpoint, anomalous.

*Further reading:*
Allan, Keith 2001. *Natural Language Semantics.* Oxford & Malden MA: Blackwell.
Coulson, Seana 2001. *Semantic Leaps: Frame-shifting and Conceptual Blending in Meaning Construction.* Cambridge: Cambridge University Press.

**Word** English speakers sometimes define the *word* as a 'collection of letters separated by spaces' but this did not apply to Ancient Greek. Part of the Greek inscription from the Rosetta Stone reads ΒΑΣΙΛΕΥΟΝΤΟΣΤΟΥΝΕΟΥΚ ΑΙΠΑΡΑΛΑΒΟΝΤΟΣ… "The new king, having received …" Nor does it apply to languages like Chinese: 他在读书。Tazaidushu. "He is reading." And, of course, spoken words are not bounded by either spaces or pauses.

Preliterate language users have a concept of the word, and it is often the case that phonological words are isolable constituents of language. But this is problematic because some words have more than one pronunciation; for example *either* can be pronounced /iðə/ or /aɪðə/ and *the* is mostly /ðə/, but /ði/ before vowels. Then there are homophones like *too*, *two*, *to* which are all pronounced /tu/; and homographs like *lead* "metal" /lɛd/ vs "leash" /lid/. Some of these are distinguished by meaning, but /iðə/ and /aɪðə/ are in free variation and have the same meaning.

If you consider the set *happy*, *unhappy*, *wrap* and *unwrap* you may determine that there are two pairs of words distinguished from each other by meaning and they share a common segment, *un–*. English speakers will support the idea that *un–* has an identifiable meaning, but not that it is a word, because it is unable to stand on its own.

If *don't* consists of *do* and *n't* or *not*, how about *won't*? Is *wo* a form of *will* just as *n't* is a form of *not*? Presumably it is.

Is each of *son-in-law*, *put up with* ("tolerate"), and *kick the bucket* ("die") one word or three? Are alphabetisms like *S.O.B.* and *U.S.A.* words? Are proper names like *Marilyn Monroe* and *Norma Jean Baker* words?

It seems that there is no single certain criterion for identifying a word.

*Further reading:* Chapter 2.3 and
Katamba, Francis 2005. *English Words: Structure, History, Usage*. London: Routledge.

**Word classes** See **Morphosyntactic classes, lexical classes, word classes** or **parts of speech**.

# 4 some key linguists

Austin, John Langshaw (1911–1960) [247] ¦ Bickerton, Derek
(b. 1926) [247] ¦ Bloomfield, Leonard (1887–1949) [248] ¦
Chomsky, Avram Noam (b. 1928) [249] ¦ Fodor, Jerry Alan
(b. 1935) [250] ¦ Grice, Herbert Paul (1913–1988) [251] ¦
Halliday, Michael Alexander Kirkwood (b. 1925) [252] ¦ Hymes, Dell
Hathaway (b. 1927) [254] ¦ Jackendoff, Ray S. (b. 1945) [255] ¦
Jakobson, Roman Osipovich (1896–1982) [256] ¦ Jespersen, Otto
(1860–1943) [257] ¦ Katz, Jerrold Jacob (1932–2002) [257] ¦
Labov, William (b. 1927) [258] ¦ Lakoff, George (b. 1941) [259] ¦
Sapir, Edward (1884–1939) [260] ¦ Saussure, Ferdinand de
(1857–1913) [261] ¦ Searle, John Rogers (b. 1932) [262] ¦
Wittgenstein, Ludvig Josef Johann (1889–1951) [263] ¦
Whorf, Benjamin Lee (1897–1941) [264] ¦

This section gives brief critical appreciations of a handful of people who have engaged in the study of language. The list could easily be ten times as long. There are several hundred such critical appreciations to be found in:

Brown, E. Keith (General editor) 2006. *Encyclopedia of Languages and Linguistics*. 2nd edn. 14 vols. Oxford: Elsevier.

## Austin, John Langshaw (1911–1960)

J. L. Austin was a philosopher of language who taught at Oxford University in the years after World War II. He was one of a group of philosophers associated with 'ordinary language philosophy'. These thinkers and scholars became increasingly uneasy with the prevailing logical positivism of the day propounded by philosophers such as Alfred J. Ayer. According to Ayer, the only question we could really ask of utterances was whether or not they were a correct representation of reality, i.e. were they true or false. Austin challenged this by arguing that this approach ignored the function of utterances in everyday speech. In his seminal book *How to do Things with Words*, based on the William James lectures delivered at Harvard University in 1955, he demonstrated that utterances can be regarded as events or acts.

There are three types of speech acts which Austin argues utterances can be said to perform: a locutionary act, an illocutionary act, and a perlocutionary act. A locutionary act, or locution, refers simply to the act of saying something that makes sense in the language; in other words, that follows the grammatical rules of language. An illocutionary act is one which is performed through the locution: stating, warning, wishing, promising, and so on. And finally, a perlocutionary act is the effect the illocutionary act has on the listener: such as persuading, convincing, deterring, misleading, surprising, and so forth. Speech act theory tends to concentrate largely on illocutions. Locutions and perlocutions, coming before and after the illocutionary act, although important, are of less central interest. When Austin first began his study of speech acts he attempted first of all to distinguish between a class of utterances which he called performatives and those which he termed constatives. Performatives are a special group of utterances the saying of which actually performs the action named by the verb: e.g. *I pronounce you man and wife* (an act of marriage); *I apologize* (an act of apology). In order for these utterances to count as performatives, various conditions have to be met. Only certain people can pronounce you man and wife, for example, whilst if you apologize and clearly don't mean it you have not really apologized. The right situation has to be matched with the right form of words. Austin defined this matching process in terms of 'felicity conditions'.

Constatives consist of all those other utterances, such as statements and questions, where actions are being described or asked about rather than explicitly performed, as in *I cooked the cake* and *Can you cook the cake?* Austin quickly realized, however, that the distinction between performatives and constatives was artificial, since even constatives are performing some kind of act, although of a more purely linguistic kind than performatives. *I cooked the cake* performs the illocutionary act of stating a fact. And similarly, *Can you cook the cake?* is performing the illocutionary act of inquiring. But certain illocutionary acts use explicit performatives. Explicit performatives have a performative verb, a verb which names the action being performed, e.g. *affirm, allege, assert, forecast, predict, announce, insist, order, state*. These are sometimes referred to as speech act verbs.

We thus arrive at the view that all utterances constitute speech acts of one kind or another. Since Austin's early work on speech acts, much effort has been directed towards categorizing the types of acts possible in language, principally by the linguistic philosopher John Searle (q.v.).

### Key texts
> *Sense and Sensibilia* (Oxford: Oxford University Press, 1964)
> *Philosophical Papers* (ed. by James O. Urmson and Geoffrey J. Warnock, Oxford: Oxford University Press, 1961)
> *How To Do Things With Words: The William James Lectures delivered at Harvard University in 1955* (ed. by James O. Urmson, Oxford: Clarendon, 1962)
> *How To Do Things With Words* (2nd edn, ed. by James O. Urmson and Marina Sbisà, Oxford: Oxford University Press, 1975)

## Bickerton, Derek (b. 1926)

Derek Bickerton is Professor Emeritus at the University of Hawaii. Much of Bickerton's work has centred on the study of creole languages, particularly in Guyana and Hawaii, which has provided the basis for some powerful and influential ideas about the evolution of language. Bickerton was struck early on in his research by two significant features of the process of creolization. The first was the similarity of creoles all over the world in terms of their grammatical structures and processes of word formation, and the second was the speed with which creoles developed, particularly in slave colonies or among immigrant workers from different language backgrounds using pidgin to communicate. Given that children of pidgin speakers had access to limited linguistic resources, their ability to generate a new language seemed little short of miraculous. Bickerton's solution to this conundrum was to suggest that children are biologically programmed to produce language; this is known as the bioprogram hypothesis. In contact communities with no education, and with only a simple pidgin as material, children were able to generate a fully functional language within a generation. Bickerton's research provided additional support for those who believe, like Chomsky (q.v.), that language is hard-wired into the brain, and that the principles of grammar are universal.

Bickerton's work was published in *The Roots of Language* (1981), after which he extended his research to consider how language evolved in the human species. In *Language and Species* (1990) he argued that crucial to the evolution of language is the emergence of three central mental capacities: symbolization, predication, and voluntary expansion. The first of these involves the evolution of representational systems in which a sequence of sounds stands for something in the outside world. Symbolic thinking of this kind represents a significant advance on animal cries. The second involves the ability to predicate something about the outside world, i.e. to comment on it. Putting together the two words *dog* and *barks* makes a meaningful sequence which is not derivable from the two words considered in isolation. This again distinguishes language from animal cries where there is no indication that one sound influences another in the same way. The third capacity, voluntary expansion, is the ability to innovate and add to sequences at will, as compared with animal cries which are generally fixed and formulaic. These three capacities make possible a proto-language which, for Bickerton, is the beginning of syntax. In more recent work, published in 2000 with William Calvin, *Lingua ex Machina*, Bickerton has pushed the argument further in an attempt to use discoveries about neurological structures in the brain to link the development of symbolic

thinking with human biology and Darwinian theories of natural selection.

**Key texts**
> *Roots of Language* (Ann Arbor: Karoma, 1981)
> *Language and Species* (Chicago: University of Chicago Press, 1990)
> *Language and Human Behavior* (London: Routledge, 1995)
> With William Colvin, *Lingua ex Machina: Reconciling Darwin and Chomsky with the Human Brain* (Cambridge MA: MIT Press, 2000)

## Bloomfield, Leonard (1887–1949)

Bloomfield was an American linguist who held professorial posts at Ohio State University, the University of Chicago and, from 1940, Yale University. He began his career as a teacher of German. His interest in linguistics was aroused by Eduard Prokosch, a philologist in the German department of the University of Wisconsin where Bloomfield studied as a postgraduate. It was sealed by a period he spent in Leipzig from 1913 to 1914; there he came under the influence of the German neogrammarian scholars who had revolutionized the study of historical philology by demonstrating that sound changes in any language are regular and predictable, rather than idiosyncratic, as had earlier been supposed.

Bloomfield used the scientific methodology he had learnt in Leipzig to study non-Indo-European languages, firstly, Tagalog, a Malayo-Polynesian language, and subsequently, Algonquin, a Native American language. In so doing, he was following in the footsteps of Franz Boas, an anthropological linguist, who was the first linguist of significance to attempt a descriptive analysis of non-Indo-European languages. Bloomfield's own descriptive approach was influenced by the work of Ferdinand de Saussure (q.v.) whose concept of language structure he adopted. Like Saussure, he argued that languages are autonomous systems in which lexis, syntax, and phonology are all interrelated and capable of precise empirical description. He accepted Saussure's distinction between diachronic and synchronic language states but, while he never lost interest in historical linguistics, his major concern was with synchronic descriptive linguistics.

Bloomfield's major work, *Language*, was

published in 1933. In it, Bloomfield developed what he considered would be a complete scientific methodology for describing linguistic phenomena. Because speech is prior to writing phylogenetically (in the development of the human species), ontogenetically (in the development of an individual human), and in terms of frequency, he considered it axiomatic that language study must always be focused on spoken rather than written language and that morphological and syntactic analysis should be independent of semantic content. The task of linguists, as he saw it, was to collect data from native speakers of the language and then to analyse them by studying phonological and syntactic patterns. Bloomfield argued that one of the principal ways in which items are structured in a language was in terms of their constituency. Any sentence could be analysed in terms of its immediate constituents. These, in turn, could be analysed into further constituents, and so on, down to the level of morphemes, which are the smallest constituents. A sentence is thus conceived of as a hierarchy of interlocking constituents, each of which can either be replaced by a similar constituent, or redistributed to construct other sentences. The important task for the linguist was to discover the individual constituents of the language being observed. This was achieved through discovery procedures, a set of principles which covered the distribution and substitutability of items.

Bloomfield's descriptive methodology was preeminent from the 1930s until its influence waned with the rise of generative linguistics after the publication of Noam Chomsky's *Syntactic Structures* in 1957, which turned a new generation of linguists from mere description towards explanation. This meant penetrating beyond the surface structures of language and understanding the mental system which produced them.

**Key texts**

> *Introduction to the Study of Language* (New York: Henry Holt, 1914)
> A set of postulates for the science of language (*Language* 2: 153–64, 1926)
> *Language* (New York: Holt, Rinehart and Winston, 1933)
> *Linguistic Aspects of Science* (Chicago: University of Chicago Press, 1939)
> *Outline Guide for the Practical Study of Foreign Languages* (Baltimore: Linguistic Society of America, 1942)

## Chomsky, Avram Noam (b. 1928)

More than any other linguist, Noam Chomsky dominates contemporary linguistics. From his first book, *Syntactic Structures*, published in 1957, he has constantly challenged the orthodoxies of linguistic inquiry. In many cases his most searching ideas have developed from what, on the face of it, are fairly simple observations. In contrast to many descriptive linguists, for example, he claimed that it was not enough for a grammar simply to take account of existing sentences. It must also be able to account for sentences which have not yet been uttered. What struck him about language was its creativity, that is, the capacity of language speakers to generate completely novel sentences endlessly. This could only be possible if speakers had an internalized set of rules, or generative grammar, that specifies which sequences of a language are grammatical and thus possible, and which are not. This mental grammar comprises a speaker's 'competence', and the task of the linguist, as he saw it, was to explain linguistic competence and, in so doing, to penetrate the mysteries of the human mind.

An early target for Chomsky was the behaviourist theory of language acquisition associated with Burrhus F. Skinner. To Skinner, language consists of a set of habits built up over years by a process of trial and error. Children learn it in much the same way that rats learn how to find food pellets in laboratory experiments. In opposition to this, Chomsky argued that the conditioning process of approval and reward was counterproductive in language acquisition. Parents tend to approve statements by their children which are true, rather than those which are grammatically correct. Moreover, the language that children hear around them which, according to Skinner they are copying, is full of so-called 'performance errors': unfinished sentences, mistakes, and slips of the tongue. Yet, despite this, children manage to learn the rules for correct clause construction. Chomsky argued that the only way to explain this is to suppose that children are genetically programmed to acquire language. They are born with a universal grammar applicable to all languages, which it is the task of the linguist to map.

Of course, the difficulty in such a task is that the mind is not open to immediate inspection. The linguist has to proceed indirectly, by examining actual language use and working backwards to the mental system responsible for its production. One thing which Chomsky saw immediately was that a description of the surface structure of sentences alone is not sufficient to achieve this. There are pairs of sentences, such as *John is eager to please* and *John is easy to please*, which have the same surface structure but which have entirely different underlying structures, as revealed by the fact that the second may be paraphrased *To please John is easy* (or *It is easy to please John*) whereas the first may not, cf. *To please John is eager*. Observations such as this led Chomsky to posit two levels of structure: deep and surface structure. This meant that there are two components to grammar – the first consisting of rules for combining constituents and controlling the input into the deep structure, and the second specifying the rules by which the surface structure is derived. The two were connected by transformational rules. The deep~surface divide proved useful in providing an explanation for a number of linguistic features which descriptive linguistics on its own could not. At the same time it made syntax into a highly elaborate study – arguably too elaborate, in that linguists began seeing transformations everywhere, with the consequence that the concept became troublesome. In recent times, Chomsky has simplified the transformational approach and slimmed the processes down to just a few central operations. The terms 'deep' and 'surface' have also been refined so that Chomsky now refers to 'D' structure and 'S' structure. In 1995, Chomsky radically overhauled his approach in the Minimalist Program. This effectively stripped away all but the most necessary elements, and emphasized the principles of economy and optimal design in grammar.

Universal grammar remains the Holy Grail of Chomskyan linguistics and, in this respect, the Minimalist Program has been useful in discovering linguistic universals, that is, constructions and processes which all languages have in common. Clearly, when children are born, they do not come into the world with knowledge of a particular language. Nevertheless, if Chomsky is right, their knowledge must be of a kind which can develop into whatever language exists in the community around them. Language acquisition in this model becomes more like tuning a television receiver than the old model of learning by imitation and reinforcement. It's a model which underlies his Principles and Parameters approach, outlined in 1979, and which continues to be productive.

**Key texts**
> *Syntactic Structures* (The Hague: Mouton, 1957)
> *Aspects of the Theory of Syntax* (Cambridge MA: MIT Press, 1965)
> With Morris Halle, *The Sound Pattern of English* (New York: Harper & Row, 1968)
> *Language and Mind* (New York: Harcourt Brace and World, 1968)
> *Reflections on Language* (New York: Pantheon Books, 1975)
> *Lectures on Government and Binding: The Pisa Lectures* (Dordrecht: Foris, 1981)
> *Language and the Study of Mind* (Tokyo: Sansyusya Publishing Co. Ltd, 1982)
> *Modular Approaches to the Study of the Mind* (San Diego: State University Press, 1984)
> *Knowledge of Language: Its Nature, Origin, and Use* (New York: Praeger, 1986)
> *Language and Thought* (Wakefield RI: Moyer Bell, 1993)
> *The Minimalist Program* (Cambridge MA: MIT Press, 1995)
> *On Language* (New York: The New Press, 1998)
> *New Horizons in the Study of Language and Mind* (Cambridge: Cambridge University Press, 2000)
> *On Nature and Language*, Adriana Belletti and Luigi Rizzi (eds) (Cambridge: Cambridge University Press, 2002)
> *The Architecture of Language*, Nirmalangshu Mukherji, et al. (eds) (New Delhi: Oxford University Press, 2006)

### Fodor, Jerry Alan (b. 1935)

Jerry Fodor is an American linguistic philosopher and cognitive scientist currently teaching at Rutgers University in New Jersey. He began his academic career at the Massachusetts Institute of Technology, where he taught for 27 years. At MIT he came into contact with the work on generative linguistics pioneered by Noam Chomsky (q.v.). Fodor was quick to realize the importance of such work for cognitive science. Like Chomsky, Fodor developed a strong commitment to the idea of psychological nativism, the idea that many cognitive functions and concepts are innate. And, like Chomsky, he was highly critical of behaviourist models of cognition.

Much of Fodor's work has been devoted to studying the philosophy of language, in particular, to the relation between thought and language. Probably, his most contentious proposal has been to argue that thought has a prior existence to language and possesses a semantic structure which can be described in a way similar to that of language. The language of thought (LOT), or 'mentalese', is deduced by Fodor from the way in which natural languages work. If we take language to be the expression of thought, and given that language is systematic, then thought also must be systematic. For Fodor, LOT is an innate capability of the human mind. It is what enables us to represent the world to ourselves and thus to think about it. Mental representations are the outcome of LOT and are imagined by Fodor to have a syntactic structure comparable to that of natural languages. The model that underlies Fodor's view of the mind is heavily computational. Thinking is a consequence of the mind running central programs on the propositions that make up LOT and generating the beliefs and desires that make up our mental states. He rejects, however, the reductive concept of the mind that this might lead to by arguing that mental states can be realized in many different ways. In order to be described as a language, LOT must have the productivity and combinatorial properties which are constitutive of natural languages. Creativity is thus constitutive of our mental life.

Fodor has also been influential in developing the idea that the mind has a modular structure. According to this view, the mind is organized in terms of modules, or 'organs', which are responsible for certain domain-specific activities, such as creating well-formed sequences of sounds, or matching words to sounds. It has long been clear to observers that speakers can experience localized impairment in one part of their physical linguistic apparatus without any necessary impairment of their general linguistic competence. Modularity seems to offer a principled way of accounting for this. At the same time, however, Fodor has been critical of psycholinguists like Steven Pinker, who,

in his view, have taken modularity too far. Fodor is still concerned to argue that there is a large part of the mind governed by general cognitive processes operating across the mind as a whole.

**Key texts**
> *Psychological Explanation* (New York: Random House, 1968)
> With T. Bever and M. Garrett, *The Psychology of Language* (New York: McGraw Hill, 1974)
> *The Language of Thought* (Cambridge MA: Harvard University Press, 1975)
> *The Modularity of Mind: An Essay on Faculty Psychology* (Cambridge MA: MIT Press, 1983)
> *Psychosemantics: The Problem of Meaning in the Philosophy of Mind* (Cambridge MA: MIT Press, 1987)
> *A Theory of Content and Other Essays* (Cambridge MA: MIT Press, 1990)
> *The Elm and the Expert, Mentalese and its Semantics*. The 1993 Jean Nicod Lectures (Cambridge MA: MIT Press, 1994)
> *Concepts: Where Cognitive Science Went Wrong*. The 1996 John Locke Lectures (Oxford: Oxford University Press, 1998)
> *In Critical Condition* (Cambridge MA: MIT Press, 1998)
> *The Mind Doesn't Work That Way: The Scope and Limits of Computational Psychology* (Cambridge MA: MIT Press, 2000)
> With Ernest Lepore, *The Compositionality Papers* (Oxford: Oxford University Press, 2002)

## Grice, Herbert Paul (1913–1988)

Paul Grice was a British-born philosopher of language who taught in Britain, at Oxford University, and America, at the University of California. His work has been central to the modern study of pragmatics. For Grice, the problem with verbal communication lies in the fact that language underspecifies meaning. As a consequence, studying the encoded meaning of an utterance alone is insufficient to explain its full meaning. Grice was particularly interested in the way in which speakers and listeners depend on processes of natural, rather than formal, logic in order to understand utterances. For example, the negator *not* works in formal logic so that statements like *John is happy* and *John is not happy* are mutually exclusive. However, in natural language, denying that John is happy doesn't necessarily mean that he is unhappy; we recognize possible states which exist between the two. It is because of this that we can create formulations such as *John is not unhappy*. Similarly, in formal logic, the quantifier *some* does not exclude the possibility of *all*, so that *Some students passed the exam* does not contradict the statement *All students passed the exam*. However, if you ask a friend how many people passed the exam and the answer came back *some*, you would naturally conclude that not everyone had passed. Examples like these encouraged the idea that language has its own natural logic, in addition to the formal kind proposed by logicians and certain semanticists. Natural logic allows for certain things to be implied beyond those which are obviously stated. Grice termed these implicatures.

Grice distinguished two main kinds of implicatures, conventional and conversational. Conventional implicatures are inferences that we draw from our competence in the language itself, whereas conversational implicatures arise from the common ground and hence our communicative competence. So, for example, in the utterance *Paul is an Englishman, therefore he is brave* the linguistic context would enable us to access the conventional implicature (arising from the connective 'therefore') that Paul is brave because he is an Englishman – a somewhat dubious assumption. An utterance of *The picnic was ruined. Someone forgot the corkscrew* conversationally implicates that the picnic was spoiled because there was no alcohol available. Accounting for the intention of speakers was where Grice felt semantic analyses of meaning fell short. In response to this he developed the *cooperative principle*, the basic assumption of which is that speakers will normally try to cooperate in the process of communication. The principle itself states, 'Make your contribution such as is required, at the stage at which it occurs, by the accepted purpose or direction of the talk exchange in which you are engaged' ('Logic and conversation', 1975). In order to comply with this principle, speakers need to follow a number of sub-principles, which Grice called maxims. These fall into four categories, of quantity, relation, manner and quality (for details see Chapter 3.1 'Cooperative principle' and Grice 'Logic and conversation' 1975).

The cooperative principle and its associated maxims represent a kind of baseline for talking. Unless there is evidence to the contrary, we assume, as listeners, that speakers will tell the truth, estimate what we need to know, package the material accordingly, keep to the topic, and give some thought to our being able to understand them. The maxims, then, are best regarded not as rules but as implicit principles on which successful communication is built. They can be departed from in two main ways. Speakers can choose either to flout or to violate them. Floutings are different from violations. Violating a maxim involves some element of communication failure: providing too little, or too much, detail, being irrelevant, or too vague. Floutings, however, are apparent rather than real violations. They enable us to comply with the maxims indirectly rather than directly. So, for example, sarcasm, calling out *Clever!* when someone has done something stupid, can be viewed as a form of flouting since it only seems to violate the maxim of quality. Although Grice's theory of meaning has been deeply influential in modern pragmatics, it has been challenged, principally by Dan Sperber and Deirdre Wilson in *Relevance: Communication and Cognition*, Oxford: Blackwell, 1986.

**Key texts**

> Meaning (*The Philosophical Review* 66: 377–88, 1957)
> Utterer's meaning and intention (*The Philosophical Review* 78: 147–77, 1969)
> Logic and conversation (in Peter Cole and Jerry Morgan (eds) *Syntax and Semantics, Vol. 3*. New York: Academic Press, 1975)
> *Studies in the Way of Words* (Cambridge MA: Harvard University Press, 1989)
> *The Conception of Value* (Oxford: Oxford University Press, 1991)
> *Aspects of Reason* (Oxford: Oxford University Press, 2001)

## Halliday, Michael Alexander Kirkwood (b. 1925)

Michael Halliday is a British linguist who, in 1976, moved to Australia where he became Foundation Professor at the University of Sydney; he remained there until his retirement. He is currently Distinguished Visiting Professor at the University of Hong Kong. Halliday is principally important for developing a model of grammar known as *systemic functional grammar*. A functional grammar is one which seeks to derive the formal structures of language from the functions it is said to perform. 'Systemic' here means viewing language as a set of interacting systems for expressing meanings. The development of this kind of grammar was, in part, a reaction to more formal approaches associated with Chomskyan transformational grammar. For Chomsky, the grammar of a language operates separately from meaning, which is why nonsense sentences can still be grammatical. For Halliday, however, grammar is essentially the encoding of meaning. Speakers begin with a meaning they wish to convey and then are offered a series of choices within the linguistic system. The context within which these choices are made consists of three overarching functions which language is said to fulfil:

1. The ideational function: the use we make of language to conceptualize the world. This function emphasizes language as an instrument of thought, a symbolic code, with which we represent the world to ourselves.
2. The interpersonal function: the use we make of language as a personal medium. This function emphasizes language as an instrument of transaction by which we represent ourselves to others.
3. The textual function: the use we make of language to form texts, whether spoken or written. This function emphasizes language as an instrument of communication with which we construct cohesive and coherent sequences.

According to Halliday, these functions relate to three central purposes which govern the form clauses take. A clause acts as a representation (ideational function), an exchange (interpersonal function), and a message (textual function). Halliday's procedure is to take each of these in turn and describe the choices open to users of the language in their construction of utterances.

Systemic functional grammar has appealed to applied linguists because it stresses the importance of social context in determining the choices language users make. Speakers are constrained by 'field' (the subject being talked about), 'tenor' (the relationships between the participants and the social roles they adopt), and 'mode' (the

channel of communication). In stressing the importance of context, Halliday was following in the footsteps of the British linguist John R. Firth, who famously said 'We know a word by the company it keeps'. Halliday's work has also been important in the study of language acquisition. According to Halliday, children develop language in order to fulfil certain communicative functions. From his observations of his son Nigel, he identified seven main functions:

1. Instrumental: 'I want.'
2. Regulatory: 'Do as I tell you.'
3. Interactional: 'Me and you.'
4. Personal: 'Here I come.'
5. Heuristic: 'Tell me why.'
6. Imaginative: 'Let's pretend.'
7. Informative: 'I've got something to tell you.'

Systemic functional grammar has established itself as a useful model for analysing language, and it is seen as complementary, rather than opposed, to more formal models.

### Key texts
> *Intonation and Grammar in British English* (The Hague: Mouton, 1967)
> *Explorations in the Functions of Language* (London: Edward Arnold, 1973)
> *Learning How to Mean* (London: Edward Arnold, 1975)
> With Ruqaiya Hasan, *Cohesion in English* (London: Longman, 1976)
> *Language as Social Semiotic: The Social Interpretation of Language and Meaning* (London: Edward Arnold, 1978)
> *The Semiotics of Culture and Language* (London: Pinter, 1984)
> *Spoken and Written Language* (Waurn Ponds: Deakin University Press, 1985)
> *An Introduction to Functional Grammar* (London: Edward Arnold, 1985)
> With Ruqaiya Hasan, *Language, Context and Text: A Social Semiotic Perspective* (Waurn Ponds: Deakin University Press, 1985)
> *New Developments in Systemic Linguistics* (London: Pinter, 1987–1988)
> *Current Ideas in Systemic Practice and Theory* (London: Pinter, 1991)
> *The Collected Works of M.A.K. Halliday*, ed. by Jonathan J. Webster. Vol. 1: *On Grammar*; 2:

*Linguistic Studies of Text and Discourse*; 3: *On Language and Linguistics*; 4: *The Language of Early Childhood*; 5: *The Language of Science*; 6: *Computational and Quantitative Studies*; 7: *Studies in English Language*; 8: *Studies in Chinese Language*; 9: *Language and Education*; 10: *Language and Society* (London: Continuum, 2002–2007)

## Hymes, Dell Hathaway (b. 1927)

Dell Hymes is an American linguist who has taught at the universities of Yale, Berkeley, Pennsylvania, and latterly Virginia, from which he retired in 1996. He is principally known for his pioneering work in the ethnography of communication, a field which he largely created. Edward Sapir (q.v.) and Frank Boas were formative influences, and Hymes began his career as a linguist by studying the structure of Native American languages. As a consequence, he became deeply interested in the part played by folklore and oral narrative in the culture and society of Native American life. In contrast to Chomsky (q.v.), for whom the purpose and function of language has always been of secondary importance, Hymes argues that considerations of usage are a prerequisite to understanding linguistic form.

In 1962, Hymes published an essay entitled, 'The ethnography of speaking' which was an attempt to synthesize the study of culture (ethnography) and linguistics in a new discipline. Hymes argued that interpreting human behaviour involves understanding how language is used in particular social settings. This, in turn, is dependent on understanding the rules and conventions underlying such interactions. 'The ethnography of speaking,' Hymes 1962: 101 said, 'is concerned with the situations and uses, the patterns and functions, of speaking as an activity in its own right.' He called the knowledge that speakers deploy in negotiating such interactions 'communicative competence'. The focus of activity for ethnographers like Hymes is in identifying speech communities: social groupings that share rules of speaking, and (for Hymes) at least one language variety. A fundamental tenet of such an approach is the recognition that most individuals belong to several speech communities. The purpose of the ethnographer is first to describe communicative behaviour in these culturally specific settings, and then to use the knowledge gained to build a metatheory about human communication.

Hymes's particular contribution to research in this area has been to identify and classify the components which are salient in the social use of language. For ease of remembering, he labelled each of the main groups with one of the letters from the word *speaking*. What these components aim to do is to establish the parameters within which the various speech acts we perform can be described:

S SITUATION: composed of 'setting' (location, venue and time), and 'scene' (the particular cultural event)
P PARTICIPANTS: the addressor and addressee
E ENDS: purposes, goals and outcomes
A ACT SEQUENCE: the form and order of the interaction
K KEY: tone and manner
I INSTRUMENTALITIES: the channel of communication (e.g. telephone, fax, email) and the medium (e.g. gestures, facial expressions, language)
N NORMS: cultural expectations about the amount, style, and form of speech
G GENRES: the linguistic modes in which messages are couched (e.g. adverts, sermons, poems)

Hymes's work has been especially influential in those branches of linguistics which are concerned with the social functions of language; in particular, with the way in which different language patterns and behaviours reflect different ways of experiencing the world. Sociolinguists, discourse analysts, and pragmaticists have benefited greatly from the insights generated by the link he forged between ethnography and linguistics.

**Key texts**

> The ethnography of speaking (in Thomas Gladwin and William C. Sturtevant (eds), *Anthropology and Human Behavior*, Washington: The Anthropology Society of Washington, pp. 13–53, 1962)
> With John J. Gumperz (eds), *The Ethnography of Communication* (Menasha WI: American Anthropological Association, 1964)
> *Language in Culture and Society* (New York: Harper and Row, 1964)

> *Foundations in Sociolinguistics: An Ethnographic Approach* (Philadelphia: University of Pennsylvania Press, 1974)
> *"In Vain I Tried to Tell You": Essays in Native American Ethnopoetics* (Philadelphia: University of Pennsylvania Press, 1981)
> *Studies in the History of Linguistic Anthropology* (Amsterdam: John Benjamins, 1983)
> *Ethnography, Linguistics, Inequality: Essays in Education, 1978–1994* (London: Taylor & Francis, 1997)
> *Now I Know Only So Far: Essays in Ethnopoetics* (Lincoln: University of Nebraska Press, 2003)

## Jackendoff, Ray S. (b. 1945)

Ray Jackendoff is Seth Merrin Professor of Philosophy at Tufts University after many years as Professor of Linguistics at Brandeis University. Jackendoff's principal contribution has been in the field of cognitive linguistics. This particular branch of the discipline is concerned with the way in which language relates to human perception and understanding. Our conception of the world is mediated through language, in particular through lexical and syntactic expression. It is the nature of this mediation which cognitive linguists are concerned to explore and map. Much of Jackendoff's critical work has been spent in trying to develop just such a map and, from this, arrive at an explanatory model of the semantics, or meaning structure, of natural languages.

Jackendoff studied at the Massachusetts Institute of Technology under Noam Chomsky (q.v.) and Morris Halle. He was profoundly influenced by the model of generative grammar developed by Chomsky, the essential goal of which was to account for the mental processes involved in the production and comprehension of language. But in contrast to Chomsky, Jackendoff's approach has not centred solely on syntax. Over the years, Chomsky has put forward many versions of generative grammar, but they have all privileged syntax as the major component of language. Jackendoff, however, treats phonology, syntax, and semantics as three parallel generative processes. These three components are coordinated through interfaces. The production of language begins with the semantic component – we have a thought. The reception of language begins with the phonological component – we hear a sound. But in practice all the components work in parallel to process the linguistic input and output. In Jackendoff's model each component is located within a separate area of the mind and contains within it various subroutines. The phonological component, for example, has separate routines which deal with word recognition, intonation and voice recognition. It is these that enable us to understand the tone in which something is said, or recognize someone's voice, even when we do not understand the language.

Like that advanced by Jerry A. Fodor (q.v.), Jackendoff's conception of the language faculty is modular in structure, though he differs from Fodor in the way it works. For Jackendoff, the various language components operate their own individual computational processes, only communicating with each other through message-passing interfaces. He differs from Fodor in asserting that there is limited access to the internal states of the cognitive process, and claiming that there is no 'language of thought'. Jackendoff argues strongly against the existence of 'mentalese'. Language is not simply the expression of some prior existing thought. Crucially, it brings thought into consciousness, and in so doing gives it a shape and a coherence it could never have pre-linguistically. For Jackendoff, language is a form of thinking. It has no direct relation to the world, but is mediated through the various conceptual schemas or mental models which make up the semantic component of language users. Much of the work of cognitive linguistics, under the influence of Jackendoff, has been concerned with identifying these schemas from naturally occurring language.

**Key texts**

> *Semantic Interpretation in Generative Grammar* (Cambridge MA: MIT Press, 1972)
> *Semantics and Cognition* (Cambridge MA: MIT Press, 1983)
> *Consciousness and the Computational Mind* (Cambridge MA: MIT Press, 1987)
> *Semantic Structures* (Cambridge MA: MIT Press, 1990)
> *Languages of the Mind: Essays on Mental Representation* (Cambridge MA: MIT Press, 1992)
> *Patterns in the Mind: Language and Human Nature* (New York: Basic Books, 1994)
> *Foundations of Language: Brain, Meaning,*

Grammar, Evolution (New York: Oxford University Press, 2002)

> Language, Consciousness, Culture: Essays on Mental Structure (Jean Nicod Lectures) (Cambridge MA: MIT Press, 2007)

## Jakobson, Roman Osipovich (1896–1982)

Roman Jakobson was a Russian-born linguist who became a key figure in the development of structuralist approaches to linguistics in the early part of the twentieth century. He was a leading member of the Moscow Linguistic Circle. Linguistics in that period was heavily influenced by neogrammarian methodology, the main concern of which was with tracing the history and development of language across time. Jakobson, however, had come into contact with the work of Ferdinand de Saussure (q.v.), and, like Saussure, he was more interested in studying the structure and function of language for contemporary users – what Saussure termed the synchronic state of language. In 1920 Jakobson went to live in Prague, where he became one of the founders of the Prague School of Linguistics. It was in Czechoslovakia that Jakobson developed his structural-functional approach to linguistics. He introduced into phonetics the concept of distinctive feature analysis, whereby sounds are distinguished from each other by articulatory and acoustic features which together compose a sound's identity. Sounds that possess a certain feature are conceived of as marked, as opposed to those that do not, which are unmarked. Jakobson extended the theory of markedness into analyses of syntactic and semantic structure. Unmarked structures are considered more 'natural' than marked ones, and languages differ according to the grammatical choices they made. Jakobson used this structuralist methodology to develop a typology of languages and establish a set of linguistic universals, or general features, which languages across the world share.

With the start of World War II, Jakobson took his ideas to Scandinavia, and then on to the USA, where he remained for the rest of his life. In America he came into contact with Morris Halle, who was profoundly influenced by Jakobson's distinctive-feature theory of phonology. This became the basis of generative approaches to phonology, which were dominant during the late twentieth century. In the later stages of his career Jakobson turned his attention to communication theory. He had always been interested in the relation between the structure of language and its basic communicative function and, in the 1960s, he began writing about the communicative process. Jakobson distinguished six communication functions, each of which was associated with a dimension of the communication process.

1. Referential function is linked to context (contextual information).
2. Poetic function is linked to message (autotelic).
3. Emotive function is linked to sender (self-expression).
4. Conative function is linked to receiver (vocative or imperative addressing of receiver).
5. Phatic function is linked to channel (checking channel working).
6. Metalinguistic function is linked to code (checking code working).

Jakobson's work has had an influence outside the confines of pure linguistics. Apart from his contribution to communication theory, his structuralist methodology has assisted in the diagnosis and treatment of a number of speech disorders, in particular aphasia, a condition where speakers struggle to make meaningful sequences. Jakobson linked the two main forms of this disorder to the two axes of language identified by Saussure, the 'associative' and the 'syntagmatic'. More recent studies of the way the brain organizes grammatical information have suggested a physiological basis to this distinction.

**Key texts**
> Lectures on Sound and Meaning (Cambridge MA: MIT Press, 1937)
> Child Language, Aphasia and Phonological Universals (Berlin: Mouton de Gruyter, 1941)
> With Morris Halle, Fundamentals of Language (Berlin: Mouton de Gruyter, 1956)
> The Framework of Language (Michigan: Oxon Publishing Ltd, 1980)
> Verbal Art, Verbal Sign, Verbal Time (ed. by Krystyna Pomorska and Stephen Rudy, Minneapolis: University of Minnesota Press, 1985)
> With Linda Waugh, The Sound Shape of Language (Berlin: Mouton de Gruyter, 1979)
> Dialogues with Krystyna Pomorska (Cambridge: Cambridge University Press, 1983)
> On language/Roman Jakobson (ed. by Linda

R. Waugh and Monique Monville-Burston, Cambridge MA: Harvard University Press, 1990)
> *Selected Writings: Phonological Studies* (Berlin: Mouton de Gruyter, 2002)

## Jespersen, Otto (1860–1943)

Otto Jespersen was a Danish linguist whose specialty was the grammar of the English language. For much of his career he was a professor of English at Copenhagen University. Among his claims to fame is his founding, along with Paul Passy, of the International Phonetic Association, which has been of seminal importance in the study of phonetics. When Jespersen was studying phonetics in the late nineteenth century, the 'neogrammarians' held sway in much of northern Europe. They argued that sound changes in a language were systematic, rule-governed, and independent of semantic content. Jespersen, however, believed that sound and sense were closely connected and argued that many sound changes are due to semantic factors. The interdependence of form and meaning at all linguistic levels became a distinctive feature of his own methodology. In the case of phonetics, it led him in later life to become a proponent of phonosemanticism, the idea that the phonetic form of words is not arbitrary but semantically motivated.

Jespersen took a broadly functional view of language. Language was chiefly an instrument for people to communicate and understand one another. Probably his most original contribution to grammatical theory was to set up two new grammatical categories, *Rank* and *Nexus*. The theory of ranks effectively removes the concept of word classes (parts of speech) from grammatical analysis. Being more notional, ranks are strictly functional. Words in a sequence are categorized into 'primaries', 'secondaries', and 'tertiaries'. In the phrase *closely guarded secret*, 'secret' is a primary, which is defined by a secondary, 'guarded', which in turn is defined by a tertiary 'closely'. There is the possibility of a fourth rank, or quaternary, e.g. *very*, but in practice three ranks were considered sufficient. The interesting point about Jespersen's methodology is that it allows words to be described in terms of what they do in a sentence, rather than what they are perceived to be in terms of conventional morphological classification.

The term 'nexus' applies to structures such as sentences, or sentences in embryo, where two ideas are expressed in one unit: for example, in the sentence, *I saw the man fall*, there are two ideas – 'I saw' and 'the man fall' which are part of the same nexus. In this particular example 'nexus' coincides with the term 'clause', but this need not be the case. For Jespersen, the grammar of sentences is fundamentally semantic. Sentences exist to express ideas. Jespersen contrasts a nexus, in which two concepts are expressed by a single unit with a 'junction' in which one concept is expressed by two units (e.g. *it's raining* vs Latin *pluvit*).

Jespersen expounded these and related ideas in his *Modern English Grammar* and *The Growth and Structure of the English Language*. Both books have had a significant influence on linguistics, particularly the field of functional linguistics, where Jespersen's arguments about the interrelationship of form and function still continue to resonate.

### Key texts

> *The Articulations of Speech Sounds Represented by Means of Analphabetic Symbols* (Marburg: Elwert, 1889)
> *Progress in Language* (London: Swan Sonnenschein & Co., 1894)
> *Growth and Structure of the English Language* (Leipzig, 1905 [9th edn Oxford: Blackwell, 1938])
> *Language: Its Nature, Development, and Origin* (London: Allen and Unwin, 1922)
> *The Philosophy of Grammar* (London: Allen and Unwin, 1924)
> *A Modern English Grammar on Historical Principles: Part I. Sounds and Spellings. Part II. Syntax. First Volume. Part III. Syntax. Second Volume. Part IV. Syntax. Third Volume. Part V. Syntax. Fourth Volume. Part VI. Morphology. Part VII. Syntax* (London: Allen and Unwin, 1909–1949)
> *An International Language* (London: Allen and Unwin, 1928)
> *Essentials of English Grammar* (London: Allen and Unwin, 1933)
> *Analytic Syntax* (London: Allen and Unwin, 1937)

## Katz, Jerrold Jacob (1932–2002)

Jerry Katz was Distinguished Professor of Philosophy and Linguistics at the City University of New York. Prior to that he was Assistant Professor and then Professor of Philosophy at the Massachus-setts Institute of Technology. Katz was an early pioneer in the development of semantic theory. Throughout his career he was preoccupied with the nature of meaning and with the way in which we can assign a truth value to linguistic struc-tures. When he began his work in the mid-1960s, semantics was still heavily influenced by the logical positivism of Gottlob Frege and Bertrand Russell, who were primarily interested in the denotational meaning of words and with trying to construct a formal logic which would express the propositional content of language free from the distractions of usage. Katz was aware, right from the beginning, that such a reductionist view of meaning in natural language was insufficient to fit with the radical work on generative syntax being pioneered by Noam Chomsky (q.v.) in the early 1960s. Researching at MIT alongside Chomsky, Katz set out first to try to supplement Chomsky's work with a corresponding theory of semantics.

Together with Jerry A. Fodor (q.v.), Katz proposed that semantics was a component of generative grammar – in particular, that lexi-cal senses were mapped onto lexical items via projection rules. Lexical items were marked semantically in such a way that their meanings corresponded structurally to the concepts or ideas they represented. This enabled the deep structure of sentences to be expressed in semantic terms, and provided a justification for the argument that transformations to surface structures were meaning-preserving. Chomsky incorporated Katz's semantic component into the standard theory of generative grammar which he formulated in 1965. But despite Katz's concurrence with generative principles, he nonetheless felt that the mentalism on which it was based was not robust enough to support the natural logic of words and sentences. For Chomsky, the study of language was funda-mentally a way of studying the human mind. Language was a psychological reality. Linguists were concerned with language as a form of know-ledge. The inevitable consequence of this was to make it difficult to escape the circle of language and view it in relation to the real world. Katz eventually departed from this view in favour of a form of 'realism' associated with Plato, in which language was seen as an object in its own right. In Katz's revised position, the linguist is concerned with the relationship between language and the real world rather than with its relationship to the human mind. In his mature work he is preoccupied with the way in which the abstractions of language are mapped onto ordinary reality. Nowhere is this more evident than in his concern to argue against the standard account, from Frege, that sense determines reference. Since the total sense set of lexical items could never be arrived at, it seemed logically wrong to Katz to suppose that sense could determine reference. Instead he argued for a weaker relationship in which sense mediates refer-ence. This effectively leaves the way open for a theoretical explanation of semantic and pragmatic features such as presupposition, indeterminacy, and the meaning of names – which have reference but little definable sense.

### Key texts
> With Paul M. Postal, *An Integrated Theory of Linguistic Descriptions* (Cambridge MA: MIT Press, 1964)
> *The Philosophy of Language* (New York: Harper & Row, 1966)
> *Semantic Theory* (New York: Harper & Row, 1972)
> *Propositional Structure and Illocutionary Force: A Study of the Contribution of Sentence Meaning to Speech Acts* (New York: T.Y. Crowell, 1977)
> *Language and Other Abstract Objects* (Oxford: Blackwell, 1981)
> *The Philosophy of Linguistics* (ed. by J. Katz, Oxford: Oxford University Press, 1985)
> *The Metaphysics of Meaning* (Cambridge MA: MIT Press, 1990)
> *Realistic Rationalism* (Cambridge MA: MIT Press, 1998)
> *Sense, Reference, and Philosophy* (New York: Oxford University Press, 2004)

### Labov, William (b. 1927)
William Labov is Professor of Linguistics at the University of Pennsylvania. More than any other linguist, he has been responsible for developing the branch of linguistics known as sociolinguis-tics. Before Labov began his pioneering work, the standard methodology for investigating language use was to examine idealized samples of speech, free from interference from local dialect, or the influence of social context. The work carried

out on regional and geographical varieties was usually confined to vanishing rural dialects; Labov, however, focused on the everyday speech of ordinary people, in particular, the language of the streets. In so doing he gave recognition to forms of speech such as Black English Vernacular (also known as AAVE, see below), which had been little studied in linguistics.

For his dissertation, which he completed in 1964, Labov studied the dialect of New York City. His methodology depended on the mapping of what he termed 'linguistic variables'. These are recognizable dialect features, the use of which varies according to such things as age, social class and gender. Since Labov, this has become a standard method for investigating linguistic diversity and change. Labov was particularly interested in the fact that many of the inhabitants of New York don't use features of the prestige accent. To investigate this phenomenon he developed a range of innovative techniques for interviewing and for measuring change quantitatively (see Chapters 2.7 and 5.8) One of the aims of these techniques was to overcome the besetting problem of the 'observer's paradox' (see Chapter 3.1). In addition to interviews conducted in the home, Labov collected data informally (see Chapter 3.1, Observer's paradox, for a discussion of the department store study).

Labov went on to study the linguistic features of African American Vernacular English (AAVE), spoken in Harlem. One of his concerns was to understand the failure of many black children to learn to read. The outcome of this was a seminal paper 'The Logic of Nonstandard English' which defended AAVE as grammatically well-formed and perfectly able to serve as a basis for learning. Labov also investigated the way Black teenagers structured narrative stories of their own lives. The narrative model that emerged from this is widely used by narratologists today (see Chapter 2.11). Labov has also done extensive work studying sound change in progress, initially in Martha's Vineyard and more recently throughout America. He has identified and described a process of 'chain shifting', wherein one sound replaces a second sound, replacing a third sound, in a complete shift. He found a Southern shift in Appalachia and southern coastal regions, and a Northern Cities shift in urban areas around the Great Lakes. Labov's achievement has been to develop systematic techniques for gathering and analysing sociolinguistic data and, in so doing, inspire a generation of linguists interested in why and how languages vary and change.

**Key texts**

> *The Social Stratification of English in New York City* (Washington DC: Center for Applied Linguistics, 1966)
> *The Study of Non-Standard English* (Champaign IL: National Council of Teachers of English, 1970)
> *Sociolinguistic Patterns* (Philadelphia: University of Pennsylvania Press, 1972)
> *Language in the Inner City* (Philadelphia: University of Pennsylvania Press, 1972)
> With David Fanshel, *Therapeutic Discourse: Psychotherapy as Conversation* (New York: Academic Press, 1977)
> *Locating Language in Time and Space* (ed.) (New York: Academic Press, 1980)
> *Principles of Linguistic Change. Volume I: Internal Factors* (Oxford: Basil Blackwell, 1994)
> *Principles of Linguistic Change. Volume II: Social Factors* (Oxford: Basil Blackwell, 2000)
> With Sharon Ash and Charles Boberg, *Atlas of North American English: Phonology and Phonetics* (Berlin: Mouton de Gruyter, 2006)

## Lakoff, George (b. 1941)

George Lakoff is a professor of Cognitive Linguistics at the University of California, where he has taught since 1972, having previously taught at Harvard University and the University of Michigan. Lakoff has had a major influence on the development of cognitive linguistics, a discipline which is primarily concerned with linking linguistic structures and processes with fundamental cognitive functions such as perception and understanding. Lakoff started out as a student of Noam Chomsky at the Massachusetts Institute of Technology. Like many other linguists of the time he was initially persuaded by Chomsky's formal approach to syntax, in particular by the theory of transformational grammar. Basic to Chomskyan linguistics is the separation of syntax from semantics and pragmatics: sentences are constructed according to syntactic rules which are independent of meaning. Lakoff, however, came increasingly to believe that many syntactic constructions were the output of central cognitive processes. This in turn led him, along with other linguists, to develop an alternative model of linguistics which gave greater prominence to semantics.

Fundamental to this change in direction was Lakoff's work on metaphor. Prior to Lakoff, linguists generally viewed metaphor as an anomaly, something outside of normal language, requiring special forms of interpretation. Lakoff argued that metaphor, far from being a decorative addition to utterances, was at the heart of all language construction. For Lakoff, metaphors are ways in which we conceptualize experience. They are hidden from us only because they are deeply embedded within language. So, for example, Lakoff argues that expressions such as *time flies* and *time passes* express the underlying metaphor 'time is a moving object'. There is nothing inevitable about this way of perceiving time. Another culture might well conceive of time as stationary, while people do the moving. In this way, Lakoff maintains, a culture's metaphors are an invaluable guide to its values and attitudes.

More particularly, Lakoff's work led him to view our sensorimotor system, especially our spatial awareness, as crucially important in the way we use language. For Lakoff, prepositions such as *up, down, in*, and *out*, take on figurative meanings in expressions like *Things are looking up, I'm feeling down* and *Count me in/out*. They reflect the biological importance we attach to standing up as opposed to lying down, and the priority we give to the inside of our bodies as opposed to the exterior. Together with fellow cognitive scientists, Mark Johnson and Rafael Núñez, Lakoff has argued for something which he calls the 'embodied mind'. By this he seems to mean that cognitive awareness is structured by the neural system. Our minds do not work independently from our bodies, rather, they take their input from the rest of our bodies. In recent years Lakoff has extended this approach to other areas of knowledge such as mathematics and science, questioning the assumed objective basis of these modes of inquiry. Such an approach has incurred criticism, notably from the linguist Steven Pinker, who has accused Lakoff of 'cognitive relativism' (in the *New Republic Online* http://pinker.wjh.harvard.edu/articles/media/2006_09_30_thenewrepublic.html) according to which all knowledge becomes

unverifiable. Like Chomsky before him, Lakoff's views about language have led him into the field of political science and to a radical questioning of the USA's foreign and domestic policies.

**Key texts**

> *Irregularity in Syntax* (New York: Holt, Rinehart and Winston, 1970)
> With Mark Johnson, *Metaphors We Live By* (Chicago: University of Chicago Press, 1980)
> *Women, Fire, and Dangerous Things: What Categories Reveal About the Mind* (Chicago: University of Chicago Press, 1987)
> With Mark Turner, *More Than Cool Reason: A Field Guide to Poetic Metaphor* (Chicago: University of Chicago Press, 1989)
> With Mark Johnson, *Philosophy In The Flesh: the Embodied Mind and its Challenge to Western Thought* (New York: Basic Books, 1999)
> With Rafael E. Núñez, *Where Mathematics Comes From: How the Embodied Mind Brings Mathematics into Being* (New York: Basic Books, 2000)

## Sapir, Edward (1884–1939)

Edward Sapir was an American anthropologist and linguist who had a seminal influence on the development of linguistics as a discipline in twentieth-century America. The son of an immigrant family from Eastern Europe, he first made his mark academically at Columbia University, where he studied Germanic philology and anthropology. At Columbia he studied under the anthropologist Frank Boas, who inspired Sapir to undertake the recording and analysing of endangered Native American languages. During his career Sapir was to record 39 different Native American languages. These recordings formed the substance of his extensive studies of the relationship between linguistic structure and culture.

Sapir was innovative in applying the comparative methods used in studying Indo-European languages to the investigation of Native American languages. He believed firmly in the functional equivalence of all human languages, including those previously termed 'primitive', and placed written and unwritten languages on an equal footing. In his many scholarly writings, he demonstrated the grammatical intricacies and subtleties of languages which were on the verge of extinction. At the time he was writing there was little direct evidence of (North) American prehistory but, using linguistic evidence, Sapir was able to show the genetic relationships between different languages and to develop a classificatory system which could be used by anthropologists to investigate the relationships among Native American peoples.

The latter part of Sapir's career was spent as Sterling Professor of Anthropology at Yale University, where he came into contact with Leonard Bloomfield. The younger Bloomfield was engaged in developing a descriptive model of linguistic analysis which largely excluded semantics. By contrast, Sapir had become firmly convinced through his study of Native American languages that meaning is integral to any theory of grammar. He developed the view that our perception of the world is shaped by our language: 'Human beings do not live in the objective world alone, nor alone in the world of social activity as ordinarily understood, but are very much at the mercy of the particular language which has become the medium of expression for their society. ... We see and hear and otherwise experience very largely as we do because the language habits of our community predispose certain choices of interpretation' (The status of linguistics as a science, *Language* 5: 207–14, 1929). It was this view of language, taken up enthusiastically by a student of Sapir's, Benjamin Lee Whorf (q.v.), which subsequently became known as the 'Sapir-Whorf Hypothesis'.

In the field of linguistic theory, Sapir's most important contributions were, arguably, in phonology. In a paper published in 1925 entitled 'Sound patterns in language', he argued that the phoneme should be defined in terms of its contrastive relationships with other sounds, rather than in terms of any supposed objective qualities. He followed this up in 1933 by suggesting that the importance of the phoneme resided in its 'psychological reality', in other words, in the intuitions of native speakers about the sound structure of their language. This distinction between phonetics and phonology was arrived at independently of parallel work on phonemics by the Prague School linguists in Europe, and had a profound impact on American linguistics. The concept of 'psychological reality', in particular, echoes through the early work of Chomsky.

Sapir died at the early age of 55, just before the outbreak of the World War II, and having only completed one sole-authored book, *Language: An Introduction to the Study of Speech*. But he left behind a core of devoted followers, one of whom, Zellig Harris, was to become the mentor of Noam Chomsky (q.v.).

**Key texts**

> *Language: An introduction to the Study of Speech* (New York: Harcourt, Brace and company, 1921)
> *Selected Writings in Language, Culture and Personality* (ed. by D. Mandelbaum Berkeley: University of California Press, 1949)
> *The Collected Works of Edward Sapir 5–6: American Indian Languages* (ed. by William Bright and Victor Golla, Berlin: Mouton de Gruyter, 1990–1)
> *The Collected Works of Edward Sapir 3: Culture* (ed. by Regna Darnell et al., Berlin: Mouton de Gruyter, 1999)

## Saussure, Ferdinand de (1857–1913)

Ferdinand de Saussure, sometimes called 'the father of modern linguistics', was a Swiss linguist who taught at the University of Geneva. After his death, his students collected his lecture notes together and published them in a small volume entitled *Cours de linguistique générale*. It was a slim volume but had, and continues to have, a seminal influence on linguistics. Saussure was instrumental in the development of structural linguistics. He likened language to a game of chess, in which each piece is defined by both its situation on the board and its relationship with the other pieces. For Saussure, words define themselves in contrast to each other; they are continuously adjusting their 'value' according to the state of play in the system as a whole.

This particular insight is intimately connected with Saussure's treatment of words as signs. Signs have no natural relationship to the things they represent. The word *dog*, for instance, has no intrinsic connection with the animal it symbolizes; any other word would do equally well to represent it. For Saussure, the relationship is essentially arbitrary: it's a consequence of the way in which the language has evolved. Since Saussure, the principle of arbitrariness has been much discussed, and various refinements have been made to it, but it remains a fundamental idea of modern linguistics. Saussurean linguistics approaches language as an enclosed system. Words are related to each other as signs and can be strung together in various combinations to form sentences. The extent of a word's capacity to form sentences is seen as the sum of its potential to combine with, or substitute for, others. Saussure imagined sentences as having two axes on which items could be sorted in these ways. The axis of substitution he termed 'associative', and that of combination he termed 'syntagmatic'. Saussure's 'associative' relations are today known as 'paradigmatic' relations, thanks to Louis Hjelmslev.

Basic to Saussure's view of language is the separation between language as substance and language as concept. The separation is there in the notion of the sign. A sign has two component parts: a physical token of some sort, such as a cross, a string of sounds (as in /tri/ 'tree'), or the colour green; and a concept which is attached to it – the crucifixion, 'treeness', permission to proceed. The conceptual level of language, the abstract system of rules which compose it, Saussure referred to as *langue*; the substance side, the representation of those rules in actual sentences or utterances, he termed *parole*. Saussure himself concentrated on *langue* and had very little to say about *parole*, but in recent times the spotlight has moved more favourably to *parole*. Like much that is contained in Saussure's book, these terms have been subject to considerable debate, but the distinction that he described between these two dimensions of language has been very influential. Most modern linguists accept a distinction between an abstract and a concrete side of language, although the boundary which separates them may be difficult to determine.

Saussure's methodology typically involves working with two-term oppositions: paradigmatic~syntagmatic, *langue~parole*, and there are others – notably, diachronic~synchronic. This binary model of language, in which two opposing terms interact dynamically, is distinctive of Saussure and has had widespread influence beyond linguistics. It has been particularly productive in related fields of inquiry, e.g. in the arts and social sciences, where it is possible to discern a similar set of sign-making features capable of being viewed as a system. This is sometimes known as structuralism and, while it has been somewhat overtaken by rival theoretical approaches, it remains a powerful influence in contemporary thinking about language.

**Key texts**

> *Mémoire sur le système primitif des voyelles dans les langues indo-européenes* (On the original system of vowels in Indo-European Languages) (Leipzig: Teubner, 1878)
> *Cours de linguistique générale* (ed. by Charles Bally and Albert Sechehaye, with the collaboration of Albert Riedlinger, Lausanne and Paris: Payot, 1916 [The third edition of 1931 is regarded as the standard edition.])
> *Édition Critique du Cours de Linguistique Générale de Ferdinand de Saussure*, 2 vols (ed. by Rudolf Engler, Wiesbaden: Harrassowitz, 1968–74)
> *A Course in General Linguistics* (transl. by Wade Baskin, Glasgow: Fontana/Collins, 1974)
> *Saussure's Third Course of Lectures in General Linguistics (1910–1911)* (Emile Constantin ders notlarından, Language and Communication series, volume 12, transl. and ed. by Eisuke Komatsu and Roy Harris, Oxford: Pergamon, 1993)
> *Écrits de Linguistique Générale* (Writings on general linguistics) (Établis et édités par Simon Bouquet et Rudolf Engler, avec la collaboration d'Antoinette Weil, Paris: Gallimard, 2002)

## Searle, John Rogers (b. 1932)

John Searle, whose writings on the philosophy of language have been deeply influential in the field of pragmatics, is Professor Emeritus of Philosophy at the University of California. Searle was educated at Oxford University in the mid-twentieth century, where he came into contact with 'the ordinary language philosophy', of John L. Austin (q.v.) and Peter F. Strawson, both of whom were his teachers. Like Austin, he believed that the meaning of utterances depends not simply on their propositional content but on the particular acts which speakers are attempting to perform. Austin's *How to do Things with Words*, published in 1962, had established the ground rules for determining the act status of utterances. By the end of his book Austin had revised his earlier categorization of utterances into performatives and constatives in favour of illocutionary acts, some of which employ explicit performative clauses. Searle further developed what became known as *speech act theory* by categorizing illocutionary acts into their various types and establishing the social prerequisites, or felicity conditions, which determine the appropriateness of their performance.

In his essay 'The classification of illocutionary acts' (1975), Searle divided speech acts into the following types:

> REPRESENTATIVES: these commit the speaker to the truth of the expressed proposition (paradigm cases: asserting, concluding, telling, claiming)
> DIRECTIVES: these are attempts by the speaker to get the addressee to do something (paradigm cases: requesting, ordering, pleading, inviting)
> COMMISSIVES: these commit the speaker to some future course of action (paradigm cases: promising, threatening, offering, vowing)
> EXPRESSIVES: these express a psychological state (paradigm cases: thanking, apologizing, welcoming, congratulating)
> DECLARATIONS: these effect immediate changes in the institutional state of affairs (paradigm cases: excommunicating, marrying, naming a ship)

Under Searle, speech act theory set out to match utterances against the situational context and the relationship between the people communicating with one another. Thus, pleading, commanding, and requesting are all directives, but they differ according to the relationship between speaker and hearer. The act of commanding, for example, requires the speaker to be in a position of authority, while that of pleading requires the reverse; the act of requesting requires either that they are peers, or else that the hearer is in authority. Similarly, suggesting, insisting and hypothesizing all belong to the class of representatives, but they differ in the degree of commitment towards the truth of what is being represented. All of these can be expressed as differences in felicity conditions. It's the felicity conditions which enable us to know that the sentence *You must have another piece of cake* uttered by the hostess at a tea party is an invitation, not a command. The situation simply doesn't fit the paradigm for giving a command.

In his later work, Searle developed the concept of intentionality – the assigning of meaning to actions – into a series of propositions about how we interpret anything in social life, from getting married to ordering a meal in a restaurant. In his book *The Construction of Social Reality* (1995), he argues that social life is constituted by a collective intentionality, or set of agreements, and that the language we use about them depends crucially on such implicit intentionalities.

**Key texts**

> *Speech Acts: An Essay in the Philosophy of Language* (Cambridge: Cambridge University Press, 1969)
> *Expression and Meaning: Studies in the Theory of Speech Acts* (Cambridge: Cambridge University Press, 1979)
> *Intentionality: An Essay in the Philosophy of Mind* (Cambridge: Cambridge University Press, 1983)
> *Minds, Brains and Science* (London: Penguin, 1984)
> *The Rediscovery of the Mind* (Cambridge MA: MIT Press, 1992)
> *The Construction of Social Reality* (Harmondsworth: Penguin, 1995)
> *The Mystery of Consciousness* (London: Granta, 1997)
> *Mind, Language and Society, Philosophy in the Real World* (New York: Basic Books, 1998)
> *Rationality in Action* (Cambridge MA: MIT Press, 2001)
> *Consciousness and Language* (Cambridge: Cambridge University Press, 2002)
> *Mind, A Brief Introduction* (Oxford: Oxford University Press, 2004)

## Wittgenstein, Ludvig Josef Johann (1889–1951)

Ludvig Wittgenstein was one of the foremost linguistic philosophers of the twentieth century. An Austrian by birth, he spent a significant part of his life at the University of Cambridge, where he was appointed to the Chair of Philosophy in 1939. Wittgenstein began his philosophical career under the influence of the logical positivism espoused by Bertrand Russell, but he later came to reject Russell's positivism, particularly its view of the relationship between language and the world. In his *Tractatus*, which belongs to his early career, Wittgenstein adopted the view that language provides us with a mental picture of the external world. The purpose of philosophy was thus to demonstrate the truth or falsity of this picture by subjecting it to the logical processes of verification. Wittgenstein realized, however, that this view of language meant there were certain experiences, for example religious and aesthetic ones, about which philosophy had nothing significant to say. What processes of verification could meaningfully be applied to statements about a belief in beauty or in God? Accordingly, the *Tractatus* ends with the sobering statement 'Whereof one cannot speak thereof one must be silent.'

Wittgenstein later abandoned this view of language, and with it the positivistic outlook which underlay it. In his most enduring work, *Philosophical Investigations*, published after his death, he rejected the idea that words contain some definable essence in favour of a view which saw meaning in terms of use: 'The meaning of a word is its use in the language,' he says (*Philosophical Investigations*, 1963: 43). Wittgenstein argued that we can never stand outside language and verify the truth or otherwise of claims about God, or truth, or beauty because all arguments rest on language – the way we choose to use words. On this view, language becomes a game. In games, whether chess or football, there are rules which players follow. While these rules may be formalized in manuals, they are essentially simply agreements among the players about the way the game is to be played. Such is the case, Wittgenstein argued with language. In order to discuss science, religion, or the weather speakers need to understand the rules which are being implicitly invoked. Just as one wouldn't use the language of football to talk about tennis, one wouldn't talk about God in the language of molecular biology. The corollary of Wittgenstein's argument is that words have meaning only in the context in which they are used. They exist within a network of terms that mutually sustain each other, as do the rules of a game. It is sometimes thought that Wittgenstein's account of language is relativistic, a kind of 'anything goes' approach, but he points out clearly that individuals can't simply make up rules. Just as a footballer can't decide to carry on after the whistle has blown, so speakers are not free to use words just as they like. A private language, he argues, is not a language. For Wittgenstein all language use is dependent on tacit public agreements of some kind. Language is 'a form of life', he states, meaning that language is a construction arising out of the process of living, rather than a neutral instrument or tool which we objectively apply to the world.

Linguistic philosophy has sometimes been criticized for abandoning the pursuit of truth for the pursuit of statements about truth. But Wittgenstein was instrumental in realizing that the old model of philosophy did not really fit the new insights about language emerging from the discipline of linguistics. His own career as a philosopher reflects that shift.

### Key texts

> *Tractatus Logico-Philosophicus* (London: Kegan Paul, Trench, Trübner, 1922)
> *Preliminary Studies for the 'Philosophical Investigations' Generally Known as the Blue and Brown Books* (Oxford: Basil Blackwell, 1958)
> *Philosophical Investigations = Philosophische Untersuchungen* (transl. by Gertrude E.M. Anscombe, Basil Blackwell: Oxford 1963)
> *On Certainty* (ed. by Gertrude E.M. Anscombe and Georg H. von Wright; transl. by Denis Paul and G.E.M. Anscombe, Oxford: Basil Blackwell, 1969)

### Whorf, Benjamin Lee (1897–1941)

Benjamin Whorf is principally known in linguistics for giving his name, along with that of Edward Sapir (q.v.), to the 'Sapir-Whorf Hypothesis'. This states that,

> We dissect nature along lines laid down by our native languages. The categories and types that we isolate from the world of phenomena we do not find there because they stare every observer in the face; on the contrary, the world is presented in a kaleidoscopic flux of impressions which has to be organized by our minds—and this means largely by the linguistic systems in our minds. (*Language, Thought and Reality*, p. 212)

This view of languages as structuring the way we perceive the world has been variously interpreted in the years since Whorf's death, at the early age of 44, and is still the subject of contentious debate. Whorf became interested in linguistics while working as a fire prevention engineer for the Hartford Fire Insurance company. He claimed that his early interest in what came to be known as linguistic relativity began as a consequence of writing reports on insurance losses. These alerted him to the way in which misunderstandings can arise from the use of language. At Yale University he was taught by the anthropologist and linguist Edward Sapir. Sapir encouraged Whorf to further study Native American languages. Whorf became more convinced than ever that the grammatical and lexical structure of a language was systematically related to the world view of the people who spoke it. Whorf claimed, for example, that the Hopi Indians of northern Arizona had a different way of conceptualizing time from Europeans and that this was reflected in their language. Instead of visualizing time as Europeans do, the Hopi perceive it more organically, in terms of processes and change. In recent years, however, these claims have been challenged, and it has been shown that the Hopi language contains tense and words for units of time such as days, weeks, and months, and also for quantifying time ('quick', 'long time' and 'finished'). They also have traditional devices for measuring time.

Probably the most direct attack on the linguistic relativity hypothesis has been by Steven Pinker in the *Language Instinct* (1994). Pinker incorrectly claims that Whorf took a fairly modest proposition of Sapir's about the relationship between language and thought and inflated it by means of flawed, even bogus, research, into a form of linguistic determinism. Whorf's view, he suggested, would mean that certain thoughts and perceptions would be denied to us unless our language allowed them. In fact a careful reading of Whorf's work shows that Whorf was less extreme than Sapir (see Keith Allan, *The Western Classical Tradition in Linguistics*, London: Equinox, 2009). No linguist or anthropologist of significance has ever accepted the strongly deterministic form of the hypothesis. However, many are attracted to a softer version of it, in line with Whorf's own observations about linguistic relativism 'The statement that "thinking is a matter of LANGUAGE" is an incorrect generalization of the more nearly correct idea that "thinking is a matter of different tongues"' (Whorf 1956: 339). This allows us to say that languages do differ in the way they relate to the experiential world, as we know from the difficulty of finding exact translation equivalents, and it's only to be expected that these differences reflect cultural and social ones in some shape or form. In fact, rather than language controlling thought, it merely influences thought.

**Key text**

> *Language, Thought, and Reality: Selected Writings of Benjamin Lee Whorf* (ed. by John B Carroll, Cambridge MA: MIT Press, 1956)

4

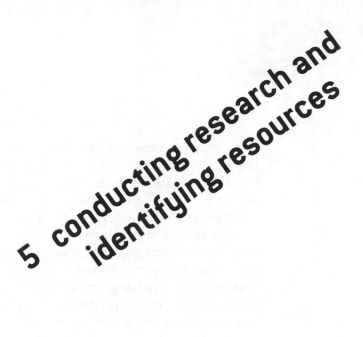

# 5 conducting research and identifying resources

**5.1**   doing ethical research

**5.2**   researching general and theoretical linguistics

**5.3**   researching phonetics and phonology

**5.4**   researching morphology

**5.5**   researching syntax

**5.6**   researching the history of language(s)

**5.7**   researching semantics and pragmatics

**5.8**   researching sociolinguistics

**5.9**   researching psycholinguistics

**5.10**   researching applied linguistics

**5.11**   researching cognitive linguistics

**5.12**   researching functional approaches to language

**5.13**   researching discourse and conversation

**5.14**   researching forensic linguistics

5

Part 5 introduces some techniques in linguistic research including observation and introspection, the use of questionnaires and interviews, recording and transcribing language data, and working with corpus data. It also examines ethical issues in collecting language data. It then goes on to describe the approaches taken in selected studies in the sub-disciplines of general and theoretical linguistics, phonetics and phonology, morphology, syntax, the history of language(s), semantics and pragmatics, sociolinguistics, psycholinguistics, applied linguistics, cognitive linguistics, functional approaches to language, discourse and conversation, and forensic linguistics. Each chapter recommends a range of relevant resources for linguistic inquiry and the study of language and languages.

5

# 5.1 **doing ethical research**

## chapter contents

> Collecting data through observation and introspection     271
> Questionnaires and interviews     272
> Recording and transcribing language data     272
> Corpus data     273
> Statistics     275
> Overview     275
> Key points     275
> References     276

This chapter introduces the conventions governing ethical research in linguistics, and summarizes some key data collection methods. Linguists draw on empirical evidence to construct hypotheses about the structure of languages, and the quality of the hypotheses depends on the accuracy of the data. As you go on in the study of linguistics you will increasingly need to collect language data of your own. Data may be of many kinds: linguists work on the language of novels, business letters, billboards or stockmarket reports. We analyse emails and internet language (including what can be found on social networking websites such as MySpace and Facebook), radio broadcasts, parliamentary debates and telephone conversations. Some of the data are in the public domain, published or broadcast, and accessible to everyone. However we are also interested in other more private data such as personal emails, letters or conversations and here we need to ensure that we collect data in an ethical manner.

Your university will have a set of guidelines for ethical research and you need to familiarize yourself with these. Your lecturer will be able to give you precise details. However, certain ethical principles apply to all linguistic work. It is not appropriate to collect data from people in a dependent relationship to the researcher (such as an employee). No personal or identifying information can be disclosed in transcripts or reports, and participants must be given pseudonyms or code numbers so their identities cannot be discovered. Covert data collection is not acceptable. Before interviewing anyone, before administering a questionnaire and before recording conversations (or collecting personal emails or letters), you must obtain the consent of all participants. This consent must be based on a clear understanding of the nature of the research and the way in which the material is to be used. University ethics procedures usually require us to give all participants an explanatory statement written in plain language, and obtain their signed consent. An example of what an explanatory statement might look like is given below.

Another ethical issue is the extent to which the research may have positive or negative implications for the participants or their community. Cameron, Frazer, Harvey et al. 1992 argue that linguists need to take careful account of the relationship between their own research goals and those of the community being studied. We need to consider whether we are exploiting a community by doing work on them, infantilizing a community by doing work for them, or working with a community and following a research agenda that is set by the community itself. Researchers need to provide feedback and share their findings so that the research is 'empowering' for the actual research subjects themselves.

Li Wei argues that different styles of research

> can carry with them a political ideology, a view of the person and a philosophy of knowledge. For example, surveys often aim for participative democracy, whereas experiments are often about control; qualitative ethnographic observation aims for a holistic view of the person, while quantitative variationist studies tend to fragment the person into variables; tape-recordings and detailed transcription of them aim for a 'mirror reflection', or a 'positivistic' picture, of what actually happens, whereas in-depth interviews and critical analyses of them want to (re)construct particular versions of experience and reality. (Li 2000: 481)

Language scholars therefore need to be mindful of their underlying assumptions and possible impact of the methods we choose to employ. For more information on ethical research see Brown 2006 and Dornyei 2007.

## EXPLANATORY STATEMENT

### Experiences and Attitudes Concerning the English Apostrophe

My name is Phineas Bloggs and I am conducting a research project with Andy Conda, a professor in the Department of Linguistics, towards a BA (Honours) at Fucitol University. This means that I will be writing a thesis that is the equivalent of a short book. You have been selected to take part in this survey as a user of English in Bootlegger Crossing.

**Aims**
I am conducting this research to find out how much English users care about the apostrophe, the consequences of ignoring apostrophes, and whether reform in this area would benefit users of English.

*Possible benefits*
The study hopes to give an indication of trends in society, and will also have implications for whether apostrophe reform in English is desirable.

**What does the research involve?**
The study involves a brief questionnaire that should take approximately 15 minutes to complete.

*Inconvenience/discomfort*
The risk of inconvenience or discomfort through participation is not beyond that of the normal experience of everyday life.

**Can I withdraw from the research?**
Being in this study is voluntary and you are under no obligation to consent to participation. However, if you do consent to participate, you may only withdraw prior to the questionnaire being submitted.

## Collecting data through observation and introspection

Language data are collected in a number of ways. A simple method is introspection. That is, the linguist reflects on their own usage, or applies judgements to sets of sample sentences to determine which they find grammatical or ungrammatical (or elicits judgements from language informants in a similar way). Look at the examples given below and decide whether they are acceptable/grammatical ($\sqrt{}$), unacceptable/ungrammatical ($*$) or a bit odd (?) (i.e. you are unsure about the grammaticality).

(1) I ought to leave before the traffic builds up.
(2) Ought I to leave before the traffic builds up?
(3) Ought I leave before the traffic builds up?
(4) Did I ought to leave before the traffic builds up?
(5) Oughtn't I leave before the traffic builds up?
(6) Oughtn't I to leave before the traffic builds up.
(7) I oughtn't to leave before the traffic eases.
(8) I oughtn't leave before the traffic eases.

Introspection is a very rapid method of collecting information about language, and is widely used by field linguists as the basis on which they will write grammars and dictionaries of previously undescribed languages. However it is not always reliable. Labov's work in New York City, and Trudgill's research in Norwich have shown that speakers' intuitions about their own usage do not always correspond to their actual usage, especially when there are social evaluations attached to particular forms. This point is discussed further in Chapter 2.7, Sociolinguistics.

## Questionnaires and interviews

There are many areas in the study of language where questionnaires (written or spoken) are useful, particularly when data are sought from a large number of informants. They might be used for sociolinguistic research (e.g. eliciting speech samples, or investigating attitudes towards a linguistic feature such as accent, slang, pronunciation, non-standard usage) or in language survey work (e.g. exploring when and where a language is used and its speakers' proficiency). Often questionnaires are used to complement other types of data-gathering methods, such as a focus-group interview, in order to get a fuller picture.

Questionnaires need to be carefully planned, especially when it comes to drafting the questions. It is useful to carry out a pilot study to determine whether the questions produce the targeted responses, and to rephrase any which are complicated or ambiguous. There are many practical books available that can help you in the selection of subjects and in the successful design, presentation and administration of a questionnaire; see, for example, Dörnyei 2003. The analysis of questionnaire data involves collating responses, and tabulating them, often requiring statistical analysis to determine whether the results are significant (see section below).

An interview can be used for many different purposes. It might aid a researcher who is trying to access speakers' intuitions about certain language forms (perhaps even to elicit the forms themselves) or it might be aimed at gaining insights into the attitudes and opinions of the participants with respect to certain topics; i.e. using the interview as a kind of spoken questionnaire. People can be interviewed individually or in groups (for instance, special focus groups where members are carefully selected). Both methods have their strengths and weaknesses. Group interviews allow researchers to collect information from a lot of people at one time, and the group interaction itself provides additional insights. Moreover, when participants get to hear each other's views, they are often more motivated to speak up. On the other hand, the presence of others and their opinions can be inhibiting, and some people are more motivated to speak their mind when they are not part of a group. Interviews offer richer data than questionnaires, but also involve considerably more work. They require the initial recruiting of participants and the careful framing of questions, taking into account the same pitfalls as described earlier for the questionnaire. Interviews are generally recorded using audio- and/or video-recording, and the recorded material then needs to be transcribed. The purpose of the interview will dictate the type of transcription conventions, whether phonetic, phonemic, conversational analytic or other.

## Recording and transcribing language data

One of the most reliable methods of collecting language data is by audio-recording, and linguists record naturally occurring talk as well as interviews. Recording data allows the researcher to listen repeatedly and make accurate transcriptions of what was said. It also allows other researchers, and the original speaker, to check and verify the transcription and interpretation. Some researchers prefer to use video-recording in order to record all the non-verbal communication associated with or replacing talk; others, however, find this more intrusive. One of the goals of much linguistic work is to record and describe normal talk and minimize the participant's awareness of being recorded (see Chapters 2.7 and 3.1 for a discussion of the observer's paradox). As technology becomes more sophisticated, the possibilities for unintrusive recording become greater.

In order to analyse recorded language data, we need to transcribe the talk. Written transcripts allow us to work across a set of data very easily. Transcripts fall into two broad groups depending on the type of analysis intended. Scholars working on phonological questions or describing an unknown language will need a phonemic or phonetic transcript using IPA symbols (see Chapters 2.1 and 2.2). Those working on discourse or conversational structure will use normal orthography and special symbols to indicate aspects of conversational organization (see Chapter 2.12). The format of the transcript also depends on the purpose of the analysis. People working with adult–child interactions often use a column format with each participant in a separate column, allowing the child language data to be isolated. Most discourse and conversational analysis works with a sequential format resembling a play script. If you are planning to transcribe data, read the work of scholars working in the area you are studying, and pay close attention to the kind of transcripts they use. All transcripts are selective, and you need to ask why the writers have chosen to set out the data the way they have. A good starting point is Ochs 1999, a reprint of a very influential article originally published in 1979. Ochs advises researchers on layout and the use of symbols in the transcription of both verbal and non-verbal actions from audio- and video-recordings. As she argues, transcription is in fact the first stage of analysis, and imposes a theoretical framework on the data. She argues that 'One of the consequences of ignoring transcription procedure is that researchers rarely produce a transcript that does reflect their research goals and the state of the field' (Ochs 1999: 168). Transcription becomes more difficult as the number of participants increases: with three or more speakers (as in a group interview) it is often not easy to tell who is talking and what is being said.

There is a wide variety of equipment available for recording, including digital recorders, tape recorders, analogue recorders, disk recorders and memory recorders. The selection of appropriate audio recorders and microphones will depend very much on the nature of your work and also its purpose. Digital recordings are used by many language professionals because of the quality of the soundtrack, and also because they allow the use of transcription software such as Transcriber. However, this is an area of rapidly changing technology, and anything we advise here will rapidly become out of date. Therefore, the best recommendation is that you check with your lecturers or tutors to find out which equipment and software programs they recommend. They may be able to give you access to appropriate recording devices and software programs. There are also many useful websites that help to keep you up to date: for example, the Department of Speech, Hearing and Phonetic Sciences at the University College London has a very useful website (http://www.phon.ucl.ac.uk/resource/audio/recording.html).

## Corpus data

Another application of technology to language research is the development of large corpora of language data (see Chapter 2.13). These might contain collections of different types of written texts, transcriptions of spoken language or perhaps both. There are vast numbers of English texts available on the internet, and the number is growing. Accessing the material in these electronic collections can often be done free of charge, but if there is a charge you might want to involve your institution. The following are just some of the well-known examples of electronic corpora that can be used for scholarly research:

**Corpora of written texts**

The Lancaster-Oslo/Bergen Corpus (LOB, British English texts from 1961)

The Freiburg-Lancaster-Oslo/Bergen Corpus (FLOB, British English texts from 1991)

The Brown Corpus (BC, 500 written samples of American English)

The Australian Corpus of English (ACE, texts from 1986)

The Wellington Corpus of Written New Zealand texts (WC, texts from 1986)

The Helsinki Corpus of English Texts (HC, texts from *c.* 750 to *c.* 1700 and transcripts of interviews with speakers of British rural dialects from the 1970s)

**Corpora of spoken texts**

The (Bergen) Corpus of London Teenager Talk (COLT, speech of 13 17-year-olds from different boroughs of London, collected in 1993)

The Australian Radio Talkback Corpus (ART, from Australia-wide ABC and commercial radio stations)

The Wellington Corpus of Spoken New Zealand English (WSC, formal, semi-formal and informal speech collected 1 January to December 31, 1988)

The CHILDES Archive, http://www.childes.psy.cmu.edu (Corpus of child language data)

**Corpora of spoken and written texts**

The International Corpus of English (ICE) is a collection of electronic corpora of material from English worldwide. Each ICE corpus consists of one million words of spoken and written English produced after 1989 (http://www.ucl.ac.uk/english-usage/ice/).

Some corpora are simply plain text, but most will be annotated to some degree. The most basic annotation includes the context, the type of language used, and some background information about the speakers or authors. Texts of conversations will typically also indicate where speakers begin and end their turns. Depending on the nature of the linguistic research, corpus annotation might also be more detailed to incorporate grammatical tagging, whereby words are marked up as corresponding to a particular part of speech or word-class (information is supplied in the form of tags) and even details of the syntactic structure of phrases and sentences (parsing) and pronoun reference (anaphoric annotation). Richer annotation includes phonetic and prosodic transcription and information to do with morphology, semantics and pragmatics.

Databases such as the ones just listed make the investigation of linguistic phenomena far more exciting and far easier than was ever possible in dark precomputational times. Imagine you want to investigate swearing patterns across different Englishes, or the different functions of the discourse particle *well*; or perhaps you are interested in how many times J.K. Rowling begins a sentence in *The Philosopher's Stone* with *and* or *but*. Computers can supply large amounts of information quickly and accurately. They can tell you how frequently certain words occur in a text and the context of words (e.g. the collocations they enter into). They can even help you to ascertain an author's style (useful in stylistics and forensic linguistics, especially when there are questions of disputed authorship). For more on the applications of corpora in language studies see McEnery and Wilson 2001 and Hunston 2002. These books also include comprehensive lists of available corpora. A useful online resource is Michael Barlow's corpus linguistics website (http://www.athel.com/corpus.html) with up-to-date details of corpora, tools and applications.

## Statistics

Although not all language studies require the use of statistics, it is becoming increasingly common for researchers to use basic statistical testing in their work, particularly with questionnaire, survey or corpus-based studies. A knowledge of statistical concepts and terminology (deviation, mean, average, frequency, range, graphs and so on) is essential for accurately interpreting your language data, as well as making knowledgeable judgements about the relative quality of other people's data. The functions and uses of statistics are varied. Descriptive statistics show us ways of displaying data. It deals with frequencies, central tendency and measures of variability. On the other hand, inferential statistics are used in order to prove or disprove a certain hypothesis adopted by the researcher. Tests such as Chi-square tests, $t$-tests and the ANOVA can be used for this purpose.

There are many helpful books to guide you through the bewildering array of different statistical techniques. You are strongly advised to select one that is specially tailored for linguistics. Brown 1988 focuses on the skills and processes necessary for understanding statistical research in language learning. Hatch and Lazaraton 1991 is a comprehensive and useful resource that covers both research design and statistics in applied linguistics. Oakes 1998 is a readable and sensible introduction to statistics used in corpus linguistics. Two recent texts are Baayen 2008 and Johnson 2008. Both books are fairly advanced practical guides with a range of real data sets that teach the reader by example. The first introduces linguists and psycholinguists to the basic principles and methods of statistical analysis, with a specific focus on the interactive software package 'R'. Johnson's book is an interdisciplinary introduction to a number of the most widely used statistical methods in language research, including 'R'.

## Overview

We cannot do justice here to the range of different skills, tools and techniques you may need when undertaking a piece of language research. However, there are many very practical guides that are available for students. One of the most comprehensive is Wray and Bloomer 2006. It provides very helpful advice on choosing research topics, collecting data and the use of corpora, as well as guidance on how to analyse data and write up results. It also contains around 250 suggestions for project ideas.

In the following chapters we will explore selected research studies in the main subdisciplines of linguistics, showing how researchers approach the collection of data and construction of hypotheses and models.

## Key points

> Research in linguistics needs to conform to ethical guidelines.

> Ethical research requires informed consent of participants, and needs to consider the possible impact of the research on the community studied.

> Data collection methods include the use of introspection, questionnaires, interviews, and audio- or video-recording and transcription.

> Corpus data may also be used as the basis for research.

> Appropriate statistical methods need to be used.

## References

Baayen, R. Harald 2008. *Analyzing Linguistic Data: A Practical Introduction to Statistics Using R*. Cambridge: Cambridge University Press.

Brown, James D. 1988. *Understanding Research in Second Language Acquisition: A Teacher's Guide to Statistics and Research Design*. Cambridge: Cambridge University Press.

Brown, James D. 2006. Research methods for applied linguistics. In *The Handbook of Applied Linguistics*, ed. by Alan Davies and Catherine Elder. Oxford: Blackwell, pp. 476–500.

Cameron, Deborah, Elizabeth Frazer, Penelope Harvey, M.B.H. Rampton, and Kay Richardson 1992. *Researching Language: Issues of Power and Method*. London: Routledge.

Dornyei, Zoltan 2003. *Questionnaires in Second Language Research: Construction, Administration, and Processing*. Mahwah NJ: Lawrence Erlbaum.

Dornyei, Zoltan 2007. *Research Methods in Applied Linguistics: Quantitative, Qualitative, and Mixed Methodologies*. Oxford: Oxford University Press.

Hatch, Evelyn and Ann Lazaraton 1991. *Research Manual: Design and Statistics for Applied Linguistics*. New York: Newbury House.

Hunston, Susan 2002. *Corpora in Applied Linguistics*. Cambridge: Cambridge University Press.

Johnson, Keith 2008. *Quantitative Methods in Linguistics*. Oxford: Blackwell.

Li, Wei 2000. Methodological questions in the study of bilingualism. In *The Bilingualism Reader*, ed. by Wei Li. London: Routledge, pp. 438–48.

McEnery, Tony and Andrew Wilson 2001. *Corpus Linguistics*. Edinburgh: Edinburgh University Press.

Oakes, Michael P. 1998. *Statistics for Corpus Linguistics*. Edinburgh: Edinburgh University Press.

Ochs, Eleanor 1999. Transcription as theory. In *The Discourse Reader*, ed. by Adam Jaworski and Nikolas Coupland. London: Routledge, pp. 167–82.

Wray, Alison and Aileen Bloomer 2006. *Projects in Linguistics: A Practical Guide to Researching Language*. London: Hodder Arnold.

# 5.2 researching general and theoretical linguistics

## chapter contents

> Ferdinand de Saussure          277
> Noam Chomsky                    279
> John Lyons                      281
> Key points                      281
> References                      281
> Resources                       282

This chapter shows how the work of key theorists has shaped the way theoretical linguists conduct research. How does one research general and/or theoretical linguistics? Not with a questionnaire, but by assembling data and ideas from a wide range of sources and abducing hypotheses from them. It is largely an exercise in 'armchair linguistics', making use of introspection. In this chapter we review work by three theoretical linguists: Ferdinand de Saussure, Noam Chomsky, and John Lyons.

## Ferdinand de Saussure

Twentieth-century European linguistics was greatly influenced by the work of Ferdinand de Saussure (1857–1913). As Professor of Comparative Linguistics at Geneva University, Saussure famously gave three courses in general linguistics in the sessions 1906–7, 1908–9, and 1910–11. Saussure destroyed most of his notes as he went along, but after his death in 1913 Charles Bally and Charles Albert Sechehaye, assisted by Albert Riedlinger, collated what remained of Saussure's notes and those of several members of his audience under the title *Cours de Linguistique Générale* (*CLG*) (Saussure 1916), known in English as *A Course in General Linguistics* (Saussure 1974). Because of its construction, and because the lecture notes were taken from three different periods during which Saussure developed his ideas, the book cannot be judged a definitive account of his theories about language. *CLG* has been augmented by the publication of a handful of Saussure's own jottings discovered in 1996 (Saussure 2002), and additional notes from members of his audience. Nevertheless it is on *CLG* that Saussure's reputation rests.

   *CLG* is permeated by Saussure's belief that linguistics is just a part of 'semiology', better known as *semiotics*, which studies how signs make meaning (see Chapter 3.1, 'Sign'). Crucial to linguistics is the double articulation, a dyadic relation between signifier (*signifiant*) and signified (*signifié*) – a distinction which goes back to the Stoic difference between *sēmainon* and *sēmainomenon* in Ancient Greece (see Allan 2009). Saussure very probably took the idea directly from *La Vie du Langage* (Whitney 1875a), the translation of William Whitney's *Life and Growth of Language* (Whitney 1875b).

Saussure recognized the arbitrariness of the sign. He could have been taking his cue from Plato in *Letter VII* (Plato 1997) or Aristotle in *On Interpretation* (Aristotle 1984), but in fact he mentions Whitney. Saussure's associative and syntagmatic relations were very possibly conceived under influence from Hermann Paul's (1846–1921) *stoffliche und formale Gruppen* "material and formal groups" (Paul 1880 §§75–78). Associative relations are 'vertical', i.e. relations between linguistic elements that can operate at one constituent place in the syntagm. Syntagmatic relations are those which hold 'horizontally' along the chain of speech between constituents in a string. Saussure's associative and syntagmatic relations were carried over into American descriptivist linguistics as 'constituent analysis', 'immediate constituent analysis', 'slot and filler analysis', 'distributional analysis', and so on. They apply to phonological, morphological, and syntactic data.

Following the lead of Henry Sweet (e.g. Sweet 1899), and in concert with Sechehaye 1908, Saussure champions the priority of spoken over written language; it is one of the ways in which he leads linguistics out of the nineteenth century. For him the signifier is not pure physical phonological form but an 'acoustic/auditory image'. We may compare Saussure's auditory image to the cognitive (psychological) counterparts of a phoneme or the combination of phonemes into a morpheme: it is an abstract categorization. Saussure is celebrated for his distinction between *langue*, a system of signs (which we will therefore render into English as "language system"), and *parole* "speech", which together constitute *langage* "language". Once again there is influence from Paul's *Prinzipien* (Paul 1880 §§17, 22, 286, 293). The notion that the language system is characteristically an expression of social interaction among humans, Saussure picked up directly from Whitney, who represented a tradition stretching back through Humboldt (1767–1835), Herder (1744–1803), and Locke (1632–1704) to Lucretius (95–55 BCE) and Epicurus (341–270 BCE). Saussure makes grammar the study of the language system in the brains of individuals who constitute the language community. The relationship between *langue* and *parole* is comparable to that of chicken and egg: no one knows how many tens of thousands of years *langue* has existed as a resource for individual speakers; yet it must have originated from the *parole* of (earlier) individual speakers. *Parole* is the contextually relevant application of *langue*. *Langue* is learnt from the *parole* of others, and it is *parole* that causes language to evolve and gives rise to *langue*. Hence they, like chicken and egg, are interdependent.

The only book Saussure ever published (when he was twenty-one) was on the vowel system of Proto-Indo-European – his *Mémoire sur le système primitif des voyelles dans les langues Indo-européennes* (Saussure 1879). Proto-languages are hypothesized on the basis of evidence of current forms in related languages, and the sound changes that must have taken place to produce contemporary forms (see Chapter 5.6). Saussure studied among the neogrammarians in Leipzig, and received his doctorate from there in 1881. But whereas the neogrammarians were rigidly inductive, the *Mémoire* is based on abstract morphophonemic analysis (study of the phonemic differences among allomorphs – see Chapter 5.5), in which the postulated abstract elements are defined in terms of structural function rather than phonetic shape. Emphasis on the function of an element within a linguistic system remained characteristic of Saussurean linguistics throughout his life. Saussure's approach to linguistics in the *Mémoire* is more like Chomsky's in the later twentieth century than of the neogrammarians before him or the Bloomfieldians of the first half of the twentieth century. But Saussure never lost sight of the social and cognitive aspects of language as a system for communication among people; and in that respect he has more in common with functionalist grammarians than with Chomsky. The emphasis on language as a structured system makes it appropriate to label Saussure a *structuralist*, although the term was not in use during his lifetime.

So why was Saussurean linguistics paradigmatic in the sense that for a time it provided model problems and solutions to a community of practitioners (Kuhn 1970: viii)? Saussure brought together in the lectures that gave rise to *CLG* the various ideas of his illustrious contemporaries and immediate predecessors, fashioning them into what was thought to be a workable theory. Saussure's insistence that linguistics is an independent science that should study language (*langue*) as a self-contained structured system came to characterize twentieth-century linguistics, and it remains an ideological force in linguistics today. His discussion of syntagmatic and associative relations was influential. His explications of the distinction between *langue* and *parole* as different manifestations of *langage* were better articulated than those presented by Hermann Paul. Chomsky's discussions of 'competence' and 'performance' owe much to Saussure (Chomsky 1964: 10f). Today Saussure's semiology is influential in fields outside linguistics; and his vision of language as a socially shared, psychologically real structured system is shared by today's functionalists.

As with any good theoretical linguist, Saussure's legacy is a set of valuable insights into the nature and structure of language that provide his successors with a set of principles and procedures to be used in the analysis of language.

## Noam Chomsky

Noam Chomsky (b. 1928) was trained by Zellig Harris in the distributional analysis of language described in Harris 1951. While working on his master's thesis, Chomsky became frustrated by the procedures of segmentation and classification that Harris described.

> They were designed to isolate classes of phones, sequences of these classes, classes of these sequences, etc., until, ultimately, sentences are characterized in terms of their constituents. But the elements that were needed in the optimal generative grammar simply did not have this character. They were not classes, sequences of classes, or anything of the sort, but were simply abstract elements forming strings that could be mapped into phonetic representation by deeply ordered rules of considerable generality. (Chomsky 1975: 30)

Chomsky was soon championing the universalism and cognitivism of traditional grammar against its rejection by Bloomfieldians, and was, already in the 1950s, reanalysing the traditional concerns with the new tools of mathematical logic and transformational grammar under Harris's tutelage (see Harris 1970). The true revolution that Chomsky bequeathed was the shift from discovering grammars inductively to axiomatizing them in a top-down hypothetico-deductive process and setting up adequacy conditions for evaluating them.

> It became increasingly clear to me that the methodological limitation of procedures based on substitution, matching, and similar 'taxonomic' operations was arbitrary and unwarranted. One might approach the problem of projecting a corpus to a language of grammatical sentences in an entirely different way, with a procedure for evaluating a completed system of categories rather than a procedure for constructing these categories step by step by taxonomic methods. … There would now be no reason to regard phonemes, morphemes, categories, and other elements to be segments, classes of segments, sequences of classes, sets of phenomenal

properties (e.g. phonetic distinctive features), and so on. Rather they would be elements in various abstract systems of representation. (Chomsky 1975: 31)

This is what led to *Syntactic Structures* (Chomsky 1957), the book that revolutionized linguistic theory in the second half of the twentieth century. Chomsky was responsible for replacing the bottom-up structuralist analyses such as that given at (1) below (Hockett 1958: 152) with the top-down (incomplete set of) phrase structure rules given in (2); see Chapter 2.4.

(1)

| the | son- | -s | and | daughter- | -s | of | a | man | a- | -re | hi | -s | child- | -ren |
|---|---|---|---|---|---|---|---|---|---|---|---|---|---|---|
| | sons | | | daughters | | | a man | | | | | | | |
| | sons and daughters | | | | | of a man | | | | | his | | children | |
| | sons and daughters of a man | | | | | | | | are | | his children | | | |
| the sons and daughters of a man | | | | | | | | | are his children | | | | | |
| The sons and daughters of a man are his children | | | | | | | | | | | | | | |

(2)

| | | |
|---|---|---|
| S | → | NP Aux VP |
| VP | → | V (NP) |
| NP | → | Det N PP |
| PP | → | Prep NP |
| N | → | N (*and* N) |
| Aux | → | Tense |
| Tense | → | Present, Past |
| V | → | *be* |
| Det | → | *a, the, his* |
| N | → | *son, daughter, man, child* |
| Prep | → | *of* |

Rather as Saussure had distinguished *langue* from *parole*, Chomsky 1965 distinguished 'competence' or knowledge of grammar, which is what his syntactic theory aims to model, from 'performance', which was the use of language that included errors in writing and speech. Subsequent to Chomsky 1986, these were renamed I[nternalized]-language and E[xternalized]-language. Over the years Chomskyan syntactic theories have moved on from the context-sensitive phrase structure grammar of *Syntactic Structures* to the elaborate underlying structures of *Aspects of the Theory of Syntax* (Chomsky 1965) to the X-bar theory of Chomsky 1972, with its generalizations over phrase structures (noting, for instance, what NP, PP and VP have in common). The kinds and complexity of the transformational rules postulated to generate surface structures from underlying structures also changed greatly during this period. The Principles and Parameters theory of Chomsky 1982 identified certain universal principles of grammar, which are differently implemented (or not implemented at all) by the parameters imposed by learning a particular language. Finally we have the minimalist theory of Chomsky 1993, which has very few rules and only one transformation.

Since Chomsky 1964, Chomskyan linguistics has argued for an 'autonomous' syntactic component at the heart of the grammar which generates strings that need to be interpreted by a phonological component to give them regular linguistic form, and by a semantic component to assign them meaning. This counterintuitive stance is anathema to cognitive and functional linguists.

Chomsky's legacy is a different set of valuable insights into the nature and structure of language; they too provide his successors with a set of principles and procedures to be used in the analysis of language.

## John Lyons

John Lyons (b. 1932, knighted 1987) is most famously a semanticist. But in 1968, when Professor of General Linguistics at Edinburgh University, he published *Introduction to Theoretical Linguistics* (Lyons 1968). Almost immediately it became a classic introduction to the discipline. The book focuses on the core topics of general linguistics: phonetics, phonology, morphology, syntax, and semantics. Lyons's presentation is notable for its measured delivery and eclectic approach, even though the author's assumptions are those prevalent in the mid-1960s with respect to categorial and transformational grammar. Having defined linguistics, Lyons offers a scholarly critique of traditional grammar, beginning with the Ancient Greeks. He does not ignore the Indian grammatical tradition, dating back to Plato's time, but studied in the West only from the late eighteenth century. In the nineteenth century, comparative philology, which identified relations among the members of various language families but especially Indo-European, gave rise to modern linguistics. Concomitantly, as linguistic inquiry turned to focus on spoken language. Lyons offers some general remarks about the structures one discerns in language, then describes the sounds of language. However, more than half of *Introduction to Theoretical Linguistics* is devoted to aspects of grammar: problems of grammaticality versus acceptability, grammar and the lexicon, morphology, constituency, context-sensitive vs context-free grammars, primary, secondary and functional grammatical categories, transitivity and ergativity. The last part of the book surveys traditional and modern semantics, sense and reference, lexical relations, and lexical versus grammatical meaning, and questions the universality of semantic components.

Although half a century old, Lyons 1968 remains a valuable resource for thoughtful students of linguistics in the twenty-first century. Lyons differs from Saussure and Chomsky in the breadth of his linguistic interest and its firm seating in a great tradition of inquiry into language.

## Key points

> The work of Saussure established a set of key concepts which became the basis of subsequent linguistic research.

> Chomsky's revolutionary approach to linguistic theory brought a new theoretical and methodological rigour to research in theoretical linguistics.

## References

Allan, Keith 2009. *The Western Classical Tradition in Linguistics*. 2nd edn. London: Equinox.

Aristotle 1984. *The Complete Works of Aristotle. The Revised Oxford Translation*, ed. by Jonathan Barnes. Bollingen Series 71. Princeton: Princeton University Press.

Chomsky, Noam 1957. *Syntactic Structures*. The Hague: Mouton.

Chomsky, Noam 1964. Current issues in linguistic theory. In *The Structure of Language: Readings in the Philosophy of Language*, ed. by Jerry A. Fodor and Jerrold J. Katz. Englewood Cliffs: Prentice-Hall.

Chomsky, Noam 1965. *Aspects of the Theory of Syntax*. Cambridge MA: MIT Press.

Chomsky, Noam 1972. *Studies on Semantics in Generative Grammar*. The Hague: Mouton.

Chomsky, Noam 1975. Introduction. *The Logical Structure of Linguistic Theory*. New York: Plenum Press.

Chomsky, Noam 1982. *Some Concepts and Consequences of the Theory of Government and Binding*. Cambridge MA: MIT Press.

Chomsky, Noam 1986. *Knowledge of Language: Its Nature, Origin, and Use*. New York: Praeger.

Chomsky, Noam 1993. A minimalist program for linguistic theory. In *The View from Building 20*, ed. by Ken Hale and Samuel J. Keyser. Cambridge MA: MIT Press, pp. 1–52.

Harris, Zellig S. 1951. *Methods in Structural Linguistics*. Chicago: University of Chicago Press.

Harris, Zellig S. 1970. *Papers in Structural and Transformational Linguistics*. Dordrecht: D. Reidel.

Hockett, Charles F. 1958. *A Course in Modern Linguistics*. New York: Macmillan – now Palgrave Macmillan.

Kuhn, Thomas S. 1970. *The Structure of Scientific Revolutions*. International Encyclopedia of Unified Science. 2nd edn. Chicago: Chicago University Press [First edn 1962].

Lyons, John 1968. *Introduction to Theoretical Linguistics*. London: Cambridge University Press.

Paul, Hermann 1880. *Prinzipien der Sprachgeschichte*. Halle: Max Niemeyer.

Plato 1997. *Complete Works*, ed. by John M. Cooper. Indianapolis: Hackett.

Saussure, Ferdinand de 1879. *Mémoire sur le système primitif des voyelles dans les langues Indo-européennes*. Leipsick: Teubner.

Saussure, Ferdinand de 1916. *Cours de Linguistique Générale* [Publié par Charles Bally et Albert Sechehaye; avec la collaboration de Albert Riedlinger]. Paris: Payot.

Saussure, Ferdinand de 1974. *A Course in General Linguistics*. Glasgow: Fontana/Collins [transl. by Wade Baskin from the 3rd edn of *Cours de Linguistique Générale*. Paris: Payot, 1931. First edn published in 1916].

Saussure, Ferdinand de 2002. *Écrits de Linguistique Générale* (Établis et édités par Simon Bouquet et Rudolf Engler, avec la collaboration d'Antoinette Weil]. Paris: Gallimard.

Sechehaye, Ch. Albert 1908. *Programme et Méthodes de la Linguistique Théorique: Psychologie du Langage*. Paris: Honoré Champion.

Sweet, Henry 1899. *The Practical Study of Languages: A Guide for Teachers and Learners*. London: J.M. Dent.

Whitney, William D. 1875a. *La Vie du Langage*. Paris: Germer Baillière.

Whitney, William D. 1875b. *The Life and Growth of Language*. London: Henry S. King.

# Resources

Relevant **journals** include:
> *Australian Journal of Linguistics*
> *Journal of Linguistics*
> *Language*
> *Language Sciences*
> *Lingua*
> *Linguistic Inquiry*
> *Linguistics*
> *Natural Language and Linguistic Theory*

Relevant **annual series** include:
> Chicago Linguistic Society Papers
> Berkeley Linguistic Society Papers
> North Eastern Linguistic Society Papers

**Useful URLs** include:
> http://www.wikipedia.org
> http://linguistlist.org/

# 5.3 researching phonetics and phonology

## chapter contents

> Key points            285
> References         285
> Resources         286

This chapter identifies the tasks for researchers in phonetics and phonology, and then recounts a history of research into these sub-disciplines of language study.

As we showed in Chapters 2.1 and 2.2, phonetics is the study of human speech sounds; phonology the study of the speech sounds used within one particular language or a family of languages. Researchers need to identify:

> the properties of speech sounds used in languages, what constitute segments of speech
> how the segments are grouped into syllables and larger structures
> what the prosodic aspects of speech are.

Consequently, researchers require ear-training. In addition, of course, there is concern with the physiological mechanisms that transmit and receive sounds. Researchers into phonetics and phonology need to identify the optimal ways to describe all these things; and they must also be able to manipulate and even invent instruments for recording, interpreting, and synthesizing speech.

The earliest phonological analysis was carried out by those who first created alphabets some five thousand years ago – because the basis for an alphabet is the phonemic inventory of a language. In India the sacred Hindu texts, the *Vedas*, the oldest of which may date from about 1500 BCE, needed to be pronounced correctly to create the desired effect. However, like all languages Sanskrit changed, and so a description of the sound system of Vedic Sanskrit was devised, principally by the fifth-century BCE grammarian Pāṇini. This gave a full and mostly accurate account of the speech mechanisms. There was a classification of speech sounds, partly in terms of place and manner of articulation, and also an appreciation that allophonic variation is sensitive to the phonetic and morphological environment (see Allen 1953). In the Western linguistic tradition it was Aristotle who, c. 340 BCE in *Poetica*, described the pronunciation of a 'letter' as 'an indivisible sound of a particular kind, one that may be a constituent of an intelligible sound [= word]' (1456[b]22). In effect, he was describing the phoneme symbolized by the letter (= grapheme).

Until the twentieth century, developments in phonemics and phonetics were largely the province of scholars interested in orthography. Around 1135 CE an Icelander, using methods such as contrasting 'minimal pairs' that were not found again until the twentieth century, made a phonemic transcription of Icelandic to accurately represent the spoken language in writing (see Haugen 1972; Allan 2009). Unfortunately his work had no impact on the development of phonology.

Others, such as Butler 1633, Holder 1669, Lodwick 1686, Champollion 1822, Ellis 1848 followed, but the great leap forward was with the work of Henry Sweet (1845–1912) whose *Handbook of Phonetics, Including a Popular Exposition of the Principles of Spelling Reform* (Sweet 1877) looks both backward and forward. Sweet championed 'phonetics as the indispensable foundation of all study of language', a view that became a mainstay of modern linguistics. Sweet's phonetic alphabet inspired Frenchman Paul Édouard Passy (1859–1940), a French teacher of English, to establish the International Phonetic Alphabet (IPA) in 1886. In addition to Sweet's Romic script, the IPA uses Greek symbols such as $\theta$ and $\lambda$, special symbols like $\int$ and $\Omega$, digraphs like $\mathit{tf}$, and assigns new values to $x$ and $q$. The IPA has been revised several times since then; for the current version see http://www.langsci.ucl.ac.uk/ipa/. Sweet's distinction between 'Broad Romic' and 'Narrow Romic' is exactly the distinction between a phonemic and a phonetic description (though Sweet himself never used the word *phoneme*). Leonard Bloomfield 1926 succinctly defined the phoneme as '[a] minimum same of vocal feature'. English phonetician Daniel Jones (1881–1967), a pupil of Passy, published his *Outline of English Phonetics* in 1918 and it ran to nine editions (Jones 1960). In it he identified the cardinal vowels at the boundaries of the vowel-making area in the mouth. You can hear the recordings he made of them in 1956 linked to http://www.let.uu.nl/ffaudiufon/data/e_cardinal_vowels.html.

During the years 1928 to 1939 the Prague Linguistic Circle (*Pražský lingvistický kroužek*) had significant influence on twentieth-century phonological theory. Basic to their method of phonological analysis is the setting up of contrasts or distinctive features – the same method as was used by the medieval Icelander whose work was mentioned earlier. The criterion for determining which sounds are significantly contrastive is meaning: phonetic differences that do not signal semantic contrasts are not contrastive. Prague School distinctive features were brought to Chomskyan grammar by Roman Jakobson (1896–1982). In *Preliminaries to Speech Analysis* (Jakobson, Fant and Halle 1952), the emphasis was on acoustic features but, in later work, distinctive features are identified primarily in articulatory terms (see Jakobson and Halle 1956; Jakobson and Waugh 1979). The *Sound Pattern of English* (hereafter *SPE*, Chomsky and Halle 1968) brought distinctive feature analysis to a wider audience. Phonology became explicitly linked with grammar following *SPE*, which postulated the transformational cycle as a means of introducing prosodic (suprasegmental) phonology into the surface realization of syntactically well-formed and semantically interpreted language structures. It was soon established that both the stress assignment rules and transformational cycle proposed in *SPE* were deeply flawed. The morphological derivations in *SPE*, which ingeniously related twentieth-century pronunciation to earlier forms (e.g. *divine* and *divinity* have the underlying form [divīn] in common), have also been criticized. One reaction to the syntactic basis for phonological structure proposed in *SPE* was the development of metrical phonology, which groups phonemes into syllables, syllables into metrical feet, feet into phonological words, and words into larger units (see Liberman and Prince 1977). There are levels of representation for segments, syllables, and High and Low tones (word tone H*, phrase tone L⁻, and boundary tone L%). As Selkirk 1980: 29 wrote: 'prosodic structure is not syntactic structure, nor is it isomorphic to it.'

With the development of digital recording and computer analysis much phonetic analysis in the twenty-first century is instrumental. You can try your hand at this by downloading PRAAT from http://www.fon.hum.uva.nl/praat/. This is a small informal program that will easily run on a home computer. It enables, among other things, speech analysis (graphic and statistical), speech synthesis, and speech manipulation.

## Key points

> Research in phonetics and phonology relies on accurate recognition of speech sounds.

> The International Phonetic Alphabet allows phoneticians to represent speech sounds orthographically

> Phonologists use the descriptions of sounds and their distribution in a language to identify the significant contrasts in the sound system of that language.

## References

Allan, Keith 2009. *The Western Classical Tradition in Linguistics*. 2nd edn. London: Equinox.

Allen, W. Sidney 1953. *Phonetics in Ancient India*. London: Oxford University Press.

Bloomfield, Leonard 1926. A set of postulates for the science of language. *Language* 2: 153–64. Reprinted in *Readings in Linguistics*, ed. by Martin Joos. Washington DC: American Council of Learned Societies. 1957: 26–31.

Butler, Charles 1633. *The English Grammar, or The institution of letters, syllables, and words, in the English tongue. Whereunto is annexed an index of words like and unlike*. Oxford: W. Turner.

Champollion, Jean-François 1822. *Lettre à M. Dacier ... : relative a l'alphabet des hiéroglyphes phonétiques employés par les Égyptiens pour inscrire sur leurs monuments les titres, les noms et les surnoms des souverains grecs et romains*. Paris: F. Didot.

Chomsky, Noam and Morris Halle 1968. *The Sound Pattern of English*. New York: Harper and Row.

Ellis, Alexander J. 1848. *The Essentials of Phonetics*. London: Pitman.

Haugen, Einar 1972. *The First Grammatical Treatise: The Earliest Germanic Phonology*. London: Longman.

Holder, William 1669. *The Elements of Speech, an Essay of Enquiry into the Natural Production of Letters: with an Appendix Concerning Persons Deaf & Dumb*. London: T.N. for J. Martyn [Menston: Scolar Press Facsimile. 1967].

Jakobson, Roman, C. Gunnar Fant and Morris Halle 1952. *Preliminaries to Speech Analysis*. Technical Report 13. Cambridge MA: Acoustics Laboratory, MIT.

Jakobson, Roman and Morris Halle 1956. *Fundamentals of Language*. The Hague: Mouton.

Jakobson, Roman and Linda R. Waugh 1979. *The Sound Shape of Language*. Brighton: Harvester.

Jones, Daniel 1960. *An Outline of English Phonetics*. 9th edn. Cambridge: Heffer [First edn, Leipzig: Teubner, 1918].

Liberman, Mark and Alan Prince 1977. On stress and linguistic rhythm. *Linguistic Inquiry* 8: 249–336.

Lodwick, Francis 1686. Essay towards an universall alphabet. In *The works of Francis Lodwick: a study of his writings in the intellectual context of the seventeenth century*, ed. by Vivian Salmon. London: Longman. 1972, pp. 235–46.

Selkirk, Elizabeth O. 1980. *On Prosodic Structure and Its Relation to Syntactic Structure*. Bloomington: Indiana University Linguistics Club.

Sweet, Henry 1877. *Handbook of Phonetics, Including a Popular Exposition of the Principles of Spelling Reform*. Oxford: Clarendon Press.

5

# Resources

There is of course much ongoing work in phonetics and phonology. Excellent introductions are:

> Ladefoged, Peter 2006. *A Course in Phonetics*. 5th edn, with CD-ROM. Boston MA: Thomson Wadsworth. See the reader reports at http://www.amazon.com/gp/product/customer-reviews/0155001736/ref=cm_cr_dp_pt/104-5564410-9609514?ie=UTF8&n=283155&s=books.

> Clark, John, Colin Yallop and Janet Fletcher 2007. *An Introduction to Phonetics and Phonology*. 3rd edn. Malden MA: Blackwell. This book provides a clear explanation of the field of phonetics and gives good examples of the different elements it covers.

Relevant **journals** include:

> *Journal of Phonetics*
> *Journal of the International Phonetic Association*
> *Phonetica. International Journal of Phonetic Science*
> *Phonology*
> *Journal of the Acoustical Society of America*
> *Journal of the Acoustical Society of Japan*
> *Journal of Speech, Language, and Hearing Research*
> *Language and Speech*

**Useful URLs** include:

> http://www.wikipedia.org
> The IPA Homepage: http://www.langsci.ucl.ac.uk/ipa.
> The IPA CHART can be downloaded free from http://www.langsci.ucl.ac.uk/ipa/fullchart.html.
> A Unicode phonetics font can be downloaded free from http://scripts.sil.org/cms/scripts/page.php?site_id=nrsi&item_id=DoulosSIL_download#FontsDownload.
> There is an interactive IPA chart on-line at http://web.uvic.ca/ling/resources/ipa/charts/IPAlab/IPAlab.htm.
> The PRAAT program for instrumental phonetic analysis can be downloaded from http://www.fon.hum.uva.nl/praat/

# 5.4 researching morphology

## chapter contents

> Key points      289
> References      289
> Resources      290

This chapter gives a brief account of how morphologists use language data to identify the rules governing word structure. Research into morphology can be restricted to investigating data from just one language but commonly extends to several. Morphology is the study of the internal structure of words and how this structure affects their phonological, syntactic and semantic properties. For example compare English *nation, national, nationalization, nationality, nationalist, nationalistic, nationalistically* which are etymologically related to *natal, native,* and *nativity.* The term *morphology* ("study of form") was first applied to the structure of animals and plants but adopted into linguistics by August Schleicher (1821–68) and applied to the study of word structure. The study of morphology was a principal part of pedagogical grammars in ancient times: the morphology of Ancient Greek was explored in the *Technē Grammatikē* attributed to Dionysius Thrax in the first century BCE and that of Latin in the *Ars Grammatica* of Aelius Donatus in the fourth century CE. Paradigms of word structures in Greek and Latin were set out and taught to generations of language learners until well into the twentieth century in what became known as 'word and paradigm' grammars.

In the twentieth century, methods of distributional analysis were demonstrated by, for example, Roman Jakobson in Jakobson 1936 and Zellig Harris in Harris 1948. Consider some examples of case forms in Latin (a declension is a formally defined noun class).

| Latin first declension (feminine) nouns | | | | |
|---|---|---|---|---|
| noun stem | —S | —PL | CASE | rough gloss |
| *fēmin-* | —*a* | —*ae* | NOMINATIVE | "the woman/women" [case of clause subject] |
| | —*ae* | —*ārum* | GENITIVE | "of the woman/women" [possessive] |
| | —*ae* | —*īs* | DATIVE | "to the woman/women" [recipient] |
| | —*am* | —*ās* | ACCUSATIVE | "the woman/women" [case of direct object] |
| | —*ā* | —*īs* | ABLATIVE | "from/with/in/by the woman/women" |

| Latin third declension nouns | | | | | | |
|---|---|---|---|---|---|---|
| CASE | MASCULINE | | FEMININE | | NEUTER | |
| | "rumor" | "rumors" | "night" | "nights" | "star" | "stars" |
| NOM | rūmor | rūmōrēs | nox | noctēs | sīdus | sīdera |
| GEN | rūmōris | rūmōrum | noctis | noctium | sīderis | sīderum |
| DAT | rūmōrī | rūmōribus | noctī | noctibus | sīderi | sīderibus |
| ACC | rūmōrem | rūmōrēs | noctem | noctēs | sīdus | sīdera |
| ABL | rūmōre | rūmōribus | nocte | noctibus | sīdere | sīderibus |

Every nominal suffix realizes four covert categories: CASE, GENDER, NUMBER, and DECLENSION. The forms of the suffixes can be predicted from the particular combination of contrastive components from each of the four categories:

| The morphology of Latin noun suffixes | |
|---|---|
| case | NOMINATIVE/GENITIVE/DATIVE/ACCUSATIVE/ABLATIVE |
| gender | MASCULINE/FEMININE/NEUTER |
| number | SINGULAR/PLURAL |
| declension | FIRST/SECOND/THIRD/FOURTH/FIFTH |

For example:

ACCUSATIVE & FEMININE & SINGULAR & FIRST $\rightarrow$ –am (e.g. fēminam)
GENITIVE & NEUTER & PLURAL & THIRD $\rightarrow$ –um (e.g. sīderum)
ABLATIVE & MASCULINE & SINGULAR & SECOND $\rightarrow$ –ō (e.g. puerō)

Some of the earliest **morphophonemic** rules were created by Priscianus Caesarensis for Latin in the early sixth century CE in *Institutiones Grammaticae* "Grammatical Doctrine" (Priscian 1961). There were rules (spelled out in words rather than the formalism below) specifying that the final –h of a verb stem changes to –x in the past tense (**P**):

$$h \rightarrow x \quad \begin{cases} veh{-} + \mathbf{P} \rightarrow vex{-} \\ trah{-} + \mathbf{P} \rightarrow trax{-} \end{cases}$$

This rule accounted for the fact that the verbs *vehere* "carry" (whence comes our word *vehicle*) has the past tense forms *vexi* "I carried", *veximus* "we carried"; *trahere* "drag" has the past forms *traxisti* "you dragged", *traxerunt* "they dragged".

In English there are morphophonemic rules for deriving the correct forms for all of the English regular plural s morpheme, the third person singular agreement suffix –s in (e.g. *gives*), and the {POSSESSIVE} –s suffix.

$$\left.\begin{array}{l} \{\text{REGULAR PLURAL}\} \\ \{\text{3.S.AGREEMENT}\} \\ \{\text{POSSESSIVE}\} \end{array}\right\} \rightarrow \begin{cases} \text{/əz/ / [+sibilant] \_\_\#} \\ \text{/s/ / [–sibilant, –voice] \_\_\#} \\ \text{/z/ elsewhere} \end{cases}$$

As we saw in the example above from the Latin grammarian Priscian, pronunciation of a stem may change in the environment of morphological change such as suffixation. For example, in English the final tense long vowel (perhaps diphthong) of a stem becomes a lax short monophthong with the accretion of –*ity* for some stems. Note that there is no stress shift.

/dɪˈvain/        /səˈɹin/        /pɹəˈfein/        /vəˈboʊs/        /pɹəˈfaʊnd/
/dɪˈvɪnɪtɪ/        /səˈɹɛnɪtɪ/        /pɹəˈfænɪtɪ/        /vəˈbɒsɪtɪ/        /pɹəˈfʌndɪtɪ/

(*Divine, serene, profane, verbose, profound; divinity,* and so on.) But not all, cf. /oʊˈbiːs ~ oʊˈbiːsɪtɪ/ (*obese, obesity*). Note that the correlations between /ai/~/ɪ/, /i/~/ɛ/, /ei/~/æ/, /oʊ/~/ɒ/, /aʊ/~/ʌ/ are signalled for the first four in traditional orthography by <i>, <e>, <a>, <o> respectively in *divine~divinity, serene~serenity,* and so on. The spelling of the relevant vowel is slightly different in *profound~profundity* (and in *pronounce~pronunciation*). In *Canada~Canadian, Newton~Newtonian* the unstressed syllable in the source becomes a stressed syllable in the derived word with consequent vowel change from /ə/ to a long tense vowel.

/ˈkænədə/        /ˈnjutən/
/kəˈneidɪən/        /njʊˈtoʊnɪən/

Once again the traditional orthography signals the connection. Such morphophonemic correlations as these were discussed in Chomsky and Halle 1968 and later in Optimality theory (see Prince and Smolensky 2002). Optimality theory provides insights into various aspects of morphology in terms of ranked constraints on rules, the violability of rules, and selecting from among possible outputs (such as between the possessives *Jesus' wounds* versus *Jesus's wounds*). Optimality theory is very much an area of ongoing research.

To sum up: morphologists research the structure of words and the structural relations among related words leading to the identification of patterns of structural change. Some illustrations of their work have been given in this chapter.

## Key points

> Morphologists examine the internal structure of words.

> Morphologists analyse the distribution of grammatical forms such as nominal suffixes, and construct morphophonemic rules to explain their different realizations.

> Morphologists study systematic relationship among words within the same language and among related languages.

5

## References

Bauer, Laurie 2003. *Introducing Linguistic Morphology*. 2nd edn. Edinburgh: Edinburgh University Press [First edn 1988].

Booij, Geert 2005. *The Grammar of Words: An Introduction to Linguistic Morphology*. Oxford: Oxford University Press.

Carstairs-McCarthy, Andrew 2002. *An Introduction to English Morphology: Words and their Structure*. Edinburgh: Edinburgh University Press.

Chomsky, Noam and Morris Halle 1968. *The Sound Pattern of English*. New York: Harper and Row.

Harris, Zellig S. 1948. Componential analysis of a Hebrew paradigm. *Language* 24: 87–91.

Jakobson, Roman 1936. Beitrag zur allgemeinen Kasuslehre. *Travaux du Cercle Linguistique de Prague* 6: 240–88.

Katamba, Francis and John T. Stonham 2006. *Morphology*. 2nd edn. Basingstoke: Palgrave Macmillan.

Prince, Alan and Paul Smolensky 2002. Optimality Theory: Constraint Interaction in Generative Grammar. http://roa.rutgers.edu/view.php3?id=845.

Priscian 1961. Institutiones Grammaticae. In *Grammatici Latini*, ed. by Heinrich Keil. 8 vols. Hildesheim: Georg Olms, pp. 2: 1–597 and 3: 1–377.

## Resources

> Bauer 2003 is an informative, scholarly and comprehensive instructional text.
> Booij 2005 is a well-organized, coherent, and clear introduction to morphological concepts that explains how to do morphological analysis theoretically. It also gives information on the acquisition of morphology, the processing of complex words, and how lexical knowledge is structured and stored in memory.
> Carstairs-McCarthy 2002 looks at historical sources of English word formation as well as English morphology today.
> Katamba and Stonham 2006 is a lively, comprehensive introduction to current morphological theory and analysis designed to take absolute beginners to a point where they can approach the current literature in the subject.

Relevant **journals** include:

> *Yearbook of Morphology* (Foris: Dordrecht) has been replaced by a journal *Morphology* which first appeared as Volume 16 (2006). Back files of the yearbooks will be made available electronically by Springer Netherlands.
> Many general linguistics journals such as *Language*, *Journal of Linguistics*, *Australian Journal of Linguistics, Language Typology* run articles on morphology.

**Useful URLs** include:

> http://www.wikipedia.org
> http://mmm.lingue.unibo.it/proc.php (online proceedings of the Mediterranean morphology meetings)
> http://www.surrey.ac.uk/LIS/SMG/index.htm (the University of Surrey morphology group)

# 5.5 **researching syntax**

## chapter contents

> Structuralism     291
> Anthropological linguistics     292
> Transformational generative grammar     293
> Systemic functional grammar     294
> Key points     294
> References     294
> Some useful resources     295

This chapter illustrates the way that the structure of sentences is researched. The data for syntactic analysis may be drawn from introspection about the possible patterns in the language being studied (if the syntactician is a native speaker) or from elicited sentences, texts or judgements by native speakers.

Many of the basic grammatical ideas of modern studies of language can be traced back to early Greek and Latin traditions (see Allan 2009). For example, it was the Ancient Greeks who gave us our notion of parts of speech, as well as the categories themselves such as *noun* and *verb*. Out of the work of these ancient scholars emerged what came to be known as 'traditional grammar'. The beliefs that were handed down viewed language as an immutable system, and grammatical endeavours, until well into the 1800s, were prescriptive in nature (see Chapter 2.4) – forms were either correct or incorrect. Scholars focused overwhelmingly on writing. They didn't concern themselves with what were the acceptable rules of syntax, but rather with grammatical and stylistic excellence. An example is the prohibition against double negatives (*She don't know nothing about syntax*). In the early twentieth century this all changed. The present chapter will focus on the ideas of five key linguists who provide some of the defining moments in syntactic research.

## Structuralism

Often described as 'the father of modern linguistics', Ferdinand de Saussure developed ideas that are generally considered to be the starting point of twentieth-century structuralism (see Chapters 3.1 and 4.1). Following his early work in philology, he was responsible for a number of major distinctions that have since become fundamental to linguistics. Central is the idea that language is a structured system that can be viewed synchronically (i.e. at a particular point in time) and diachronically (i.e. historically) (see Chapter 2.16). Saussure's work focused on synchronic relations. These he analysed as a formal system of distinct elements, which he saw as underlying the apparently disordered reality of dialects and real-time production and comprehension. His insights began what became known as structural linguistics.

Out of structuralism emerged a technique of analysing sentence structure called immediate constituent (IC) analysis. It viewed sentences as a hierarchically ordered set of structures that can be analysed by progressive divisions. For instance, a sentence like *The beginning student enjoyed syntactic theory* can be dissected into two main parts: *the beginning student* and *enjoyed syntactic theory*. These can be further divided into *the + beginning + student, syntactic + theory* and *enjoyed*; *enjoyed* into *enjoy+ed*, and so on. This method laid the foundation for the analysis of syntactic structure. Yet, because it didn't do much to help us actually understand the nature of grammatical structure by explaining how sentences relate to each other and the internal relations that hold within sentences, it spawned a number of different approaches in which linguists tried to address these issues. A number of the new approaches also started to put more emphasis on the social reality of language and the role of the human mind, aspects of language that were totally missing from the methods of structural linguistics.

## Anthropological linguistics

Another approach that emerged during this time took the study of syntax away from Saussure's abstract theoretical approach to more empirical concerns. Beginning with the work of the anthropological linguist Franz Boas, American linguists in particular became preoccupied with the extraordinary diversity in language. The Indo-European languages, which had been the focus of attention until this point, represent only a tiny proportion of the approximately 6,000 known languages of the world. The focus shifted to the indigenous languages of America and to developing reliable descriptions of the grammar and culture of these languages before they disappeared. This work pioneered a fieldwork tradition in descriptive linguistics and linguistic ethnography, which involves working in communities, observing language in use, learning the language and developing grammatical descriptions drawing on informants' judgements.

These languages presented very different structural patterns from familiar European languages such as Latin and English: what emerged during this time were techniques of grammatical description that did not force these radically new grammatical structures into the familiar Indo-European mould. In 1911, Boas's famous *Handbook of American Indian Languages* (Boas 1911) was published, and around a decade later appeared another significant anthropologically focused book by Edward Sapir called simply *Language* (Sapir 1921). Sapir's book made the claim that the different structures of languages could provide insights into the workings of the human mind. His ideas were particularly influential. They triggered an explosion of new research into the relationship between language and culture – aimed at working out how people think. This has now become a large part of the motivation for researching syntax.

A legacy of this period is field linguistics. Many linguists now work with native speakers of previously undescribed languages, often in remote locations. Their interests lie in producing careful descriptions and analyses of the world's languages, particularly those which are endangered. Many also dedicate a good deal of their time to language maintenance and language revitalization (see for example Aikhenvald 2003; 2004; 2008; Dixon 1972; Dixon 2002; 2004; Evans 1995; 2003a; 2003b).

# Transformational generative grammar

The so-called 'Chomskyan revolution' was launched by the publication of *Syntactic Structures* (Chomsky 1957) followed by *Aspects of the Theory of Syntax* (Chomsky 1965). Suddenly, the study of syntax, which up until then had received scant attention, was thrown onto centre stage. In these works, Chomsky introduced his idea of 'generative grammar' (see Chapter 2.5), which departed radically from the earlier structuralist methods of classification (see Chapter 5.2). He showed that the conventional methods of structural linguistics were not adequate for the study of syntax. While any language has a finite number of phonemes, there is no natural limit to the number of sentences in a language. Sentences, no matter how long, can always be longer – *Kate thinks that syntax is fun* can be generated again and again to produce something like *Keith said that Julie believes that Kate thinks that syntax is fun*. Generative grammar provided a device that claimed to be able to generate all (and only) the sentences of any language. It also claimed to be able to account for the underlying grammatical relations that held within sentences. This is shown by the now famous pair of sentences *John is easy to please* versus *John is eager to please* (these are superficially similar but there is an underlying difference in structure – in the first *John* functions as the object of *to please* and in the second the subject).

Chomsky also insisted on drawing a clear distinction between *competence* (= a person's knowledge of the rules of a language) and *performance* (= a person's actual use of that knowledge). This is not unlike the Saussurean dichotomy *langue* versus *parole* (Saussure 1931; 1974), except that Chomsky saw *competence* as more of a mental construct than a social one (see Chapters 3.1 and 5.2). But he shared with Saussure the belief that *competence* (or *langue*) was the focus of research, not *performance* (or *parole*). Chomsky rejected previous linguistic research that relied on collected samples of speech. He argued that no corpus, no matter how large, could capture the open-endedness of language. It would inevitably contain performance errors that would detract from the underlying generalizations that could be drawn. In Chomsky's view, the main goal of research was to capture the linguistic competence of speakers that enabled them to produce and understand sentences they had never heard before. The job of the linguist was to make conjectures about available linguistic facts and to test them against the evidence provided by native speakers of the language, generally in the form of acceptability judgements. Because Chomsky's work aimed to uncover the mental processes underlying actual performance, syntactic research suddenly became of interest to psychologists, who developed experimental methods to study language and cognition.

Chomsky argued that our language capacity is hard-wired into the brain. An assumption that naturally follows from this is that all languages have a common structural base. This knowledge is known as universal grammar or UG. His line of thinking has since triggered a spate of research aimed at uncovering the abstract structures that make up innate grammar. Studying in depth the grammars of individual languages has become the main thrust of the Chomskyan endeavour.

In summary, Chomsky's work inspired a rapid spread of new and exciting ideas, as well as sometimes spectacular clashes of views. What followed his early works was a burgeoning of alternative models of grammatical analysis, either in support of his ideas or in reaction against them, for example case grammar, relational grammar, X-bar theory, Montague grammar, generalized phrase structure grammar, functional grammar, network grammar. You can find excellent accounts of these various syntactic theories in the many encyclopedias of linguistics that are now available (Brown 2006; Crystal 2003; Frawley 2003, for example).

## Systemic functional grammar

Systemic functional grammar (SFG), led by the British linguist Michael Halliday, also emerged in the 1960s. It drew its inspiration from the intellectual tradition of European linguistics (following Saussure) and also from American anthropological linguistics. The name derives from the technical sense of grammar as a network of 'systems' of interrelated contrasts and from the emphasis on interrelated processes (functions) not merely constituency. So while it takes account of the syntactic structure of language, its orientation is practical – attempting to define what language does and how it does it. While Chomsky's approach was formal, abstract, and unconcerned with the meaning and use of utterances, SFG adopts a pragmatic view of language as a social phenomenon. It is therefore not so much concerned with the workings of the human mind, but rather with humans who, as social beings, exchange meanings through the use of language. In this approach syntactic accounts are functional, with a focus not so much on grammaticality but on usage and the semantic and pragmatic aspects of analysis. Not surprisingly, in SFG, the text rather than the sentence has become the main object of study.

Works such as Halliday 1973; 1978; Halliday and Hasan 1976 and more recently Halliday and Matthiessen 2004 have been hugely influential in applied linguistic research, especially the fields of stylistics, education and language learning in the classroom. Many have applied systemic-functional principles to children's language development and to second language acquisition.

### Key points

> Syntacticians research the structure of sentences in a language, identifying and analysing the possible patterns.

> The structures of different languages are compared, based on data collected by field linguists.

> Syntacticians such as Chomsky seek to identify the underlying principles that govern the structure of all human languages.

> Systemic-functional linguists explore how language works as a system of choices which speakers can draw on in context.

## References

Aikhenvald, Alexandra Y. 2003. *A Grammar of Tariana, from Northwest Amazonia*. Cambridge: Cambridge University Press.

Aikhenvald, Alexandra Y. 2004. *Evidentiality*. Oxford: Oxford University Press.

Aikhenvald, Alexandra Y. 2008. *The Manambu Language, from East Sepik, Papua New Guinea*. Oxford: Oxford University Press.

Allan, Keith 2009. *The Western Classical Tradition in Linguistics*. 2nd edn. London: Equinox.

Boas, Franz 1911. *Handbook of American Indian Languages. Volume 1*. Washington DC: Smithsonian Institution [The Introduction was published separately as *Introduction to the Handbook of American Indian Languages*. Washington DC: Georgetown University Press, 1963].

Brown, E. Keith (General editor) 2006. *Encyclopedia of Languages and Linguistics*. 2nd edn. 14 vols. Oxford: Elsevier.

Brown, E. Keith and Jim Miller (eds) 1996. *Concise Encyclopedia of Syntactic Theories*. Oxford: Pergamon.

Chomsky, Noam 1957. *Syntactic Structures*. The Hague: Mouton.

Chomsky, Noam 1965. *Aspects of the Theory of Syntax*. Cambridge MA: MIT Press.

Crystal, David 2003. *The Cambridge Encyclopedia of the English Language*. 2nd edn. Cambridge: Cambridge University Press.

Dixon, Robert M.W. 1972. *The Dyirbal Language of North Queensland*. Cambridge: Cambridge University Press.

Dixon, Robert M.W. 2002. *Australian Languages: Their Nature and Development*. Cambridge: Cambridge University Press.

Dixon, Robert M.W. 2004. *The Jarawara Language of Southern Amazonia*. Oxford: Oxford University Press.

Evans, Nicholas R.D. 1995. *A Grammar of Kayardild*. Berlin: Mouton de Gruyter.

Evans, Nicholas R.D. 2003a. *Bininj Gun-wok: A Pan-dialectal Grammar of Mayali, Kunwinjku and Kune*. 2 vols. Canberra: Pacific Linguistics.

Evans, Nicholas R.D. (ed.) 2003b. *The Non-Pama-Nyungan Languages of Northern Australia: Comparative Studies of the Continent's Most Linguistically Complex Region*. Canberra: Pacific Linguistics.

Frawley, William J. (General editor) 2003. *International Encyclopedia of Linguistics*. 2nd edn. Oxford: Oxford University Press.

Halliday, Michael A.K. 1973. *Explorations in the Functions of Language*. London: Edward Arnold.

Halliday, Michael A.K. 1978. *Language as a Social Semiotic*. London: Edward Arnold.

Halliday, Michael A.K. and Ruqaiya Hasan 1976. *Cohesion in English*. London: Longman.

Halliday, Michael A.K. and Christian M.I.M. Matthiessen 2004. *An Introduction to Functional Grammar*. 3rd edn. London: Arnold.

Pinker, Steven 1994. *The Language Instinct: The New Science of Language and Mind*. London: Allen Lane.

Pinker, Steven 1999. *Words and Rules: The Ingredients of Language*. New York: Basic Books.

Sapir, Edward 1921. *Language: An Introduction to the Study of Speech*. New York: Harcourt, Brace.

Saussure, Ferdinand de 1931. *Cours de Linguistique Générale*. Publié par Charles Bally et Albert Sechehaye avec la collaboration de Albert Riedlinger. 3rd edn. Paris: Payot [First edn published 1916].

Saussure, Ferdinand de 1974. *A Course in General Linguistics*. Glasgow: Fontana/Collins [transl. by Wade Baskin from the 3rd edition of *Cours de Linguistique Générale*. Paris: Payot, 1931. First edn published in 1916].

Wray, Alison and Aileen Bloomer 2006. *Projects in Linguistics: A Practical Guide to Researching Language*. London: Hodder Arnold.

## Some useful resources

The sorts of articles that appear in journals like *Language, Linguistic Inquiry* and *Journal of Linguistics* can be very difficult to read, but this should not discourage you from looking through these journals. You may well find some ideas there that are quite inspirational for your own research. Just be warned that a lot of the writing on syntax is very technical indeed and often takes for granted a good understanding of linguistic theory. However, there are occasional works that are extremely accessible and engaging, even for the non-linguist. The works of Pinker 1994; 1999 for example, provide clear (at times even humorous) explanations of a number of quite difficult topics in syntactic research and make excellent bedtime reading. There are also some very good general treatments of syntactic theory. For example, Brown and Miller (eds) 1996 is a useful starting point. It is a comprehensive reference work that provides an overview of the different theories of syntax and of the wider issues involved.

There are all sorts of interesting questions that would make for worthwhile research into syntactic structure. If you are looking for inspiration for projects of your own, you might think of consulting the Wray and Bloomer 2006 book *Projects in Linguistics*. As the title implies, it is a handy guide to researching language, and it offers an array of practical suggestions for students looking for projects on structure and indeed many other sub-disciplines. It also gives hands-on advice on techniques of collecting data.

# 5.6 researching the history of language(s)

## chapter contents

> Sir William Jones      298
> Sound laws      298
> Diachrony and synchrony      299
> Grammaticalization      299
> Linguistic universals      300
> Variation as a sign of language change      301
> Into the twenty-first century      301
> Key points      302
> References      302
> Resources      303

This chapter summarizes the key areas of research into history of languages, notably the identification of processes of sound change and grammaticalization, typological universals and the role of variation. The basic aim of historical research in linguistics is to investigate change in language. At first researchers concentrated their endeavours on identifying the facts of language evolution. They concerned themselves with the features of language that had changed in the past (largely sound changes) and the processes by which these had changed – in other words, the 'what' and 'how' of change. In modern times, the focus of research has shifted more to explanation – in other words, the 'why' of change. Research into the history of language and languages these days could be thought of as having three main goals:

> the collection of historical information
> the discovery of common patterns of change
> the testing of hypotheses about the causes of change.

Ideally, these three goals give rise to the foundation of an explicit theory of language change that will provide universal laws for the explanation of any change that takes place, and thus predict the direction of change.

Research in historical linguistics is wide-ranging. It includes contributions on phonological change, syntactic and morphological change, grammaticalization (creation of grammar), lexical and semantic change, linguistic reconstruction, and even input from other disciplines such as prehistory, philology and sociology. It is impossible to do justice to the range of achievements of such an enormous field in one chapter. What we offer here is a brief outline of some of the key moments of research in the area from the early days of the comparative philologists through to modern times.

## Sir William Jones

The period towards the end of the eighteenth century was a turning point in historical linguistics. In 1786 a British scholar, Sir William Jones, argued that the only way to account for the similarity between the classical languages Sanskrit, Ancient Greek and Latin was to assume that they were related and descended from a common ancestor (which later came to be known as Proto-Indo-European). As he described it, these languages of India and Europe:

> [share] a stronger affinity ... than could possibly have been produced by accident; so strong, indeed, that no philologer could examine them all three, without believing them to have sprung from some common source, which, perhaps, no longer exists. (Jones 1786)

These words are now famous. They suggested for the first time the notion of an ancestral (or proto) language. Jones's ideas triggered similar thinking by a number of scholars, and an explosion of research into language evolution followed. The work carried out by European linguists (dubbed the neogrammarians) in the course of the next century established the study of historical linguistics as a separate discipline.

## Sound laws

In the nineteenth century, focus was overwhelmingly on sound change. On the basis of what they observed in the ancient languages, the early linguists (then known as 'philologists') believed that sounds changed in a totally systematic manner, and they identified what they described as sound 'laws'. The most significant of these was a set of sound changes we now know as Grimm's law, named after one of the famous brothers Grimm of fairytale fame. Jacob Grimm noticed that where a Sanskrit, Latin or Greek word began with a stopped consonant like [p] or [k], these corresponded to fricatives [f] and [x] in Germanic; hence *piscis* in Latin corresponds to *fish* in English. The Danish scholar Rasmus Rask had in fact identified these sound correspondences earlier (Rask 1818; 1993); yet Jacob Grimm (rather unfairly) is always given the credit (Grimm 1822). In all there were nine correspondence sets of this nature. The only way to account for them was to assume that the ancestor of all the Germanic languages had split off from the Indo-European languages in a regular way. The work of Rask and Grimm in the early 1800s did much to shed light on the complex relationship between Germanic and Indo-European.

Until 1877, there was a niggling group of exceptions to Grimm's law that undermined the idea of exceptionless sound change; then Karl Verner discovered that there was regularity in these irregularities (Verner 1877). He determined that Grimm's law was affected by the accent (stress) pattern of a word. When the stress fell on something other than the root syllable the consonant changed in a different way; for example, [p] and [k] didn't become [f] and [x] but rather [b] and [g]. By discovering a principled explanation for these irregularities, Verner had rescued what came to be known as the 'neogrammarian (or regularity) hypothesis'. Exceptions to sound change were not random, but could be accounted for by examining other factors such as the phonological environment (in this case stress). Verner's work had a profound effect on research in historical linguistics, particularly in the areas of phonological change and the comparative method (see Chapter 2.10). As a result, researchers started to pay more attention to the phonetic conditions under which the sound changes took place and, as historical linguists Hock and Joseph 1996: 126 point out, it has now become common practice 'to look more carefully at linguistic change in order to explain apparent irregularities'. Many systematic sound changes have since been discovered in languages around the world and even though the hypothesis is still considered contentious, most linguists now acknowledge the systematic nature of sound change.

## Diachrony and synchrony

Any account of trends in historical linguistics must pay heed to the Swiss linguist Ferdinand de Saussure. Many of the theoretical notions contained in his *Cours de linguistique générale* ("Course in General Linguistics" Saussure 1931; 1974) have become basic to modern linguistics, and two pairs of concepts in particular are especially significant for the development of historical linguistic thinking.

The first is the distinction between 'diachrony' (= historical) and 'synchrony' (= non-historical) (see Chapters 3.1, 5.5, and others). A diachronic approach to language study views language across time as a continually evolving medium. A synchronic study investigates the whole linguistic system as a state existing at a particular point in time, in either the past or the present (for example, you could have a synchronic study of each of Old, Middle and Modern English). This widely accepted dichotomy stymied rather than facilitated historical linguistic endeavour in the early days. Saussure viewed synchronic linguistics as more important than diachronic linguistics. Linguists interested in the historical study of a language could do no more than investigate the language at various points in time; that is, as a continuing succession of synchronic states. With this approach, it would only be possible to study which features changed as the language moved from state to state. It would reveal little of the 'how' and the 'why' of these changes.

Saussure's second dichotomy distinguished between *langue* (= the language system) and *parole* (= performance) (see Chapters 3.1 and 4.1). Saussure's focus was very much on the discovery of the underlying system. However, since the actual social act of speaking holds the key to a proper understanding of language change, to ignore *parole* is to ignore the clues to where a language might be heading. It took another few years for linguists to realize that it was actually possible to view change in progress.

## Grammaticalization

In 1912 the French Indo-Europeanist Antoine Meillet coined the term *grammaticalization* (Meillet 1912: 385). He described it roughly as this: the acquisition of grammatical characteristics by formerly independent words. He wasn't the first to point this out. A number of linguists in the nineteenth century had also argued that lexical words (with independent meanings) shift to become grammatical markers (such as prepositions and conjunctions) or bound grammatical morphemes (such as tense suffixes and other inflections). Grammaticalization describes, for example, the shift from Old English *lic* "body" (as in *lichgate* "the roof covered gateway at the entrance to a church yard") to Modern English *like* and *–ly* (as in *godly*).

Although grammaticalization can be considered a useful cover term to describe the interaction of a range of different linguistic changes (including sound change, semantic change and reanalysis), the concept has also stimulated an explosion of new research into grammatical change, a previously rather neglected area in historical linguistics. It started in the 1970s with Talmy Givón 1971. His slogan 'Today's morphology is yesterday's syntax' became a kind of catchphrase of the time. It highlighted the fact that the only way to understand the grammar of a language was to know something about its early stages of development. As more people began to explore the process of grammaticalization, more exciting descriptive and explanatory studies of grammaticalization changes appeared, especially towards the end of the twentieth century. These have now given us a much better idea of the typical pathways a language takes in creating its grammar (its history and also future development) and the types of changes that are involved. There is now a wealth of books and articles on the subject (for general treatments see Traugott and Heine 1991 and Hopper and Traugott 2003).

## Linguistic universals

As just explained, until quite recently emphasis within historical linguistics was very much on sounds and the way they changed over time. As a consequence, historical grammar, more particularly syntax, remained a relatively neglected area of study. The problem was that linguists didn't have the same knowledge about syntax and its workings as they did about sounds. There were also practical problems that made it easier to study sound change than syntactic change. The nature of sounds means that they can be listed, and because of the finite nature of their inventories, full descriptions can be gained of lost sound systems, sometimes on the basis of a very limited corpus. This is not the case for syntax– no finite corpus of utterances, no matter how large, will provide full descriptions of early syntactic systems. There will always be gaps in our knowledge, and uncertainty about any conclusions made will always be greater for syntax than for phonology.

It was during the 1960s that the American linguist Joseph Greenberg produced his now famous essay 'Some universals of grammar with particular reference to the order of meaningful elements' (Greenberg 1963). This proved to be a turning point in the study of diachronic syntax in that it provided a useful synchronic framework for a theory of syntactic change to emerge. This approach, and those which it has inspired, uses typology and typological universals to account for existing syntactic patterns and their historical development. Greenberg examined selected grammatical features (mainly word order patterns) from 30 of the world's languages. He divided these languages into three basic types – S(ubject)V(erb)O(bject), SOV and VSO. Data in his research showed correlations between certain word order patterns and other grammatical properties. From his findings, he listed 45 implicational universals of the type – 'If a language A has feature F1, then (with more than chance frequency) it also has feature F2'. Here are two examples:

*Universal 3*: Languages with dominant VSO order are always prepositional.
*Universal 4*: With overwhelmingly greater than chance frequency, languages with normal SOV order are postpositional.

For example, Irish is a VSO language and has prepositions: *tá sí ag an fárk* is she at the park "she's at the park". Japanese is a SOV language and has postpositions: *watashi-wa ofisu-ni imasu* I-NOM office-in be "I am in the office".

Implicational statements of this sort seek to establish constant relationships between different grammatical features of language. They represent tendencies based on those properties which emerge from the data as being the statistically predominant ones, and against which patterns of change may be studied.

Since the appearance of Greenberg's work, there have been a number of proposals that seek to account for these word order correlations by appealing to the existence of a basic ordering of elements to which all languages naturally conform. The pressure to conform to this basic ordering is viewed as strong enough to initiate change. The work of two linguists in particular exemplifies this position; namely Lehmann 1973 and Vennemann 1974. More recently Hawkins 1983; 1988, using a sample of 350 languages, has attempted to refine and further clarify the original implicational universals and, in addition, find a rationale for them.

Typology also has important consequences for the reconstruction of past grammatical systems. By showing us the preferred avenues of change, linguists can use their knowledge of syntactic types in reconstructing earlier stages. While there are problems with this approach (cf. Watkins 1976), it follows that, as our understanding of typology and typological universals grows, so too will our understanding of grammatical change and also the role of typology in the reconstruction process for syntax.

## Variation as a sign of language change

As earlier discussed, for a long time it was believed that we couldn't actually observe languages changing. As Jean Aitchison 2001 once put it, it was believed that linguistic change was something that crept up so gradually as to be imperceptible – much like the getting of wrinkles or the opening of a flower. One day you look in the mirror and the wrinkles are there; suddenly the flower is blooming but you never saw the petals actually open. In fact these early linguists didn't know where to look. The key to observing language change is identifying variation in certain social groups, but until quite recently not much attention was paid to it. In the main, linguists based their linguistic descriptions on the fairly careful and formal speech of educated people. Anything that wouldn't fit nicely into neat lists and tidy paradigms was ignored.

In the mid 1960s this all changed. It was the American linguist William Labov who first demonstrated that the relationship between society, linguistic variation and change could be studied in a systematic way. People had always realized of course that members of different social classes had different linguistic behaviour, but it was Labov's 1966 study of New York English that showed for the first time that these differences could be quantified (see Chapters 2.7 and 5.8). He started out by identifying a number of linguistic features that were used variably within the New York speech community. They include sociolinguistic variables such as post-vocalic *r* in words like *beer* and *pork*, the pronunciation of *–ing* in words like *cooking* and *eating* and the pronunciation of *th* in words like *thirty* and *this*. Labov's work showed that the earlier view of change was incorrect. Language change always occurs in the presence of socially relevant variation – and it is directly observable. Labov's novel view of language change sparked a thriving new line of research into linguistic evolution.

## Into the twenty-first century

Despite the wealth of descriptive and theoretical studies in historical linguistics, all sorts of questions about language and its history are still to be explored. This is true even for English, undoubtedly the most researched and best-documented language of all. (If you are interested in the history of English we recommend consulting Bauer 1994 – it offers some excellent suggestions for research projects for students.) Janda and Joseph 2003: 131 conclude, in the introduction to their handbook on historical linguistics, that 'we believe that the greatest achievements of historical linguistics are still to come'. And as research in historical linguistics progresses, so more and more exciting avenues and approaches for investigating language change come to light. Moreover, in recent years there has been a flourishing of databases that help us to find out what languages used to be like and how they are now. At our fingertips are major corpora comprising millions of running words (see Chapter 2.13). For example, for English there is the *London-Lund Corpus of Spoken British English* (a computer corpus of educated spoken British English), the *Helsinki Corpus of English Texts: Diachronic and Dialectal* (a computerized collection of extracts of continuous text from Old, Middle and Early Modern English), *Early English Books Online* (scanned images of around 100,000 books published between 1473 and 1700) and many more, all available to researchers anywhere in the world. In some ways, the diachronic study of language has never been easier. There is much that will inspire you.

## Key points

> Research into the history of languages draws on the methods of comparing languages pioneered by Sir William Jones.

> Reconstruction, pioneered by Rasmus Rask, allowed the identification of sound 'laws': the regular processes governing sound change.

> Research into grammaticalization explores the process by which independent lexical items develop into grammatical markers.

> The identification of typological universals underpins research into syntactic change.

> The study of language change is also the study of language variation, as variation indicates change in progress.

## References

Aitchison, Jean 2001. *Language Change: Progress or Decay?* 3rd edn. Cambridge: Cambridge University Press.

Bauer, Laurie 1994. *Watching English Change: An Introduction to the Study of Linguistic Change in Standard Englishes in the Twentieth Century*. London: Longman.

Givón, Talmy 1971. Historical syntax and synchronic morphology: an archeologist's field trip. In *Papers from the Seventh Regional Meeting of the Chicago Linguistics Society. April 16–18, 1971*, ed. by Chicago Linguistics Society. Chicago: Chicago Linguistics Society.

Greenberg, Joseph H. 1963. Some universals of grammar with particular reference to the order of meaningful elements. In *Universals of Language*, ed. by Joseph H. Greenberg. Cambridge MA: MIT Press, pp. 73–113.

Grimm, Jakob 1822. *Deutsche Grammatik Vol. I*. 2nd edn. Göttingen: Dieterich.

Hawkins, John A. 1983. *Word Order Universals*. New York: Academic Press.

Hawkins, John A. (ed.) 1988. *Explaining Language Universals*. Oxford: Basil Blackwell.

Hock, Hans H. and Brian D. Joseph 1996. *Language History, Language Change, and Language Relationship: An Introduction to Historical and Comparative Linguistics*. Berlin: Mouton de Gruyter.

Hopper, Paul J. and Elizabeth C. Traugott 2003. *Grammaticalization*. 2nd edn. Cambridge: Cambridge University Press.

Janda, Richard and Brian Joseph 2003. On language, change, and language change – or, of history, linguistics, and historical linguistics. In *The Handbook of Historical Linguistics*, ed. by Brian Joseph and Richard Janda. Malden MA: Blaackwell, pp. 1–181.

Jones, William 1786. The Third Anniversary Discourse delivered to the Asiatick Society 2 February, 1786. *The Works of Sir William Jones in Six Volumes: Vol. I*. London: G.G. and J. Robinson, and R.H. Evans. 1799, pp. 19–34.

Labov, William 1966. *The Social Stratification of English in New York City*. Washington DC: Center for Applied Linguistics.

Lehmann, Winfred P. 1973. A structural principle of language and its implications. *Language* 49: 47–66.

Meillet, Antoine 1912. L'évolution des formes grammaticales. *Scientia (Rivista di Scienza)* 12 (6): 384–400.

Rask, Rasmus K. 1818. *Undersögelse om det gamle Nordiske eller Islandske Sprogs Oprindelse. Et af det kongelige Danske Videnskabers-Selskab kronet Prisskrift*. Copenhagen: Gyldendal.

Rask, Rasmus K. 1993. *Investigation of the Origin of the Old Norse or Icelandic Language*. Transl. by Niels Ege. Copenhagen: Linguistic Circle of Copenhagen.

Saussure, Ferdinand de 1931. *Cours de Linguistique Générale*. Publié par Charles Bally et Albert Sechehaye avec la collaboration de Albert Riedlinger. 3rd edn. Paris: Payot [First edn published 1916].

Saussure, Ferdinand de 1974. *A Course in General Linguistics*. Glasgow: Fontana/Collins [transl. by Wade Baskin from the 3rd edition of *Cours de Linguistique Générale*. Paris: Payot, 1931. First edn published in 1916].

Traugott, Elizabeth C. and Bernd Heine (eds) 1991. *Approaches to Grammaticalization*. 2 vols. Amsterdam: John Benjamins.

Vennemann, Theo 1974. Topics, subjects and word order: from SXV to SVX via TVX. In *Historical Linguistics: Proceedings of the First International Conference on Historical Linguistics, Edinburgh, 2nd–7th September 1973*, ed. by John M. Anderson and Charles Jones. Amsterdam: North Holland, pp. 339–76.

Verner, Karl A.B. 1877. Eine Ausnahme der ersten Lautverschiebung. *Zeitschrift für vergleichende Sprachforschung auf dem Gebiete der indogermanischen Sprachen* 23 (3): 97–130. ["An exception to the first consonant shift". Transl. by Winfred P. Lehmann in *A Reader in Nineteenth Century Historical Indo-European Linguistics*. Bloomington: Indiana University Press. 1967, pp. 132–63.]

Watkins, Calvert 1976. Towards Proto-Indo-European syntax: problems and pseudo-problems. In *Papers from the Parasession on Diachronic Syntax*, ed. by Sanford B. Steever, Carol A. Walker and Salikoko S. Mufwene. Chicago: Chicago Linguistics Society, pp. 305–26.

## Resources

Much of the research into historical linguistics (such as you might find in journals like *Diachronica* and *Transactions of the Philological Society*) is highly technical and assumes a good understanding of linguistic theory. However, there have recently appeared some excellent overviews of the disciplines. In addition to those included in the reference list, a number of useful textbooks and handbooks are listed below:

> Aitchison, Jean 2001. *Language Change: Progress or Decay?* 3rd edn. Cambridge: Cambridge University Press.

> Campbell, Lyle 2004. *Historical Linguistics: An Introduction*. 2nd edn. Edinburgh: Edinburgh University Press.

> Crowley, Terry 1997. *An Introduction to Historical Linguistics*. 3rd edn. Auckland: Oxford University Press.

> Harris, Alice C. 1995. *Historical Linguistics in Cross-Linguistic Perspective*. Cambridge: Cambridge University Press.

> Hock, Hans H. 1991. *Principles of Historical Linguistics*. 2nd edn. Berlin: Mouton de Gruyter.
> Hopper, Paul J. and Elizabeth C. Traugott 2003. *Grammaticalization*. 2nd edn. Cambridge: Cambridge University Press.
> Jeffers, Robert J. and Ilse Lehiste 1979. *Principles and Methods for Historical Linguistics*. Cambridge: MIT Press.
> Jones, Charles (ed.) 1993. *Historical Linguistics: Problems and Perspectives*. London: Longman.
> Joseph, Brian and Richard Janda (eds) 2003. *The Handbook of Historical Linguistics*. Malden MA: Blackwell.
> Lehmann, Winfred P. 1992. *Historical Linguistics: An Introduction*. 3rd edn. London: Routledge.
> McMahon, April M.S. 1994. *Understanding Language Change*. Cambridge: Cambridge University Press.
> Trask, Robert L. 1996. *Historical Linguistics*. London: Arnold.

# 5.7 researching semantics and pragmatics

## chapter contents

> Introduction                          305
> Lexical semantics                     306
> Pragmatics – meaning in context       307
> Key points                            307
> References                            307
> Resources                             308

## Introduction

This chapter examines how research in semantics and pragmatics explores the way meaning is assigned to words and utterances. Research in semantics and pragmatics has primarily been based on introspection, though some scholars such as Rosch, and Labov, working on prototype theory, have used experimental methods to elicit data. Research into the meaning of language began in Ancient Greece, and Aristotle's contribution (*c.* 350 BCE) is of particular interest. In *Categories* he wrote about the use of language in categorizing reality, and much of what he says addresses the semantic relations between the terms used in naming things. In *On Interpretation*, *Prior Analytics* and *Metaphysics* he discussed (to use modern terminology) linguistic aspects of forming a proposition, the nature of appropriate inference from one or more premises, and the different effects of negation over terms quantified by universals and particulars. His ideas were later developed to a more sophisticated level by the Stoics. Aristotle includes a brief discussion of homonymy and polysemy in *Categories* 1$^a$1, 15$^b$18; lengthy discussion of and tests for homonyms in *Topics* 106$^a$1; and an examination of what is criterial in constructing a definition in *Topics* (139$^a$28–139$^b$12). In the literary vein, he looks at the use of language in rhetorical argument in *Rhetoric*, where he has interesting things to say about metaphor and about the structure of certain kinds of discourse, and he touches upon matters that re-emerge in Grice 1975 as maxims of the cooperative principle. The Stoics (second century BCE to second century CE) identified something very like illocutionary type, and they clearly distinguished between what we would now call intension and extension (see Allan 2009).

Despite some interesting observations on semantics made during the Middle Ages (e.g. by Walter Burleigh in the early fourteenth century) we can skip to the birth of modern semantics in the work of Gottlob Frege (1848–1925), a mathematician who more or less invented predicate logic. Frege recognized the compositionality of meaning, clearly distinguishing concept from denotatum and sense from reference. These were not original distinctions: they were recognized in the Middle Ages if not earlier, but what

Frege 1892 did was establish a way of talking about them which inspired modern linguistics. Post-Fregean semantics influenced the work of Bertrand Russell 1905, Wittgenstein 1953, Carnap 1959, Montague 1974, and the ensuing Discourse Representation Theory (Kamp and Reyle 1993), Dynamic Semantics (Groenendijk and Stokhof 1991), and Default Semantics (Jaszczolt 2005). These formal semanticists focus on the meanings of sentences. For instance the sentence *If a farmer owns a donkey, then he beats it* can be represented as the Discourse Representation Structure:

<table>
<tr><td>x  y<br><br>farmer(x)<br>donkey(y)<br>x owns y</td><td>⇒</td><td>u  v<br><br>u = x<br>v = y<br>u beats v</td></tr>
</table>

Which can be spelled out in predicate logic as:

$$\forall xy((\text{FARMER}(x) \,\&\, \text{DONKEY}(y) \,\&\, \text{OWNS}(x,y)) \to \exists uv(u = x \,\&\, v = y \,\&\, \text{BEATS}(u,v))).$$

In both models (systems of logic), every variable x is assigned the meaning "farmer" and every variable y the meaning "donkey"; for some variables u and v, if u = x and y = v, then u beats v (see the resources listed below for more explanation).

## Lexical semantics

Lexical semantics, which is primarily concerned with the semantics of listemes (see Chapter 3.1), tends to be less formal. For example, Labov 1978 investigated the defining characteristics of *cup* versus *mug* by getting people to name a sequence of gradually differentiated drinking vessels drawn with characteristics ranging from cups, to bowls, goblets and mugs. He found that people chose the appropriate name on the basis of (a) the shape and configuration of the container – proportion of height to width, whether or not the container is tapered, whether or not it has a handle; (b) the material from which the container is made; and (c) the purpose to which the container is put. Most people add that the potential accompaniment of a saucer is criterial in distinguishing a cup from a mug. This is one practical experimental method to identify the semantic characteristics of a listeme that denotes a physical object. A most succinct definition of *cup* is given by Katz 1977: 49:

Physical object
Inanimate
Vertical orientation
Upwardly concave
Height about equal to top diameter
Top diameter greater than bottom diameter
Artefact
Made to serve as a container from which to drink liquid

This contrasts with the 831-word definition given by Wierzbicka 1984: 222–24. These different sets of specifications raise the question of what a semantic definition aims to do and who it is designed for.

## Pragmatics – meaning in context

Pragmatics is said to derive from the work of Charles Peirce (1839–1914), though modern uses of the term are rather different from his, which referred essentially to the 'practical bearings' that a denotatum has (Peirce 1958 5: 438). Today, research into pragmatics looks at meaning in context, or more exactly meaning in the light of what the speaker takes to be common ground. It is now almost universally accepted that meaning is underspecified by speakers (and expected to be by hearers); consequently, hearers are expected to make a lot of inferences on the basis of the words actually uttered. If someone says *Max has broken a toe* the standard implicature is that it is his own toe (Grice 1975; Levinson 2000) (See Chapters 2.6 and 4.1). Some guides to implicature are: the Q[uantity]-principle 'What isn't said, isn't [the case]'; the I[nformativeness]-principle 'What is said simply is stereotypically exemplified'; and the M[anner]-principle 'What is said in an abnormal way is not normal.' As rules of thumb, these work well: *I think Max has a new girlfriend* Q-implicates that I don't know this for a fact or I would have said so; *Sally got pregnant and married George* I-implicates that the events followed this sequence (compare *Sally got pregnant and married George – but not in that order*); *Maggie's not an unlikeable girl* M-implicates that she is not very likeable. According to Bach 1994 *Bex and Posh are married* has the standard 'impliciture' that they are married to each other because this is the default meaning (it is called 'explicature' by Carston 2002). But others, like Allan 2000; Levinson 2000, call it an implicature (in fact an I-implicature). These controversies are currently under discussion in, for example, Bach 2006; Carston 2002; Jaszczolt 2002; Recanati 2004.

---

## Key points

> Modern semantics builds on Frege's work on predicate logic.

> Lexical semantics draws on the names people give to objects, and identifies the underlying criteria.

> Research in pragmatics explores how speakers and hearers draw on common ground to interpret underspecified utterances.

---

## References

Allan, Keith 2000. Quantity implicatures and the lexicon. In *The Lexicon-Encyclopedia Interface*, ed. by Bert Peeters. Amsterdam: Elsevier, pp. 169–218.

Allan, Keith 2009. *The Western Classical Tradition in Linguistics*. 2nd edn. London: Equinox.

Bach, Kent 1994. Conversational impliciture. *Mind and Language* 9: 124–62.

Bach, Kent 2006. Impliciture vs explicature: what's the difference? <http://userwww.sfsu.edu/~kbach/Bach.ImplExpl.pdf>.

Carnap, Rudolf 1959. *Introduction to Semantics: Formalization of Logic*. Cambridge MA: Harvard University Press.

Carston, Robyn 2002. *Thoughts and Utterances: The Pragmatics of Explicit Communication*. Oxford & Malden MA: Blackwell.

Frege, Gottlob 1892. Über Sinn und Bedeutung. *Zeitschrift für Philosophie und philosophische Kritik* 100: 25–50. Reprinted as 'On sense and reference'. In *Translations from the Philosophical Writings of Gottlob Frege*, ed. by Peter Geach and Max Black. Oxford: Blackwell. 1960: 56–78.

Grice, H. Paul 1975. Logic and conversation. In *Syntax and Semantics 3: Speech Acts*, ed. by Peter Cole and Jerry L. Morgan. New York: Academic Press, pp. 41–58. Reprinted in H. Paul Grice *Studies in the Way of Words*. Cambridge MA: Harvard University Press. 1986.

Groenendijk, Jeroen A.G. and Martin J.B. Stokhof 1991. Dynamic predicate logic. *Linguistics and Philosophy* 14: 39–100.

Jaszczolt, Katarzyna M. 2002. *Semantics and Pragmatics: Meaning in Language and Discourse*. Harlow: Longman.

Jaszczolt, Katarzyna M. 2005. *Default Semantics: Foundations of a Compositional Theory of Acts of Communication*. Oxford: Oxford University Press.

Kamp, Hans and Uwe Reyle 1993. *From Discourse to Logic: Introduction to Modeltheoretic Semantics of Natural Language, Formal Logic and Discourse Representation Theory*. Dordrecht: Kluwer.

Katz, Jerrold J. 1977. A proper theory of names. *Philosophical Studies* 31: 1–80.

Labov, William 1978. Denotational structure. In *Papers from the Parasession on the Lexicon*, ed. by Donka Farkas, Wesley M. Jacobsen and Karol W. Todrys. Chicago: Chicago Linguistics Society, pp. 220–60.

Levinson, Stephen C. 2000. *Presumptive Meanings: The Theory of Generalized Conversational Implicature*. Cambridge MA: MIT Press.

Montague, Richard 1974. *Formal Philosophy*, ed. by Richmond Thomason. New Haven: Yale University Press.

Peirce, Charles S. 1958. *Collected Papers of Charles Sanders Peirce*. 8 vols. Cambridge MA: Harvard University Press.

Recanati, François 2004. *Literal Meaning*. Cambridge: Cambridge University Press.

Russell, Bertrand 1905. On denoting. *Mind* 14: 479–93. Reprinted in *Logic and Knowledge*, ed. by Robert C. Marsh. London: Allen and Unwin. 1956: 39–56.

Wierzbicka, Anna 1984. Cups and mugs: lexicography and conceptual analysis. *Australian Journal of Linguistics* 4: 257–81.

Wittgenstein, Ludwig 1953. *Philosophical Investigations*. Oxford: Blackwell.

## Resources

Good introductions to semantics and pragmatics include:
> Allan, Keith 2001. *Natural Language Semantics*. Oxford & Malden MA: Blackwell.
> Chierchia, Gennaro and Sally McConnell-Ginet 2000. *Meaning and Grammar: An Introduction to Semantics*. 2nd edn. Cambridge MA: MIT Press [First edn 1990].
> Cruse, D. Alan 2004. *Meaning In Language: An Introduction to Semantics and Pragmatics*. 2nd edn. Oxford: Oxford University Press.
> Frawley, William J. 1992. *Linguistic Semantics*. Hillsdale: Lawrence Erlbaum.
> Gamut, L.T.F. 1991. *Language Logic and Meaning. Vol. 1, Introduction to Logic. Vol. 2, Intensional Logic and Logical Grammar*. Chicago: Chicago University Press.
> Goddard, Cliff 1998. *Semantic Analysis: A Practical Introduction*. Oxford: Oxford University Press.
> Huang, Yan 2007. *Pragmatics*. Oxford: Oxford University Press.
> Jaszczolt, Katarzyna M. 2002. *Semantics and Pragmatics: Meaning in Language and Discourse*. Harlow: Longman.
> Levinson, Stephen C. 1983. *Pragmatics*. Cambridge: Cambridge University Press.
> Lyons, John 1977. *Semantics*. 2 vols. Cambridge: Cambridge University Press.

> Östman, Jan-Ola, Jef Verschueren and Eline Versluys (eds) 2006. *Handbook of Pragmatics*. Amsterdam: John Benjamins [Online at http://www.benjamins.com/online/hop/].
> Saeed, John I. 2003. *Semantics*. 2nd edn. Oxford: Blackwell.

Relevant **journals** include:
> *Journal of Semantics*
> *Natural Language Semantics*
> *Linguistics and Philosophy*
> *Journal of Pragmatics*
> *Pragmatics and Cognition*
> *Journal of Intercultural Pragmatics*

But many general journals include articles on semantics and pragmatics.

**Useful URLs** include:
> http://www.wikipedia.org
> http://ipra.ua.ac.be/ (International Pragmatics Association)
> http://semanticsarchive.net/links.html

# 5.8 **researching sociolinguistics**

## chapter contents

> Correlational sociolinguistics      310
> Linguistic ethnography      313
> Narrative, and negotiation of power      315
> Language and gender      316
> Key points      317
> References      318
> Resources      319

In this chapter a range of sociolinguistic methods are illustrated using examples of research studies in dialectology, correlational sociolinguistics and linguistic ethnography. While introspection and elicitation are the main data collection methods used in much of the research discussed in previous chapters, sociolinguists are much more cautious about the value of such data. In this chapter we show how sociolinguists approach research, by describing in detail the methods used in some representative sociolinguistic studies.

Sociolinguistics grew out of an earlier tradition of dialectology, in which field researchers used questionnaires to construct regional dialect maps. Examples of the questions used in a dialect survey of England (Orton and Wright 1974) are given below.

1. What's in my pocket? (empty pocket)
2. What berries do children go picking along the hedgerows in the early autumn?
3. There's yesterday, there's today, and the 24 hours after today you call ___
4. If you were asked: How did you know it was me talking outside when you couldn't see me? You might reply ___
5. We say today it snowed, yesterday it also ___

Some answers given in different regions of England:
1. *nothing/naught*
2. *blackberries/brambles*
3. *morrow/the morn/tomorn/tomorrow*
4. I *kenned/knew/owned* your voice.
5. *snowed/snew*

## Correlational sociolinguistics

More sophisticated survey methods and a new theoretical framework were developed by William Labov (Labov 1972; 1997) for the study of urban varieties of a language (see Chapters 2.7, 4.1 and 5.7). Labov observed that language use in cities is socially stratified. While the linguistic rules that speakers use will mostly be shared with other members of the speech community, there will be variation in some linguistic features, and this variation carries social meaning.

In his work on variation in New York City, Labov noted that speakers vary in the use of the (r) variable, that is 'the presence or absence of consonantal constriction for post-vocalic, word-final and pre-consonantal /r/' (Labov 1972: 72) in words such as *beer, bar, board, flower*. He labels the variants as *(r-1)* where there is consonantal restriction, whether weak or strong, and *(r-0)* where there is no constriction. Labov collected data on this and other variables in New York, including *(eh)*, in *cap, badge, pass, dance, (oh)* in *off, lost, wash, caught,* and *(th)* and *(dh)* in *thing* and *then*.

On the basis of exploratory interviews, Labov hypothesized that:

> if any two subgroups of New York City speakers are ranked in a scale of social stratification then they will be ranked in the same order by their differential use of (r). (Labov 1972: 44)

Labov collected data by rapid anonymous observation (see Labov 1997 for an account of his very cleverly designed department store study) and he conducted a more extensive survey of the Lower East Side of New York. In the survey he recorded extended interviews with the participants, in the course of which he tried to move them from a careful, formal speech style to a more relaxed and natural way of speaking. He argued that every speaker has a vernacular speech style, acquired in childhood and used in intimate and informal interactions. Overlaid on this style are more formal, careful speech varieties for use with strangers or superiors, or in formal settings. Labov wanted to elicit the vernacular speech style, but he notes that speakers will shift to their careful speech style when observed or interviewed. He calls this phenomenon the **observer's paradox** (see Chapter 3.1), and he developed interview techniques designed to overcome it.

He began the interview by asking participants to read a list of carefully selected words and then a text. Both word list and text included words containing the relevant variables, plus some distractors (words with no sociolinguistic variables in them, to divert attention from the variables of interest). There were also minimal pairs: pairs of words distinguished by only one phoneme (e.g. *pin~pen, dock~dark, guard~god*; in New York these last two pairs are distinguished not by the vowel but by the presence of /r/). He then moved to an interview, with questions becoming increasingly open-ended, including questions about the games which participants had played in childhood. He reasoned that as the participants became used to him and the tape recorder they would begin to relax, and when talking about childhood games they would shift towards a vernacular speech style. He also asked participants whether they had ever been in danger of being killed, as narratives about danger of death were likely to elicit emotional language, moving them even further away from careful attention to speech. Any incidental conversation after the formal interview was recorded as well.

He was thus able to compare the speakers' use of the linguistic variables across a number of speech styles (minimal pairs, word list, reading passage, interview and casual speech). In addition, he asked participants to listen to recorded samples of speech containing the sociolinguistic variables, and elicited their judgements.

He then coded all relevant words and produced a score reflecting the proportion of use of the sociolinguistic variables for each speaker in each style. Using information about education, occupation and income, he assigned participants to ten levels which were mapped onto four social class groupings: lower class, working class, lower middle class, upper middle class (Ash 2002: 406f). See Figure 5.1 (from Labov 1972: 114, Figure 4.2).

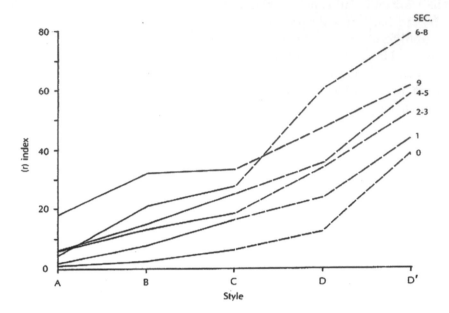

Figure 5.1 *Class stratification of a linguistic variable in process of change: (r) in* guard, car, beer, beard, board, *etc. SEC (Socioeconomic class) scale: 0–1, lower class; 2–4, working-class; 5–6, 7–8, lower middle class; 9, upper middle class. A, casual speech; B, careful speech; C, reading style; D, word lists; D', minimal pairs.*

The results show that the frequency with which the linguistic variants are used correlates with social class membership. That is, the higher the social class, the more likely a speaker is to use (r-1) rather than (r-0). Thus Labov was able to show that use of linguistic variables is socially stratified within a community. He argued that certain forms are used more by members of higher social classes, and thereby attract the prestige associated with those speakers.

Supporting evidence for this claim comes from the speech style data. Labov showed that in the more formal styles (i.e. reading words or texts) speakers made greater use of the variants associated with the social classes above them (see Figure 5.1). Labov's model thus links the three dimensions of attention to speech, formality of context and social class membership, to explain the differential use of the linguistic variables. He posits that speakers have internalized variable rules which allow them to produce the appropriate proportion of realizations of the linguistic variable to match the social context and the social class in which they are locating themselves, shifting to a higher prestige variety in careful speech.

Figure 5.1 above shows that in more formal styles, lower-middle-class speakers increase their usage beyond the level used by the social class above them (upper middle class, group 9). Labov attributes this crossover to linguistic insecurity. He argues that lower-middle-class speakers are very anxious to improve their status, and do this by overshooting the proportion of (r) used by the target group.

For a detailed account of sociolinguistic survey methods, see Tagliamonte 2006.

# Linguistic ethnography

Linguistics ethnography is the observation of naturally occurring speech in order to understand the rules governing language behaviour (see Chapter 2.7). An example of this approach is the Blum-Kulka 1993 study of the dinner table conversations of eight middle-class Jewish-American families and eight comparable Israeli families. There were similarities: both groups told tales of personal experience, engaged in multi-party construction of narratives, and respected the rights of children to tell stories. However, cultural differences emerged in the location of the stories in time and space. Israeli stories were typically about events close to home, but distant in time, while Jewish-American stories were about the day's events outside the home, often elicited by a formulaic question such as *How was your day?* The example below (Blum-Kulka 1993: 377) displays the Jewish-American family's cultural expectation that every family member has a right to retell the day's events.

American family 4: The children are Jordan (age 7.5, male) and Sandra (4, female). Sandra's initiation takes place half an hour into dinner. ( # indicates a pause, xxx indicates indecipherable speech)
1. Sandra:    *Mommy to who will I tell how my day goes?*
2. Mother:    *Okay let's hear your day.*
3. Sandra:    *Well # I xxx played puzzles xxx I made xxx*

Blum-Kulka identifies this as a ritual. Participants have the right to offer their day's story, as a gift which must be accepted, as the mother does in line 2. Stories belong to the teller and are told in monologic mode, whereas at the Israeli dinner tables the family fables are often told collaboratively, even by participants unfamiliar with the story.

In a larger scale ethnographic study Shirley Brice Heath 1982; 1983 studied three neighbouring North Carolina communities, a white working-class community, which she called Roadville, a black working-class community, Trackton, and Maintown, a middle-class community of both ethnicities. Over a ten-year period she and her team of students observed the way adults in the three communities interacted with pre-school children, particularly in what she called literacy events, i.e. activities associated with reading and writing.

Her observations showed that the children acquired different ways of communicating, and different approaches to literacy, reflecting diverse interaction patterns in the three communities. One part of her study examined the speech event of the bedtime story. In Trackton, children were not read bedtime stories, nor explicitly encouraged to develop literacy. Oral storytelling was an important part of the culture, and the children were expected to develop verbal skills, and engage in language play, wit and creativity, embellishing stories for entertainment.

Books were the source of Roadville children's stories. Roadville parents read to their children and asked them factual questions about content. Children were encouraged to learn and recite texts, often Bible stories, with a focus on getting it right. Heath argues that neither background equips children for the culture of school. Trackton children are not prepared to recount factual information, while Roadville children have not learnt to go beyond the facts to evaluate the information.

In Maintown, parents engaged in bedtime reading activities, asked factual questions but also went beyond the factual, encouraging children to explain, classify and compare what they were reading to previous knowledge. This approach develops the literacy skills that the children will need to function well in the classroom.

Much recent ethnographic work examines interactions in schools. An important example is the work of Rampton 1995 who studied the language use of students of English, African-Caribbean, Indian and Pakistani heritages in a school in the South Midlands of England. There were co-ethnic friendship groups, among whom ethnic languages or dialects (Jamaican Creole, Asian English, Panjabi) were often used (in addition to the local variety of English) to mark solidarity. Friendship groups also crossed over ethnic boundaries, and Rampton was interested in the phenomenon of language **crossing**: using the language varieties of social or ethnic groups other than one's own. This crossing involved the use of greetings, swear words, insults and other common expressions.

Rampton suggested that the exchange of language was a means of establishing solidarity in multi-ethnic friendship groups. Crossing was used more by boys than girls, as was the exchange of insults used to express solidarity. Language crossing resembles more general findings of the use of insulting language in male subcultures: what is acceptable among friendship group members may be offensive when used with outsiders. More recent work (Rampton 2006) again uses ethnographic methods to study 13- and 14-year-old London schoolchildren. He observes the emergence of a style of classroom discourse interwoven with features of popular culture, particularly music. There are also recurrent references to the speech styles of different social classes (including *Cockney* and *posh*), which are stylized, being performed in heightened fashion. Children use these linguistic elements and fragments of German drawn from their language classes to locate themselves at that point in the interaction, projecting an image and a stance. This focus on performative aspects of language use is central to current work in sociolinguistics.

In another school-based study, Heller 1999; 2001 explored the use of language to express in-group identity and solidarity among bilingual members of a linguistic minority. Her study was conducted in a French medium secondary school in Ontario, a predominantly English-speaking part of Canada. She was interested in the use of forms of French and other languages both in the classroom and around the school, among members of different social groups. To discover what those choices meant for group affiliation and identity, Heller collected data by means of observation over four years. She also recorded classes and conducted interviews with students. The main linguistic groups in the school were French speakers from Ontario and Quebec, English-speaking Canadians, and Somali immigrants. Friendship groups formed partly on linguistic lines: groups differed in the language they used for casual conversation (Canadian French, Parisian French, or English) and the value they assigned to those languages. While the school valued Standard French, the wider community valued English. Heller draws on Bourdieu's notion of the linguistic marketplace (Bourdieu 1977), and examines the value assigned to certain forms of language use, including bilingualism. Languages are seen as resources which provide symbolic power and access to valued domains. Bilingualism in Standard French and English is seen as bestowing a Toronto/Ontario/international identity, while a more local identity is associated with monolingualism in the vernacular Québecois dialect of French (which also conveys an image of tough masculinity). Language use in the school shows a complex interrelation between symbolic power, gender and language use. Heller 2001 observed that boys controlled the public discourse in the school, while girls played marginal roles. Also on the margins of the student body were immigrant students, speakers of the non-standard Quebec dialect, and gay students. One group of girls resisted marginality and the silent, passive, decorative role assigned to girls in the school culture, by designating themselves as *nerds*. Their resistance was displayed linguistically, as the girls chose English rather than French, spoke out in class, and labelled themselves as lesbians.

## Narrative, and negotiation of power

Recent sociolinguistic work collects personal narratives to show how speakers employ language to project identity and affiliation. In an 18-month ethnographic study of a high school in Bolton, in the north-west of England, Moore 2006 used students' narratives to explore the operation of power and inequality among Year 8 to Year 10 students. Patterns of association, activities, attitudes and clothing choices served as the basis for classifying girls into different communities of practice. Moore discusses two groups in particular: the *Populars*, who socialized with males from the school peer group, and the *Townies*, who socialized with older males, and engaged in more extreme activities such as drinking, smoking, drug use, and sex. Moore examined the relationship between group membership and storytelling rights. In one conversation, Kim, a peripheral member of the Townies, Ellie, a core Townie with high status in the group, and Meg, another core member, negotiate storytelling rights.

In the extract from Moore's data given below, Ellie uses a different voice in lines 185–189 to enact a lie she told to her mother. In doing so she is able to evoke family roles, norms and authority structure, and her attempts to evade sanction. (Note: The transcription is slightly modified, and <Q_ ..._Q> indicates a quotational quality; [  ] marks overlapping sections; (2) is a two second pause.)

| 184 | Ellie: | And then we got home ... my mum like asked me |
| | Meg: | (Cough) |
| 185 | Ellie: | what had happened. I went, <Q_Roughley crew came round. |
| 186 | Ellie: | There was, like, a big rumble, [you know. I] got a few things |
| | Meg: | [[(laugh)]] |
| 187: | Ellie: | here and there._Q> And then I told my sister what really |
| 188 | Ellie: | happened so my sister like when we fell out told my mum that |
| 189 | Ellie: | she bottled me.                              (['she' = Kim]) |
| | Meg: | [[(inaudible)]] |
| | Kim: | (sharp intake of breath) Yeah! [And her mum and Dad have |
| 190 | Ellie: | [Oh yeah] |
| | Kim: | disowned her. [Cos they said –] they said, erm ... She came |
| 191 | Kim: | home and they said. We're going out for a meal, and she |
| 192 | Ellie | [No, what it – I'll tell] the story, |
| | Kim: | said, Well,    [er, we're sorry to – |
| 193 | Ellie: | [cos I know it!]                         [[Cos I know it!]] |
| | Meg: |                                                  [[I know!]] |
| | Kim: | [Oooohhh! You] tell all the stories.    [[I'm better at telling |
| 194 | Ellie: | You're shit at telling [stories!] |
| | Kim: | stories than you!]]              [I'm well] good |
| 195 | Ellie: | [You've missed the whole beginning bit.] |
| | Meg: | [By the way, Ally's still after] me ... (2) |
| | Kim: | at [telling stories!] |

(Moore 2006: 630f)

In this extract we see Ellie and Kim tussling for the right to narrate a story known to all of them (apart from the researcher, to whom it is being told). Ellie claims the right on the basis of having been the participant in this part of the event, while Kim attempts to claim rights as a better storyteller, a claim disputed by Ellie. Ellie, supported by Meg, positions Kim outside the storytelling. The analysis gives us insights into the way power is constructed locally in discourse.

## Language and gender

Research on language and gender has used the correlational methods developed by Labov, ethnographic approaches (as in Heller's work above), and more recently, narrative methods to explore the construction of identity. Jenny Cheshire 1978; 1998 studied grammatical variation in the British city of Reading, and spent nine months collecting data through participant observation of adolescents in playgrounds. She examined nine non-standard variables, including the use of the present tense suffix with subjects other than third-person singular, and *what* in place of standard English *who, whom, which* and *that*.

| Some non-standard grammatical forms used in Reading (Cheshire 1998) | |
|---|---|
| the present tense suffix | We **goes** shopping on Saturdays. |
| non-standard *what* | Are you the boy **what's** just come? |
| non-standard *never* | I **never** done it, it was him. |
| non-standard *come* | I **come** down here yesterday. |
| non-standard *was* | You **was** outside. |
| *ain't* | I **ain't** got any. |

Cheshire found greater use of non-standard grammatical variants by male participants, and also noted that girls and boys had largely separate social networks, with different norms. Vernacular loyalty, the degree of identification with the values of the subculture, was signalled among boys by the use of non-standard *never* and *what*, and among girls by non-standard *come* and *ain't*. Both groups used non-standard present tense verb forms, non-standard *was* and *never*.

Cheshire's data show differences in linguistic behaviour between the 'good' girls (defined as those who did not swear, steal or set fire to the playground) and the others, who make greater use of non-standard variants such as *come* and *ain't*.

The link between propriety and the use of standard forms of language is highlighted in Gordon's work in New Zealand. Gordon 1997 reports playing recordings of anonymous male and female speakers of different ages and social classes to a group of seventh-form students, aged 17–18. A recording of a middle-aged working-class woman provoked the judgement from some boys that she was a *slut* and a *slag*, whereas an upper-middle-class speaker was described as *proud* and *snobbish*. While the latter are also evaluative judgements, there is no reference to sexual morality. Gordon argues that:

> [t]he belief that certain activities or modes of appearance can also be indicators of possible sexual promiscuity underlies many of the unwritten rules for middle-class female behaviour. (Gordon 1997. 48)

This would explain why women shift towards middle-class norms in formal situations where they are talking to a stranger and are likely to be judged.

Gordon's hypothesis might also explain an apparent anomaly in findings by Eisikovits 1987 in Sydney – that older girls use fewer non-standard forms than younger ones. As earlier studies had found, she observed greater use of non-standard variants by boys than by girls. Both groups increased the use of standard forms when interacting with the standard speaking researcher. Girls used more standard forms, and this increased when talking to the researcher. In false starts, the girls self-corrected towards the standard form while the boys self-corrected away from the standard.

| Self-correction (Eisikovits 1987) | |
|---|---|
| Girl: | *An me an Kerry – or should I say, Kerry and I – are the only ones who've done the project.* |
| Boy: | *I didn't know what I did – what I done.* |

Eisikovits suggests that overt and covert prestige may account for this difference (see Chapter 2.7), but also notes the effect of the female interviewer, with empathy leading to greater convergence by girls. Her data include two age groups, 14-year-olds and 16-year-olds, and the older girls used significantly fewer non-standard forms than the younger ones, while no decline in use with age was observed across the two groups of boys (Eisikovits 1998: 44). From interview data she concludes that the older girls see themselves as growing up, settling down and becoming less rebellious while, for the boys, growing up is associated with greater self-assertion and toughness.

What these studies show is that the large-scale statistical findings of Labov and others reveal major patterns of variation. More subtle and diverse patterning within communities of practice and the ways in which conversational participants negotiate identity can be revealed by ethnographic methods, with researchers using a combination of observations, interviews and analysis of narratives.

## Key points

> Regional dialects have been surveyed using questionnaires.

> Social variation is studied by extended interviews with a sample of the community, and by rapid anonymous observation.

> The sociolinguist interview attempts to overcome the observer's paradox and elicit the kind of language that speakers use when not being observed.

> In stratified communities language use is also stratified: the frequency of use of sociolinguistic variants correlates with social class, and with the degree of care and attention paid to speech style.

> Linguistic ethnographers observe naturally occurring interactions in order to reveal the culture-specific norms governing talk.

> In multilingual contexts, norms emerge to govern crossing (the use of out-group language).

> Ethnographic studies reveal the ways in which speakers use linguistic resources to present images of themselves, or display a stance in relation to the current interaction.

> The cultural expectations of male and female behaviour, as well as local construction of identity in communities of practice, are displayed and enacted in the language choices which speakers make.

## References

Ash, Sharon 2002. Social class. In *The Handbook of Language Variation and Change*, ed. by J.K. Chambers, Peter Trudgill and Natalie Schilling-Estes. Oxford: Blackwell, pp. 402–22.

Blum-Kulka, Shoshana 1993. 'You gotta know how to tell a story': Telling, tales and tellers in American and Israeli narrative events at dinner. *Language in Society* 22.

Bourdieu, Pierre 1977. The economics of linguistic exchanges. *Social Sciences Information* 16: 645–68.

Cheshire, Jenny 1978. Present tense verbs in Reading English. In *Sociolinguistic Patterns in British English*, ed. by Peter Trudgill. London: Edward Arnold, pp. 52–68.

Cheshire, Jenny 1998. Linguistic variation and social function. In *Language and Gender: A Reader*, ed. by Jennifer Coates. Oxford: Blackwell, pp. 29–41.

Eisikovits, Edina 1987. Sex differences in inter-group and intra-group interaction among adolescents. In *Women and Language in Australian and New Zealand Society*, ed. by Anne Pauwels. Mosman: Australian Professional Publications, pp. 45–58.

Eisikovits, Edina 1998. Girl-talk/Boy-talk: sex differences in adolescent speech. In *Language and Gender: A Reader,* ed. by Jennifer Coates. Oxford: Basil Blackwell, pp. 42–53.

Gordon, Elizabeth 1997. Sex, speech and stereotypes: why women use prestige forms more than men. *Language in Society* 26: 47–63.

Heath, Shirley Brice 1982. What no bedtime story means: narrative skills at home and school. *Language in Society* 11 (2): 49–76.

Heath, Shirley Brice 1983. *Ways with Words: Language, Life and Work in Communities and Classrooms*. Cambridge: Cambridge University Press.

Heller, Monica 1999. *Linguistic Minorities and Modernity: A Sociolinguistic Ethnography*. London: Longman.

Heller, Monica 2001. Gender and public space in a bilingual school. In *Multilingualism, Second Language Learning and Gender*, ed. by Aneta Pavlenko, Adrian Blackledge and Marya Teutsch-Dwyer. Berlin: Mouton de Gruyter, pp. 257–82.

Labov, William 1972. *Sociolinguistic Patterns*. Oxford: Basil Blackwell.

Labov, William 1997. The social stratification of (r) in New York City department stores. In *Sociolinguistics: A Reader and Coursebook*, ed. by Nikolas Coupland and Adam Jaworski. New York: St. Martin's Press, pp. 168–78.

Mesthrie, Rajend, Joan Swann, Andrea Deumert and William L. Leap 2000. *Introducing Sociolinguistics*. Edinburgh: Edinburgh University Press.

Moore, Emma 2006. 'You tell all the stories': using narrative to explore hierarchy within a community of practice. *Journal of Sociolinguistics* 10: 611–40.

Orton, Harold and Nathalia Wright 1974. *A Word Geography of England*. London: Seminar Press.

Rampton, Ben 1995. *Crossing: Language and Ethnicity among Adolescents*. London: Longman.

Rampton, Ben 2006. *Language in Late Modernity: Interaction in an Urban School*. Cambridge: Cambridge University Press.

Tagliamonte, Sali A. 2006. *Analysing Sociolinguistic Variation*. Cambridge: Cambridge University Press.

## Resources

Some useful **journals** are:
> *Language in Society*
> *Journal of Sociolinguistics*
> *Journal of Multilingual and Multicultural Development*

The field of sociolinguistics changes very rapidly so textbooks quickly become out of date. An excellent introduction to the field is:
> Mesthrie, Rajend, Joan Swann, Andrea Deumert and William L. Leap 2009. *Introducing Sociolinguistics*. 2nd edn. Edinburgh: Edinburgh University Press.

Useful **reference texts** include:
> Chambers, J.K., Peter Trudgill and Natalie Schilling-Estes (eds) 2002. *The Handbook of Language Variation and Change*. Oxford: Blackwell.
> Coulmas, Florian (ed.) (1997) *The Handbook of Sociolinguistics*. Oxford: Blackwell.
> Holmes, Janet and Miriam Meyerhoff (eds) 2005. *The Handbook of Language and Gender*. Oxford: Blackwell.
> Meyerhoff, Miriam 2006. *Introducing Sociolinguistics*. London: Routledge.
> Swann, Joan, Ana Deumert, Theresa Lillis and Rajend Mesthrie 2004. *A Dictionary of Sociolinguistics*. Edinburgh: Edinburgh University Press.
> Trudgill, Peter 2003. *A Glossary of Sociolinguistics*. Edinburgh: Edinburgh University Press.

## chapter contents

> Experimental or observational methods     320
> Neurolinguistic research     321
> Key points     322
> References     322
> Resources     322

This chapter illustrates how child language data are elicited, and gives an example of experimental research in neurolinguistics.

## Experimental or observational methods

Most research in psycholinguistics, and in particular child language research, relies largely on experimental or observational methods. Experimental methods are designed to elicit targeted responses in controlled and replicable settings, allowing a measure of the child's stage of development and comparison with other children. A famous test, the Wug Test, was developed by Jean Berko in the 1950s, to examine the development of inflectional morphology (Berko 1958). Children between 4 and 7 years old were given made-up words, such as the noun *wug*. They were shown a picture and told 'this is a wug'. Then they were shown two, and were asked 'Now there is another one. There are two of them. There are two _____'.

THIS IS A WUG.

NOW THERE IS ANOTHER ONE. THERE ARE TWO OF THEM. THERE ARE TWO _____.

*Figure 5.2 The Wug Test*

Children who answered *wugs*, as most did, displayed evidence of having acquired the rule for plural formation. This was evidence of rule-governed behaviour, and it supported a theory of syntactic construction of underlying rules rather than imitation as the basis for language learning.

With a similar test frame, the children were given a range of nouns with different endings. Berko found that the children were generally able to apply the appropriate allomorph, [s] or [z], depending on the whether the final consonant was voiceless or voiced (cf. *cats* or *dogs*). However the rule for the [ɪz] allomorph, required after final sibilants [s], [z], [ʃ], [ʒ], [tʃ], or [dʒ] (cf. *horses, witches, bridges,* and so on), was mastered a little later in development. This shows that children create rules which may initially be too general, and that these are subsequently refined, gradually approaching adult rules.

## Neurolinguistic research

Experimental clinical studies are the basis of most neurolinguistic research. An example of research into neurolinguistic disorders is a study of acquired foreign accent syndrome (FAS). This is a relatively uncommon disorder, in which a native speaker of a language begins to speak with a foreign accent, usually as a result of brain injury or illness. Miller, Lowit and O'Sullivan 2006 describe the case of a 60-year-old woman from Tyneside in the north of England, whose speech changed some time after a brain haemorrhage. Interlocutors began to perceive her as Italian, although she had never travelled or studied a foreign language, and had no contact with foreigners. She was aware of this perception and found it distressing.

> I went through this door; when I came through it the next morning it was not me. … People ask me where I come from. I say S. They say: I never heard anyone in S talk like that before. I think: that's right. I come from here, but I don't come from here any more. Where do I come from, where did I go to? (Miller, Lowit and O'Sullivan 2006: 406)

Miller and colleagues investigated which features of the woman's speech led to this perception. They recorded words and sentences produced by her, and by comparable speakers with Pakistani, French, Italian and Greek accents, as well as another native Tynesider, and a person with mild stroke-affected speech. They then played the recorded words and sentences to ten listeners who were asked to rate their foreignness on a five-point scale ranging from 'definitely sure this is a native speaker' to 'definitely sure this is not a native speaker'. The researchers described the phonological and syntactic differences between the FAS speaker and the other native Tynesider, and used statistical methods to determine which differences contributed to her speech being seen as foreign, and in particular as Italian. They concluded that her use of lengthened vowels in place of schwa /ə/, leading to a shift from stress-timed to syllable-timed speech, seemed to make a large contribution to this perception. There were many other changes in her speech but not all of these led to listeners identifying her speech as foreign. By contrast, the stroke-affected speaker's utterances were heard as disordered but not foreign.

When the FAS speaker was asked to imitate other accents ('pretend you are speaking with an American/French/the Queen's English accent'), she was not able to do so. A feature of a number of brain disorders is **apraxia**, the inability to make intentional changes. Therapists were thus unable to teach her to change her accent. However, her speech was completely intelligible and in time, as her family and friends became used to her new way of speaking, she learnt to live with it.

Scovel 1998 provides a good basic introduction to child language and neurolinguistic research.

## References

Berko, Jean 1958. A child's learning of English morphology. *Word* 14: 150–77.

Miller, Nick, Anja Lowit and Helen O'Sullivan 2006. What makes acquired foreign accent syndrome foreign? *Journal of Neurolinguistics* 19: 385–409.

Scovel, Thomas 1998. *Psycholinguistics*. Oxford: Oxford University Press.

## Resources

Reading:
> Fletcher, Paul and Brian MacWhinney (eds) 1995. *The Handbook of Child Language*. Oxford: Blackwell.
> MacWhinney, Brian 2000. *The CHILDES Project: Tools for Analyzing Talk*. 3rd edn. Mahwah NJ: Lawrence Erlbaum.
> O'Grady, William D. 2005. *How Children Learn Language*. Cambridge: Cambridge University Press.

Useful **URL**:
> CHILDES Archive, http://www.childes.psy.cmu.edu.

# 5.10 **researching applied linguistics**

## chapter contents

> Researching second language acquisition    323
> Researching translation    324
> Key points    325
> References    325
> Resources    325

This chapter gives two brief examples, chosen from the wide range of research tools used in applied linguistics: an experimental study from the area of second language acquisition (SLA), and a comparative study of translations of the same text into two different languages.

## Researching second language acquisition

The wide range of methods used in applied linguistics reflects the range of research interests covered by this discipline. Work includes experimental, observational and narrative methods of data gathering.

Important early work in second language acquisition was done by Dulay and Burt 1973; 1974, who studied the acquisition of eight grammatical morphemes by 60 Spanish and 55 Chinese L1 children learning English as a second language. They showed the children pictures and asked them questions designed to elicit answers containing obligatory contexts for the use of the target forms (e.g. *There are three cat__ in the garden*). They were thus able to assign a score for use of the target forms. They found a common order of acquisition across the Spanish and Chinese-speaking children learning English, providing evidence for the existence of universal developmental sequences for different L1 children learning English as a second language.

A recent study by Ellis, Loewen and Erlam 2006 exemplifies a widespread approach to research in SLA. They explored different forms of corrective feedback provided to learners who made grammatical errors, to see what effect they had. Corrective feedback may be explicit or implicit: explicit feedback may consist of either an indication that there has been an error, or metalinguistic information about the error; implicit feedback is given when the researcher supplies the corrected form, or **recast**, of the flawed utterance. In this case the learner may not be aware that an error is being indicated. Examples of a partial recast and metalinguistic input are given below.

**Partial recast**

Learner:      ... they saw and they follow follow follow him
Researcher:      Followed
Learner:      Followed him and attached him.

Ellis and colleagues examined the effect of implicit corrective feedback in the form of partial recasts of the learners' utterances, and explicit feedback where the error was repeated and metalinguistic information supplied. Three groups, one receiving implicit feedback, one receiving explicit feedback, and a control group receiving neither, were assessed on their performance on tests of the past tense *–ed* form. They were tested on oral imitation, grammatical judgement, and metalinguistic knowledge before the treatment, a day later, and twelve days later. Both experimental groups had an hour of communicative tasks over two consecutive days, requiring them to work with picture sequences and retell the story.

The responses of the 34 students were analysed statistically to determine the contribution of the two forms of corrective feedback to their performance in the tests. The students began with relatively high scores on explicit knowledge of the grammatical form, but they made limited use of it, suggesting low implicit knowledge. The post-tests, particularly the later one, indicated that the learners' implicit knowledge improved significantly as a result of the treatment, and this improvement was greater among those who received explicit, metalinguistic feedback. The researchers argue that 'the awareness generated by metalinguistic feedback promotes the kind of synergy between explicit and implicit knowledge that is hypothesized to underlie L2 learning' (Ellis, Loewen and Erlam 2006: 364).

The study demonstrates how SLA theory is built through hypothesis testing. As well as contributing to theory building, such work provides evidence-based guidance to classroom teachers on how to provide effective corrective feedback.

## Researching translation

Munday 2001: 121ff presents a case study comparing the approach of Spanish and Italian translators of J.K. Rowling's children's book *Harry Potter and the Philosopher's Stone*. He draws on a three-stage approach proposed by Toury 1995. This involves first identifying the cultural systems of the target language, then specifying target language equivalents of source language segments, and then identifying the strategies employed by the translators and the norms governing those strategies.

Rowling drew on English and Latin morphology and phonesthetics to create names for the school, *Hogwarts*, or the houses (e.g. *Ravenclaw, Gryffindor, Slytherin*) and for characters (e.g. *Hagrid, Snape, Albus Dumbledore, Draco Malfoy*). These names exploit the connotations of the morphemes (sound symbolism) to create an effect, giving a clue to the nature of the referent. The Spanish and the Italian target texts (TTs) reveal very different strategies for dealing with these names. The Spanish TT simply uses the names created by Rowling, with one bracketed explanatory note on *Draco (dragòn) Malfoy*. The Italian TT transfers some names directly (*Hogwarts, Hagrid*) but in other cases attempts to translate the sense of the name (*Slytherin > Serpeverde, Ravenclaw > Pecoranera, Snape > Piton*, and so on). *Gryffindor* is changed to *Grifondoro* to retain pronunciation. *Quentin*

*Tremble*, author of the book *The Dark Forces* becomes *Dante Tremante*, drawing on the Italian word for "tremble" and alluding to Dante's Inferno.

Munday concludes that the translators drew on different norms, the Spanish TT being oriented to the English source text, despite the potential loss of meaning for readers, and the Italian TT orienting to target language norms, attempting to create an amusing effect similar to that of the original.

## Key points

> Applied linguists gather data using experimental, observational and narrative approaches.

> In the study of second language acquisition, work such as the experimental study illustrated here contributes to theory building.

> Research in translation studies explores the kinds of choices that confront translators, and the strategies they employ to represent the source text.

## References

Dulay, Heidi C. and Marina K. Burt 1973. Should we teach children syntax? *Language Learning* 23: 245–58.

Dulay, Heidi C. and Marina K. Burt 1974. Natural sequence in child second language acquisition. *Language Learning* 24: 37–53.

Ellis, Rod, Shawn Loewen and Rosemary Erlam 2006. Implicit and explicit corrective feedback and the acquisition of L2 grammar. *Studies in Second Language Acquisition* 28: 339–68.

Munday, Jeremy 2001. *Introducing Translation Studies: Theories and Applications*. London: Routledge.

Toury, Gideon 1995. *Descriptive Translation Studies and Beyond*. Amsterdam: John Benjamins.

## Resources

An accessible and up-to-date book on researching applied linguistics is:
> Dörnyei, Zoltán 2007. *Research Methods in Applied Linguistics*. Oxford: Oxford University Press.

Other useful titles include:
> Davies, Alan and Catherine Elder (eds) 2004. *The Handbook of Applied Linguistics*. Oxford: Blackwell.
> Ellis, Rod 1997. *Second Language Acquisition*. Oxford: Oxford University Press.
> Hinkel, Eli 2005. *Handbook of Research in Second Language Teaching and Learning*. Mahwah NJ: Lawrence Erlbaum Associates.
> Johnson, Keith and Helen Johnson (eds) 1998. *Encyclopedic Dictionary of Applied Linguistics*. Oxford: Blackwell.
> Lightbown, Patsy M. and Nina Spada 2006. *How Languages are Learned*. 3rd edn. Oxford: Oxford University Press.
> Mackey, Alison and Susan M. Gass 2005. *Second Language Research: Methodology and Design*. Mahwah NJ: Lawrence Erlbaum Associates.
> Mitchell, Rosamond and Florence Myles 2004. *Second Language Learning Theories*. 2nd edn. London: Hodder Arnold.

Useful **journals** in the field include:
> *Applied Linguistics*
> *Studies in Second Language Acquisition*
> *TESOL Quarterly*

# 5.11 **researching cognitive linguistics**

## chapter contents

> The anthropocentricity of language     326
> Categorization, prototypes, and stereotypes     327
> Metaphor     329
> Figure and ground     329
> Key points     330
> References     330
> Resources     330

This chapter summarizes key approaches taken by cognitive linguists to the specification of the categories which human languages use to represent the world.

Cognitive linguistics is the systematic study of language under the assumption that language is constrained and informed by the relations that human beings (a) perceive in nature – particularly in relation to themselves; (b) have experience of in the world they inhabit; (c) conceive of in abstract and metaphysical domains. In other words, research into cognitive linguistics seeks to ascertain whether language categories are randomly created in a completely arbitrary fashion, or whether they reflect human perceptions and conceptions about the things humans use language to refer to. The latter is expected to be found as the norm. Consider some of the evidence.

## The anthropocentricity of language

Language is anthropocentric: humans necessarily describe the world of their experience with reference to the human body and its everyday experiences. All speech communities use the human body and its parts as a basis for describing and measuring other things in the world around them, thus demonstrating the human-centredness of language and, indirectly, of the human cognition that language reflects. For example, traditional units of measurement such as English *inch, hand, foot, yard, fathom, mile* are determined by the human body.

Traditional counting systems are mostly based on the numbers 4, 5, 10, or 20, because of the structure of our hands and feet. Bunte and Franklin 1988 record that in San Juan Southern Paiute (Uto-Aztecan):

| | | |
|---|---|---|
| *ma-nuxi-y* | *shu - roxo - mai - y* | *toxo - mai - y* |
| hand-?-NOM | nearly-complete-hand-NOM | complete-hand-NOM |
| "five" | "nine" | "ten" |

Most people are right-handed, and in many cultures the right hand is regarded more positively than the left hand – used in many cultures to handle the impure. Latin *sinisteritas* "left-hand" is the source for *sinister*. English *cackhanded* and *gauche* derive from Germanic and French words for "left-handed". Whether gender terms are assigned to animals (cow~bull, mare~stallion, hen~cock/rooster) is often determined by whether or not the sex of the animal is of significance to a sizeable proportion of the language community.

The form of a listeme is arbitrary with respect to what the listeme denotes. In contrast, the scope of a listeme's denotation is motivated, and essentially determined, by human perception (i.e. the categorizing of sensory data using both biologically and culturally determined criteria). Thus, possible words are the English phrasal verb *put up with*, the Maasai verb *abol* "to hold a cow/bull by the mouth", and the Chinook word *ania'lot* meaning "I give him to her". Impossible in any language would be a verb *\*mimp* meaning "marry a woman allergic to": there can be no sentence *I mimped cats* with the meaning "I married a woman allergic to cats" (McCawley 1971). The partial noun phrase *a woman allergic to*, consisting of a head noun phrase and part of its restrictive relative clause, is an incomplete notion – which is not the case with any normal noun phrase. In many languages there is a verb with the meaning "marry a woman, take a wife" (e.g. Maasai *ayam*). In theory, there could be a language that has a verb meaning "marry a woman who is rich" because this is a complete notion. If *\*zamp* were to mean "marry a woman allergic to cats", then *I zamped* would be acceptable, and *I zamped cats* would be a tautology similar to *I bought it for money*.

## Categorization, prototypes, and stereotypes

The fact that the scope of a lexeme's denotation is motivated explains why there is no possibility of a naturally occurring noun *voogs* denoting the membership of the set {your-eye, the-Vatican, *b*, a-night-with-Brigitte-Bardot, $\sqrt{2}$}. No such motley collection, lacking any common physical, functional, or even metaphysical attribute, would be named by a root listeme in any natural language. Category names such as *bird* serve to differentiate a class of entities with one or more common or closely related attributes (a family resemblance or semantic chain) from some other class of entities such as bats. However, categories like rugs and carpets, or cups and mugs, or shrubs, bushes, and small trees seem to merge gradually one into another rather than starkly abut one another; so that, although the prototypical exemplars of each category are clearly different, there is a fuzzy boundary between, say, a small carpet and a large rug. Prototype semantics (see Chapter 3.1) was developed to investigate these matters.

There is a division among cognitive semanticists between those who make the decomposition assumption, and those who do not. The decomposition assumption is that the meaning of a listeme or more complex expression *e* can be exhaustively decomposed into a finite set of semantic or conceptual primitives that are together necessary and sufficient to determine the sense and denotation of every instance of *e*. The prototype hypothesis is that some denotata are better exemplars of the meaning of a listeme than others, therefore members of the category denoted by the listeme are graded with respect to one another. It follows that some senses of a listeme are more salient than others.

Battig and Montague 1969 asked students to list as many Vegetables, or Fruits, or Diseases, or Toys, and so forth as they could in 30 seconds. They hypothesized that the most salient members in each category would be (a) frequently listed and (b) high on the list. They found, for instance, that a carrot is the prototype for Vegetable, i.e. the best exemplar of the category because frequently listed near the top. The prototype in no way defines the category: as we said before, no one believes that a vegetable is a carrot! Furthermore, categories are independent of related categories with respect to prototypicality. For instance, a swordtail (*Xiphophorus helleri*) is a good exemplar of the category Pet Fish, but it is not a good exemplar of either of the categories Pet and Fish. All in all, prototype semantics has failed to deliver startling insights into semantics. Its greatest value has been to make respectable the correlation of semantics with cognitive processes.

An alternative approach to discovering the prototype is to present subjects with a variety of drawings of objects and ask the name for them (see Chapter 5.7). The drawings morph the characteristics from, for example, cups to mugs to bowls to goblets to vases, and then subjects must pick the best examples of a cup, a mug, and so on, perhaps on the basis of the figure alone, or imagining that someone was drinking coffee from the container, or else it was full of mashed potatoes, soup, or cut flowers. It turns out that a prototype is simply as-good-an-exemplar-as-can-be-found among the class of things denoted by the listeme (*cup, fish, mushroom, chair,* or whatever) (Allan 2001).

Just how important to language studies is this? One's interpretation of the noun *tomato* does not, even on reflection, lead to the thought that we are dealing with something nearly five times more of a vegetable than a fruit. What is more important is that the tomato's ambiguous status is captured in the semantic frame that reflects our conceptualization of *tomato*.

(a) A tomato is vegetable-like because it is eaten, often with other vegetables, as part of an hors d'oeuvre or main course. It is not eaten, alone or with other fruits, for dessert.
(b) A tomato is fruit-like because it grows as a fruit well above the ground and not on or below it. Also, it is often eaten raw and the extracted juice is drunk like fruit juices.
(c) Flowers are cultivated for ornamentation, but tomatoes are cultivated for food.

Our practice of eating tomatoes as if they are vegetables rather than as if they are fruit is what explains the relative ranking in each category (as revealed in the Battig and Montague figures).

The weakness in relying on experimental evidence for prototypes is that establishing the prototype depends upon the experiences and beliefs of the population investigated. The claimed prototypicality ranking might be valid for the community surveyed, but not for all speakers of the language, or even the same speakers on a different occasion. Experiments to identify prototypes may indeed identify salient exemplars of a category, but there is no reason to assume that these are necessarily what we think of, or are subconsciously aware of, when a category is named. The meaning of the linguistic expression naming a category is *not* identical with the prototype of that category. If semantic structure reflects conceptual structure, we have yet to discover exactly what the latter is.

Prototype semantics selects a particular denotatum or a particular sense as the most typical exemplar for a lexeme (Rosch 1978). Stereotype semantics (Putnam 1975) holds that the meaning of a language expression is not a well-defined set of properties necessarily found in every denotatum, but is rather a minimum set of stereotypical facts about the typical denotatum. The stereotype is a mental image, mental construct, idealized cognitive model (Lakoff 1987) or Gestalt (holistic mental image) with the attributes of the typical denotatum (Allan 2001). For example, the stereotypical bird flies, even though emus and penguins don't. The stereotypical politician is economical with the truth when his or her power or credibility is threatened. Putnam expressly allows for experts to have considerably more knowledge at their command than their fellows, which raises the interesting question: Do the words *elm* and *beech* have the same stereotype and meaning for a botanist as they do for an inner-city dweller who can't distinguish an elm from a beech? Presumably not: the expert has different (mental) encyclopedia entries from the lay person. However, if the botanist were to point out and name an elm, the inner-city dweller would know it is not a beech, even if s/he could still not recognize another elm thereafter. Putnam's notion of a stereotype incorporates connotation: a male chauvinist and a radical feminist will possibly have quite different stereotypes for *man* and *woman* and yet have no difficulty picking the denotatum of one from the other.

A problem that no one has resolved is how a (stereo)typical denotatum of *e* is distinguishable from as-good-an-exemplar-as-can-be-found among the class of things denoted by *e*. One possibility is that the stereotype properly includes the prototype. For instance, whatever the stereotype of *vegetable* may be, it presumably properly includes the prototype carrot and the peripheral onion. The stereotypical *vehicle* includes both the prototypical car and bus and the peripheral horse-drawn wagon. If this is correct, then it is obvious we should favour the stereotype in giving the semantics of listemes.

## Metaphor

Instead of the view current among Chomskyan linguists that syntax is 'autonomous', cognitive linguistics offers a conceptual characterization of syntax and morphology. These, like semantics, are taken to be conceptualizations, i.e. mental processes (Langacker 1987). All linguistic expressions are profiled against relevant background knowledge that is encyclopedic in scope. For example, the various meanings (construals) of the English word *back* are profiled against the characteristics of the human back (Allan 1995). The *back of a horse* corresponds to the back of a human in being where the spine is; the *back of a computer* is the opposite side from the side that a human mostly interacts with; the *back of a shirt* is the part in contact with the human back; *back there* and *back then* lie in the direction the human back has moved from. The notion of being behind someone to cover their back gets figuratively extended to *backing someone up* (supporting them) and even further extended in *backing a horse* – which is, loosely speaking, to support it. Since *Metaphors We Live By* (Lakoff and Johnson 1980), cognitive linguists have spent a great deal of effort studying the metaphors of everyday language.

## Figure and ground

There is also the ubiquitous figure~ground relation found in *the book is on the table* where the book is the figure and the table ground. Note how strange it would be to express the converse relation: *the table is under the book* – from which it would be construed that the book was massive and table very small. The active~passive alternation is another example of different figure and ground relations: compare *the assassin drove this car* against *this car was driven by the assassin*.

Because language is a creation of human beings for the purpose of communicating with other human beings, the communicative function of a language expression arises directly from, and is informed by, the speaker's cognitive awareness of its intended effect upon the hearer(s). As we have seen, researchers of cognitive linguistics seek to capture the ways to bring this about.

## Key points

> Researchers in cognitive linguistics seek to establish whether perceptual categories reflect properties inherent in humans and the things they use language to refer to in the world.

> Categories can be identified by citing prototypical exemplars, and researchers conduct experiments to elicit these.

> Data are collected by eliciting the names for objects represented in a graduated series (of, for instance, pictures).

> Stereotype semantics identifies a denotatum by specifying the minimum set of stereotypical properties of a typical exemplar.

## References

Allan, Keith 1995. The anthropocentricity of the English word(s) back. *Cognitive Linguistics* 6: 11–31.

Allan, Keith 2001. *Natural Language Semantics*. Oxford & Malden MA: Blackwell.

Battig, William F. and William E. Montague 1969. Category norms for verbal items in 56 categories. *Journal of Experimental Psychology Monograph 80*.

Bunte, Pamela A. and Robert J. Franklin 1988. San Juan Southern Paiute numerals and mathematics. In *In Honor of Mary Haas*, ed. by Willam Shipley. Berlin: Mouton de Gruyter, pp. 15–36.

Lakoff, George 1987. *Women, Fire, and Dangerous Things*. Chicago: University of Chicago Press.

Lakoff, George and Mark Johnson 1980. *Metaphors We Live By*. Chicago: University of Chicago Press.

Langacker, Ronald W. 1987. *Foundations of Cognitive Grammar. Vol. 1, Theoretical Prerequisites*. Stanford: Stanford University Press.

McCawley, James D. 1971. Prelexical syntax. In *Monograph Series on Languages and Linguistics No.24. Report of the Twenty-Second Round Table Meeting on Linguistics and Language Studies*, ed. by Richard J. O'Brien. Washington DC: Georgetown University Press, pp. 19–33. Reprinted in James D. McCawley *Grammar and Meaning*. Tokyo: Taikushan. 1973: 343–56.

Putnam, Hilary 1975. The meaning of 'meaning'. In *Minnesota Studies in Philosophy*, ed. by Keith Gunderson. Minneapolis: University of Minnesota Press. Reprinted in *Mind, Language, and Reality: Philosophical Papers. Vol. 2*. Cambridge: Cambridge University Press. 1975: 215–71.

Rosch, Eleanor 1978. Principles of categorization. In *Cognition and Categorization*, ed. by Eleanor Rosch and Barbara B. Lloyd. Hillsdale NJ: Lawrence Erlbaum, pp. 27–48.

## Resources

Just a few of the many books on cognitive linguistics are listed here.
> Croft, William and D. Alan Cruse 2004. *Cognitive Linguistics*. New York: Cambridge University Press.
> Geeraerts, Dirk 2006. *Cognitive Linguistics: Basic Readings*. Berlin: Mouton de Gruyter.
> Goddard, Cliff and Anna Wierzbicka (eds) 2002. *Meaning and Universal Grammar*. Amsterdam/Philadelphia: John Benjamins.
> Lakoff, George 1987. *Women, Fire, and Dangerous Things*. Chicago: University of Chicago Press.
> Langacker, Ronald W. 1987. *Foundations of Cognitive Grammar. Vol. 1, Theoretical Prerequisites*. Stanford: Stanford University Press.

> Langacker, Ronald W. 1991. *Foundations of Cognitive Grammar. Vol. 2*. Stanford: Stanford University Press.
> Langacker, Ronald W. 1999. *Grammar and Conceptualization*. Berlin: Mouton de Gruyter.
> Langacker, Ronald W. 2002. *Concept, Image and Symbol: The Cognitive Basis of Grammar*. 2nd edn. Berlin: Mouton de Gruyter.
> Talmy, Leonard 2000. *Toward a Cognitive Semantics. Volume I: Concept Structuring Systems. Volume II: Typology and Process in Concept Structuring*. Cambridge MA: MIT Press.
> Taylor, John R. 2002. *Cognitive Grammar*. Oxford. Oxford University Press.

Relevant **Journals** include:
> *Cognition*
> *Cognitive Linguistics*
> *Pragmatics and Cognition*

Useful **URLs** include:
> http://www.wikipedia.org
> http://www.cognitivelinguistics.org/

# 5.12 **researching functionalist approaches to language**

## chapter contents

> Saussure and the Prague School     332
> Systemic functional grammar     334
> Other functionalist theories     334
> Key points     335
> References     335
> Resources     336

This chapter outlines how functionalist approaches place the use of language for social interaction at the centre of a theory of language. Researchers who take a functionalist approach to language analysis aspire to such tenets as the following, though no single functionalist theory achieves the full set of ideals.

> Functionalists hold that linguistic structures can only be understood and explained with reference to the semantic and communicative functions of language, whose primary function is to be a vehicle for social interaction among human beings.
> Functionalism presupposes that communication influences, but does not necessarily determine, the forms that language takes.
> Cognitive and sociocultural factors explain linguistic phenomena.
> Language acquisition is part of general cognitive learning ability.
> Syntax allows people to combine elements of meaning in a variety of ways; it is semantically and pragmatically motivated.
> The social significance of language makes discourse more relevant to functionalist theorizing than decontextualized sentences.
> Linguistic corpora are a better source for language data than sentences contrived by the analyst in the course of modelling language.
> A functionalist theory should comprehensively model language, incorporating discourse, morphology, phonology, pragmatics, semantics, and syntax.
> A functionalist theory should apply to the complete spectrum of typologically distinct languages.

## Saussure and the Prague School

Ferdinand de Saussure (see Chapters 4.1 and 5.2) held some of the same aims as the functionalists. Vilém Mathesius (1882–1945) wrote, in 1936, the very Saussurean:

> The relative importance of a linguistic fact within the grammatical system of a given language can be ascertained only from the point of view of the whole system, that is

by considering its real function within the system, and may well be set off by a well considered use of foreign comparative material. (Mathesius 1964b: 307)

The reference to 'the grammatical system of a given language' is surely Saussure's *langue*; and Saussurean, too, is requiring the essence of linguistic analysis to depend on the function of linguistic elements within the grammatical system. However, the last clause is pure Prague School – of which Mathesius was a founding member. Members of the Prague Linguistic Circle developed phonological theory, functionalist linguistics, methods of structuralist literary analysis, text linguistics, and semiotics which were publicized through the journal *Travaux du Cercle Linguistique de Prague*. In the article quoted above Mathesius also said:

If we are to apply analytical comparison with profit, the only way of approach to different languages as strictly comparable systems is the functional point of view, since general needs of expression and communication, common to all mankind, are the only common denominators to which means of expression and communication, varying from language to language, can reasonably be brought. (Mathesius 1964b: 306)

Functionalists believe that, as a check on the naturalness of the descriptive categories, a language can be analysed effectively only in comparison with other languages. Most linguistic categories that are to be found in one language will also be found in others; so when choosing between two models of grammar with equal descriptive power, the model applicable to more than one language is to be preferred. Thus, a functional grammar includes aspects of universal grammar, but functionalists base their universalism on the assumption that because all human communities use language for social interaction, all languages must serve the same kinds of functions. This notion stretches back through the Western Classical Tradition to Epicurus. It is an idea that associates culture with language.

The Prague School find linguistic communication to be goal-oriented (Vachek 1964: 33) and look to the link between syntax and what came to be called 'communicative dynamism', 'functional sentence perspective', and later 'information structure', i.e. the distribution of theme and rheme, given and new, topic and focus. In a paper written in 1928, Mathesius 1964a drew attention to the different clause constituent orders and grammatical choices that are used in Czech, English, and German as the result of different norms for information structures in these languages. The choice between (1) to (3), is a matter of functional sentence perspective in the light of the discourse context.

(1) Max bought the car from Sally.
(2) Sally sold the car to Max.
(3) The car was bought from Sally.

Functional sentence perspective also has prosodic effects: compare the different nuances of (4) to (6) in which **BOLD SMALL CAPITALS** indicate stressed syllables.

(4) Maisie **SHOT** her lover [she didn't knife him].
(5) Maisie shot **HER** lover [not mine].
(6) Maisie shot her **LOV**er [not her husband].

Prague School phonology studied the function of speech sounds: distinctive feature analysis concentrates on the functional differences that contribute to difference in meaning. Out of it came markedness theory. Originally, it was applied to privative differences between phonemes; e.g. French /a/ and /ã/ can be distinguished by saying the former is unmarked and the latter marked by nasalization. Markedness is now recognized in all fields of linguistics and the criterion is that the unmarked form is 'more natural' – in other words, it is usually the default (citation) form, is typically more frequent, and is acquired earlier by children learning the language as a mother tongue. In many languages a singular noun is unmarked, the plural marked, cf. English *cat~cats*. The active is usually unmarked by comparison with the passive *I washed the car~The car was washed by me.* Topicalization is marked; compare *Poodles I abhor~I abhor poodles.* The standard interrogative *Has John gone to New York?* is unmarked compared with *John's gone to New York?*

## Systemic functional grammar

The Prague School functionalists influenced Michael Halliday (b. 1925) (see Chapters 4.1 and 5.5), who worked on prosody and also developed a polysystemic grammatical theory, originally called System-Structure Grammar, then Scale and Category Grammar, and now Systemic Functional Grammar (SFG), see *The Collected Works of M.A.K. Halliday* (Halliday 2002–2009). Halliday and his school have always been interested in the grammatical analysis of text and discourse, and Hallidayan theory has been adopted by critical discourse analysts (see Chapters 2.7 and 2.12; also Leeuwen 2005). Hallidayan grammar uses Saussure's associative relations as paradigmatic systems realized through syntagmatic structures. A grammatical system (there are said to be around 1,000) offers a number of choices. For a given structure, the choices form lattices. An important Hallidayan contribution to linguistic terminology is the labelling of *metafunctions*. First, languages reflect the speakers' construal of experience in terms of an 'ideational metafunction', which expresses experiential and 'logical' aspects of meaning (*logical* refers to functional and constituency relations within and between categories). Essentially it captures the propositional content of a text. Second, there is the 'interpersonal metafunction', which captures aspects of illocutionary and perlocutionary force and generally responds to pragmatic matters such as politeness and cooperation in social interaction. The 'textual metafunction' relates to the informational structure (theme~rheme, given~new, topic~focus aspects) of the text. This allows texts to be constructed to express ideational and interpersonal meanings.

## Other functionalist theories

There are many other branches of functionalist linguistics, including: Tagmemics (Pike 1967); Functional Grammar (Dik 1997; Siewierska 1991); West Coast Functionalism (Givón 1995; Goldberg 1995; Mann and Thompson 1988); Lexical Functional Grammar (Bresnan 2001); and Role and Reference Grammar (Van Valin 2001; 2005).

Common to Saussurean and functionalist approaches to language is the initial assumption that the primary function of human language is social interactive communication, and that linguistic elements can be explained by reference to their functions within the structural system of a language. The motivation for language structures is their communicative potential; so the analysis is meaning-based and compatible with what is known about psychological mechanisms used in language processing. Thus, the whole monostratal analysis that integrates morphology, syntax, semantics, and pragmatics into a single representation, such as is found in, say, Role and Reference Grammar, is as close to being psychologically real as any linguistic analysis can be, and the analysis demonstrably has cross-language applicability.

## Key points

> Functionalist linguists see language as a vehicle for social interaction, and identify the ways in which communicative functions are realized.

> These models see syntax as motivated by semantics and pragmatics.

> Researchers describe languages in comparison with other languages, and assume that since languages are used to perform the same functions, they will share functional categories.

> Hallidayan grammar identifies three key metafunctions: ideational, interpersonal and textual.

## References

Bresnan, Joan 2001. *Lexical-Functional Syntax*. Malden MA: Blackwell.

Dik, Simon C. 1997. *The Theory of Functional Grammar*, ed. by Kees Hengeveld. 2nd revised edn. 2 vols. Berlin: Mouton de Gruyter.

Givón, Talmy 1995. *Functionalism and Grammar*. Amsterdam: John Benjamins.

Goldberg, Adele E. 1995. *Constructions: A Construction Grammar Approach to Argument Structure*. Chicago: University of Chicago Press.

Halliday, Michael A.K. 2002–2009. *The Collected Works of M.A.K. Halliday,* ed. by Jonathan J. Webster. Vol. 1: *On Grammar*; 2: *Linguistic Studies of Text and Discourse*; 3: *On Language and Linguistics*; 4: *The Language of Early Childhood*; 5: *The Language of Science*; 6: *Computational and Quantitative Studies*; 7: *Studies in English Language*; 8: *Studies in Chinese Language*; 9: *Language and Education*; 10: *Language and Society*. London: Continuum.

Leeuwen, Theo van 2005. *Introducing Social Semiotics*. London: Routledge.

Mann, William C. and Sandra A. Thompson 1988. Rhetorical Structure Theory: toward a functional theory of text organisation. *Text* 8: 243–281.

Mathesius, Vilém 1964a. On linguistic characterology with illustrations from Modern English. In *A Prague School Reader in Linguistics*, ed. by Josef Vachek. Bloomington: Indiana University Press, pp. 59–67. First published in *Actes du Premier Congrès International de Linguistes à La Haye, du 10-15 Avril, 1928*, Leiden: A.W. Sijthoff, 1928: 56–63.

Mathesius, Vilém 1964b. On some problems of the systematic analysis of grammar. In *A Prague School Reader in Linguistics*, ed. by Josef Vachek. Bloomington: Indiana University Press, pp. 306–19. First published in *Travaux du Cercle Linguistique de Prague* 6, 1936: 95–107.

Pike, Kenneth L. 1967. *Language in Relation to a Unified Theory of the Structure of Human Behavior*. 2nd edn, revised. The Hague: Mouton.

Siewierska, Anna M. 1991. *Functional Grammar*. London: Routledge.

Vachek, J. 1964. *A Prague School Reader in Linguistics*. Bloomington: Indiana University Press.

Van Valin, Robert D. Jr 2001. *An Introduction to Syntax*. Cambridge: Cambridge University Press.

Van Valin, Robert D. Jr 2005. *Exploring the Syntax–Semantics Interface*. Cambridge: Cambridge University Press.

## Resources

There is a useful review of functional theories in:

> Butler, Christopher S. 2003. *Structure and Function: A Guide to Three Major Structural-functional Theories*. 2 vols. Amsterdam: John Benjamins.

**Useful URLs** include:

> http://www.wikipedia.org
> http://www.functionalgrammar.com
> http://wings.buffalo.edu/linguistics/research/rrg.html

**researching discourse and conversation**

## chapter contents

> Conversation analysis 337
> Discourse analysis 338
> Critical discourse analysis (CDA) 338
> Key points 339
> References 339
> Resources 340

In this chapter the contrasting methodological approaches of conversation analysis and discourse analysis are summarized.

In the Western, Greco-Roman tradition, research into the nature of discourse and conversation has one of the longest and best documented histories of any branch of linguistics. A structured approach to language through the study of rhetoric and dialectic emerged with the theories of human knowledge expounded by the philosopher Empedocles (*c.* 495–435 BCE), and other, later members of the Sophist school of philosophy. Early research into the structure and functions of discourse, as seen in the work of such luminaries as Plato and Aristotle, has a strong emphasis on the search for truth, the power of persuasion and the moral or ethical properties of speech. Yet this did not preclude the analysis of logic and meaning using methods that would be familiar to modern semanticists. The tradition of rhetoric and literature analysis was continued by Roman scholars and formed a centrepiece of the classical education in Western Europe until the second half of the twentieth century. It was then largely replaced by the study of mass media and communication, though in many ways retaining an interest in issues of persuasion, ethics, and truth.

## Conversation analysis

From a modern perspective, the analysis of discourse has tended to differ substantially from the analysis of conversation. Whereas discourse analysis may be characterized by the segmenting of the data into hierarchical structures, conversation analysis is concerned with structures and features of talk that emerge as each speaker makes a contribution. A typical conversation analysis (CA) research paper will examine closely an interaction between two or more speakers, and describe the way in which the speakers negotiate various parts of the conversation and identify any rules which appear to be governing their speech. CA researchers try to avoid deciding beforehand what these rules might be, but instead, allow the speakers to indicate, through their interaction, the rules of conversation. In this way, researchers have identified the rules for selecting who should speak next in a conversation (Sacks, Schegloff and Jefferson 1974), the rules for moving to a new topic (Jefferson 1988; Sacks 1992), the rules for offering and responding to greetings, invitations, accusations, requests, leave takings and other such conversational routines (see Wolfram and Schilling-Estes 2006), and the rules for interruption and the use of silence (Okamoto, Rashotte and Smith-Lovin 2002; Tannen and Saville-Troike 1985). All these rules are revealed by the way in which speakers themselves behave in such situations. For example, if one speaker interrupts another, he or she may apologize for doing so, which indicates that a rule has been violated. It is for this reason that CA methodologies are described as data-driven, or 'bottom-up' approaches. CA research depends on detailed transcriptions of naturally occurring talk.

## Discourse analysis

Discourse analysis, in its many forms, has tended to operate in a 'top-down' fashion: researchers identify rules that they believe may govern the structure of the discourse, and then attempt to validate these rules by finding evidence for them in the characteristics of the data.

Analysts may divide the text into 'speech acts', such as thanking or requesting, or attempt to correlate form with function, for example by identifying words used to express politeness. The analysis of storytelling has yielded rich results, and permits the elements of a typical story, or narrative, to be identified (Labov and Waletzky 1967; Mandler 1984; Polanyi 1985; Propp 1968; Rumelhart 1977; Thorndyke 1977; see also Chapters 2.11 and 2.12 in this volume). This can be a useful indicator of language acquisition, or it may be used to compare the structures of different languages.

Discourse may be categorized according to its genre, such as a movie script, a medical consultation, a newspaper editorial or a textbook. Considerable research has been undertaken that describes the various genres employed by speakers and writers in producing coherent texts, and attempts to interpret the genre choices made and the impact on the listener or reader. Similarly, the structures of texts that belong to specific genres, such as abstracts for academic publications, have been carefully analysed and described using frameworks developed for the purpose (see Swales 1990). This research has made a significant contribution to language learning and teaching as it provides guidelines for students constructing texts in these genres.

## Critical discourse analysis (CDA)

A critical approach to discourse analysis is used to describe the way that a text can be produced to serve a specific political or social purpose. Critical discourse analysts apply the methods of discourse analysis described above in order to expose underlying biases or prejudice in discourse (see Bloor and Bloor 2007, and Chapters 2.7 and 2.12 in this volume). The result of this approach is that while CDA research is reasonably consistent in applying the principles of critical discourse analysis identified by early theorists (see Fairclough and Wodak 1997), there are almost as many methods used to analyse the textual features as there are researchers. Some, like Fairclough 2000 and Dijk 1996, have broadly analysed discourse features without an articulation of a specific methodology, while others have relied on a narrower or more rigid methodology to uncover the relevant features of the text. In the latter category we might find research that draws on interactional sociolinguistics (Wodak 1996) or pedagogical linguistics (Pennycook 2001). Common to all of the methodologies developed in critical discourse analysis is the application of a 'higher' level of analysis, the critique of social and political themes which are expressed through the features identified in the texts.

## Key points

> Conversation analysts examine the sequential organization of talk, using detailed transcripts to identify how speakers have assigned meaning to the utterances to which they are responding.

> Discourse analysts identify the hierarchical organization of spoken or written texts, classifying texts by type into genres, and identifying the structures and speech acts which are employed.

> Critical discourse analysts attempt to reveal underlying ideological assumptions or persuasive goals of texts.

## References

Bloor, Meriel and Thomas Bloor 2007. *The Practice of Critical Discourse Analysis: An Introduction*. London: Hodder Arnold.

Dijk, Teun A. van 1996. Discourse, power and access. In *Texts and Practices: Readings in Critical Discourse Analysis*, ed. by Carmen R. Caldas-Coulthard and Malcolm Coulthard. London: Routledge, pp. 84–104.

Fairclough, Norman 2000. *New Labour, New language?* London: Routledge.

Fairclough, Norman and Ruth Wodak 1997. Critical Discourse Analysis. In *Discourse as Social Interaction*, ed. by Teun A. van Dijk. London: Sage, pp. 258–84.

Jefferson, Gail 1988. On the sequential organization of troubles-talk in ordinary conversation *Social Problems* 35: 418–41.

Labov, William and Joshua Waletzky 1967. Narrative analysis: oral versions of personal experience. In *Essays on the Verbal and Visual Arts*, ed. by June Helm. Seattle: American Ethnological Society, pp. 12–44.

Mandler, Jean M. 1984. *Stories, Scripts, and Scenes: Aspects of Schema Theory*. Hillsdale NJ: Lawrence Erlbaum.

Okamoto, Dina G., Lisa S. Rashotte and Lynn Smith-Lovin 2002. Measuring interruption: syntactic and contextual methods of coding conversation. *Social Psychology Quarterly* 65: 38–55.

Pennycook, Alastair 2001. *Critical Applied Linguistics: A Critical Introduction*. Mahwah NJ: Lawrence Erlbaum.

Polanyi, Livia 1985. *Telling the American Story: A Structural and Cultural Analysis of Conversational Storytelling*. Norwood NJ: Ablex.

Propp, Vladimir I. 1968. *Morphology of the Folktale*. Transl. by Laurence Scott. Austin: University of Texas Press.

Rumelhart, David E. 1977. Understanding and summarizing brief stories. In *Basic Processes in Reading: Perception and Comprehension*, ed. by David LaBerge and S. Jay Samuels. Hillsdale NJ: Lawrence Erlbaum, pp. 265–303.

Sacks, Harvey 1992. *Lectures on Conversation*. Oxford: Blackwell.

Sacks, Harvey, Emmanuel Schegloff and Gail Jefferson 1974. A simplest systematics for the organization of turn-taking for conversation. *Language* 50: 696–735.

Swales, John M. 1990. *Genre Analysis: English in Academic and Research Settings*. Cambridge: Cambridge University Press.

Tannen, Deborah and Muriel Saville-Troike (eds) 1985. *Perspectives on Silence*. Norwood NJ: Ablex.

Thorndyke, Perry W. 1977. Cognitive structures in comprehension and memory of narrative discourse. *Cognitive Psychology* 9: 77–110.

Wodak, Ruth 1996. *Disorders of Discourse*. London: Longman.

Wolfram, Walt and Natalie Schilling-Estes 2006. *American English: Dialects and Variation*. 2nd edn. Malden MA: Blackwell.

## Resources

Relevant **journals** include:
> *Critical Discourse Studies*
> *Discourse Analysis Online*
> *Discourse and Society*
> *Discourse Processes*
> *Discourse Studies*

# 5.14 **researching forensic linguistics**

## chapter contents

> Authentification                          342
> Legal language and discourse analysis     342
> Key points                                343
> References                                343
> Resources                                 343

This chapter outlines two main areas of research in forensic linguistics: authentification, and discourse analysis of legal language.

As will be clear from the forensic linguistics chapter in this volume (see Chapter 2.15), research in this area has tended to be practice-driven. In fact, it is possible to argue that forensic linguistics does not actually exist as a distinct area of research, and that it is merely the application of linguistic knowledge to a specific (namely, forensic) investigation. However, this assumes a narrow definition of forensic linguistics based solely on the role played by expert witnesses in a court case, and it ignores the important influence that legal cases have had in driving more general linguistic research. A famous example is the work of sociolinguist William Labov, whose ground-breaking investigation into the features of Black English Vernacular (BEV) was motivated by his desire to show that some black children in North American schools were being disadvantaged by a failure of the state educational institutions to recognize BEV as a rule-governed variety of English, just like any other. He was able to show that in specific cases, such as the marking of some past tenses, BEV differed systematically from standard American English, and that for BEV-speaking students to use the standard form, they would need to learn two distinct varieties of English. This then formed the basis of a discrimination hearing on behalf of the affected students, and it is widely regarded as the first forensic linguistics case, at least in the United States of America.

Most practitioners and specialists in the field would today recognize that forensic linguistics includes a wide range of study and research interests, such as legal and police discourse, the language of international law and diplomacy, translation and interpretation in a legal setting and all kinds of legal disputes about the use of language in society. This is of course supplemented by research in all fields of linguistics, perhaps especially in phonetics, which can be drawn on by forensic linguists when they are called upon to provide expert testimony in a court case.

In fact there are many categories of research in forensic linguistics – the website for the International Association of Forensic Linguists (www.iafl.org) arranges its bibliography into 16 main topics with more than 75 sub-topics of published research. This makes it a useful resource for readers who are interested in a particular branch of forensic linguistics. Here, just two of the most common areas of forensic linguist research are described.

## Authentification

Much of the forensic linguistic research published in the area of authentification relates to either voice or handwriting recognition. Linguists have worked steadily over the past three decades to provide reliable indicators of identity for the authors of spoken and written texts. In both cases, the research has yet to confirm the reliability of any tool that will enable foolproof, automated identification, but a number of publications have presented some possible authentification indicators, such as formant values for particular vowels, the length of syllables or other segments, the pitch range of voice samples, and, for written texts, patterns of punctuation marks.

The methods used in this type of research are largely quantitative, as the aim is to establish the statistical validity of potential indicators of identity. A key element in this research is calculating the probability that a given feature of language is common to many speakers, versus the probability that it is shared by very few, or even confined to one speaker. It is therefore very important for researchers to amass linguistic 'population data', that is, data about the linguistic characteristics of the broader population, covering as many features as possible. It will be of no help in solving a case to say that two voice samples contain identical patterns of pitch variation if we don't know how common those patterns of pitch variation are among the general population: it may be no more useful than saying that the suspect was wearing a size nine shoe.

A related area of research is concerned with tests that aim to identify a person's place of origin (typically in refugee casework). However, such tests are highly contentious, and condemned publicly by the IAFL as unreliable and methodologically flawed.

## Legal language and discourse analysis

Research into the language of the legal system has usually taken a discourse analysis approach. Researchers are typically interested in identifying patterns of language use in whole texts, such as transcripts of court cases, police records of interview (audio-recorded or transcribed), and legal documents. The analysis of these texts may be aimed at uncovering institutionalized bias (Barksy 1994; Eades 2002; Watson 1997), detecting excessive use of legal jargon that may confound lay participants (Cotterill 2000; Eades 2000; Rock 2007; Russell 2000; Shuy 1987), monitoring the shift from one speaker to another and the access each speaker has to the floor in a courtroom (Pomerantz and Atkinson 1984; Drew 1985; Eades 1996) or identifying patterns of questioning used by police interrogators (Heydon 2004).

A related area of research investigates the work of interpreters and translators in courts, diplomatic assemblies, government hearings (particularly refugee and immigration tribunals) and police interviews. Of particular interest is the translation and interpretation of legal jargon, and ensuring the adequate administration of justice when an interpreter is used.

## References

Barksy, Robert F. 1994. *Constructing a Productive Other: Discourse Theory and the Convention Refugee Hearing*. Amsterdam & Philadelphia: John Benjamins.

Cotterill, Janet 2000. Reading the rights: a cautionary tale of comprehension and comprehensibility. *Forensic Linguistics* 7: 4–25.

Drew, Paul 1985. Analyzing the use of language in courtroom interaction. In *Handbook of Discourse Analysis. Volume III*, ed. by Teun A. van Dijk. London: Academic Press, pp. 133–47.

Eades, Diana 1996. Verbatim courtroom transcripts and discourse analysis. In *Recent Developments in Forensic Linguistics*, ed. by Hannes Kniffka. Frankfurt: Peter Lang, pp. 241–54.

Eades, Diana 2000. I don't think it's an answer to the question: Silencing Aboriginal Witnesses in Court. *Language in Society* 29: 161–95.

Eades, Diana 2002. The politics of misunderstanding in the legal process: Aboriginal English in Queensland. In *Misunderstanding in Spoken Discourse*, ed. by Juliane House, Gabriele Kasper and Steven Ross. London: Longman, pp. 196–223.

Heydon, Georgina 2004. *The Language of Police Interviewing: A Critical Analysis*. Basingstoke: Palgrave Macmillan.

Pomerantz, Anita M. and J. Maxwell Atkinson 1984. Ethnomethodology, conversation analysis, and the study of courtroom interaction. In *Psychology and Law: Topics from an International Conference*, ed. by Dave J. Müller, Derek B. Blackman and Antony J. Chapman. New York: Wiley, pp. 283–97.

Rock, Frances 2007. *Communicating Rights: The Language of Arrest and Detention*. Basingstoke: Palgrave Macmillan.

Russell, Sonia 2000. 'Let me put it simply ...': The case for a standard translation of the police caution and its explanation. *Forensic Linguistics* 7: 26–48.

Shuy, Roger W. 1987. Comprehensibility in the DWI Arrest. *The Champion* May: 23–46.

Watson, D.R. 1997. The presentation of victim and motive in discourse: the case of police interrogation and interviews. In *Law In Action: Ethnomethodological and Conversation Analytic Approaches to Law*, ed. by Max Travers and John F. Manzo. Aldershot: Dartmouth, pp. 77–99 [First published in *Victimology* 8, 1983: 31–52].

## Resources

The International Association of Forensic Linguists (IAFL) is an organization which primarily consists of linguists whose work involves them in the law. The URL is http://www.iafl.org/.

# 6  career pathways

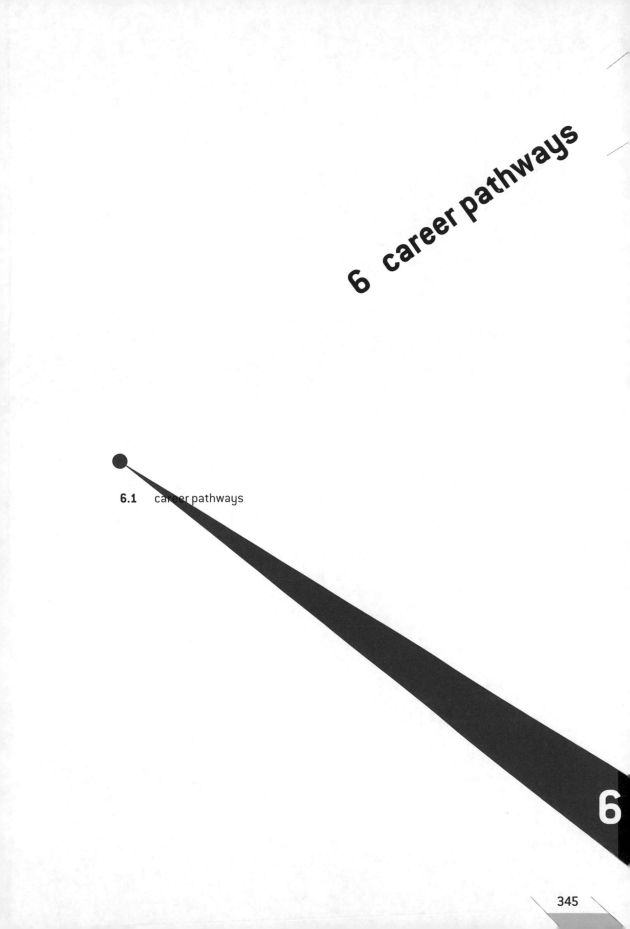

**6.1**   career pathways

**6**

# 6.1 **career pathways**

## chapter contents

> Using your linguistics 347
> Linguistics and education 348
> Linguistics, medicine, and therapy 350
> Linguistics and the law 350
> Linguistics and writing 351
> Linguistics in your degree 352
> The voice of experience – the careers linguists have 353
> Useful career websites 356
> A final note 357
> References 357

## Using your linguistics

We all attach enormous importance to language and everyone can benefit in some way from the study of linguistics. Language is, after all, essential to human life. It is central to the way we think, and it is the basis of social cohesion. But what practical use can be made of the linguistic information and linguistic theory that you learn in your studies – where in later life can you apply your knowledge of phonetics and phonology, or syntax and semantics? Here are some applications of linguistic scholarship that you might not have thought about.

> ### The film industry

Have you ever wondered who invents all those artificial languages used in science fiction films? Many of you will be familiar with the invented language Klingon used in *Star Trek* movies. Its creator, Mark Okrand, is a linguist. Phonetics training is also essential for dialect coaches who work with actors to master accents other than their own.

> ### Information technology

With speech-based applications now used increasingly in human–computer interfaces, natural language processing and speech recognition technology have become two very significant areas of IT. Linguistic research is the key to progress in these areas, and training in linguistics is a necessity for these new career paths.

> ### Advertising and marketing

Increasingly companies consult linguists when they are creating product names and preparing sales campaigns. Research into sound symbolism tells us that voiceless stops (such as [p] and [k]) have connotations of compactness and speediness – useful to know if you are a company seeking promising brand names for a new car. Such information becomes even more important for products being sold globally. An Australian wine company might want to promote its wine in China. What are the culturally appropriate metaphors that could be used in the tasting notes? ('An alluring nose with coffee and chocolate combined with forest floor aromas' might not carry the desired message for potential consumers outside the West.)

### ⟩ Safety measures

There are all sorts of applications of linguistics to safety in the workplace, especially the study of discourse. Language is not a precise notation like logic but is plagued with vagueness, indeterminacy, variability and ambiguity. The consequences can be dire. In the airline industry, a number of disasters have occurred because of misunderstandings between control towers and pilots. While faulty communication is a linguistic fact of life, there is much that can be done to avoid such communication tragedies. Applied linguists were involved in the design of Airspeak and Seaspeak, the official international codes for air and sea traffic control.

### ⟩ Preserving languages

The world's languages are dying at an unprecedented rate. In a report by the Australian National Board of Employment, Education and Training (McKay 1996) it is estimated that at the present rate of destruction by the year 2100 only 10% of the world's languages (estimated to be roughly six thousand at the end of the twentieth century) will still be spoken. That is roughly one language dying each week! Efforts are now being made to reverse this trend. Many linguists find themselves working together with governments and speech communities to document, preserve and even revive endangered languages and cultures.

Linguistic knowledge has a range of applications in the workplace, and is useful in a variety of jobs both inside and outside the university setting. Linguistics is concerned with such things as problem solving, the collection of data, the analysis and reporting of findings, and with recommending approaches to the solution of problems. Not surprisingly, many linguistic graduates have found themselves well trained for careers within administration, industry and public service. It is now well recognized that linguistics is useful in business, in financial institutions, in marketing, in personnel work and in industrial relations – indeed, in any careers where what is called for is clear and effective communication and an understanding of the sorts of tensions and problems that can arise from human interaction. In an increasingly globalized world, international business and trade require people with knowledge of languages, but also with an awareness of the ways languages differ socially and culturally. Cross-cultural awareness training is commonly provided to international business people. Those with linguistic training are equipped with a great deal of knowledge in this area.

The following are some of the other fields that require people with linguistic knowledge. They give you a taste of the sorts of enterprising things you can do with the material you acquire in your introductory linguistics classes.

## Linguistics and education

Traditionally a good proportion of linguistics graduates enter the teaching profession, especially foreign and second language teaching. Linguistics trains students to think about a language in a scientific way: this metalinguistic knowledge is very different from the sort of unconscious knowledge a person has by simply being a speaker of a language. This offers all sorts of practical advantages in language teaching and learning. You will find, for example, that the knowledge of English syntax and phonology is particularly helpful if you are having to teach the structures of another language, or having to learn them yourselves – especially if you are an adult. Adults are often more interested in foreign languages than children are, especially if the other language is required for work. Learning a language later in life is far easier if you already come equipped with some explicit understanding of how languages work.

There are many areas where linguistics is relevant in the classroom. Of particular importance are the fields of sociolinguistics and discourse analysis. Speaking other languages involves much more than learning words, their meanings, their pronunciation and the order in which they occur. Being a competent speaker of a language also means knowing the correct distance to stand from someone, how much to look that person in the eye, when to talk and when not to, what to talk about and how to talk about it, when to interrupt, how much to talk, when and how to compliment someone and so on. This is known as 'communicative competence' and current linguistic research in this area has shown that interesting differences exist between speakers even of the same language. Men and women, for instance, can have very different interactional styles (see Tannen 1990). It is not surprising that language pedagogy is now attaching great importance to discourse and conversational issues.

Classrooms these days can include children from vastly different linguistic and cultural backgrounds, and this can place some of them at a disadvantage, especially if teachers are ignorant about concepts such as dialect, accent, and standard language. Imagine the potential misunderstanding when an Australian Aboriginal child says to a teacher – *You gotta gimme paper? Gotta* in many varieties of Aboriginal English functions as a marker of future time (much like *gonna* in other dialects). A teacher unaware of this feature would interpret the sentence not as a request, which is what it is, but as a directive – and a rather impolite one at that; see Eagleson, Kaldor and Malcolm 1982. Students might even be improperly assessed because they do not speak the standard variety of English. All too frequently non-standard dialects are viewed as corrupt, inadequate, even illogical, and a reflection of cognitive deficiencies or perhaps even perversity on the part of the speaker. It is widely seen as the job of schools to eradicate all signs of these non-standard 'blots' on the English language landscape. Yet teaching the school language will be much more effective if it builds on what the child already knows about his or her home language. Approaching this home language as a legitimate and rich variety, instead of as a collection of endless mistakes, helps a child to learn the standard more effectively. Linguists have done much to draw attention to the complexity of non-standard varieties of English, and have highlighted the educational benefits of a bidialectal policy. In linguistics you learn that children can easily develop two accents, two vocabularies, two dialects even – one for school and one for home. They become very skilled at codeswitching – switching between varieties according to context (see, for example, Labov 2001; Trudgill 1975).

There are all sorts of other ways that linguistics can contribute to the education setting. An awareness of different discourse styles can make for more effective teaching and student engagement in classroom. There are also some fairly specialized applications of linguistics to teaching (e.g. in reading, composition, and literature). If you are interested in exploring this further, we recommend you read Oaks 2001, which contains a number of chapters that explore the relationship between linguistic research and education.

## Linguistics, medicine, and therapy

Speech therapy and the more general study of communication disorders are concerned with people whose language use is abnormal in some way. This can be due to developmental problems or to an illness or accident that damages a language faculty that had previously been fully developed. An important task for speech therapists is to diagnose the problem and develop techniques to help such people improve their communicative abilities. In order to study and describe language that is 'not normal', it is important to know what the structure of 'normal' language is, and to master the terminology used to describe it. The methods and scholarship of linguistics teach you this, supply the tools you need, and provide an excellent foundation to subsequent professional training in speech therapy.

There are many other ways that linguistics can be used to improve the medical care of patients. One area of growing importance is doctor–patient (or practitioner–client) communication, especially breakdowns in this communication (see, for example, Cordella 2004). Misunderstandings in medical settings can arise from different languages or even different varieties of the same language. They can also result from the dissimilar discourse styles of doctors and patients. Linguistic research has shown that different ways of breaking bad news to patients can even result in radically different medical outcomes. Doctors need to be especially aware of the impact of language they use when recommending treatment. Healthcare professionals who have an appreciation of language issues (better still a knowledge of discourse analysis) can more easily identify the kinds of discourse tensions that occur between caregivers and patients, especially in complex intercultural contexts.

## Linguistics and the law

There are a number of applications of linguistics to the legal profession. As Oaks 2001: 1 points out, 'it is becoming more common for court cases to involve expert testimony by linguists who draw on their specific areas of expertise'. For example, a phonetician might be called on for speaker profiling and voice comparison (comparing, say, the taped recording of a telephone conversation with samples of the defendant's speech). A linguist might also be employed to perform handwriting and stylistic analyses of documents and so develop writer profiles to determine authorship (resolving, for example, whether it was the deceased who actually wrote the suicide note). Linguists are frequently called on to provide expert opinion when a trademark infringement has been alleged. Brand names often become household words (such as to hoover coming to mean "to vacuum") and while some corporations don't mind this, they do mind when other corporations transgress what they see as their trademark territory. This is where trained linguists come in.

These are all prototypical cases of so-called forensic linguistics (see Chapter 2.15). But there are plenty of other places where linguistic knowledge can be applied. The Plain English movement is a good example. Language in legal settings is characterized by a highly technical vocabulary and convoluted syntax. Expert evidence in and outside the courtroom, police warnings, even jury instructions, have been shown to be notoriously difficult for non-lawyers to understand. Lay people are often unable to comprehend the documents in which their legal and professional rights are set out. Since the late 1970s, there have been social and political movements pushing for clear and simple language, and for some time now linguists have been helping to translate legal language into a form that is more accessible to non-specialists. Misunderstandings in courtrooms can result not only from unintelligible legal language but also from cultural differences. For example, many linguists work hard to expose the kinds of miscommunication that can arise when defendants speak a non-standard form of English (perhaps even a creole lexically related to English); in other words, a separate linguistic variety that is not properly recognized or understood outside their speech community. Such misunderstandings can have serious consequences; see, for example, the work described in Koch 1985; Eades 2000; 2006a; 2006b. Linguists also work on problems which may arise with courtroom interpreting.

This is just a glimpse of some of the ways that linguistics can contribute to legal processes. You will find that all the major areas of the discipline – phonetics, phonology, syntax, semantics and sociolinguistics – are playing an increasingly important role.

## Linguistics and writing

There are really three groups of people who have careers in writing. There are of course the authors who produce material for print and online media. There are the technical writers who specialize in producing materials such as instruction manuals and software documentation. And there are the editors who appraise and select content for publication. These are people with a keen eye for ill-chosen words, grammatical errors, and infelicities of style and punctuation.

At first blush you might think that linguistics, writing, and editing have very little in common. After all, represented here are two very different camps of people when it comes to their approach to language: linguistics is descriptive, while writing and editing are prescriptive. In fact the two camps have a lot in common. Both are interested in acceptability, ambiguity and intelligibility; in other words, effective communication. Linguistic misdemeanours like aberrant apostrophes or misplaced adverbials are distracting to people, and, if they are distracting, they disrupt effective writing. It is not surprising that as the discipline of linguistics has become better known over the years, many employers now choose to hire writers and editors with qualifications in linguistics.

When people are trained to examine how language works, they become more skilled in handling their own language. This is particularly true when it comes to good writing. In linguistics you learn useful tools like grammatical analysis. You also learn about registers and jargons; in other words, varieties associated with particular contexts or purposes. Science reports, departmental memos, video instruction manuals and emails all have very different grammatical features, and a knowledge of discourse analysis and stylistics can help writers choose appropriate language for these different situations.

We are not claiming here that linguistic awareness will instantly turn you into effective communicators. There are enough examples of bad linguistic prose around to show that this is not the case. Nor will an ignorance of linguistics prevent you from becoming effective communicators. If that were the case William Shakespeare might well have ended up a wool dealer like his father John! Nonetheless, research has revealed the beneficial links between language awareness and language skills, especially in writing. Unlike speech, writing is not a natural activity – it has to be explicitly taught after the sounds of the language, much vocabulary, and most of the grammar have been acquired. With a feeling for sentence patterning, we can better evaluate the different choices that confront us when we draft something written, such as a speech or a report. (On the research evidence for this, see Hudson 2001.)

## Linguistics in your degree

Linguistics is in an interesting position, because it is basic to so many different disciplines, not simply the ones that have language as their main object of study. As we have just described, linguistics crosses over many of the traditional boundaries of arts, social science, science, technology and business. Because of this, you will find that you can combine linguistics in your studies with many other subjects to create an interesting degree programme.

> Linguistics complements English and other languages (e.g. Romance, Slavic, Germanic, Asian languages). Any formal linguistic training will make you a much more effective language learner and teacher. As a side advantage, linguistics (combined with a qualification to teach a language) offers graduates opportunities for travel and employment overseas. Teachers of English, in particular, can find employment in most parts of the world.

> Linguistics can be of great use to people who study literature. Literature in any form, be it prose, poetry or drama, uses language, and a detailed study of the language found in any piece of literature can be very revealing. There is one branch of linguistics called stylistics, which is devoted mainly to the study of how language is used in literature. In composing non-literary texts you will also find linguistic analysis a useful tool.

> Linguistics is an integral part of social science disciplines such as sociology, anthropology, and psychology, and also sociocultural studies like history, ethnomusicology, European studies, Asian studies, and studies of indigenous languages and cultures.

> Linguistics is useful to students of law, especially in the light of current debates about language and the law, cross-cultural communication and multilingualism.

> Linguistics is a discipline at the forefront of cognitive science; and so, along with philosophy, computer science, and psychology, it is a cornerstone of cognitive studies courses.

> Linguistics is vital for any work in computer science that aims to make it possible for humans to interact with computers using natural language, including speech recognition, natural language processing, and knowledge retrieval. Analysis of formal languages is also an area in which linguistics and computer science overlap.

> There can be no trade or business activity without communication. Knowledge of foreign languages is an undisputed asset for business people, but perhaps even more crucial is an understanding of the principles of successful communication and an ability to effectively use the language expertise already available in the community. Some departments of linguistics even offer specialist subjects, such as Linguistics for Business, which examine these issues.

> Linguistics is recommended or even required by numerous Faculties of Education. Teachers of English and of foreign languages must frequently select curriculum materials and adapt these for use in their individual classes – all of which presupposes a solid grounding in key linguistic concepts.

> There will also be people who are interested in linguistics for its own sake. Many graduates may wish to become linguists themselves, or at least take their studies in linguistics further – they might want to be phoneticians, grammarians, or syntacticians. Many universities offer postgraduate programmes at the Master's level both by coursework and thesis, as well as PhD degrees, usually by research alone.

## The voice of experience – the careers linguists have

The following are some of the typical careers where linguists are required:

> Administration
> Audiology
> Computers, engineering and technology
> Information technology
> Communications and signals
> Creative arts
> Editing and publishing
> Education
> Field linguistics
> Foreign affairs
> Immigration and ethnic affairs
> Indigenous language study, maintenance, and development
> Journalism
> Language planning and policy work
> Language teaching (including teaching English as a second or foreign language)
> Law
> Media
> Social work and counselling
> Speech pathology
> Translating and interpreting

Here is what some former linguistic students have to say about the value of learning about language (for privacy reasons their names have been changed). Some of these recent graduates are based in Australia, but their work experiences are applicable to linguistics graduates in other countries.

**Siobhan** studied linguistics at undergraduate honours level. She currently works in a cochlear implant clinic. Her job as a research assistant is varied but includes clinical testing of subjects with cochlear implants, analysing their speech perception and production abilities, and studying ways to improve their communication skills in everyday life.

I got my job in cochlear implants precisely because I *had* studied linguistics. They were looking for somebody to assess the communication abilities of children with cochlear implants so my experience in describing and analysing language was exactly what they were after. In linguistics, you learn to analyse language from a variety of angles – there's the sounds of the language, its rules for how to conduct a conversation, the grammar and so on. Linguistics also taught me how to direct my writing for an audience – I quite often write technical reports about language abilities for health professionals, then rewrite the same report in everyday language to send to parents. It's great to think that something I enjoyed studying can bring direct benefits to the community.

**Zelda** did undergraduate honours then a Master's in linguistics and is currently writing a PhD analysing political discourse. She has worked as a qualitative researcher in the fields of telecommunications, tertiary education, and healthcare.

Her knowledge of linguistics has been applied in a diverse range of jobs, including:

> Socio-technical researcher at a major telephone company's research laboratories where she conducted studies in the late 1980s and early 1990s on mediated communication, using the then emerging technologies of desktop videoconferencing and corporate email systems.

> Consultant to industry training boards. She conducted a feasibility study on the Australian bush-food industry: linguistic awareness of Aboriginal English and paralinguistic features was useful when collaborating with Aboriginal community groups.

> Researcher at a university Institute of Health Services Research: she looked at use of medical jargon and healthcare department bureaucratese in various contexts of communication with patients.

In all fields, linguistic awareness is useful for questionnaire and focus group discussion design for ensuring that questions are not ambiguous or subject to misinterpretation. It is also useful in many corporate contexts for identifying areas of miscommunication and their underlying causes.

**Faith** has worked as a writer, editor, and teacher. She now works for the State government where her role requires high-level communication skills.

Linguistics taught me about the structure of language, and particularly about the relationship between structure and meaning. This has been invaluable in all my working roles, but especially in editing and in teaching writing, where a detailed understanding of the way language works and the ability to explain the impact of subtle variations in structure to an author or a student have been very practical and useful outcomes. My continuing interest in language in all its variety is due to the enthusiasm of my teachers.

**Grace** currently holds a senior managerial role in one of Australia's leading providers of multicultural language, employment and settlement services.

I came to linguistics mid-career when I was moving from a direct English language teaching role into a support role for other teachers. I've found having the Master's in linguistics a great advantage. As well as providing a solid technical background for my work, it gives me confidence in working with others on curriculum and language resources.

**Euphemia** graduated in 2006 with an honours degree in linguistics. Since then she has been working at a regional Aboriginal Language Centre.

A major study in linguistics is the least prerequisite for endangered language work in most language centres across Australia. Often Honours is also required. The top end of Australia has recently been identified as a global 'hot spot' for endangered languages – many of our Australian languages are the most endangered in the world. In addition to this, there is little known about many of these languages. There is a great deal of urgent documentation, maintenance, revitalization and analysis to be done. Aside from working with endangered languages, regional language centre work provides opportunities to study emerging languages such as the Northern Territory's Kriol.

Specifically, I am privileged to work with the last fluent speakers of the Mangarrayi language at Jilkminggan community – two sisters who are the elders of the community. This work includes documenting dreaming stories, learning one of the most endangered languages in the world, working with the community to develop possible revitalization strategies, and providing support for a new school language programme.

I am also involved in the development and delivery of translation and interpreting services. A background in linguistics is essential to identifying the intricate and subtle pragmatic differences in language and culture which is key to delivering quality service in these areas.

**Phillipa** is now a lecturer in Criminal Justice at an Australian university.

My linguistics degrees (BA Hons and PhD) have certainly offered many career opportunities, some less predictable than others. Like many, I have had the chance to teach English linguistics at a foreign university (Denmark) in addition to teaching linguistics and public relations writing in Australia. Less conventionally, I have offered expert opinions in court cases involving linguistic evidence and attracted a certain amount of media attention because of my specialization in the language of police interviewing. I present seminars on language in the workplace to corporate audiences where the pressure is high but there's always a touch of glamour and star treatment! Finally, I am working to revise police training materials to include linguistic perspectives on the interrogation of suspects.

**John** studied linguistics at the University of Pittsburgh. He has provided translation/interpretive support to US and British naval vessels in the Persian Gulf, created and taught language courses for the US Navy and taught English in Indonesia.

Linguistics opens the door to a number of careers both in your home country and overseas. I had always sought an intellectually challenging career which would also offer the chance to travel. Linguistics has been good to me on both fronts. I first worked in the Middle East, interpreting the region's linguistic and sociocultural complexities for the US government. Then, I made the move to the classroom, developing and teaching Farsi and English courses in varying locales and contexts. Most recently, I've been working on a PhD exploring stylistic language variation, the way that humans strategically vary their language to accomplish goals. In the future I hope to work with skilled migrants and refugees, helping them to linguistically adapt to new work and social contexts. A background in linguistics has afforded me vast opportunities to teach, travel and learn in the world-at-large – opportunities I surely would not have had without such a background.

**Max** read English at Leeds University, where he took some classes in linguistics. On graduating he went directly to teach English at Achimota School, a prestigious co-educational secondary school located at Achimota in Accra, Ghana.

Achimota educated several presidents of Ghana: Kwame Nkrumah, Edward Akufo-Addo, Jerry Rawlings, John Atta Mills as well as Robert Mugabe who became President of Zimbabwe and his wife Sally, and Alhaji Sir Dauda Jawara, first Head of State of The Gambia. While at Achimota, I was able to use my knowledge of grammar and phonology to develop classes in English language. I also took the opportunity of successfully trialling English pronunciation classes in the associated primary school. Later I went on to teach English linguistics in Nigeria and Kenya. Studying linguistics was absolutely the best training for anyone thinking of teaching a language.

## Useful career websites

Just as the internet has revolutionized the study of linguistics, it has also dramatically changed the way university graduates may seek careers advice and assistance. Employment information and job opportunities in linguistics can be readily accessed online. Here are details of just a few of the many career websites offering information about linguistics education and general careers advice and assistance for graduates in linguistics around the world. It is also worthwhile visiting individual university websites. Many include employment and careers information and also profile some of their recent graduates.

> **The LINGUIST List** http://www.linguistlist.org/

This site offers a searchable archive of jobs postings for academic and professional positions for linguists. It also includes information on graduate and research assistantships (financial support for graduate and postgraduate work) and has a link to some of the frequently-asked questions that relate to linguistics as a career.

> **The Linguistic Society of America** http://lsadc.org/

The LSA offers general employment advice and assistance for linguists. While the job listings are restricted to members of the LSA, it has an open page that provides tips for job applications and interviewing, as well as a list of useful career resources.

> **The Linguistics Association of Great Britain** http://www.lagb.org.uk/

Although careers advice is not provided here, the LAGB website includes a useful linguistics facts sheet and also has links to UK university linguistics departments, as well as a number of learned societies and organizations for linguistics in the UK and elsewhere.

> **Subject Centre for Languages, Linguistics and Area Studies**
  http://www.llas.ac.uk/resources/paper/2124#toc_24579

This is one of 24 Subject Centres funded by the UK Higher Education Academy. Their primary aim is to outline employability in the area of languages, linguistics and area studies across higher education in the UK.

> **Career View on Linguistics**
  http://www.graduatecareers.com.au/content/view/full/211

This is part of a series produced by Career Development and Employment at Victoria University of Wellington in New Zealand. Though the booklet was originally developed for a New Zealand audience, it contains generally relevant and useful information on linguistics and the range of skills that it develops. It also outlines the fields where linguistic graduates are most sought after.

> **World Wide Learn** http://www.worldwidelearn.com/online-education-guide/
  social-science/linguistics-major.htm

This website offers information about education in linguistics (general details about undergraduate, graduate degree and certificate programmes and also scholarship information). It outlines job opportunities, and especially focuses on those that lie beyond the usual academic careers in teaching and research.

## A final note

'Language must take its place alongside diet, traffic safety, and the cost of living as something that everyone thinks about and talks about,' said Dwight Bolinger 1980: 188. There are tangible everyday benefits to the study of language. As we have outlined, those who are trained to examine how language works become more skilful in handling their own language. They are also better equipped to conduct their lives more effectively in the public sphere. The linguist Dwight Bolinger was right – it should be as natural to comment on the linguistic probity of courts, advertisers, businesses, and offices as it is to comment on their financial probity. In his own writing Bolinger constantly addressed issues to do with correctness, truth, social class and dialect, manipulation through advertising and propaganda, the influences of language on our thinking and behaviour, linguistic discrimination and, in particular, official obfuscation and the maintenance of power. Language is the property of everyone, and we all need to pay more attention to the way it affects our lives.

## References

Bolinger, Dwight 1980. *Language: The Loaded Weapon*. London: Longman.

Cordella, Marisa 2004. *The Dynamic Consultations: A discourse analytical study of doctor–patient communication*. Amsterdam: John Benjamins.

Eades, Diana 2000. I don't think it's an answer to the question: Silencing Aboriginal Witnesses in Court. *Language in Society* 29: 161–95.

Eades, Diana 2006a. Interviewing and examining vulnerable witnesses. In *Encyclopedia of Languages and Linguistics*. 2nd edn, ed. by E. Keith Brown. 14 vols. Oxford: Elsevier, pp. 5: 772–77.

Eades, Diana 2006b. Lexical struggle in court: Aboriginal Australians versus the state. *Journal of Sociolinguistics* 10: 153–81.

Eagleson, Robert D., Susan Kaldor and Ian G. Malcolm (eds) 1982. *English and the Aboriginal Child*. Canberra: Curriculum Dvelopment Centre.

Hudson, Richard 2001. Grammar teaching and writing skills: the research evidence. *Syntax in the Schools* 17: 1–6.

Koch, Harold 1985. Non-Standard English in an Aboriginal land claim. In *Cross-Cultural Encounters: Communication and Miscommunication*, ed. by John B. Pride. Melbourne: River Seine, pp. 176–95.

Labov, William 2001. *Principles of Linguistic Change. Volume 2: Social factors*. Oxford: Blackwell.

McKay, Graham 1996. *The Land Still Speaks: Review of Aboriginal and Torres Strait Islander Language Maintenance and Development Needs*. Canberra: Australian Government Publishing Service.

Oaks, Dallin D. (ed.) 2001. *Linguistics at Work: A Reader of Applications*. Cambridge MA: Heinle & Heinle.

Tannen, Deborah 1990. *You Just Don't Understand: Women and Men in Conversation*. New York: William Morrow/Milsons Point NSW: Random House.

Trudgill, Peter 1975. *Accent, Dialect and the School*. London: Edward Arnold.

# index

**A**

abstract 4, 15, 42, 50, 53, 63, 64, 75, 88, 89, 135–7, 142–4, 148, 151, 154, 160, 171, 175, 189, 205, 211, 216, 217, 220, 221, 227, 228, 258, 262, 278–80, 292–4, 326, 338

accent 32, 93, 129, 168, 179, 180, 198, 259, 272, 298, 321, 347, 349

acceptability 8, 11, 13, 15, 21, 22, 24, 64, 180, 185, 186, 199, 236, 239, 242, 269, 271, 281, 291, 293, 327, 351

accusative 51, 55, 241, 287, 288

acoustics 31, 42, 105, 160, 188, 210, 221, 256, 278, 284

addressing 7, 17, 48, 77, 86, 89, 91, 92, 96, 99, 101, 107, 123, 134, 137, 145, 167, 180, 181, 187, 189, 192, 223, 231, 254, 256, 263

adjacency pairs 141, 146, 148

adjective 8, 50–4, 58, 59, 61, 63, 94, 97, 102, 167, 181–3, 212, 215, 217, 219, 221, 228

adverb(ial) 51, 58, 59, 182, 183, 187, 192, 215, 217, 221, 222, 233, 351

affix 50, 54, 55, 131, 183. *See also* prefix, infix, suffix, circumfix.

affricate 32, 37, 38

allomorph 49, 50, 53, 55, 94, 216, 278, 320, 321

allophone 40–4, 48, 53, 198, 199, 204, 221, 283

alphabet 8, 34, 42, 170, 172–5, 198, 227, 243, 283, 284

anaphora 72–4, 183, 189, 194, 208, 274

Ancient Greek 49, 57, 119, 130, 172–5, 183, 196, 217, 242, 281, 287, 291, 298

animal language 3–7, 13, 224, 248

anthropocentricity 326

anthropological linguistics 248, 260, 261, 265, 291, 292, 294

antonymy 75, 79, 84, 184

applied linguistics 9, 10, 14, 18, 115–25, 209, 253, 275, 276, 294, 323–5, 348

approximant 32, 38

Arabic 38, 92, 97, 123, 172, 173, 199

arbitrariness 6, 13, 123, 129, 189, 210, 257, 261, 278, 279, 326, 327

argument (logical) 184, 186, 212, 217, 236, 237

argument (point of view) 17–20, 22, 25, 135, 136, 150, 192, 264, 305

Aristotle 208, 214, 239, 278, 283, 305, 337

Arrernte 8

articulation 6, 13, 31–3, 35, 37–9, 38, 40, 42, 44, 45, 47, 107, 166, 186, 192, 193, 221, 256, 277, 283, 284, 338

artificial intelligence 158, 162

aspect (grammatical) 51, 99, 111, 123, 167, 184, 185, 217, 240

aspiration 32, 38, 40, 41, 44

assimilation 37, 44, 45, 53

attributive 181, 182

auditory 31, 33, 104, 106, 179, 210, 221, 278

Austin, J.L. 82, 84, 206, 227, 231, 247, 262

authentification 342

auxiliary verb 7, 59, 63, 179, 185, 202, 215–17, 240–2, 280

**B**

backchannel 96, 145, 146

back-formation 54

behaviourism 112, 116, 120, 121, 249, 251

Bickerton 98, 100, 196, 247, 248

bilabial 32, 37, 38, 41, 42, 44, 201

bilingualism 95, 97, 100, 104, 115, 117, 121, 189, 314

blend 54, 185, 242

Bloomfield 11, 248, 249, 261, 278, 279, 284

body language 3, 4, 17, 148, 188

Bolinger 180, 182, 209, 357
borrowing 46, 54, 129
bound morpheme 50–2, 54, 216
Bourdieu 91, 92, 100, 314, 318

C

cardinal vowel 36, 242, 284
career xv, 121, 347–57
case (grammatical) 51, 55, 202, 217, 218, 287, 288, 293
causative 50, 183
channel 91, 134, 135, 186, 213, 235, 253, 254, 256
Chinook 54, 210, 327
Chomsky 7, 8, 11, 12, 14, 21, 61, 64, 66, 89, 101, 112, 113, 116, 117, 120, 126, 150, 180, 190, 191, 201–3, 210, 211, 220, 229, 234, 235, 237–40, 248–51, 253–5, 258–61, 277–82, 284, 285, 289, 290, 293–5, 329
circumfix 50, 55, 183
classifier 52, 98
clause 5, 8, 14, 59, 64, 78, 83, 122, 136, 138, 142, 143, 146, 182–8, 191–3, 202, 207, 213, 216, 217, 219–24, 229, 230, 233, 236–41, 249, 253, 257, 263, 287, 327, 333
clause-type 187, 216. *See also* mood.
click 32, 33
coalescence 45
coarticulation 38
coda 137–9, 144, 232
code 4, 5, 7, 15, 91, 92, 97–9, 122, 162, 188, 253, 256, 348
codeswitching 97, 98, 100, 188, 349
cognition 9, 72, 73, 83, 103, 106–8, 112, 113, 139, 158, 162, 189, 191, 204, 215, 225, 235, 250, 251, 255, 259, 260, 278, 279, 281, 293, 326–30, 332, 349, 352
coherence 7, 19, 72, 74, 136, 189, 190, 221, 227, 253, 338
cohesion 7, 25, 122, 189, 190, 253, 347
collocation 153, 156, 157, 190, 226, 227, 233, 274
common ground 69, 71, 72, 74, 77, 81, 84, 142, 143, 148, 188, 190, 193, 206, 224, 252, 307
communication xv, 2–7, 11, 12, 14, 73, 80, 82, 89, 93, 98, 118, 120, 125, 153, 167, 181, 186, 188, 190, 191, 196, 210, 213, 222, 224, 230, 251–4, 256, 272, 278, 332–4, 337, 348, 350–4
communicative competence 9, 13, 89, 90, 109, 120, 191, 252, 254, 349
comparative (adjective) 51, 182
comparative linguistics 10, 14, 116, 122, 128, 129, 132, 260, 277, 281, 297, 298, 333
competence 8, 9, 13, 58, 60, 63, 65, 93, 94, 116, 118, 119, 180, 190, 191, 210, 220, 239, 249, 251, 252, 254, 279, 280, 293
complementary distribution 41–3, 48, 199, 221
compositionality 67–9, 74, 175, 305, 327, 350
compounding 54, 186, 229
computers in linguistics 8, 10, 14, 30, 31, 107, 150, 153, 156–62, 164–6, 186, 274, 284, 285, 302, 347, 352, 353
conditioning 48, 53, 249
conjunction 7, 59, 191, 192, 217, 229, 299
connotation 7, 75–7, 83, 88, 139, 192, 195, 210, 233, 324, 329, 347
consonant 32, 35, 37–9, 44–6, 53, 88, 107, 110, 111, 127, 139, 173, 175, 192, 200, 218, 242, 298, 311, 320
constituency 42, 49, 59–69, 74, 78, 107, 112, 148, 160, 193, 203, 211, 212, 219, 220, 227, 229, 232–4, 238, 242, 249, 250, 278, 279, 281, 283, 292, 294, 333, 334
context 6, 9–12, 24, 53, 57, 58, 64, 67, 69–77, 80, 82, 83, 86, 87, 89, 90, 97, 110, 116, 119, 120, 122, 124, 128, 134–6, 138, 140, 173, 185, 188–95, 198–200, 202, 203, 206, 208, 213, 219, 223, 227–9, 231–3, 235, 237, 240, 252, 253, 256, 258, 263, 264, 274, 278, 280, 281, 294, 307, 312, 318, 323, 332, 333, 349–51, 354, 355
contradictory 79, 83, 84, 184
contraries 79, 83, 84, 184, 194, 205
convention 6, 7, 12, 14, 20, 22–4, 34, 45, 50, 61, 71, 72, 77, 80, 81, 84, 91, 94, 96, 124, 137, 145, 148, 170–2, 190, 192, 194, 195, 198, 199, 201, 214, 230, 232, 252, 254, 257, 269, 272, 293
conversation analysis (CA) 11, 30, 144, 145, 148, 337, 339
converse predicates 78, 184
conversion 10, 50, 131, 211

cooperative principle (maxims) 75, 77, 79–81, 84, 91, 180, 190, 194, 206, 252, 305, 334

coreferentiality 14

corpus linguistics 11, 98, 150–5, 157, 158, 231, 268, 273–6, 293, 300, 302

cotext 69, 72–4, 183, 193, 194, 197

covert prestige 88, 195, 196, 317

creativity 6, 13, 21, 65, 116, 117, 120, 139, 140, 191, 203, 224, 249, 251, 313, 353

creole 97, 99, 196, 199, 222, 247, 248, 314, 351. *See also* pidgin.

critical discourse analysis (CDA) 90, 91, 93, 94, 139, 144, 148, 234, 334, 338, 339

Crystal 22, 27, 179, 180, 199, 214, 236, 294, 295

Cyrillic 173

**D**

data mining 156, 162

declarative 51, 69, 187, 216, 237

declension 55, 202, 287, 288

deixis 73, 74, 136, 193, 196, 197, 236. *See also* indexicality.

denotation 32, 58, 68, 69, 73, 75, 76, 83, 129, 139, 175, 176, 181, 183, 192, 212, 217, 224, 227–30, 240, 258, 305–7, 327–30

dénouement 143, 148

dental 32, 37, 40, 130

derivational morphology 52, 55, 58, 109

determiner 59, 61, 182, 183, 193, 197, 217, 238

Devanāgarī 172

diachrony 152, 197, 198, 248, 262, 291, 299, 300, 302

diacritic 32, 35, 173, 198

dialect 6, 34, 35, 37, 38, 40, 53, 87, 89, 92–5, 97, 122, 129, 130, 132, 152, 166, 168, 179, 188, 189, 195, 198, 199, 201, 205, 217, 218, 232, 240–2, 258, 259, 274, 291, 310, 314, 315, 317, 337, 347, 349, 357. *See also* regional variation.

dictionary 18, 51, 67, 68, 75, 92, 151, 153, 154, 157, 188, 199, 202, 205, 211–13, 228, 231, 232, 271. *See also* lexicon.

digital tools. *See* computers in linguistics.

diglossia 97, 199

Dinka 7

diphthong 36, 37, 39, 198, 201, 242, 289

discourse 7, 10, 11, 13, 14, 25, 30, 90, 93, 94, 96, 97, 109, 124, 141, 144–6, 148, 153, 165, 167, 168, 183, 187, 189–91, 193, 194, 209, 213, 220, 224, 229, 231, 233–6, 254, 268, 273, 274, 305, 314, 316, 332–4, 337–9, 341–3

disjuncture 47, 48, 145

displacement 4, 13, 197

dispreferred 147, 192

distinctive feature 44, 186, 193, 201, 202, 256, 257, 280, 284, 333

domain 7, 11, 87, 92, 97, 100, 139, 153, 161, 189, 204, 209, 251, 269, 314, 326

double articulation 6, 13, 32, 277

Dutch 8, 129, 130, 199

Dyirbal 51, 52

**E**

Egyptian 170, 172, 174

elicitation 109, 219, 271, 272, 291, 305, 310, 311, 313, 317, 320, 322, 323, 330

elision 45, 200, 229

emic 42, 46, 50, 217, 221

encyclopedia 76, 77, 83, 142, 192, 212, 294, 329

entailment 77–9, 83, 84, 86, 200–2, 207, 227, 233

epenthesis 45, 53, 201, 226

equivalence 5, 6, 59, 69, 76, 115, 122, 123, 125, 174, 176, 192, 226, 228, 260, 265, 324

essay writing 15, 16, 18–26

ethnography of communication 12, 14, 89, 90, 254, 292, 310, 313

ethnomethodology 145

expert system 161

**F**

face 25, 81, 84, 145, 192

field (mode and tenor) 134, 135, 137, 209, 235, 253

figurative language 128, 139, 159, 185, 215, 242, 260, 329

finite clause 142, 143, 186, 202, 233

finite set 6, 13, 65, 69, 74, 327

flap 32, 35, 37

Fodor 113, 126, 214, 250, 251, 255, 258, 281

forensic linguistics 10, 30, 31, 153, 164–9, 274, 341–3, 350

fossilization 118, 224

frame 111, 142, 143, 148, 189, 208, 225, 227, 320, 328
free morpheme 50, 51, 55, 216
free variation 41, 45, 49, 242
French 6, 7, 35, 38, 91, 92, 97, 98, 116, 119, 121, 123, 124, 128, 159, 188, 198–200, 208, 222, 228, 230, 233, 284, 299, 314, 315, 321, 327, 334
fricative 32, 37, 38, 130, 193, 298
functionalist linguistics 13, 54, 120, 124, 136, 187, 190, 204, 217, 233, 235, 236, 238, 248, 253, 256, 257, 260, 278, 281, 293, 294, 332, 335, 336

**G**

gender (grammatical) 51, 55, 93, 116, 123, 202, 218, 288, 327
gender (language and) 25, 76, 86, 88, 93–7, 100, 124, 152, 240, 259, 314, 316
generativity 69
genre 11, 91, 94, 124, 136, 138, 139, 151–4, 209, 214, 254, 338, 339
German 6, 42, 43, 50, 92, 95, 97, 129–31, 199, 207, 248, 314, 333
Germanic 129–31, 224, 240, 260, 298, 327, 352
gesture 3, 4, 146, 254
glide 37, 38, 242
glottal/glottis 32, 38, 39, 179, 201
glottis 33, 39, 201
Goffman 181
grammaticalization 99, 297, 299, 300, 302
Grice 79–81, 85, 194, 195, 206, 207, 251, 252, 305, 307, 308

**H**

Halliday 5, 9, 14, 65, 66, 124, 134–6, 140, 188–90, 214, 233–5, 252, 253, 294, 295, 334, 335
historical linguistics 10, 14, 30, 87, 127–32, 197, 198, 207, 248, 290, 291, 297–303
homograph 49, 160, 204, 242
homonymy 75, 83, 204, 205, 305
homophone 49, 88, 171, 172, 204, 242
homorganic 44
Humboldt 11, 226, 278
Hymes 89, 90, 100–2, 120, 126, 191, 254
hypotheticality 70, 130, 132, 187, 216, 236

**I**

ideational 4, 6, 253, 334, 335
idiom 16, 128, 159, 188
illocution(ary force) 21, 82–4, 202, 206, 231, 247, 263, 305, 334
immersion 119, 121
imperative 51, 187, 216, 237, 256
implicature 71, 72, 77, 78, 81, 83, 84, 192, 206, 207, 252, 307
indeterminability 79, 84, 258, 348
indexicality 73, 74. *See also* deixis.
Indo-European 130–2, 173, 197, 248, 260, 278, 281, 292, 298, 299
inference 71, 72, 74, 76, 77, 80, 188, 190, 206–8, 252, 275, 305, 307
infix 50, 55, 183
inflectional morphology 52, 58, 108, 109, 111, 213, 217, 222, 241, 299, 320
instrumental phonetics 31
interaction 7, 16, 25, 73, 80, 81, 90, 91, 95, 97, 109, 110, 112, 113, 118, 119, 125, 134, 143, 145, 156, 165, 186, 191, 213, 218, 229, 253, 254, 272, 273, 278, 299, 311, 313, 314, 317, 318, 332–5, 337, 339, 348, 349
interlanguage 117, 118, 124, 125
international phonetic alphabet (IPA) 5, 31, 32, 34, 37, 39, 42, 198, 208, 209, 273, 284–6
interpersonal 6, 13, 134, 135, 236, 253, 334, 335
interrogative 51, 187, 216, 224, 237, 334
intonation 8, 12, 25, 32, 46–8, 104, 109, 110, 120, 145, 146, 160, 186, 188, 201, 202, 209, 213, 223, 235, 255
isogloss 87

**J**

Jackendoff 184, 212, 255
Jakobson 122, 126, 202, 256, 284, 285, 287, 290
Japanese 8, 46, 49, 90, 98, 117, 171, 172, 192, 300
jargon 18, 50, 87, 131, 165, 186, 209, 210, 228, 240, 342, 351, 354
Jespersen 257
Jones, D. 35, 284, 285
Jones, W. 130, 131, 297, 302, 303

**K**

Kalkatungu 40

Katz 113, 126, 214, 257, 258, 281, 306, 308
Krashen 118, 119, 126

**L**

labiodental 32, 37
Labov 88, 94, 95, 102, 136–8, 140, 199, 218,
 219, 225, 258, 159, 271, 301, 303, 305, 306,
 308, 310–12, 316–18, 338, 339, 341, 349, 357
Lakoff, G. 215, 225, 259, 260, 328–30
Lakoff, R. 96, 102
language acquisition 4, 99, 103, 104, 108, 112,
 113, 115–18, 120, 124, 125, 168, 234, 240,
 249, 250, 253, 294, 323, 325, 332, 338
language attitudes 92, 93
language change 10, 30, 100, 128, 130, 131, 199,
 211, 297, 299, 301, 302
language contact 92, 97, 99, 100
language disorders 10, 106–8, 256, 321, 322,
 350
language rights 92, 97, 313, 315, 316
language teaching xv, 2, 9, 14, 31, 115, 116,
 119–21, 125, 150, 151, 234, 338, 348, 349,
 350, 353, 354, 356, 357
language variation 10, 86, 121, 302
*langue* 210, 211, 220, 262, 278–80, 293, 299,
 333
lateral 32, 37, 38
lateralization 104, 113, 117, 125
Latin 55, 57, 119, 130, 132, 171, 173, 199, 202,
 207, 217, 218, 233, 241, 287–9, 291, 292,
 298, 324, 327
law xv, 2, 10, 14, 30, 164–9, 196, 210, 231, 232,
 341–3, 350–3
Lenneberg 104, 114, 117, 126
lexeme 18, 50–2, 54, 55, 68, 210–12, 225, 233,
 241, 327, 328
lexicon 54, 68, 75, 81, 83, 132, 159, 184, 211,
 212, 226, 231, 232, 237, 281
Linear B 172
lingua franca 98, 99, 222
linguistic relativity 225, 226, 265
listeme 68, 69, 74, 75, 83, 188, 204, 205,
 211–13, 226–8, 236, 306, 327–9
literacy 90, 213, 313, 314
locution 81, 82, 84, 206, 231, 247
logic 57, 208, 223, 242, 251, 252, 258, 279,
 305–7, 337, 348

logograph 170–2, 175
Lyons 197, 199, 213, 220, 228, 277, 281, 282,
 308

**M**

Maasai 8, 13, 67, 327
machine translation 122, 159, 160, 162
Mandarin 35, 46, 92, 231
manner adverb 58, 182, 183, 222
manner of articulation 37, 39, 40, 42, 192, 283
manner (maxim) 80, 84, 195, 252
markedness 21, 46, 51, 53, 146, 147, 154, 173,
 174, 179, 183, 184, 186–8, 213, 217, 227,
 236, 241, 256, 258, 274, 334
matched guise 93
McCawley 227, 327, 330
metalanguage 69, 74
metaphor 104, 128, 135, 139, 205, 214, 215,
 235, 260, 305, 329, 348
metrical feet 45, 284
Milroy 88, 89, 95, 102, 219
minimal pair 41, 43, 283, 311, 312
modality 136, 215–17, 232, 236,
mode (*see* field)
model 8, 21, 69, 70, 72–4, 76, 89, 92, 105–7,
 109, 111, 112, 115–20, 136, 158, 186, 189,
 193, 204, 208, 212, 225, 227, 229, 237, 250,
 251, 253, 255, 259–64, 275, 279, 280, 293,
 306, 312, 328, 332, 333, 335
monophthong 36, 37, 39, 242, 289
mood 51, 202, 216, 217, 233. *See also*
 clause-type.
morph 18, 50, 53, 132, 216, 217, 328
morpheme 18, 50–5, 58, 65, 68, 88, 109–12,
 117, 118, 123, 171, 183, 188, 193, 199, 200,
 216, 217, 236, 249, 278, 288, 299, 323, 324
morpheme acquisition order 118
morphology 8, 14, 30, 49, 50–5, 108, 109, 111,
 118, 128, 202–4, 216, 217, 226, 233, 236,
 240, 249, 257, 274, 278, 281, 283, 284,
 287–90, 297, 299, 300, 320, 324, 329, 332,
 334
morphosyntax 8, 9, 51, 55, 58, 60, 65, 68, 159,
 182, 212, 217
motivation 13, 15, 57, 77, 95, 105, 106, 121, 142,
 192, 210, 257, 272, 292, 327, 332, 334, 335
Mycenaean 172

**N**

naming 4, 5, 8, 13, 43, 54, 58, 59, 77, 82, 92, 94, 110, 142, 143, 159, 160, 162, 164, 168, 174, 176, 185, 192, 194, 206, 213, 216, 217, 228, 231, 243, 247, 258, 263, 294, 298, 305–7, 324, 327–30, 347, 350

narrative 13, 73, 94, 135–8, 140, 141, 144, 181, 192, 254, 259, 311, 313, 315–17, 323, 325, 338

nasal 32, 35, 37–9, 44–6, 88, 193, 201, 334

negative 7, 45, 49, 50, 57, 68, 81, 89, 112, 117, 119, 121, 132, 147, 183, 187, 192, 200, 201, 216, 223, 232, 237, 240, 242, 251, 270, 291, 305

neurolinguistics 10, 103, 320–2

neutralization 45

Nida 123, 126

non-factuality 70

nonfinite 142, 143

non-standard 88, 89, 93, 95, 182, 189, 195, 199, 232, 272, 315–17, 349, 351

note-taking xv, 16, 17, 19

noun phrase (NP) 14, 53, 59–63, 65, 69, 78, 158, 181, 182, 186, 193, 197, 203, 208, 217–19, 222–4, 226, 227, 237, 238, 241, 242, 280, 327

number (grammatical) 51, 55, 111, 197, 202, 217, 240, 288

**O**

object language 69, 74, 77, 78, 233

observer's paradox 218, 259, 273, 311, 317

obstruent 35, 37

**P**

palatal 32, 35, 36, 38, 39, 45

Pāṇini 283

papyrus 174

parameters (*see* universal grammar)

parsing 158, 234, 274

part of speech 217, 274

participle 51, 128, 202, 217, 240, 241

pathology 31, 153, 353

performative 83, 84, 247, 263, 314

perlocution 82–4, 231, 247, 334

pharyngeal 32, 35, 38, 39, 173

philology 11, 128, 197, 248, 260, 281, 291, 297, 298

phoneme 5, 8, 40–6, 48, 53, 61, 104, 106, 107, 166, 172, 173, 175, 198–200, 204, 219–21, 226, 227, 261, 272, 273, 278, 281, 283, 284, 293, 311, 334

phone 31–7, 39–45, 47, 48, 53, 160, 173, 175, 192, 198, 201, 204, 209, 213, 220, 221, 279

phonestheme 68, 324

phonetics 8, 9, 14, 30–43, 45, 46, 48, 107, 129, 164, 166, 169, 172, 203, 221, 232, 237, 256, 257, 261, 272–4, 279–86, 298, 341, 347, 351

phonology 8, 9, 14, 15, 18, 30, 40, 42, 48, 53, 55, 61, 81, 87, 93, 107, 108, 110, 128, 132, 139, 160, 170, 172, 188, 189, 191, 197–9, 201, 203, 204, 209, 211, 213, 220, 221, 230, 231, 233, 235, 237, 242, 248, 249, 255, 256, 261, 273, 278, 280, 281, 283–7, 297, 298, 300, 332, 333, 347, 349, 351

phonotactics 44, 48, 201, 219

phrasal verb 51, 327

pictograph 170, 171, 173, 175

pidgin 98–100, 196, 199, 210, 222, 228, 248

pitch 8, 12, 25, 31, 34, 46, 48, 109, 166, 179, 186, 209, 342

place of articulation 37, 44, 45, 192

planning 10, 18–20, 146, 220, 231, 253

plosive 32, 37, 201

plot 143

plural 50–5, 57, 68, 91, 92, 99, 111, 112, 117, 132, 183, 193, 211, 213, 216–18, 222, 224, 288, 320, 334

Polish 35

polysemy 75, 83, 139, 204, 205, 305

postalveolar 32, 38, 45

power (and language use) 12, 90–4, 96, 100, 124, 135, 144, 199, 232, 270, 314–16, 329, 357

pragmatics 7, 9, 14, 30, 67, 73–7, 83, 84, 106, 108, 109, 120, 139, 164, 183, 190, 191, 192, 202, 208, 220, 223, 224, 229, 235, 251, 253, 254, 258, 259, 262, 274, 294, 305–9, 332, 334, 335, 355

Prague school 256, 261, 284, 332–4

predicate 7, 78, 83, 143, 158, 183–6, 217, 227, 233, 239, 240, 248

predicative 181, 182

prefix 50, 55, 68, 94, 183, 224

prestige (*see* social variation)

presupposition 70, 80, 200, 201, 213, 223, 224, 239, 258, 332, 352

pronoun 8, 14, 51, 59, 61, 64, 72, 73, 91, 94, 99, 111, 112, 117, 123, 129, 136, 168, 179, 180, 182, 183, 193, 194, 197, 217, 219, 224, 274

proper name 77, 142, 143, 159, 174, 192, 217, 243

prosody 104, 334

proto-language 5, 6, 129, 278

prototype semantics 224, 225, 305, 327–9

psycholinguistics 9, 10, 14, 30, 103–13, 185, 220, 251, 275, 320, 322

psychology 2, 3, 10, 11, 14, 18, 30, 31, 91, 93, 103, 112, 120, 125, 210, 236, 251, 258, 261, 263, 278, 279, 293, 334, 335, 352

punctuation 21, 47, 167, 169, 173, 174, 176, 342, 351

**Q**

quality (maxim) 80, 84, 195, 252

quantity (maxim) 79, 84, 194, 252

**R**

Rampton 27, 89, 90, 102, 276, 314, 319

received pronunciation (RP) 93, 179, 180, 195

recursion 158

reduplication 54

reference (referring to) 8, 13, 14, 70–7, 80–4, 88, 93, 94, 111, 122, 123, 128, 134–6, 141–4, 148, 150, 154, 158, 167, 175, 179, 181, 183–6, 189–92, 196–8, 201–3, 205, 206, 209, 210, 212–14, 217, 219, 220, 223, 224, 226, 228–31, 233, 237, 240–2, 247, 250, 256, 258, 262, 271, 284, 300, 305, 307, 317, 324, 326, 330, 333–5

referencing 2, 20–2, 24

regional variation 87, 132, 151, 168, 198

register 87, 135, 138, 139, 165, 169, 186, 209, 240, 351. *See also* jargon.

relation (maxim) 80, 84, 195, 252

repertoire 6, 25, 88, 89

rhetoric 11, 21, 98, 144, 214, 233, 305, 337

rhotic 32, 37, 232

rhythm 7, 8, 45, 139, 179, 180, 232

Role and Reference Grammar 334, 335

root (morphological) 50, 55, 173, 183, 211, 298, 327

Rosetta Stone 49, 172, 173, 242

Russian 46, 55, 92, 112, 173, 232

**S**

Sapir 11, 49, 56, 93, 225, 226, 254, 260, 261, 264, 265, 292, 295

Saussure 11, 122, 126, 188, 210, 211, 219, 220, 228, 230, 248, 256, 261, 262, 277–82, 291–5, 299, 303, 332–4

schwa 36, 53, 226

*scripta continua* 173, 174, 176

script (Schankian) 77, 158, 208

script (writing system) 34, 171–5, 209, 284

Searle 21, 23, 24, 206, 247, 262, 263

second language 99, 104, 115–20, 124, 125, 191, 294, 323, 325, 348

secondary grammatical category 51, 55, 222, 236

selection restriction 187, 215, 226, 227, 237

Selinker 117, 125, 126

semantic field 124, 214, 227, 228

semantic relation 77, 83, 200, 305

semantics 9, 14, 30, 67–9, 73, 74, 76, 81, 132, 158, 183, 188, 202, 208, 223, 224, 225, 227, 231, 235, 239, 255, 258–61, 274, 281, 305–9, 327–30, 332, 334, 335, 347, 351

Semitic 172, 173, 175

semivowel 38, 201

sense (meaning) 6, 9, 11, 17, 42, 46, 48, 68, 73, 75, 83, 122, 125, 139, 146, 154, 161, 184, 187, 188, 192, 194, 198–207, 209–11, 213, 214, 220, 221, 223, 224, 228–30, 232, 233, 236, 247, 257, 258, 279, 281, 294, 305, 324, 327, 328

Serbo-Croat 7

Shoebox 158, 159

sibilant 38, 53, 288, 321

sign 3, 96, 122, 171, 188, 210, 230, 261, 262, 277, 278, 301, 349

situation of utterance 69, 73, 193, 194, 196

social networks 88, 152, 269, 316

social variation 87, 88, 169, 317. *See also* sociolect.

sociocultural theory 112

sociolect 88, 240. *See also* social variation.

sociolinguistics 7, 9, 10, 12, 14, 30, 86–100, 120, 164, 166, 168, 181, 191, 195, 199, 205, 209,

240, 254, 258, 272, 301, 310–12, 314, 315, 317, 319, 339, 341, 349, 351

sociology 10, 11, 14, 31, 297, 352

sonorant 37, 45, 48, 201

sound laws 298

sound symbolism 13, 54, 129, 324, 347

source text 122, 123, 325

speech act 75, 81–4, 91, 146, 231, 247, 254, 263, 338, 339

speech community 10, 12, 57, 88, 89, 128, 129, 134, 188, 199, 205, 210, 232, 254, 301, 311, 326, 348, 351

speech disorders (*see* language disorders)

speech organs 33, 220

speech processing 10, 105

speech production 107, 166

speech sounds 5, 6, 31, 39, 40, 42, 104, 107, 108, 201, 209, 220, 221, 283, 285, 333

speech synthesis 10, 160, 162, 285

speech therapy 11, 350

spell-checking 156, 157

standard language/variety 92, 93, 95, 96, 199, 231, 232, 349

stem 50, 52, 54, 55, 58, 94, 108, 183, 241, 287–9

stereotype semantics 76, 77, 95, 195, 307, 327–30

stop consonant 35, 37, 38, 40, 41, 44, 45, 47, 107, 173, 179, 193, 201, 347

stress (prosodic) 8, 32, 38, 44, 46, 48, 110, 120, 139, 145, 179, 188, 198, 202, 223, 284, 289, 298, 321

structuralism 90, 91, 120, 230, 256, 262, 279, 280, 291–3, 333

study skill xv, 15–28

style 10, 11, 14, 19, 21, 22, 30, 77, 80, 81, 86, 87, 93, 95, 96, 122, 125, 128, 134–40, 165, 169, 179–81, 183, 186, 192, 195, 196, 205, 209, 213, 218, 224, 229, 232, 233, 235, 236, 240, 254, 274, 291, 294, 311, 312, 314, 318, 349–52

stylistics (*see* style)

subjunctive 51, 187, 216, 236

subordinate clause 142, 143, 202, 230

suffix 50, 51, 53, 55, 68, 94, 182, 183, 224, 288, 289, 299, 316

Sumerian 171, 172

superlative 51, 182

syllabary 172, 175

syllable 32, 38, 41–6, 48, 107, 110, 139, 172, 174, 175, 179, 185, 198–200, 209, 219, 232, 283, 284, 289, 298, 321, 333, 342

symmetric predicates 78, 83

synonymy 78, 83, 189, 190, 200, 233

syntax 8, 9, 11, 14, 30, 50–2, 55, 57–66, 87, 98, 99, 105, 109, 110–12, 117, 121, 128, 132, 139, 148, 154, 158, 164, 165, 169, 183, 188, 190, 191, 196, 197, 204, 212, 216, 217, 219, 221, 226, 227, 232–5, 237, 240–2, 248–51, 255, 256, 258, 259, 274, 278, 280, 281, 284, 287, 291–7, 300–2, 320, 321, 329, 332–5, 347, 349–51

systemic functional grammar (SFG) 124, 136, 187, 233, 234, 253, 294, 334

**T**

table of comparison 43, 48

target text (*see* source text)

teacher education 11

tenor (*see* field)

tense (grammatical) 50–5, 68, 73, 83, 99, 111, 112, 138, 158, 168, 184, 185, 193, 197, 202, 203, 217, 222, 232, 236, 240, 241, 265, 280, 288, 289, 299, 316, 324, 341

text generation 160, 162, 233, 234

textual function 7, 13, 73, 253

thematic (theta) role 69, 184, 212, 236, 237

thematic subject 142–4, 148

title 19, 23, 72, 73, 92, 142, 143, 148

tone 32, 46–8, 91, 146, 202, 254, 255, 284

tongue 32, 33, 35–9, 198, 201, 242

transcription 42, 43, 45, 48, 96, 137, 145, 148, 152, 162, 165, 232, 269, 270, 272–4, 276, 283, 315, 338, 339, 342

transformational (generative) grammar (TG) 63, 187, 204, 237, 241, 250, 253, 258, 259, 271, 280, 281, 284, 293

transition relevance place (TRP) 146

transitivity 60, 65, 184, 187, 212, 226, 237, 238, 241, 281

translation 23, 63, 69, 112, 119, 122–5, 127, 128, 159, 160, 162, 174, 176, 192, 210, 214, 228, 241, 265, 323–5, 341, 342, 351, 353

trill 32, 35, 37, 38

triphthong 36, 37, 39, 201, 242

Turkish 55
turn-taking 90, 91, 109, 145, 148
typology 54, 256, 297, 300–2, 332

**U**
underspecification 71, 73, 74, 158, 251, 307
universal grammar 10, 64, 65, 71, 99, 109, 112,
    116, 117, 188, 204, 216, 239, 240, 248–50,
    256, 279–81, 293, 297, 300–2, 333
uvula/uvular 32, 38, 39

**V**
velar/velum 32, 33, 35, 38, 39, 44, 45, 88, 192,
    198, 201
verbal language 3–6
Vietnamese 54
vocal cords 33, 34, 38. *See also* glottal/glottis.
voice (grammatical) 51, 240, 241
voicing (voiced/voiceless) 32, 33, 37, 38, 40, 41,
    44, 45, 53, 107, 130, 173, 192, 198, 201, 213,
    288, 320, 321, 347

vowel 32, 34–9, 43, 45, 46, 48, 49, 53, 88, 89,
    127, 129, 130, 139, 152, 166, 173–5, 179,
    192, 198, 200, 201, 226, 232, 242, 262, 278,
    284, 289, 311, 321, 342
Vygotsky 112, 114

**W**
West Greenlandic Eskimo 54
Whorf 93, 225, 226, 261, 264, 265
Wittgenstein 12, 14, 263, 264, 306, 308
word formation 54, 63, 211, 248, 290
writing xv, 8, 10, 11, 16–19, 21, 22, 25–7, 30, 34,
    49, 57, 67, 74, 93, 120, 129, 135, 136, 139,
    140, 152, 153, 170, 171, 175, 176, 185, 186,
    191, 199, 204, 208, 211, 213, 214, 223, 229,
    231, 249, 270, 280, 284, 291, 295, 313, 351,
    352

**Z**
zero morph 50, 53, 216